ANTITRUST LAW AMIDST FINANCIAL CRISES

ANTITRUST LAW AMIDST FINANCIAL CRISES

IOANNIS KOKKORIS AND
RODRIGO OLIVARES-CAMINAL

CAMBRIDGE UNIVERSITY PRESS
Cambridge, New York, Melbourne, Madrid, Cape Town, Singapore,
São Paulo, Delhi, Dubai, Tokyo, Mexico City

Cambridge University Press
The Edinburgh Building, Cambridge CB2 8RU, UK

Published in the United States of America by Cambridge University Press, New York

www.cambridge.org
Information on this title: www.cambridge.org/9780521194839

First published 2010

Printed in the United Kingdom at the University Press, Cambridge

A catalogue record for this publication is available from the British Library

ISBN 978-0-521-19483-9 Hardback

To our families, for providing us with moral support during our academic and professional endeavours . . .

CONTENTS

FOREWORD

PHILIP LOWE, FORMER DIRECTOR GENERAL, DIRECTORATE GENERAL COMPETITION, CURRENTLY DIRECTOR GENERAL FOR ENERGY, EUROPEAN COMMISSION

The recent financial and economic crisis has created significant challenges for the economy and for business, as well as for policy-makers. Competition policy has a central role to play in responding to the crisis and, as Dr Kokkoris and Dr Olivares-Caminal discuss in their extremely timely book, competition authorities around the world have faced their own specific challenges.

In the face of wholesale government intervention in the market, the European Commission's objective in ensuring compliance with EU competition rules, and specifically the rules on state aid, has been to help maintain a level playing field in the European financial sector, and to help preserve the achievements of the single market. At the outset of the crisis we sought to ensure that rescue measures respected fundamental competition principles by setting out how we would apply state aid rules in the Commission's four Communications on rescue and restructuring of the financial sector. And the introduction of the Temporary Framework for state aid provided member states with the necessary flexibility to act to target specific problems within their territory by facilitating programmes of access to finance for the real economy. These measures were key in ensuring the coherence of rescue and recovery measures across the EU and, crucially, helped keep any disruptions to the level playing field to an absolute minimum.

And as we consider how to create the right conditions for recovery and economic growth, the long-term benefits of pursuing an effective competition policy have become more, and not less, relevant. Looking ahead, a strong competition policy will help increase our economic fitness and create the competitive and efficient markets that encourage innovation, boost productivity and create jobs.

The European Commission's firm stance on the importance of maintaining competition rules and principles has also held true for our approach to antitrust rules and merger control, in spite of some pressure to set aside or amend our rules. To differing degrees, we have seen failing-firm defences in merger control, attempts to justify cartels, and calls for more state aid to remedy crisis-related market failures. However, I believe we have the right rules in place to deal with the crisis. The Commission has been able to show flexibility on procedure in order to respond to crisis conditions, while at the same time standing firm on the principles.

The EC Merger Regulation is a good example of where recent reforms have stood us in good stead in terms of ensuring that merger control instruments are based on sound economic principles and are flexible enough to take account of evolving market conditions. And the Commission has maintained a strong focus on cartel enforcement during the downturn in view of the serious harm cartels cause to the whole economy. Indeed, as Neelie Kroes, the outgoing Commissioner for Competition, recently put it, no matter what the rate of economic growth, cartels are harmful to the consumer.

This book tackles many of the issues I have mentioned above and raises interesting questions about how flexible competition enforcement should be in view of the difficulties faced by companies in the global downturn.

In this unprecedented situation of economic difficulty, I am sure many of my colleagues in Directorate General Competition would agree with me that it is important to look at all sides of the debate; it is only through a lively exchange of views that we can determine the best set of policy tools to continue to respond effectively to the crisis and create the conditions for future sustainable growth. For this reason, I welcome Dr Kokkoris and Dr Olivares-Caminal's contribution to this discussion and I hope that they will agree with my belief that ultimately the way out of this crisis – for the financial sector and the wider economy – lies in making sure that markets remain competitive, with a robust enforcement of the competition rules but with an approach which is informed and realistic on what can be achieved.

FOREWORD

FREDERIC JENNY, PROFESSOR OF ECONOMICS, ESSEC;
CHAIRMAN, OECD COMPETITION COMMITTEE

The financial crisis has had a considerable impact on competition policy and competition law enforcement.

First, questions were raised about the trust that one could put in free and competitive markets. It was recognized that for markets, such as the financial markets which have a systemic risk component, strict prudential regulation is a necessary complement of competition. Inadequate regulation or regulation which did not keep up with innovation in the financial markets was considered to be at the heart of the financial crisis. The political rhetoric of the 1990s against regulation was replaced by a more pragmatic approach to regulation.

Second, questions arose about whether and how competition law enforcement should be modified in a time of financial and economic crisis.

A consensus had emerged toward the end of the twentieth century that the enforcement of competition law should move toward an 'effects-based approach'. This approach requires that the competitive and efficiency effects of business practices or transactions be analysed in the context in which they are implemented to determine whether they should be prohibited.

This move away from an ideological or formalistic approach to competition law enforcement and towards a method of enforcement based on applied economic analysis put competition authorities in a much better position to face the challenges of the economic and financial crisis.

What changed drastically with the financial and economic crisis was the context of markets. All of a sudden, because credit was scarce, the competitive pressure from new entrants, from hostile takeovers or from small competitors became less constraining. Because the financing of international trade also experienced difficulties and because of the protectionist tendencies of a few governments, international trade decreased and so did the pressure of international competition. Because the real crisis, which was a consequence of the financial crisis, was severe; some industries were faced with rapidly decreasing demand and very few opportunities to redeploy their resources in other sectors. Consolidations in some industries seemed to be the only possible solution to avoid bankruptcy. To try to alleviate the pain due to the rapidity of the collapse of the economy and a dramatic rise in unemployment, governments started intervening both to stimulate demand and to subsidize failing firms.

There were calls for competition authorities to modify their standards of competition law enforcement (and to move towards a more permissive attitude recognizing the need to meet sociopolitical goals such as keeping employment up or to avoid the failure of firms which may have been badly managed but were at risk of disappearing altogether). Other voices were heard saying that the goals and the standards of competition law enforcement should be kept intact, but that enforcement should take into consideration the new macroeconomic context of markets (including the existence of a systemic risk in the financial sector, the difficulty of reallocating resources in the real sector, the potential collapse of large segments of industries due to rapidly declining demand, the increase in state aids, and so on).

This book is the first comprehensive analysis of the responses of competition authorities to these challenges.

It explains how a number of new themes (or themes which had been forgotten because the economy had grown more or less smoothly for several decades) emerged in antitrust enforcement – for example, the conditions under which an efficiency defence could be accepted for mergers raising competition issues, the failing-firm defence for anti-competitive mergers, the benefits and costs of crisis cartels, and the conditions under which state aids could be accepted on a temporary basis. These themes became central concerns of competition authorities and this book thoroughly discusses the emergence of these new enforcement issues.

Also, as the book argues, by commenting on a vast number of decisions, competition law enforcement has, on the whole, been adapted intelligently and pragmatically to the challenges raised by a rapid and dramatic economic downturn without compromising the goals of competition law (the protection of consumer surplus) and without lowering the standards of competition law enforcement, unlike what happened after the 1929 economic crisis.

It is heartening to see that, as a result, competition law and competition policy are now seen as part of the solution to the economic crisis, rather than as part of the problem.

PREFACE

The idea for this book can be traced back to the events that occurred during the weekend of 13–14 September 2008 when discussions were being held on both sides of the Atlantic to rescue troubled financial institutions. The outcome of these discussions was the emergency deal between Bank of America and Merrill Lynch, the filing for bankruptcy of Lehman Brothers and the announcement of the merger between Lloyds and HBOS.

As a result of a crisis threatening the stability of an economy, competition policy may be set aside due to special and exceptional circumstances. Therefore it is important to have a clear understanding of the rules (i.e. competition law) and the exceptions to those rules, especially in the presence of such exceptional circumstances. In addition, it is important for distressed entities and policy-makers to clearly understand the array of options that they have in advance since these can be used as part of their 'crisis toolkit'. The aim of this book is to provide an analysis of such exceptions to competition law and policy, particularly in the context of a financial crisis.

The topics analysed herein include the failing-firm defence, efficiency defence, crisis cartels and state aids. During a crisis, concepts such as failing-firm defence and efficiency defence are essential in effective and pragmatic enforcement of merger legislation. In addition, the treatment of state aids as well as crisis cartels is also essential in ensuring the sustainability of undertakings and of whole industries.

The key issue that this book addresses is whether a crisis can justify the adoption of a more lenient approach to established legal standards as a result of the risks of the systemic crisis to the entire market. In summary, the book provides a comprehensive understanding of the rationale of competition law in the light of conflicting interests (promoting competition versus the collapse of a firm that might result in a systemic crisis). This book provides a valuable practical guide for policy-makers as well as practitioners in the field of competition policy.

The book has immensely benefited from the contribution of Phedon Nicolaides on the treatment of state aids. His insightful approach has been invaluable to the completeness of the arguments of this book.

We would also like to express our gratitude to Philip Lowe, Director General for Competition, European Commission, as well as Frederic Jenny, Chairman of the OECD Competition Committee, for writing the forewords to this book.

Finally, we are indebted to Cambridge University Press and specifically to Kim Hughes and Richard Woodham for their essential assistance in the process of publishing this book. Gratitude is also owed to Kiriakos E. Papadakis for providing us access to the data that he has collected over the years.

The views expressed herein are strictly personal and do not necessarily reflect any views of the affiliated institutions.

Ioannis Kokkoris and Rodrigo Olivares-Caminal
London and Geneva,
15 January 2010

TABLE OF CASES

European Union

Chiemiefarma see Quinine Cartel
Commission v. Italy, Case C-173/73 359n
Commission v. Italy, Case C-35/96, [1998] ECR I-03851 354n
Commission v. Spain, Case C-499/99, [2002] ECR I-16031 344
Compagnie de Saint Gobain, Case C-307/97, [1999] ECR I-06161 364n
Compagnie Maritime Belge, Case C-395/96, [2000] ECR 1-1365 494n
Compagnie Maritime Belge, Cases T-24, 25, 26 and 28/93, [1996] ECR II-1211 494n
Compagnie Maritime Belge, Commission Decision of 23 December 1993, [1993] OJ L34/20 494n
Competition Authority v. The Beef Industry Development Society Ltd (BIDS) and Barry Brothers (Carrigmore) Meats Ltd, Case C-209/07, [2008] 6 ECC 113, [2008] ECR 00 324–31, 460n
Confederación Española de Transporte de Mercancias (CETM) v. Commission, Case T-55/99, [2000] ECR II-3207 357–8, 362n
Continental Can see *Europemballage Corp.*
Continental/Phoenix, Case M3436 445n
Cooperatieve 'Suiker Unie' UA v. Commission (Sugar Cartel), Cases 40-48/73, [1975] ECR 1663, (1975) E Comm Ct J Rep 1663 23n, 24n, 280
Corus UK Ltd v. Commission, Case T-48/00 335n
Crédit Lyonnais, Case C-47/96, Commission Decision 98/490/EC, [1998] OJ L221/28 483n
Credit Union Provision of Access to Basic Financial Services – Scotland, Commission Decision of 6 April 2005, N244/2003 United Kingdom 354n
Dalmine SpA v. Commission, Case T-50/00 335n
Danish Crown/Steff-Houlberg, Case COMP/M2662 [2002] 162–3
Danish Crown/Vestjyske Slagterier, Case COMP IV/M1313, 9 March 1999 163, 228
Danske Busvognmaend v. Commission, Case T-157/01, [2004] ECR II-917 355n
Degussa AG v. Commission, Case C-250/99 P 304n
Deloitte & Touche/Andersen UK, Case COMP/M2810 128–9
Dexia – Restructuring aid (Belgium), Case C9/2009, [2009] OJ C181/42 487
Distribution of Package Tours during

France

Germany

Italy

Netherlands

Sweden

United Kingdom

United States

Board, Approval of Proposal by Wells Fargo & Company to Acquire Wachovia Corporation, (12 October 2008) 428

Whirlpool/Maytag, Press Release, US Department of Justice, Department of Justice Antitrust Division Statement on the Closing of Its Investigation of Whirlpool's Acquisition of Maytag (29 March 2006) 247, 255–6

TABLE OF TREATIES AND OTHER INTERNATIONAL INSTRUMENTS

Germany

Italy

Japan

New Zealand

Spain

United Kingdom

United States

Introduction

> As freak legislation, the antitrust laws stand alone. Nobody knows what it is they forbid.
>
> Isabelle Paterson (1866–1961)[1]

As result of the recent crisis it has been argued that competition policy may be set aside due to special and exceptional circumstances.[2] These special and exceptional circumstances can be, inter alia, the collapse of a bank that can trigger a systemic crisis. Therefore it is important to have a clear understanding of the rules (i.e. competition law) and the exceptions to those rules, especially in the presence of such exceptional circumstances.[3] In addition, it is important for distressed entities and policy-makers to understand clearly the array of options that they have in advance since these can be used as part of their 'crisis toolkit'. The aim of this book is to provide an analysis of such exceptions to competition law and policy, particularly in the context of a financial crisis.

Promotion of consumer welfare has traditionally been considered one of the aims, not the sole aim, of antitrust, both in the United States and in Europe.[4] In the United States of America the Federal Trade Commission (FTC) acts to ensure that markets operate efficiently to benefit consumers. In the United Kingdom the Office of Fair Trading (OFT) declares that the its goal is to make markets work well *for consumers*. Most

[1] Isabel Paterson was a Canadian-American journalist, author, political philosopher and leading literary critic of her day. Along with Rose Wilder Lane and Ayn Rand, who both acknowledged an intellectual debt to Paterson, she is one of the three founding mothers of American libertarianism.

[2] The views of this book are strictly personal and do not reflect the views of the Office of Fair Trading, UNCTAD or any other affiliated institutions.

[3] This chapter will mainly use the term 'competition', which is interchangeable with 'antitrust' as used in the US for the law or authorities that protect trade and commerce from restraints, monopolies, price-fixing and price discrimination. See *Black's Law Dictionary*, 8th ed., Thomson West, 2004, p. 92, for the definition of antitrust law.

[4] R. Whish, *Competition Law*, 5th ed., Butterworths, 2003, at pp. 15 et seq.

academics seem to agree that consumer protection is the prevailing aim of antitrust legislation.[5] This book will provide a comprehensive understanding of the rationale of competition law in the light of conflicting interests (promoting competition versus the collapse of a firm that might result in a systemic crisis). The key issue that this book aims to address is whether the risk of a systemic crisis can justify the adoption of a more lenient approach to established antitrust legal standards. The European Union, UK and USA perspectives will be analysed to reflect a comprehensive understanding.

Nowadays we face global restructuring of industries that may represent the most significant economic change of the last decades. Fierce competition from imports, severe overcapacity in some industries and technological advancements are only some of the features that characterize markets nowadays. Distressed companies on the verge of insolvency are a common phenomenon that is observed in both developed and developing economies. Companies that are in distressed financial conditions may choose to embark on a merger as a means to ensure their viability and profitability. A strategic response for struggling firms and one of the means of implementing a successful debt restructuring process is to combine in order to achieve competitively necessary efficiencies.[6] Either a failing firm within a booming industry or firms in a distressed industry will choose to merge/acquire/be acquired (or choose to sell loss-making divisions) in order to enhance the firm's viability and profitability. Given these wrenching transformations, the applicability and importance of the failing-firm defence and failing-division defence might be crucial.[7]

The importance of mergers (and thus of the failing-firm defence) for the restructuring process is indicated, inter alia, by the US Supreme Court in the *United States v. General Dynamics Corp.* case.[8] The Court upheld that three groups – private parties, shareholders and creditors – benefit from the merger of a failing firm. The shareholders are unlikely to lose the investment and are likely to reap benefits if the merger proves

[5] The report prepared by the ICN (International Competition Network) Unilateral Conduct Working Group (ICN Report) for the 6th Annual Conference of the ICN in May 2007 includes a table of the objectives of unilateral conduct laws identified in the responses of the jurisdictions which were surveyed as part of the ICN Report.

[6] D. Valentine, 'Horizontal Issues: What's Happening and What's on the Horizon' (1995), available at www.ftc.gov/speeches/other/dvhorizontalissues.htm.

[7] An equivalent term is failing-company defence.

[8] *United States v. General Dynamics Corp.*, (1974) 415 U.S. 486.

profitable. The creditors will benefit as a result of retaining their rights against the debtor and are likely to be reimbursed for the credit they have provided to the firm. On the other hand, in insolvency proceedings they are not as likely to be fully reimbursed.

The restructuring process can thus be used as a tool to determine if a division of a firm or the whole firm must be merged or acquired by another undertaking in order to maintain its viability and its future prospects for profitability. In such a case the only possible means of restructuring is through a successful merger/acquisition. This merger may need to be assessed by the relevant competition authorities. If the authorities consider that the merger will have anti-competitive effects, they may block it, thus resulting in the unsuccessful completion of the restructuring procedure. The US and the EU have their own criteria for assessing the argument of failing-firm defence. The satisfaction of these criteria is an essential factor for a merger which is likely to have anti-competitive effects to be allowed to proceed. The failing-firm defence refers to the supposedly neutral effect on competition of concentrations where one (or both) of the merging parties (the acquirer and/or the target) are failing or will fail due to poor financial performance.[9]

As mentioned above, a significant and frequent, in certain economies, reason for engaging in mergers is the restructuring of debt of a company which is on the verge of insolvency. There is a growing literature on the effect of insolvency procedures on *ex ante* decisions by firms and shareholders. The restructuring of the debt may entail the sale of a loss-making division and, if the company has subsidiaries, the sale of the subsidiary or subsidiaries as a whole. Thus the failing-firm defence and failing-division defence can be invoked in cases where this sale is assessed by the relevant competition authorities. However, the failing-division defence has not been given much acceptance and accreditation by the above-mentioned competition authorities and courts.

Turning to efficiencies, there can be cases where efficiencies are being alleged and the mergers are occurring in a period of crisis. Important questions are being asked regarding whether the assessment of efficiencies should be different in these cases. Mergers can induce both beneficial and adverse effects in a market. The importance of considering efficiencies in mergers cannot be underestimated.

Efficiencies contribute a great deal towards achieving the goals of a

[9] V. Baccaro, 'Failing Firm Defence and Lack of Causality: Doctrine and Practice in Europe of Two Closely Related Concepts' (2004) 1 *ECLR* 11, at p. 11.

competition system – promoting consumer welfare and total welfare, and providing a genuine benefit to society. In addition, efficiencies which increase competition in the market should unambiguously be encouraged. Mergers consolidate the ownership and control of business assets, including physical assets (for example, a plant) and intangibles (for example, brand reputation). They can enhance corporate (and wider economic) performance by improving the efficiency with which business assets are used. Further reasons for firms to engage in mergers and acquisitions include efficiencies arising from the mergers,[10] and the tendency of some countries to endorse the concept of 'national champions'.[11] In the absence of the European Commission's ('the Commission') decisions and of judgments of the Community courts that would clarify problematic issues of the practical application of the efficiency defence,[12] the parties and their advisers rely on guidelines. In order to successfully present and sustain their efficiency claims, merging parties should have a clear understanding of at which stage of the merger assessment they should be introduced, how efficiencies will be assessed in relation to anti-competitive concerns and what kind of evidence should be produced.

Advocates of a more lenient approach advocate placing increased emphasis on preventing inefficiencies that may result from the

[10] In the form of, inter alia, economies of scale and economies of scope. 'Economies of scale' refers to the situation where long-run average costs of production decrease as output rises. See further D. Begg, S. Fischer and R. Dornbusch, *Economics*, 5th ed., McGraw-Hill, 1997, p. 109. The term applies to efficiencies associated with increasing or decreasing the scale of production and refers to changes in the output of a single product type. 'Economies of scope' refers to situations where the joint output of a single firm is greater than the output that could be achieved by two different firms each producing a single product (with equivalent production inputs allocated between the two firms). See further R. Pindyck and D. Rubinfeld, *Microeconomics*, 4th ed., Prentice Hall International, 1998, p. 227. The term refers to efficiencies associated with increasing or deceasing the scope of marketing and distribution and to changes in the number of different types of product. In addition, economies of scale relate primarily to supply-side changes (such as level of production) whereas economies of scope relate to demand-side changes (such as marketing and distribution).

[11] The concept of 'national champion' refers to domestic firms that are able, post-merger, to successfully compete in international markets.

[12] The European Commission is the executive body of the European Union. Alongside the European Parliament and the Council of the European Union, it is one of the three main institutions governing the Union. Its primary roles are to propose and implement legislation, and to act as 'guardian of the treaties' which provide the legal basis for the EU. The Commission consists of twenty-seven commissioners, one from each member state of the EU.

prevention of the merger. Thus, rather than an efficiency defence, we may need to consider an inefficiency defence as well. This is an important consideration that was clearly taken into account in a number of cases. In the penultimate chapter, we shall analyse the circumstances under which the authorities should place significant emphasis on the continuity of service or product, so significant that in certain cases even if the criteria of efficiency defence may not be strictly satisfied, the merger should be cleared on the basis of the prevention of the resulting inefficiencies from discontinuing the product or service. This argument is similar to that analysed in the discussion of the failing-firm defence regarding circumstances in which the authorities should be more lenient towards accepting arguments based on the failing-firm defence.

The book will also address cartel agreements. Such agreements generally involve price-fixing, market division, control of output, mitigation of technological improvement and limitation of production. Through cartels, 'private' interests may determine the level and distribution of the national income, the level of employment and the stability of markets, as well as general economic and political stability. Cartel justifications that have been proposed include that a cartel will prevent cut-throat competition. In industries where fierce competition would yield below-cost pricing, the cartel guarantees a 'reasonable' price. In addition, it has been argued that a cartel sustains needed capacity and prevents excess capacity. Furthermore, a cartel reduces uncertainty as regards the average price of a product. It also assists in financing desirable activities, such as research and development (R & D), and in providing countervailing power, since if there is a single buyer (monopsonist/oligopsonist) or supplier (monopolist/oligopolist), there is unequal bargaining power that a cartel can address.

Without the industry-wide agreement on capacity reduction that can be achieved through a crisis cartel, smaller firms may exit the market, thus leaving a limited number of choices for customers as well as inducing unemployment. In such conditions, undertakings may operate at inefficient output levels and may even incur losses. The Treaty of Rome did not contain any clauses regarding crisis conditions. When the Treaty of Rome was signed, economic expansion seemed to be likely to continue. Due to the lack of express clauses in the Treaty of Rome the Commission could not justify applying the Article 81(3) criteria.[13] Thus

[13] Pursuant to the Treaty on the Functioning of the European Union (Lisbon Treaty) (EC Official Journal C 306/2 of 17 December 2007, p. 1) the provisions on

the Commission initially reduced fines on cartels existing in situations of crisis. German legislation, the Treaty of Rome and the Treaty of Paris had adopted different attitudes to the existence of crises in the economy. The German statute was more lenient towards crisis cartels by allowing structural crisis agreements. The Treaty of Paris, although not exempting crisis cartels, allows for intervention by Community institutions to ensure minimum prices.[14] In contrast, the Treaty of Rome adopts a stricter approach and does not contain any exemptions for crisis cartels.

As the case law illustrates, crisis cartels are likely to appear in industries where production facilities are durable and specialized and consumer demand falls due to adverse market conditions. The Commission and the Court of First Instance (CFI) or European Court of Justice (ECJ) will authorize a restructuring plan involving sectoral agreements if it is believed that the Article 101(3) criteria are met. These criteria will be met if the reduction in the capacity of the sector will, in the long term, lead to more efficent capacity utilization enhancing the competitiveness of the sector and thus benefiting consumers. In addition, the Commission interestingly argues that a factor that will be taken into account is the impact of the capacity co-ordination on the mitigation of the adverse impact of the crisis on employment.[15] The Commission explicitly states that reorganization operations should also be used to stabilize and secure the employment situation in the sector concerned.[16] Again, the Commission uses the positive impact on employment of the co-ordination of the business conduct of competitors as a factor favouring exemption. Thus a detailed plan of plant closures as well as avoidance of the creation of new capacity are also necessary factors in the agreement being accepted by the Commission.

In addition, the agreement must constitute indispensable means of achieving the necessary capacity reduction. The limited duration of the agreement, the existence of firms in the industry which are not party to

Footnote 13 (*cont.*)
anticompetitive agreements (formerly Article 81) are now in Article 101, abuse of dominance (formerly Article 82) now in Article 102, public undertakings (formerly Article 86) now in Article 106, and state aid (formerly Articles 87–8) now in Articles 107–8. The European Court of Justice is now the Court of Justice, and the Court of First Instance is now the General Court. The terms European Court of Justice or ECJ and Court of First Instance or CFI will be used herein.

[14] R. Joliet, 'Cartelisation, Dirigism and Crisis in the European Community' (1981) 3 *World Economy* 403, p. 405.

[15] Twenty-third Report on Competition Policy, para. 85.

[16] Twenty-third Report on Competition Policy, para. 88.

the agreement and the fact that the co-ordinated reduction in capacity is only an element in the business strategy of firms constitute reassurances that competition will not be eliminated.

In addition, the 'financial constraints' consideration reflects a concern that high fines might force an offending firm into insolvency. The European Commission and the US antitrust authorities have wide discretion and apparent lack of transparency in awarding discounts. However, factors external to competition policy – in particular the social objectives of the Treaty on the Functioning of the European Union (TFEU) – may determine how they are granted. Thus firms can be involved in cartels and not end up paying a fine in crisis situations, increasing both their profits from collusion and their tendency to be in cartels (in the absence of criminal sanctions like those the UK's competition authorities can impose).

In the past, economic recessions have often been followed by efforts to change the legal framework of competition, in order to preserve people's faith in the free-market system. Perhaps the most prominent example of such efforts was the National Industrial Recovery Act (NIRA) in the United States at the time of the Great Depression in the early 1930s. In trying to contain the damage of the Great Depression, this Act allowed hundreds of industries legally to meet and agree upon rules limiting 'excessive' competition. However, subsequent historical analysis has shown that some serious harm to the economy was the actual result of these efforts.[17] Pursuant to this legislation, there was a full suspension of the enforcement of competition law, combined with collective bargaining in setting wages. Had there not been full suspension and had the EC policy on crisis cartels of the 1980s and 1990s been followed, the recovery of the economy might not have been so slow.

Turning to state aid enforcement, the control of state aid is an important component of the competition policy of the European Union. State intervention influences the way markets operate by favouring certain undertakings and causing, as a result, serious damage to their competitors operating in the same and/or different member states. State intervention may thus undermine the achievement of a market economy with free and undistorted competition. Indeed, Protocol 27 of the Treaty on the European Union (TEU) and TFEU recognizes that the establishment of an internal market, as provided by Article 3 TEU, requires 'a system

[17] See K. Heyer and S. Kimmel, 'Merger Review of Firms in Financial Distress' (2009), available from: www.usdoj.gov/atr/public/eag/244098.htm.

ensuring that competition is not distorted'. Therefore the state aid policy of the EU prohibits in principle state aid and allows exceptionally only the kind and amounts of state aid that pursue common policy aims and do not cause excessive distortion between member states.

The concept of state aid is evolving. Public authorities have been quite adept in devising new measures to support companies or whole industrial sectors. As a consequence, EU courts have had to refine the definition of what constitutes state aid and the Commission has had to sharpen its investigative methods. Not surprisingly, state aid policy has played an important role during the financial crisis. It has allowed member states to support, initially, financial institutions and then the real economy while at the same time it has strived to prevent excessive distortion of competition and disruption to the flow of resources between member states.

Member states have not been allowed to discriminate in favour of their banks. They have not been allowed to grant unlimited amounts of aid. They have been required to submit realistic restructuring plans which in some cases have led to the sale of the beneficiaries or even to their closure.[18] The Commission has issued special rules as a result of this crisis. These rules are without doubt accommodating. Given that similar and even more generous measures have been adopted by countries outside the European Union, it is not unreasonable to conclude that the special rules merely reflected the exceptional nature and unprecedented magnitude of the crisis.

In every crisis, there will be a push for a regulatory response and a political response, which would lead to a restructuring of regulation but may restrict competition even further.[19] It is obvious that the European Commission (and all competition authorities in the EU), under the current economic crisis, have to be cautious with the application of competition rules. They must consider not only the short-term restabilization of the economy but the long-term development of competition as well.

According to Nadia Calvino, deputy director-general for competition at the European Commission,

[18] For example, the liquidation aid to Roskilde Bank in Denmark (NN 39/2008).

[19] See Professor Petzman's speech at the OECD, Summary Record of the Discussion on Competition and Financial Markets, DAF/COMP/M(2009)1/ANN5, 10 April 2009, Roundtable 4 on Going Forward: Adaptation of Competition Rules, Processes and Institutions to Current Financial Sector Issues, available at www.oecd.org.

> There are clear challenges in the policy landscape: there is a financial crisis which leads to systemic risks and is now turning also into a real economic recession. The European Commission has a significant role to play in the current economic environment, but we have to protect the short-term stability of markets while also keeping in mind the importance of a long-term perspective.[20]

Competition authorities should be pragmatic in enforcing competition legislation against mergers, cartels and state aid in periods of crisis. In adopting a pragmatic approach, competition authorities should aim at minimizing adverse precedential issues as well as adverse effects on competition, effects that can sustain after the crisis is over. Competition policy needs to be pragmatic, and flexible enough to address sudden exogenous shocks and the wide-ranging implications of such shocks to whole markets. After all, the ultimate and undoubted aim of the Commission should be to enhance the degree of competition in a market, leading to improvement of consumer welfare. On a number of occasions, it is thus essential to subordinate competition policy if such an approach will ensure sustainability and enhancement of consumer welfare, or alternatively if such an approach will prevent a deterioration of consumer welfare through means irrelevant to competition policy (e.g. systemic crisis, macroeconomic instability and so on).

Turning to each chapter in detail, the first chapter will present an overview of competition law and policy and will place significant emphasis on US and EU legislation regarding mergers and cartels. This chapter will not purport to provide an exhaustive analysis, but an overview of the legislative means that are employed in these jurisdictions to address anti-competitive conduct. The origin of the competition legislation in these jurisdictions is essential to understanding the approach that they take in dealing with mergers, cartels and state aid in periods of crisis. This approach will be the subject of the chapters that will follow.

The second chapter will address the occurrence of a crisis. The origins and causes of crises can be quite diverse and they pose serious threats to the economy of a country or region or to the entire world. Therefore this chapter will try to identify a working matrix to understand the different

[20] EU, Competition and Public Law Report, Brussels focus (2009), 'Brussels: Part of the Problem or Part of the Cure', available from www.abreuadvogados.com/xms/files/05_Comunicacao/Artigos_na_Imprensa/Iberian_Lawyer_Artigo_MMP_Fev.2009.pdf.

types of crisis and their common factors. Also, this chapter will attempt to demonstrate the detrimental effects of financial and other crises in the economy.

The third chapter will then present the application of the failing-firm defence. This chapter will address in detail one of the main considerations (defences) which competition authorities can take into account in assessing an anti-competitive merger. The failing-firm defence refers to the supposedly neutral effect on competition of concentrations where one (or both) of the merging parties (the acquirer and/or the target) are failing due to poor financial performance. There is a growing literature on the effect of insolvency procedures on *ex ante* decisions by firms and shareholders. Restructuring of a company may entail the sale of a loss-making division, and if the company has a subsidiary, the sale of the subsidiary as a whole. Thus the failing-firm defence and the failing-division defence can be invoked in cases where this sale is assessed by the relevant competition authorities. However, the failing-division defence has not been given great acceptance and accreditation by competition authorities and courts. We should note that in declining-industry conditions it is more likely that firms which are currently failing will continue to be in an adverse financial situation and will not be viable at all in the near future, thus causing an industry-wide crisis.

The fourth chapter will present the efficiency defence, which is relevant in the enforcement of merger legislation. Mergers may eliminate any competition that exists between the merging parties and may lead to a reduction in the number of firms competing in the market. Where this reduction has a substantial adverse effect on overall market competition, the market will be less oriented to consumer and efficiency goals, even in the absence of breaches of competition legislation. The importance of considering efficiencies in mergers cannot be underestimated. Efficiencies contribute a great deal towards achieving the goals of an antitrust system – whether promoting consumer welfare or total welfare, or providing genuine benefit to society. In addition, efficiencies which increase competition in the market should unambiguously be encouraged.

The term 'efficiency defence' is a statutory defence whereby a merger must be permitted – even if it will lessen competition – if efficiency gains due to the merger exceed or offset the effects of reduced competition. The efficiency defence is closely related to the welfare standard. In reality, however, the choice of a welfare standard does not reflect the findings of economic science, but rather has the nature of a political choice, which works against the adoption of the total surplus standard. The European Commission seems to have adopted a consumer welfare standard. A merger between two undertakings which induces harm to competition can be cleared by the competition authorities if the merger leads to efficiencies. In the presence of a banking crisis, it is debatable whether under the consumer welfare standard an efficiency-enhancing merger is in fact a strategy to avoid a bank run. The chapter will analyse the strict criteria for accepting an efficiency defence, and under what conditions these criteria could be relaxed.

Subsequently, the fifth chapter presents 'crisis cartels'. Crisis cartels are allegedly justified by the fact that collusive behaviour was the only means for the survival of the cartelists. In addition, the 'financial constraints' consideration reflects a concern that high fines might force an offending firm into insolvency.

The sixth chapter will explain the concept of state aid. State aid policy has played an important role during the financial crisis. The chapter presents the latest statistics on the amount of state aid granted by member states.

The penultimate chapter will present a detailed analysis of the treatment of mergers, cartels and state aid in periods of crisis. Mergers have been one of the most preferred methods for firms to avoid insolvency. Firms in distress prefer to be merged with or acquired by stronger, more solvent undertakings in order to avoid a likely insolvency. A strategic response for struggling firms and one of the means of implementing a successful restructuring process is to combine in order to achieve competitively necessary efficiencies. Given these wrenching transformations, the applicability and importance of the failing-firm/division defence, as well as the efficiency defence, might be crucial. In addition, the chapter reviews the state aid guidelines issued by the Commission in response to the financial crisis and considers how the Commission has treated the various measures taken by member states. A number of landmark cases are reviewed in more detail. The chapter also evaluates the application of state aid policy during the financial crisis and will conclude with a critical assessment of the role and effectiveness of state aid policy during the crisis. The chapter will analyse the circumstances under which crisis cartel agreements should be accepted as a means to mitigate the adverse impact of crisis in a given sector. This chapter will also present the welfare objectives as well as the aims of competition policy in major jurisdictions. The aim of the chapter in a nutshell is to analyse how an anti-competitive merger, a crisis cartel or a particular type of aid can provide the means to tide companies over a financial crisis.

A large number of cases will be analysed throughout this book in an attempt to present fully the concepts addressed herein, as well as their implications for competition enforcement during periods of both non-crisis and crisis.

The concept of this book is unique. It will present the latest developments in competition law and policy in relation to a crisis situation and the possibility of competition laws being circumvented. Competition enforcement is an area that is enormously dynamic and has recently undergone substantial modifications due to the development of new case studies and exceptional circumstances that have the potential to redraft the entire competition policy map. The book will provide a comprehensive understanding of the rationale of competition law in the light of conflicting interests.

One of the aims of this book is to provide a full account of these concepts, as illustrated in Figure 0.1. It analyses the legislation and the case law which have developed these concepts.

The book will provide a detailed analysis of competition enforcement in times of crises. Competition enforcement is likely to be relevant in circumstances where the sustainability of markets, as well as of whole economies, is adversely affected. Such circumstances include, inter alia, economic and financial crises. The analysis herein will employ the global financial crisis that was initiated in 2007 as a working example. The key issue that this book aims to address is whether a crisis can justify the adoption of a more lenient approach to established legal standards as a result of the risks, to the entire economy, of a systemic crisis. The EU but also the UK, German and US perspectives will be analysed to reflect a comprehensive understanding.

Overall, the book aims to provide a legal analysis of defences (and exceptions) to competition law and policy, particularly in the context of a financial crisis. The book will provide a detailed analysis of the rationale of competition law in the light of conflicting interests and will be a valuable practical guide for policy-makers as well as for practitioners in the fields of competition law and policy.

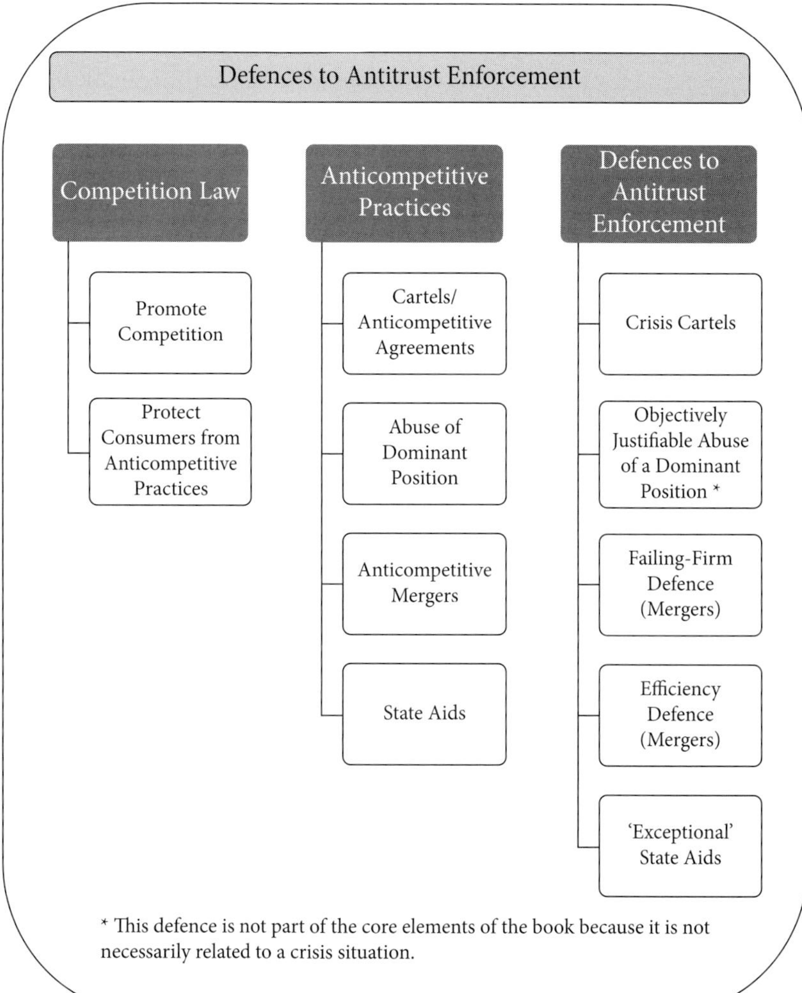

Figure 0.1. Defences against antitrust enforcement.

1

Introduction to competition law: EU, US and UK

> Ronald [Coase[1]] said he had gotten tired of antitrust because when the prices went up the judges said it was monopoly, when the prices went down they said it was predatory pricing, and when they stayed the same they said it was tacit collusion.
>
> Prof. William M. Landes[2]

1.1 Introduction

Competition law is a set of rules, disciplines and judicial decisions maintained by governments relating either to agreements between firms that restrict competition or to the concentration or abuse of market power on the part of private firms.[3] This chapter will briefly present the competition legislation in the three jurisdictions: the EU, the USA and the UK. The chapter will not purport to provide an exhaustive analysis, but an overview of the legislative means that are employed in these jurisdictions to address anti-competitive conduct. The subsequent chapters will analyse certain issues of relevance in greater detail (e.g. failing-firm defence, efficiency assessment, crisis cartels, state aid).

Before analysing the competition legislation in the three jurisdictions mentioned above, it is worth noting the development of competition legislation in some other jurisdictions. In Canada in 1910 the Parliament enacted the Combines Investigation Act, which was superseded in 1919 by the Combines and Fair Prices Acts and the Board of Commerce Act. These last were replaced in 1923 by the Combines Investigation Act.[4]

[1] Ronald Harry Coase (born 29 December 1910) is a Nobel laureate economist.

[2] W. Landes, 'The Fire of Truth: A Remembrance of Law and Economics at Chicago: 1932–1970' (1981) *Journal of Law and Economics* 193.

[3] B. Hoekman and P. Holmes, Competition Policy, Developing Countries and WTO, World Bank Working Paper, Washington D.C., 1999.

[4] The Competition Act contains both criminal and civil provisions aimed at preventing anticompetitive practices in the marketplace. Its purpose is to maintain and encourage

In New Zealand, the 1914 Cost of Living Act was followed in 1919 by the Board of Trade Act. A Board of Trade would be established with investigatory powers concerning monopolies, unfair competition and other conduct harming public welfare. In 1923, an amendment to this Act abolished the Board of Trade and transferred its competences to the Ministry of Industries and Commerce.

Across jurisdictions there are two principles which govern the approach that competition legislation takes towards anti-competitive conduct. The first principle is the 'prohibition' principle, under which restrictive business practices and the acquisition of monopoly power or a dominant position are prohibited per se. According to the second principle, employed by most European countries, restrictive business practices or a dominant market position may be permitted to some extent following a rule-of-reason approach.

The reason behind these different principles reflects the social policy behind the various jurisdictions' antitrust laws. The United States' adoption of the per se approach stemmed from the nineteenth-century Populist movement that resented the anti-competitive activities of various trusts, and therefore sought free competition at any cost.[5] In the European Union and Germany, however, the need for economic and technical development and efficiency is reflected in adopting the rule-of-reason principle having a supervisory antitrust role addressing abuses of a dominant position rather than the dominant position per se.

Under the per se approach, it would not be necessary to show any effect of anti-competitive conduct. For example, fixing prices is illegal per se. An argument that the pricing agreement would benefit society and/or consumers would not mitigate the illegality of the agreement.

There are advantages and disadvantages to the per se approach. The per se approach provides certainty as regards conducts which are prohibited. The disadvantages of this approach include that kinds of certain

competition in Canada in order to promote the efficiency and adaptability of the Canadian economy, expand opportunities for Canadian participation in world markets while at the same time recognizing the role of foreign competition in Canada, ensure that small and medium-sized enterprises have an equitable opportunity to participate in the Canadian economy, and provide consumers with competitive prices and product choices. See www.competitionbureau.gc.ca/eic/site/cb-bc.nsf/eng/h_00148.html.

[5] T.J. Grendell, 'The Antitrust Legislation of the United States, the European Economic Community, Germany and Japan' (1980) *The International and Comparative Law Quarterly* 29(1) 64. See www.jstor.org/stable/758753.

possibly pro-competitive conduct are branded anti-competitive without assessment of their effects.

In several jurisdictions there are exemptions which provide a uniform means of exempting certain kinds of conduct from competition legislation. Industries benefited from these exemptions because of an overriding socioeconomic necessity.

In addition, there is a third important aspect of antitrust legislation: enforcement, as well as penalties for violation. The US, the UK and Ireland, for example, have criminal and civil penalties for corporate and/or individual violations of certain antitrust laws, while the Commission can impose a civil penalty only against companies. Finally, the antitrust laws of a majority of countries provide for enforcement by administrative agencies, with review by the courts.

We shall analyse the legislation in Germany in greater detail since the treatment of crisis cartels in Germany will be addressed in the following chapters. In Germany, agreements to restrict competition generally were held to be legal under the principle of freedom of contract until the mid-twentieth century. The Penal, the Industrial and the Civil Codes, as well as the Law against Unfair Competition of 1909, have been applied by the German courts from time to time against monopolistic practices. An exhaustive investigation of German cartels was made by the German government between 1903 and 1906. In 1923, Chancellor Stresemann promulgated the Decree against the Abuse of Economic Power. This decree represented the first cartel law enacted in Germany acknowledging the legality of cartels not adversely affecting public welfare by committing abusive practices. A cartel court would be established, with exclusive jurisdiction in cartel matters. Cartels were put under the final authority of the minister of the economy. This cartel court represented the first court with exclusive jurisdiction in matters relating to cartels.

The Act against Restraints of Competition (ARC, or Gesetz gegen Wettbewerbsbeschränkungen – GWB),[6] was enacted in 1957. This law replaced the postwar decartelization orders. The GWB permitted 'agreements made for a common purpose by enterprises or associations of enterprises . . . of no effect in so far as they are likely to influence, by restraining competition, production or marketing conditions'. Several minor amendments to the law were adopted in 1965 while substantial alterations were made by the Amending Act of 1973.

[6] Available from the Bundeskartellamt website: www.bundeskartellamt.de/WEnglisch/Legal_bases/Legal_basesW3Dnavidw2625.php.

The German legislator of the seventh amendment of the GWB, which came into force in 2005, opted for a far-reaching harmonization of the German cartel prohibition and its exemptions with European competition law even for cases which stay below the threshold of affecting trade between member states. As a consequence, the wording of the current Chapter 1 GWB is very close to that of Article 101(1), and Chapter 1(2) GWB mirrors Article 101(3). In addition, §2(2) GWB specifies that Regulations of the Council or the Commission of the European Community on the application of Article 101(3) of the treaty to agreements of certain categories, decisions by associations of undertakings and concerted practices ('block-exemption regulations') shall apply *mutatis mutandis* when applying Chapter 1(2) GWB. The provisions expressly state that this shall also apply where the agreements, decisions and practices mentioned in Chapter 1(2) GWB are inadequate to affect trade between member states.

The almost complete harmonization of Chapter 1(1) and (2) of the GWB with European competition law has rendered many decisions of the German authorities and courts of former times obsolete. There are still a few existing peculiarities of German competition law, such as Chapter 1(3) GWB, which provides exemption from the cartel prohibition for cartels of small or medium-sized enterprises, or the exemption of the prohibition of resale price maintenance for newspapers and magazines provided by §30 GWB.[7]

The Act prohibits the abusive exploitation of a dominant position by one or several undertakings. Section 19(2) of the GWB states, 'Two or more undertakings are dominant in so far as no substantial competition exists between them with respect to certain kinds of goods or commercial services and they jointly satisfy the conditions of sentence 1.'

The Bundeskartellamt is the sole institution concerned with merger control. Where the Bundeskartellamt has prohibited the merger, this decision can in exceptional cases be overridden by the federal minister for economic affairs and technology, provided the conditions established in law are fulfilled. In regulated sectors, other institutions may be involved.

Germany's use of antitrust exemptions establishes an additional rule of reason in its antitrust legislation. Chapter 3 of the GWB provides

[7] R. Bechtold and U. Denzel, 'Germany', in I. Kokkoris (ed.), *Competition Cases from the European Union: The Ultimate Guide to Leading Cases of the EU and All 27 Member States*, Sweet and Maxwell, 2007.

an additional exemption for co-operation between small and medium enterprises (SMEs) which rationalize economic processes. In so far as this exceeds the limits permissible under Article 101(3) (and therefore §2(1) of the GWB), it is evident that this exemption is limited to cases in which Article 101 is inapplicable for lack of an effect on trade between member states. As soon as there is such an effect, Article 101 and Article 3(1) of the Regulation 1/2003 will override §3 of the GWB. The criteria under §3 of the GWB are: (1) there is a co-operation between SMEs, (2) that co-operation rationalizes economic processes through co-operation between undertakings, (3) competition in the market is not substantially restricted and (4) the agreement or decision serves the purpose of improving the competitiveness of SMEs. The rationalization exemption is intended to provide Germany with resource maximization on a national level.

After this brief account of the competition legislation in Germany, this introductory chapter will analyse in detail legislation in the EU, the US and the UK.

1.2 The European Union

The European Union has its origins in the common market established by the European Coal and Steel (ECSC) Treaty in 1952.[8] The aim of the ECSC Treaty, as stated in its Article 2, was to contribute, through the common market for coal and steel, to economic expansion, growth of employment and a rising standard of living. In the light of the establishment of the common market, the ECSC Treaty introduced the free movement of products without customs duties or taxes. It prohibited discriminatory measures or practices, subsidies, aids granted by states, special charges imposed by states and restrictive practices. The treaty dealt specifically with three elements which could distort competition: agreements,[9] concentrations and the abuse of dominant position.

[8] The ECSC Treaty expired on 23 July 2002. Thus the coal and steel sectors are now subject to Articles 101 and 102 TFEU, rather than Articles 65 and 66 ECSC. The consequences of this expiry are explained in the Commission's document Communication from the Commission Concerning Certain Aspects of the Treatment of Competition Cases Resulting from the Expiry of the ECSC Treaty, [2002] OJ C152/5, [2002] 5 CMLR 1036, section 2; see http://europa.eu.int/eur-lex/pri/en/oj/dat/2002/c_152/c_15220020626en00050012.pdf.

[9] Agreements or associations between undertakings could be cancelled by the High Authority if they directly or indirectly prevented, restricted or distorted normal competition.

The Treaty of Rome established the European Economic Community (EEC), and was signed in Rome on 25 March 1957, entering into force on 1 January 1958.[10]

According to Article 3a of the Treaty of Rome,

> 1. For the purposes set out in Article 2, the activities of the Member States and the Community shall include, as provided in this Treaty and in accordance with the timetable set out therein, the adoption of an economic policy which is based on the close coordination of Member States' economic policies, on the internal market and on the definition of common objectives, and conducted in accordance with the principle of an open market economy with free competition.

The ECJ has argued that the Articles in the EC Treaty ensuring that competition is unhindered are 'a fundamental provision . . . essential for the accomplishment of the tasks entrusted to the Community and, in particular, for the functioning of the internal market'.[11] The rationale behind the European competition policy is to allow firms to compete on a level playing field in all EU member states.

The Lisbon Treaty came into force on 1 December 2009. The Lisbon Treaty aims at a more democratic, efficient and transparent union. The treaty rewrote the EU's internal rules and introduced institutional changes designed to streamline decision-making. The treaty redistributed voting weights between member states and removed national vetoes in a number of areas. It expanded the Commission's powers and increased the Parliament's involvement in the legislative process. In addition, the human rights charter became legally binding. The Lisbon Treaty amended the Rome and Maastricht treaties, giving the EU a new legal framework and tools to tackle challenges in an increasingly interlinked world.[12] The treaty created the function of president of the European Council,[13] elected for two and a half years, and the position of the new high representative for the union in foreign affairs and security policy.

[10] The treaty establishing the European Atomic Energy Community (Euratom) was signed at the same time and the two are therefore jointly known as the Treaties of Rome. See further http://europa.eu/abc/treaties/index_en.htm.

[11] *Eco Swiss China Time Ltd v. Benetton International NV*, Case C126/97 [2000] 5 CMLR 816, para. 36.

[12] See http://ec.europa.eu/news/eu_explained/091201_en.htm.

[13] The European Council is a meeting of the heads of state or government of the European Union, and the president of the European Commission. On average four European Councils are held each year. Discussion and decisions take place on the matters of key issues and direction of the EU.

According to Article 3 of the Treaty on the Functioning of the European Union,[14]

> 1. The Union shall have exclusive competence in the following areas:
>   (a) customs union;
>   (b) the establishment of the competition rules necessary for the functioning of the internal market;
>   (c) monetary policy for the Member States whose currency is the euro;
>   (d) the conservation of marine biological resources under the common fisheries policy;
>   (e) common commercial policy.

According to Article 3(3) of the consolidated version of the Treaty on European Union,[15]

> The Union shall establish an internal market. It shall work for the sustainable development of Europe based on balanced economic growth and price stability, a highly competitive social market economy, aiming at full employment and social progress, and a high level of protection and improvement of the quality of the environment. It shall promote scientific and technological advance.

Article 3 of the Lisbon Treaty no longer includes 'a system ensuring that competition in the internal market is not distorted' as a policy objective of the EU. Instead, the reference to undistorted competition has been moved to a protocol annexed to the treaty. The Lisbon Treaty now refers to 'competition rules necessary for the functioning of the internal market'.

The Lisbon Treaty no longer specifies 'a single market where competition is free and undistorted' as an objective for the EU. The reference to competition is now included in the legally binding Protocol on the Internal Market and Competition, which is annexed to the treaty and states that 'the internal market as set out in Article 2 of the Treaty on European Union includes a system ensuring that competition is not distorted'. Article 3(1)(g) of the EC Treaty, which listed one of the EU's objectives as the implementation of 'a system ensuring that competition in the internal market is not distorted', has been repealed by the Treaty of Lisbon. Furthermore, the European Council's Legal Service has issued an opinion stating that the removal of Article 3(1)(g) would not prevent the

[14] See http://eur-lex.europa.eu/LexUriServ/LexUriServ.do?uri=OJ:C:2008:115:0001:01:EN:HTML.

[15] See http://eur-lex.europa.eu/LexUriServ/LexUriServ.do?uri=OJ:C:2008:115:0001:01:EN:HTML.

legislator from acting to ensure that competition in the internal market is not distorted. The real effect of this change may therefore be limited.[16]

With the Lisbon Treaty coming into force on 1 December 2009, interpretative issues could also arise due to the stronger references to full employment and social objectives, including the reference to a 'highly competitive social market economy', in amended Article 3 of the Treaty on European Union. This might induce arguments that a broader industrial policy standard should apply.[17]

We turn now to the wording of the competition provisions in the Lisbon Treaty.

1.2.1 Anti-competitive agreements

According to the wording of Article 101,

> 1. The following shall be prohibited as incompatible with the common market: all agreements between undertakings, decisions by associations of undertakings and concerted practices which may affect trade between Member States and which have as their object or effect the prevention, restriction or distortion of competition within the common market, and in particular those which:
>   (a) directly or indirectly fix purchase or selling prices or any other trading conditions;
>   (b) limit or control production, markets, technical development, or investment;
>   (c) share markets or sources of supply;
>   (d) apply dissimilar conditions to equivalent transactions with other trading parties, thereby placing them at a competitive disadvantage;
>   (e) make the conclusion of contracts subject to acceptance by the other parties of supplementary obligations which, by their nature or according to commercial usage, have no connection with the subject of such contracts.
> 2. Any agreements or decisions prohibited pursuant to this Article shall be automatically void.
> 3. The provisions of paragraph 1 may, however, be declared inapplicable in the case of:
>   • any agreement or category of agreements between undertakings,
>   • any decision or category of decisions by associations of undertakings,
>   • any concerted practice or category of concerted practices,

[16] See further www.mayerbrown.com/publications/article.asp?id=8198&nid=6, www.debrauw.com/News/LegalAlerts/Pages/CompetitionExtraDecember2009.aspx.

[17] See www.wilmerhale.com/publications/whPubsDetail.aspx?publication=9321.

which contributes to improving the production or distribution of goods or to promoting technical or economic progress, while allowing consumers a fair share of the resulting benefit, and which does not:

(a) impose on the undertakings concerned restrictions which are not indispensable to the attainment of these objectives;
(b) afford such undertakings the possibility of eliminating competition in respect of a substantial part of the products in question.

Article 101 of the Lisbon Treaty has three basic parts. First, Article 101(1) imposes a broad prohibition on agreements 'which may affect trade between member states and which have as their object or effect the prevention, restriction or distortion of competition within the common market'. Article 101(2) then provides that any such agreement is automatically void.[18] Finally, Article 101(3) allows the European Commission to exempt agreements from the broad prohibition if those agreements are found to have certain pro-competitive effects. Article 101(3) provides that the prohibition in Article 101(1) may be declared inapplicable to agreements that satisfy certain conditions. Notification is now abolished under regulation 1/2003, where it is provided that agreements which satisfy the conditions of Article 101(3) will not be prohibited. They will be valid and enforceable *ab initio*, without the adoption of an exemption decision. Article 101(3) is also applicable to categories of agreements.[19] The object of such exemptions is to exclude a generic type of agreement from the ambit of Article 101(1), thereby avoiding the need for separate and time-consuming individual exemptions.[20]

Article 101 prohibits anti-competitive conduct – such as the creation of restrictive agreements including price-fixing and market-sharing

[18] *STM v. Maschinebau Ulm*, [1966] ECR 235.

[19] Commission Regulation (EC) No 2790/1999 on the application of Article 101(3) of the Treaty to vertical agreements and concerted practices, [1999] OJ L336/21, [2000] 4 CMLR 398.

[20] For main cases involving the application of Article 101(3) see further: Commission's Guidelines on the Application of Article 101(3) of the Treaty, OJ 2004 C101/97, paras. 1–31; Cases 56 and 58–64, *Établissements Consten Sàrl and Grundig-Verkaufs-Gmbh v. Commission of the European Economic Community*, [1966] ECR 299; Case 56/65, *Société Technique Minière v. Maschinenbau Ulm GmbH*, [1966] ECR 235; Case C-234/89 *Stergios Delimitis v. Henninger Bräu AG*, [1991] ECR I 935; joined cases T-374/94, T-375/94, T-384/94, T-388/94, *European Night Services v. Commission*, [1998] ECR II 3141; Case T-112/99, *Métropole Télévision (M6) v. Commission*, [2001] ECR II 2459; Case C-309/99 *Wouters v. Algemene Raad Van de Nederlandse Orde Van Advocaten (Raad Van de Balies Van de Europese Gemeenschap, Intervening)* [2002] ECR I 1577; Case C-519/04 P *Meca Medina v. Commission* 18 July 2006, Commission Decision *CECED*, OJ 2000 L187/47.

– and covers horizontal agreements between firms in the same industry and vertical agreements between companies along the supply chain. Article 101(1) provides that agreements, decisions and concerted practices which directly or indirectly fix purchase or selling prices or any other trading conditions may be caught. Such agreements have as their object the restriction of competition.[21] Competition may also be eliminated when firms agree to apportion particular markets between themselves. Geographical market-sharing agreements may be more effective than price-fixing from the cartel's point of view, because the expense and difficulties of fixing common prices are avoided. Such agreements are restrictive from the consumer's point of view since they diminish choice.[22] A further way in which a cartel might be able to earn supra-competitive profits is by agreeing to restrict its members' output.[23] Restrictive agreements include collusive tendering or bid-rigging, where the undertakings collaborate on responses to invitations to tender for the supply of goods and services.

Any form of entity which engages in economic activity will be considered by the Commission and the ECJ to be an undertaking.[24] The concept of undertaking covers corporations, partnerships, individuals, trade associations, liberal professions and state-owned corporations.[25]

Article 101(1) distinguishes three forms of collusion: agreements between undertakings (the concept of agreement includes contract, but is broader),[26] unilateral conduct (the general principle is that Article

[21] E.g. T-202/98, *Tale & Lyle v. Commission*, [2001] ECR II-2035.

[22] *Peroxygen Products* (Commission Decision 85/74), [1985] OJ L35/1, [1985] 1 CMLR 481; *Quinine Cartel* (Commission Decision 69/240), OJ L192/5, [1969] CMLR D41, 41/69; *ACF Chiemiefarma NV v. Commission*, [1970] ECR 661 *(Quinine Cartel)*, 40–48/73 *Suiker Unie v. Commission*, [1975] ECR 1663 (Sugar Cartel).

[23] *Peroxygen Products* (Commission Decision 85/74), [1985] OJ L35/1, [1985] 1 CMLR 481, *White Lead* (Commission Decision 79/90), [1979] OJ L21/16, [1979] 1 CLMR 464.

[24] C-41/90 *Höfner v. Elser v. Macroton GmbH*, [1991] ECR I-1979.

[25] C-159 & 160/91 *Christian Poucet v. Assurances Generals De France (AGP)* [1993] ECR I-637; *Reuter/BASF* 76/743/EEC, (1976) OJ L254/40; *UNITEL* 78/516/EEC, (1978) OJ L157/39; *Distribution of Package Tours during the 1990 World Cup* 92/521/EEC, (1992) OJ L326/31; *Coapi* 95/188, (1995) OJ L122/37; T-319/99, *FENIN v. Commission*, [2003] 5 CMLR 1; C-309/99, *Wouters, Save Bergh and Price Waterhouse v. Algemene Raad Van de Nederlandse Orde van Advocaten*, [2002] ECR I-1577; C-180/98, *P. Pavlov and Another v. Stichting Pensioenfond Medische Specialisten*, [2000] ECR I-6451; 170/83, *Hydrotherm v. Andreoli*, [1984] ECR 2999; C-73/95P, *Viho v. Commission*, [1996] ECR I-5457; 6 & 7/73 *Commercial Solvents*, [1974] ECR 223; C-497/99R, *Irish Sugar*, [2001] ECR I-5332.

[26] 41/69 *Chiemiefarma NV v. Commission*, [1970] ECR 661 (*Quinine Cartel*), T-1/89 *Rhone-Poulenc SA v. Commission (Polypropylene)* [1991] ECR II-867, *Hercules v. Commission*, [1991] ECR II-1711, *BP Kemi* 79/934/EEC, (1979) OJ L286/32, [1979] 3 CMLR 684.

101 applies to activities of two or more undertakings and is thereby to be distinguished from Article 102),[27] and decisions by associations of undertakings (such associations are typically trade associations but could also include other organizations). Decisions and recommendations would fall within the scope of Article 101(1).[28] In addition, Article 101 applies to concerted practices – forms of co-operation which are more amorphous than a formal oral or written agreement,[29] including concerted practice in vertical arrangements.[30] Horizontal agreements could result in elimination or restriction of *inter*brand competition; vertical agreements could result in elimination or reduction of *intra*brand competition.

The test for determining whether Community antitrust law is applicable is whether it 'may affect trade between Member States'. Community courts have established that three elements must be proven under this test.

An agreement confined to activities in a single member state may infringe Article 101(1) if there is an impact on cross-border economic activity involving at least two member states. The concept of trade is broad, and covers all economic activities related to goods and services. If behaviour can affect trade between member states then it is within the scope of the EC Treaty. The expression 'may affect' means that there is a reasonable probability that an agreement or practice will have an actual

[27] C-107/82 *AEG-Telefunken v. Commission*, [1983] ECR 3151, 25 & 26/84 *Ford Werke AG v. Commission*, [1985] ECR 2725, C-277/87 *Sandoz*, [1990] ECR I-45, T-41/96 *Bayer AG v. Commission*, [2000] ECR II-3383, Cases 56 and 58–64 *Établissements Consten Sàrl and Grundig-Verkaufs-Gmbh v. Commission of the European Economic Community*, [1966] ECR 299.

[28] 8/72 *Vereeniging van Cementhandelaren v. Commission*, [1972] ECR 977, *Coapi* 95/188, (1995) OJ L122/37, T-25/95 *Cimenteries et al.*

[29] *ICI v. Commission*, [1972] ECR 619 (Dyestuffs), *Cooperatieve 'Suiker Unie' UA v. Commission*, [1975] ECR 1663 (Sugar), T-49/95 *Van Megen Sports v. Commission*, [1996] ECR II-1799, 100/80 *Musique Diffusion Francaise v. Commission (Pioneer Case)* [1983] ECR 1825.

[30] C-89, 104, 114, 116, 117 and 125-129/85 *Wood Pulp – A Ahlstrom OY and others v. Commission*, [1988] ECR 5193, *Ferry operators – currency surcharge* 97/84/EEC, (1997) OJ L26/23, *Commission Guidelines on Vertical Restraints*, [2000] OJ C291/01, 26/76 *Metro v. Commission (No 1)* [1977] ECR 1875 paras. 20–1, *Consten and Grundig v. Commission*, [1966] ECR 299, [1966] CMLR 418, *STM v. Maschinenbau Ulm*, [1966] ECR 235, [1966] CMLR 357, *Stergios Delimitis v. Henninger Bräu*, [1991] ECR 1–935, [1992] 5 CMLR 210, *Ford v. Commission*, [1985] ECR 2725, [1985] 3 CMLR 528, *Viho v. Commission*, [1996] ECR I-5457, [1997] 4 CMLR 419, *Bayer v. Commission*, [2000] ECR II-3383, [2001] 4 CMLR 176; this judgment is on appeal to the ECJ, Cases C-2/01 P etc. *Commission v. Bayer, Metro v. Commission (No 1)* [1977] ECR 1875, [1978] 2 CMLR 1.

or potential influence on trade, either directly or indirectly. It is not required that the agreement or practice will have or has had an actual effect on trade.[31]

Finally, the action or agreement must have a potential appreciable effect on trade between member states. Appreciability is evaluated by considering the absolute turnover and market share of the companies involved in view of other market players.[32]

If an agreement is clearly designed to prevent, restrict or distort competition, then there will be no need to prove anti-competitive behaviour. Any such agreement will be a per se breach Article 101(1).[33] Otherwise, following a rule-of-reason approach, the effects of the conduct need to be assessed.[34] In the case of agreements that are assessed under a rule-of-reason approach, competition authorities and courts will determine their validity on the basis of a realistic assessment of their impact on competition.[35]

[31] See Commission Notice: Guidelines on the Effect on Trade Concept Contained in Article 101 and 82 of the Treaty. This document can be downloaded form the Commission's website at http://europa.eu.int/comm/competition/antitrust/legislation. See also the following cases: *STM v. Maschinenbau Ulm*, [1966] ECR 235, 8/72 *Vereeniging van Cementhandelaren v. Commission*, [1972] ECR 977, 246/86 *Belasco v. Commission*, [1989] ECR I-2117. Read the opinion of Advocate General Mischo at p. 2174, 193/83 *Windsurfing International v. Commission*, [1986] ECR 611, C-216/96 *Bagnasco (Italian Banks)* [1999] ECR I-135, 56 & 58/64 *Consten and Grundig v. Commission*, [1966] ECR 299, Case 56/65 *Société Technique Minière v. Maschinenbau Ulm Gmbh (Mbu)* [1966] ECR 235.

[32] *Völk v. Vervaecke*, [1969] ECR 295, see *Commision De minimis Notice on Agreements of Minor Importance*, 2001 OJ C368/13. This document can be downloaded from the Commission's website at http://europa.eu.int/comm/competition/antitrust/deminimis.

[33] 56/65 *STM v. Maschinenbau Ulm*, [1966] ECR 235, 56 & 58/64 *Consten & Grundig v. Commission*, [1966] ECR 299, 23/67 *Brasserie de Haecht SA v. Wilkin*, [1967] ECR 407, T-374, 375, 384, 388/94 *European Night Services v. Commission*, [1998] ECR II-3141, C-234/89 *Delimitis v. Henninger Brau*, [1991] ECR I-935.

[34] 26/76 *Metro SB-Grossmarkte v. Commission*, [1977] ECR 1875, 161/84 *Pronuptia de Paris v. Schillgalis*, [1986] ECR 353, T-112/99 *Metropole Television (M6) and Others v. Commission*, [2001] ECR II-2459, C-309/99 *Wouters v. Algemene Raad van de Nederlandsche Orde van Advocaten*, [2002] ECR I-1577.

[35] Cases at the Community level that, on the basis of a detailed effects analysis, have reversed the Commission's anti-competition analysis include Case T-328/03 *O2 (Germany) v. Commission*, judgment of 2 May 2006 and Case T-168/01 *GlaxoSmithKline Services v. Commission*, judgment of 27 September 2006.

1.2.2 Unilateral conduct

According to the wording of Article 102,[36]

> Any abuse by one or more undertakings of a dominant position within the common market or in a substantial part of it shall be prohibited as incompatible with the common market in so far as it may affect trade between Member States.
>
> Such abuse may, in particular, consist in:
>
> (a) directly or indirectly imposing unfair purchase or selling prices or other unfair trading conditions;
> (b) limiting production, markets or technical development to the prejudice of consumers;
> (c) applying dissimilar conditions to equivalent transactions with other trading parties, thereby placing them at a competitive disadvantage;
> (d) making the conclusion of contracts subject to acceptance by the other parties of supplementary obligations which, by their nature or according to commercial usage, have no connection with the subject of such contracts.

Article 66(7) of the ECSC Treaty was based on dominance.[37] The origins of the notion of dominance can be traced back to German competition law. The German competition law (the GWB) used the term 'dominance' in §22(1); it was a familiar concept due to the previous Abuse Regulation of 1923.[38] One reason for adopting the term 'dominance', rather than the term 'monopolization' which is used in the Sherman Act,[39] is the influence that the German competition law had on the drafter of the ECSC Treaty, Jean Monnet.

[36] This section draws from I. Kokkoris, *A Gap in the Enforcement of Article 102*, British Institute of International and Comparative Law, 2009.

[37] Article 66(7) was concerned with the concept of a dominant position: 'If the High Authority finds that public or private undertakings which, in law or in fact, hold or acquire in the market for one of the products within its jurisdiction a dominant position shielding them against effective competition in a substantial part of the common market are using that position for purposes contrary to the objectives of this Treaty, it shall make to them such recommendations as may be appropriate to prevent the position from being so used. If these recommendations are not implemented satisfactorily within a reasonable time, the High Authority shall, by decisions taken in consultation with the Government concerned, determine the prices and conditions of sale to be applied by the undertaking in question or draw up production or delivery programmes with which it must comply, subject to liability to the penalties provided for in Articles 58, 59 and 64.'

[38] Verordnung Gegen Missbrauch Wirtschaftlicher Machtstellungen, 1923, Reichsbesetzblatt, [R6B.1] I, 1067, 2 November 1923.

[39] 15 U.S.C. §2: Monopolizing trade a felony; penalty: 'Every person who shall monopolize, or attempt to monopolize, or combine or conspire with any other person or persons, to

The notion of dominance has been addressed both in law and in economics. In the realm of economics, dominance has been addressed by theories dealing with oligopolistic and monopolistic market structures. In the realm of law, the concept of dominance is found in two sets of legal provisions, namely Article 102[40] and the EC Merger Regulation (ECMR).[41] The legal definition of dominance has been an issue of intense debate which was laid down by the ECJ in *United Brands*.

The ECJ stated that

> The dominant position thus referred to (by Article [82]) relates to a position of economic strength enjoyed by an undertaking which enables it to prevent effective competition being maintained on the relevant market by affording it the power to behave to an appreciable extent independently of its competitors, customers and ultimately of its consumers.[42]

In *Hoffmann-La Roche*[43] the ECJ defined the notion of dominance as 'a position of economic strength enjoyed by an undertaking, which enables it to behave to an appreciable extent independently of its competitors, its customers and ultimately of consumers'.

The ECJ further stated in *Hoffman-La Roche*:

> Furthermore, although the importance of the market shares may vary from one market to another the view may legitimately be taken that very large shares are in themselves, and save in exceptional circumstances, evidence of the existence of a dominant position. An undertaking which has a very large market share and holds it for some time . . . is by virtue of that share in a position of strength . . .[44]

The statement from *Hoffman-La Roche* contains no definition of what is implied by the term 'some time'. Thus the lack of a consistent definition might result in arbitrary interpretation.

monopolize any part of the trade or commerce among the several States, or with foreign nations, shall be deemed guilty of a felony, and, on conviction thereof, shall be punished by fine not exceeding $10,000,000 if a corporation, or, if any other person, $350,000, or by imprisonment not exceeding three years, or by both said punishments, in the discretion of the court.'

[40] Articles 81 and 82 of the EC Treaty (ex 85 and 86 prior to the Treaty of Amsterdam which came into force on 1 May 1999). The EC Treaty was signed on 25 March 1957.

[41] Article 102 deals with the abuse of an already existing dominant position (*ex post*), whereas the ECMR deals with the prospective assessment of dominance (*ex ante*).

[42] Case 27/76, *United Brands Co. and United Brands Continental BV v. Commission*, [1978], ECR I-207. At §65.

[43] Case 85/76, *Hoffmann-La Roche & Co. AG v. Commission*, [1979] ECR I-461, at §38.

[44] Case 85/76 *Hoffman-La Roche & Co. AG v. Commission*, [1979] ECR-461 at §41.

The legal definition of dominance has been addressed by several cases brought before the ECJ. In *Continental Can*,[45] the Commission, in defining a 'dominant position', focused on the ability of entities to behave independently in making decisions that affect the market as a whole. Regarding its definition in merger cases, the formulation of the concept of dominance in *United Brands* was echoed in the ECJ's *Kali-Salz*[46] decision with respect to collective dominance.[47]

The legal definition of dominance as it has emerged through the case law still entails certain drawbacks. The essence of the ECJ's definition of dominance is the ability to act, to an appreciable extent, independently of competitors, customers and consumers. It is this essence that entails problems. One of the criticisms of the definition of dominance is that firms cannot act to an appreciable extent independently of their consumers due to the downward-sloping demand curve which implies that the higher the price of the product the lower the quantity demanded. We should note that this inverse relationship between price and quantity may not hold for products such as medicines that are price-inelastic, meaning that the increase in price may not affect the quantity demanded. This argument holds for both dominant and non-dominant firms, and as Azevedo and Walker argue, 'trying to define dominance with respect to the ability of a firm to behave to an appreciable extent independently of its consumers will not distinguish adequately between dominant and non-dominant firms'.[48]

[45] Case 6/72 *Europemballage Corp. and Continental Can Co. Inc. v. Commission (Continental Can)*, [1973] ECR I-215. At §3.

[46] Case M308 *Kali und Salz/MdK/Treuhand*, [1998] OJ C275/3; on appeal Cases 68/94 and C-30/95 *France v. Commission, Société Commerciale des Potasses et de l'Azore (SCPA) v. Commission*, [1998] ECR I-1375.

[47] See §221 of case C-68/94 and C-30/95 *France v. Commission, Société Commerciale des Potasses et de l'Azore (SCPA) v. Commission*, [1998] ECR I-1375. According to this paragraph, in the case of an alleged collective dominant position, the Commission is therefore obliged to assess, using a prospective analysis of the reference market, whether the concentration which has been referred to it leads to a situation in which effective competition in the relevant market is significantly impeded by the undertakings involved in the concentration and one or more other undertakings which together, in particular because of correlative factors which exist between them, are able to adopt a common policy on the market and act to a considerable extent independently of their competitors, their customers, and also of consumers.

[48] J.P. Azevedo and M. Walker, 'Dominance: Meaning and Measurement' (2002) 23(7) *ECLR* 363, at p. 364. Additional work on the same definition on dominance includes F. Dethmers and N. Dodoo, 'The Abuse of Hoffmann-La Roche: The Meaning of Dominance under EC Competition Law' (2006) 27(10) *ECLR* 537; A. Jones and B. Sufrin, *EC Competition Law*, 2nd ed., Oxford University Press, 2004, at p. 264; J. Church and

A further criticism relates to the difficulty of measuring the ability of firms to behave independently of competitors. Every firm that faces competitors (i.e. all firms apart from monopolists) is constrained to some extent by the conduct of these competitors. The pricing policy of even a dominant firm is dependent on the pricing of its competitors. A dominant firm will raise prices above the competitive level to a point that will be determined by its demand curve, as well as by the constraints imposed on the firm by its competitors' strategy. A firm's commercial decisions will take into account its rivals' likely reactions and it may adapt its strategy accordingly. So a dominant firm does not act independently of its competitors. This argument is also true in cases where the market is focused on other dimensions of competition, such as quality and innovation.[49]

Azevedo and Walker argue that the definition of dominance as was outlined in *United Brands* could be made more economically coherent by replacing 'behave to an appreciable extent independently' with 'restrained by the independent actions'.[50] They also suggest an approach that mitigates the drawbacks related to the definition of dominance in *United Brands*. They argue that dominance can be defined as the ability to restrict output substantially in the marketplace.[51] Dominant firms have power over price and thus, by restricting output in the market, decrease consumer welfare. According to the authors, focusing on output restriction is consistent with most of the standard factors that are usually considered relevant in the appraisal of dominance.[52] In addition, in cases where the observation of price and costs cannot be easily achieved, concentrating on the ability to reduce quantity may provide an alternative means of

R. Ware, *Industrial Organization Strategic Approach*, McGraw-Hill, 2000, at p. 603; L. Cabral, *Introduction to Industrial Organization*, The MIT Press, 2000, at pp. 72–5, I. Dobbs and P. Richards, 'Output Restriction as a Measure of Market Power' (2005) 26(10) *ECLR* 572.

49 As regards the possibility of firms lowering quality (and hence costs), but not price, up to the point at which further reductions in quality would not be profitable. As regards the possibility of firms slowing the pace of innovation (and hence R & D expenditure) as far as is consistent with maintaining long-run profits. See further J.P. Azevedo and M. Walker, Dominance: Meaning and Measurement, CRA Competition Policy Discussion Papers, 2001, pp. 1–8, at p. 4, available from www.crai.co.uk.

50 Azevedo and Walker 2002, at p. 366.

51 The authors clarify that the definition refers to the restriction of total output in the market below its current level.

52 Factors such as market shares, barriers to entry, barriers to expansion, spare capacity, substitute products. Azevedo and Walker 2002, at p. 6.

assessing dominance. Thus, according to the authors, this definition would be consistent with current practice and would have a firm economic foundation.

However, focusing the definition of dominance on the restriction of output may be considered too narrow and possibly inadequate to incorporate conduct that has an adverse impact on competition entailing limited or no output restriction. Adverse effects on competition can be induced due to, among other things, lower quality. Notwithstanding the criticisms mentioned above, for the purposes of this book dominance is defined according to the ECJ's definition in *United Brands*. In the context of Article 102,[53] as the ECJ in *Continental Can* argued, 'there is no need for a causal link to be established between the dominant position and the abuse. It is necessary only that the conduct strengthens the undertaking's dominant position and fetters competition on the market.'[54]

The International Competition Network (ICN) Unilateral Conduct Working Group (UCWG) was established in May 2006, and its primary objectives are to examine the challenges involved in addressing anticompetitive unilateral conduct of dominant firms and firms with market power, as well as to promote greater convergence and sound enforcement of laws governing unilateral conduct.[55] The respondents to the ICN Report cited two basic legal definitions of single-firm dominance / substantial market power – structural and behavioural. Behavioural definitions share a focus on a firm's appreciable freedom from competitive constraints or the ability to act in ways that a competitively constrained firm could not. The structural definition identifies substantial market power by an established market-share threshold that may allow for possible situation-specific deviations.

As regards the definition of 'abuse', although there is no definition of the concept in the legislation, the ECJ has on numerous occasions dealt

[53] On the contrary, as the ECJ confirmed in *Kali und Salz*, there must be a causal link between the creation or the strengthening of dominance under the original ECMR and the adverse impact on effective competition. This distinction in the necessity of the 'causal link' illustrates the different application of the dominance test under Article 102 and ECMR. Case M308 *Kali und Salz/MdK/Treuhand*, [1998] OJ C275/3; on appeal Cases 68/94 and C-30/95 *France v. Commission, Société Commerciale des Potasses et de l'Azore (SCPA) v. Commission*, [1998] ECR I-1375.

[54] Case 6/72 *Europemballage Corp. and Continental Can Co. Inc. v. Commission* (*Continental Can*), [1973] ECR I-215, at §§26–7.

[55] See www.internationalcompetitionnetwork.org/working-groups/current/unilateral.aspx.

with this concept; for instance, in *Continental Can*,[56] it stated that 'abuse may occur if an undertaking in a dominant position strengths such position in such a way that the degree of dominance reached substantially fetters competition [that] only undertakings remain in the market whose behaviour depends on the dominant one'.

In *Hoffmann-La Roche*,[57] the ECJ widened the concept by holding it to be an 'objective concept' relating to the behaviour of a dominant undertaking which influences the structure of the market thereby weakening competition through methods different from those of normal practice and having an effect of hindering the maintenance and the growth of competition. A dominant undertaking can protect its commercial interests, but the behaviour must be proportionate and not intended to strengthen the dominant position and thereby abuse it.[58]

As mentioned above, the definition of dominance contains two elements, the ability to prevent effective competition and the ability to behave independently. However, what is unclear is how these two elements relate to each other. From an economic perspective independent actions do not distinguish between dominant firms and non-dominant firms. No firm can act to an appreciable extent independently of its consumers or customers. This is because each firm is constrained by the demand curve it faces. Firms typically face downward-sloping demand curves, indicating that a firm can only charge a higher price if it is willing to make fewer sales. It is not open to the firm to raise prices and sell the same quantity as before. This argument holds both for a dominant and for a non-dominant firm.

Four requirements must be met for the application of Article 102. One or more undertakings must be in a dominant position, and such position must be held within the common market or a substantial part of it. In addition, there must be an abuse and this must have an effect on interstate trade.[59] Dominance is analysed in relation to three variables: the product market, the geographical market and the temporal

[56] *Europemballage Corp. and Continental Can Co. Inc. v. Commission (Continental Can)*, at §26.

[57] Case 85/76, *Hoffmann-La Roche & Co. AG v. Commission*, [1979] ECR I-461, at §91, repeated in e.g. Case 322/81, *Michelin v. Commission*, [1983] ECR 3461, at §70.

[58] See e.g. *Europemballage Corp. and Continental Can Co. Inc. v. Commission (Continental Can)*, at §189.

[59] A. Jones and B. Sufrin, *EC Competition Law: Text, Cases and Materials*, 2nd ed., Oxford University Press, 2004, at p. 255.

market.[60] Article 102 does not prohibit the existence of a dominant position, rather it only prohibits its abuse.[61]

The main types of abuse include: excessive pricing (*United Brands*),[62] predatory pricing (*AKZO*[63]),[64] discriminatory pricing (*United Brands*),[65]

[60] P. Craig and G. De Burca, *EU Law: Text, Cases and Materials*, 3rd ed., Oxford University Press, 2003, at p. 993.

[61] V. Korah, *An Introductory Guide to EC Competition Law and Practice*, 5th ed., Hart, 1994, at p. 83.

[62] On excessive pricing see, indicatively, D. Elliott, 'What is an Excessive Price?' (2007) 6(8) *Comp. L.I.* 13; S. Kon and S. Turnbull, 'Pricing and the Dominant Firm: Implications of the Competition Commission Appeal Tribunal's Judgment in the Napp case' (2003) 24(2) *ECLR* 70; M. Glader and S. Larsen, 'Article 102: Excessive Pricing' (2006) 5(7) *Comp. L.I.* 3; D. Geradin and M. Rato M., 'Excessive Pricing: In Reply' (2006) 5(10) *Comp. L.I.* 3; P. Oliver, 'The Concept of "Abuse" of a Dominant Position under Article 82 EC: Recent Developments in Relation to Pricing' (2006) 1(2) *Euro. C.J.* 315.

[63] Case C-62/86, *AKZO Chemie BV v. Commission*, [1991] ECR I-3359.

[64] On predatory pricing see indicatively: M. Gal, 'Below-Cost Price Alignment: Meeting or Beating Competition? The France Telecom Case' (2007) 28(6) *ECLR* 382; M. Gravengaard, 'The Meeting Competition Defence Principle – A Defence for Price Discrimination and Predatory Pricing?' (2006) 27(12) *ECLR* 658; P. Andrews, 'Is Meeting Competition a Defence to Predatory Pricing? The Irish Sugar Decision Suggests a New Approach' (1998) 49 *ECLR*; T. Eilmansberger, 'How to Distinguish Good from Bad Competition under Article 82 EC: In Search of Clearer and More Coherent Standards for Anti-Competitive Abuses' (2005) *CMLR* (PP) 129, OECD, Competition Policy Roundtable on Predatory Foreclosure, 15 March 2005, at pp. 1–279.

[65] On price discrimination/rebates see, indicatively, OECD, Competition Policy Roundtable on Loyalty and Fidelity Discounts and Rebates, 4 March 2003, at pp. 1–239; J.T. Lang, (2005) 'Fundamental Issues Concerning Abuse under Article 82 EC', Regulatory Policy Institute 19; J.T. Lang, 'Defining Legitimate Competition: How to Clarify Pricing Abuses under Article 102' (2002) *FILJ* 83; M. Lorenz, M. Lübbig and A. Russel, 'Price Discrimination: A Tender Story' (2005) *ECLR* 355; P. Akman, 'To Abuse, or Not to Abuse: Discrimination between Consumers' (2007) 32(4) *E.L. Rev.* 492; D. Gerard, 'Price Discrimination under Article 102(c) EC: Clearing up the Ambiguities' (July 2005) *Global Competition Law Centre Research Papers on Article 82 EC* 133; J.T. Lang and R. O'Donoghue, 'Defining Legitimate Competition: How to Clarify Pricing Abuses under Article 102 EC, (2002) 26 *Fordham International Law Journal* 83; M. Armstrong and J. Vickers, 'Price Discrimination, Competition and Regulation' (1993) 41 *Journal of Industrial Economics* 335; A. Perrot, 'Towards an Effects-Based Approach of Price Discrimination', in *The Pros and Cons of Price Discrimination*, Swedish Competition Authority, 2005; D. Ridyard, 'Exclusionary Pricing and Price Discrimination Abuses under Article 102: An Economic Analysis' (2002) 6 *ECLR* 286; M. Armstrong, Recent Developments in the Economics of Price Discrimination, October 2005 Working Paper, http://129.3.20.41/eps/io/papers/0511/0511004.pdf; R. Schmalensee, 'Output and Welfare Implications of Monopolistic Third-Degree Price Discrimination' (1981) 71 *American Economic Review* 242; H.R. Varian, 'Price Discrimination and Social Welfare' (1985) 75 *American Economic Review* 870; P. Muysert, 'Price Discrimination: An Unreliable Indicator of Market Power' (2004) 6 *ECLR* 350.

refusal to supply (*Commercial Solvents*[66]),[67] tying in (*Hilti*,[68] *Tetra Pak II*[69]),[70] loyalty rebates (*Hoffman-La Roche*), abuse of intellectual property

66 Cases 6 & 7/73, *Instituto Chemioterapico Italiano SpA and Commercial Solvents Corp. v. Commission (Commercial Solvents)* [1974] ECR 223.

67 On refusal to deal / essential facilities see, indicatively, C. Nagy, 'Refusal to Deal and the Doctrine of Essential Facilities in US and EC Competition Law: A Comparative Perspective and a Proposal for a Workable Analytical Framework' (2007) 32(5) *E.L. Rev* 664; D. Carlton, A General Analysis of Exclusionary Conduct and Refusal to Deal: Why Aspen and Kodak Are Misguided, NBER Working Paper No 8105, 2001, www.nber.org/papers/w8105; Z. Chen, T. Ross and W.T. Stanbury 'Refusals to Deal and Aftermarkets' (1998) 13 *Review of Industrial Organization* 131; B. Doherty, 'Just What Are Essential Facilities?' (2001) 38 *CMLR* 397; A. Jones, 'A Dominant Firm's Duty to Deal: EC and US Antitrust Law Compared', in Philip Marsden, ed., *Handbook of Research in Transatlantic Antitrust*, BIICL, 2006; J.T. Lang, 'Defining Legitimate Competition: Companies' Duties to Supply Competitors and Access to Essential Facilities' (1994) 18 *Fordham International Law Journal* 437; M. Lao, 'Aspen Skiing and Trinko: Antitrust Intent and Sacrifice' (2005) 73 *Antitrust Law Journal* 171; OECD, 'The Essential Facilities Concept', Background Note, OECD/GD(96)113; G. Robinson, 'On Refusing to Deal with Rivals' (2002) 87 *Cornell Law Review* 1177; A. Stratakis, 'Comparative Analysis of the US and EU Approach and Enforcement of the Essential Facilities Doctrine' (2006) 27 *ECLR* 434; J. Venit, 'Article 102: The Last Frontier – Fighting Fire with Fire?' (2005) 28 *Fordham International Law Journal* 1157.

68 Case T-30/89, *Hilti v. Commission,* [1991], ECR II-1439, confirmed C-53/92P, [1994] ECR I-666.

69 Case T-83/91, *Tetra Pak Rausing SA v. Commission (Tetra Pak II),* [1994] ECR II-755.

70 On tying and bundling see, indicatively, D. Spector, 'From Harm to Competitors to Harm to Competition: One More Effort, Please!', (2006) 2(1) *Euro. C.J.*, Supp. (special issue) 145; K.-U. Kuhn, R. Stillman and C. Caffarra, 'Economic Theories of Bundling and their Policy Implications in Abuse Cases: An Assessment in Light of the Microsoft Case' (2005) 1(1) *Euro. C.J.* 85; D. Ridyard, 'Tying and Bundling: Cause for Complaint?' (2005) 26(6) *ECLR* 316; M. Furse 'Article 102, Microsoft and Bundling, or "The Half Monti"' (2004) 3(3) *Comp. L.J.* 169; J. Tirole, 'The Analysis of Tying Cases: A Primer' (2005) 1 *Comp. Policy Int'l* 1; C. Bellamy and R. Child, *European Community Law of Competition*, 6th ed., Oxford University Press, 2008, paras. 10.119–10.120; Bishop and Walker, *The Economics of EC Competition Law*, 2nd ed., Sweet and Maxwell, 2002, at p. 209; B. Nalebuff, Bundling, Tying and Portfolio Effects, DTI Economics Paper No 1, February 2003; E. Iacobucci, Tying as Quality Control: A Legal and Economic Analysis, University of Toronto, Faculty of Law, Law and Economics Research Paper No 01–09, http://papers.ssrn.com/abstract=293602; W.S. Bowman, 'Tying Arrangements and the Leverage Problem' (1957) 67 *Yale L.R.* 19; K.N. Hylton and M. Salinger, 'Tying Law and Policy: A Decision-Theoretic Approach' 69 *Antitrust Law Journal* 469; C. Ahlborn, D.S. Evans and A. Jorge Padilla, 'The Antitrust Economics of Tying: A Farewell to Per Se Illegality' (Spring–Summer 2004) *Antitrust Bulletin* 287; D.W. Carlton and M. Waldman, 'The Strategic Use of Tying to Preserve and Create Market Power in Evolving Industries' (2002) 33 *Rand J. Econ.* 194; J. Carbajo, D. de Meza and D.J. Seidmann, 'A Strategic Motivation for Commodity Bundling' (1990) 38 *Journal of Industrial Economics* 283; D.J. Seidmann, 'Bundling as a Facilitating Device: A Reinterpretation of Leverage Theory' (1991) 58 *Economica* 491; Yongmin Chen, 'Equilibrium Product Bundling'

rights (*Magill*[71]) and vexatious litigation (*Promedia*[72]). As the judgment in *Continental Can* clarified, though,[73] Article 102 did not set out an exhaustive enumeration of the types of abuse of a dominant position prohibited by the EC Treaty.[74]

The concept of abuse is related to the behaviour of an undertaking which is such as to influence the degree of competition through methods different from those ensuring normal competition. Normal competition refers to a situation where an undertaking has a substantial market share resulting from efficient performance regarding quality of product or of service, and efficient marketing and distribution. The first two paragraphs of Article 102 refer to exploitative abuse of market power inducing harm to consumers. The final two refer to methods detrimental to consumers through their impact on effective competition structures.[75]

The existence of a dominant position is a necessary condition for application of Article 102; however, it is not necessary for there to be a link between dominance and abuse. As mentioned above, the CFI in *Continental Can* argued, 'there is no need for a causal link to be established between the dominant position and the abuse. It is necessary only that the conduct strengthens the undertaking's dominant position and fetters competition on the market'.[76] Consequently, a dominant undertaking can abuse its position without using the market power that the position confers, but by ordinary commercial practices also engaged

Footnote 70 (*cont.*)

(1997) 70 *J. Bus.* 85; R.P. McAfee, J. McMillan and M.D. Whinston, 'Multiproduct Monopoly, Commodity Bundling and Correlation of Values' (1989) 104 *Q.J. Econ.* 371; W.J. Adams and J.L. Yellen, 'Commodity Bundling and the Burden of Monopoly (1976) 90 *Q.J. Econ.* 475; R.L. Schmalensee 'Gaussian Demand and Commodity Bundling' (1984) 57 *J. Bus.* 211; M.A. Salinger, 'A Graphical Analysis of Bundling' (1995) 68 *J. Bus.* 85; K.-U. Kühn, R. Stillman and C. Caffarra, Economic Theories of Bundling and their Policy Implication in Abuse Cases: An Assessment in Light of the Microsoft Case, CEPR Discussion Paper No 4756 (2005), T.A. Lampert, 'Evaluating Bundled Discounts' (2004–5) 89 *Minn. L. Rev.* 1688, at pp. 1700–5; D.A. Crane, 'Multiproduct Discounting: A Myth of Nonprice Predation' (2005) 72 *U. Chi. L. Rev.* 27.

71 *Magill TV Guide*, [1989] OJ L78/43.

72 Case T-111/96, *ITT Promedia NV v. Commission (Promedia)*, [1998] ECR II-2937.

73 Case 72/71 *Re Continental Can Co. Inc.*, [1972] OJ L7/25.

74 See further *Europemballage Corp. and Continental Can Co. Inc. v. Commission (Continental Can)*, supra note 62, at §26.

75 *Europemballage Corp. and Continental Can Co. Inc. v. Commission (Continental Can)*, at §26.

76 *Europemballage Corp. and Continental Can Co. Inc. v. Commission (Continental Can)*, at §§26–7.

in by non-dominant undertakings.[77] The market on which the abusive conduct takes place need not be the same as that on which the dominant position is held.[78] Although the alleged abusive conduct is normally found on the dominated market, it may also be found on a distinct but closely associated market, likely to strengthen the position on the dominated market.[79]

The Commission issued guidelines on the enforcement priorities in Article 102 cases in an attempt to clarify its approach in the enforcement of Article 102.[80]

The enforcement guidelines are less 'radical' than the approach considered when reform of Article 102 was raised in the Discussion Paper.[81] The guidelines seek to distinguish between competition on the merits, which has beneficial effects for consumers and should therefore be promoted, and competition that is liable to lead to harmful foreclosure. The assessment of market power will be dependent on the dynamics of the market and on the extent to which products are differentiated. A 'soft' safe harbour of 40 per cent market share is established (in the 2004 BA/Virgin case). The Commission will also consider barriers to entry and countervailing buyer power. The Commission will only penalize conduct that is likely to harm competition, and ultimately consumers, rather than conduct that is likely to harm competitors. The Commission will examine direct evidence of any exclusionary strategy, including internal documents which may be helpful to interpret the dominant company's conduct. In assessing potentially abusive pricing conduct, the Commission will intervene if the behaviour excludes or impedes an 'as-efficient' competitor. A dominant firm will be able to rely on an 'efficiency' defence if conduct generates 'efficiencies' so that there is a net benefit to consumers. The burden of proof is on the dominant company.

[77] *Europemballage Corp. and Continental Can Co. Inc. v. Commission (Continental Can)*, at §27; Case 85/76, *Hoffmann-La Roche & Co. AG v. Commission*, [1979] ECR I-461, at §91 and §120.

[78] Case T-51/89, *Tetra Pak Rausing SA v. Commission (Tetra Pak I)* [1990] ECR II-309, [1991] 4 CMLR 334, §25.

[79] Case T-83/91, *Tetra Pak Rausing SA v. Commission (Tetra Pak II)*, [1994] ECR II-755, §§23–8.

[80] Guidance on the Commission's Enforcement Priorities in Applying Article 82 EC Treaty to Abusive Exclusionary Conduct by Dominant Undertakings. http://ec.europa.eu/competition/antitrust/art82/guidance.pdf.

[81] Guidance on the Commission's Enforcement Priorities in Applying Article 82 EC Treaty to Abusive Exclusionary Conduct by Dominant Undertakings. http://ec.europa.eu/competition/antitrust/art82/guidance.pdf.

National competition authorities have to apply Articles 101 and 102 when they are applying the respective national legislations. According to Article 3(1) of Regulation 1/2003,[82]

> Where the competition authorities of the Member States or national courts apply national competition law to agreements, decisions by associations of undertakings or concerted practices within the meaning of Article 81(1) of the Treaty which may affect trade between Member States within the meaning of that provision, they shall also apply Article 81 of the Treaty to such agreements, decisions or concerted practices. Where the competition authorities of the Member States or national courts apply national competition law to any abuse prohibited by Article 82 of the Treaty, they shall also apply Article 82 of the Treaty.

Article 3(2) of Regulation 1/2003 states that

> The application of national competition law may not lead to the prohibition of agreements, decisions by associations of undertakings or concerted practices which may affect trade between Member States but which do not restrict competition within the meaning of Article 81(1) of the Treaty, or which fulfil the conditions of Article 81(3) of the Treaty or which are covered by a Regulation for the application of Article 81(3) of the Treaty. Member States shall not under this Regulation be precluded from adopting and applying on their territory stricter national laws which prohibit or sanction unilateral conduct engaged in by undertakings.

Thus when an anti-competitive agreement or practice may have an effect on trade between member states, the national competition authorities and courts must apply Articles 101 and 102 to the conduct in addition to their national laws.

1.2.3 Merger assessment

The Treaty of Rome of 25 March 1957 (the EC Treaty)[83] did not provide any specific provision for the control of mergers. Articles 81 (or 101 after the Lisbon Treaty) and 82 (or 102 after the Lisbon Treaty) of the EC Treaty focus on controlling the behaviour of undertakings rather than on dealing with mergers. The European Commission (the Commission) steered by such omission sought to persuade the European Council (the

[82] See http://eur-lex.europa.eu/LexUriServ/LexUriServ.do?uri=OJ:L:2003:001:0001:0025:EN:PDF.

[83] The Treaty of Rome established the European Economic Community (EEC) and was signed by France, West Germany, Italy, Belgium, the Netherlands and Luxembourg (the latter three as part of the Benelux) on 25 March 1957.

Council) to enact a merger-control provision, while at the same time it attempted in some instances to apply Articles 101 and 102 to prevent anti-competitive conduct arising from some mergers.

The application of Articles 81 and 82 on mergers entails certain drawbacks. Motivated by such shortcomings the Council of Ministers of the EU,[84] on 21 December 1989, adopted Council Regulation 4064/89,[85] which came into force on 21 September 1990. Regulation 4064/89 is based both on Article 103, which provides for the making of Council Regulations to implement the provisions of Articles 101 and 102, which grants the Council the residual power to take appropriate measures where action proves necessary in order to attain one of the Commission's objectives and the EC Treaty has not provided the necessary powers.[86] The main aim of 4064/89 is to provide means for the prevention of anti-competitive concentrations as well as to provide a single framework (the 'one-stop-shop' principle[87]) within which such transactions can be assessed.[88]

According to Article 2(3) of 4064/89, 'a concentration which creates or strengthens a dominant position as a result of which effective

[84] The Council of the European Union forms, along with the European Parliament, the legislative arm of the European Union. The Council of the European Union contains ministers of the governments of each of the European Union member states.

[85] Council Regulation (EEC) 4064/89 of 21 December 1989 on the control of concentrations between undertakings, [1989] OJ L395/1, corrigendum, [1990] OJ LL257/14. Council Regulation (EC) No 1310/97 (OJ L 180, 9/7/97) amended 4064/89 on the control of concentrations between undertakings, focusing mainly on issues such as multiple notifications, joint ventures, remedies and referrals to member states.

[86] Articles 81, 82, 83 and 232 of the EC Treaty (ex 85, 86, 87 and 235 of the EC Treaty prior to the Treaty of Amsterdam). Pursuant to the Lisbon Treaty (EC Official Journal C 306/2 of 17 December 2007, p. 1), the provisions on anti-competitive agreements (formerly Article 81) are now in Article 101, abuse of dominance (formerly Article 82) now in Article 102, public undertakings (formerly Article 86) now in Article 106, and state aid (formerly Articles 87–8) now in Articles 107–8. The European Court of Justice is now the Court of Justice and the Court of First Instance is now the General Court. The terms European Court of Justice or ECJ and Court of First Instance or CFI will be used herein.

[87] According to the 'one-stop-shop' principle, a single authority, this being the Commission, assesses mergers having a Community dimension within a strict and short timetable and has exclusive Community-wide competence.

[88] The Commission will consider whether the adverse effect of the transaction on effective competition is transitory or permanent and will only initiate an investigation in the latter case, as the approach in *Aerospatiale* indicated. See further: Case No IV/M53 *Aerospatiale-Alenia/De Havilland*, [1991] OJ L 334/42, [1992] 4 CMLR M2. This case was the first prohibition decision concerning single dominance. See, further, D. Livingston and J. Scott, 'Competition Law and Practice', *FT Law & Tax*, 1995, at p. 768.

competition would be significantly impeded in the common market or in a substantial part of it shall be declared incompatible with the common market'. A merger may lead either to unilateral effects or to co-ordinated effects. These two effects are mutually inconsistent,[89] since non-co-ordinated effects (or unilateral effects) arise when the merged group enjoys market power without depending for its success and profitability on co-ordinated interaction with other the firms in the market, whereas co-ordinated effects depend on the successful co-ordinated interaction of the merged entity with the other firms in the market. A merger may lead either to the post-merger firm unilaterally engaging in anti-competitive conduct or to the remaining firms after the merger collectively co-ordinating their behaviour.

Article 1(4) of 4064/89 required the Commission to report to the Council before 1 July 2000 on the operation of the thresholds and on the criteria for determining whether a concentration has a Community dimension. The Commission submitted a report which considered several jurisdictional, procedural and substantive issues that needed to be addressed. The Commission published these issues in a Green Paper in December 2001.[90] In December 2002 the Commission published its proposals for reform of 4064/89,[91] together with a draft notice on the appraisal of horizontal mergers,[92] as well as draft best practices on the conduct of EC merger control proceedings.[93] The draft notice was the response of the Commission to a widespread demand for enhanced legal certainty surrounding the Commission's merger decisions. The reforms aimed at clarifying the criteria applied by the Commission in the appraisal of concentrations in situations where the undertakings

[89] Europe Economics, 'Study on Assessment Criteria for Distinguishing between Competitive and Dominant Oligopolies in Merger Control' (2001), europa.eu.int/comm/enterprise/library/lib-competition/libr-competition.html, at pp. vi, 62, 63.

[90] See, further, Green Paper on the Review of Council Regulation (EEC) No 4064/89, COM(2001) 745/6, 11 December 2001. It should be noted that the Commission issued a Green Paper rather than a White Paper. Green Papers are typically issued at an early stage in the legislative process, setting out the various options for change under discussion and establishing the overall framework of debate.

[91] Proposal for a Council Regulation on the control of Concentrations between Undertakings, COM/2002/0711 final – CNS 2002/0296. Official Journal C 020, 28 January 2003 pp. 4–57.

[92] Commission Notice on the appraisal of horizontal mergers under the Council Regulation on the control of concentration between undertakings, COM/2002, 11 December 2002.

[93] See DG Competition Best Practices on the conduct of EC merger control proceedings, available from the DG Competition website at europa.eu.int/comm/competition/index_en.html.

concerned are active sellers in the same relevant market or potential competitors in that market (horizontal mergers).[94]

The analysis continues with the reforms proposed in the Green Paper and adopted in the Council Regulation (EC) No 139/2004 of 20 January 2004 on the control of concentrations between undertakings (the ECMR).[95] The new regulation entered into force in May 2004, coinciding with the expansion of the EU from fifteen to twenty-five member states. The reform aimed at improving the parties' rights of defence and the Commission's decision-making process,[96] both essential for the application of the ECMR especially in an enlarged EU of twenty-five member states. The ECMR reform further aimed at minimizing transaction costs for firms through the 'one-stop-shop' principle, and at augmenting the transparency and the speediness of the assessment procedure of concentrations, leading thus to enhanced legal certainty.

The adopted reforms concerned procedural, jurisdictional and substantive issues. This part of this chapter will deal with the substantive reforms and will only briefly address the jurisdictional and procedural reforms. The substantive proposed reforms concerned the change from the dominance test to the substantial lessening of competition (SLC) test. The Commission proposed, and the Council accepted, an altered version of the dominance test in the ECMR as the substantive legal standard for assessing mergers.[97] The Commission considered that the aim of improving legal certainty and enhancing transparency regarding the scope of the dominance test is best served by clarifying the ECMR itself. The new test is outlined in Article 2(3) of the ECMR, which states that 'a concentration which would significantly impede effective competition, in the common market or in a substantial part of it, in particular

[94] For further details on the history of the debate concerning the change of the legal substantive test see, further, K. Fountoukakos and S. Ryan, 'A New Substantive Test for EU Merger Control' (2005) 5 *ECLR* 277. For a definition of the concept of horizontal as well as of vertical and conglomerate mergers see the relevant section of this chapter below on the Guidelines on the Assessment of Horizontal Mergers under the Council Regulation on the Control of Concentrations between Undertakings, Official Journal C 31, 5 February 2004, pp. 5–18 (Horizontal Merger Guidelines or Guidelines).

[95] Official Journal L 24, 29 January 2004, pp. 1–22: the 'recast ECMR'.

[96] William, Cutler and Pickering, 'The European Commission Adopts Merger Control Reform Package' (2002), www.wilmerhale.com/files/Publication/7178d077-068a-4bd2-9976-cb2dcf73db4d/Presentation/PublicationAttachment/bef3d442-7bcc-48a2-99a9-50a85b9c7490/ACFD854.pdf.

[97] Official Journal L 24, 29 January 2004, pp. 1–22, 139/2004.

as a result of the creation or strengthening of a dominant position, shall be declared incompatible with the common market'.[98] Thus the creation or strengthening of a dominant position is only one example, although the principal example, of a significant impediment to effective competition. The significant impediment to effective competition (SIEC) test is a hybrid of the dominance test and the SLC test. The new legal substantive test is regarded as a compromise between the two tests.[99]

There was considerable debate in the Council, with Germany, Italy and the Netherlands being in favour of the current dominance test whereas the United Kingdom, Ireland and Sweden preferred a move to SLC. Denmark and Portugal supported the Commission's proposal, while France and Spain suggested a compromise wording based on their own domestic tests. Finally, the Franco-Spanish compromise prevailed, supplemented by a last-minute German addition to a recital which provided that the SIEC test will only be applied to non-dominance situations for the purpose of catching non-collusive oligopolies.[100] Since most EU member states adhere to the dominance test it would have been unreasonable for the Commission to switch to the SLC test, since such a move would inhibit the harmonization of national competition laws and would enhance legal uncertainty.

The legal substantive test in the ECMR, the SIEC test, is intended to fill the perceived 'gap' in the dominance test which was illustrated by such cases as *Airtours* and *Heinz*.[101] The 'gap' corresponds to the situation where the post-merger entity's market share falls below the level required for dominance but the merger may lead to unilateral effects. Recital 25 of the ECMR states that the notion of the SIEC test 'should be interpreted as extending, beyond the concept of dominance, only

98 Article 2(3), Council Regulation (EC) No 139/2004 of 20 January 2004 on the control of concentrations between undertakings (the EC Merger Regulation), (139/2004), Official Journal L 24, 29 January 2004, pp. 1–22.

99 For a fuller analysis of the reforms as well as of the debate between the 'dominance test' and the 'substantial lessening of competition' test that the Green Paper induced see I. Kokkoris, 'The Reform of the European Control Merger Regulation in the Aftermath of the Airtours Case: The Eagerly Expected Debate: SLC v. Dominance Test' (2005) 26(1) *ECLR* 37.

100 When interpreting provisions of regulations and directives, the European courts look at the aim of the provision and frequently examine recitals to elicit that aim. It is therefore likely that the German amendment will have the effect of narrowing the plain meaning of the SIEC test. See, further, www.internationallawoffice.com/ld.cfm?Newsletters__Ref=7850#substantive.

101 Case T-342/99 *Airtours v. Commission*, [2002] 5 CMLR 317; US District Court, Columbia, *FTC v. HF Heinz Company et al.*, 00–5362a (2000).

to the anti-competitive effects of a concentration resulting from the non-co-ordinated behaviour of undertakings which would not have a dominant position in the market concerned'.[102] According to this Recital, the SIEC test extends, in a disciplined way, beyond dominance, and makes clear that the new test covers non-co-ordinated effects, thus rectifying the problem of the 'gap'. In the formulation of Recital 25, the Commission has attempted to enhance legal certainty by creating the impression that the interpretation of the SIEC test is compatible with former court judgments.[103]

Even though the new wording of the legal substantive test rectifies the 'gap', the application of the SIEC test may be quite wide and allow increased scrutiny of smaller transactions between smaller firms in concentrated markets, where the reduction in the number of players may lead to a possible reduction in competition due to the loss of competitive constraints on the remaining firms in the post-merger market. Although the wording used in the new provision could be read as extending the reach of the ECMR further than the SLC test would have,[104] Voigt and Schmidt argue the SIEC test, in rectifying the 'gap', does not make European merger policy more restrictive; however, it gives the Commission more discretion in its assessment of concentrations. According to Voigt and Schmidt, the enhancement of the restrictiveness of European merger policy due to the introduction of the new substantive test is mitigated and balanced by the explicit introduction of the efficiency defence,[105] including the failing-firm defence. However, both the new test and the efficiency defence increase the Commission's discretion and, hence, make merger policy less predictable.

Apart from substantive reforms there were also procedural and jurisdictional reforms adopted in the ECMR. An extensive account of

[102] Recital 25 of Council Regulation (EC) No 139/2004 of 20 January 2004 on the control of concentrations between undertakings (the EC Merger Regulation), (139/2004), OJ L 24, 29 January 2004, pp. 1–22. See also I. Kokkoris (2009), 'Was There a Gap in the ECMR', in *Concurrences*, 1–2009.

[103] S. Voigt and A. Schmidt, 'Switching to Substantial Impediments to Competition (SIC) can have substantial costs' (2004) *ECLR* 25(9) 584, at p. 587.

[104] Using such wording as 'appreciable' rather than 'substantial', as well as a reference to foreclosure of competitors. See further William, Cutler and Pickering, 'The European Commission Adopts Merger Control Reform Package' (2002), available at www.wilmerhale.com/files/Publication/7178d077-068a-4bd2-9976-cb2dcf73db4d/Presentation/PublicationAttachment/bef3d442-7bcc-48a2-99a9-50a85b9c7490/ACFD854.pdf.

[105] See further Voigt and Schmidt 2004, at p. 589.

these reforms is outside the scope of this chapter. Procedural changes included enhanced flexibility for companies in deciding when to file merger notifications, allowing firms to better organize their transactions without being obliged to fit their planning around unnecessary regulatory rigidities and deadlines for Commission decisions. In addition, amendments to the time schedule provide more time to the Commission to consider remedies proposed by firms (this 'stop-the-clock' provision will operate at the parties' request). In combination with the new regulation for the enforcement of Articles 81 and 82 (or 101 and 102 after the Lisbon Treaty) – that is, Council Regulation 1/2003[106] – the procedural and jurisdictional reforms to the ECMR strengthen the Commission's enforcement powers.

Regarding jurisdictional issues, a pre-notification process would determine the allocation of jurisdiction between the Commission and national competition authorities (NCAs) and would tackle the phenomenon of intra-EU multi-jurisdictional filings, whilst at the same time enhancing the effectiveness of the 'one-stop-shop' principle according to which parties may request the Commission to take jurisdiction in cases where the turnover thresholds are not met but the merger needs to be notified to at least three member states. The 'one-stop-shop' principle is essential for the efficient application of the ECMR, especially in the enlarged EU.[107]

Apart from substantive procedural and jurisdictional reforms, the Commission also published Guidelines on the Assessment of Horizontal Mergers under the Council Regulation on the Control of Concentrations between Undertakings (EU Guidelines).[108] The Commission, with its EU Guidelines, aims to clarify the criteria it would apply in the assessment of concentrations under the ECMR. The next section will provide a detailed analysis of the EU Guidelines.

[106] Council Regulation (EC) No 1/2003 of 16 December 2002 on the implementation of the rules on competition laid down in Articles 81 and 82 of the Treaty, Official Journal L 1, 4 January 2003, at pp. 1–25.

[107] See further William, Cutler and Pickering 2002.

[108] Guidelines on the Assessment of Horizontal Mergers under the Council Regulation on the Control of Concentrations between Undertakings, Official Journal C 31, 5 February 2004, at pp. 5–18. Although the Commission's notices and guidelines are not legally binding, they strongly indicate the Commission's position on a variety of important issues. In this chapter we analyse the failing-firm defence as regards horizontal mergers. We argue, though, that the same principles that apply to the failing-firm defence in horizontal mergers apply to vertical and conglomerate mergers.

1.2.4 *The Horizontal Merger Guidelines*

In a world of multiple sovereign jurisdictions there is no guarantee that all jurisdictions will adopt the same approach in the assessment of a concentration. The Horizontal Merger Guidelines (the EU Guidelines) help expose similarities and differences such as diverse approaches to market definition and entry conditions, various analyses of co-ordinated and non-co-ordinated effects, and different treatment of efficiencies. Such an exposure is a first step towards harmonization of merger legislation across different jurisdictions.

The Commission issued the EU Guidelines setting out the Commission's approach to transactions commonly known as horizontal mergers, clarifying the applicability of the ECMR and explaining the economic rationale the Commission employs in assessing horizontal mergers. Before analysing the EU Guidelines, it is useful to define briefly the concepts of horizontal, vertical and conglomerate mergers that will be used throughout in this book.[109]

Horizontal mergers are mergers between parties who operate in the same relevant market. Such mergers can increase the market power of the merging firms so that they can unilaterally impose a profitable post-merger price increase. Other firms in the market might raise their prices in response, also unilaterally. Thus rivalry might weaken. Moreover, a horizontal merger may increase the likelihood (and/or stability and sustainability) of collusion, either tacit or explicit, between the remaining firms in the market.

Vertical mergers are mergers between parties who operate at different levels of an industry. Such mergers, though often pro-competitive, may in some circumstances reduce competitive constraints faced by the merged firm as a result of increased barriers to entry, raising rivals' costs, causing substantial market foreclosure or increasing the likelihood of collusion. This risk is, however, unlikely to arise except in the presence of existing market power or in markets where there is already significant vertical integration as well as vertical restraints.

Conglomerate mergers are mergers between firms in apparently unrelated markets which would rarely significantly impede effective

[109] For the respective definitions, see further ICN Merger Working Group, Analytical Framework Sub-group, 'The Analytical Framework for Merger Control', final paper for ICN annual conference on 28–9 September 2002, Office of Fair Trading, London, available at www.internationalcompetitionnetwork.org/afsguk.pdf.

competition. However, in some jurisdictions, mergers of this type have been found to create competition problems, such as through the exercise of 'portfolio power'.

The EU Guidelines describe both the theoretical basis and the analytical methodology for evaluating the potential for anti-competitive effects resulting from a horizontal merger. More importantly, in line with the desire to improve economic reasoning, the EU Guidelines focus on the nature of the analysis needed to identify the competitive constraints that each of the merging parties currently poses on the other. The aim is to provide greater predictability with a view to increasing legal certainty for all parties concerned.

The EU Guidelines explore the possible anti-competitive effects of horizontal mergers and consider the main ways in which a horizontal merger may significantly impede competition. By eliminating the competitive constraints between the parties, a horizontal merger may allow the merged firm to increase its prices regardless of the response of its remaining competitors, and thus may lead to non-co-ordinated effects. In addition, a horizontal merger may lead to co-ordinated effects by creating an environment favourable to sustainable tacit collusion, thus reducing the effectiveness of competition and consequently leading to price increases.

It has been argued that the new substantive test and the accompanying EU Guidelines are an indication of the Commission's likely intention to adopt a more interventionist approach towards mergers. The EU Guidelines widen the potential scope of the ECMR below the traditional threshold associated with findings of single-firm dominance. By removing the safe harbour previously implicit in the definition of single-firm dominance, the EU Guidelines may be regarded as implying that the Commission will intervene in a significantly large number of transactions.

The purpose of the ECMR is to sustain an effective and well-functioning internal market by effectively ensuring that reorganizations in the market will not have any anti-competitive impact on markets. Mergers eliminate any competition that exists between the merging parties and reduce the number of firms competing in the market. Where this reduction has a substantial effect on overall market competition, the market will be less oriented to consumer and efficiency goals, even in the absence of breaches of competition law.

In order to assess the impact of a merger on the structure of competition, a number of elements are taken into account, including the market position of the merging companies, the existence and degree of actual and potential competition, demand and supply trends, barriers to entry, the buying power of customers of the relevant goods and services, the interests of intermediate and ultimate consumers, and the development of technical and economic progress provided that it is to consumers' advantage and does not form an obstacle to competition.[110] In addition, efficiencies resulting from the merger and the existence of failing firms among the merging parties will also be taken into account.

The European Commission has also issued guidelines for the assessment of non-horizontal mergers.[111] The Commission admits that the majority of vertical and conglomerate mergers do not raise problems, and they can bring about efficiency gains that benefit both businesses and consumers. The Guidelines provide examples, based on established economic principles, of where vertical and conglomerate mergers may significantly impede effective competition in the markets concerned. For instance, they outline the circumstances under which a vertical merger could be likely to result in competing companies being denied access to an important supplier or facing increased prices for their inputs and thus ultimately lead to higher prices for consumers.[112] The Guidelines also indicate levels of market share and concentration below which the Commission is unlikely to identify competition concerns (so-called 'safe harbours'). This will help interested parties to identify such mergers more easily.[113]

Advocate Kirschner, in the opinion in *Tetra Pak*,[114] argued that there are substantial differences between the elements that comprise US and EU law, resulting in problems that one jurisdiction faces not having a counterpart in the other jurisdiction. After the analysis of competition legislation in the EU, this chapter turns now to the analysis of US antitrust legislation.

[110] Article 2(1)b of Regulation 139/2004.

[111] Guidelines on the Assessment of Non-Horizontal Mergers under the Council Regulation on the Control of Concentrations between Undertakings, Official Journal C 265, 18 October 2008.

[112] See the Commission's press release at http://europa.eu/rapid/pressReleasesAction.do?reference=IP/07/1780.

[113] The text of the Guidelines is available on the Commission's website at http://ec.europa.eu/comm/competition/mergers/legislation/legislation.html.

[114] T-51/89 *Tetra Pak Rausing SA v. Commission*, [1991] 4 CMLR 334, at 343–4.

1.3 The United States of America

The Sherman Act of 1890 is frequently considered the origin of competition law. Senator Sherman himself acknowledged this fact when he stated that the bill did 'not announce a new principle of law, but applies old and well-recognized principles of the common law to the complicated jurisdiction of our State and Federal Government'.[115]

Following the American Civil War, large trusts emerged in industries such as railroads, petroleum, sugar, steel and cotton. These trusts and combinations were deemed to be responsible for the unfair prices and wages paid to farmers. This led to concern about the impact of anti-competitive conduct on growth, and then to the enactment of the Sherman Act of 1890. The Sherman Act is a broad prohibition of structural anti-competitive arrangements, such as business trusts, monopolistic combinations and certain mergers. The Sherman Act carries criminal sanctions. It also permits private suits for treble damages (note that if the government brings and wins an action, a plaintiff can use that victory to pursue their own damages – it is prima facie evidence of a violation) as well as injunctive relief.

Faced with the question of how to restrict the interpretation of the broad terms of the Sherman Act, the Supreme Court initially, in *United States v. Joint Traffic Association*,[116] employed the concept of ancillary restraints.[117]

In 1911 in *Standard Oil v. United States*,[118] the Supreme Court adopted a rule-of-reason approach. Chief Justice White's statement of the rule of reason, as outlined in *Standard Oil* and *American Tobacco*

[115] Cited in M. Furse, *Competition Law of the EC and UK*, Oxford University Press, 2006, p. 3.

[116] *United States v. Joint Traffic Association*, (1898) 171 U.S. 505, 568.

[117] R. Bork, 'The Rule of Reason and the Per Se Concept: Price Fixing and Market Division' (January 1966) 75(3) *Yale Law Journal* 373, notes that a horizontal market-division or price-fixing agreement should be lawful when four conditions are met: the agreement accompanies a contract integration (the co-ordination of other productive or distributive efforts of the parties), the agreement is ancillary to the contract integration (capable of increasing the integration's efficiency and no broader than required for that purpose), the aggregate market share of the parties does not make restriction of output a realistic threat, and the parties have not demonstrated that their primary purpose was the restriction of output. If either of the first two conditions is not met, the agreement is properly classified as illegal per se. When a horizontal group agrees to employ vertical restraints the legality of the vertical restraints should be judged by whether the horizontal agreement meets the four conditions above.

[118] *Standard Oil v. United States*, (1911) 221 U.S. 1.

Co. v. United States,[119] includes three tests: the per se concept, the intention of the parties and the effect of the agreement. According to Bork the three tests are better viewed as guides for the litigation process than as logically separate criteria. Bork maintains that there is only one test, which is the effect of the agreement.[120] Bork stresses that the misuse of the per se concept destroys efficiency and hence misallocates resources. Bork even notes that the extending the per se concept may have the same adverse impact on consumers as do cartel agreements.[121]

A review of the cases decided by the US courts indicates that the courts generally did not apply the rule of reason to cartel agreements. The courts started applying the rule of reason in 1927 with *United States v. Trenton Potteries*,[122] wherein the Supreme Court held that the rule-of-reason test, as applied in trusts,[123] is not also applicable to price-fixing agreements (cartels). This view was confirmed in several cases, including *United States v. Socony Vacuum Oil*,[124] *American Tobacco Co. v. United States*[125] and *United States v. Paramount Pictures*.[126] *Appalachian Coals, Inc. v. United States*[127] is one of the small number of cases where the Supreme Court adopted a rule-of-reason approach. This case involved price-fixing under emergency circumstances in the coal industry.

The Supreme Court has applied a two-tiered analysis to the assessment of an antitrust action. First, the Court examines the facts to determine whether the purpose for such conduct is itself anti-competitive by analysing its impact on the competitive market. Horizontal arrangements, such as price-fixing, are per se illegal. For conduct that is not per se illegal the Court may assess any pro-competitive effects of a conduct and balance them against likely anti-competitive effects of that conduct. A court will not apply the rule of reason to the case if under the first step of the analysis such an arrangement is deemed a per se violation. It should be emphasized that the adoption of the per se or rule-of-reason approach depends upon the outlook of the particular Supreme Court

[119] *American Tobacco Co. v. United States*, (1946) 328 U.S. 781 .

[120] Bork 1966.

[121] Ibid.

[122] *United States v. Trenton Potteries*, (1927) 273 U.S. 392.

[123] *Standard Oil v. United States*, (1911) 221 U.S. 1 ; *United States v. American Tobacco*, (1911) 221 U.S. 106.

[124] *United States v. Socony Vacuum Oil*, (1940) 310 U.S. 150.

[125] *American Tobacco Co. v. United States*, (1946) 328 U.S. 781.

[126] *United States v. Paramount Pictures*, (1948) 334 U.S. 131.

[127] *Appalachian Coals, Inc. v. United States*, (1933) 288 U.S. 344.

justices. Grendell argues that according to the US statutes free competition is paramount. The US rule of reason merely balances the benefits and burdens on competition.[128]

Congress has utilized the exemption approach by enumerating certain classes that are exempt from the antitrust statutes. Congressional exemptions can be awarded to individual enterprises or entire categories of restrictive arrangements.

In 1914, Congress enacted the Clayton Act (1914, 15 U.S.C. §§12–27), which enumerated certain types of practice as being illegal under the Sherman Act. The Clayton Act addresses price discrimination (§2), tying and exclusive dealing (§3), mergers (§7) and interlocking directorates (§8). The price-discrimination section of the Clayton Act was amended by the Robinson-Patman Act of 1936.

In addition, §5 of the FTC Act enables the Federal Trade Commission (FTC) to capture conduct that cannot be addressed by the Sherman Act.[129] According to Section 5 of the FTC Act,

> Unfair methods of competition unlawful; prevention by Commission
> (a) Declaration of unlawfulness; power to prohibit unfair practices; inapplicability to foreign trade
>   (1) Unfair methods of competition in or affecting commerce, and unfair or deceptive acts or practices in or affecting commerce, are hereby declared unlawful.
>   (2) The Commission is hereby empowered and directed to prevent persons, partnerships, or corporations, except banks, savings and loan institutions described in section 57a(f)(3) of this title, Federal credit unions described in section 57a(f)(4) of this title, common carriers subject to the Acts to regulate commerce, air carriers and foreign air carriers subject to part A of subtitle VII of title 49, and persons, partnerships, or corporations insofar as they are subject to the Packers and Stockyards Act, 1921, as amended (7 U.S.C. 181 et seq.), except as provided in section 406(b) of said Act (7 U.S.C. 227(b)), from using unfair methods of competition in or affecting commerce and unfair or deceptive acts or practices in or affecting commerce.
>   (3) This subsection shall not apply to unfair methods of competition involving commerce with foreign nations (other than import commerce) unless (A)

[128] T.J. Grendell, 'The Antitrust Legislation of the United States, the European Economic Community, Germany and Japan' (January 1980) 29(1) *International and Comparative Law Quarterly* 64, available at www.jstor.org/stable/758753.

[129] For a more detailed analysis of the FTC Act see Kokkoris 2009.

– such methods of competition have a direct, substantial, and reasonably foreseeable effect –
(i) on commerce which is not commerce with foreign nations, or on import commerce with foreign nations; or
(ii) on export commerce with foreign nations, of a person engaged in such commerce in the United States; and
(B) such effect gives rise to a claim under the provisions of this subsection, other than this paragraph. If this subsection applies to such methods of competition only because of the operation of subparagraph (A)(ii), this subsection shall apply to such conduct only for injury to export business in the United States.

Commissioner Leibowitz mentions that Senator Cummins of Iowa, one of the main proponents of the FTC Act, emphasized that the reason for the law was 'to go further and make some things offenses' that were not condemned by the antitrust laws. He added that 'the only purpose of Section 5 [is] to make some things punishable, to prevent some things, that cannot be punished or prevented under antitrust law'.[130] And Leibowitz adds that 'Congress could have simply given the Commission the ability to enforce the Sherman Act. But it didn't. Instead, the plain text of the statute makes it clear that Congress intended to create an agency with authority that extended well beyond the limits of the antitrust laws.'

The US courts in cases such as *Keppel Brothers*,[131] *FTC v. Brown Shoe Company*[132] and *FTC v. Motion Picture Advertising Service Company*[133] have affirmed the ability of the FTC to apply the FTC Act.

In *FTC v. Sperry & Hutchinson*, Justice White, speaking for a unanimous view of the Court, posed and answered two questions:

> The question [of the reach of Section 5] is a double one: first, does Section 5 empower the Commission to define and proscribe an unfair competitive practice, even though the practice does not infringe either the letter or the spirit of the antitrust laws. Second, does Section 5 empower the Commission to proscribe practices as unfair or deceptive in their effect upon consumers regardless of their nature or quality as competition? We think the statute, its legislative history and prior cases compel an affirmative answer to both questions.

130 J. Leibowitz, 'Tales from the Crypt', FTC Workshop on Section 5, 17 October 2008, available at www.ftc.gov.

131 *FTC v. R.F. Keppel & Bros., Inc.*, (1934) 291 U.S. 304, 310.

132 *FTC v. Brown Shoe Co.*, (1966) 384 U.S. 316, 321.

133 *Federal Trade Commission v. Motion Picture Advertising Service Co.*, (1953) 344 U.S. 392.

> Legislative and judicial authorities alike convince us that the Federal Trade Commission does not arrogate excessive power to itself if, in measuring a practice against the elusive, considers public values beyond simply those enshrined in the letter or encompassed in the spirit of the antitrust laws.[134]

The Supreme Court's decision in this case adopted an expansive reading of section 5 of the FTC Act. The Supreme Court held that §5 enabled the FTC to 'define and proscribe an unfair competitive practice, even though the practice does not infringe either the letter or the spirit of the antitrust laws' and to 'proscribe practices as unfair or deceptive in their effect on competition'.[135]

In addition, the majority Statement for the FTC in the Matter of Negotiated Data Solutions LLC states that the Act reaches 'not only practices that violate the Sherman Act and other antitrust laws, but also practices that the Commission determines are against public policy for other reasons'.[136]

Salinger argues that §5 can fill in gaps left by the other statutes.[137] As examples of such gaps he mentions invitations to collude, as well as facilitating practices. He adds that because §2 outlaws only monopolization, another possible gap in the Sherman Act is anti-competitive behaviour that creates market power short of monopoly. This is very similar to the

[134] *FTC v. Sperry & Hutchinson*, (1972) 405 U.S. 223, 239, 244. The Court in *FTC v. Brown Shoe Co.*, (1966) 384 U.S. 316, 321, stated that this 'broad power of the Commission is particularly well established with regard to trade practices which conflict with the basic policies of the Sherman Act and Clayton Acts even though such practices may not actually violate these laws'. In *FTC v. Independent Federation of Dentists*, (1986) 476 U.S. 447, 454, the Court observed that the standard for 'unfairness' under the FTC Act is, 'by necessity, an elusive one, encompassing not only practices that violate the Sherman Act and the other antitrust laws, but also practices that the Commission determines are against public policy for other reasons'. See further D. Balto (2008), 'A Section 5 Enforcement Agenda that even Bill O'Reilly Could Love', FTC Workshop on Section 5, 17 October 2008, available at www.ftc.gov.

[135] Supreme Court decision, at 239.

[136] See Statement of the Commission, in the matter of Negotiated Data Solutions LLC, F.T.C. File No 051 0094 (January 23, 2008), available at www.ftc.gov/os/caselist/0510094/080122statement.pdf; dissenting statement of Chairman Majoras, in the matter of Negotiated Data Solutions LLC, F.T.C. File No 051 0094 (January 23, 2008), available at www.ftc.gov/os/caselist/0510094/080122majoras.pdf; dissenting statement of Commissioner Kovacic, in the matter of Negotiated Data Solutions LLC, F.T.C. File No 051 0094 (January 23, 2008), available at www.ftc.gov/os/caselist/0510094/080122kovacic.pdf.

[137] Remarks of Michael Salinger at the FTC Workshop on Section 5, 17 October 2008, www.ftc.gov.

gap in Article 102 due to its inability to apply to anti-competitive conducts of non-dominant firms. He adds that when the FTC uses §5 alone, it should do so to attack anti-competitive behaviour that falls into gaps left by the Sherman and Clayton Acts.

US antitrust law can be enforced concurrently by the courts and by the FTC, which has been given extensive administrative powers to prevent adverse impact on competition. The statutes subject violators to criminal prosecution under the Sherman Act and civil liability under both the Sherman and Clayton Acts.

1.3.1 Anti-competitive agreements

According to the wording of section 1 of the Sherman Act (Trusts, etc., in restraint of trade illegal; penalty),

> Every contract, combination in the form of trust or otherwise, or conspiracy, in restraint of trade or commerce among the several States, or with foreign nations, is declared to be illegal. Every person who shall make any contract or engage in any combination or conspiracy hereby declared to be illegal shall be deemed guilty of a felony, and, on conviction thereof, shall be punished by fine not exceeding $10,000,000 if a corporation, or, if any other person, $350,000, or by imprisonment not exceeding three years, or by both said punishments, in the discretion of the court.

In assessing criminal responsibility under the Sherman Act, the Court has had to arrive at approximations and to test the 'good' against the 'bad', reaching wide decisions of guilty or not guilty, which often could not prevent the specific antisocial practices pursued.[138]

In *United States v. United States Shoe Machinery Co. of New Jersey*,[139] the question arose whether that company had monopolized or attempted to monopolize. United States Shoe Machinery maintained its position through a leasing system penalizing those who used the machines of other companies by refusing the use of their own patented

[138] M. Tobriner and L. Jaffe, 'Revision of the Anti-Trust Laws' (September 1932) *California Law Review* 20(6) 585, at p. 594, mention an article by J.L. Young, 'Who Shall Administer the Anti-Trust Laws?' (1930) 147 *Annals* 171. James L. Young tells the authors of a friend who sat on a jury in an antitrust suit for damages and told him, 'We were so dazed by the deluge of evidence and the uncertainty of the term "restraint of trade" that we had to find for the defendant.' The case was apparently a clear one of liability. See also *Pulpwood Co. v. Green Bay Paper Co.*, (1919) 168 Wis. 400, 411, 170 N. W. 230, 235.

[139] *United States v. United States Shoe Machinery Co. of New Jersey*, (1918) 247 U.S. 32, 38 Sup. Ct. 473.

machines. The Court could not find enough harmful intent therein to counterbalance the absence of wrongful intent in the general existence of the company, which it was unwilling to declare a monopolistic conspiracy. The ideal solution would have allowed the company to continue intact and to have done away with the abuse of the leasing system. As it was, the Court was intent on deciding whether the shoe company was or was not a criminal.

Tobriner and Jaffe argue that the 'rule of reason' was devised in answer to the contention that it was absurd to hold every restraint of trade illegal no matter how harmless it might be and in the face of the fact that though at common law all covenants to compete were called in 'restraint of trade' they were only condemned when unreasonable.[140]

For conduct which violates the antitrust laws, where even its perpetrators know it is illegal and will seek under all circumstances to keep it secret, the punitive principle is appropriate. But the legality of many plans, having nothing fraudulent or immoral in them, may turn on questions of degree, particularly if non-monopolistic price agreements may under some circumstances be within the 'rule of reason'. Economic progress may be mitigated due to uncertainty whether legal conduct will lead to criminal penalties.

According to the Sherman Act, conducts that are per se illegal include horizontal price-fixing (*Socony*),[141] horizontal market division, group boycotts and tying arrangements (if substantial – *International Salt*,[142] *Northern Pacific*[143]).

In the early years of the Sherman Act there was no significant case law. In 1910, in the *Standard Oil*[144] and *American Tobacco* cases,[145] the Court announced the 'rule of reason', that the act only applied to unreasonable restraints. Due to the adoption of the 'rule-of-reason' approach, the assessment of a given conduct may differ based on subjective reasons. Thus the Sherman Act is rarely used to pursue criminal sanctions.

Section 1 of the Sherman Act forbids contracts, conspiracies, agreements and so on that are in restraint of trade; therefore, for there to be a

140 Tobriner and Jaffe 1932, at p. 594. See also *Pulpwood Co. v. Green Bay Paper Co.*, (1919) 168 Wis. 400, 411, 170 N. W. 230, 235.

141 *United States v. Socony-Vacuum Oil Co., Inc.*, (1940) 310 U.S. 150.

142 *International Salt Co., Inc. v. United States*, (1947) 332 U.S. 392.

143 *Northern Pacific Railway Co. v. United States*, (1942) 316 U.S. 346.

144 *Standard Oil Co. of New Jersey v. United States*, (1910) 221 U.S. 1.

145 *American Tobacco Co. v. Werckmeister*, (1907) 207 U.S. 284.

§1 violation, there must be at least two parties involved (i.e. not *restraints* but *agreements in restraint* of trade).

In the early case of *United States v. Trans-Missouri Railroad* (1897),[146] eighteen railroads agreed to set rates west of the Mississippi River. The Court found a violation of §1 and noted that courts will not look to reasonableness.

In *United States v. Addyston Pipe & Steel* (1899; 6th Cir.),[147] pipe manufacturers entered an agreement to raise prices for three-quarters of the US market. The Court held that agreements among competitors not to compete were prohibited unless they were 'merely ancillary' to a legitimate transaction. An interesting paradox is that after this case the railroad companies started merging, but there was no Sherman Act action.

In *United States v. Joint Traffic Association* (1898),[148] the Court held that the Sherman Act's application must be 'reasonable'. Only contracts with 'direct and immediate effect' were an actionable restraint of trade.

The rule-of-reason approach was developed through a number of cases. In *Standard Oil v. United States* (1910) Standard Oil coerced railroads into giving it preferential rates. The Court used this case to outline the rule-of-reason approach. The Court stated that only 'unduly' restrictive agreements or those with a bad 'inherent nature or effect' were prohibited.

In *Chicago Board of Trade v. United States* (1918),[149] the 'call rule' prohibited purchasing grain after the market closed for any price other than the closing price. The Court said that according to the rule-of-reason approach the agreement's effect on competition is assessed. In this case, the Court argued that the conduct related to one type of commodity and one stock exchange and thus the harm to competition was minimal.

In *United States v. Trenton Potteries* (1927),[150] vitreous pottery makers agreed to fix prices and limit their output, and the Court argued that the §1 violation was met if the agreement (rather than the prices) was unreasonable.

In *United States v. Socony Vacuum Oil* (1940),[151] large oil companies agreed to buy surplus oil, resulting from overproduction, from small

[146] *United States v. Trans-Missouri Freight Association*, (1897) 166 U.S. 290.

[147] *Addyston Pipe & Steel Co. v. United States*, (1899) 175 U.S. 211.

[148] *United States v. Joint Traffic Association*, (1898) 171 U.S. 505.

[149] *Chicago Board of Trade v. United States*, (1918) 246 U.S. 231.

[150] *United States v. Trenton Potteries Co.*, (1927) 273 U.S. 392.

[151] *United States v. Socony-Vacuum Oil Co., Inc.*, (1940) 310 U.S. 150.

oil producers in order to raise oil prices. The Court established the per se illegality of horizontal price-fixing. The Court emphasized that what was important was conspiring to fix prices, not whether prices were ultimately fixed. The Court distinguished prior cases. It distinguished *Chicago Board of Trade* due to the fact that the conduct was not designed to affect prices and only affected a small part of the trading market.

In *Arizona v. Maricopa County Medical Society* (1987),[152] 1,700 physicians agreed on the maximum price they would charge insurance companies for their services, to help the insurance companies evaluate risk. The Court found that the agreement was a per se violation since it involved horizontal price-fixing.

In *National Society of Professional Engineers v. United States* (1978),[153] the Court held that there had been a violation evaluated under the rule of reason and argued that only pro-competitive effects were valid justifications under the rule. This case narrowed the rule-of-reason approach to pro-competitive justifications.

According to the case law concerning §1 of the Sherman Act, an agreement includes a spectrum of action, from express agreements to interdependent behaviour to entirely independent action.

In *Interstate Circuit v. United States* (1939),[154] the Court found that acceptance by competitors, knowing that concerted action is contemplated, of an invitation to participate in a plan the necessary consequence of which, if carried out, is restraint of interstate commerce is sufficient to establish an unlawful conspiracy under the Sherman Act.

American Column & Lumber v. United States (1921)[155] involved facilitating practices. The American Hardwood Manufacturer's Association had an 'open competition plan' which acted as a clearing-house for current and future prices as well as for production data.

In *United States v. Container Corp. of America* (1969),[156] corrugated box manufacturers agreed to exchange past, current and future price data, but there was no agreement to adhere to those prices. The Court found that there was a per se violation, because the effects of the agreements were to stabilize prices, which was considered to be per se illegal.

[152] *Arizona v. Maricopa County Medical Soc.*, (1982) 457 U.S. 332.
[153] *National Society of Professional Engineers v. United States*, (1978) 435 U.S. 679.
[154] *Interstate Circuit, Inc. v. United States*, (1939) 306 U.S. 208.
[155] *American Column & Lumber Co. v. United States*, (1921) 257 U.S. 377.
[156] *United States v. Container Corp.*, (1969) 393 U.S. 333.

1.3.2 Unilateral conduct

We turn briefly now to §2 of the Sherman Act, which prohibits three things: monopolization, attempt to monopolize and conspiracy to monopolize. Monopoly as such is not condemned by common law or by the Sherman Act. When it results from 'normal growth' it does not offend the law. 'Monopolization' (prohibited by the Sherman Act) is the act of controlling a market.

The wording of §2 of the Sherman Act (Monopolizing trade a felony; penalty) is as follows:

> Every person who shall monopolize, or attempt to monopolize, or combine or conspire with any other person or persons, to monopolize any part of the trade or commerce among the several States, or with foreign nations, shall be deemed guilty of a felony, and, on conviction thereof, shall be punished by fine not exceeding $10,000,000 if a corporation, or, if any other person, $350,000, or by imprisonment not exceeding three years, or by both said punishments, in the discretion of the court.

Early cases that have to do with monopolization included *Standard Oil v. United States* (1910),[157] where predatory pricing was alleged. In *United States v. Aluminum Co. of America*,[158] ALCOA had a monopoly on 'virgin' ingot production. The Court found that ALCOA's conduct was monopolization, and was thus a violation of §2.

ALCOA is also the largest case in the history of antitrust by every measure except cost. Four Supreme Court justices had to recuse themselves because of their involvement in the case earlier in their careers. ALCOA had over 90 per cent of the nation's aluminium sales and all of the nation's ingot production. The origin of the monopoly becomes important in this assessment.

Justice Hand argued that a company that acquires a monopoly position via means other than industry, skill and foresight has monopolized. In other words, there must be some exclusion of competitors, something other than 'natural' growth. The Court added that the intent was clearly to exclude competitors. According to *ALCOA*, to commit the offence of monopolization one has to have a monopoly plus some accompanying bad conduct – conduct which shows no motive except to exclude others.

[157] *Standard Oil Co. of New Jersey v. United States*, (1910) 221 U.S. 1.
[158] *ALCOA S. S. Co. v. United States*, 338 U.S. 421 (1949).

In *ALCOA*, the Court broke the company up, forcing divestiture of some of its plants. Whatever remedy is used, it is geared toward three things: ending the combination or conspiracy, depriving the defendant of the benefit of the combination or conspiracy and rendering the monopoly power impotent.

In *United States v. United Shoe Machinery* (1954) (Dist. Ct.),[159] United Shoe had a market share of between 75 and 85 per cent of all shoemaking machinery. United Shoe leased, rather than sold, its machines. The Court held that the lease-only agreement was a violation of §2. The Court gave three possible interpretations of what constitutes a §2 violation: an undertaking's monopoly power and conduct violating §1, an undertaking's power to use any exclusionary practice and actual exercise of that power, and finally an undertaking's overwhelming market power which is not the result of skill, industry or foresight.

According to the *United Shoe* case, practices not otherwise in violation of the antitrust laws can violate §2 if they are in conjunction with enhanced market power.

Referring briefly to important case law, the *United States v. Grinnell Corp.* (1966)[160] case defined the monopolization offence as possession of a monopoly in the relevant market, and wilful acquisition or maintenance of that power (as opposed to growth from a superior product, business acumen or accident).

Two of the most common antitrust monopolization allegations are predatory pricing and refusal to deal. As regards predatory pricing, the Areeda approach has been adopted in every circuit after the publication of a very influential article.[161] In *Barry Wright Corp. v. ITT Grinnell Corp.* (1983, 1st Cir.) the Court adopted the Areeda approach.

In *Brooke Group Ltd v. Brown & Williamson Tobacco* (1993), Ligget sued B&W over its pricing of generic cigarettes but the Court held that there was no violation. Court stipulated use of the Areeda-Turner predatory pricing theory and argued that the ability to recoup losses needs to be proved.

Section 2 renders attempts to monopolize an antitrust offence. To prove such an offence one must have both the intent to commit the attempt to monopolize and a dangerous probability of success. In *Lorain*

[159] *United Shoe Machinery Corp. v. United States*, (1954) 347 U.S. 521.

[160] *United States v. Grinnell Corp.*, (1966) 384 U.S. 563.

[161] P. Areeda and D. Turner, 'Predatory Pricing and Related Practices under Section 2 of the Sherman Act' (1975) 88 *Harv. L. Rev.* 697.

Journal v. United States (1951), a newspaper refused to sell advertising to anyone buying advertising on a new radio station. The Court argued that *Lorain Journal* was guilty of an attempt to monopolize. This case was not a case of monopolization due to a radio station which had entered the market recently and led *Lorain Journal* to attempt to regain its market position.

In *Spectrum Sports v. McQuillan* (1993),[162] the Court found that there must be some degree of market power for liability for attempts to monopolize. Case law seems to imply that 40 to 50 per cent was not enough market power for attempt-to-monopolize cases and that a market share of higher than 50 per cent would make a claim more likely to succeed.

Turning briefly to the Clayton Act, this Act prohibits (in §3) making a sale of goods with a condition not to deal in a competitor's goods, where the effect is to substantially lessen competition or to tend to create a monopoly. The Clayton Act is more prohibitive than the Sherman Act in aiming to prevent acts from becoming Sherman violations. The Clayton Act, §2, restricts price discrimination. In *Standard Oil Co. of California v. United States (Standard Stations)* (1949),[163] Standard Oil sold to stations with the requirement that they only purchased their gasoline from Standard. The Court argued that Standard Oil had about 6.7 per cent of the California market and concluded that this was a violation of §3 of the Clayton Act.

1.3.3 *Merger Assessment*

The assessment of whether the planned merger would significantly increase concentration and result in a concentrated market and whether the merger, in the light of concentration, raises concern about potential harmful competitive effects, is based on the SLC test. The 1992 Horizontal Merger Guidelines (hereafter US Guidelines)[164] reflect the analytical framework of analysis of horizontal mergers under US merger law. Section 7 of the 1914 Clayton Antitrust Act[165] (15 U.S.C. §18) prohibits mergers and acquisitions that may substantially lessen competition or tend to create a monopoly.

[162] *Spectrum Sports v. McQuillan*, (1993) 506 U.S. 447.

[163] *Standard Oil Co. of California v. United States*, (1949) 337 U.S. 293.

[164] 1992 Horizontal Merger Guidelines, available at www.usdoj.gov/atr/public/guidelines/horiz_book/toc.html.

[165] The Clayton Antitrust Act comprises §§12, 13, 14–19, 20, 21, 22–7 of Title 15 of the U.S.C. Some sections have been edited or eliminated because of space concerns.

According to §7 (Acquisition by one corporation of stock of another),

> No person engaged in commerce or in any activity affecting commerce shall acquire, directly or indirectly, the whole or any part of the stock or other share capital and no person subject to the jurisdiction of the FTC shall acquire the whole or any part of the assets of another person engaged also in commerce or in any activity affecting commerce, where in any line of commerce or in any activity affecting commerce in any section of the country, the effect of such acquisition may be substantially to lessen competition, or to tend to create a monopoly.
>
> No person shall acquire, directly or indirectly, the whole or any part of the stock or other share capital and no person subject to the jurisdiction of the FTC shall acquire the whole or any part of the assets of one or more persons engaged in commerce or in any activity affecting commerce, where in any line of commerce or in any activity affecting commerce in any section of the country, the effect of such acquisition, of such stocks or assets, or of the use of such stock by the voting or granting of proxies or otherwise, may be substantially to lessen competition, or to tend to create a monopoly.

The government gains its authority to review mergers and acquisitions before the parties are allowed to consummate the transaction under §7A of the Clayton Act (15 U.S.C. §18a), or the Hart-Scott-Rodino Antitrust Improvements (HSR) Act of 1976.[166] Although §7 of the Clayton Act refers to mergers that may 'lessen' competition, mergers that worsen the competitive situation of markets that already exhibit weak competition and mergers that, while preserving the status quo, forestall future competition will also be prohibited.[167] Under the wording of §7, it is not necessary to prove that the competition has been restrained; it is enough that it 'may' tend to substantially lessen competition. A transaction could also be challenged on the basis that it is an agreement in restraint of trade (§1 of the 1890 Sherman Antitrust

[166] See http://profs.lp.findlaw.com/mergers. According to the FTC website (www.ftc.gov), the Hart-Scott-Rodino (HSR) Act established the federal pre-merger notification programme, which provides the FTC and the Department of Justice with information about large mergers and acquisitions before they occur. The parties to certain proposed transactions must submit pre-merger notification to the FTC and the DOJ. Pre-merger notification involves completing an HSR form, also called a 'Notification and Report Form for Certain Mergers and Acquisitions', with information about each company's business. The parties may not close their deal until the waiting period outlined in the HSR Act has passed, or the government has granted early termination of the waiting period.

[167] OECD, 'Substantive Criteria Used for the Assessment of Mergers', available at www.oecd.org/dataoecd/54/3/2500227.pdf, at p. 295.

Act[168]) or alternatively that it is an 'unfair method of competition' (§5 of the Federal Trade Act).[169]

The 1992 Horizontal Merger Guidelines provide the analysis of merger enforcement and aim at providing guidance in the planning of mergers. The Department of Justice (DOJ) first released merger guidelines in 1968, which needed to be replaced due to developments in legal and economic thinking about mergers. In 1982, the DOJ released revised merger guidelines which were significantly different to the 1968 guidelines and in 1984 the DOJ issued a refinement of the 1982 Guidelines. The 1992 Horizontal Merger Guidelines clarify certain aspects of the 1984 Merger Guidelines that proved to be ambiguous or were interpreted by observers in ways that were inconsistent with the actual policy of the agencies.[170]

In order for the antitrust authorities to assess the anti-competitive impact of a merger they must determine the products that belong in the same market as the products of the merging firms. Market definition and the evaluation of market shares and concentration provide the starting framework for analysing the competitive impact of a proposed merger.

When determining whether a product can be substituted for another product, the agencies will consider evidence of whether the buyers perceive the products as substitutes, the price movements in the products involved, similarities or differences in design and use of the products, consumer preferences, the seller's perception of the substitutability of the products, and the barriers and costs associated with switching demand to potential substitutes. For each product market, the enforcement agencies must identify the geographic markets in which the firms sell their products. When determining whether geographic substitutability exists, the agencies will consider diversion of orders to other areas, basic demand characteristics, views of customers and competitors, the shipment patterns of the merging firms and competitors, and the barriers and switching costs associated with diverting orders to companies located in other areas and the excess capacity of firms outside the location of the merging firms.

Market power for a seller is the ability profitably to maintain prices

[168] 15 U.S.C. §1–7.

[169] Global Legal Group, 'The European and US Merger Control Rules: Issues for Private Equity Investors' (2006), available at www.sjberwin.com/media/pdf/publications/eu/mergercontrol2006.pdf.

[170] See www.ftc.gov/bc/docs/horizmer.htm.

above competitive levels for a significant period of time.[171] Once the product and geographic markets have been established, the individual market shares of the merging firms are examined. Market concentration is a function of the number of firms in a market and their respective market shares. The Herfindahl–Hirschman Index (HHI) is used for the calculation of market concentration. The HHI is calculated by summing the squares of the individual market shares of all the participants. Thus a market with only one participant (a pure monopoly) will have the HHI of 10,000, while a market with ten equal participants will have an HHI of 1,000. If there were only four firms in a particular market, each with 25 per cent of the market, the HHI would be 2,500 ($25^2 \times 4$). Any market with an HHI of over 1,800 is considered highly concentrated, between 1,800 and 1,000 the market is considered moderately concentrated, and below 1,000 the market is considered to be unconcentrated.

Mergers producing an increase in the HHI of more than fifty points in highly concentrated markets will raise significant antitrust concerns. A merger that increases the HHI by more than one hundred points in highly concentrated markets is considered to create market power and is likely to be challenged by the enforcement agencies.[172]

In addition, a merger is unlikely to create or enhance market power if entry into the relevant market is relatively easy. For entry to be considered a sufficient competitive constraint on the merging parties it must be shown to be likely, timely (within two years) and sufficient to deter or defeat any potential anti-competitive effects of the merger. Under the US Guidelines, the enforcement agencies will also examine whether there exists a lessening of competition through either 'co-ordinated interaction' or 'unilateral effects'. If a merger does not pose a serious threat to competition, it is unlikely to be challenged. If a substantial threat is present, however, the enforcement agencies will assess whether net efficiencies (e.g. economies of scale, cost reductions and/or technological advancements) outweigh the likely adverse impact on competition.

In the US, the agencies take an economically driven, consumer welfare approach to merger review whereby the agencies evaluate the likely net effect of a transaction on price and output. The agencies assess whether the merger, in light of market concentration and other factors that characterize the market, raises concern about potential adverse competitive effects. A merger may diminish competition by enabling the incumbent

[171] OECD, 'Substantive Criteria Used for the Assessment of Mergers', at p. 293.

[172] See http://profs.lp.findlaw.com/mergers.

firms more successfully and more completely to engage in co-ordinated interaction that harms consumers.[173]

After the analysis of the legislation in the EU and the US, this chapter will provide a brief analysis of the competition legislation in the UK. Similar to the analysis of the EU and the US legislation, the aim is to present the basis of the application of competition legislation in the UK.

1.4 United Kingdom

There are events and developments under the English common law which could be considered the root of competition law. At the time of the Magna Carta (in 1215), legislation provided that all monopolies were to be contrary to the law because of their harmful effect on individual freedom. The common-law doctrine of restraint of trade provided that covenants in restraint of trade were not enforceable.[174] Between the late nineteenth century and 1948, UK monopolies were not assessed. In February 1918, the minister of reconstruction appointed a special committee to investigate trusts in England in order to suggest means necessary to safeguard the public interest due to probable extension of trade organizations and combinations. The committee suggested that the Board of Trade should obtain information relating to trusts and combinations and report annually to Parliament. In addition, a tribunal of between three and seven members would be set up to which complaints by the Board of Trade would be referred (following an investigation in order to assess whether public interest would be harmed). This tribunal would recommend remedial action to the state in cases of harm to public interests.[175] In 1947 legislation was enacted for assessing anti-competitive conduct.

The core of the regulation of anti-competitive behaviour in UK domestic law is closely modelled upon EC law. Chapters I and II of the Competition Act 1998 are almost identical to Articles 101 and 102 of the Lisbon Treaty. UK courts and agencies are instructed to apply those

[173] OECD, 'Substantive Criteria Used for the Assessment of Mergers', at p. 293.

[174] *John Dyer's Case* (1414) YB 2 Hen 5. This is the first case on record of restraint of trade. The *Horner v. Graves* (1831 131 ER 284) case focused on the public interest as the test for assessing restraint of trade. The *Utopia* (1516) case was where the word 'monopoly' was first used. M. Furse, 2006, at p. 4.

[175] W. Notz, 'Recent Developments in Foreign Anti-Trust Legislation' (December 1924) 34(2) *Yale Law Journal* 159, available at www.jstor.org/stable/788664.

provisions in a way that achieves consistency with EC law.[176] UK merger control law also retains the distinctive character that it has enjoyed since its introduction in 1964. The principal features that set it apart from the ECMR are the facts that notification is voluntary and that the concept of a concentration includes the acquisition of material influence.[177]

As regards anti-competitive conduct (anti-competitive agreements, unilateral conduct), the functions of the Office of Fair Trading (OFT) include the investigation of competition law infringements and the adoption of decisions to punish and prohibit such infringements.[178] Complementary to the OFT, there are a number of sectoral regulators who have parallel powers to enforce competition law within their sectors.[179] The OFT's and the other regulators' decisions are reviewable by the Competition Appeals Tribunal (CAT).[180] Section 60 of the Competition Act ensures that questions arising under UK competition law are dealt with in a manner which is consistent with the treatment of corresponding questions arising in EC law. The obligation to follow analysis of the European Commission has been addressed in *Iberian U.K. Ltd v. BPB Industries plc*, and *Crehan v. Inntrepreneur Pub Co.*

As far as merger control is concerned, the central figures are the OFT, which has competence to conduct the first-phase assessment of a merger, and the Competition Commission (the Commission), which has responsibility for conducting second-phase merger investigations and determining the remedies required where it concludes that a merger gives rise to a substantial lessening of competition. In addition, it conducts second-phase merger reviews.[181] The Secretary of

[176] Competition Act 1998, §60. The analysis draws from B. Alan, 'United Kingdom', in I. Kokkoris, *Competition Cases from the European Union: The Ultimate Guide to Leading Cases of the EU and All 27 Member States*, Sweet and Maxwell, 2007.

[177] The concept of material influence captures influence that is weaker than that required to establish control for the purpose of EC law.

[178] OFT decisions are available from www.oft.gov.uk. Competition Commission decisions are available at www.competition-commission.org.uk.

[179] Principal examples are the Office of Communications (Ofcom), with responsibility in this respect for telecommunications; the Gas and Electricity Markets Authority (Ofgem); the Water Services Regulation Authority (Ofwat); and the Office of the Rail Regulator (ORR).

[180] Further information and judgments are available at www.catribunal.org.uk.

[181] See §§188 and 189. In addition, the provisions for market investigations by the Competition Commission have no equivalent in EC law. The Enterprise Act 2002, §§131 et seq., provides for the investigation of markets which may present structural or behavioural anti-competitive features. The Competition Commission can impose remedies where it establishes that such features exist.

State may assume a decisive role in cases of 'exceptional public interest', currently limited to those that concern national security, financial stability and the media. The Lloyds/HBOS merger, which will be analysed in this book, provides an example of an issue of 'exceptional public interest'.

1.4.1 *Anti-competitive practices*

In the UK, anti-competitive practices are mainly prescribed in Chapter I of the Competition Act 1998. The relevant parts of this chapter read as follows:

> Competition Act 1998, Part I, Chapter I – Agreements
> Section 2: Agreements etc. preventing, restricting or distorting competition
>
> (1) Subject to section 3, agreements between undertakings, decisions by associations of undertakings or concerted practices which
>   (a) may affect trade within the United Kingdom, and
>   (b) have as their object or effect the prevention, restriction or distortion of competition within the United Kingdom, are prohibited unless they are exempt in accordance with the provisions of this Part.
>
> (2) Subsection (1) applies, in particular, to agreements, decisions or practices which
>   (a) directly or indirectly fix purchase or selling prices or any other trading conditions;
>   (b) limit or control production, markets, technical development or investment;
>   (c) share markets or sources of supply;
>   (d) apply dissimilar conditions to equivalent transactions with other trading parties, thereby placing them at a competitive disadvantage;
>   (e) make the conclusion of contracts subject to acceptance by the other parties of supplementary obligations which, by their nature or according to commercial usage, have no connection with the subject of such contracts.
>
> (3) Subsection (1) applies only if the agreement, decision or practice is, or is intended to be, implemented in the United Kingdom.
>
> (4) Any agreement or decision which is prohibited by subsection (1) is void.
>
> (5) A provision of this Part which is expressed to apply to, or in relation to, an agreement is to be read as applying equally to, or in relation to, a decision by an association of undertakings or a concerted practice (but with any necessary modifications).
>
> (6) Subsection (5) does not apply where the context otherwise requires.

(7) In this section 'the United Kingdom' means, in relation to an agreement which operates or is intended to operate only in a part of the United Kingdom, that part.
(8) The prohibition imposed by subsection (1) is referred to in this Act as 'the Chapter I prohibition'.

Section 3: Excluded agreements

(1) The Chapter I prohibition does not apply in any of the cases in which it is excluded by or as a result of
  (a) Schedule 1 (mergers and concentrations);
  (b) Schedule 2 (competition scrutiny under other enactments);
  (c) Schedule 3 (planning obligations and other general exclusions);
  ...
  (d) [repealed].
(2–6) [Omitted]

Exemptions
Section 9: Exempt agreements

(1) An agreement is exempt from the Chapter I prohibition if it
  (a) contributes to
    (i) improving production or distribution, or
    (ii) promoting technical or economic progress, while allowing consumers a fair share of the resulting benefit; and
  (b) does not
    (i) impose on the undertakings concerned restrictions which are not indispensable to the attainment of those objectives; or
    (ii) afford the undertakings concerned the possibility of eliminating competition in respect of a substantial part of the products in question.
(2) In any proceedings in which it is alleged that the Chapter I prohibition is being or has been infringed by an agreement, any undertaking or association of undertakings claiming the benefit of subsection (1) shall bear the burden of proving that the conditions of that subsection are satisfied.

UK law includes provisions that have no equivalent provision in EC law. The most important such provision is the criminal sanctions for cartel behaviour in the Enterprise Act 2002.

Enterprise Act 2002, Part 6 – Cartel offence
Section 188: Cartel offence

(1) An individual is guilty of an offence if he dishonestly agrees with one or more other persons to make or implement, or to cause to be made or implemented, arrangements of the following kind relating to at least two undertakings (A and B).

(2) The arrangements must be ones which, if operating as the parties to the agreement intend, would –
 (a) directly or indirectly fix a price for the supply by A in the United Kingdom (otherwise than to B) of a product or service,
 (b) limit or prevent supply by A in the United Kingdom of a product or service,
 (c) limit or prevent production by A in the United Kingdom of a product,
 (d) divide between A and B the supply in the United Kingdom of a product or service to a customer or customers,
 (e) divide between A and B customers for the supply in the United Kingdom of a product or service, or
 (f) be bid-rigging arrangements.

(3) Unless subsection (2)(d), (e) or (f) applies, the arrangements must also be ones which, if operating as the parties to the agreement intend, would
 (a) directly or indirectly fix a price for the supply by B in the United Kingdom (otherwise than to A) of a product or service,
 (b) limit or prevent supply by B in the United Kingdom of a product or service, or
 (c) limit or prevent production by B in the United Kingdom of a product.

(4) In subsections (2)(a) to (d) and (3), references to supply or production are to supply or production in the appropriate circumstances (for which see section 189).

(5) 'Bid-rigging arrangements' are arrangements under which, in response to a request for bids for the supply of a product or service in the United Kingdom, or for the production of a product in the United Kingdom
 (a) A but not B may make a bid, or
 (b) A and B may each make a bid but, in one case or both, only a bid arrived at in accordance with the arrangements.

(6) But arrangements are not bid-rigging arrangements if, under them, the person requesting bids would be informed of them at or before the time when a bid is made.

(7) 'Undertaking' has the same meaning as in Part 1 of the 1998 Act.

In the development of competition enforcement through case law,[182] a number of decisions have been set aside for failure to achieve the standard of full and meticulous assembly and analysis of the facts.[183]

[182] This draws from the excellent critical analysis of UK case law in Alan 2007.

[183] *Albion Water v. Water Services Regulation Authority* (www.catribunal.org.uk/237-610/1046-2-4-04-Albion-Water-Limited--Albion-Water-Group-Limited.html). In *Toys and Games* inadequate records of witness interviews led to remittance of the case to the OFT for reconsideration (www.oft.gov.uk). In *Claymore Dairies v. Office of Fair Trading*

When assessing matters of fact, UK authorities and courts will place greater weight on direct evidence (such as contemporaneous documents, observed behaviour, witness evidence when seeking leniency) than on indirect evidence (such as expert economic analysis).[184] Strong and compelling evidence will need to be presented to substantiate an infringement, especially where penalties are in issue.[185] In price-fixing cases, direct evidence of communication about prices between competitors will establish infringement unless an explanation of innocence can be convincingly provided.[186] There is greater uncertainty about the position where the communication occurs indirectly through an intermediary with whom a firm has a legitimate reason to communicate about prices. There will be an infringement where the communication with an intermediary is intended to form part of a chain of communication between competitors.[187] In the case of agreements that are assessed under a rule-of-reason approach, courts will determine their validity on the basis of a realistic assessment of their impact on competition.[188]

As regards specific concepts and how they have been addressed in the jurisprudence, the concept of an undertaking has been addressed in detail in *BetterCare v. Director General of Fair Trading*; and the standard of proof in *Napp Pharmaceutical Ltd v. Director General of Fair Trading*, *Replica Football Kits (JJB Sports v. Office of Fair Trading and Others)*, and *Burgess v. Office of Fair Trading*.

The concept of agreement and concerted practice was clearly addressed in *Apex v. Office of Fair Trading*, *Makers v. Office of Fair Trading*, *Replica Football Kits (JJB Sports v. Office of Fair Trading and others)* and *Toys and Games (Argos and Littlewoods v. Office of Fair*

Footnote 183 (*cont.*)

the shortness of the decision was criticized ((2005) All ER (D) 27 (Sep)). In *IBA Health v. Office of Fair Trading* (1023/4/1/03) the same concern was echoed, although the Court of Appeal added that the OFT only need record the essential elements of its decision. Detailed analysis of these cases can be found in Alan 2007.

184 See further *Replica Football Kits* (www.oft.gov.uk) and *Aberdeen Journals v. Director General of Fair Trading* (1005/1/1/01).

185 See further *Napp Pharmaceutical v. Director General of Fair Trading* (1001/1/1/01) and *Replica Football Kits*.

186 See further *Apex v. Office of Fair Trading* (1032/1/1/04) and *Makers v. Office of Fair Trading* (1061/1/1/06).

187 See further *Toys and Games* (www.oft.gov.uk).

188 See further *Racecourse Association v. Office of Fair Trading*, [2005] CAT 29 (collective selling of media rights found not to infringe Chapter 1), and *Crehan v. Inntrepreneur Pub Co.* (beer tie found not to infringe Article 101(1) despite Commission decision to the contrary in parallel case).

Trading). The above-mentioned cases involved horizontal price-fixing. The concept of agreement and concerted practice has also been addressed in vertical cases including *Unipart v. O2.*

As regards the definition of the concept of an agreement found to infringe Article 101 / Chapter I, significant cases include, inter alia, *General Insurance Standards Council (Independent Insurance Brokers v. Director General of Fair Trading).*

1.4.2 *Unilateral conduct*

According to the wording of Chapter II of the Competition Act, unilateral conduct in the UK can be considered an abuse of a dominant position. The relevant part of these provisions reads as follows:

> Part I, Chapter II – Abuse of Dominant Position
> Section 18: Abuse of dominant position
>
> (1) Subject to section 19, any conduct on the part of one or more undertakings which amounts to the abuse of a dominant position in a market is prohibited if it may affect trade within the United Kingdom.
> (2) Conduct may, in particular, constitute such an abuse if it consists in
>   (a) directly or indirectly imposing unfair purchase or selling prices or other unfair trading conditions;
>   (b) limiting production, markets or technical development to the prejudice of consumers;
>   (c) applying dissimilar conditions to equivalent transactions with other trading parties, thereby placing them at a competitive disadvantage;
>   (d) making the conclusion of contracts subject to acceptance by the other parties of supplementary obligations which, by their nature or according to commercial usage, have no connection with the subject of the contracts.
> (3) In this section 'dominant position' means a dominant position within the United Kingdom; and 'the United Kingdom' means the United Kingdom or any part of it.
> (4) The prohibition imposed by subsection (1) is referred to in this Act as 'the Chapter II prohibition'.
>
> Section 19: Excluded cases
>
> (1) The Chapter II prohibition does not apply in any of the cases in which it is excluded by or as a result of
>   (a) Schedule 1 (mergers and concentrations); or
>   (b) Schedule 3 (general exclusions).
> (2–4) [Omitted]

As regards specific abuses, similar to the application of Article 102, Chapter II applies, inter alia, to exclusive dealing (*Associated Newspapers*, *Claymore Dairies v. Office of Fair Trading*), predatory pricing (*Napp Pharmaceutical Ltd v. Director General of Fair Trading*, *Aberdeen Journals Ltd v. Director General of Fair Trading*, *First Edinburgh/Lothian*, *Claymore Dairies v. Office of Fair Trading*, *Brannigan v. Office of Fair Trading*), margin squeeze (*Genzyme v. OFT and Healthcare at Home v. Genzyme*, *BSkyB*), bundled pricing (*Genzyme v. OFT and Healthcare at Home v. Genzyme*, *BSkyB*), excessive pricing (*Napp Pharmaceutical Ltd v. Director General of Fair Trading*, *Attheraces and Another v. British Horseracing Board and Another*, *Albion Water v. Water Services Regulation Authority*), refusal to supply (*Burgess v. OFT*).[189]

In circumstances where the dominant firm enjoys a position of overwhelming market power, the protection of consumer choice takes priority, as does the preservation of opportunities to the dominant firm's rivals, both as a goal in itself[190] and as a means of fostering dynamic competition over the long term even if that may mean a sacrifice in short-term productive efficiency.[191] Courts will, however, be less willing to intervene for the benefit of competitors where there is no impact upon consumer welfare.[192]

1.4.3 Merger assessment

Turning to merger enforcement, relevant merger situations producing an effect on competition are prescribed under the Enterprise Act 2002. The relevant parts of this Act read as follows:

> Part 3 (Mergers), Chapter 1 – Duty to Make Reference
> Section 22: Duty to make references in relation to completed mergers
>
> (1) The OFT shall, subject to subsections (2) and (3), make a reference to the Commission if the OFT believes that it is or may be the case that
> (a) a relevant merger situation has been created; and
> (b) the creation of that situation has resulted, or may be expected to result, in a substantial lessening of competition within any market or markets in the United Kingdom for goods or services.

189 For these cases please see further www.oft.gov.uk, www.competitionappealstribunal.org.
190 See further *Genzyme v. Office of Fair Trading* (1016/1/1/03) and *Burgess v. Office of Fair Trading* (1038/2/1/04).
191 See further *Albion Water v. Water Services Regulatory Authority*.
192 See further *Attheraces v. British Horseracing Board*, [2007] EWCA Civ 38; Alan 2007.

(2) The OFT may decide not to make a reference under this section if it believes that
(a) the market concerned is not, or the markets concerned are not, of sufficient importance to justify the making of a reference to the Commission; or
(b) any relevant customer benefits in relation to the creation of the relevant merger situation concerned outweigh the substantial lessening of competition concerned and any adverse effects of the substantial lessening of competition concerned.
(3–5) [Omitted]
(6) In this Part 'market in the United Kingdom' includes
(a) so far as it operates in the United Kingdom or a part of the United Kingdom, any market which operates there and in another country or territory or in a part of another country or territory; and
(b) any market which operates only in a part of the United Kingdom; and references to a market for goods or services include references to a market for goods and services.
(7) [Omitted]

Section 33: Duty to make references in relation to anticipated mergers

(1) The OFT shall, subject to subsections (2) and (3), make a reference to the Commission if the OFT believes that it is or may be the case that
(a) arrangements are in progress or in contemplation which, if carried into effect, will result in the creation of a relevant merger situation; and
(b) the creation of that situation may be expected to result in a substantial lessening of competition within any market or markets in the United Kingdom for goods or services.
(2–3A) [Omitted]

With respect to merger-control cases, there is relatively limited judicial intervention. The principal point of challenge has been as to the OFT's exercise of its discretion to refer mergers for a second-phase investigation by the Commission. Significant merger cases[193] include *IBA Health v. Office of Fair Trading* (on the reference test). In this case the Court endorsed the OFT's margin of appreciation in determining whether a reference is required. The OFT argued that the reference test is whether a significant prospect of a substantial lessening of competition results from the merger. The CAT said that it was sufficient that there was a

[193] For a more detailed analysis see further Alan 2007. In addition, *Co-operative Group (CWS) v. Office of Fair Trading* (1081/4/1/07) related to the decision-making process of providing to the OFT undertakings in lieu of a reference to the Competition Commission.

credible view that that would be the case. A merger should be referred where the OFT believed either that there was indeed a significant prospect that the merger may be expected to give rise to an SLC or that there was a significant prospect that the Commission might reach an alternative view to that effect after a fuller investigation.

The Court of Appeal rejected the second limb of the CAT's test.[194] The Court of Appeal said that the relevant test was the test set out in the statute, and added the following explanatory remarks:

- the duty only arises where the OFT forms the relevant belief which connotes a more positive state of mind than a mere suspicion;
- the belief must be reasonable and objectively justified by relevant facts;
- the words 'may be expected to result' do connote a greater than 50 per cent chance;
- the reference test clearly embraces a lower degree of likelihood than an expectation on the part of the OFT that an SLC will be created. That expectation must be more than merely fanciful.

In *Celesio AG v. Office of Fair Trading*,[195] the CAT rejected the notion that the OFT has a wide discretion whether to refer. The CAT argued that once a merger's prospect of a substantial lessening of competition exceeds the fanciful, the OFT is likely to refer the merger.

In *Somerfield plc v. Competition Commission*, the CAT assessed whether the Commission in imposing remedies is only entitled to go so far as is necessary to remove the substantial lessening of competition or whether it is entitled to go further and remove any lessening of competition. The Commission's normal practice appears to be to require full divestment, presumably on the basis that that is necessary to ensure full and effective competition between the two enterprises. The CAT noted that the Commission should consider alternative solutions where the merging parties could substantiate that they would be as effective in meeting the Commission's statutory duties to remedy the SLC.

1.5 Concluding remarks

This chapter briefly presented the competition legislation of Germany, the EU, the US and the UK, in an attempt to provide the background for the analysis of the complicated and controversial issues that this book will address. The origin of the competition legislation in these

[194] Alan 2007.

[195] Appeal against the OFT's decision in *Boots/Alliance UniChem* (www.catribunal.org.uk).

jurisdictions is essential to understanding the approach that they take in dealing with mergers, cartels and state aid, in periods of crisis. This approach will be the subject of the chapters that follow. These chapters will elaborate in detail on the approach that these jurisdictions take on these controversial issues, in periods of crisis, affecting the stability of whole economies.

2

Some notes on crises

What we know about the global financial crisis is that we don't know very much.

Paul A. Samuelson (1915–2009)[1]

Global capital markets pose the same kinds of problems that jet planes do. They are faster, more comfortable, and they get you where you are going better. But the crashes are much more spectacular.

Lawrence H. Summer[2]

2.1 Introduction

In September 2006, Professor Nouriel Roubini, better known by the nickname of 'Dr Doom' he had acquired through pessimistic and gloomy predictions, announced to an audience mainly of economists at the International Monetary Fund (IMF) that a crisis was imminent: the bursting of the housing bubble would seriously affect the US, causing a broad, international recession.[3] His audience was largely sceptical and even dismissive.[4] In the year that followed, the world was swept by the most severe financial crisis in several generations.[5]

In view of the magnitude of the crisis and its relevance, this chapter seeks to explain what a crisis is. First, the chapter attempts to define a crisis, analysing its characteristic elements. Second, it explores different

[1] Paul A. Samulson was a Nobel-laureate economist.

[2] Lawrence H. Summer is an economist, academic and former US Treasury deputy secretary. Interview in *Time* magazine, 15 February 1999.

[3] See Dr Doom, *IMF Survey*, 16 October 2006. *Fortune* magazine claims that Roubini's predictions were made in October 2005. In its August 2008 issue it stated that in 2005, 'Roubini said home prices were riding a speculative wave that would soon sink the economy. See '8 Who Saw this Crisis Coming . . .', *Fortune* magazine, August 2008.

[4] See Stephen Mihm, Dr. Doom, The New York Times, 17 August 2008.

[5] S. Figlewski, 'Viewing the Financial Crisis from 20,000 Feet Up' (Spring 2009) 16(3) *Journal of Derivatives* 56.

types of crisis, such as social, political, environmental, financial, economic and so on. Third, it analyses the similarities and differences between financial and economic crises. In this analysis, it is observed that there are no precise parameters for the existence or imminence of a crisis, only rather warnings of it. Fourth, the chapter will examine the most relevant financial and economic crises in the twentieth and twenty-first centuries prior to the US subprime mortgage crisis that resulted in the worldwide credit crunch. This short recount of crisis will go from the Great Depression in the US in 1929 to the 2001 crisis in Argentina. Fifth, the chapter will study the financial and economic crisis that began in 2007, starting with an account of the milestones of the crisis and continuing with an attempt to understand what really happened. Sixth, the chapter will look into different business opportunities that have been triggered by most recent crises, from innovation to distress investment. Finally, there will be a note on the regulatory changes relating to the crisis, including the likelihood of an overregulation scenario.

2.2 What is a crisis?

The word 'crisis' comes from the Greek *krisis*, meaning 'decision', from *krinein*, 'decide'. Its first use was by Hippocrates,[6] in a medical context, which was then continued by Galen.[7] According to the Hippocratic school, illnesses were the result of an imbalance in the body's four fluids or 'humours' (blood, black bile, yellow bile and phlegm) of the body. Followers of the Hippocratic school believed that these four humours are naturally equal in proportion; otherwise a person becomes sick until the balance is restored. This imbalance can eventually lead to a crisis, a point in the progression of disease where it becomes life-threatening.[8]

According to the *Oxford English Dictionary*, a crisis is a 'time of intense difficulty or danger', or 'the turning point of a disease, when it becomes clear whether the patient will recover or not'.[9] When

[6] Hippocrates of Cos (c.460 BC– c.370BC) was an ancient Greek physician of the age of Pericles, and is considered one of the most outstanding figures in the history of medicine.

[7] Aelius Galenus or Claudius Galenus (c.130 AD–c.200 AD), better known as Galen of Pergamum, was a Roman physician and philosopher of Greek origin and probably the most accomplished medical researcher of the Roman period, second only to Hippocrates of Cos in his importance to the development of medicine.

[8] F.H. Garrison, *History of Medicine*, W.B. Saunders Company, 1966.

[9] *Oxford English Dictionary*, available at www.askoxford.com.

looking at the two definitions, it becomes clear that emergency and decision-making will necessarily be part of the context: one has to decide quickly how to solve or escape the intense difficulty, and the physician needs to take a swift decision in order to define whether and how the patient will recover.[10] The different components of a crisis (intense difficulty, turning point, emergency and decision-making) will apply differently according to the type of crisis and who faces it. An example of the interplay of these components can be found in the Argentine economic crisis of 2001–2:[11] for its choice of incompliance with international contracts (decision) in order to react to the brutal downturn of its economy (intense difficulty), the government invoked the defence of necessity, or 'the only way for the State to safeguard an essential interest against a grave and imminent peril'[12] (turning point and emergency).

2.3 What are the different types of crisis?

A crisis can be either personal or societal;[13] thus there are many different types of crisis. This chapter will focus on the societal type of crisis, such as social, political, environmental, financial, economic and so on. Furthermore, certain types of crisis bring further crises, depending on the rapidity and quality of the decision-making process involved in solving each of these. For instance, a drought (environmental crisis) can lead to a drop in production and the growth of poverty (economic and social crisis), which can bring mistrust in the government (political crisis), which can lead to civil war (humanitarian crisis). In order to understand better these types of crisis, one can explore examples of their respective intense difficulties, turning points, emergencies and decision-making. This analysis is provided below.

[10] D.W. Levy, 'A Legal History of Irrational Exuberance' (Summer 1998) 48 *Case Western Law Review* 799.

[11] S.F. Hill, 'The "Necessity Defense" and the Emerging Arbitral Conflict in its Application to the U.S.–Argentina Bilateral Investment Treaty' (Summer 2007) 13(3) *Law and Business Review of the Americas* 547.

[12] International Law Commission (ILC), Draft Articles on Responsibility of States for Internationally Wrongful Acts, with commentaries, Article 25, UN GAOR, 56th Sess., Supp. No 10, UN Doc. A/56/10, 12 December 2001.

[13] Societal in the sense that it affects a group of people.

2.3.1 *Social crisis*

A social crisis is a crisis related to society, its organization or its hierarchy.[14] Many causes have been cited that can trigger a social crisis, such as a multiplication of difficult personal situations and frustrations, weak adhesion to power or incomprehension of public policies, the absence of credible political alternatives, the rise of conflicts between employers and employees and the feeling of growing social injustice.[15] This creates a link between social crisis and elements of economic crisis and political crisis; however, a social crisis can develop without an economic or a political crisis taking place. Actors in the social crisis are commonly defined as trade unions and employers,[16] as well as the government. The former call for some decisions to be taken regarding the society, its organization or its hierarchy, and the latter participate in the negotiation, taking, or not taking, the decisions in question. However, every member of civil society acting independently can also be an actor in a social crisis, at least by demanding solutions to improve a status quo.

An example of social crisis can be seen in Guadeloupe, an overseas territory of France located in the Caribbean, in early 2009, which extended to other overseas *départements*. Thousands of persons demonstrated and there were mass strikes, escalating into rioting in Pointe-à-Pitre, Guadeloupe's main city.[17] People protested against living costs resulting from economic and structural conditions. The archipelago depends on imports, thus living costs are elevated, and they endure the repercussions of the world economic crisis. Demonstrators also complained about unemployment, bad public transport, low access to water and poor education.[18] The overseas *départements* are ex-colonies, and have suffered from slavery. Still, in Guadeloupe, most economic power is in the hands of white people.[19] One much-repeated slogan of the demonstrations was 'Guadeloupe is ours and not theirs'.[20] Thus elements

[14] According to the *Oxford English Dictionary*'s definition of 'social' (available at www.askoxford.com).

[15] 'Entreprises: les DRH français craignent une crise sociale', *Le nouvel observateur*, 7 October 2008 – an article about Jean-Marc Le Gall, Olivier Théophile and Jean-Marie Pernot.

[16] 'Les acteurs de la crise sociale en France', *Le nouvel observateur*, 24 March 2009.

[17] 'Strike in Guadeloupe Escalates into Rioting', *New York Times*, 17 February 2009.

[18] 'Les revendications du LKP', *Le nouvel observateur*, 19 February 2009.

[19] 'Strike in Guadeloupe Escalates into Rioting' *New York Times*, 17 February 2009.

[20] 'Les négociations vont reprendre en Guadeloupe et en Martinique', *Le Parisien*, 9 February 2009, available at www.leparisien.fr/economie/les-negociations-vont-reprendre-en-guadeloupe-et-en-martinique-09-02-2009-404917.php.

were present for a social crisis to erupt, which developed into an identity crisis. Intense negotiations were undertaken by the representatives of government with trade unions and other associations in order to put an end to the crisis. An agreement was finally signed in Guadeloupe, giving in to many of the claims of the social movements.[21]

2.3.2 *Political crisis*

According to the definition of politics,[22] a political crisis affects activities associated with governing a country or area, or the political relations between states. Thus, in a national context, a political crisis challenges political authority, the rules organizing the state or the organization of power. It can bring the emergence of a new political system (such as monarchy, democracy etc.) if it is an institutional crisis, or a new government within the same political system (the resignation of a president or prime minister or a call for new elections). The political crisis can be initiated by a wide range of actors, such as members of civil society, the opposition, the military or governing political parties who cannot reach an agreement amongst themselves. A political crisis thus can be understood as a problematic phase in the evolution of the political system of a country. A political crisis can be so serious that its uncertain outcome can trigger the dissolution of legislative power or social unrest that can end in civil war.

Honduras has undergone a severe political crisis between the middle and the end of 2009, when President Zelaya was expelled from the country by the military. Roberto Micheletti, constitutionally second in line for the presidency, was sworn in as interim president. Before his removal, Zelaya had planned a non-binding public consultation to ask people whether they supported moves to amend the Constitution. It has been widely said that the purpose was to allow Zelaya to stand again for president and be re-elected.[23] However, the institutional crisis in Honduras had started before Zelaya's ousting, with serious

[21] 'Accord de sortie de crise en Guadeloupe, la Réunion se dirige vers la grève', *L'Outre-Mer*, 6 March 2009, available at www.outre-mer.gouv.fr.

[22] See the *Oxford English Dictionary*: • plural noun usu. treated as sing. 1 the activities associated with governing a country or area, and with the political relations between states. 2 a particular set of political beliefs or principles. 3 activities aimed at gaining power within an organization: *office politics*. 4 the principles relating to or inherent in a sphere or activity, especially when concerned with power and status: *the politics of gender*.

[23] 'Zelaya's Scrap of Paper', *The Economist*, 5 November 2009.

disagreements within the executive, legislative and judicial powers and the military.[24] Examples of these disagreements include (1) the order issued by the Supreme Court to reinstate the commander-in-chief of the armed forces after the decision of Zelaya to remove him; (2) the fact that the non-binding public consultation had been declared illegal by the Supreme Court and Congress, and was opposed by the military; (3) the fact that Congress had voted to remove Mr Zelaya for repeated violations of the Constitution and the law; and (4) the fact that the Supreme Court had ordered the president to be removed from office to protect law and order.[25] After the removal of Zelaya from the presidency, two accounts of events have been current:[26] first, that Zelaya's removal was a coup d'état and that he should be reinstated; second, that Zelaya's ousting was constitutional and that the country should have new elections. This is an example of a political crisis. However, Zelaya managed to return to the country and sheltered in the Brazilian embassy. This ignited clashes between both camps, supporters of the ousted Zelaya and of the interim president Micheletti, provoking roadblocks, riots and several deaths, as tourism and public investment fell sharply.[27] This is an example of a political crisis that turns into a social crisis, and which can also expand into an economic crisis if detriment to the economy continues. Challenges to the executive power have not ceased, although presidential elections have brought some stability.

2.3.3 *Environmental crisis*

The *Oxford English Dictionary* defines environment as the surroundings or conditions in which a person, animal or plant lives or operates, or as the natural world, especially as affected by human activity.[28] An environmental crisis is thus generally a time of intense difficulty altering the natural world due to human activity. An environmental crisis should not be confused with a natural disaster, which is not caused by mankind but derives from nature. An environmental crisis can be created by any

[24] See Elisabeth Malkin and Marc Lacey, 'Battle for Honduras Echoes Loudly in Media', *New York Times*, 24 September 2009.

[25] See US Congress, Honduras Constitutional Law Issues, Report for Congress 2009, Directorate of Legal Research, LL File No 2009-002965, available at http://schock.house.gov/UploadedFiles/Schock_CRS_Report_Honduras_FINAL.pdf.

[26] 'Zelaya's Scrap of Paper', *The Economist*, 5 November 2009.

[27] Ibid.

[28] Available at www.askoxford.com.

kind of human activity, such as production (nuclear accident), transport (oil spill) or energy consumption (greenhouse effect). As other crises, it can have widespread consequences if no decision is taken swiftly: it can trigger disease or death of humans, animals and plants – even the extinction of certain species. It can also expand into crises of other types – social, political etc.

Global warming is considered an Armageddon of an environmental crisis by most specialists.[29] At the beginning of 2007, the United Nations Intergovernmental Panel on Climate Change (IPCC) declared that the evidence of a warming trend is 'unequivocal', and that human activity has 'very likely' been the driving force in that change over the last fifty years.[30] This reflected evidence that the release of carbon dioxide and other heat-trapping gases has played a central role in raising the world's average surface temperature. Since 1970, temperatures have risen at nearly three times the average rate for the twentieth century, and melting ice sheets could lead to a rapid rise in sea levels and to the extinction of large numbers of species. The consequences are already upsetting: snow and ice on mountains such as Kilimanjaro or Everest are reputedly melting,[31] desertification has already pushed people to migrate in order to avoid hunger and frontiers between some countries have become unclear due to the alteration of natural borders.[32] Countries have adopted regulations in order to solve the environmental crisis, but as the emergency needs to be addressed at a global level, the international community is also making efforts to act jointly.[33] There is criticism of the depth and rapidity of decisions to resolve the current situation, which, as in all crises, are crucial for the mitigation of the effects of crisis.[34]

[29] Jonathan Wheatley, interview with Marina Silva, *Financial Times*, 5 October 2009.

[30] See IPCC, *Summary for Policymakers, in Climate Change 2007: The Physical Science Basis, Contribution of Working Group I to the Fourth Assessment Report of the Intergovernmental Panel on Climate Change* (ed. S. Solomon, D. Qin, M. Manning, Z. Chen, M. Marquis, K.B. Averyt, M.Tignor and H.L. Miller), Cambridge University Press, 2007.

[31] Sindya N. Bhanoo, 'Mt. Kilimanjaro Ice Cap Continues Rapid Retreat', *New York Times*, 2 November 2009.

[32] 'Lines in the Sand', *The Economist*, 13 June 2009.

[33] Edward Luce, 'Agenda Hijacked by Global Warming', *Financial Times*, 25 September 2009. See also in general the website of the United Nations Climate Change Conference, 7–18 December 2009, at http://en.cop15.dk.

[34] John Vidal, Allegra Stratton and Suzanne Goldenberg, 'No Global Climate Change Treaty Likely for up to a Year, Negotiators Admit', *The Guardian*, 5 November 2009.

2.3.4 *Economic and financial crises*

References to 'financial crisis' or 'economic crisis' are frequent, and usually the phrases are used interchangeably. However, technically speaking, these crises are different. The word 'finance' is defined as the management of large amounts of money, especially by governments or large companies,[35] thus a 'financial crisis', in a national or international context, affects the management of large amounts of money and monetary resources. In this order of ideas, the definition of 'economy' is the state of a country or region in terms of the production and consumption of goods and services and the supply of money.[36]

The world has faced what has been referred to as financial and economic crises several times over the past decades; particularly resonant is that of 2007 – the US subprime mortgage crisis that derived in what is known as the credit crunch. The similarities between these two types of crisis first lay in the interplay of the different components described above (intense difficulty, turning point, emergency and decision-making). However, further similarities and differences have led to much confusion. Thus both financial and economic crises affect monetary resources, on different scales. What can start with a situation affecting the management of large amounts of public money and monetary resources can end up disturbing the whole state of a country in terms of the supply of money, the production and consumption of goods and services: a financial crisis can lead to an economic crisis.

Kindleberger famously discerned a pattern for financial crisis which can easily be followed by an economic crisis:

> What happens, basically, is that some event changes the economic outlook. New opportunities for profits are seized, and overdone, in ways so closely resembling irrationality as to constitute a mania. Once the excessive character of the upswing is realized, the financial system experiences a sort of 'distress', in the course of which the rush to reverse the expansion process may become so precipitous as to resemble panic. In the manic phase, people of wealth or credit switch out of money or borrow to buy real or illiquid financial assets. In panic, the reverse movement takes place, from real or financial assets to money, or repayment of debt, with a crash in the prices of commodities, houses, buildings, land, stocks, bonds – in short, in whatever has been the subject of the mania.[37]

[35] *Oxford English Dictionary*, available at www.askoxford.com.

[36] Ibid.

[37] Charles P. Kindleberger, *Manias, Panics, and Crashes: A History of Financial Crises*, Wiley, 2000, at pp. 2–3.

This has been illustrated by the chief economist of the Organisation for Economic Co-operation and Development (OECD), who, referring to the situation in 2008, stated that what happens is that money markets, inter-bank lending and commercial-paper lending come to a standstill; lending to corporations and households freezes (financial crisis); and spending, production, and employment potentially collapse (economic crisis).[38]

Financial crisis

When financial intermediation (the process by which resources are allocated from those individuals who wish to save some of their income for future consumption to those individuals and firms who wish to borrow to invest[39]) is disturbed, the financial crisis becomes evident. When banks, the financial intermediaries, become insolvent or nearly so (intense difficulty and emergency), they are less able to perform their intermediary function.[40] Individuals may not recover all their savings and financial constraints increase,[41] preventing firms and individuals from borrowing (intense difficulty and emergency): a credit crunch has developed. This can lead to a disruption of the management of money and monetary resources and to events such as bank runs, stock market crashes and/or bursting of speculative bubbles. The government has to choose how to react (decision-making), for instance by bailing out a bank to avert its being declared insolvent (turning point).

Economic crisis

An economic crisis arises when the four above-mentioned components of a crisis (intense difficulty and emergency, decision-making, turning point) disturb the state of affairs of a country in terms of (1) production and consumption of goods and services, and (2) the supply of money. An economic crisis can start with a fall in the money supply.[42] This can lead to a decrease in consumption and production. If demand falls, output is low and unemployment rises. The gross domestic product (GDP) of the country falls, which can trigger a recession or, if it is more severe, a depression (intense difficulty and emergency). The

[38] OECD, interview with the new OECD chief economist, Klaus Schmidt-Hebbel, Financial Crisis and the Economy, *OECD Observer* No 269, October 2008.

[39] N. Gregory Mankiw, *Macroeconomics*, 6th ed., Worth Publishers, 2007.

[40] Ibid.

[41] Ibid.

[42] Ibid.

right decisions need to be taken to escape the recession – or depression – (decision-making and turning point). Interestingly, according to some new Keynesian economists,[43] a recession results from a failure of co-ordination among decision-makers: when people, firms and the government have failed to reach a solution that is feasible and that everyone prefers to a recession, then members of society have failed to co-ordinate their behaviour.

2.4 How do we know that we are in a crisis?

Excepting the four elements found in every crisis (intense difficulty, turning point, emergency and decision-making), no common parameters can be set that determine that a crisis has erupted. However, there are certain warning signs for each type of crisis. Civil unrest and a general feeling of injustice are the symptoms of a social crisis. A political crisis can be perceived when established power is significantly challenged or there are strong disagreements within this power. When a human activity severally threatens to alter the natural world, there is an indication of the imminence of an environmental crisis. A financial crisis can be diagnosed when the sound management of public and private money is deeply affected. An economic crisis can be identified when the supply of money and the production and consumption of goods and services are on the verge of collapse. These respective signs, accompanied by a feeling of emergency that becomes overwhelming, should trigger immediate awareness of a crisis situation, entailing quick decisions to mitigate its possible consequences. Based on these elements and signs, and although there are no precise parameters, the determination of a crisis (or at least a distress scenario) can still be made accurately.

2.5 Some financial and economic crises of the twentieth and twenty-first centuries

The world has faced several financial and economic crises.[44] Examining some of the most notorious, such as the Great Depression of 1929, the

[43] See Gregory Mankiw and David Romer, eds., *New Keynesian Economics*, Vol. 2: *Coordination Failures and Real Rigidities*, MIT Press, 1991.

[44] For a recount of different crises see e.g. Kindleberger 2000, at pp. 2–3. There are other studies that provide an account of specific industry crises, for example Laeven and Valencia have identified 124 banking crises over the period from 1970 to 2007.

stock market crash of 1987, the Mexican crisis starting in 1994, the 1997 Asian crisis that provoked the Russian crisis of 1998, and the Argentine crisis of 2001–2, can help us better understand their idiosyncrasies.

2.5.1 The Great Depression

The Great Depression started in the US in August 1929,[45] when the recession began and production started falling.[46] The stock market crash reached its peak on 29 October, commonly referred to as 'Black Tuesday', when the Dow Jones Industrial Average (DJIA) fell almost 23 per cent and the market lost between US$8 billion and US$9 billion in value. The US financial crisis spread to the economy, contributing to falling production and employment, and accelerating deflation.[47] The public lost faith in banks and started withdrawing its savings, pushing banks which had not yet collapsed to lend less in order to avoid failing.[48] The US economic crisis turned into a global depression as Europe, by the summer of 1931, saw its prices falling and suffered from a lack of demand and growing unemployment.[49] The crash of the Austrian bank Creditanstalt in 1931 became a symbol of the Great Depression.[50] In the end, over nine thousand banks failed, devastating deflation set in, millions of homeless lived in the streets and

Footnote 44 (*cont.*)
See Luc Laeven and Fabian Valencia, Systemic Banking Crises: A New Database, International Monetary Fund Working Paper 08/224, 2008.

45 For a detail recount of the Great Depression, see Milton Friedman and Anna J. Schwartz, *A Monetary History of the United States, 1867–1960*, Princeton University Press for NBER, 1963.

46 A recession can be understood as a marked slowdown in economic activity. Many countries consider that two or more consecutive quarters of declining GDP should be considered a recession. For example, the National Bureau of Economic Research considers that a recession is a significant decline in economic activity spread across the economy; lasting more than a few months; and normally visible in production, employment, real income and other indicators. However, economists disagree on what precisely constitutes a recession.

47 See Directorate-General for Economic and Financial Affairs, European Commission, Economic Crisis in Europe: Causes, Consequences and Responses, European Economy 7 (provisional version), European Communities, 2009.

48 See Paul Krugman, 'Who was Milton Friedman?', *New York Review of Books*, February 2007.

49 See Directorate-General for Economic and Financial Affairs 2009.

50 'What if? If Lehman Had Not Failed, Would the Crisis Have Happened Anyway?', *The Economist*, 10 September 2009.

unemployment rose to rates as high as 25 per cent in the US and 43 per cent in Germany.[51]

Although many governmental measures were launched in order to fight the global financial, economical and social crisis, such as President Franklin D. Roosevelt's New Deal,[52] or the abandonment of the gold standard by some countries starting in 1931, many economists agree that it was the war effort linked to the Second World War that brought the Great Depression to an end.[53]

The causes of the 1929 crisis are widely debated. The monetarist and the Keynesian explanations are two of the most prominent theories. The former, led by Friedman and Schwartz,[54] claims that the US Federal Reserve turned the recession into a depression by failing to prevent the fall in money supply.[55] This theory is preferred by free-market allies.[56] The latter, based on John Maynard Keynes's theories,[57] considers that monetary policy had little effect in times of low interest rates, and that it was rather fiscal policies (especially government spending) which could have helped countries out of the depression.[58] This theory is rather promoted by free-market opponents.

2.5.2 *The stock market crash of 1987*

The stock market crash of 1987 is a less catastrophic example, considering its time span and social consequences. On 'Black Monday', 19 October 1987, the DJIA plunged nearly 23 per cent in a day. The crash had begun in Hong Kong, spread through Europe and then hit the United States. Several reasons have been suggested for this sudden crash, such as computer trading, the interplay of stock markets with

[51] See Directorate-General for Economic and Financial Affairs 2009.

[52] The New Deal was the name of a complex package of economic programmes instituted by Roosevelt between 1933 and 1936 aiming at the 'three Rs': relief, reform and recovery of the economy during the Great Depression.

[53] See Directorate-General for Economic and Financial Affairs 2009.

[54] Friedman and Schwartz 1963.

[55] See, for instance, B. Bernanke, 'Money, Gold and the Great Depression', the H. Parker Willis Lecture in Economic Policy, Washington and Lee University, Lexington, VA, 2 March 2004, available at www.federalreserve.gov.

[56] See P. Krugman, 'How Did Economists Get It So Wrong?', *New York Times*, 6 September 2009.

[57] John Maynard Keynes, *The General Theory of Employment, Interest and Money*, Macmillan, 1936, reprinted 2007.

[58] See Krugman 2009.

derivatives markets or the overvaluation of stock prices.[59] The central banks promptly reacted by loosening monetary policies, and the recession was avoided.[60] This financial crisis was confined to equity markets and was over in weeks, and thus did not develop into an economic crisis.[61]

2.5.3 *The Mexican crisis (the tequila effect)*[62]

In December 1994, the newly elected president of Mexico, Ernesto Zedillo, resolved to devalue the Mexican peso. The main reason behind this decision was that the current-account deficit represented 7 per cent of Mexico's GDP, seriously affecting its foreign-exchange reserves.[63] This resulted in a steep plunge of the Mexican peso – about 50 per cent within six months.[64] In turn, it caused the local-currency value of government dollar-linked debts to increase and sent Mexico into a deep recession. The financial crisis expanded into an economic crisis. Prices rose, credit was interrupted and unemployment increased due to the fall in production.[65] This devaluation triggered what has been called the tequila effect, which made other currencies decline during 1995, mainly in Latin America. An emergency plan was put in place to bail out Mexico from a free fall. This plan was articulated by the then president of the United States, Bill Clinton, through the North American Free Trade Agreement. A US$17.1 billion assistance programme was provided to Mexico by the IMF.[66] However, the stock market did not regain its 1994 value in dollar terms until early 2004.[67]

[59] See, for instance, Didier Sornette, *Why Stock Markets Crash: Critical Events in Complex Financial Systems*, Princeton University Press, 2002.

[60] 'Paint It Black, The Stockmarket Crash Has Lessons for Today's Market', *The Economist*, 18 October 2007.

[61] 'Credit Crunch in a Century's Context', *Financial Times*, 7 August 2009.

[62] For a detailed description of the Mexican crisis see D. Arner and T. Slover, 'The Mexican Currency Crisis of 1995', in D. Arner, M. Yokio-Arai and Zhongfei Zhou, eds., *Financial Crises in the 1990s: A Global Perspective*, British Institute of International and Comparative Law, 2002.

[63] 'Tequila Slammer', *The Economist*, 29 December 2004.

[64] Ibid.

[65] S. Dillon, 'Peso Crisis Bites Into Mexico's Long-Ruling Party', *New York Times*, 4 July 1997.

[66] J.E. Stiglitz, 'The Broken Promise of Nafta', *New York Times*, 6 January 2004.

[67] 'Tequila Slammer', *The Economist*, 29 December 2004.

2.5.4 The Asian crisis, 1997–1998

In 1997 and 1998 private investors pulled more than US$100 billion out of East Asian countries.[68] The countries were also affected by enormous currency devaluations, high inflation and a crash on stock markets. Unemployment rose hugely as wages dropped and millions of people fell into poverty.[69] A financial crisis had once again developed into an economic and social crisis. The grounds for the crisis are disputed, but it has been widely reported that banks took on too much foreign-currency external debt.[70] With the devaluation, the burden of repaying the foreign debt then became too heavy.[71] In order to avoid default, one of the utmost consequences of an economic crisis, the countries concluded big 'rescue packages' with the IMF.[72] These were later criticized.[73] The countries affected by the 1997–8 Asian economic, currency and financial crises were Indonesia, Hong Kong, Malaysia, the Philippines, South Korea and Thailand.

The crisis expanded to various countries, such as Russia, where, starting in August 1998, a financial crisis erupted, soon to become an economic crisis: the ruble fell in value, the country defaulted on domestic and private debt and most of Russia's financial system collapsed.[74] Despite the intervention of the IMF,[75] the rapid recovery of Russia is said to have been due to the increase in oil prices in 1999 and 2000.[76] This crisis also seriously affected Ukraine and Pakistan. These three countries had to restructure their external debt.

[68] For an enlargement on the Asian crisis see G. Corsetti, P. Pesenti and N. Roubini, 'What Caused the Asian Currency and Financial Crises? Part I: A Macroeconomic View', available at www.nber.org/papers/w6833, and 'What Caused the Asian Currency and Financial Crises? Part II: The Policy Debate', available at http://ideas.repec.org/p/nbr/nberwo/6834.html.

[69] The World Bank, 'East Asia 10 Years after the Financial Crisis, News & Broadcast', 5 April 2007, available at http://web.worldbank.org.

[70] Ibid.

[71] 'Swan Song', *The Economist*, 19 December 2007.

[72] Jack Boorman, 'For the IMF and Others, Lessons from the Asian Crisis', *New York Times*, 20 January 1999.

[73] 'New Fund, Old Fundamentals', *The Economist*, 30 April 2009.

[74] 'As Winter Draws In', *The Economist*, 22 October 1998.

[75] 'Argentina, Turkey and the IMF', *The Economist*, 5 March 2001.

[76] 'Good in Part', *The Economist*, 19 July 2001.

2.5.5 *The Argentine crisis, 2001–2002*[77]

Argentina had outperformed most countries in the region in 1997, in terms of growth per capita. The IMF even referred to Argentina as a 'star performer'.[78] However, between 2001 and 2002, output fell by 20 per cent, inflation reignited, the government defaulted on its external debt obligations and the banking system was largely paralysed.[79] The financial and economic crisis left more than half of the population in poverty and triggered civil unrest and political instability, thus exploding in both a social and a political crisis.

The causes of the downturn are debated, but one of the most frequently cited causes is monetary policy.[80] In 1991, Argentina's economic ministry decided to peg the Argentine peso to the US dollar. This was useful in order to fight hyperinflation, but caused Argentina to become less competitive in its exports and to lose control over its monetary policy. The peso was finally devalued in 2002.

The main consequences of the devaluation were (1) a nominal devaluation of the peso to US$0.25, finally stabilized at approximately US$0.33; (2) an inflationary impact that resulted in real salaries shrinking by 30 per cent; (3) a domestic redistribution of wealth in the order of US$30 billion which were diverted from savers' bank deposits and pension funds to private-sector debtors and provincial governments;[81] (4) in US dollar terms, GDP in 2003 falling to less than 50 per cent of that of 2001; (5) as a result of the *corralito*,[82] and of the mandatory conversion

[77] For an enlargement on this issue, see US Congress, Joint Economic Committee, Argentina's Economic Crisis: Causes and Cures (June 2003), available at www.house.gov/jec.

[78] See e.g. International Monetary Fund, IMF Executive Board Discusses Lessons from the Crisis in Argentina, Public Information Notice (PIN) No 04/26, 24 March 2004.

[79] S.F. Hill, 'The "Necessity Defense" and the Emerging Arbitral Conflict in its Application to the U.S.–Argentina Bilateral Investment Treaty' (Summer 2007) 13(3) *Law and Business Review of the Americas* 547.

[80] G. Perry and L. Servén, 'The Anatomy of a Multiple Crisis: Why Was Argentina Special and What Can We Learn from It?', in V. Alexander, G.M. von Furstenberg and J. Mélitz, eds., *Monetary Unions and Hard Pegs*, Oxford Scholarship Online Monographs, 2004.

[81] For causes (1), (2) and (3) see D.F. Cavallo, 'The New "Washington Consensus" that Triggered the Argentine Crisis', delivered to conference at the Real Instituto Elcano, Madrid, Spain, 11–12 December 2003, during the series La Seguridad Jurídica y las Inversiones Extranjeras en América Latina – El Caso Argentino', available at www.cavallo.com.ar/papers/Elcanodic03ingles.html.

[82] The *corralito* or 'little corral' was a set of measures adopted that worked as a fence put around bank deposits to avoid money from escaping the banking system.

of US dollar bank deposits into pesos at an exchange rate different to the free-market rate, there was seizure of property that ended in a crisis of the judicial system due to the lack of an apolitical response.[83] Under general discomfort due to the mandatory conversion into pesos of bank deposits, and facing daily demonstrations, the temporary elected president brought forward elections to 27 April 2003. According to US courts entertaining claims against the Argentine government, Argentina suffered 'the worst economic crisis in its history'.[84] Since the default on its external obligations in 2001–2 Argentina has not been able to regain access to international capital markets until 2010.

Argentina's crises triggered a confidence crisis in Uruguay that could have become a financial crises, had this not been averted by comprehensive debt re-profiling.

2.5.6 The recent US subprime mortgage crisis and the credit crunch

The crisis timeline

The actual economic crisis, no different to the ones above, started with a financial crisis.[85] What began as a subprime mortgage lending crisis in the US in mid-2007 intensified following Lehman Brothers' insolvency in September 2008 and gradually spread into other markets and countries, triggering a worldwide economic downturn.

The first event or sign of what we now know as a crisis (and which at the time went completely unnoticed) was HSBC's announcement of a US$10.7 billion write-down on 7 February 2007, largely associated with subprime loans. This was followed by an announcement made on 27 February 2007 by the Federal Home Loan Mortgage Corporation (Freddie Mac), ceasing to buy the most risky subprime mortgages and mortgage-related securities. In April, New Century Finance filed for US

[83] See 'Por una Mayor Transparencia Judicial', *La Nación* newspaper, 27 February 2005, available at www.lanacion.com.ar/herramientas/printfriendly/printfriendly.asp?origen=3ra¬a_id=683190.

[84] See *Applestein TTEE FBO D.C.A. Grantor Trust v. Republic of Argentina*, 2003 US Dist. LEXIS 20922, No 02 Civ. 4124, 2003 WL 22743762, (S.D.N.Y. 2003); also *Lightwater Corp. v. Republic of Argentina*, 2003 US Dist. LEXIS 6156, No 02 Civ. 3804, 2003 WL 1878420 (S.D.N.Y. 2003).

[85] See M. Hewitt, 'The Financial Crisis Timeline (30 May 2007–4 February 2009)', *DollarDaze*, 10 February 2009, available at www.dollardaze.org/blog/?post_id=00578. See also 'Timeline: Credit Crunch to Downturn', BBC News, 7 August 2009, available at http://news.bbc.co.uk/2/hi/7521250.stm.

Chapter 11 bankruptcy protection. By late April, the subprime market squeeze started to be felt, not only in the US but also around the world. In June, the investment bank Bear Stearns suspended redemptions from its High-Grade Structured Credit Strategies Enhanced Leverage Fund and – after rival banks refused to help bail it out – in August liquidated two funds that had invested in mortgage-backed securities. After this, American Home Mortgage Investments filed for Chapter 11 bankruptcy protection. On 9 August 2007, investment bank BNP Paribas halted redemption on three funds because it was not able to value their assets. The shares of the largest United States mortgage lender, Countrywide, plunged 13 per cent on fears of insolvency and the company drew down its entire US$11.5 billion credit line the next day. At the end of August, the German Sachsen Landesbank's collapse was adverted by Baden-Württemberg's takeover.

In mid-September 2007, the Bank of England provided liquidity to Northern Rock as depositors withdrew their money in the biggest run on a British bank for over a century. On 1 October 2007, Swiss bank UBS announced US$3.4 billion in losses from subprime-related investments. In mid-October, banking giant Citigroup unveiled a US$6.5 billion write-off for subprime exposure. Between the end of October and the beginning of November, Merrill Lynch reported US$7.9 billion losses as a consequence of what was known as the US subprime mortgage crisis. Deutsche Bank revealed a US$3 billion write-down on bad debt and Credit Suisse announced US$1 billion losses on bad loans. In November 2007, Citigroup reported additional losses in the amount of between US$8 billion and US$11 billion from exposure to the US subprime market. Wachovia Securities wrote down US$1.7 billion on bad loans. Bank of America reported US$3 billion in subprime losses. Barclays wrote down US$2.6 billion in subprime losses and UBS reported a further US$10 billion write-down caused by bad loans. On 12 December 2007, the US Federal Reserve established a Term Auction Facility and authorized temporary reciprocal currency arrangements with foreign banks. Liquidity was scarce and while governments were trying to assure that liquidity would be provided if it were required , an over-leveraged situation forced the need to sacrifice certain positions. Later that month, Morgan Stanley wrote off US$9.4 billion in subprime losses and sold a 9.9 per cent stake to the Chinese Investment Corporation.

In January 2008, Bear Stearns announced an additional US$1.9 billion in subprime losses, Citigroup wrote down US$18 billion in subprime losses, Merrill Lynch reported a US$14.1 billion write-down for investments related to subprime mortgages and bond insurer MBIA reported US$2.3 billion losses. In February 2008 UBS increased its total losses to US$18.4 billion and Northern Rock was nationalized by the UK government. At the beginning of March 2008, HSBC reported US$17.2 billion in losses mainly linked to the United States housing market. Later that month, the Term Securities Lending Facility was established to lend up to US$200 billion in Treasury securities, the Primary Dealer Credit Facility was established to extend credit at the primary credit rate against a broad range of investment-grade securities, and Maiden Lane LLC was set up to facilitate the acquisition of the Bear Stearns Companies by JP Morgan Chase & Co. In the middle of these measures, Carlyle Capital's creditors seized assets of mortgage-backed funds after it failed to meet more than US$400 million of margin calls. In April, UBS revealed a further US$19 billion of asset write-down above the US$18.4 billion announced for 2007; Citigroup reported additional US$12 billion in subprime losses, bringing its total to US$40 billion; Merrill Lynch revealed additional losses, bringing its total to US$31.7 billion, and RBS reported US$12 billion in write-down, the largest in UK corporate history.

In June 2008, Standard and Poor's downgraded bond insurers AMBAC and MBIA's rating from AAA to AA. In July, the Office of Thrift Supervisor closed IndyMac Federal Bank, and the US Treasury and the US Federal Reserve Board authorized lending to the Federal National Mortgage Association (Fannie Mae) and to Freddie Mac. Despite several attempts to transmit confidence to the markets,[86] in September 2008 things got even worse: (1) Fannie Mae and Freddie Mac were both placed into government conservatorship in one of the largest bail-outs in US history; (2) Lehman Brothers filed for Chapter 11 bankruptcy protection, becoming the first major bank to collapse since the start of the credit crisis; (3) a merger between Merrill Lynch and Bank of America was agreed; (4) the US Federal Reserve announced a rescue package for the American Insurance Group (AIG) in the amount of US$85 billion to save it from insolvency in exchange for an 80 per cent stake in the firm; and (5) Washington Mutual, a giant US mortgage lender, was closed down by regulators and sold to JP Morgan Chase. Also in September,

[86] See, for example, Henry Paulson (US Treasury Secretary), who stated on the *Face the Nation* television programme on Sunday 19 July 2008 that 'it's a safe banking system, a sound banking system . . . regulators are on top of it'. He also added, 'our economy has got very strong long-term fundamentals, solid fundamentals'. See CBS News at www.cbsnews.com/stories/2008/07/20/ftn/main4276028.shtml?tag=contentMain;contentBody.

the US Federal Reserve set an Asset-Backed Commercial Paper Money Market Mutual Fund Liquidity Facility (AMLF) and Treasury Secretary Henry Paulson and US Federal Reserve chairman Ben Bernanke proposed a US$700 billion stabilization programme.

In early October 2008, the DJIA fell 18.15 per cent in its all-time worst weekly performance. Two new facilities were also established in the US during October: the Commercial Paper Funding Facility, to provide a liquidity backstop to US issuers of commercial paper, and the Money Market Investor Funding Facility. A new facility was established in November, the Term Asset-Backed Securities Lending Facility. New Maiden Lanes were set up to assist in the restructuring of AIG: Maiden Lane II and Maiden Lane III. In December 2008, US federal funds were set to a historic low target of between zero and 0.25 per cent, and the US Federal Reserve began to purchase mortgage-backed securities from Fannie Mae, Freddie Mac and the Government National Mortgage Association (Ginnie Mae). In January 2009, the US Treasury and the Federal Deposit Insurance Corporation announced guarantees, liquidity access and capital for Bank of America.

What happened?

The most important question is, how could falling housing prices create the biggest crisis since the Great Depression?[87] A closer look at the mechanics of the crisis allows a better comprehension of its severity and degree of proliferation. As housing prices started to deflate,[88] defaults on subprime mortgages sharply increased and the value of mortgage-based securities started to fall. This brought losses among banks and other financial institutions. The complexity of the securitized assets also created uncertainty, first on the extent of losses and then regarding the distribution of losses among financial institutions.[89] As noted by Elmeskov, this situation led to 'runs on individual institutions, rising prices of insuring against default and a general seizing up of securities and inter-bank

[87] This has been asked repeatedly by economists such as Nouriel Roubini. See for instance 'A Proposal to Prevent Wholesale Financial Failure by Lasse H. Pedersen and Nouriel Roubini', NYU Stern Finance website, 18 February 2009, available at http://sternfinance.blogspot.com.

[88] J. Elmeskov, 'The General Economic Background to the Crisis', paper for Session 1 on How the Global Economy Headed to the Crisis at the G20 Workshop on the Causes of the Crisis: Key Lessons, Mumbai, 24–6 May 2009.

[89] See T. Philippon, 'Overview of the Crisis, NYU Stern Finance website, 14 October 2008, available at http://sternfinance.blogspot.com.

markets and a hardening of lending attitudes among banks'.[90] The collapse of many banks and financial institutions added to the panic in the inter-bank loan market. With reduced capital and less ability to bear risk, financing became very hard to obtain,[91] making production more difficult. Consumers cut their spending, due both to general circumstances and to increasing unemployment: demand fell. International trade dropped, as well as commodity prices. The European Union declared in November 2008 that many of its member states had slipped into recession.[92] In December 2008, the National Bureau of Economic Research declared that the US had been in recession since December 2007.[93]

Market failure and regulatory weakness are the most often cited causes of the propagation of the downturn.[94] A market failure takes place when prices do not reflect all publicly available information and the market does not operate efficiently. Possible causes of market failure include monopoly practices or government regulation. According to Schmidt-Hebbel, markets failed in the actual crisis 'in poor governance and the structures of executive incentives that were inappropriate for the stability of financial firms . . . in the opacity of financial instruments and their trading, and a lack of public information about balance sheets of financial institutions and their off-balance sheet vehicles'.[95] This leads to the second cited cause, regulatory weakness, which allowed the market failure. According to economists such as Krugman,[96] the reason for the weakness or deregulation of financial markets is based on a belief in efficient and self-correcting financial markets, which do not need to be regulated. In the view of the crisis, advocates of deregulation, such as Greenspan, partially admitted that they were wrong,[97] stating that 'those of us who have looked to the self-interest of lending institutions to protect shareholders' equity, myself included, are in a state of shocked disbelief'. This brings many to say that there is no failure in the market

[90] Elmeskov 2009.

[91] Figlewski 2009.

[92] See Directorate-General for Economic and Financial Affairs, European Commission, Economic Forecast Autumn 2008, European Economy 6, European Communities, 2008.

[93] See National Bureau of Economic Research Press Release, Determination of the December 2007 Peak in Economic Activity, version 11 December 2008, available at www.nber.org/cycles/dec2008.html.

[94] OECD interview with Klaus Schmidt-Hebbel 2008.

[95] Ibid.

[96] See Krugman 2009.

[97] E.L. Andrews, 'Greenspan Concedes Error on Regulation', *New York Times*, 23 October 2008.

system, simply a failure in financial regulation.[98] The OECD has itself called for more effective monitoring and regulation of the market.[99]

Measures of several types have been undertaken to fight the crisis, calm the global panic and restore stability. Some of the most important are the provision of liquidity to the system[100] (mainly to central banks) and the provision of assurances to depositors and creditors of banks. There have been massive injections of liquidity by central banks to stimulate lending and counterbalance the doubtful value of mortgage-backed securities.[101] The illiquidity of major firms and financial institutions such as Bear Stearns, AIG or Fannie Mae and Freddy Mac has been managed in order to protect the financial system, often through spectacular bank intervention strategies.[102] They simply were too big to fail, too interconnected to fail or too important to fail. The scale and speed of these expansionary policy responses have been considered to be the biggest difference between the current crisis and the Great Depression, and crucial to avoiding total financial meltdown.[103]

2.6 Business opportunities in a crisis period

2.6.1 Taking business opportunities

As John F. Kennedy famously stated, 'The Chinese use two brush strokes to write the word "crisis." One brush stroke stands for danger; the other for opportunity. In a crisis, be aware of the danger – but recognize the opportunity.' Since a crisis implies a turning point, it also represents a chance for improvement. This is true for business: if the right decisions are taken, a crisis is an opportunity to innovate, create products better tailored to customers' needs and make profit. This has been the case throughout history: companies who took off during the Great Depression include Revlon and

[98] See United Nations Conference on Trade and Development, *The Global Economic Crisis: System Failures and Multilateral Remedies*, United Nations Publications, 2009, at p. 22.

[99] A. Gurría, 'From the Financial Crisis to the Economic Downturn, Restoring Growth Is a Key Challenge', *OECD Observer*, October 2008. See also Chapter 2, section 2.7, below in this volume.

[100] C. Stephanou, Dealing with the Crisis, Taking Stock of the Global Policy Response, Crisis Response No 1, The World Bank Group, Financial and Private Sector Development Vice-Presidency, June 2009.

[101] Figlewski 2009.

[102] Stephanou 2009.

[103] See Directorate-General for Economic and Financial Affairs 2009.

Hewlett-Packard.[104] In the current crisis, it is already possible to distinguish which companies are having good results.

The most obvious successes are the very big companies.[105] They are able to reduce prices, adapting to the fact that customers have less money to spend, hence winning market from their competitors. To achieve this goal, they can restrict their costs by making bargain acquisitions from their providers. Furthermore, they have normally entered the crisis with cash and sound management strategies and they attract investors worried by more fragile rivals. Only two stocks on the DJIA rose in 2008: Wal-Mart and McDonalds.[106] A senior executive of Burger King also believed that the recession had been positive for his firm.[107]

Many companies find their road to success through innovation. According to some managers, you need to 'invest your way out' of recession.[108] Many companies, such as IBM, hold innovation sessions with their employees.[109] New assets can be bought at lower costs than in non-crisis times and talented persons can be hired cheaply: this increases the companies' potential to take off in a new direction. It might also be the right time for a change towards a greener business[110] and reinforced corporate social responsibility.[111] People suffering from a crisis have special needs, and firms able to innovate to meet those needs might find themselves in a fine position: companies that provide distraction for people staying home have seen their business pick up, such as film libraries or online booksellers such as Amazon.[112] Some businesspeople also take advantage of the moment simply to start up their own companies,[113] understanding market changes and new customers' needs quicker than do already established companies. New or smaller companies have potential, since consumers pressed by budget cuts are more likely to give chances to innovative and cheaper products by unknown firms.

[104] 'Thriving on Adversity', *The Economist*, 1 October 2009.

[105] Ibid.

[106] 'Trading Down', *The Economist*, 28 May 2009.

[107] Ibid.

[108] 'Thriving on Adversity', *The Economist*, 1 October 2009.

[109] Ibid.

[110] A. Seager, 'We Must Not Resort to Protectionism, Warns Brown', *The Guardian*, 30 January 2009.

[111] Belén Fernández-Feijóo Souto, 'Crisis and Corporate Social Responsibility: Threat or Opportunity?' (2009) 1 *International Journal of Economic Sciences and Applied Research* 36, available at www.ceeol.com.

[112] 'Trading Down', *The Economist*, 28 May 2009.

[113] 'Thriving on Adversity', *The Economist*, 1 October 2009.

For some firms, the crisis is also a good occasion to 'clean up'. They reposition themselves in the market, getting rid of their less profitable branches and strategies while they concentrate on advantageous activities.[114] As countries tend to adopt protectionist policies in difficult times, some markets become inaccessible, and firms are obliged to try new markets.[115] This can be beneficial and can increase their independence in the future. Moreover, bad management and cash-flow strategies, such as incautious debts and credits, are exposed by the crisis, and must be replaced urgently by more efficient policies.[116] Some costs on unnecessary travel, goods or services are cut, and this might develop into good habits that will be maintained in better times. Moreover, turnaround specialists and companies generally helping others make better use of their resources or choose more competitive providers see their own businesses expand.[117] Hence a firm surviving the crisis can be stronger and more efficient than it was before the turmoil.[118]

2.6.2 Opportunities in distress

As Napoleon marched on Waterloo, Baron Rothschild, a British nobleman and member of the Rothschild banking family, is said to have declared that 'the time to buy is when there's blood in the streets'.[119] This is applicable to an economic crisis period, when many companies and people are in great economic trouble and desperate to save themselves from the turmoil: all kind of financial assets are being sold for much less than they had been valued at months ago. The combination of credit crisis and property slump has opened new bargain opportunities,[120] and the slow economy can be a catalyst for corporate consolidation and capital restructuring.[121] Profits can be made, and some firms, called

[114] Ibid.

[115] Seager 2009.

[116] 'Thriving on Adversity', *The Economist*, 1 October 2009.

[117] 'The Vultures Take Wing', *The Economist*, 29 May 2007.

[118] 'Surviving the Slump', *The Economist*, 28 May 2009.

[119] L. Story, 'Investors Stalk the Wounded of Wall Street', *New York Times*, 4 April 2008.

[120] D. Thomas, 'Credit Crisis Throws Up Profitable Opportunities', *Financial Times*, 12 September 2008.

[121] S. Nayar, 'Specialist Hedge Funds Benefit from Global Turn of Events, *Financial Times*, 15 November 2009.

'special-situation funds', 'distressed-debt funds' or, more harshly, 'vulture funds' or 'grave-dancers' have specialized in this business.

As banks retreat from fund management,[122] the special-situation firms are often hedge funds or private equity funds.[123] Nevertheless, any company can take advantage of the downturn to buy cheap assets, becoming de facto a distressed-debt investor. Hedge funds and private equity funds are advantageous as they are loosely regulated.[124] Although additional regulation applies when they take over some companies such as banks,[125] these funds are often able to set up legal structures to avoid extra regulations.[126] According to Hedge Fund Research, as the mortgage crisis erupted in 2007, about US$21 billion flowed into hedge funds specialized in distressed investments.[127] Private equity has abundance of unallocated capital, raised in the boom years of 2006–7,[128] and private equity funds have been launched by firms such as Carlyle or Morgan Stanley to pursue high-risk and -return strategies on distressed debt.[129]

The vulture funds' objective is to buy assets at a steep discount, i.e. bargain prices. Usual examples of these opportunities include unsold real estate, companies or assets of companies that seem to be heading towards insolvency, mortgages of pressed homeowners or bank loans of firms that are experiencing financial constraints.[130] The process itself can be lucrative, for instance when it includes mergers and acquisitions.[131] Then the funds hope to resell these assets at a higher price, make profit on reorganized firms or collect the full face value of what they had acquired at a discount on its par value.

Crashing prices, bank repossessions and empty units have made the real-estate sector very attractive to these so-called special-situation funds,[132] as they hope for high returns when prices pick up. The Marriott

[122] 'Wasting Assets', *The Economist*, 18 June 2009.
[123] Nayar 2009.
[124] Story 2008.
[125] 'Return of the Grave-Dancers', *The Economist*, 4 July 2009.
[126] Ibid.
[127] Story 2008.
[128] 'Wasting Assets', *The Economist*, 18 June 2009.
[129] Thomas 2008.
[130] Story 2008.
[131] See Nayar 2009. Vincent Boland, 'Crisis Creates Opportunities for Mergers', *Financial Times*, 25 March 2009.
[132] Kevin Brass, 'Looking to Profit from a Glut of Unsold Apartments', *New York Times*, 1 October 2009.

company,[133] a de facto distressed-debt investor, owns few properties but receives franchise fees from many. It has not been affected by the crisis and is in a good position to look for troubled hotels at bargain prices, in order to exploit or resell them in the future; the company's president said that many hotels might soon be on sale for half their price.[134]

An interesting strategy of distressed-debt funds is to buy cheap debt and rework the terms. In the US, vulture funds buy at steep discount distressed debts auctioned by the Federal Deposit Insurance Corporation after it has seized a failed bank.[135] Then, they renegotiate the terms of the debt with the borrowers in order to recover as soon as possible the amount invested and make additional profits. When the debt cannot be collected swiftly, the vulture creditor usually files a foreclosure lawsuit in order to seize the collateral.[136] The strategy can also be beneficial for the borrower, when a special-situation fund creditor agrees to refinance and reduces the borrower's debt, in order to resell the debt gainfully with a guarantee of state agency, for instance the Federal Housing Administration in the United States.[137]

Some of these vulture or special-situation funds address the shortage of cash: many investors and lenders need loans to develop or survive, but banks are capital-constrained and need to reimburse their own debts.[138] Hence the situation creates an optimal situation to speculate with others' needs, allowing these funds to lend cash and demand high interest rates.[139] Some offer low interest rates, in exchange for the right to buy the firm in a distress situation.[140]

The vulture or special-situation funds' business is speculative. It entails great risk and has attracted a great deal of scepticism. Nobody can be sure that their speculative expectations will be met in an uncertain and volatile market, when distressed assets are not necessarily good investments.[141] Furthermore, since the value might not increase in the

133 'Trading Down', *The Economist*, 28 May 2009.

134 Ibid.

135 Eric Lipton, 'After the Bank Failure Comes the Debt Collector', *New York Times*, 17 April 2009.

136 Eric Lipton, 'After the Bank Failure Comes the Debt Collector', *New York Times*, 17 April 2009.

137 L. Story, 'Wall St. Finds Profits by Reducing Mortgages', *New York Times*, 22 November 2009.

138 'Return of the Grave-Dancers', *The Economist*, 4 July 2009.

139 Thomas 2008.

140 'The Vultures Take Wing', *The Economist*, 29 May 2007.

141 Story 2008.

short term, special-situation funds need to maintain the assets in the medium or long term at their own expense,[142] and lock their liquidities in until conditions improve – if they improve.[143]

In the US, the Treasury has tried to push financial institutions to sell toxic assets, and private institutions to buy them, in order to clean up bank balance sheets. It can be argued that, to a certain extent, the Treasury is thereby promoting business practices similar to those of the vulture or special-situation funds, encouraging them to become regulated banks or to lend directly to get the economy on its feet.[144] Despite their opportunistic and often harsh approach, special-situation funds are useful vehicles for tidying up the finance markets, discarding weak elements and recycling them into more profitable investments.

2.7 Overregulation after the crisis?

Regulatory weakness has been considered one of the foremost causes of the recent crisis, whether due to trust in the free market[145] or to the fact that demand for regulation declines in prolonged good times.[146] Governments have to supervise the entities and the elements or practices that have contributed to the economic downturn. Entities and practices have even received incentives to persist in risky conduct.

Many of the entities undertaking banking-type functions are not traditional banks. Thus they slip through regulatory safe harbours, becoming entities over which regulators have no jurisdiction.[147] For instance, Lehman Brothers, being an investment bank, was free from the national regulations applying to traditional banks, which would have prevented it from becoming over-leveraged.[148] Regulatory weakness has also allowed the existence of different behaviours that have led to or worsened the crisis. For instance, bankers and investors in general receive great

[142] Brass 2009.

[143] Nayar 2009.

[144] Phillip Inman, 'Governments Banks Failing to Sell off Assets to Private Equity Firms', *The Guardian*, 18 October 2008.

[145] See Krugman 2009.

[146] J. Aizenman, Financial Crisis and the Paradox of Under- and Over-Regulation, NBER Working Paper No 15018, National Bureau of Economic Research, May 2009.

[147] N.M. Barofsky, E.R. Dinallo, K.R. Feinberg and S.A. Kelsey, 'On Regulation and Capital Markets', 2009 Global Economy Forum and Law Alumni Association Fall Lecture, New York University, 2009, available at www.law.nyu.edu/news/GLOBAL_ECONOMIC_POLICY_FORUM.

[148] Ibid.

incentives to take risks in order to generate greater profit, which exposes the economy to possible meltdown.[149] Moreover, tax policies encourage household and company indebtedness.[150] In addition, the principle of 'too big to fail' generates moral hazard. Although there are solid reasons not to announce bail-out policies, the optimal choice is to offer support when crisis strikes.[151] Similarly, once risk-taking entities reach a certain size, they become 'too big to fail' and the entities holding their liabilities can start to rely on a state guarantee, if needed.[152] As result of the recent crisis, besides the concept of an entity being too big to fail, we have seen new concepts, such as too interconected to fail or too important to fail.

2.7.1 What needs to be re-regulated?

There is a general belief this regulatory weakness needs to be addressed to prevent a crisis from happening again.[153] In September 2009, at the G20 Summit in Pittsburgh, it was agreed that since 'reckless behaviour and a lack of responsibility led to crisis, we will not allow a return to banking as usual'.[154]

In order to avoid a new downturn, economists call for the regulation of many areas that were previously unregulated.[155] Some consider that it is the structure of the entities undertaking banking activities that should be modified.[156] Some believe that these entities should simply be allowed to fail.[157] But the majority opinion is that there is a need to make banking activities themselves safer.[158] The most cited areas, those allegedly needing most urgent action, are the inclusion in the regulation of all important financial entities, such as hedge funds, or the setting of minimum capital requirements for all relevant entities (not just banks) in order to avoid excessive leverage. Also encouraged are the promotion of transparent accounting standards, the placing of limits on derivatives

149 J.B. Berk, 'Incentives and the Financial Crisis', *Financial Times*, 3 December 2008.

150 C. Crook, 'Congress Misses the Point on Reform', *Financial Times*, 1 November 2009.

151 B. Weder di Mauro, 'The Dog That Didn't Bark', *The Economist*, 1 October 2009.

152 Berk 2008.

153 Andrews 2008.

154 G20 Leaders' Statement, the Pittsburgh Summit, 25 September 2009, available at www.pittsburghsummit.gov/mediacenter/129639.htm.

155 See, for instance, Steve Schifferes, 'Striving for a New World Economic Order', BBC News, 4 April 2009.

156 Berk 2008.

157 'Death Warmed Up', *The Economist*, 1 October 2009.

158 Ibid.

and the establishment of a cap on executive bonus payments. On the same lines, the G20 leaders, endorsing their former London meeting's declaration,[159] stated in Pittsburgh that they were

> committed to act together to raise capital standards, to implement strong international compensation standards aimed at ending practices that lead to excessive risk-taking, to improve the over-the-counter derivatives market and to create more powerful tools to hold large global firms to account for the risks they take. Standards for large global financial firms should be commensurate with the cost of their failure.[160]

2.7.2 *How to re-regulate*

There seems to be wide agreement that some areas should be re-regulated; the issue is, by whom.[161] Efforts have been seen and are being seen at firm, agency and parliament levels, as well as at the international level.

At the most micro level, according to the Institute for International Finance, firms are engaging in substantial internal reforms, in areas such as risk management, liquidity management or compensation, in order to avoid similar failures.[162]

At the national level, countries are in the process of re-regulating banking and finance activities. Some countries have adopted tougher regulations, such as the criminalization in Hong Kong of insider trading.[163] The US Senate is close to producing draft legislation on financial regulation, which would address derivatives, systemic risk, resolution authority for failing companies and consumer protection.[164] The bill would consolidate the four banking regulators, take power from the US Federal Reserve and create a single supervisory body,[165] the Financial Institutions Regulatory Authority.[166] Furthermore, the US Federal

[159] G20 Leaders' Statement 2009.

[160] Ibid.

[161] 'When Fortune Frowned', *The Economist*, 9 October 2008.

[162] Institute for International Finance, Financial Industry Calls for a New Phase of Systematic Dialogue on Global Regulation, New IIF Report Sees Recovery in Global Capital after Year of Intense Strain, Press Release, 3 October 2009, available at www.iif.com/press/press+119.php.

[163] 'To the Dungeon', *The Economist*, 17 September 2009.

[164] T. Braithwaite, 'US Senate to Introduce Financial Bill', *Financial Times*, 1 November 2009.

[165] Ibid.

[166] 'Régulation bancaire: l'étonnante ambition du Sénat américain', *Le Monde*, 12 November 2009.

Reserve has been creating new rules in the last two years, directed at abusive mortgage practices, opaque home equity loans and predatory loans.[167] It has also been targeting misleading information about credit and debit cards, such as recent rules on restriction on overdraft fees.[168]

Since global regulation reform can be internationally consistent, transparent and co-ordinated, there has been a call for regulation at the international level. This would prevent the fragmentation of the financial system, thus avoiding the rise of protectionism in some countries or the concentration of speculative flows in others. The financial principles announced by the G20 on prudential regulation, compensation or international co-operation,[169] as well as the work of the Basel Committee on Banking Supervision on capital requirement or leverage ratios,[170] are examples of succesful global regulation attempts.

There have also been calls for the creation of supranational entities, to which countries would delegate regulatory power. Accordingly, the G20 has expanded the Financial Stability Board,[171] and the European Union has announced the creation of macro-prudential supervision at the EU level and the establishment of the European Systemic Risk Board.[172]

2.7.3 *Danger of overregulation?*

Zanny Minto Beddoes, economics editor of *The Economist*, stated, 'How much control will be imposed will depend less on ideology . . . than on the severity of the economic downturn.'[173] Indeed, measures taken while in the middle of a crisis might have been rushed and might not have contemplated the full range of their consequences. Furthermore, the parties that would suffer from these measures might be underrepresented in the

[167] Stephen Labaton, 'New Rules Would Restrict Overdraft Fees on Debit Cards', *New York Times*, 13 November 2009.

[168] Ibid.

[169] G20 Declaration on strengthening the financial system, London, 2 April 2009, available at www.g20.org/Documents/Fin_Deps_Fin_Reg_Annex_020409_-_1615_final.pdf.

[170] See Bank for International Settlement, Comprehensive Response to the Global Banking Crisis, press release, 7 September 2009, available at www.bis.org/press/p090907.htm.

[171] G20 Declaration on strengthening the financial system 2009.

[172] Europa, Gateway to the European Union, New Financial Supervision Architecture: Q&A on the European Systemic Risk Board / the macro-supervision part of the package, Brussels, 23 September 2009, available at http://europa.eu/rapid/pressReleasesAction.do?reference=MEMO/09/405.

[173] 'When Fortune Frowned', *The Economist*, 9 October 2008.

decision-making process.[174] There is a risk of overregulation, through excessive regulatory reform, or through tackling the wrong issues.

Overregulation has been a repeated criticism of the actual regulatory effort and has touched many domains. First, there are numerous examples of how overregulation might affect the areas to be regulated. If banks are asked to hold higher levels of capital, they will lend less, especially to borrowers that appear weaker, and banks might retract from emerging-market lending.[175] Asking banks to replace short-term with more expensive long-term borrowing might deprive banks of millions in profit and thus further affect their ability to lend.[176] Prohibiting derivatives, which were at the core of many failures, such as that of AIG, would deprive the world of an excellent risk-management tool.[177] Regulating 'non-banking' entities in the same way as banks can be off the point: if hedge funds, unlike traditional banks, do not affect taxpayers in case of failure, then regulating their managers' compensation to try to prevent risky behaviour might be irrelevant.[178] The creation of the United States Financial Institutions Regulatory Authority might allegedly lead to a weaker or uncertain regulatory situation if this entity is not provided with the right resources, competencies and powers.[179] There has also been concern that the US Federal Reserve's new rules restricting overdraft fees might incite Community banks simply to stop offering overdraft protection to consumers and reduce their financing possibilities.[180] Hence economists fundamentally worry that overregulation, provoked by the quest for financial stability, will negatively affect economic growth and innovation.

The trend towards international regulation has been criticized by certain economists.[181] They consider it unfeasible or unrealistic that

[174] Aizenman 2009.

[175] Institute for International Finance, Financial Industry Calls for a New Phase of Systematic Dialogue on Global Regulation, New IIF Report Sees Recovery in Global Capital After Year of Intense Strain, Press Release, 3 October 2009, available at www.iif.com/press/press+119.php.

[176] 'Parting Shot', *The Economist*, 8 October 2009.

[177] 'Over the Counter, Out of Sight', *The Economist*, 12 November 2009.

[178] P. Brianҫon, 'Smash the Pinata', Breakingviews.com, 12 November 2009, available at www.breakingviews.com/2009/11/12/eu%20hedge%20fund%20regulation.aspx?sg=archive.

[179] 'Régulation bancaire: l'étonnante ambition du Sénat américain', *Le Monde*, 12 November 2009.

[180] Labaton 2009.

[181] D. Rodrik, 'A Plan B for Global Finance', *The Economist*, 12 March 2009.

countries delegate their sovereignty to international bodies, especially considering that power will be vested in parliaments when national taxpayers are likely to be affected.[182] Some are concerned that erroneous financial measures could be taken and then imposed internationally, thereby multiplying their harmful consequences at a global level.[183] Moreover, advocates of national regulatory reforms often consider that one size does not fit all. Each state should decide whether it wants to take measures and in which area, itself being responsible for deciding whether to favour financial stability over growth or innovation.[184]

2.8 Concluding remarks

Although there are many different types of crisis, a crisis is always composed of four elements: intense difficulty, emergency, turning point and decision-making. It is difficult to know with precision when a crisis starts and ends. The rapidity and accuracy of the decisions taken will be crucial to escaping the crisis.

Each type of crisis can lead to another type. The financial and economic crises that the world faced in 2007 are typical examples of a chain of crises: the banking crisis developed into a global financial crisis that in turn developed into an economic crisis. Like any type of crisis, although this economic crisis has caused significant damage, there are still opportunities for whoever is ready to seize them, by innovating and repositioning, or by taking advantage of economic distress. There is hope that a similar crisis might be avoided in the future, thanks to regulatory efforts; discussion is still open as to how these efforts should be undertaken and how to avoid the negative effects of overregulation.

[182] Weder di Mauro 2009.
[183] Rodrik 2009.
[184] Ibid.

3

Failing-firm defence

Capitalism without bankruptcy is like Christianity without hell.

Frank Borman[1]

Today, certain people file for bankruptcy, businesses and individuals, and it no longer has the stigma it once had. Now it's almost considered wise, a way to regroup and come back again.

David Dinkins[2]

Acquisition of a failing firm is always efficient.

Prof. Fred S. McChesney[3]

3.1 Introduction

Nowadays, during this period of crisis, we face global restructuring of industries that may be the most significant economic change of the last decades. Fierce competition from imports, severe overcapacity in some industries and technological advancements are only some of the features that characterize contemporary markets. Distressed companies on the verge of insolvency are a common phenomenon observed in both developed and developing economies. Companies that are in distressed financial conditions may choose to embark on a restructuring process in order to ensure their viability and profitability.

Restructuring is often done as part of insolvency procedures. Restructuring is the term for the act of fully or partially dismantling and reorganizing a company. It might involve the selling of sectors or units

[1] Frank F. Borman is a retired NASA astronaut and engineer, best remembered as the commander of Apollo 8. He was also the chief executive officer of Eastern Airlines from 1975 to 1986.

[2] David Norman Dinkins is a politician who held the position of Mayor of New York City from 1990 to 1993.

[3] See Fred S. McChesney, 'Defending the Failing Firm Defence' (1986) 65 *Nebraska Law Review* 1.

of the company and severe job losses. Restructuring of the liability and of stockholders' equity components of a financial balance sheet is normally undertaken because the company does not generate enough cash flow to service its debt and other liabilities. Restructuring may include deferral of the principal or of interest payments on debt, the equalization of debt or other liabilities, and, in insolvency, the modification or termination of burdensome contractual commitments. Restructuring is normally done with reference to the outcome that would ensue in a insolvency proceeding even where no such proceeding occurs.[4]

Debt restructuring aims at enabling the company to continue business operation without danger from debt. One of the costs associated with a business debt restructuring is the time required to negotiate with bankers, creditors, tax authorities and suppliers. According to Norton,[5] if a company decides to restructure its debt, it will be faced, inter alia, with three alternatives that are negotiated and implemented out of court: out-of-court reorganization, pre-packaged reorganization plans and pre-negotiated reorganization plans. An out-of-court reorganization is the financial restructuring of the debt of the company by means of a contractual voluntary agreement without the intervention of any court or regulatory authority. According to the pre-packaged reorganization plan, the company designs and negotiates a settlement with its creditors without having the need to file a full court-supervised reorganization procedure. Then the approved plan is filed with the court for homologation in order to make it binding upon the dissenting minority. A pre-negotiated plan is negotiated between the debtor and its creditors on an out-of-court basis and then is filed with a court who will summon a creditors' meeting to obtain their consent and approval. If the plan is adopted by the required majority, the court will approve it and it will become mandatory for all comprising parties.[6]

A strategic response for struggling firms and one of the means of implementing a successful debt restructuring process is to combine in order to achieve competitively necessary efficiencies.[7] Either a failing

[4] See www.cmra.com/html/body_glossary.html.

[5] W.L. Norton Jr., *Norton Bankruptcy Law and Practice*, 2nd ed., Thomson, 1994, §86(1).

[6] R. Olivares-Caminal, 'Recognition of Corporate Debt Restructuring Procedures in Latin America under US Law: Lessons from the Multicanal Case' (2005) 2(3) *International Corporate Rescue* 143. Also see I. Kokkoris, 'Weak-Form Tests of Market Efficiency in Corporate Debt Restructuring' (2005) 2(6) *International Corporate Rescue* 337.

[7] D. Valentine, 'Horizontal Issues: What's Happening and What's on the Horizon' (1995), at www.ftc.gov/speeches/other/dvhorizontalissues.htm.

firm within a booming industry or firms in a distressed industry will choose to merge, acquire or be acquired, or choose to sell loss-making divisions in order to enhance the firm's viability and profitability. Given these wrenching transformations, the applicability and importance of the failing-firm defence and failing-division defence might be crucial.[8]

As this chapter will illustrate, a merger or acquisition is one of the means by which a company may wish to implement a restructuring procedure.[9] Merger control has a significant role in today's economies, a fact which is underlined by the ever-increasing number of mergers that are completed. The purpose of merger legislation is to capture mergers that may have anti-competitive effects on the market structure.

There are several reasons for firms to engage in mergers. A merger or an acquisition is a common method that firms choose in order to be profitable and sustain their viability and profitability through time. Mergers consolidate the ownership and control of business assets, including physical assets (e.g. plant) and intangibles (e.g. brand reputation). They can enhance corporate – and wider economic – performance by improving the efficiency with which business assets are used. Further reasons for firms to engage in mergers and acquisitions include economies of scale and economies of scope that firms benefit from, as well as efficiencies stemming from the tendency of some countries to endorse the concept of 'national champions'. In addition, mergers provide means to a firm to exit the industry and at the same time reap monetary reward or compensation for the risks and the initial investments. Furthermore, mergers may also satisfy the ambitions of executives for more power and greater control.[10]

The importance of mergers (and thus of the failing-firm defence) for the restructuring process is indicated, inter alia, by the US Supreme Court in the case *United States v. General Dynamics Corp.*[11] The Supreme Court upheld that three groups – private parties, shareholders and creditors – benefit from the merger of a failing firm. The shareholders

[8] An equivalent term is 'failing-company defence'.

[9] For the purposes of this chapter, the terms 'merger' and 'acquisition' will be used interchangeably and will refer to the term 'concentration'.

[10] Managers may be interested in the size, growth or risk diversification of the company they run. Owners of firms may sometimes give managers incentives in their contracts to achieve some of these targets (i.e. increasing the firm's size in the marketplace). See further M. Motta, *Competition Policy: Theory and Practice*, Cambridge University Press, 2004, at p. 243.

[11] *United States v. General Dynamics Corp.*, (1974) 415 U.S. 486.

are unlikely to lose the investment and are likely to reap benefits if the merger proves profitable. The creditors will benefit as a result of retaining their rights against the debtor and are likely to be reimbursed for the credit they have provided to the firm. On the contrary, in insolvency proceedings they are not as likely to be fully reimbursed.

The restructuring process can thus be used as a tool to determine if a division of the firm or the whole firm must be merged or acquired by another undertaking in order to maintain its viability and its future prospects for profitability. In such a case the only possible means of restructuring is through a successful merger or acquisition. This merger may need to be assessed by the relevant competition authorities.[12] If the authorities consider that the merger will have anti-competitive effects, they may block it, resulting thus in the unsuccessful completion of the restructuring procedure.

The US and the EU have their own criteria for assessing the argument for the failing-firm defence. The satisfaction of these criteria is an essential factor for a merger which is likely to have anti-competitive effects to be allowed to proceed. In addition, each of the above jurisdictions has its own legislation regarding merger assessment. It will be necessary for the purposes of this chapter and for a complete understanding of the implications of merger legislation, as they are identified through the failing-firm defence, to provide a brief analysis of the legislation concerning the assessment of mergers in these jurisdictions. Thus for each of the above jurisdictions an analysis of the relevant legislation will be provided. It is imperative to tie the analysis of the relevant legislation with its actual application in cases where the failing-firm defence has been invoked. For each jurisdiction the landmark cases related to failing-firm defence will be analysed in order to evaluate how the competition authorities and the courts have assessed the failing-firm defence.

Apart from the analysis of competition legislation surrounding mergers, this chapter will also include a brief analysis of the restructuring process during which the failing-firm defence may be invoked if it is decided that the means of viability of the firm are through a merger or acquisition. Therefore an analysis of the basic concepts surrounding corporate debt restructuring is imperative.

[12] This chapter will mainly use the term 'competition', which is interchangeable with 'antitrust' as used in the US for the law or authorities that protect trade and commerce from restraints, monopolies, price-fixing and price discrimination. See *Black's Law Dictionary* (8th ed. 2004) for the definition of antitrust law, at p. 92.

This chapter will begin with a brief analysis of corporate restructuring and then proceed to address the notion of failing-firm defence. Subsequently, it will deal with the concepts of failing-firm defence and failing-division defence as these two have been developed in the legislation and case law of the EU, other European national competition authorities and the US. The chapter will expose some of the controversial issues surrounding the success of the failing-firm defence. Finally, concluding remarks regarding failing-firm defence and failing-division defence will be presented.

3.2 Corporate restructuring

In the analysis of companies with financial difficulties or that are on the verge of insolvency it is essential to assess the plan of reorganization and the prospects of the reorganized company as regards profitability and viability. Changes in market conditions which may affect the future prospects of a company's viability should also be taken into account.

The concept of insolvency consists in a debtor's ultimate inability to meet financial commitments.[13] Liabilities exceed assets, with the consequence that it is impossible for all liabilities to be discharged in full. Insolvency as such is not a condition to which legal consequences can be attached. These occur only after there has been some formal proceeding, such as winding up or the appointment of an administrator or administrative receiver. A formal insolvency proceeding is necessary, at which point transactions entered into by the company at a time when it was insolvent will in certain conditions be void or liable to be set aside. A winding-up or administration order gives retroactive legal significance to an earlier state of insolvency which at the time it first arose had no impact in law.[14]

Significant adjustments are often made to the assets and liabilities by the time a company completes its reorganization process. These adjustments are noticeable when assets are sold during the reorganization process and also when the asset values are compared with estimates of the liquidation value of the assets. In planning the reorganization, a failing firm with one or more subsidiaries must decide if the plan will

[13] I. Fletcher, *The Law of Insolvency*, Sweet and Maxwell, 1990, at p. 1.

[14] R.M. Goode, *Principles of Corporate Insolvency Law*, 2nd ed., Sweet and Maxwell, 1997, at p. 65.

incorporate substantive consolidation of the subsidiaries. Under substantive consolidation, all of the assets and liabilities of the entities in question are pooled and used collectively to pay debts. In order for substantive consolidation to be granted by a court, proponents must prove that the parent and the subsidiaries in question operated as a single unit. This can be proved by such means as intercompany guarantees and transfers of assets.[15]

In general, there are different approaches that can be used to invest in the distressed market. Large and aggressive investors may buy a substantial block of the debtor's bonds and try to become a significant player in the reorganization plan. Moreover, investors may pool their resources in distressed-debt funds ('vulture funds'), which invest in the securities of insolvent companies. Such funds often operate by acquiring large blocks of securities of a particular class and use their leverage in the reorganization process to formulate a plan favourable to their position. In addition, individual investors may buy specific securities in an insolvent company. Not all such strategies are profitable.[16]

The analysis of insolvent companies that have filed plans of reorganization should be approached in a systematic way. The analysis must place more emphasis on pro formas and less on historical results. Often the relative rates of return among old securities are substantially reordered under the reorganization plans. The analysis must therefore value all securities of debtors and purchase those that offer the highest potential returns.[17]

As mentioned above, significant adjustments are often made to the assets and liabilities by the time a company completes its reorganization process, which, inter alia, concern assets that are sold during the reorganization process. In such cases, the success of the failing-firm defence may prove invaluable. The concept of the failing-firm defence is the focus of the next part of this chapter.

3.3 Failing-firm defence

The failing-firm defence refers to the supposedly neutral effect on competition of concentrations where one (or both) of the merging parties

[15] F. Fabozzi, *The Handbook of Fixed Income Securities*, 3rd ed., Business One Irwin, 1991, at p. 399.

[16] Ibid., at p. 401.

[17] Ibid., at p. 406.

(the acquirer and/or the target) are failing or will fail, due to poor financial performance.[18]

As mentioned above, a significant and frequent, in certain economies, reason for engaging in mergers is the restructuring of debt of a company which is on the verge of insolvency. There is a growing literature on the effect of insolvency procedures on *ex ante* decisions by firms and shareholders. The restructuring of the debt may entail the sale of a loss-making division and, if the company has subsidiaries, the sale of the subsidiary or subsidiaries as a whole. Thus failing-firm defence and failing-division defence can be invoked in cases where this sale is assessed by the relevant competition authorities. However, the failing-division defence has not been given much accreditation by competition authorities and courts. One would hope that in periods of crisis this trend will change.

Weeds and Mason argue that the policy towards failing firms that competition authorities may adopt affects entry decisions.[19] A firm entering a market also considers its ease of exit, foreseeing that it may later wish to leave should market conditions deteriorate. A way of entering a market is the acquisition of or merger with an incumbent. Such a merger or acquisition will allow the entrant to benefit from the infrastructure, expertise and customer base of the incumbent in the market. In addition, by facilitating exit in times of financial distress, the failing-firm defence can encourage entry so as to increase welfare overall. Even if welfare is decreased when the firm enters the market by merging with or acquiring an incumbent, the increase in welfare resulting from earlier entry may more than offset this loss.

Apart from the importance and implications of entry in a merger involving a failing firm, in the assessment of a merger in a failing industry the competition authorities should also pay attention to potential dynamic or innovative efficiencies. Dynamic or innovative efficiencies may make a particularly powerful contribution to competitive dynamics, R & D and welfare, but are not readily verifiable and quantifiable because they tend to focus on future products. Merger analysis should give efficiencies more weight if the profitability of a failing industry can be improved by the merger (e.g. by lowering fixed costs) even if the price effects are not immediate. Thus there is a trade-off between the viability

[18] V. Baccaro, 'Failing Firm Defence and Lack of Causality: Doctrine and Practice in Europe of Two Closely Related Concepts' (2004) 1 *ECLR* 11, at p. 11.

[19] R. Mason and H. Weeds (2003), 'The Failing Firm Defence: Merger Policy and Entry', at repec.org/res2003/Mason.pdf.

of the failing firm and the positive impact that it may have on competition due to the existence of one additional competitor in the market and further consolidation in the market (if a competitor merges with or acquires the failing firm) due to the merger, which may also result, however, from the exit of the failing firm from the market.

Competition authorities have recognized the importance of a merger or acquisition in avoiding insolvency, the impact of the failing-firm defence on entry in the market, and the role of potential dynamic or innovative efficiencies, and have taken into account the financial distress in which a company may be in the assessment of mergers involving the said company. Both in the EU and the US the 'failing-firm defence' is addressed in the merger guidelines. The case law has provided further impetus to the development of the defence in both jurisdictions.

In order to accomplish the target of sustaining the competitive structure of the post-merger market, the competition authority must apply a legal substantive test in order to determine the likelihood of the anticompetitive impact of the merger, as well as to determine the level and quality of evidence it needs in its assessment of whether the merger should be prohibited.

After analysing the fundamentals and the rationale behind corporate debt restructuring, in the next parts of this chapter the argument for failing-firm defence, how it can be taken into account and how it can influence the assessment of a merger will be addressed. We will analyse the criteria that need to be satisfied in order for such a defence to be acceptable and examine how the defence has been invoked in practice in the assessment of merger cases and whether it has been successful. The analysis of merger legislation provided in this chapter will focus on EU and US law.

In order to acquire a complete understanding of the implications of merger legislation for corporate debt restructuring, a brief background of the competition legislation and the implementing structure of the competition legislation in the EU and the US is necessary. After briefly examining these issues, the chapter will analyse cases where the failing-firm defence has been invoked and assess the criteria that need to be satisfied in order for such a defence to be successful.

3.4 The European Union perspective

For the achievement of the aims of the treaty, Article 3(1)(g) gives the Community the objective of instituting a system ensuring that

> competition in the internal market is not distorted. Article 4(1) of the treaty provides that the activities of the member states and the Community are to be conducted in accordance with the principle of an open market economy with free competition. These principles are essential for the further development of the internal market.
>
> The completion of the internal market and of economic and monetary union, the enlargement of the European Union and the lowering of international barriers to trade and investment will continue to result in major corporate reorganizations, particularly in the form of concentrations.[20]
>
> Council Regulation (EC) No 139/2004 of 20 January 2004 on the control of concentrations between undertakings (the EC Merger Regulation)[21]

3.4.1 Legislation

The Commission will, in line with the case law of the European Court of Justice (ECJ),[22] consider the 'failing-firm defence'. In vigorously competitive markets, mergers involving failing firms may often enhance general welfare, either through increasing the efficiency of existing capacity, redeploying that capacity to socially more valued uses, or preserving jobs and having other socially beneficial advantages.[23] Moreover, there might be, on economic grounds, beneficial effects resulting from, inter alia, economies of scale, economies of scope, or other efficiencies, so that prohibiting the deal would add new detrimental economic and social effects to the effect on competition which would exist in any case. The burden of proof of such welfare benefits lies with the party that claims the defence. If one of the companies in the merger is a 'failing firm' and would leave the market anyway, then the merger may be deemed not significantly to impede effective competition. The basic requirement is that the deterioration of the

[20] Recitals 2 and 3 of the preamble of Council Regulation (EC) No 139/2004 of 20 January 2004 on the control of concentrations between undertakings (the EC Merger Regulation), Official Journal L 24, 29 January 2004, at pp. 1–22.

[21] Ibid.

[22] Applied in IV/M308 *Kali und Salz/MdK/Treuhand*, [1994] OJ L186/30; on appeal Cases C-68/94 and C-30/95 *France v. Commission, Société Commerciale des Potasses et de l'Azore (SCPA) v. Commission*, [1998] ECR I-1375, [1998] 4 CMLR 829.

[23] G. Hewitt, 'The Failing Firm Defence' (1999) 1(2) *OECD Journal of Competition Law and Policy* 113, at p. 115.

competitive structure that follows the merger cannot be said to be caused by the merger.[24]

The 'lack of causality' between the merger and the possible worsening of the competitive structure due to the merger plays a major role in assessing the acceptability of the failing-firm defence. The analysis of the counterfactual, a comparison between the competitive conditions occurring due to the merger and the conditions that would prevail if the merger were blocked, are crucial in assessing the acceptance of a failing-firm defence.

The Commission considers the following three criteria as relevant for the application of a 'failing-firm defence'.[25] First, the allegedly failing firm will in the near future be forced out of the market because of financial difficulties if not taken over by another undertaking. Second, there is no alternative purchase less anti-competitive than the notified merger. There may be the case that buyers are interested in buying the failing firm's assets after the firm exits the market. A firm's exit may also provide the means for new entry into the market. In addition, it may be more beneficial for competition for more than one firm to acquire the assets of the failing firm rather than a single firm acquiring the total of the failing firm's assets. Third, in the absence of a merger, the assets of the failing firm will inevitably exit the market. Once the conditions for the application of the failing-firm defence are fulfilled the merger would not be considered to cause a significant impediment to effective competition in the common market. The three criteria outlined in the Horizontal Merger Guidelines[26] appear to be the cumulative requirements in order to prove lack of causality between the merger and the worsening of the competitive structure that it would otherwise create.[27]

Thus if one of the parties is failing financially, the Horizontal Merger Guidelines would permit an otherwise anti-competitive merger.[28] The rationale is that the competitive structure would deteriorate equally

[24] Guidelines on the Assessment of Non-Horizontal Mergers under the Council Regulation on the Control of Concentrations between Undertakings, Official Journal C 265 of 18 October 2008 (hereafter Guidelines), §89.

[25] Guidelines, §90.

[26] Guidelines on the Assessment of Horizontal Mergers under the Council Regulation on the Control of Concentrations between Undertakings, Official Journal C 31, 5 February 2004, at pp. 5–18.

[27] Baccaro 2004, at p. 23.

[28] Firms on the verge of administration may not meet the criterion of exit of the firm in the near future. Firms in liquidation, though, are more likely to satisfy the criterion. It should be noted that decisions by an in-profit parent company to shut down loss-making subsidiaries are not likely to be accepted as a credible failing-firm defence.

absent the merger. The future market structure would be equally detrimental to competition irrespective of whether the deal were cleared or blocked. Thus there is no link of causality between the merger and the negative effects on competition and therefore no legal ground for prohibiting the merger. The Commission made it clear in the *Kali und Salz*[29] decision that the acceptance of the failing-firm defence is an exceptional situation. Normally, there would be a presumption that a concentration which results in a significant impediment to effective competition is the cause of this deterioration in the competitive structure. The burden of proof that the requirements of the failing-firm defence are fulfilled and that there is no causal link between the merger and the deterioration of the competitive structure is upon the parties.

Firms on the verge of administration may not meet the criterion of exit of the firm in the near future. Firms in liquidation, though, are more likely to satisfy the criterion. Decisions by a parent company which is profitable to shut down its loss-making subsidiaries are not likely to be accepted as a credible failing-firm defence.

3.4.2 *Application of the failing-firm defence*

Even before the prior Regulation 4064/89 came into force,[30] the Commission dealt with firms acquiring bankrupt companies. In 1989, the Commission authorized Mannesmannröhrenwerke AG, Klöckner Stahl GmbH, Krupp Stahl AG, Lech Stahlwerke GmbH, Thyssen Stahl AG, Thyssen Edelstahlwerke AG and the Land of Bavaria to form a new company under the name Neue Maxhütte Stahlwerke GmbH. The new company would take over part of the facilities and workforce of Eisenwerk Gesellschaft Maximilianschütte mbH, which was declared bankrupt on 16 April 1987. The Land of Bavaria would hold 45 per cent of the shares in the new company, with the remaining 55 per cent being divided among the other companies that formed the Neue Maxhütte Stahlwerke Gmbh. A restructuring plan was devised that provided for production cuts and closure of the Haidhof works. The plan was expected to help the company return to viability, as well as to contribute to the restructuring of the steel industry in the European Community.[31]

[29] IV/M308 *Kali und Salz/MdK/Treuhand*, [1994] OJ L186/30.

[30] 4064/89 entered into force on 21 September 1990.

[31] Nineteenth Report on Competition Policy, at p. 86, europa.eu.int/comm/competition/publications/publications/#PORTS.

The Commission's approach to situations where the failure of a firm is imminent unless the merger is consummated will be analysed below in this chapter. In such cases, the parties can request derogation under Article 7(3) of the ECMR, as is indicated by the *Kelt/American Express* case analysed below.

The previous ECMR, 4064/89, did not include any reference to the failing-firm defence. However, the defence had been invoked and dealt with in a number of Commission decisions, the most important of which are analysed below.

Aerospatiale-Alenia/De Havilland

Initially, the failing-firm defence was invoked in *Aerospatiale*.[32] Alenia-Aeritalia e Selenia Spa (hereafter Alenia) and Aerospatiale SNI (hereafter Aerospatiale) would have acquired De Havilland, Boeing's regional aircraft division (hereafter De Havilland). Aérospatiale and Alenia were already active through Avions de Transport Régional (hereafter ATR) in the relevant markets for regional turboprop aircraft (three different markets were defined according to the size of the aircraft). The activities of ATR and De Havilland were overlapping in the market for medium-size turboprops, where the new entity would have reached a 64 per cent market share worldwide. The parties invoking the failing-firm defence argued that Boeing would shut down De Havilland. The Commission questioned the relevance, for the assessment of dominance under 4064/89, of De Havilland facing liquidation if it were not taken over by Aerospatiale-Alenia. The Commission argued that such elimination was not probable.[33] In addition, the Commission argued that even if De Havilland exited the market, the parties were not the only potential purchasers.

In assessing the likelihood of De Havilland leaving the market in the absence of the merger, the Commission took into account a number of factors including that De Havilland produced good-quality, well-known and highly respected products; that the net selling price of its aircraft had increased; and that production costs had decreased while there was still room for further increase of productivity.[34] Although the Commission did not expressly mention this aspect, the burden of proof is heavier for

[32] Case IV/M.053 *Aerospatiale-Alenia/De Havilland*, [1991] OJ L334/42.

[33] Ibid., para. 31.

[34] OECD, 'Failing firm defence' (1996), www.oecd.org/dataoecd/35/6/1920253.pdf, at p. 93.

the merging firms in the case of a failing division than in the case of a failing firm.

Kali und Salz[35]

The concept and the condition of the failing-firm defence were discussed at length in the Commission's decision in *Kali und Salz*. The case concerned the joint venture between Kali, Salz and Treuhandanstalt (hereafter Treuhand) and the concentration of the rock salt and potash activities of Kali and Salz, a subsidiary of the German chemical company BASF Aktiengesellschaft, and MdK, a state-owned company of the former German Democratic Republic. The above-mentioned concentration would create a monopoly on the market (98 per cent in the market for potash products).

The economic situation of MdK was critical and the firm was on the verge of bankruptcy. MdK's current economic situation was mainly a result of the firm's operating structure and of a crisis in sales attributable primarily to the collapse of markets in Eastern Europe. In addition, MdK's sales on the German market had fallen quite substantially, and MdK would not be able to dispose of an efficient distribution system. The undertaking could not continue to operate without Treuhand, which had been covering the losses.

Hence the Commission, in its appraisal of the notified proposal of merger, examined whether the requirements of the failing-firm defence were met. The parties argued that, without the merger, MdK would soon be forced out of the market and that the market shares that would become available would be acquired by Kali and Salz.

Without an acquisition by a private industrial partner with the necessary management expertise and in the absence of synergies, a rescue of MdK appeared to be unlikely. The Commission stated that the costs of restructuring would be higher than the aid provided for the merger. An administration charged with privatization cannot be expected to rescue with extraordinarily high aid one of its own undertakings that cannot be expected to survive and to hold it in the long term as a state-owned company. The Commission concluded, then, that there was sufficient proof that MdK would withdraw from the market if it were not taken over by a private undertaking.

In addition, due to the fact that the structural factors of the German potash market had isolated it from competitors from other countries,

[35] IV/M308 *Kali und Salz/MdK/Treuhand*, [1994] OJ L186/30.

the Commission accepted that MdK's share of the German potash market would accrue to Kali and Salz since the latter could increase its potash production without any further expenditure and become the sole supplier in the German market.

The Commission further accepted that a purchase of all or a substantial part of MdK by companies other than Kali and Salz could be discounted. The Commission concluded that Goldman Sachs had made a substantial effort to interest as many firms as possible in purchasing MdK. According to the Commission, the lack of alternative buyers was objectively justified by a number of factors: the operating structure of MdK, the existence of overcapacities, the generally depressed state of the potash market and the absence of significant synergies as a result of the acquisition.

The Commission stated that a merger which should normally be considered to lead to the creation or reinforcement of a dominant position on the part of the acquiring firm can be regarded as not causing such a position in the market if, even in the event of the merger being prohibited, the acquirer would inevitably achieve or reinforce a dominant position.

Thus, there is a lack of causality between the concentration and the deterioration of the competitive structure if:[36]

(1) the acquired undertaking would in the near future be forced out of the market if not taken over by another undertaking,
(2) the acquiring undertaking would take over the market share of the acquired undertaking if it were forced out of the market,
(3) there is no alternative, less anti-competitive, purchase.

The first criterion reveals an exclusive focus on the failing firm's market. If the failing firm's assets exit the market, there will be a tendency for supply in that market to decrease. Such reductions and the welfare-reducing price increases they entail are very likely where there was little or no excess capacity in the pre-merger situation. Furthermore, the negative effects of decreased supply may not be quickly reversed through the addition and use of new capacity.[37]

The lack of causality implies that it is the disappearance of the failing company (which would be unavoidable even in the event of the

[36] This chapter refers to these three criteria as the *Kali und Salz* criteria.

[37] See further OECD, 'Failing firm defence' (1996), www.oecd.org/dataoecd/35/6/1920253.pdf, at p. 19.

concentration being prohibited) and not the concentration itself which creates or strengthens the dominant position. The burden of proof for a missing link of causality lies with the merging undertakings.

In assessing the merger the Commission concluded that after the proposed merger a dominant position in the German market for agricultural potash would be strengthened. However, it also concluded that Kali and Salz's dominant position would be reinforced even in the absence of the merger, because MdK would withdraw from the market in the foreseeable future if it were not acquired by another undertaking, and its market share would then accrue to Kali and Salz. Furthermore, it could be practically ruled out that an undertaking other than Kali and Salz would acquire all or a substantial part of MdK. The Commission concluded that the merger was not therefore the cause of the reinforcement of a dominant position in the German market and cleared the merger.[38]

The Commission further stated,

> bearing in mind the causality considerations outlined above, a merger leading to the creation or reinforcement of a dominant position must take place in such a way as to cause the least possible damage to competition. This means that any alternative partial disposal of the target company which will reduce the deterioration of the competitive structure must as a rule be carried out if the rest of the merger is to be accepted under merger law.[39]

The Commission's decision was appealed by the French government and the Société Commerciale des Potasses et de l'Azote

[38] Recital 23 of the Merger Regulation (139/2004, or Recital 13 of 4064/89) mentions the objective of strengthening the Community's economic and social cohesion. Recital 23 states that it is necessary to establish whether or not concentrations with a Community dimension are compatible with the common market in terms of the need to maintain and develop effective competition in the common market. In so doing, the Commission must place its appraisal within the general framework of the achievement of the fundamental objectives referred to in Article 2 of the Treaty establishing the European Community and Article 2 of the Treaty on European Union. In the *Kali und Salz* decision, after concluding that the 'rescue merger' (or 'failing-firm defence') principle applied, the Commission stated that given the severe structural weakness of the regions in East Germany which were affected by the merger and the likelihood of serious consequences for them of the closure of MdK, this conclusion would also be in line with the objective mentioned in Recital 23. Again, this was not a criterion for the application of the failing-firm defence, whose requirements were anyway met in *Kali und Salz*, but an additional factor pointing in the same direction. See further OECD, 'Failing firm defence' (1996), www.oecd.org/dataoecd/35/6/1920253.pdf, at p. 93.

[39] IV/M308 *Kali und Salz/MdK/Treuhand*, [1994] OJ L186/30, para. 87.

(SCPA), subsidiary of EMC Group, and by EMC in *French Republic v. Commission*.[40] The French government, SCPA and EMC applied to the ECJ for the annulment of the Commission's decision on the grounds that it was incompatible with the common market in the way the Commission had examined the merger in highly concentrated markets, that the Merger Regulation had been applied incorrectly and also that the concept of the failing company defence was used incorrectly.

The French government stated, inter alia, that the Commission had wrongly applied the failing-firm defence, without taking into account all the requirements used in US antitrust law. The Commission stated that in the contested decision it did not adopt the American failing-firm defence in its entirety. Nevertheless, the ECJ stated that it is not apparent how that could have affected the lawfulness of the Commission's decision. The ECJ confirmed that the failing-firm defence was relevant for the assessment of whether the concentration was compatible with the common market. The discrepancy in the requirements between the Commission and the US antitrust divisions did not in itself constitute the ground of invalidity of the contested decision. According to the ECJ, the Commission proved that MdK was very likely to close down in the near future if not taken over by a private undertaking and that the failing-firm defence was applied correctly.

The French government challenged the Commission's inclusion of the criterion that the acquiring party need absorb all the market share of the target if the latter exited the market. The ECJ held that the above-mentioned criterion was intended to ensure the existence of a causal link between the concentration and the deterioration of the competitive structure of the market. According to the ECJ, a failing-firm defence could be accepted if the competitive structure resulting from the concentration would deteriorate in a similar fashion even if the concentration did not proceed. The ECJ further stated that

> the criterion of absorption of market shares, although not considered by the Commission as sufficient in itself to preclude any adverse effect of the concentration on competition, therefore helps to ensure the neutral effects of the concentration as regards the deterioration of the competitive structure of the market. This is consistent with the concept of causal connection set out in Article 2(2) of the Regulation.[41]

[40] Cases C-68/94 and C-30/95 *France v. Commission, Société Commerciale des Potasses et de l'Azore (SCPA) v. Commission*, [1998] ECR I-1375, [1998] 4 CMLR 829.

[41] See further Cases C-68/94 and C-30/95 *France v. Commission, Société Commerciale des Potasses et de l'Azore (SCPA) v. Commission*, [1998] ECR I-1375, [1998] 4 CMLR

Thus the approach taken by the ECJ was wider than the conditions set out in the Commission's *Kali und Salz* decision. The ECJ's reasoning seems unduly restrictive since it could permit the approval of a monopoly but block transactions that give rise to less-concentrated markets.[42]

Saint Gobain

This case concerned the creation of a joint venture in the silicon carbide sector between Société Européenne des Produits Réfractaires (SEPR), which belonged to the Saint Gobain group from France, Elektroschmelzwerk Kempten (ESK), which belonged to the Wacker-Chemie group from Germany, and Nom, a private investment and development company for the northern provinces of the Netherlands (owned by the Dutch state).[43] The operation would have brought together the two largest producers of silicon carbide and would have enabled them to secure market shares of more than 60 per cent in the markets for silicon carbide for abrasive and for heat-resistant applications.

The Commission rejected the failing-firm defence since it considered that the *Kali und Salz* criteria were not satisfied. The Commission did not expect the financial difficulties of Wacker-Chemie to lead to the exit of the firm from the market. In addition, it claimed that Saint Gobain would not acquire Wacker-Chemie's market share if the latter exited the market. Thus the competitive structure after the merger was likely to be worse than the competitive structure if the merger were blocked. Finally, the Commission claimed that there were alternative purchasers for Wacker-Chemie than Saint Gobain, and less anti-competitive solutions such as the sale of one of the most advanced processing plants in the world (belonging to Wacker-Chemie), whose processing capacities would remain in the market, competing with Saint Gobain.

The Commission could not establish a lack of causality between the merger and its effects on the market. According to the *Kali und Salz* criteria, there has to be no causal link between the merger and the deterioration of the competitive market structure. It can be argued that the *Kali und Salz* criteria that the Commission has defined as necessary for

829, para. 116. The ECJ annulled the Commission's decision due to erroneous findings concerning the collective dominant position on the non-German markets within the Community.

[42] N. Levy, 'The Control of Concentrations between Undertakings', in V. Korah, *Cases and Materials on EC Competition Law*, 2nd ed., Hart Publishing, 2001, at p. 614.

[43] Case No IV/M.774, *Saint Gobain/Wacker-Chemie/NOM*, [1997] OJ L247/1.

a successful failing-firm defence are defined very narrowly and thus cannot easily be met in practice.

Blokker/Toys 'R' Us

In *Blokker/Toys 'R' Us*,[44] the Commission adopted the ECJ approach in *Kali und Salz* in the necessity of lack of causation between the concentration and the creation or strengthening of a dominant position (under 4064/89) or of significant impediment to competition (under the ECMR). An increase of 4 per cent was sufficient to cause the Commission to block the concentration outright. In this case, the Commission argued that the undertaking would go out of business in the near future.

However, lack of causality was not established as the total market share of Toys 'R' Us Inc. was not likely to be obtained by Blokker Holding BV, and alternative, more pro-competitive solutions compared to the merger could be found. It is essential for the acquirer to obtain the market share of the target firm even in the absence of the acquisition.[45] Thus the failing-firm defence was not accepted. As mentioned above, the 'failing-company' doctrine is based on a lack of causality between the concentration and the creation or strengthening of a dominant position. As Baccaro mentions, the defence was technically a 'failing-division defence', but was assessed by the Commission according to the *Kali und Salz* criteria.[46]

Boeing[47]

The *Boeing/McDonnell Douglas* case had both a US antitrust law and a Community dimension. The parties invoked the failing-firm defence in order to have the merger approved by the US Federal Trade Commission (FTC) and the EU Commission.

Boeing US (hereafter Boeing) operates in two principal areas: commercial aircraft as well as defence and space. Commercial aircraft operations involve development, production and marketing of commercial jet aircraft and providing related support services to the commercial airline industry worldwide. McDonnell Douglas Co. (MDC) is a US corporation which operates in four principal areas: military aircraft; missiles, space and electronic systems; commercial aircraft; and financial

[44] Case No IV/M.890, *Blokker/Toys 'R' Us*, [1998] OJ L 316/1.

[45] C.J. Cook and C.S. Kersey, *E.C. Merger Control*, 3rd ed., Sweet and Maxwell, 2000, London, at p. 279.

[46] Baccaro 2004, at p. 15.

[47] Case No IV/M.877, *Boeing/McDonnell Douglas*, [1997] OJ L336/16.

services. In 1996, Boeing and MDC entered into an agreement by which the corporation would merge and MDC would become a wholly owned subsidiary of Boeing.

The market shares of Boeing in the relevant product market would increase from 64 per cent to 70 per cent. By acquiring MDC, Boeing would be faced with only one competitor in the relevant market and its capacity in commercial aircraft, particularly the skilled work force, would also be increased. The notified merger would also strengthen the ability of Boeing to induce airlines to enter into exclusivity deals, thereby further foreclosing the market. The Commission concluded that Boeing already enjoyed a dominant position on the overall market for large commercial aircraft. The proposed concentration would lead to the strengthening of this dominant position through which effective competition would be significantly impeded in the common market.

According to Boeing, MDC was a failing firm regarding its civil section, Douglas Aircraft Company (DAC). Failure of a competitive R & D recovery programme, as well as a threefold fall in its market shares, caused the company's weakness. Due to the fact that, at the time of the merger notification, MDC held 6 per cent of global orders for large civil aircraft, production and revenues from its aircraft servicing operation kept DAC profitable. This profitability clearly precluded the application of the failing-firm defence. The Commission accepted that no existing aircraft manufacturer was interested in acquiring DAC and was unable to prove the existence of a potential entrant who could use DAC as a means of entering the market.[48] Thus the failing-firm defence argument was not accepted.

The FTC, taking into account the consumer welfare evaluation, approved the merger. In its view, the decision prohibiting the proposed merger could harm important US defence interests.[49]

Bertelsmann[50]

CLT-UFA SA (CLT-UFA) and Taurus Beteiligungs-GmbH & Co. KG (Taurus) would acquire joint control of Premiere Medien GmbH & Co. KG (Premiere), BetaDigital Gesellschaft für digitale Fernsehdienste

[48] S. Bishop and M. Walker, *The Economics of EC Competition Law: Concepts, Application and Measurement*, Sweet and Maxwell, 2002, at p. 308.

[49] See, for example, para. 12 of Case No IV/M.877, *Boeing/McDonnell Douglas*, [1997] OJ L336/16.

[50] Case No IV/M.993, *Bertelsmann/Kirch/Premiere*, [1999] OJ L 053/1.

mbH (BetaDigital) and BetaResearch Gesellschaft für Entwicklung und Vermarktung digitaler Infrastrukturen mbH (BetaResearch). The proposed concentration was to be effected through the purchase of shares.

Bertelsmann AG was the common parent company of the leading German media group. The Bertelsmann group had activities primarily in book and magazine publishing, book clubs, printing, music publishing and sound recording, and had holdings in commercial television. CLT-UFA was a joint venture between Bertelsmann and Audiofina SA, in which the parent companies had merged their European television interests. These included the shareholding in Premiere. Taurus was a holding company belonging to the Kirch group. Kirch was the leading German supplier of feature films and entertainment programmes for television and was also active in commercial television.[51]

The merger between the two German pay-TV platforms was prohibited as it would have led to a near monopolistic structure of the German pay-TV market.

Unlike *Kali und Salz*, this case did not involve a whole company being on the verge of exiting the market. In fact, DF 1 GmbH & Co. KG (hereafter DF 1) formed only part of Kirch's pay-TV business. Closure by Kirch of its pay-TV business would not imply that Kirch as a whole would be dissolved. Kirch's decision to shut down the pay-TV market was simply a management decision to give up an area of its business that had not performed as expected. As the Commission emphasized,

> Where the 'failing division defence' and not the 'failing company defence' is invoked, particularly high standards must be set for establishing that the conditions for a defence on the grounds of lack of a causal link have been met. If this were not so, any concentration involving the disposal of an allegedly unprofitable area of a business could be justified for merger-control purposes by a declaration on the part of the seller that, without the merger, it would be necessary to close down the seller's business in that area.[52]

The Commission claimed that the parties' arguments do not suffice to establish the defence of lack of a causal link. The parties had failed to provide evidence that the DF 1 division was likely to exit the market. Even if Kirch were to decide that it would close down DF 1 in view of the high initial losses and failure to live up to expected growth rates for subscribers, its withdrawal from the pay-TV market would not

[51] Ibid., para. 7.
[52] Ibid., para. 71.

automatically follow, since DF 1 was merely the marketing platform for Kirch's digital offer. In the Commission's view, the parties' arguments that the market shares relinquished by DF 1 would in any case fall to Premiere were inconclusive. The competitive situation which would arise, with or without the proposed concentration, was not the same. In addition, the parties' arguments were insufficient to establish that the failing-firm/failing-division criteria requirements had been fulfilled. They had not proved that the acquisition of DF 1, in its entirety or in significant parts, by businesses other than Premiere could be excluded.

Even if Kirch terminated the operations of DF 1, the negative effects on competition would be less severe than if the merger were allowed, since DF 1's assets and all of its pay-TV distribution rights would not be transferred to Premiere, allowing competing pay-TV organizations to acquire Kirch's pay-TV distribution rights and enter the pay-TV market in competition with Premiere. Accordingly the parties did not fulfil any of the *Kali und Salz* criteria in order to establish a defence on the ground of lack of a causal link.

The Commission's rationale was that if the criteria for a successful failing-division defence were not stricter than those for failing-firm defence, then any merger or acquisition involving the disposal of an allegedly unprofitable business could be justified by a declaration that the division in question would be closed.[53]

The European Commission might have considered being less restrictive to a merger involving a division of a firm. However, some assurance that the division's failing status is not merely a reflection of creative accounting as regards issues like transfer payments and the allocation of common costs should have been necessary.

Rewe/Meinl

In this case, the German company Rewe wanted to acquire all the shares of the Austrian company Julius Meinl AG (hereafter Meinl).[54] The concentration would cause the creation or strengthening of a dominant position and thus was cleared after commitments were accepted by the Commission.

The parties, in invoking failing-division defence, argued that Meinl was experiencing severe competitive disadvantages compared to larger

[53] Extract from Levy 2001, at p. 614.

[54] Case No IV M.1221, *Rewe/Meinl*, [1999] OJ L 274/1.

competitors. Similar to *Bertelsman*,[55] the decision to sell Meinl was a management decision to give up an area of business that had not performed as expected. It was not based on the grounds of Meinl's quasi-insolvency. The parties' arguments were not such as to justify applying the defence based on lack of causality. The parties had not proved that in the absence of a takeover by another firm Meinl would in any event withdraw from the market in the near future and that in such a case its market share would accrue mainly to Rewe. The parties' contention that there was no less anti-competitive alternative to the sale to Rewe/Billa, Spar being ineligible owing to its market position, was unsubstantiated. Therefore the competitive situation which would arise with or without the proposed operation was not the same.

The parties therefore satisfied none of the *Kali und Salz* criteria for sustaining the defence of lack of causality. The Commission concluded that the proposed operation gave rise for this reason to the creation of a dominant position. As in the Bertelsmann merger, the European Commission might have considered being less restrictive towards a merger involving a division of a firm.

BASF

For the Commission, a fundamental step in the development of the failing-firm defence was the *BASF/Eurodiol/Pantochim* case.[56] The case was decided before the publication of the EU Horizontal Merger Guidelines.

BASF Aktiengesellschaft would acquire control of Pantochim SA, Eurodiol SA and ProvironFtal NV by purchase of assets from the parent company SISAS SpA. Although BASF would have a market share of 70 per cent, the Commission took into account that the acquiring companies were facing financial difficulties and allowed the merger on the basis that it would have less harmful impact on the market than the counterfactual of the undertakings exiting the market.

BASF stated that Eurodiol and Pantochim were on the verge of bankruptcy and would have been forced out of the market had they not been acquired. On 18 September 2000, Eurodiol and Pantochim were placed under a pre-bankruptcy regime (*concordat judiciaire*) by the Commercial Court (Tribunal de Commerce) of Charleroi in Belgium. In the same judgment, the Court nominated four court commissioners (*commissaires*

[55] Case No IV/M.993, *Bertelsmann/Kirch/Premiere*, [1999] OJ L053/1.

[56] Case COMP/M.2314 *BASF/ Eurodiol/Pantochim*, [2002] OJ L132/45.

au sursis) to supervise the management of Eurodiol and Pantochim during the period of pre-bankruptcy proceedings. In addition, the Italian parent company SISAS was also in bankruptcy proceedings.[57]

During the observation period (*période d'observation*) under this pre-bankruptcy regime, the Tribunal de Commerce ordered the provisional postponement of debts (*sursis provisoire*); that is, a preliminary suspension of the rights of the creditors. Due to the lack of liquidity and the significant amount of the companies' debts, a restructuring plan (*plan de redressement*) which would theoretically have allowed the Tribunal de Commerce to prolong the *concordat judiciaire* and the suspension of the rights of the creditors by means of a *sursis définitif* (stay of execution) was not proposed in this case. Therefore the danger of bankruptcy of both Eurodiol and Pantochim was obvious. The Tribunal de Commerce of Charleroi, responsible for the pre-bankruptcy proceedings, had confirmed to the Commission that both undertakings would have to be declared bankrupt if a buyer for Eurodiol and Pantochim were not approved before the expiry of the observation period. Once BASF had terminated financial support they would inevitably have been forced out of the market.[58] Thus the first *Kali und Salz* criterion was satisfied.

BASF argued that there was no alternative buyer for Eurodiol and Pantochim. Since a restructuring plan could be excluded, the Tribunal de Commerce of Charleroi authorized the *commissaires au sursis* to find a suitable buyer. Subsequently, a number of competitors were contacted. Apart from BASF, no other company approached by the *commissaires au sursis* was ready to submit a viable offer for these companies. The Commission decided to inquire further as to the possibility of an acquisition by an alternative purchaser and concluded that no other, less anti-competitive, solution was available. Thus the second condition identified in the *Kali und Salz* decision was met.

BASF argued that as far as the third condition of the *Kali und Salz* decision, namely the accrual to the acquiring company of the entire market share of the acquired undertaking, was concerned, it is sufficient that only a part of the market share is accrued to the acquiring company. The Commission recognized that the assets of the failing firm would definitely exit the market. This exit would most probably have led to a considerable deterioration of market conditions, to the disadvantage of the customers. The Commission argued that an immediate takeover

[57] Ibid., para. 5.
[58] Ibid., para. 144.

of Eurodiol and Pantochim, after bankruptcy, by a third party seemed unlikely. In addition, a restart of the plants at a later stage, after the expiry of six months, would be relatively expensive compared with an immediate takeover since, inter alia, the shutdown of production would cause additional costs for new catalysts when the plant was restarted. Finally, it was not likely that a third party would buy specific assets of the two companies after their shutdown following a bankruptcy judgment. The Commission concluded that it was very likely that the assets of Eurodiol, as well as those of Pantochim, would definitely exit the market. However, in slightly departing from the *Kali und Salz* criteria, the Commission noted,

> Nor can it be expected that BASF would absorb merely all of Eurodiol's market share since their main competitors are likely to gain significant parts of this share as well. However, the Commission recognises that the assets of the failing firm would definitely exit from the market in this case. This exit would most probably lead to a considerable deterioration of market conditions, to the disadvantage of the customers. The Commission considers that these elements are equally relevant for the application of the rescue merger concept.[59]

The Commission, in clearing the merger, which nominally gave BASF a market share of around 70 per cent in certain markets, placed importance on a series of factors. It took into account the particular and exceptional circumstances of the case, which were characterized by the imminent bankruptcy of the failing companies in the absence of the merger, the absence of a timely alternative offer under the Belgian bankruptcy proceedings, and the inevitable exit from the market of the assets to be acquired, combined with capital-intensive plants, tight capacity constraints in the industry and demand inelasticity.[60] In its decision the Commission stated that the exit of assets and the production capacities of the failing companies would cause 'a significant capacity shortage for products, which were already offered on the market under very tight capacity constraints'. Given this reduction in capacity, at least for a considerable transitional period of time, market conditions would be adversely affected as a direct consequence of the exit of Eurodiol's capacity. As mentioned above, if the failing firm's assets exit the market, there will be a tendency for the supply in that market to decrease, inducing price increases which are very likely where there was little or

[59] Ibid., para. 151.
[60] Ibid., para. 163.

no excess capacity in the pre-merger situation.[61] The Commission concluded that the deterioration of the competitive structure resulting from the notified operation would be less significant than in the absence of the merger and that market conditions could be expected to be more favourable than in the case of the assets to be acquired exiting the market.

In *BASF* the Commission refined the *Kali und Salz* criteria. The Commission indicated that the approach taken by the Court of Justice in *Kali und Salz* was wider than the criteria set out in the Commission's decision. According to the Court of Justice, the existence of a causal link between the concentration and the deterioration of the competitive structure of the market can be excluded and so a merger can be regarded as a rescue merger[62] only if the competitive structure resulting from the concentration is expected to deteriorate in similar fashion even if the concentration were not allowed to proceed; that is to say, even if the concentration were prohibited.[63]

Although the Commission left the first two *Kali und Salz* criteria unaltered, it argued that it was not necessary for BASF to obtain the total market shares of Eurodiol and Pantochim, contrary to the *Kali und Salz* requirement that the acquirer would acquire the market share of the acquired undertaking if the latter exited the market. The approach in *Kali und Salz* is not suitable in a situation where, after bankruptcy, a monopoly situation would not be created as was the case in *Kali und Salz*. Thus the third *Kali und Salz* criterion was changed from the requirement of the acquirer to gain the whole market share to the requirement that the assets of the acquired are likely to exit the market. The Commission stated that for the application of the rescue merger, two conditions must be satisfied:

(1) the acquired undertaking would in the near future be forced out of the market if not taken over by another undertaking, and
(2) there is no alternative, less anti-competitive, purchase.

In *BASF*, the Commission decided that, in addition to the first two criteria, it was necessary to establish that:

(3) the assets to be purchased would inevitably disappear or exit from the market in the absence of the merger.[64]

[61] See further OECD, 'Failing firm defence' (1996), www.oecd.org/dataoecd/35/6/1920253.pdf, at p. 19.

[62] I.e. application of the failing-firm defence.

[63] Case COMP/M.2876, *Newscorp/Telepiù*, [2004] OJ L110/73, para. 207.

[64] Case COMP/M.2876, *Newscorp/Telepiù*, [2004] OJ L110/73, paras. 207–8.

The Commission cleared the merger after comparing the level of competition likely to result from the merger with that likely to result from the exit of the failing firm, and not with the status quo.[65] The Commission once more stated that the application of the concept of the 'rescue merger' requires that the deterioration of the competitive structure through the merger is at least no worse than in the absence of the merger.[66]

The *Arthur Andersen* cases

The *Arthur Andersen* cases were a result of the disintegration of the Andersen network in the aftermath of the Enron scandal.[67] These cases, it can be argued, were decided based on the doctrine of 'failing-firm defence'. However, the issue of failing-firm defence was not addressed and the assessment was focused on the 'causality' issue.[68] The Commission's investigation showed that Andersen Worldwide was no longer able to discharge its core contractual obligations of co-ordinating the global development of member firms. In these mergers there were significant overlaps in the market for audit and accounting services to listed and large companies at national level.

In *Deloitte & Touche/Andersen UK*,[69] the Commission stated that no conceivable alternative to the proposed merger would be less harmful for competition and thus there was no causal link between the proposed operation and any possible deterioration of the competitive structure in the market resulting from the present operation. The parties argued that Arthur Andersen in the United Kingdom (hereafter Andersen UK) was no longer an effective top-tier audit competitor, and hence that the reduction in the number of top-tier suppliers of audit services would inevitably be reduced from five to four, irrespective of the merger. The rapid disintegration of Andersen's worldwide network had compounded the difficulty of any possibility of reversal of Andersen's demise, or of another organization using the individual Andersen units to recreate a fifth force for the provision of audit and accounting services. The Commission argued that even if Andersen UK could continue as an independent audit and accounting services

[65] Bishop and Walker 2002, at p. 309.

[66] Case COMP/M.2314, *BASF/ Eurodiol/Pantochim*, [2002] OJ L132/45, para. 143.

[67] COMP/M.2810, *Deloitte & Touche/Andersen UK*; COMP/M.2824, *Ernst & Young/ Andersen Germany*; COMP/M.2816, *Ernst & Young/Andersen France*.

[68] Baccaro 2004, at p. 19.

[69] COMP/M.2810, *Deloitte & Touche/Andersen UK*, para. 61.

firm, the market investigation had shown that Andersen UK could no longer exist as a viable competitor in the market for audit and accounting services to quoted and large companies.[70]

The Commission in *Ernst & Young/Andersen France* argued that there was no causal link between the proposed operation and the possible situation of collective dominance.[71] As the Commission had already found in *Deloitte Touche Tohmatsu/Andersen UK*, the reasons for excluding this causal link were:

(1) that the reduction from five to four global accounting networks was inevitable;
(2) that the proposed merger was no more harmful for competition than other possible scenarios as regards the risk of collective dominance of the market for audit and accounting services to large and quoted companies.

In addition, the Commission argued that if the transaction proposed did not take place for any conceivable reason (such as withdrawal of the notification or regulatory prohibition), only two possible alternative scenarios to the proposed transaction could be established. These two scenarios were:

(1) the takeover of Andersen France by one of the other remaining 'big four' audit and accounting firms;
(2) no takeover would take place and the existing clients would be dispersed between the remaining 'big four' firms (with two sub-scenarios for the attribution of shares).[72]

Therefore the Commission concluded that there was no causal link between the proposed operation and the risk of collective dominance that would result from it. In addition, the Commission considered all the alternative scenarios and concluded that the mergers did not lead to a more harmful outcome than the alternatives.

Although there was no firm in clear financial hardship, the Commission took into account the *Kali und Salz* criterion (lack of causality) and the counterfactual to the mergers and cleared all the mergers.

[70] Ibid., paras. 45, 46.
[71] COMP/M.2816 *Ernst & Young/Andersen France*, para. 75.
[72] Ibid., para. 80.

Newscorp[73]

This case was a combination of a change from joint to sole control of Stream by one of its parent companies, Newscorp, and its merger with another company, Telepiù. As Stream was a separate division of one company, Newscorp, this merger raised the question whether the failing-firm defence applied when the acquiring firm was financially healthy but one of its divisions, which was failing, was merging with another entity. Thus it referred to whether the failing-division defence can be accepted.

Newscorp argued that Stream was currently a 'failing firm' which would exit the market in the absence of the merger because there were no realistic prospects of Stream becoming profitable as a stand-alone entity. The acquirer of sole control of the failing company was one of its parent companies, which was also acquiring sole control of Telepiù. The whole firm (i.e. Newscorp) was not likely to exit the market. Stream's withdrawal from the Italian pay-TV market would accordingly take the form of a management decision to abandon a business activity whose development had not lived up to the expectations of the firm's managing board.[74]

Newscorp further argued that in the absence of substantial synergies, there was no realistic prospect of a less anti-competitive purchaser emerging because it was very difficult to imagine somebody having synergies large enough to substantially change the financial outlook for Stream. Newscorp had indicated neither the potential buyers with whom Newscorp and the Vivendi group had entered into negotiations to sell their respective companies in Italy nor the reasons for which the negotiations had failed. According to the information available to the Commission, neither Newscorp nor Telecom Italia had ever put Stream on public offer.

According to Newscorp, the assets to be acquired would inevitably exit the market. As regards Stream's premium rights, Newscorp argued that they would most likely be acquired by Telepiù. Following Stream's bankruptcy, the rights would be returned to the right-holders, who would be able to put them up for sale again. Newscorp further stated that there was no causal link between the merger and the deterioration of the competitive structure of the market as a result of the transaction.

The Commission considered that Newscorp had not been able to

[73] Case COMP/M.2876, *Newscorp/Telepiù* [2004], OJ L110/73.

[74] The Commission also took into account the fact that the parties raised this argument at a very late stage, which created further doubts on the probative value of their claim as nothing had fundamentally changed since the notification.

demonstrate that there was no causal link between the concentration and the effect on competition, because conditions of competition could be expected to deteriorate to a similar or identical extent even without the concentration in question. However, the Commission took into account that allowing the merger subject to appropriate conditions would be more beneficial to consumers than the disruption caused by the potential closure of Stream. Thus the Commission took into account the overall market conditions (the chronic financial difficulties of both companies, specific features of the Italian market) in clearing the merger. In this case, the European Commission adopted a more lenient approach in this merger involving a division of a firm. It took into account the specific conditions and features of the market in clearing the merger.

The lack of causality between the merger and the adverse impact on the competitive situation in the market was not substantiated, thus the failing-division defence was not successful. Baccaro suggests an additional criterion to the criteria for failing-firm defence: that the lack of causality as regards the deterioration of the competitive structure of the market should be satisfied if a failing-division defence is invoked.[75] The importance of proving lack of causality is even greater in the case of a claimed 'failing division' which is actually the acquiring company.[76] Otherwise, every merger involving an allegedly unprofitable division could be justified under merger control law by the declaration that, without the merger, the division would cease to operate.

3.5 Derogation: removing the suspension

According to Article 7(3) of Regulation 139/2004,[77]

> The Commission may, on request, grant a derogation from the obligations imposed in paragraphs 1[78] or 2.[79] The request to grant

[75] Baccaro 2004, at p. 16.

[76] Case COMP/M.2876, *Newscorp/Telepiù*, [2004] OJ L110/73, para. 212.

[77] Official Journal L 24/1, 29 January 2004. The respective Article in Regulation 4064/89 was 7(4).

[78] 'A concentration with a Community dimension as defined in Article 1, or which is to be examined by the Commission pursuant to Article 4(5), shall not be implemented either before its notification or until it has been declared compatible with the common market pursuant to a decision under Articles 6(1)(b), 8(1) or 8(2), or on the basis of a presumption according to Article 10(6).'

[79] 'Paragraph 1 shall not prevent the implementation of a public bid or of a series of transactions in securities including those convertible into other securities admitted to trading on a market such as a stock exchange, by which control within the meaning of Article 3

> a derogation must be reasoned. In deciding on the request, the Commission shall take into account inter alia the effects of the suspension on one or more undertakings concerned by the concentration or on a third party and the threat to competition posed by the concentration. Such a derogation may be made subject to conditions and obligations in order to ensure conditions of effective competition. A derogation may be applied for and granted at any time, be it before notification or after the transaction.

This Article provides an exemption from the general rule of suspension of the concentration's realization: the derogation is approved by a European Commission decision, which is taken after a request by the participating (to the concentration) undertakings or even after a request by interested third parties,[80] intending to avoid harm to their interests. In cases where a derogation has been requested, the European Commission, in order to decide if the realization of the concentration should be permissible or not, is obliged to balance not only the interest of the merging parties and those of interested third parties, but also the possible harm to competition as a consequence of the immediate completion of the merger.[81]

Between September 1990 and November 2008, the European Commission has issued around a hundred decisions about derogation from suspension of concentrations.[82] According to Article 7(3) of Regulation 139/2004, derogation constitutes the European Commission's practice only in exceptional circumstances. Nevertheless, derogation has been issued for a variety of reasons that interested undertakings usually provide.[83]

Footnote 79 (*cont.*)

is acquired from various sellers, provided that: (a) the concentration is notified to the Commission pursuant to Article 4 without delay; and (b) the acquirer does not exercise the voting rights attached to the securities in question or does so only to maintain the full value of its investments based on a derogation granted by the Commission under paragraph 3.' See V. Korah, *An Introductory Guide to EC Competition Law and Practice*, 9th ed., Hart Publishing, 2007, at p. 396.

[80] For instance, as interested third parties could be considered creditors, employees and so on.

[81] This is the reason why 'such a derogation may be made subject to conditions and obligations in order to ensure conditions of effective competition'. Compare G. Karydis, 'Le controle des concentrations entre entreprises en vertu du règlement 4064/89 et la protection des intérêts légitimes des tiers' (1997) 1–2 *Cahiers de droit europeen* 81, *passim*, and mainly at p. 92, point 24.

[82] See Article 7(4) of the precedent Regulation 4064/1989. Compare http://ec.europa.eu/comm/competition/mergers/statistics.pdf.

[83] See further O. Blanco, ed., *EC Competition Procedure*, 2nd ed., Oxford University Press, 2006, paras. 16.07–16.09; and N. Levy, *The Control of Concentrations between Undertakings*, Matthew Bender, 2002, para. 5.13.

For instance, there were cases where the European Commission offered derogation in cases of urgent interim measures to ensure the success of the operation,[84] in cases of lack of harmful effects on competition,[85] in cases of fulfilment of prior commitments,[86] in cases of the need to fulfil legal requirements,[87] in cases of the difficult economic situation of the target,[88] or in cases of the need to comply with certain conditions of a bid.[89]

In deciding on the request, the Commission shall take into account, inter alia, the effects of the suspension on one or more undertakings concerned by the concentration or on a third party and the threat to competition posed by the concentration. Such derogation may be made subject to conditions and obligations in order to ensure conditions of effective competition. Derogation may be applied for and granted at any time, be it before notification or after the transaction.[90] If derogation is granted, the concentration will be put into effect before the decision of the Commission regarding its compatibility with the common market.

There may be particular circumstances regarding the financial viability of the merging parties that may necessitate a quick assessment of the merger. If that is the case, then derogation may be granted according to Article 7(3) of the ECMR. The Commission has granted such derogation in *Kelt/American Express*[91] and *ING/Barings*.[92] In *Kelt/American Express* the Commission examined the latest annual accounts and was satisfied of the very serious nature of the undertaking's financial position.

[84] Case COMP/JV.3, *BT/Airtel*, 1998; Case M1865 *France Telecom/Global One*, 2000.

[85] COMP/M.1358 (in Philips/Lucent Technologies (Deconcentration)), 6 January 1999, Case M497 *Matra Marconi Space/Satcoms*, 1994.

[86] See COMP/M.1820 (BP/JV Dissolution, para. 2) and COMP/M.1822 (Mobil/JV Dissolution, para. 2), 2 February 2000, both combined with COMP/M.1383 (Exxon/Mobil, 29 September 1999). See also Case M1419 *Groupe Cofinoga/BNP*, 1999.

[87] See COMP/M.1667 (BBL/BT/ISP Belgium, 23 September 1999), IV/JV.2 (ENEL/FT/DT, 22 June 1998, para. 8) and IV/M.538 (OMNITEL, 27 March 1995, para. 6).

[88] Case M573 *ING/Barings*, 1995. See also Case M3418 *Siemens/Alstom Gas and Steam Turbines*, 2003, Case No IV/M.116, *Kelt/American Express*, [1991] OJ L223/0.

[89] See COMP/M.3007 (E.ON/TXU Europe Group, 18 December 2002, para. 2) and COMP/M.2777 (Cinven Ltd/Angel Street Holdings, 8 May 2002, para. 2). This includes derogations according to Article 7(4) (under 4064/89). An Article 7(4) derogation was allowed in COMP/M.2621, *SEB/Moulinex* (the equivalent of Article 7(3) under 139/2004 is Article 7(4) under 4064/89).

[90] See further Article 7(3) of Regulation 139/2004.

[91] Case No IV/M.116, *Kelt/American Express*, [1991] OJ L223/0.

[92] Case M573 *ING/Barings*, 1995.

Given the specific circumstances of the case it was convinced of the need to effect the restructuring operation swiftly in order to prevent serious damage to one or more undertakings concerned by the concentration. For this reason it granted, on being requested, a derogation in accordance with the terms of Article 7(4) of Regulation 4064/89 allowing the concentration to be put into effect.

In *ING/Barings*, the notification concerned the acquisition of all the assets and liabilities of Baring Brothers & Co. Ltd. Barings Holdings was subject to insolvency proceedings. The operation concerned the acquisition, by ING, of Barings, together with Barings Securities (Japan) Ltd, from their administrators. This involved the assumption of certain liabilities of Barings together with the recapitalization of the new group owned by ING. The Commission granted a derogation, on the basis of Article 7(4) of Regulation 4064/89, given the need to effect a rapid completion of the operation in order to prevent serious damage to Barings and third parties. In view of the market shares resulting from the concentration and the structure of the various markets concerned, the Commission concluded that the operation would not create or strengthen a dominant position such as to impede effective competition within the common market.

In *Siemens/Alstom Gas and Steam Turbines*,[93] Siemens was granted by the Commission derogation from Article 7(1) for the acquisition of the small gas turbines (SGT) business, so that this transaction could be implemented immediately in order to avert serious harm to Alstom and the SGT business. Siemens is a diversified industrial corporation, based in Germany, active in numerous fields including information and communication, automation and control, power generation, transmission products and related services, transport, lighting and medical applications. Alstom is a French company whose main activities are the production of equipment for energy generation, transmission and distribution; power conversion; shipbuilding; and railways. The Commission defined markets for gas turbines as well as industrial steam turbines and large steam turbines which at least covered the entire European Economic Area (EEA) and were probably worldwide.

Interestingly in this case, in order to remove any potential concerns raised by the operation, Siemens submitted undertakings regarding the anti-competitive effects of the proposed concentration in relation to the industrial steam turbine market. However, the Commission came to

[93] Case M3418 *Siemens/Alstom Gas and Steam Turbines*, 2003.

the conclusion that the concentration did not give rise to serious doubts as to the creation or strengthening of a dominant position. On that basis the parties withdrew their remedies proposal.

3.5.1 *EADS/Astrium (II)*

In *EADS/Astrium (II)*,[94] the Commission decided not to oppose the plan of the European Aeronautic Defence and Space Company (EADS NV) to acquire sole control over Astrium NV by purchasing all the shares held by BAE Systems in Astrium.[95] Both EADS and Astrium conducted business in the aircraft and spacecraft industry. EADS was involved in the 'construction of commercial aircraft, telecommunications equipment, civil and military helicopters, space vehicles and orbital infrastructures, guided weapons and guided weapons sub-systems, drones, military aircraft and defence electronics and systems'; Astrium was involved in the 'design, development and manufacture and supply of space systems, including satellites and their payloads, sub-systems for launchers and manned space flight vehicles, ground stations, and various other subsystems and technologies'.[96]

The Commission was convinced of the urgency of the situation and was therefore satisfied that the aim of implementing the restructuring of EADS/Astrium was to remedy the difficult financial situation of Astrium.[97] The Commission therefore granted the parties derogation under Article 7(4) of the EC Merger Regulation, as requested.

3.5.2 *WPP/Cordiant*

In *WPP/Cordiant*,[98] the Commission granted derogation from the suspension obligations provided for in Article 7(1) pursuant to Article 7(4) of the Merger Regulation due to the conditions of financial distress faced by the target company. WPP offered international communication services and Cordiant, the target company, provided advertising and integrated marketing and specialist communication services.

[94] Case No COMP/M.3156, *EADS/Astrium (II)*.

[95] BAES own 25 per cent of Astrium and EADS 75 per cent. Both shareholders jointly control Astrium.

[96] Case No COMP/M.3156, *EADS/Astrium (II)*, http://ec.europa.eu/competition/mergers/cases/decisions/m3156_en.pdf, at p. 2.

[97] Ibid.

[98] Case No COMP/M.3209, *WPP/Cordiant*.

The competitive analysis of the marketing communication services indicated the existence of five national affected markets where the combined share would be below the threshold for dominance. Thus the notified concentration was compatible with the common market pursuant to Article 6(1)(b) of Council Regulation 4064/89.

3.5.3 *Orica/Dyno*

In *Orica/Dyno*,[99] the Commission granted a partial derogation from Article 7(3) of the EC Regulation 139/2004 to Orica, enabling it to acquire sole control of Dyno. Both companies are manufacturers of commercial explosives and initiating systems. The relevant geographic retail or wholesale market for bulk explosives was national. The geographic market for initiating systems was EEA-wide for wholesale purposes and national for retail purposes. The activities of the two companies overlapped in Sweden and Norway, where they both had dominant positions, which would, by the transaction, be strengthened, thus significantly impeding effective competition. However, though shares of both parties to the concentration were high, they were slowly declining due to fierce competitors in the market.

The derogation was made subject to conditions and obligations so as to remove the overlaps of party activity in all of the markets. In accordance with the terms of Article 7(3) of Regulation 139/2004, the concentration was allowed to be put into effect.

3.5.4 *BT/Airtel*

Airtel, a telephony services company in Spain, would be jointly controlled by five shareholders.[100] Under the joint-control agreement, Airtouch, BT and Groupo would be able to vote on any strategic decision. This transaction raised concern whether Airtel would perform all the functions of an autonomous economic entity in the sense of the ECMR.

The Commission granted the parties derogation from the obligation to suspend the concentration laid down in Article 7(1) of the Merger Regulation. This derogation was granted in order to facilitate some of the preliminary actions which the parties need to take immediately to ensure the success of the operation.

[99] Case No COMP/M.4151, *Orica/Dyno*.
[100] Case No IV/JV.3, *BT/Airtel*.

3.5.5 *Cinven Ltd/Angel Street Holdings*

The buyer, Cinven Ltd, is a venture capital company that was engaged in investment management, advice and services to a number of funds (including pension funds and private equity funds).[101] The seller company, Nomura International plc, was an integrated international securities and financial services business that owned Angel Street Holdings. The geographic product market was considered to be the UK. As far as the competitive assessment of the merger is concerned, neither Cinven nor any of the other companies in which it had a controlling interest were active in the same business sectors.

Therefore the Commission granted the request for derogation from the suspension obligation in Article 7(1) of the Merger Regulation on 15 March 2002. As a result of the lack of overlap between the two parties, the Commission found this decision compatible with the common market and with the EEA agreement.

3.5.6 *Teneo/Merrill Lynch/Bankers Trust*

The parties involved in the case[102] were MLE, a subsidiary of the American undertaking Merrill Lynch & Co., Inc., which provides investment, financing, insurance and related services on a global basis; BT, a subsidiary of Bankers Trust Company; Teneo, an autonomous holding company with interests in the energy, air transport, aerospace, engineering and construction, aluminium, cellulose and sea transport sectors; and AA, an airline principally operating between locations in Argentina and various parts of the world.

Teneo SA, Merrill Lynch Europe plc and Bankers Trust Foreign Investment Corporation (BT) established a joint venture to be named Andes Holding BV (Andes). In the above case the operation was under consideration as a state aid in the sense of Article 92(1) of the EC Treaty.

The Commission granted the parties derogation from the obligation to suspend the concentration imposed by Article 7 of the Merger Regulation of Council Regulation 4064/89. The Commission concluded that the notified operation did not constitute a concentration within the meaning of Article 3 of the Merger Regulation and consequently did not fall within its scope.

[101] Case No COMP/M.2777, *Cinven Ltd/Angel Street Holdings*.
[102] Case No IV/M.722, *Teneo/Merrill Lynch/Bankers Trust*.

As the case law analysis of the application of the failing-firm defence indicates, arguments such as that the target company will exit the market if it becomes independent, or that jobs will be lost, will not provide reasons for clearance of the concentration. However, as Ritter and Braun argued, revitalization of the target company to operate more efficiently may constitute a reason for the concentration to be assessed under Article 1(b), which calls for an evaluation of the 'development of technical and economic progress' possibly in the light of 'economic and social cohesion' as referred to in Article 158 (ex 130(a)).[103] With the Lisbon Treaty having come into force on 1 December 2009, interpretative issues could also arise due to the stronger references to full employment and social objectives, including the reference to a 'highly competitive social market economy' in amended Article 3 of the Treaty on European Union. This might induce arguments that a broader industrial policy standard should apply.[104]

3.6 Failing-firm defence cases before the UK competition authorities

The OFT applies four criteria in assessing the failing-firm defence.[105] Pursuant to the OFT's substantive merger guidance,[106] in order to satisfy the failing-firm defence the following conditions need to be met:

- First, in order to rely on a failing-firm defence, the firm must be in such a parlous situation that without the merger it and its assets would exit the market in the near future. Firms on the verge of administration may not meet this criterion, whereas firms in liquidation will usually do so. Decisions by profitable parent companies to close down loss-making subsidiaries are unlikely to meet this criterion.
- Second, there must be no serious prospect of reorganizing the business. Identifying the appropriate counterfactual in such a situation is often very difficult. For example, even companies in receivership often survive and recover.
- Third, there should be no alternative to the merger that is less

[103] L. Ritter and D. Braun, *European Competition Law: A Practitioner's Guide*, 3rd ed., Kluwer Law International, 2004, at p. 597.

[104] See www.wilmerhale.com/publications/whPubsDetail.aspx?publication=9321.

[105] The analysis of the cases draws on Competition Commission Reports, as well as on OFT decisions.

[106] See www.oft.gov.uk/shared_oft/business_leaflets/enterprise_act/oft516.pdf.

anti-competitive. Even if a sale is inevitable, there may be other realistic buyers whose acquisition of the plant or assets would produce a better outcome for competition. These buyers may be interested in obtaining the plant or assets should the merger not proceed: that could indeed be a means by which new entrants can come into the market. It may also be better for competition that the firm fails and the remaining players compete for its share and assets than that the failing firm's share and assets are transferred wholesale to a single purchaser.

The OFT has applied the failing-firm defence in a number of cases under the Enterprise Act 2002: (i) *Anticipated acquisition by First West Yorkshire Ltd of Black Prince Buses Ltd*, where the failing-firm defence applied in respect of a bus business as a whole; (ii) *Anticipated acquisition by Tesco Stores Ltd of Five Former Kwik Save Stores*, where the failing-firm defence applied in respect of individual local grocery stores; (iii) *Completed acquisition by the CdMG group of companies of Ferryways NV and Searoad Stevedores NV*,[107] where the failing-firm defence applied in respect of the target business, and (iv) *Completed acquisition by Home Retail Group plc of 27 leasehold properties from Focus (DIY) Ltd*,[108] where the failing-firm defence applied in respect of an individual DIY store. In this part of the chapter we shall analyse some of the above cases where the failing-firm defence was successfully invoked, as well as important cases where the defence was invoked but not accepted by the UK competition authorities.

3.6.1 *Anticipated acquisition by Menzies Distribution Ltd of Grays Newsagents (York) Ltd*[109]

This case concerned the acquisition of the entire issued share capital of Grays Newsagents (York) Ltd (an independent newspaper wholesaler of national and some regional newspapers) by Menzies Distribution Ltd (a leading British newspaper and magazine wholesaler).[110] The OFT had reason to believe that if this transaction were effected, it would create a relevant merger situation in which the resulting commonly owned

[107] *CdMG/Ferryways NV/Searoad Stevedores NV*, www.oft.gov.uk.

[108] *Home Retail Group/Focus*, www.oft.gov.uk.

[109] *Anticipated acquisition by Menzies Distribution Ltd of Grays Newsagents (York) Ltd*, Office of Fair Trading, 10 August 2007, www.oft.gov.uk/advice_and_resources/resource_base/Mergers_home/decisions/2007/Menzies2.

[110] Ibid., paras. 1, 2 and 3.

wholesale newspaper distribution business would exceed 25 per cent of the supply share in the UK. This satisfies §23 of the Enterprise Act 2002.[111] The OFT decided that the merger would not 'be expected to result in a substantial lessening of the competition within a market or markets in the United Kingdom',[112] and that it would therefore not be referred to the Competition Commission under §33(1) of the Act.[113]

In assessing the competitive constraints on the parties, the OFT considered the service market on the basis of newspaper and magazines wholesaling together and each separately. It decided that the outcome of the assessment would be the same on either basis. It also decided that it was unnecessary to sub-segment newspapers into different types – national, regional and so on – as the outcome would again be the same.[114] In terms of the geographical market, it was found that the 'multiples' (Dawson News, Smiths News and Menzies) are able to supply wholesaling services across the UK since they have a distribution contract of sufficient scale and duration. The OFT adopted a cautious approach in this case by assessing the transaction at a regional market level on the assumption that if there are no concerns regionally in this transaction, then it follows that there will be no concerns nationally.[115]

The OFT decided that no competition concerns arose with regard to magazines since Grays had only bid for two magazine contracts in the York area in seventeen years, after which Grays began to focus on newspapers only.[116] With regard to newspapers, the OFT concluded that the 'merger does not present a realistic prospect of a substantial lessening of competition with respect to large publishers post-merger, relative to a reasonable definition of the counterfactual, that is the competitive outcome absent the merger'.[117]

It was considered that Grays never competed on a newspaper contract outside York, so the possible merger effects were limited to the York area. Menzies had only made three bids for newspaper contracts in twelve years, so absent the merger the constraint imposed by Menzies on Grays' wholesaling activity would be relatively limited.[118] The OFT

[111] Ibid., para. 6.
[112] Ibid., para. 37.
[113] Ibid., para. 38.
[114] Ibid., para. 10.
[115] Ibid., paras. 14 and 15.
[116] Ibid., para. 18.
[117] Ibid., para. 23.
[118] Ibid., paras. 19 and 32.

considered that large publishers would be able to replicate the competitive constraint imposed by Menzies as an alternative bidder on newspaper contracts.[119] They were able to protect themselves from adverse merger effects through constraints such as sponsored entry of other multiple, self-supply and publisher 'change-of-control' clauses.[120] The OFT also decided that the critical precondition to entry is a wholesaling contract of sufficient scale and duration, and thus it is left to the large publishers to facilitate new entry.

In terms of competition between the parties for small or medium publishers, the OFT took the view that this was driven by the wholesalers' agreements with large publishers. Negotiations were unlikely to be driven by the small proportion of business that small or medium publishers represent. This limited the parameters of the competition between the parties for this small proportion of business, and therefore the parameters of a possible merger concern. The OFT was concerned, however, whether these small or medium publishers would have sufficient buyer power post-merger. It was therefore important whether, absent the merger, these publishers would have chosen from two newspaper distributors in York. The OFT concluded there was evidence that this would not occur because Mr Gray was in ill health and would retire instead of continuing the business and investing capital in new equipment. Finally, the OFT did not consider that the potential buying of the residual Grays business or the liquidation of the business were realistic scenarios, and it would have been inappropriate to adopt a counterfactual in which the Grays business would pass to a supplier other than Menzies.[121] Therefore 'any reduction in choice for small/medium publishers should not be attributed to the merger as such'.[122] Thus the criteria for failing-firm defence were taken into consideration in clearing this case but the defence was not formally assessed as a defence to a substantial lessening of competition.

[119] The top four large newspaper publishers account for nearly 75 per cent in terms of Grays' turnover in the York area.

[120] *Anticipated acquisition by Menzies Distribution Ltd of Grays Newsagents (York) Ltd*, Office of Fair Trading, 10 August 2007, www.oft.gov.uk/advice_and_resources/resource_base/Mergers_home/decisions/2007/Menzies2, paras. 20 and 32.

[121] Ibid., paras. 24, 25, 26 and 35.

[122] Ibid., para. 26. In addition, retailers did not have a choice of wholesaler, and this would not change as a result of the merger, so their position would remain unaffected. The OFT also found some benefits in the merger for retailers.

3.6.2 *Anticipated acquisition by Lloyds TSB Group plc (Lloyds) of sole control of HBOS plc (HBOS)*

This proposed merger was announced on 18 September 2008.[123] On the same date, the Secretary of State, under §42(2) of the Enterprise Act 2002, issued a notice of public intervention to the OFT requiring investigation and report, in accordance with §44 of the referred Act. The OFT received an informal merger submission from the parties on 8 October 2008.

On the same date, the Treasury announced some further measures concerning the stability of the financial system, stating that it was the government's intention to provide liquidity, make available capital and take any other measure required to ensure that the banking system was able to overcome the crisis. On 13 October 2008, the Treasury announced that it would implement these measures, particularly to help support the long-term strength of the economy. In particular, it stated that capital investments were going to be made in HBOS and Lloyds, subject to the completion of their proposed merger.

On 24 October 2008, there came into force, in §58 of the Act, the specification of the stability of the financial market as a public interest.

Regarding the counterfactual analysis of the case, the OFT considered that there was a prospect of substantial lessening in competition in three areas:

- personal current accounts,
- small- and medium-enterprise (SME) banking and
- mortgages.

Moreover, the OFT had medium- to long-term concerns (analysed below as the stage II counterfactual) in relation to these product areas, and short-term concerns (analysed below as the stage I counterfactual) in relation to the first two areas.

Failure or inevitable exit of HBOS

In cases where one of the parties involved in a merger is failing, certain pre-merger conditions of competition may not prevail. In this regard, the parties argued that particular care should be had regarding HBOS, the failure of which would have disastrous consequences on financial stability. The parties stated that it was impossible to evaluate the possibility that HBOS be allowed to fail.

[123] See www.oft.gov.uk/advice_and_resources/resource_base/Mergers_home/LloydsTSB.

The OFT decided that it was not appropriate in this case to apply the failing-firm defence, since it was realistic that HBOS would be allowed to fail or its assets to exit the market.

Private-sector solution: HBOS remaining independent without (HBOS-specific) government support

The parties argued that neither was it realistic to consider the prospect of reorganizing HBOS's business. In this regard, they also stated that it would have been possible to sell off its assets; however, such measure would have necessarily meant incurring substantial losses. This counterfactual is analysed below as the stage II counterfactual.

Private-sector solution: acquisition by a third party

Also, the OFT analysed the possibility of a third party, other than Lloyds, purchasing HBOS. The OFT's conclusion in this regard would be similar to the stage II counterfactual analysis below.

Public-sector solution: (HBOS-specific) government support and intervention – stage I counterfactual

The parties argued that a more realistic counterfactual scenario (to HBOS remaining independent) is that the government would intervene absent the proposed merger (most likely by nationalizing HBOS), and that this would probably lead to structural limitations on the ability of HBOS to compete.

In this regard, the OFT considered, despite the fact that some state-aid restrictions could be applied with a negative impact in HBOS's competing ability, that it would still be an effective competing force in the market, even in the case of receiving such government aid.

Private-sector solution following (HBOS-specific) government support and intervention: stage II counterfactual

The OFT considered that in the short or medium term the government would have withdrawn its financial support to HBOS once the financial crisis was over, leaving HBOS an independent entity again. Hence the OFT considered that any purchaser of the bank after this process would be a 'no-overlap' bidder. In addition, any merger which could give rise to competition problems could be cleared with remedies.

This counterfactual is referred to as stage II as it would be subsequent to the stage I counterfactual. Considerations arising in the stage I counterfactual would be primarily short-term, while those arising in stage II would be medium- to long-term.

The OFT considered that HBOS would have represented a significant competitor in the market in the case of being owned by a no-overlap third party, after government aid.

Conclusion on the counterfactual

The OFT considered mainly the two counterfactuals:

- HBOS would not be allowed to fail, and the government would intervene with some form of aid. In this case, the OFT considered that HBOS would still represent an important competitive force in the market.
- However, the government would eventually withdraw such support, either leaving HBOS independent or in the hands of a third party. In this case, the OFT considered that it would still represent a significant competitive force in the market.

Hence the OFT made an analysis of the proposed merger in order to determine if it could be expected to result in a substantial lessening of competition. As previously stated, in both stages HBOS would continue to exert a relevant competitive pressure in the market, although in Stage I it might be weakened.

Conclusion

The OFT concluded that:

- there is a real possibility of the creation of a relevant merger situation,
- that situation may be expected to result in a substantial lessening of competition in the UK,
- it is justified to make a reference to the Competition Commission under §33 of the Act, and
- it would not be appropriate to deal with the matter by way of undertakings under paragraph 3 of Schedule 7 to the Act.

The OFT advised the Secretary of State under §44 of the Act that the test for reference was met on competition grounds. The Secretary of State did not adopt the OFT's recommendation and instead cleared the merger in order to enhance the stability of the financial market. This merger did not satisfy the failing-firm defence criteria, although such criteria were eloquently made by the parties. The OFT received responses from consumer-interest groups which recognized that the merger may be necessary to restore viability but also expressed concerns about the long-term implications.

3.6.3 Completed acquisition of GV Instruments Ltd by Thermo Electron Manufacturing Ltd

GVI and Thermo were the two largest suppliers of isotope ratio mass spectronomy (IRMS) and there were no other companies of similar size.[124] Mass spectronomy is an analytical technique used to measure the masses of individual molecules that have been converted into ions. This technique has applications in many areas of science and technology – university departments, pharmaceuticals, environmental control, the nuclear industry, the oil industry, forensic science, earth sciences and more.

The isotope ratio of an element is the quantity of different isotopes in a sample. Measurements of isotope ratios can provide information about a chemical sample, such as its source or age. For example, IRMS can be used to distinguish naturally occurring testosterone from synthetic testosterone for use in sports doping investigations. There are four categories of IRMS instruments: gas IRMS, TIMS, MC-ICP-MS, and noble gas MS. Product specification and functionality play an important role in defining the product market.

The IRMS sector is small and mature, with global sales of approximately US$50 million a year. GVI, a UK-based company, and Thermo, based in the USA, export the bigger percentage of its production. The products in the market under consideration are supplied on a worldwide basis, therefore the Competition Commission (the Commission) treated the relevant markets (each of the four IRMS instruments identifies different markets) as global.

Prior to notification to the competition authorities,[125] Thermo Electron Manufacturing Ltd, a subsidiary of Thermo, acquired 100 per cent of the issued share capital of GVI for UK£11.6 million. Thermo argued that even though was already a leading IRMS manufacturer, the acquisition would enable the company to offer additional solutions; in particular, GVI will add the capability of noble gas isotope mass spectronomy to Thermo's product offering. The Commission concluded that

[124] See www.competition-commission.org.uk/press_rel/2007/march/pdf/13-07.pdf.

[125] Merger notification is voluntary in the UK.

there is a relevant merger situation within the meaning of the Enterprise Act 2002.

In discussing the counterfactual to the merger situation created by Thermo's acquisition of GVI, Thermo submitted that GVI would have imminently failed and gone into liquidation. Thermo recognized the possibility that some of GVI's assets would have been bought by small IRMS competitors in the UK, but argued that the increase in the competitive constraints on Thermo which would arise from those acquisitions would not be material. Therefore Thermo believed that its acquisition of GVI did not induce substantial lessening of competition compared with the counterfactual.[126]

As regards the criteria for the failing-firm defence, the provided evidence indicated that the business was in rapid decline and led to the conclusion that in the absence of significant restructuring or sale it would fail in the near future. In order to survive, GVI needed to enter into two types of restructuring – operational and financial. However, prior to the sale to Thermo, both options were explored but there was no evidence that any decision would occur quickly enough. In the Commission's view, unless the company received significant equity investment it remained highly likely that the company would fail.

As regards the non-existence of less anti-competitive alternatives, Thermo submitted that it was only approached after a year of discussions that GVI had had with other firms. Thermo was the only interested firm in the deal and was the most likely prospect for GVI to prevent bankruptcy. In addition, there was no strong prospect that the failure of GVI would have brought a more competitive market structure.

As regards the economic conditions in the industry, although there was no element of critical conditions, one of the factors that could have had an impact on the industry was the rapid growth in oil prices, as IRMS is widely applied in the oil industry.[127]

The Commission concluded that the acquisition of GVI by Thermo might result in an SLC in two of the concerned markets and cleared the completed merger after requiring the divestment of the overlap in the two concerned markets.

[126] See further the Competition Commission Report on this merger.

[127] Dave Shellock, 'Global Overview: Geopolitical Concerns Keep Markets on Edge', *Financial Times*, available at www.ft.com/cms/s/0/eba9de10-dee7-11db-b5c9-000b5df10621.html?nclick_check=1, accessed 18 February 2009.

3.6.4 *CdMG/Ferryways NV & Searoad Stevedores NV*

In June 2007, two wholly owned subsidiaries of CdMG,[128] LineCo NV and TerminalCo NV, acquired Ferryways and Searoad respectively.[129] Although the transaction combined two competitors in the short-sea freight sector routes between UK and Continental ports (with a combined share of approximately 30 per cent), the OFT decided that this merger would not be referred to the Competition Commission under §33(1) of the Act on the ground that the merger would not result in a substantial lessening of competition within a market or markets in the United Kingdom.

The particularly novel circumstances surrounding this transaction were that the financial collapse of the target occurred following its acquisition by Cobelfret, even though Cobelfret claimed that the target was insolvent and had been trading on a fraudulent basis for some time prior to the transaction. Given this special conduct, the OFT considered whether it would be justified in departing from its standard counterfactual of prevailing conditions of competition and assessing the transaction on the basis that the target would have stopped trading irrespective of its acquisition by Cobelfret. The OFT requested significant supporting evidence in deciding this departure from past practice.

Cobelfret claimed that the target would have faced serious liquidity issues and could have become insolvent. A number of third parties contacted by the OFT suggested that Ferryways was in a perilous financial position prior to the acquisition.

A post-acquisition audit report undertaken by Ernst & Young found that there were a number of material irregularities in the financial accounts of the target as of 31 May 2007. Based on this evidence, the OFT concluded that the target would have exited the market regardless of its acquisition by Cobelfret.

Based on a series of events, including the loss of loan arrangements and port access arrangements in Belgium and the UK, the OFT concluded that there would have been no materially different outcome from the present case in the absence of the merger and thus accepted the failing-firm defence.

[128] The CdMG group of companies is controlled by the Cobelfret Group of companies. For the purposes of assessing the relevant market and for the competitive assessment, the OFT has used the term 'Cobelfret' to collectively describe both CdMG and the Cobelfret Group.

[129] See www.oft.gov.uk/shared_oft/mergers_ea02/2008/CdMG.pdf.

3.6.5 James Budgett Sugars Ltd and Napier Brown Foods PLC

This case[130] concerned the acquisition of James Budgett Sugars Ltd (JBS), the second-largest non-producing distributor of sugar in the UK, by Napier Brown Foods plc (NBF), the largest non-producing distributor of sugar in the UK. Because of the transaction, NBF and JBS were no longer distinct. The transaction was referred to the Competition Commission by the Office of Fair Trading under §22 of the Enterprise Act 2002.[131] The UK turnover of JBS was greater than UK£70 million, which satisfied the turnover test in §23(1)(b) of the Enterprise Act, giving rise to a relevant merger situation.[132] The Competition Commission came to the finding that the acquisition has not resulted in a substantial lessening of competition.[133]

NBF acquired the entire issued share capital of JBS from ED&F Man Holdings Ltd and Greencore Group plc. British Sugar plc is the sole UK producer of sugar from beet in the UK. Tate & Lyle plc is the sole UK producer of cane sugar.[134]

This case was considered within the context of the European Union sugar regime, established in 1968 as part of the Common Agricultural Policy.[135] The Competition Commission's decision has also taken into account changes that have already occurred in anticipation of the significant reforms, such as proposals for future legislation in May or June 2005 that were announced on 23 November 2004 by the European Competition Commission.[136]

The product market was said by the Competition Commission to be the supply of sugar products to industrial customers.[137] Sweeteners were not seen to be included in the same product market due to problems with the technical feasibility of substitution, the economic viability of substitution, and regulatory restrictions.[138] The supply of sugar to industrial users was considered to be a separate market from retail due

[130] A Report on the Acquisition by Napier Brown Foods PLC of James Budgett Sugars Ltd, Competition Commission, March 2005, www.competition-commission.org.uk/rep_pub/reports/2005/fulltext/500.pdf.

[131] Ibid., paras. 1.1, 2.4 and 2.6.

[132] Ibid., para. 3.11.

[133] Ibid., para. 6.1.

[134] Ibid., paras. 3.2 and 3.7.

[135] Ibid., para. 3.1.

[136] Ibid., para. 3.5.

[137] Ibid., para. 4.10.

[138] Ibid., para. 4.8.

to differences in packaging and branding, which enable the two groups to be priced differently.[139] Different types of sugar (such as white granulated sugar, liquid sugar and specialty sugars) were not separate product markets due to the high degree of supply-side substitutability.[140]

The geographical market was determined to be Great Britain. It was found that the most important constraint on imports from other EU countries comes from the pricing policy of British Sugar, which acts as a barrier to entry and ensures that price levels prevent the existence of any sustainable financial incentive for the import of large amounts of sugar into the UK. As a result, the imports of sugar into the UK by other EU sugar producers had not proved to be a significant constraint on sugar suppliers in the UK, and it followed that the geographic market cannot be said to be wider than the UK. The Competition Commission also followed a decision by the European Competition Commission, which deemed that Northern Ireland was not included in the same geographic market as Great Britain.[141]

The Competition Commission found that JBS was not a failing firm. NBF argued that JBS purchased sugar from British Sugar and Tate & Lyle at prices that were significantly higher than those of NBF, which made it less competitive towards customers. It had also seen a decline in volumes and total profits over recent years. JBS insisted that it had been following a strategy focused on gross margins and overall profitability, and it believed that, absent the merger, the business would have declined continually to a certain level but would then continue as a profitable going concern at this level. The Competition Commission found that although JBS would have struggled to maintain its previous scale of operations, JBS was competing effectively before the merger, despite its decline in scale.[142]

In assessing the counterfactual, the Competition Commission considered the possibility that ED&F Man might have encouraged JBS to pursue a different strategy and to take advantage of the opportunities that it could provide. It also considered what might have happened if ED&F Man had partaken in the sale of JBS and what might have happened had there been potential purchasers other than NBF. It was concluded that there was no basis on which it was likely that either of these possibilities would occur in place of JBS continuing to compete under its existing strategy. The relevant counterfactual was found to be that it

139 Ibid., para. 4.9.

140 Ibid., para. 4.11.

141 Ibid., paras. 4.14 and 4.15.

142 Ibid., paras. 5.2, 5.3 and 5.7.

would have continued to compete with its existing strategy and under the continued ownership of ED&F Man and Greencore.[143] Thus the failing-firm defence was not accepted.

Competition in the relevant market was such that the extent of competition between the UK sugar producers and resellers was affected by the decisions of the producers, who were relied on for sugar supply by the resellers. Price discrimination existed and UK sugar producers could target customers and impact the ability of resellers to compete with producers as well as with each other.[144] In this market, resellers negotiated with customers in competition with their suppliers for the sugar they needed to supply those customers. Although considerations such as the volume of sugar purchased and transport costs were included when establishing prices, there was no real volumetric pricing relationship. Instead it was a process of bilateral negotiation in which the relative strength of the parties involved could be vital. NBF and JBS would have a competitive advantage over other resellers due to their greater scale of operations if producers chose to price volumetrically.

The effect of the acquisition was that it would reduce the choice of suppliers that was available to customers. However, the new company would have limited capacity to raise prices unilaterally where it competed with British Sugar and Tate & Lyle. It would also have limited capacity to raise prices in some cases where it would be constrained by competition from other resellers and importers. The Competition Commission therefore concluded, in clearing the merger, that the acquisition would have limited impact on the overall market, that there would not be a general rise in prices and that prices would not be higher than otherwise would have been the case. The Competition Commission also found that the merger would not induce a reduction in service, support, product choice or innovation.[145]

3.6.6 SCR – Sibelco SA and Fife Silica Sands Ltd and Fife Resources Ltd

This case[146] involves the acquisition of Fife Silica Sands Ltd (FSS) and Fife Resources Ltd (together referred to as 'the Fife companies') by

143 Ibid., paras. 5.9, 5.10 and 5.11.

144 Ibid., para. 5.28.

145 Ibid., para. 5.43.

146 SCR – Sibelco SA and Fife Silica Sands Ltd and Fife Resources Ltd – A Report on the Merger Situation, May 2001, Competition Commission, www.competition-commission.org.uk/rep_pub/reports/2001/fulltext/455c1.pdf.

SCR Sibelco, a global producer of silica sand, products derived from silica sand, and other industrial minerals and clays. It was referred to the Competition Commission for investigation by the Secretary of State for Trade and Industry.[147] In the year 2000, Sibelco acquired Hepworth Minerals & Chemicals Ltd and renamed it Sibelco Minerals and Chemicals Ltd. Before this acquisition the company was referred to as HMC; after it as SMC.[148] Before being acquired by Sibelco, the Fife companies were owned by a company called Anglo Pacific Group plc.[149]

There are two broad types of sand product: construction sand and industrial or silica sand. Silica sand is used for glassmaking, but it also includes grades of sand used for several other industrial purposes. The case primarily revolved around the supply of sand for glass manufacture rather than for other industrial purposes. There are three general types of glass for which this sand is used: clear-container glass, float or flat glass (for making windows), and coloured-container glass.[150] Glass sand is considered to be a scarce resource,[151] and the reason why Sibelco acquired the Fife companies was because of the potential for significant glass sand supplies over the long term. In the parts of the Fife companies' site where Sibelco had mineral extraction rights and planning permission, there were potentially large amounts of glass sand.[152]

FSS was making losses before tax during the years 1997–9, and Anglo Pacific attempted to dispose of the Fife companies through auction by way of tender. Several companies, including Sibelco, demonstrated an interest, but Anglo Pacific did not accept any of the offers made. In the year 2000, following a series of discussions, Sibelco acquired the Fife companies.[153]

It was decided by the Competition Commission that the relevant market was that for all glass sand. This was because there was no scope for substitution on the supply side, and on the demand side it was possible to substitute glass sand for some other manufacturing uses.[154] The geographic market was decided to be England and Scotland, but not beyond. The main users of glass sand are the glass production plants in

[147] Ibid., paras. 3.1, 3.2 and 3.5.
[148] Ibid., para. 3.3.
[149] Ibid., para. 3.18.
[150] Ibid., paras. 4.3, 4.4 and 4.6.
[151] Ibid., para. 4.8.
[152] Ibid., paras. 4.9 and 4.10.
[153] Ibid., paras. 3.30–3.32.
[154] Ibid., paras. 4.33 and 4.55.

Yorkshire, but these have in the past been supplied from quarries such as Fife in Scotland and Reigate in Surrey. Due to the costs of transport, international trade in glass sand between Great Britain and continental Europe was virtually non-existent. This means that there was no constraint on UK glass sand prices from imports.[155]

It was argued by Sibelco that FSS had lost almost all of its Yorkshire business and had therefore not been an effective competitor to HMC/SMC prior to the merger. Thus the merger did not result in any loss of competition.[156] In the winter of 1999/2000, FSS lost two of its former customers, and a third customer reduced its purchases from the company. The loss of these contracts was a result of quality problems with sand that FSS had delivered to these customers the year before, and also of rising haulage costs, which were reducing the competitiveness of FSS's sand. The Competition Commission rejected this argument and found that, despite the loss of much of its Yorkshire business, FSS had in fact been competing with HMC/SMC before the merger. Although it was experiencing quality problems, it was still actively negotiating with its customers for orders in 1999/2000. Competition between HMC/SMC and FSS prior to the merger ensured that HMC/SMC's prices were lower than they otherwise would have been, and without the active competition of FSS for business in the market, HMC/SMC would have been unable to offer two of these customers the favourable terms it did.[157]

Sibelco additionally argued that FSS was a failing firm prior to the merger and that absent the merger Anglo Pacific would have withdrawn financial support and the company would have failed.[158] The Competition Commission rejected this argument on the basis that FSS's sand quality problems in 1998–9 were largely due to failures of management, but by the time of the merger FSS was beginning to prosper from the new management that had been implemented in 1999. Also, FSS could have continued its operations in the short term on a cash-neutral basis. Moreover, the potential of approximately 50 million tonnes of silica sand resources in the adjacent areas to the Burrowine quarry site could have contributed to its operations in the medium to long term. These resources would have been suitable for both container and float glass manufacturing and would have been present even absent

[155] Ibid., paras. 4.43 and 4.44.
[156] Ibid., para. 3.40.
[157] Ibid., para. 2.64.
[158] Ibid., paras. 3.40 and 5.16–5.19.

the merger. The Competition Commission found that if the Fife companies had not been acquired by Sibelco, another company would have acquired them, and they would have remained a competitive force in the supply of sand for container glass and would have been a new competitive force in the supply of sand for float glass.[159]

It was concluded that glass sand prices may have been higher as a result of the transaction than they would otherwise have been. Sibelco (through HMC/SMC) had a 71 per cent share by volume of glass sand supplied to third parties in the UK in 1999–2000. Post-acquisition, those shares rose to 86 per cent, and its share by value of glass sand supplied increased significantly as well.[160] Given that prices in the UK were negotiated individually, no price lists exist,[161] and given the fact that there are severe constraints on new entry, the merger would remove the competitive constraint of FSS in the market and would likely raise prices.[162] The merger was also therefore said to operate against the public interest.[163]

The Competition Commission found that there were no benefits to be gained from the merger. The factors it assessed, some of which were argued by Sibelco, included Sibelco's reputation in the silica sand industry, the question whether the balance of FSS's production between glass sand and construction sand would have been tipped towards glass sand if Sibelco had continued to own the Fife companies rather than another company acquiring them, the environmental benefits brought by the Fife companies' site and the surrounding area, and employment prospects.[164]

The Competition Commission finally recommended that the appropriate remedy to redress the loss of competition by the merger would be the requirement for Sibelco to divest itself of the Fife companies to a purchaser approved by the Office of Fair Trading.[165]

3.6.7 *British Salt Ltd and New Cheshire Salt Works Ltd*

On 26 May 2005 the completed acquisition by British Salt Ltd of New Cheshire Salt Works Ltd was referred to the Competition

[159] Ibid., para. 2.101.
[160] Ibid., para. 4.55.
[161] Ibid., para. 4.63.
[162] Ibid., paras. 2.108–2.111.
[163] Ibid., paras. 2.124 and 2.125.
[164] Ibid, para. 2.112–2.123 and 5.65–5.69.
[165] Ibid., paras. 2.142 and 2.143.

Commission.[166] New Cheshire Salt Works (NCSW) was a small UK producer of vacuum salt, which existed prior to the merger of British Salt and New Cheshire Salt Works Ltd. British Salt and Salt Union (Ltd) were two larger UK vacuum salt producers.

Prior to the merger, British Salt and NCSW were producers of pure dried vacuum (PDV) salt and compacted salt. British Salt were also producers of undried vacuum (UV) salt and NCSW were producers of pharmaceutical salt. The market analysis used by the Competition Commission in order to analyse the effects of competition was the market for PDV and compacted salt.

British Salt and NCSW would no longer be distinct, and as a result of the merger NCSW would cease to exist. Originally the Competition Commission decided that the merger would lead to a substantial lessening of competition (SLC); however, based upon new evidence this decision was later reversed. The Competition Commission concluded that NCSW's former shareholders would have closed NCSW in late 2006 without the merger taking place. Furthermore, the acquisition of NCSW by British Salt had not been, and was not, expected to result in a substantial lessening of competition.

3.6.8 Taminco NV and the European methylamines and derivatives business of Air Products and Chemicals

The proposed acquisition which was referred on 16 July 2004 to the Competition Commission was that by Taminco NV of some particular assets from the European methylamines and derivatives (EM&D) business of Air Products and Chemicals Inc. (APCI) and its subsidiary, Air Products (Chemicals) Teesside Ltd (APCT).[167]

Control of Taminco was bestowed on Alpinvest Partners Private Equity Firm, Dutch private equity investors who were the majority holders of Taminco. Taminco specialized in the production of methylamines and derivatives, which were also produced by Air Products' EM&D business. Taminco and Air Products both produced three types of methylamine. Methylamines are chemicals which are used as feedstocks for the production of methylamine derivatives. APCI was publicly owned and was listed on the New York Stock Exchange.[168]

[166] See www.competition-commission.org.uk/inquiries/ref2005/britishsalt.

[167] See www.competition-commission.org.uk/rep_pub/reports/2004/fulltext/495.pdf.

[168] Ibid., para. 5.

The acquisition of the EM&D business by Air Products in 1998 included the production facility at Billingham, Teesside.[169] Subsequently, in September 2004, during the conduct of the inquiry by the Competition Commission, Air Products noted the closure of its Billingham facility.[170]

The parties APCI and APCT entered into a business-sale agreement with Taminco for purchase of the following assets;

- intellectual property, information, know-how and goodwill in relation to the business;
- stock (raw materials and finished goods), up to a certain monetary amount;
- all contracts and arrangements for the sale or swap of methylamines and derivatives, including sale arrangements with customers of the business; also swap agreements with two large chemical producers and the benefit and burden of the toll manufacturing agreement, and business records in relation to the business.[171]

The Competition Commission came to the conclusion that the acquisition would result in Air Products ceasing to be distinct. The share-and-supply test for the supply of derivatives and methylamines was met and the proposed merger would result in a relevant merger situation.

The Competition Commission concluded that the geographic market for methylamines was EEA-wide. The Commission came to this conclusion on the basis that methylamines and derivatives are hazardous and expensive to transport. As a result there was minimum long-distance trading.[172]

Air Products had stated that even if the merger did not take place or there was no sale of any assets, they would still take the decision to withdraw from the EM&D business.[173] An analysis was conducted on the financial performance and viability of Air Products and the EM&D business, and the Commission concluded that in the absence of the merger Air Products would have closed the Billingham facility and exited the EM&D business.[174]

The Commission also took into consideration the possibility of selling

[169] Ibid., para. 6.
[170] Ibid., para. 9.
[171] Ibid., para. 7.
[172] Ibid., para. 11.
[173] Ibid., para. 17.
[174] Ibid., para. 17.

the assets to a third party as part of the exit strategy, and came to the view that BASF would be the only likely party to purchase the assets. In the absence of the merger, there might not have been the opportunity to sell the assets to any other party.[175]

The Commission concluded that the merger would not affect competition, as the number of competitors would remain the same even in the absence of the merger. The Commission's assessment of market shares and market concentration did not indicate that there would be any difference from the counterfactual analysis.[176] Thus the Commission concluded that as a result of the proposed merger, there would be no substantial lessening of competition.

3.6.9 *Stagecoach Bus and Braddell plc*

Stagecoach Bus and Braddell[177] completed a joint-venture agreement, the subject of which was ownership of Scottish Citylink, with Stagecoach Bus having 35 per cent interest in the company and Braddell having 65 per cent interest. The rights to operate Stagecoach's Motorvator services, and Stagecoach's Megabus services in Scotland (or originating or terminating in Scotland) were transferred to Scottish Citylink, and Stagecoach became responsible for managing the day-to-day operation of Scottish Citylink.

The Competition Commission did not consider that the necessary conditions for a failing-firm defence were met, in relation either to Scottish Citylink or to the relevant Stagecoach businesses as a whole, or in relation to routes or route groups within those businesses.

Based on the financial model of the Scottish Citylink business created by the main parties, the parties argued that Scottish Citylink would have become loss-making and unable to meet its financial obligations in 2006, with no viable restructuring options.[178] The Competition Commission considered that Scottish Citylink had the financial resources to enable it to fund the cash outflow projected by the main parties for 2006, absent the joint venture.[179]

The Competition Commission considered the likelihood of successful

[175] Ibid., para. 19.

[176] Ibid., para. 20.

[177] See www.competition-commission.gov.uk/inquiries/ref2006/citylink.

[178] Competition Commission Report, www.competition-commission.gov.uk/inquiries/ref2006/citylink, para. 5.13.

[179] Ibid., para. 5.14.

restructuring both at the overall business level and on a route group or individual route level. The parties modelled two options for restructuring and argued that Scottish Citylink would not have been able to restructure itself successfully.[180] The Competition Commission noted that the main parties focused their arguments on Scottish Citylink's ability to restructure through acquisition (with and without overhead reduction) rather than through route reconfiguration. The Competition Commission did not consider that a fundamental change to Scottish Citylink's subcontracting model was the only way to restructure the Scottish Citylink business.[181] As to Scottish Citylink's service, the Competition Commission concluded that the position was unlikely to change within the period relevant to the inquiry.[182]

As regards the restructuring of the Glasgow–Edinburgh route, the Competition Commission did not expect that any of these options would have made Motorvator services profitable, for the following reasons: first, the Glasgow–Edinburgh route did not offer much scope for differentiation in terms of stopping patterns, routes, interconnections or journey; second, Motorvator had been unable to win a sufficient share of passengers; third, the Scottish Citylink Glasgow–Edinburgh service appeared to appeal to a broad range of passengers. So the Competition Commission considered it likely that Stagecoach would have withdrawn Motorvator services from the Glasgow–Edinburgh route.[183]

As regards the restructuring of the Saltire Cross route, given the interconnectivity of the route group, increasing Megabus passenger numbers and revenue, and Stagecoach's statements regarding its intentions, the Competition Commission considered that Megabus would have continued to operate at least the same level of services on the Saltire Cross route group.[184] As to Scottish Citylink's Saltire Cross services, the Competition Commission considered it likely that Scottish Citylink (or any new owner) would have attempted, and been able, to restructure or reconfigure its business.

The reasons on which the Commission based this conclusion were that Scottish Citylink might have tried to deal with its profitability problems by making similar changes that the joint venture chose absent the

[180] Ibid., para. 5.17.
[181] Ibid., para. 5.18.
[182] Ibid., para. 5.20.
[183] Ibid., paras. 5.24–5.25.
[184] Ibid., para. 5.27.

joint venture. In addition, Megabus's share of coach passengers varied considerably across the Saltire Cross flows, which represented a significant demand for Scottish Citylink's services, and this was sufficient for it to make further attempts at reconfiguration. Furthermore, there were some flows and some passengers for which the Megabus model would be unsuitable. Finally, maintaining some Saltire Cross services would have brand and reputational benefits for Scottish Citylink.[185]

Regarding the criterion of no alternative less anti-competitive than the joint venture in order to keep competition on the Saltire Cross routes, the Competition Commission considered that a trade sale of Scottish Citylink as a whole to National Express was a possible solution. The reasons were that Scottish Citylink's assets would be attractive to National Express, that National Express was released from undertakings not to expand its Scottish scheduled coach services in March 2005, that National Express would have had some ability to seek cost savings and additional revenues if it were to acquire Scottish Citylink, and finally that Scottish Citylink had not previously been on the market.[186]

Following the withdrawal of Motorvator services on the Glasgow–Edinburgh route, the Competition Commission concluded that it was more likely that Scottish Citylink would have expanded rather than that a third party would have entered. The Commission considered that withdrawal of Motorvator services would not result in termination of subcontracting arrangements, that Scottish Citylink services on this route were well established, that there were no significant seasonal peaks on this route to support temporary entry, that potential entrants would be deterred by the history of Stagecoach's failure, that any new entrant would be required to make a significant investment in frequent services to compete effectively, and lastly that fear of incumbent retaliation would also be a deterrent to entry.[187]

In the event that Scottish Citylink (or any new owner) were to withdraw Scottish Citylink Saltire Cross services, one less anti-competitive option would be to franchise these services. The Competition Commission reached this conclusion based on the fact that incumbent subcontractors would have strong incentives to enter as franchisees, that franchisees would not have to invest in back-office infrastructure themselves, that franchisees would have incentives to maintain services

[185] Ibid., para. 5.33.
[186] Ibid., para. 5.39.
[187] Ibid., para. 5.44.

at around the pre-joint-venture levels and that network benefits would not be lost.[188] Besides, even if Scottish Citylink did not seek to franchise these services, the Competition Commission considered that the sub-contractors would have incentives, and would be likely to enter to fill some of the vacuum created in the market.[189]

3.6.10 *Stagecoach Group/Eastbourne Buses Ltd–Cavendish Motor Services, Stagecoach Group/Preston Bus Ltd*

The OFT referred two mergers in the market for local bus services to the Competition Commission.[190] Stagecoach acquired first Eastbourne Buses and Cavendish Motor Services. Then, in January 2009, Stagecoach also acquired Preston Bus. The OFT methodology to study the competitive effects of transport mergers is a flow-by-flow analysis, accompanied by the use of filters to screen out the flows on which anti-competitive effects are unlikely to be felt.

Stagecoach unsuccessfully invoked the failing-firm defence to have the Preston and Eastbourne mergers cleared. In absence of the merger, Preston Bus might have probably stayed in the market, though reduced in size, or its assets might have bought by another bus operator. In Eastbourne Buses the failing-firm defence was not accepted as Stagecoach considered Cavendish a viable concern, which absent the merger would have continued trading, albeit less frequently.

3.6.11 *Anticipated acquisition by HMV of fifteen Zavvi stores*

The Office of Fair Trading (OFT) cleared HMV plc's purchase of fifteen former Zavvi stores under the failing-firm defence.[191] HMV Group plc was active in selling entertainment products. It sells prerecorded music, films, electronic games and peripherals, MP3 players and a small range of books. Zavvi Retail Ltd was also active in the sale of a broadly similar range of entertainment products to those sold by HMV as described above. The OFT reviewed this case on its own initiative. The OFT deemed that each individual Zavvi store was an enterprise.

[188] Ibid., para. 5.49.

[189] Ibid., para. 5.51.

[190] *Stagecoach Group/Eastbourne Buses Ltd–Cavendish Motor Services, Stagecoach Group/ Preston Bus Ltd*, www.oft.gov.uk.

[191] HMV/Zavvi, www.oft.gov.uk. The analysis of the case draws from the OFT decision.

The OFT also applied its discretion to treat the acquisition of all fifteen stores together as a single merger.

Zavvi entered into administration on 24 December 2008. Zavvi (and its predecessor, Virgin Megastore) had traded at a loss for a number of years. Its business was highly seasonal, with peak demand occurring across November and December. However, it experienced considerable cash flow difficulties when the sole supplier of stock to Zavvi went into administration on 27 November 2008. As a result, Zavvi was not able to source stock in its usual way and faced difficulty obtaining stock at acceptable prices or on favourable credit terms.

The OFT considered that an appropriate candidate frame of reference could be the bricks and mortar retailing of entertainment products including prerecorded music, films, electronic games and peripherals on both a national and a local basis with competition taking place at local as well as national level.

The OFT considered it appropriate in this case to focus on the applicability of an exiting-firm analysis. The OFT considered that it would be disproportionate to require the parties to carry out an in-depth analysis in relation to each of the overlap stores given the clarity of evidence indicating the application of the failing-firm defence that the OFT was able to attain at an early stage of the investigation. The OFT noted, however, that this would clearly not be the case in all failing-firm type situations.

The OFT investigated carefully with the administrator whether there was any prospect that Zavvi could have emerged from administration, potentially in a reorganized form. Zavvi had been experiencing significant losses for a number of years and failure was a possibility even before the collapse of its supplier. The OFT was informed by the administrator that a going-concern sale was not achievable for a variety of other reasons, including the difficult current economic and market conditions and the prohibitive level of investment required to turn around the Zavvi business. The OFT further believed that there was an absence of liquidity in funding markets to support an acquisition by private funds of other similar types of entity.

As regards the availability of alternative purchasers, the owners of the overlap stores informed the OFT that they did not undertake a public marketing campaign for the stores given that they were city-centre locations and only a limited number of parties were likely to be interested in them. The OFT did not consider that the closure of the overlap stores and the exit of the assets from local markets would have been a substantially better outcome than the acquisition of the stores by HMV, and did not accept that a lower purchase price was sufficient to render an alternative purchaser 'unrealistic'. As mentioned above, the OFT may also consider that the failure of a business, leaving the remaining competitors to compete for its assets and market share, is a more competitive outcome.

The HMV/Zavvi merger was cleared on the basis of failing-firm defence, although in accordance with its restated policy it had in the earlier case of the *Holland & Barrett/Julian Graves* merger decided not to accept the failing-firm defence and referred the Merger to the Competition Commission.[192] In that case, the OFT believed that the merger would result in a substantial lessening of competition. The OFT found evidence of other viable purchasers.

As the analysis of the case law in the UK illustrates, the UK competition authorities have been willing to accept failing-firm arguments. The approach they follow and the criteria they assess are almost identical to those that the European Commission uses, although the UK competition authorities frequently frame this analysis in terms of a counterfactual to the merger.[193]

3.7 Failing-firm defence cases before other national competition authorities

Apart from the European Commission and UK authorities, other national competition authorities have also addressed the failing-firm defence.[194] The Belgian competition authority in the *C&N Touristic Belgium/City Bird SA* decision[195] applied the failing-firm defence as this concept had been developed by the European Commission in *Kali und Salz*.[196] The Competition Council declared the acquisition by C&N Touristic Belgium (a tour operator now known as Thomas Cook Belgium) of City Bird (a company active in the air transport

[192] *Holland & Barrett/Julian Graves*, www.oft.gov.uk.

[193] See further Competition Commission/OFT Joint Substantive Guidelines for mergers, at www.oft.gov.uk.

[194] See the relevant chapters from I. Kokkoris, *Competition Cases from the European Union: The Ultimate Guide to Leading Cases of the EU and All 27 Member States*, Sweet and Maxwell, 2007.

[195] Competition Council Decision No 2001C/C48, 19 September 2001, *C&N Touristic Belgium/City Bird SA*, *Belgian Official Journal*, 4 April 2002, p. 13908.

[196] IV/M308 *Kali und Salz/MdK/Treuhand*, [1994] OJ L186/30.

sector) admissible, grounded on the three conditions set forth in the Commission decision in *Kali und Salz*.[197]

In particular, the Competition Council took into account the fact that City Bird had recently applied to obtain the benefits of a judicial composition proceeding (a proceeding allowing companies facing temporary financial difficulties to benefit from a provisional stay during which the company is protected from its existing creditors and is required to prepare a recovery plan) and that it mainly executed flights for Thomas Cook Belgium.

The Danish competition authorities adjudicated in *The merger between Danish Crown and Steff-Houlberg*.[198] The case concerned the merger between Danish Crown Amba and Steff-Houlberg Amba, two Danish slaughter co-operatives. The transaction was subject to notification to the European Commission; however, the Danish competition authorities requested the Commission to refer the case to Denmark under Article 9(3)(b) of the ECMR on the grounds that the merger primarily affected competition in Denmark. In its decision of 14 February 2002, in Case No COMP/M.2662, the Commission decided to partially refer the case to Denmark with regard to the markets geographically defined as Danish.

The Danish competition authorities defined very narrow markets, and due to a high level of vertical integration of the merging parties in the pork sector (the parties being active 'from stable to table') the authorities found it necessary to further segment the markets – markets for the production and sale of fresh pork for direct human consumption, production and sale of pork for industrial use, and production and sale of prepared meat products.

The merger resulted in very high market shares for the post-merger Danish Crown Amba (in some markets 90 per cent). Regarding remedies under which the merger was to be approved, however, in their assessment the Danish competition authorities also factored in the considerable deterioration of Steff-Houlberg's financial situation prior to the merger. The remedies were both structural, including divestiture of production plants, and behavioural, including that farmers should for example be allowed to supply pigs and cattle to competitive

[197] Namely (i) that the target company would have been forced out of the market if not taken over, (ii) that the market share of the failing firm would in any event accrue to the acquiring company, and (iii) that there is no alternative purchaser that is less anticompetitive.

[198] Competition Council decision of 26 April 2002, *The merger between Danish Crown and Steff-Houlberg*.

slaughterhouses, whilst Danish Crown on the other hand would be obliged to purchase pigs and cattle from all Danish farmers.

The case is one of few referrals from the European Commission to Denmark under the ECMR, and was granted despite the fact that three years previously the Commission had assessed the merger between Danish Crown and Vestjyske Slagterier.[199] Also noteworthy are the considerable remedies which illustrate that the Danish competition authorities prefer this solution to a prohibition of a transaction.

In *SEB/Moulinex*,[200] the Conseil de la Concurrence examined the acquisition by SEB of part of the assets of Moulinex. Moulinex was declared insolvent in September 2001, and a judicial turnaround procedure was opened. In this context, SEB made an offer that consisted in a takeover of all Moulinex's intangible and essential tangible assets for an amount of €15 million.

The Conseil de la Concurrence in its assessment defined twelve relevant product markets according to usage of the different appliances, and separated them from non-electric potential substitutes: electric fryers, mini ovens, toasters, electric coffee makers, espresso machines, kettles, electric barbecues and grills, rice and steam cookers, electric irons, vacuum cleaners, mixers and food processors, and equipment for informal meals.

SEB and Moulinex were major actors in France in most of these twelve markets, and the effect of the transaction on market structure varied from scarce to substantial depending on the product under consideration. The new entity's market shares ranged from 43 per cent in the espresso machine market to 82 per cent in the market for equipment for informal meals (such as raclettes, electric crêpe pans and so on). Hence the transaction could have created or strengthened a dominant position for the new entity.

The Conseil noted several characteristics of the market that suggested that SEB would not be in a position to abuse its dominant position:

(1) The main competitors in these markets were international groups with well-known brands and financial and technical resources.
(2) Some of the markets under scrutiny were characterized by the fast development of private labels or low-price unbranded products (e.g. coffee makers, kettles). The presence of such potential entrants was presumed substantially to limit price increases, at least in the lower-quality range of those markets.

[199] Case No COMP IV/M.1313.

[200] Opinions 02–A–07 of 15 May 2002, and 04–A–16 of 28 July 2004, *SEB/Moulinex*.

(3) There is important countervailing power from large retailers. Small electric appliances are mostly purchased in supermarkets and large stores dedicated to electronic and household appliances.

The retail sector being highly concentrated, it had sufficient purchasing power to prevent SEB/Moulinex from imposing either price or full product line at the expense of competitors. However, the minister of the economy concluded that the takeover would strengthen SEB's dominant position in nine markets, hence harming competition, but authorized the transaction on account of the failing-firm defence, according to which a transaction may be authorized whenever three conditions are satisfied:

(1) the target firm will disappear if it is not taken over,
(2) there is no alternative takeover that would be less harmful to competition, and
(3) the failure of the target firm is no less detrimental than its takeover in terms of competition.

This decision was annulled by the Conseil d'État. It considered that the minister had not demonstrated the third condition, namely that the disappearance of Moulinex would have been at least as harmful to competition as the takeover by SEB.

Following the annulment by the Conseil d'État, the minister of the economy referred the case to the Conseil a second time (Opinion 04–A–16), which provided an opportunity for an *ex post* assessment of the transaction that in this case confirmed the conclusions enumerated in the first Opinion (02–A–07). The originality of this case stems from the fact that it was subject to an *ex post* evaluation. It was confirmed that the transaction did not have a significant negative effect on competition. The Conseil observed that the new entity had concentrated on top-of-the-range products in response to the development of unbranded products and imports from low-cost countries.

Other French cases where the failing-firm defence argument has been successfully involved include *Alliance Santé Distribution/Ouest Répartition Pharmaceutique*[201] and *Ebsco/Rowecom*.[202]

Turning to Germany, on 24 November 2005, RTL notified the

[201] C2002–21, decision of 20 January 2003 published in the *Bulletin Officiel de La Concurrence, de la Consommation et de la Répression des Fraudes* (BOCCRF) of 11 August 2003.

[202] C2003–45, decision of 25 April 2003, published in the BOCCRF of 28 October 2003.

German competition authorities (Bundeskartellamt) of its intention to increase its stake in n-tv from 50 per cent to 100 per cent by acquiring the shares that were held by CNN/Time Warner, a co-owner of n-tv.[203] As the acquisition was for sole control, the transaction constituted a concentration within the meaning of §36(1)(2) Gesetz gegen Wettbewerbsbeschränkungen (GWB)[204] and a 'substantial strengthening of the existing affiliation between the undertakings' within the meaning of §37(2) GWB. In the first stage of its assessment of the transaction, the Bundeskartellamt held that the merger would lead to a strengthening of a collective dominant position on the German television advertising market. The Bundeskartellamt elaborated that, even pre-merger, this market was jointly dominated by the RTL group and ProSiebenSat.1. Each group held a market share of about 40–44 per cent. This triggered the presumption of a 'narrow' oligopoly according to §19(3)(2) GWB, which was further confirmed by the stability of market shares in recent years and the relative weakness of smaller competitors.

The position of RTL and ProSiebenSat.1 would further be strengthened by the transaction, since the acquisition of sole control over n-tv would allow RTL to determine n-tv's actions irrespective of CNN/Time Warner's interests. In this way, RTL would gain the possibility to fully integrate n-tv within its group. The loss of CNN/Time Warner as a shareholder influencing n-tv's entrepreneurial behaviour independently of the interests of the duopoly of RTL and ProSiebenSat.1 would result in a strengthening of their position. However, the Bundeskartellamt cleared the transaction, since it held in a second step that the merger fulfilled the requirements of the failing-firm defence and was not causal for the strengthening of the collective dominant position of RTL and ProSiebenSat.1.

In particular, the Bundeskartellamt noted that, first, n-tv had incurred negative financial results for many years and that CNN/Time Warner was not ready to continue its financial support of n-tv any longer. Consequently, the Bundeskartellamt assumed that n-tv would have been taken out of the market in the absence of the transaction in question. Second, no other potential acquirer was conceivable. In particular, smaller competitors already active in the German TV advertising market were not considered possible alternative acquirers, since their acquisition

[203] B 6–142/05, *RTL/n-tv*, 4 November 2006, WuW/E DE-V p. 1226.

[204] Available from the Bundeskartellamt website at www.bundeskartellamt.de/wEnglisch/Legal_bases/Legal_basesW3DnavidW2625.php.

of n-tv would have linked another undertaking to the duopoly consisting of RTL and ProSiebenSat.1. Third, the Bundeskartellamt was of the opinion that n-tv's market potential and advertising customers would go to RTL or to ProSiebenSat.1 even if the merger were prohibited, since the customers of n-tv had no viable alternatives.

RTL/ntv is one of the rare examples of a successful application of the failing-firm defence under German merger control law. Generally, the Bundeskartellamt and the German courts will consider the failing-firm defence if there is no causal link between the concentration notified for merger control and the creation or strengthening of a dominant position. In *RTL/ntv*, the Bundeskartellamt resorted to a threefold test which bears many similarities to the European standard:

(1) the target undertaking must not be viable without the notified transaction,
(2) no other undertaking must be interested in acquiring the target undertaking, and
(3) the market share of the target company would be absorbed by the acquiring undertaking (or by an oligopoly comprising the acquiring undertaking) even without the merger.

In another merger case, LBK Hamburg GmbH was a leading supplier of hospital services in Hamburg. Seven hospitals in the sole sponsorship of the city of Hamburg were combined within LBK. LBK was jointly controlled by the Asklepios private hospital group and the city of Hamburg. The Bundeskartellamt considered that the hospitals of the Asklepios group and of HH-Hamburg (HH) already together dominated the Hamburg hospital market. According to the Bundeskartellamt the merger would have strengthened the dominant position of the Asklepios Group and HH hospitals. The Bundeskartellamt rejected the argument that the failing-firm defence was applicable because the economic situation of Mariahilf corresponded to that of an average German hospital and third parties had shown an interest in acquiring the Mariahilf hospital. The merger also could not be justified on grounds of efficiency. Regarding the acceptance of an 'efficiency defence', the claimant argued that the merger would bring cost advantages that would benefit consumers, which Mariahilf could not realize alone or together with another acquirer. The decision makes clear that single aspects of the 'more-economic approach' are also relevant to German decision-making. However, the Bundeskartellamt takes a strict position regarding the efficiency defence.

The Italian authorities conditionally authorized the acquisition by Groupe Canal+ and its subsidiary Telepiù, the leading pay-TV operator in Italy, of the second-largest pay-TV operator in Italy, Stream.[205] Canal+ proposed buy 100 per cent of Stream's shares from the News Corporation group, which controlled Stream jointly with the Telecom Italia group. Noting that the acquisition of Stream would result in Canal+ obtaining a near monopoly in the Italian pay-TV market, the authorities conditioned their approval on numerous undertakings aimed at removing its anti-competitive effects. Canal+ did not complete the transaction, as it found these conditions unacceptable. In this case, the authorities took a position on the actual applicability of the failing-firm defence. The authorities concluded that the failing-firm defence, as submitted by the parties, was not sufficiently corroborated by the evidence, stating that

(1) Stream would not otherwise be forced to exit the market due to an irreversible crisis situation if it were not acquired by Canal+, because it was controlled by two significant financial groups (News Corporation and Telecom Italia) and its initial losses had been forecast in its business plan;
(2) the parties did not prove that, should Stream exit the market, Canal+ would capture Stream's market share; and
(3) the parties did not produce sufficient evidence that there was no alternative to the acquisition that was less restrictive of competition in the pay-TV market.

It could be argued that in this case the failing-firm defence deserved more careful consideration. The authorities, however, recognized that the Italian pay-TV market was characterized by a critical nature – because it was too small to permit two operators to recoup their own sunk costs – and that, under these circumstances, it was possible to remove the anti-competitive effects resulting from the transaction through an adequate set of undertakings.[206]

In a Swedish case, the Swedish competition authorities requested that

[205] Case C5109, *Groupe Canal+/Stream*, 13 May 2002, Bull. No 19/2002.

[206] Having regard to remedies, Law No 287/90 departs significantly from the EC Merger Regulation in one important aspect. While the Commission only has the power to assess the adequacy of remedies 'offered' by the parties, the authority also has the power to 'impose' additional remedies as a condition for clearance. The authority has used this power in a number of instances, often placing a substantial additional burden on the parties.

the District Court prohibit a transaction whereby Sveriges Television AB (SVT), Schibsted Film A/S and Nordisk Film A/S acquired joint control over Swelab Filmlaboratoriet Aktiebolag and FilmTeknik Aktiebolag.[207]

Swelab, which was jointly controlled by SVT and Nordisk Film prior to the transaction, and FilmTeknik, which was controlled by Schibsted prior to the transaction, were the only film laboratories in Sweden offering a full range of technical processing services for cinematic film. The Swedish Competition Authority (SCA) alleged that the merger of the two companies would create a dominant (near monopoly) position, which would impede effective competition. The District Court found that the relevant market should be defined as not only including cinematic film but also video and digital film. Nevertheless, the Court considered that the new entity would obtain a dominant position in the Swedish market. The Court, however, found that Swelab and FilmTeknik had not been able to keep up with technical developments, that both companies needed to make substantial investments to do so, that profitability was low, and that the companies had lost several large contracts during the last year to foreign laboratories. The Court concluded that Swelab and FilmTeknik would have difficulty surviving as independent competitors and that, under the circumstances, the competitive pressure from foreign laboratories and niche firms would be sufficient to guarantee effective competition in the market post-merger. The Court therefore denied the SCA's request.

In its decision in *Postbolagen AB*,[208] the Swedish competition authority took into account that

- the target would in the near future be forced out of the market because of financial difficulties if not taken over by the acquirer;
- there was no alternative purchaser; and
- in the absence of the acquisition, the assets of the failing firm would inevitably exit the market.

The Dutch competition authority (NMa), in the concentration of *De Telegraaf–De Limburger*,[209] stated that in order for a failing-firm defence to be successful, the following criteria need to be fulfilled:

[207] SCA: Dnr 661/96, *Sveriges Television AB, Schibsted Film A/S, Nordisk Film A/S and Skandinaviska Filmlaboratorier Holding AB*, 19 June 1996. Stockholm District Court: T 8–669–96, *SCA v. Sveriges Television AB, Schibsted Film A/S, Nordisk Film A/S and Skandinaviska Filmlaboratorier Holding AB*, 18 December 1996.

[208] 427/95 *Postbolagen AB*.

[209] *De Telegraaf–De Limburger* (Case 1538, 12 May 2000).

(1) the failing firm to be acquired would have had to leave the market shortly even without the concentration,
(2) the acquiring undertaking would also have acquired the failing firm's market share even without the concentration, and
(3) there is no alternative purchase less anti-competitive than the intended concentration.

As the above analysis of the case law illustrates, the European Commission and other national competition authorities have accepted failing-firm defence arguments, although they are more critical of failing-division defence arguments. These competition authorities are unwilling to extend the failing-firm defence or failing-firm exception to firms which have not yet failed but are less efficient competitors (so-called 'flailing firms'). If a flailing-firm defence or exception exists, parties to mergers that reduce competition (and thus are likely to be profitable to the parties) would have a strong tendency, in order to invoke the defence and be treated more leniently than they should be, to claim that they are flailing even if their situation is not as severe as that of a truly failing firm. In addition, as the OECD states, even if flailing firms can be reliably identified, competition authorities may take the view that the competition such firms provide, albeit weak, benefits consumers and should be allowed to continue as long as possible. A merger involving a flailing firm might foster a considerably better competitive environment than a similar merger involving a failing firm.[210] Similar arguments can be put forward for the unwillingness of competition authorities to accept declining-industry arguments. However, what should be taken into consideration is that in declining-industry situations it is more likely that firms which are currently flailing may continue to be in an adverse financial situation and may not be viable at all in the near future.

After analysing how the European Commission and national competition authorities in the EU have dealt with the concept of failing-firm defence, this chapter will turn now to how the US competition authorities deal with the same concepts.

[210] OECD, 'Failing firm defence' (1996), www.oecd.org/dataoecd/35/6/1920253.pdf, at p. 21.

3.7.1 The United States of America

This part of the chapter will analyse the approach that US competition authorities take in assessing the failing-firm defence. It will start with a brief analysis of the legislation and then proceed to present the most important merger cases in which failing-firm defence arguments have been raised and how they have been dealt with by the Federal Trade Commission (FTC), the Department of Justice (DOJ) and the courts.

Legislation

The US Congress recognized a failing-firm exemption in the 1950 amendments to §7 of the Clayton Act. Some have suggested that Congress intended to exempt failing firms from §7 merger analysis in order to protect private interests, such as shareholders and employees, when firms are failing, while others argue that although Congress was perhaps concerned about private interests in the situation of a failing firm, it did not intend to override the primary concern of antitrust, which is competition.[211]

The review of a proposed merger is typically conducted according to the US Guidelines, which provide guidance on how mergers are to be evaluated for potential anti-competitive effect.

The analytical framework of the US Guidelines involves the following:

- Defining the relevant product market and geographic market and identifying the firms that compete in these relevant markets.
- assessing whether the merger, in light of market concentration and other factors that characterize the market, raises concern about potential adverse competitive effects. For market concentration the Herfindahl–Hirschmann Index is used.
- Assessing the likelihood of entry by new firms into the markets.
- Assessing the likely competitive effects of the merger in light of the market concentration and other factors that characterize the markets.
- Considering any significant efficiencies resulting from the merger that could not be achieved by other means.

The US Guidelines contain a specific section on the issues of failing-firm defence and failing-division defence. The antitrust authorities assess

[211] Federal Trade Commission (FTC), 'Competition Policy in the New High-Tech, Global Marketplace' (1996), Volume 1, Chapter 3, www.ftc.gov/opp/global/report/gc_v1.pdf, at p. 4.

whether either party to the transaction would be likely to fail, causing its assets to exit the market if the merger were blocked. The theory is that a

> merger is not likely to create or enhance market power or to facilitate its exercise, if imminent failure of one of the merging firms would cause the assets of that firm to exit the relevant market. In such circumstances, post-merger performance in the relevant market may be no worse than market performance had the merger been blocked and the assets left the market.[212]

A merger is not likely to create or enhance market power or facilitate its exercise under the following circumstances:[213]

(1) if the allegedly failing firm would be unable to meet its financial obligations in the near future;
(2) if it would not be able to reorganize successfully under Chapter 11 of Title 11 of the US Code (Bankruptcy Code or USBC);
(3) if it has made unsuccessful good-faith efforts to elicit reasonable alternative offers of acquisition of the assets of the failing firm that would both keep its tangible and intangible assets in the relevant market and pose a less severe danger to competition than does the proposed merger; and
(4) if, absent the acquisition, the assets of the failing firm would exit the relevant market.

These criteria are less stringent than the equivalent criteria under EU legislation (the ECMR), since they do not require that the target company's market share be obtained by the acquirer if the failing firm exits the market.

A similar argument to that made for the failing firm can be made for a failing division of a firm. The antitrust authorities will allow the acquisition of a failing corporate division if the division has a negative cash flow on an operating basis; if there is evidence that, absent the acquisition, the assets of the division would exit the market in the near future; and if the owner of the failing division has made unsuccessful good-faith efforts to elicit reasonable alternative offers of acquisition of the assets of the failing division and has complied with the competitively preferable purchaser requirements of §5(1) of the US Guidelines.[214]

[212] Horizontal Merger Guidelines, www.justice.gov/atr/public/guidelines/hmg.htm. (US Guidelines), §5.0.

[213] US Guidelines, §5.1.

[214] US Guidelines, §5.2.

Although the US Guidelines do not recognize a distressed-industry defence, they suggest that distressed-industry conditions may be considered when assessing the degree to which a merger would create or enhance market power.[215]

It is worth noting that bankrupt entities are subject to the standard pre-merger notification thresholds under the Hart-Scott-Rodino Antitrust Improvements (HSR) Act. However, §363(b) of the USBC provides for special treatment when the target company is in bankruptcy. The USBC alters the HSR Act's filing requirements as regards who should file the notification form, and when, as well as the waiting periods before the closure of the transaction.[216]

The only exemption for violation of §7 of the Clayton Act is the failing-firm defence. A merger is not deemed to substantially lessen competition if one of the merging firms is failing and absent the merger the assets would exit the market. The rejection of the proposed merger when the target is failing might lead to the liquidation of the productive assets. The failing-firm defence was created by case law rather than by statute. The US Supreme Court first recognized this defence in 1930 in the leading case *International Shoe Co. v. FTC*. The Court allowed the merger of two firms, one of which was facing grave financial difficulties. This judgment has laid down the cornerstone for the failing-company defence. The Court aimed at a broad analysis of the competitive and the anti-competitive effect of the acquisition of a company on the edge of bankruptcy.

The legislative history of revision of the Clayton Act by the Celler-Kefauver Act of 1950 eliminated any doubts concerning the validity of the failing-firm defence. The *International Shoe* case was the base for the above-mentioned amendment. The US Supreme Court subsequently reaffirmed the validity of the defence in the case law.

A failing-company claim presents a large number of variables for consideration as well as uncertainty about the allegedly failing firm's future viability. The possibility of failure may be likely, but not imminent, reorganization cannot be ruled out and thus the eventual viability of the company may be very uncertain. Furthermore, there may

[215] Section 1.521 of the US Guidelines. See further B. Nigro, 'The Effect of Market Conditions on Merger Review – Distressed Industries, Failing Firms, and Mergers with Bankrupt Companies', www.abanet.org/antitrust/committees/communication/distressedindustry.pdf.

[216] See further Nigro, 'The Effect of Market Conditions on Merger Review'.

be an alternative purchaser but the price to be offered may be so low that it is arguably unfair or inconsistent with the goal of preserving competition.[217]

In order to invoke the failing-firm defence, the failing company should be genuinely failing. This means that the company must be insolvent, on the verge of insolvency, or in imminent danger of financial collapse. The courts have applied this requirement very strictly. The fact that the company's hopes for recovery are dim or non-existent has to be proved.[218] Furthermore, the failing company should not receive a significant share of the gains from the merger; if it does, this is an indication that the firm is not failing.

The company, if allowed to fail, can act in accordance with Chapter 11 of the USBC and still be present in the market. The reorganization process is not costless and shareholders and creditors suffer losses. The companies can be reorganized and fail, ceasing capacity and liquidating assets, thus causing competitive loss as regards output and loss of jobs. Hence the second element of the failing-firm defence requires the firm to prove that 'it would not be able to reorganize successfully'. This ensures that the firm not only faces short-term difficulties, but is also not viable in the long term.

An additional criterion for acceptance of the failing-firm defence in the US is that there be no other prospective purchaser. In other words, this condition refers to an alternative buyer that would pose less severe danger to competition. Furthermore, this buyer must make a reasonable offer. This offer is defined thus: 'any offer to purchase the assets of the failing firm for a price above the liquidation value of those assets – the highest valued use outside the relevant market or equivalent offer to purchase the stock of the failing firm – will be regarded as a reasonable alternative offer'.[219] Thus the alternative buyer need only offer more than the liquidation value to be able to keep the assets operating in the market, even though the alternative purchaser may have less to offer in the way of improving the efficiency of the failing firm than the

[217] E. Correia, 'The Failing Company Defence' (1995), www.ftc.gov/opp/global/final.htm.

[218] Correia 1995 argues that it is inconsistent with the goals of §7 to preclude consideration of a failing-firm claim unless the risks of failure are close to 100 per cent. Even based on output considerations alone, the risk of failure in the range of 75 per cent and above can be shown to result in higher expected costs than merger. In addition, the relative desirability of the acquiring competing firm and the out-of-market acquirer needs to be reassessed.

[219] Footnote 39, US Guidelines.

prospective competitor purchaser. The competition authorities should consider whether the alternative purchaser has the capability to run the failing firm as a competitive, ongoing business, including infusions of capital that will ensure the viability of the failing firm.[220]

By rating the least anti-competitive alternative in terms of liquidation value, satisfaction of the failing-firm defence criteria is biased in favour of non-market participants. Any efficiencies that a potential competitor purchaser might generate from the merger may be unnecessarily sacrificed. Furthermore, a non-market participant may simply seek a revenue stream rather than operate as an effective competitor by making long-term investment plans.[221] Many firms that purchase a distressed business may intend to ensure a revenue stream and not to compete vigorously.

The question arises why the competitor is willing to pay substantially more than the out-of-market firm. An acquiring competitor's offer is higher due to the fact that it includes a market-power premium – a payment for the expected increase in market power. The competitor purchaser's willingness to pay more than the outsider more likely reflects an efficiency premium than it does a market-power premium.[222] The reason for purchasing an unprofitable firm may be the possibility of profit from increased concentration through oligopolistic interdependence. By making an unprofitable company a good investment, the acquiring company believes that it can reduce its costs and/or improve product lines.

The lack of an alternative purchaser must be established by good-faith efforts to find another purchaser. The failing firm is required to have made good-faith efforts to obtain offers from other firms that would keep the failing firm in the market while making a less serious threat to competition. Thus the failing firm must explore alternative merger possibilities and seek out bona fide offers. Current policy towards failing-firm defence may systematically prefer alternative purchasers that are unlikely to offer the same efficiencies that a competitor purchaser may offer. In addition, the defence may induce companies to be in a severe state of decline before they qualify for the defence.

Thus the requirement to make good-faith efforts to find an alternative

220 J. McDavid, 'Efficiencies, Failing Firms and the *General Dynamics* Defence', 5 December 1995, www.ftc.gov/opp/global/194817.htm.

221 Valentine 1995.

222 Federal Trade Commission (FTC), 'Competition Policy in the New High-Tech, Global Marketplace' (1996), Volume 1, Chapter 3, www.ftc.gov/opp/global/report/gc_v1.pdf, at p. 13.

purchaser safeguards against loss in competition. However, the alternative purchaser may have much less to offer in the way of improving the efficiency of the acquired firm than the prospective competitor purchaser. In addition, there is concern that the competitor's offer may be higher because it includes a market-power premium, a payment for anticipated gains in market power. There could be a market-power premium, or an efficiency premium, or both. The problem is that it is difficult to separate them. Overestimating the market-power premium means underestimating the efficiency premium. The willingness of the acquirer to buy a company that is headed towards failure justifies giving its efficiency claims some additional credence.[223] The US Supreme Court's interpretation of the alternative-buyer condition is presented in the case of *Citizen Publishing Co. v. United States*, where failing-company claims indicate a trade-off between two scenarios that need to be considered, the company exiting the market and an anti-competitive merger. The first scenario is of great importance if the costs of the merger are balanced against the costs of blocking this merger, where there is a probability that the failing firm will survive and remain competitive. If blocking the merger implies that the failing firm's assets will exit the market and therefore the output of this firm will be lost, the clearance of the merger seems to be the only sensible solution. The loss to stockholders, and to the community where the business operates would be less severe if the merger were allowed to proceed rather than if the firm exited the market.

Looking from an economic perspective, capacity is a good predictor of output and lost output is a good measure of the competitive harm. In the case of a merger increasing concentration, it is very unlikely that the output will be reduced through the interdependence. Output is reduced more if the acquired firm's assets exit the market, thus the merger is the preferred possibility.[224] However, it should be noted that the current

[223] Correia 1995.

[224] A number of authors have compared the loss in output stemming from a firm exiting the market with the loss in output stemming from increased concentration. This literature points to the conclusion that a certain loss in output by virtue of a firm's assets leaving the market will exceed the loss in output from a merger under any realistic set of assumptions. See J. Kwoka and F. Warren-Boulton, 'Efficiencies, Failing Firms, and Alternatives to Merger: A Policy Synthesis' (1986) 31 *Antitrust Bull.* 431, at p. 445; D. Friedman, 'Untangling the Failing Company Defence' (1986) 64 *Tex. L. Rev.* 1375; F.S. McChesney, 'Defending the Failing-Firm Defence' (1986) 65 *Nebraska L. Rev.* 1. See further Correia 1995.

market share of the failing firm may overstate its future competitive significance and the anti-competitive effects of a merger. What would be of importance is whether the merged entity can unilaterally or collectively affect prices and output.

The failing-firm defence might also be applied when only a part of the company is failing. Refusal of such defence would force the parent company either to end a subsidiary or to keep it going at a loss. This requirement was widely discussed by the US Supreme Court in the case of *International Shoe Co. v. FTC*.

The *General Dynamics* case provided the definition of the 'flailing,' 'quasi-failing,' or 'weak-competitor' defence which was first applied by the lower courts in *United States v. International Harvester Co.*[225] The Court held that the acquisition did not violate §7 because the acquired company did not have sufficient financial resources to compete effectively. The claim that the firm to be acquired is a weak competitor is made in order to show that the merger is less troubling than the combined market shares. A 'weak-competitor claim' can be made in circumstances that are difficult to evaluate. In the case of *United States v. International Harvester Co.* the acquired company's 'weak-competitor claim' arose from its difficulty in borrowing capital. The Court allowed the acquisition because the acquired company lacked financial resources necessary to operate competitively. Nevertheless, a 'weak-competitor claim' does not circumvent the requirement of the alternative purchaser. In *FTC v. Warner Communications Inc.*[226] the Court noted that a weak-company defence would expand the strict limits of the failing-company doctrine.

The spirit of the *General Dynamics* decision has been incorporated into the US Guidelines by language acknowledging that 'recent or ongoing changes in the market may indicate that the current market share of a particular firm either understates or overstates the firm's competitive significance' and committing to take into consideration 'reasonably predictable effects of recent or ongoing changes in market conditions in interpreting market concentration and market share data'.[227]

In *United States v. General Dynamics Corp.*, although the US Supreme Court rejected a distressed-industry defence, it emphasized the importance of considering all relevant facts, especially in cases where the rel-

[225] *United States v. International Harvester Co.*, 564 F.2d 769 (7th Cir. 1977).

[226] 742 F.2d 1156 (9th Cir. 1984) (*per curiam*). See further Correia 1995.

[227] Nigro, 'The Effect of Market Conditions on Merger Review'.

evant market or industry exhibits fluctuations as well as dynamic features.[228] Antitrust authorities could also consider industry conditions as an argument in favour of approving a transaction. However, distressed-industry conditions could lead to increased entry barriers and, therefore, make it more difficult for a transaction to obtain approval. In spite of that, antitrust authorities take into account the impact of economic conditions on the ability of firms to raise capital and make investments, which are needed for them to be more effective competitors. Antitrust authorities should not obstruct efforts by failing or flailing firms to reorganize in order to become more efficient.

The presence of distressed-industry conditions could also affect the speed of the investigation as a prolonged merger review may harm the firm to be acquired and could weaken it to the point where the merger no longer makes sense to the purchaser.[229] The US Supreme Court rejected the failing-industry defence in *Socony-Vacuum*.[230] However, DOJ in *United States v. LTV Corp.* did consider the weakened state of the companies.[231] The LTV Corporation and Republic Steel Corporation announced plans for a merger in September of 1983 whereby LTV would acquire all the assets of Republic. The DOJ initially challenged the transaction, but agreed to settle the case, purportedly due to the weakened state of the companies and the efficiencies that would result from the transaction.[232] Thus, in this case, the US authorities accepted the failing-industry defence.

Accepting distressed-industry arguments could help revitalize failing industries by lowering their overall costs and enabling them to compete more efficiently. In moderately concentrated industries exhibiting excess capacity, ease of entry, in combination with the increased threat of import competition, would render any anti-competitive impact of the merger unlikely. However, the difficulty of identifying a distressed industry and the distinction between a distressed-industry and an industry experiencing a downturn may constitute the unlikely putting of crucial weight onto the consideration of distressed-industry circumstances. In the distressed-industry defence there is consensus

[228] *United States v. General Dynamics Corp.*, (1974) 415 U.S. 486, at pp. 504–6.

[229] Nigro, 'The Effect of Market Conditions on Merger Review'.

[230] *U.S. v. Socony-Vacuum Oil Co.*, (1940) 310 U.S. 150. See further Valentine 1995.

[231] 1984–2 Trade Cas. (CCH) 66,133 (D.D.C.) appeal dismissed, 746 F.2d 51 (D.C.Cir.1984).

[232] Stephen Labaton, 'Airlines and Antitrust: A New World. Or Not', *New York Times*, 18 November 2001, as well as Nigro, 'The Effect of Market Conditions on Merger Review'.

that mergers are strong candidates to achieve efficiencies.[233] Efficiencies which may not be credible in booming industries may be applicable when the distressed-industry defence is invoked.

The failing-firm defence has mostly been rejected in the contested proceedings in which it was raised. Some of these cases will be analysed in more detail in order to see how the defence has been invoked and applied. Such an analysis is essential in order to consider how and when the failing-firm defence should be accepted.

Application of the failing-firm defence

International Shoe

The US Supreme Court first recognized the failing-firm defence in *International Shoe Co. v. FTC*,[234] which involved an FTC challenge to the merger of two shoe manufacturers. The US Supreme Court reversed a lower court decision upholding the challenge on the grounds that the acquired company faced 'financial ruin' and argued that the anti-competitive effect that would result if the acquisition were allowed would be greater than if the failing firm exited the market.

According to the FTC the effect of such an acquisition was to substantially lessen competition between the two companies, to restrain commerce in the shoe business and to tend to create monopoly. At the time of acquisition the financial condition of the acquired company was such as to necessitate liquidation or sale, thus the prospect for future competition or restraint was entirely eliminated. The Court also upheld that the acquired company was faced with financial ruin and that the only alternative was liquidation. The company had reached the point where it could no longer pay its debts as they became due. In this case the requirement of failure of the failing-firm defence was defined.

The Court considered the alternatives for the failing company. The company might have obtained further financial help from the banks, with a resulting increased debt load which the company might have carried and finally paid. Even had it availed itself of receivership, no predictions could be made whether such a course would have meant ultimate recovery or final and complete collapse. Had it proceeded, or been proceeded against, under the USBC, holders of the preferred stock might have paid or assumed the debts and gone forward with

[233] Federal Trade Commission (FTC), 'Competition Policy in the New High-Tech, Global Marketplace' (1996), Volume 1, Chapter 3, www.ftc.gov/opp/global/report/gc_v1.pdf.

[234] *International Shoe Co. v. Federal Trade Commission*, (1930) 280 U.S. 291.

the business, or they might have considered it more prudent and less risky to accept whatever could be salvaged from the failing firm.[235] The Court concluded that between the alternatives of proceeding under the USBC and sale to the only available purchaser, the officers, stockholders and creditors, thoroughly familiar with the factors of a critical situation and more able than the FTC or court to foresee future contingencies, after much consideration, felt compelled to choose the latter alternative.

Taking into consideration the fact that the corporation's resources were so depleted and the prospect of rehabilitation was so remote, in conjunction with the fact that it was very likely to fail, with resulting loss to its stockholders and injury to the communities where its plants operated, the Court held that the purchase of its capital stock by a competitor (the only available purchaser), with the purpose of facilitating the accumulated business of the purchaser and with the effect of mitigating seriously injurious consequences otherwise probable rather than of lessening competition, neither substantially lessens competition nor is contrary to the law and prejudicial to the public.

Thus, according to the Court, the failing-company defence presupposes that the effect on competition, loss to the company's stockholders and injury to the communities where its plants operate will be less if a company continues to exist even as a party to a merger than if it disappears entirely from the market. It is, in a sense, a 'lesser of two evils' approach, in which the possible threat to competition resulting from an acquisition is deemed preferable to the adverse impact on competition if the company exits the market.

Erie Sand and Gravel Company v. *FTC*

The Erie Sand and Gravel Company were in the business of dredging and selling lake sand.[236] The Sandusky division of the Kelly Island Co. was Erie's principal competitor. Kelly was bought by two investment firms who later liquidated the entire company. The company's assets were publicly offered for sale and Erie submitted the highest bid. They acquired 92 per cent of the market in lake sand from the southern shore of Lake Erie and a total monopoly on the sale of sand from Buffalo, NY to Sandusky, Ohio. This amounted to a monopoly in three cities in the area. A complaint against Erie was issued by the Federal Trade Commission

[235] *International Shoe Co. v. Federal Trade Commission*, (1930) 280 U.S. 291, at p. 302.
[236] F.T.C. 291 F.2d 279 C.A.3 1961.

on the ground that the acquisition of the assets of a competitor violated §7 of the Clayton Act.

Erie argued that the failing-company doctrine, as enunciated in the *International Shoe* case, justified their acquisition of the Sandusky Division, citing as evidence the fact that the owners had decided to liquidate. However, this assertion was rejected by the Court, which, in referring to *International Shoe*, stated that the defence would be justifiable in circumstances where a corporation's resources were 'so depleted and the prospect of rehabilitation so remote that it faced the grave probability of a business failure with resulting loss to its stockholders and injury to the communities where its plants operated (there being no other prospective purchaser)'. It was in such circumstances that the merger was viewed as not likely to be harmful.

The Commission found that the acquisition substantially lessened competition and gave Erie a monopoly on the sale of sand. Erie was ordered to divest itself of the assets it had acquired by purchasing the Sandusky Division of the Kelly Island Co.[237]

Brown Shoe v. United States

This is an appeal for a ruling by the government of the United States against Brown Shoe at the District Court of Missouri, seeking an injunction to block a merger between Brown Shoe and G.R. Kinney Company under §7 of the Clayton Act.[238] The two companies were both in the shoemaking line of commerce and also among the top ten shoemaking businesses in the US.

The Supreme Court upheld the District Court's decision and dismissed the appeal for the following reasons:

- The District Court was correct in analysing the vertical and horizontal aspects of the merger in order to make its decision; §7 of the Clayton Act simply provided that it is important to consider economic and

[237] There was a problem defining the relevant market in this case. The question was whether the conclusion should be restricted to concrete sand and did not require differentiation between 'pit sand', 'lake sand' and 'bank sand'. However, this decision was remanded to the Federal Trade Commission on appeal since they had failed to consider the proper factors for defining the relevant market area as it related to sand. Without adequate evidence, it was impossible to adequately gauge the effect of the merger on competition as a result of differences in certain areas like production and transport costs. The order of divestiture was therefore stayed pending a review of what should constitute the relevant market area.

[238] (1962) 370 U.S. 294.

other factors to determine whether the merger might have an effect on competition.

- The vertical aspects of the merger were that the two companies were well spread in the US, and if merged would monopolize the shoe market in every state. Unlike a case where one firm is failing, which would have been acceptable, these two business were very big and played a large role in the shoe market.
- The horizontal aspect of the merger was that the two businesses conducted similar activities. Therefore if merged the cost of manufacturing the shoes would be very cheap, which would be unfair for other corporations in that line of commerce and thus lessen competition.
- The appeal judge further argued that the only exceptions are where the merger is to the benefit of the community or one of the firms is failing. Other than that, the general rule of the provision is to prevent any merger between two corporations in the same line of commerce that might have an anti-competitive effect in the market.

Therefore the Appeal Court affirmed the District Court's decision, which also issued a divestment of assets and share capital from Brown Shoe back to G.R. Kinney. The two corporations continued producing and retailing shoes separately.

As mentioned above, failing-firm defence in this case was mentioned as one of the exceptions to the general rule underlined by §7 of the Clayton Act, but the exception was not accepted in this case.

United States of America v. Lever Brothers Co. and Monsanto Chemical Co.

The government filed an injunction against Lever Brothers Co. and Monsanto Chemical Co. in which it alleged the merger of the two would substantially lessen competition and tend to create a monopoly.[239] Lever Brothers Co. is in the business of manufacturing soap and cleaning products. It made substantial profit in heavy-duty soap products but not in the detergent business. Its detergent business then deteriorated, at which stage it was approached by Monsanto with the suggestion to consider acquiring the low-sudsing detergent product. The acquisition would result in Lever's market share rising from 16.8 per cent to 22.4 per cent and Monsanto ceasing to compete in the market. After the acquisition there were three firms in the market: Procter & Gamble, Colgate

[239] 216 F. Supp. 887 D.C.N.Y. 1963.

and Lever. Lever, by virtue of their experience, expertise and substantial financial position, were in a much better position to compete in this market than Monsanto had ever been.

The government's argument that the effect of this acquisition was substantially to lessen competition was based on the assumption that the relevant market was the entire heavy-duty detergent market, ignoring the fact that there was a vigorous and rapidly growing submarket of low-sudsing detergents.

The Court highlighted that this is a situation where an acquisition by one company of a particular brand of another preserved the competitive business of the other company and promoted more active competition than would have prevailed had the acquisition not been made. The Court argued that to decide this case by the application of statistical figures, as the government would urge the District Court to do, would subordinate reality to formulae. It would mean that in the future a company with a failing brand could never transfer that brand to another company ready and able to market and distribute it in true competitive fashion. Thus the brand would disappear, and competition would be diminished. Congress undoubtedly intended, as the Supreme Court indicated, that the Court should look to the reality of the situation. The reality of the situation in 1956 was that Lever, which had no low-sudsing detergent, acquired a low-sudsing detergent from a company which was no longer an effective competitor in that submarket. By so doing the brand remained active in a competitive market.

The District Court concluded that the evidence failed to establish that in either of these lines of commerce was there any reasonable probability of substantial anti-competitive effects or a tendency to monopoly as a result of the transfer of the assets involved. The Court decided in favour of the defendants, dismissing the complaint.

Citizen Publishing Co. v. United States[240]

The owners of the *Star* and the Citizen Publishing Co. negotiated a joint operating agreement between the two newspapers for a period of twenty-five years from March 1940 that was extended in 1953 until 1990. The agreement provided, amongst other things, for the formation of Tucson Newspapers, Inc., owned in equal shares by the *Star* and the *Citizen*. The only real defence of the appellants was the failing-firm defence. The Court rejected this argument and set up strict conditions

[240] *Citizen Publishing Co. v. United States*, (1969) 394 U.S. 131, at pp. 138–9 .

under which the defence would be accepted. The Court also stated that no effort was made to sell the newspaper.

The requirements of the failing-company doctrine were not met. As the Court stated,[241]

(1) There is no indication that Citizen's owners were thinking of liquidating the company or selling the newspaper, and there is no evidence that the agreement was the last straw at which Citizen grasped.
(2) The failing company doctrine can be applied only if it is established that the acquiring company is the only available purchaser.
(3) The prospects for the failing company of reorganization through receivership or through Chapter 10 or Chapter 11 of the USBC would have to be dim or non-existent to make the failing company doctrine applicable.
(4) The burden of proving that the requirements of the doctrine are met is on those who seek refuge under it, and that burden had not been satisfied in this case.

The Court in *Citizen Publishing Co. v. United States* stated a three-part test for the applicability of the failing-company defence. The defence should be stringent, the defence is one of 'narrow scope' and the burden of proving the defence is 'on those who seek refuge under it'. The prospects of continued independent existence must be 'dim or non-existent' and it must be established that the acquiring company is the only available purchaser. The failing-company doctrine plainly cannot be applied in a merger or in any other case unless it is established that the company that acquires the failing company is the only available purchaser. If another person or group were interested, a unit in the competitive system would be preserved and not lost to monopoly power.[242] The Court restricted merging companies' abilities to invoke the failing-firm defence.

In *Citizen Publishing Co. v. United States*[243] the US Supreme Court adopted a formal test for the failing-firm defence that was similar to the test that was adopted by the FTC and the DOJ as part of the US Guidelines more than twenty years later. The Court held that an otherwise unlawful acquisition of a failing firm could be permitted if three general requirements were met:

[241] *Citizen Publishing Co. v. United States*, (1969) 394 U.S. 131, at p. 132.
[242] *Citizen Publishing Co. v. United States*, (1969) 394 U.S. 131, at p. 138.
[243] *Citizen Publishing Co. v. United States*, (1969) 394 U.S. 131, at pp. 138–9.

(1) the acquiring company must show that the target is in imminent danger of failure,
(2) the failing firm must have no realistic prospect for successful reorganization, and
(3) the failing firm must show that it has made reasonable, good-faith attempts to locate an alternative buyer and there is no viable alternative purchaser that poses less anti-competitive risk.

United States v. General Dynamics Corp.[244]

The significance of this case lies in the fact that the Court made a realistic evaluation of the probable anti-competitive effects of the merger of a firm which was neither failing nor a strong competitor. The Court upheld that the recent market shares of the acquired firm overstated its long-term market shares since its non-renewable assets were relatively low compared with those of other competitors. No claim was made that the merger would strengthen the acquired firm. The possibility of the failing-firm defence was justified on the ground that one of the firms was at least in a position of financial weakness. In addition, the company's coal reserves were depleted, or committed to long-term contracts. The Court further found that the acquired entity, standing alone, would not contribute meaningfully to further competition since virtually all its economically mineable strip reserves were committed to long-term contracts and it possessed neither the capability to obtain more strip reserves nor the expertise to develop its deep reserves.[245]

The claim was made that the future combined market shares would be smaller than the current combined market shares. The Court further argued that the combined market-share figure did not accurately reflect the firm's future competitive weakness.

The US Supreme Court allowed the acquisition of a coal mining company, which produced a company with a large market share in a concentrated industry. The profitability of the acquired company was declining but it was not in immediate danger of bankruptcy. This raised the possibility of flailing-firm defence – of justifying a merger on the grounds that one of the firms, while not in imminent danger, is at least in a position of financial weakness.

The Court further stated that since the rationale of the failing-company defence is the lack of anti-competitive consequences given that

[244] *United States v. General Dynamics Corp.*, (1974) 415 U.S. 486.

[245] *United States v. General Dynamics Corp.*, (1974) 415 U.S. 486, at p. 523.

one of the combining companies is about to disappear from the market at any rate, the viability of the 'failing company' must be assessed as of the time of the merger.

The Court in *United States v. General Dynamics Corp.* upheld that three groups of private parties benefit from the merger of a failing firm: shareholders, creditors and employees. Major shareholder losses occur only in the case of liquidation. Shareholders are unlikely to lose their investment and are likely to reap benefits in cases where the merger is profitable. The creditors will benefit as a result of retaining their rights against the debtor and are likely to be reimbursed for the credit they have provided to the firm. On the contrary, in insolvency proceedings they are not as likely to be fully reimbursed.

As McDavid states, the US Guidelines retained the *General Dynamics* concept by recognizing that

> recent or ongoing changes in the market may indicate that the current market share of a particular firm either understates or overstates the firm's competitive significance . . . The Agency will consider reasonably predictable effects of recent or ongoing changes in market conditions in interpreting market concentration and market share data.[246]

United States v. Blue Bell Inc. and Genesco Inc.

The government contended that the effect of this acquisition would substantially lessen competition or tend to create a monopoly in interstate commerce in the manufacturing and sale of industrial rental garments to unaffiliated industrial laundries.[247]

Genesco, a corporation organized and existing under the laws of Tennessee, was an international manufacturer and retailer of apparel and footwear. Blue Bell, a Delaware corporation, was a manufacturer of men's, women's and children's clothing. Blue Bell's Red Kap Industries Division manufactured and sold a line of industrial uniforms sold primarily to rental laundries. Blue Bell and Genesco were engaged in interstate commerce.

Blue Bell then acquired from Genesco substantially all of the assets used by Genesco in the operation of its industrial laundry business, i.e. the business of manufacturing and selling garments for rental laundries. Red Kap, at the time of the acquisition, was the largest firm in terms of

[246] J. McDavid, 'Efficiencies, Failing Firms and the *General Dynamics* Defence', 5 December 1995, www.ftc.gov/opp/global/194817.htm.

[247] 395 F. Supp. 538 D.C.Tenn. 1975.

industrial rental garment sales to unaffiliated laundries, and one of the two largest firms if sales to all rental laundries are taken into account. Red Kap was considered by its competitors to be one of the leading competitors, if not the leading competitor, in the manufacture and sale of industrial rental garments to the rental industry, and Hayes was considered among the leading competitors. Prior to Red Kap's acquisition of the Hayes assets, Red Kap was Hayes' most significant competitor. Hayes and Red Kap each had distribution centres located across the United States, giving them a significant advantage in competing with firms having less-extensive warehouse networks.

As regards the failing-firm defence, the fact that Genesco intended to divest itself of its industrial laundry division was immaterial. Even though earnings of its laundry and apparel and footwear retail divisions were unsatisfactory, this did not render the company a 'failing company'.

The Court held, among other things, that:

- Blue Bell's acquisition of the assets of Genesco's industrial rental garment business violated §7 of the Clayton Act because it might substantially lessen competition or create a monopoly in the manufacturing and sale of industrial rental garments to rental laundries throughout the United States.
- The plaintiff is entitled to a judgment ordering divestiture of the acquired assets under such terms and conditions as will ensure the prompt restoration of the Hayes Company as a competitive entity.

Aluminum Company v. FTC

In this case[248] the Aluminum Company and the Cleveland Company had devised a plan whereby both these companies would be joint owners of a new company that was to be formed. This new company would be called the Aluminum Rolling Mills Company. The Aluminum Company of America was the biggest player in the aluminium industry. During the time in question the Aluminum Company had no domestic competitors in the manufacture of aluminium ingots and there were three competitors in the manufacture of aluminium sheets. Two companies were active in the market for narrow sheets and one in the market for broad sheets.[249] The Cleveland Company was experiencing losses after the out-

[248] *Aluminum Co. of America v. FTC*, 284 Fed. 401 (3d Cir.).

[249] The difference in width of sheets being a factor in the breadth of the sheet market as only broad sheets are used in the manufacture of car bodies.

break of the First World War. The FTC concluded that the merger was in violation of §7 of the Clayton Act,[250] which provides,

> That no corporation engaged in commerce shall acquire, directly or indirectly, the whole or any part of the stock or other share capital of another corporation engaged also in commerce, where the effect of such acquisition may be to substantially lessen competition between the corporation whose stock is so acquired and the corporation making the acquisition, or to restrain such commerce in any section or community, or tend to create a monopoly of any line of commerce.

The Aluminum Company contended that there was no lessening of competition as 'under the exceptional conditions arising from war, there was always a sellers' market, that is, a market, where, as we understand it, sellers do not have to compete for trade but where the trade competes for sellers' products'.[251] The Aluminum Company also argued that this merger was necessary to meet the demands of war production.

However, these contentions were dismissed by the majority opinion of the Court, which held that the merger would substantially lessen competition. The Court held that

> the lessening of competition is not the only effect of the acquisition by one corporation of stock of another which Congress sought to avoid. It intended as well to prevent a transaction 'where the effect' may 'tend to create a monopoly,' which is the effect which the Commission found in the acquisition of the stock of the Rolling Mills Company. A monopoly can be created by a transaction of stock acquisition when the effect is not to lessen competition with the corporation whose stock is acquired if the effect is to end competition existing elsewhere, United States v. New England Fish Exchange (D.C.) 258 Fed. 732, 746; as for instance the ending of competition with the Cleveland Company. This is for the reason that the lessening of competition and a tendency to monopoly are not always synonymous. There may be a lessening of competition between two corporations in a stock transaction that does not tend to monopoly. But, curtailing this discussion, we are not prepared to admit the premise from which the Aluminum Company deduces its conclusion.[252]

[250] Facts mainly taken from the case.

[251] See http://uk.westlaw.com/find/default.wl?spa=ukmigrat-000&rs=WLUK9.01&ifm=NotSet&fn=_top&sv=Split&cite=284+FED+401&vr=2.0&rp=%2ffind%2fdefault.wl&mt=LawSchoolPractitioner.

[252] See http://uk.westlaw.com/find/default.wl?spa=ukmigrat-000&rs=WLUK9.01&ifm=NotSet&fn=_top&sv=Split&cite=284+FED+401&vr=2.0&rp=%2ffind%2fdefault.wl&mt=LawSchoolPractitioner.

It is interesting to note that the dissenting opinion argues that this transaction would not induce a substantial lessening of competition. However, the failing-firm defence was not successfully invoked in this case.

FTC v. Great Lakes Chemical Corp.

The defendant in this case,[253] a Delaware corporation, produced elemental bromine and its derivatives, including flame retardants, solvents and lubricants. It sought to acquire the bromine-related assets of Velsicol, which was a subsidiary of another Delaware-based business, Northwest Industries Inc. These assets comprised an R & D facility, a plant and the company's bromine fields, for which Great Lakes would pay approximately US$29 million. It is important to note that the plant had been temporarily shut down and that the research undertaken at the facility was of minimum scale.

The FTC sought an injunction against the acquisition. However, as a result of the onerous consequences of the injunction the FTC had to discharge a significant burden of proving that its suit was likely to succeed. Moreover, in addition to proving the likelihood of success, the FTC had to show that 'the equities' favour enjoining the transaction. This means that the FTC had to prove that the harm flowing from the preliminary injunction to the parties to the transaction and the public must outweigh the harm, if any, to the competition that would occur in the period between denial of the preliminary injunction and the final adjudication of the merits of the claim under §7. Courts have recognized that factors such as increased exports and benefits to local communities are important factors that can lead to denial of preliminary relief even where the FTC shows the requisite likelihood of success.

Section 7 of the Clayton Act prohibits mergers on the grounds that competition will be lessened. In order to assess the effect on competition, the state of Velsicol's bromine-related business had to be examined. According to *United States v. General Dynamics Corp.*, the competitive weakness of one of the two merging parties goes to the heart of the government's prima facie case. It was also held that the evidence presented a clear-cut case of the failing-firm defence. Alternatively, in the event that Velsicol was not considered to fall under the failing-firm defence, its weakened operational state amounted to an important factor that should be considered.

[253] *FTC v. Great Lakes Chemical Corp.*, 528 F. Supp. 84, 87 (N.D.Ill.1981).

The market that was defined in the present case was all flame retardants as opposed to brominated flame retardants. This was done in order to 'recognize competition where competition did in fact exist', according to the dicta in *Brown Shoe v. US*. Notwithstanding several inputs (including bromine) were used to make flame retardants, all retardants serve the same purpose:

> The practical indicia of Brown Shoe lead to the conclusion that the FTC's suggested brominated flame retardant market must be rejected in favor of the commercially meaningful flame retardant market. Within this market, the evidence established that the proposed acquisition is not likely to lead to a substantial lessening of competition.

In order to determine whether the proposed merger constitutes a violation of §7, one must consider the effects on consumers. In the present case, it was discovered that only small amounts of bromine were sold commercially. Several witnesses also testified that the merger would make Velsicol more competitive and strengthen its position in the market and it was asserted that Velsicol had in fact been recording increasing figures reflecting significant loss:

> It was ultimately decided that divestiture would be an effective ultimate remedy should the Commission succeed in its case on the merits. If the acquisition were permitted to go forward and Great Lakes was ultimately required to divest the Velsicol assets, competition would be improved, not lessened, because Great Lakes would be selling a more viable operation than presently exists.

FTC v. Arch Coal, Inc.

In May 2003,[254] Arch Coal Inc., owner and operator of two of Wyoming's Southern Powder River Basin (SPRB) mines (Black Thunder and Coal Creek), and New Vulcan Coal Holdings, LLC, owner of two SPRB mines (North Rochelle and Buckskin), which it operated through its subsidiary Triton Coal Company, LLC, entered into a US$364 million merger and purchase agreement under the terms of which Arch Coal would acquire all assets of Triton Coal Company, including its two SPRB mines.

A pre-merger notification of this transaction was provided to the FTC. Arch Coal consequently informed the FTC that it intended to divest one of the acquired Triton Coal mines (Buckskin) to Peter Kiewit Sons, Inc., a large company with some mining interests outside the SPRB, and in

[254] 329 F. Supp. 2d 109 (D.D.C. 2004).

January 2004 a firm asset purchase agreement was entered into by Arch Coal and Kiewit.

At the time four companies operated a Tier I mine (the SPRB mines were categorized into three tiers based on coal quality, heat content and mine location; and Tier I mines typically produced a high (8,600–8,900 British thermal unit (BTU)) coal which commanded a price premium based on its lower sulphur content and higher energy content, relative to the other tiers). These 'big four' were considered the major producers of SPRB coal, and were Arch Coal, Triton, Kennecott Energy Co., and Peabody Holding Co.[255]

At that time, over 30 per cent of the coal that was produced yearly in the United States of America was produced in the SPRB.

The FTC, on 1 April 2004, filed a complaint which sought a preliminary injunction to block Arch Coal Inc.'s proposed acquisition of Triton Coal. The Commission submitted that such an injunction is in the public interest, and that the acquisition may substantially lessen competition and/or tend to create a monopoly in coal mined from the SPRB and in 8800 BTU SPRB coal. Also, in the Commission's opinion, Arch Coal's proposed transfer of Triton's Buckskin mine assets to Kiewit (part of the subsequent terms of the transaction), was deemed insufficient to 'materially change the acquisition or its likely effect on competition'.[256]

Specifically, the FTC complaint alleged that the acquisition would:

- combine two of the four leading producers of SPRB coal, substantially increasing concentration in the SPRB market; in addition it would substantially reduce competition in the SPRB market;
- combine the two firms that hold the principal sources of excess capacity in the SPRB, and bring under Arch Coal's control the principal source of excess capacity for production of 8,800 BTU SPRB coal;
- combine two among only four producers in Tier I of the SPRB, substantially increasing concentration among 8,800 BTU SPRB coal producers; in addition it would eliminate the existing substantial

[255] See Westlaw International website at http://uk.westlaw.com/find/default.wl?spa=ukmigrat-000&rs=WLUK9.01&ifm=NotSet&fn=_top&sv=Split&cite=329+F.+Supp.+2d+109%2c+156+(D.D.C.+2004)&vr=2.0&rp=%2ffind%2fdefault.wl&mt=LawSchool Practitioner.

[256] See the US Federal Trade Commission website at www.ftc.gov/os/adjpro/d9316/index.shtm, in the Matter of Arch Coal, Inc., a corporation; New Vulcan Coal Holdings, LLC, a limited liability company; and Triton Coal Company, LLC, a limited liability company, File No 031-0191, Docket No 9316.

competition between Arch Coal and Triton, and substantially reduce competition in 8,800 BTU SPRB coal; and

- increase the likelihood of co-ordination in the market for SPRB coal – a market that was already susceptible to co-ordination.[257]

Subsequently, on 7 April 2004, the FTC also issued an administrative complaint challenging Arch Coal Inc.'s proposed acquisition of all the assets of Triton Coal Company, LLC from New Vulcan Coal Holdings, LLC. The essence of the complaint was that the proposed acquisition would make anti-competitive co-ordination more likely among the remaining coal producers in the SPRB, similar to the grounds of complaint filed under the application for preliminary injunction.

The FTC brought an action before the US District Court for the District of Columbia, under §7 of the Clayton Act and §13(b) Federal Trade Act, in a bid to enjoin the proposed merger under which Arch Coal would acquire Triton Coal and its two mines in the SPRB region.[258]

The defined product market and geographical market were concluded by the Court to be the SPRB. The FTC had the burden of proving that the merger would cause 'undue concentration in the market'.[259] The plaintiffs' submission also centred on the allegation that the merger would decrease competition by aiding co-ordinated interaction. The case was further complicated by the fact that the plaintiffs' case balanced on a novel 'theory of possible future "tacit coordination" among competitors to restrict production, as opposed to direct coordination of prices'. The Court concluded that the competition level would be the same, after the transaction. It found that the adduced evidence established ample constraint on co-ordination of the Tier I producers, by other key Tier II and Tier III players in the market.

The defendants also invoked the flailing-firm defence. They adduced evidence of Triton Coal being a firm in a weak financial position. It had over time lost its competitive edge, and was less of a competitor than any of the other big four. Evidence was adduced on its uncompetitive business practices, leading to a constant loss of money, lack of increase

[257] *FTC v. Arch Coal, Inc.*, 329 F. Supp. 2d 109, at p. 123.

[258] See the US Federal Trade Commission website at www.ftc.gov/os/adjpro/d9316/index.shtm, in the Matter of Arch Coal, Inc., a corporation; New Vulcan Coal Holdings, LLC, a limited liability company; and Triton Coal Company, LLC, a limited liability company, File No 031-0191, Docket No 9316.

[259] Ibid.

in production over a five-year period, low coal reserves, substantial shortfall in sales at one of its mines, difficulty with raising much-needed additional funds due to bad credit status, and very limited likelihood of attracting any other buyer.

The defendants may not have been able to plead successfully that Triton Coal was a failing firm, but its steadily declining business, with no 'convincing prospects for improvement', led the Court to conclude that the plaintiffs' claim of Triton's past and future competitive significance in the SPRB market had been far overstated.

Based on the above analysis, the Court found that the defendants successfully rebutted the plaintiffs' prima facie case of a §7 violation. The plaintiffs had not shown a 'reasonable probability' that the challenged transactions might substantially lessen competition in the SPRB. Moreover, the Court concluded, based on the recorded evidence, that the plaintiffs had not raised such serious and substantial questions going to the merits of the §7 claim that a preliminary injunction was warranted under §13(b) of the FTA Act to permit further review by the FTC. In short, the plaintiffs were not likely to succeed on the merits of their claim of a Clayton Act violation based on the novel theory of prospective tacit co-ordination on limiting production. As such, it was ordered that the plaintiffs' request for a preliminary injunction be denied.

The FTC subsequently applied for a motion for an injunction pending appeal in the US Court of Appeals for the District of Columbia Circuit. The motion was denied. Thereafter, on 10 September 2004, the FTC withdrew the matter from administrative litigation; and on 13 June 2005 it formally announced that it had closed its investigation of Arch Coal's acquisition of Triton Coal.[260]

Other cases

The failing-company defence in the banking sector was mentioned in the case of *United States v. Philadelphia National Bank*.[261] The case involved a horizontal merger of the second- and third-largest of the forty-two commercial banks in the metropolitan area consisting of Philadelphia and its three contiguous counties. The US Supreme Court rejected the failing-firm defence but upheld that the failing-company doctrine applied to the banking sector due to the greater public impact of a bank

[260] See www.ftc.gov/opa/2005/06/archcoal.shtm.

[261] *United States v. Philadelphia National Bank*, (1963) 374 U.S. 321.

failure compared with ordinary business failure.[262] In addition, the Court rejected the position that commercial banking is subject to a high degree of governmental regulation, or that it is somehow immune from the anti-competitive effects of undue concentration because it deals in the intangibles of credit and services rather than in the manufacture or sale of tangible commodities.[263]

As the Court argued in *United States v. Third National Bank*,[264] Congress was concerned about banks in danger of collapse – banks not so deeply in trouble as to call forth the traditional 'failing-company' defence, but nonetheless in danger of becoming, before long, financially unsound institutions. Congress seems to have felt that a bank failure is a much greater community catastrophe than the failure of an industrial or retail enterprise, and that a much smaller risk of failure than that required by the failing-company doctrine should be sufficient to justify the rather radical preventive step of an anti-competitive merger.[265] Such an argument should be taken into account in today's crisis too. The failing-firm defence was not accepted. As the Court further argued, if the gains in better service outweighed the anti-competitive detriment and the merger was essential to secure this net gain to the public interest, the merger should be approved.

In the brewing industry the failing-firm defence was applicable under the condition that all requirements are fulfilled.[266] The defence was invoked in several cases, among others in the case of *United States v. Pabst Brewing Co.*[267] The facts indicated a thirty-year decline in the number of brewers and a sharp rise in the market share controlled by the leading brewers.[268] The US Supreme Court rejected Pabst's failing-company defence due to the fact that the party failed to prove the elements of this defence.

In *United States v. Diebold Inc.*[269] the US Supreme Court argued that it was improper for the District Court to decide the applicability of that doctrine and dismiss the case on a motion for summary judgment. The failing-firm defence was not accepted.

The failing-firm defence was also held to justify the merger in *United*

[262] *United States v. Philadelphia National Bank*, (1963) 374 U.S. 321, at p. 369.

[263] *International Shoe Co. v. Federal Trade Commission*, (1930) 280 U.S. 291, at p. 368.

[264] *United States v. Third National Bank*, (1968) 390 U.S. 171.

[265] *United States v. Third National Bank*, (1968) 390 U.S. 171, at p. 187.

[266] In the case of *United States v. Pennzoil Co.*, (1965) 252 F. Supp. 962, the failing-firm defence argumentation was invoked in the oil-refining industry.

[267] *United States v. Pabst Brewing Co.*, (1966) 384 U.S. 546.

[268] *United States v. Pabst Brewing Co.*, (1966) 384 U.S. 546, at p. 551.

[269] *United States v. Diebold, Inc.*, (1962) 369 U.S. 654.

States v. Maryland & Virginia Milk Producers Assn.[270] In this case an agricultural co-operative association acquired the capital stock of Embassy Dairy, the largest milk dealer in the area which competed with the association's dealers. Finally, the failing-firm defence justified allowing the merger in *Union Leader Corp. v. Newspapers of New England*.[271]

3.8 Derogation: removing the suspension

Similar to the derogation provisions of the ECMR (Article 7(3) of Regulation 139/2004[272]) the US authorities can also in 'crisis' situations have flexibility in assessing mergers. The DOJ and the FTC can use the 'pocket decree' or 'blank cheque' when a transaction had to close before the agencies could complete a full investigation. The pocket decree or blank cheque can prove valuable when all parties are willing to be flexible and where competition problems and the potential remedies are easily identifiable.

In 2006, the DOJ permitted Mittal Steel Company to buy Arcelor SA before the expiration of the initial HSR waiting period and without a complete merger assessment by the DOJ. The companies were at that time the world's two largest steel producers. During the initial HSR waiting period the DOJ concluded that the transaction raised competition concerns in the US market for tin mill products (finely rolled steel sheets that are normally coated with tin or chrome and are used in many final consumer products such as cans).

Mittal agreed with the DOJ to divest certain assets (Arcelor's Canadian subsidiary, or certain other assets) if a substantial lessening of competition was identified. The latter agreement was accompanied by a proposed consent decree that the division of the firm could file if a divestiture were necessary.

The agreement with Mittal, similar to the concept of 'undertaking in lieu' that the UK Office of Fair Trading employs,[273] required Mittal to hold those assets separate until the completion of the investigation. The DOJ determined that this divestiture would remedy any competition concerns in the market for tin mill products.

[270] *United States v. Maryland & Virginia Milk Producers Association*, (1968) 167 F. Supp. 799, aff'd, 362 U.S. 458.

[271] *Union Leader Corp. v. Newspapers of New England*, 284 F.2d 582.

[272] OJ L24/1, 29 January 2004.

[273] Mergers, Substantive Guidance Assessment, at www.oft.gov.uk.

The then assistant attorney general Thomas O. Barnett outlined the circumstances where the DOJ's review process can affect the outcome of the competition for control of companies.[274]

Although pocket decrees have been used by the DOJ for many years, they have been and remain relatively rare. They most typically arise in fix-it-first or analogous situations where the acquiring company has an exogenous legal obligation to divest certain assets that would eliminate any competitive concern. For example, in the acquisition of radio or television stations, Federal Communications Commission (FCC) regulations might require the acquiring firm to sell a station to stay below a regulatory limit. If divestiture takes place, no further investigation would be required. If for some reason it does not take place, the pocket decree protects the ability of the division of the firm to address the competitive concern. Further, there are instances where the review process itself can affect the outcome of the marketplace competition for control of companies. For example, in some tender offer situations, the issuance of a second request can trigger foreign regulatory requirements that destroy the offeror's ability to succeed. Where such concerns arise that are not of the parties' own making, the DOJ considers whether it can minimize the impact of the review process on the competition in the marketplace consistent with the DOJ's enforcement responsibilities.

The decree allows the antitrust authorities to permit a transaction to close immediately, file a consent decree and require a remedy at a later date if the merger assessment deems it necessary.

3.9 Reflections from theory and practice

This section deals with controversial issues that surround corporate debt restructuring methods which may involve the sale or merger of a whole firm or of the loss-making division of a firm. Both the US and the EU have devised criteria against which the failing-firm defence can be assessed. In the US the firm would, among other things, not be able to reorganize successfully under Chapter 11 of the USBC and, absent the acquisition, the assets of the failing firm would exit the relevant market. In the EU the allegedly failing firm would, among other things, in the near future be forced out of the

[274] T. Barnett, 'Merger Review: A Quest for Efficiency', 25 January 2007, www.usdoj.gov/atr/public/speeches/221173.htm.

market because of financial difficulties if not taken over by another undertaking. Furthermore, in the absence of a merger the assets of the failing firm would inevitably exit the market. Thus, for the failing-firm defence to apply, a merger, acquisition and/or sale should be the only viable method of corporate restructuring. Otherwise, the failing-firm defence cannot be applicable. A tentative conclusion can be made that lack of alternative means of reorganization is a vital criterion for the success of the failing-firm defence. As Correia states, if the reorganized firm does not survive reorganization or if it does so with substantially reduced capacity, then there has been a competitive loss based on the output that will be lost.[275] However, there is substantial uncertainty surrounding the reorganization scenario. Thus a central problem in applying the reorganization criterion is that it may be impossible to make reliable predictions at the time of assessing the merger as regards the likelihood that alternative restructuring methods will be successful.

The OECD has produced a detailed report on failing-firm defence.[276] The report states that business failure can be traced to managerial inefficiency (broadly defined), market-wide excess capacity,[277] or some mixture of the two. Inefficiency should be dealt with by a reorganization or takeover designed to improve the firm's management. Redeployment is the optimal solution, however, if a firm is failing because of market-wide excess capacity.

If the reason for failure is managerial inefficiency then the merger should be reviewed by analysing and comparing all available alternatives, including liquidation. The proposed merger should be blocked only if it is inferior to one or more of the assessed alternatives. It would not be sufficient that a management decision to close down is said to be made; in order for the failing-firm defence to apply, the decision to close must be inevitable in view of economic and financial factors. The efficiencies may be more significant and verifiable if the merger enhances the managerial capacities of the failing firm. Though liquidation will change the relative market shares of incumbent firms less than various mergers would, the surviving incumbents' shares will tend to rise, and

[275] Correia 1995.

[276] OECD, 'Failing firm defence' (1996), www.oecd.org/dataoecd/35/6/1920253.pdf.

[277] This refers to a situation in which total installed capacity (the sum of outputs, assuming that each supplier produces at the minimum point of its average cost curve) exceeds the quantity demanded at the equilibrium competitive price.

they will increase most for the enterprises whose products are the closest substitutes for those of the failing firm.

If the acquired firm is failing because of adverse conditions relating to market-wide excess capacity, with the acquirer not being an actual or potential competitor of the failing firm, and after the merger all acquired assets are redeployed outside the failing firm's current market, competition authorities should consider the effects in both markets rather than exclusively concentrate on the market in which the failing firm currently operates.

As the above analysis illustrates, the main rationale for the merger will usually be to facilitate a more cost-effective redeployment of excess capacity than would occur without the merger. In this case the acquiring firm may have no intention of using or giving access to the failing firm's assets. Furthermore, the assets may be acquired merely to substantiate a threat of a likely increase in output as a means to deter new entrants or discipline rivals. Such likely motives should be taken into account by competition authorities to the extent possible.

Furthermore, if the merger or acquisition of a failing firm is not allowed and the failing firm exits the market, any technical or productive achievements of the failing firm will be lost. Hence there may be adverse welfare implications. However, exit of the failing firm may be preferable from a competition perspective since the remaining firms may compete more aggressively to counteract the decrease in supply due to the loss of the failing firm's capacity and in order to win the failing firm's customers.

Failing-company claims thus indicate a trade-off between two scenarios that need to be considered – the company exiting the market and an anti-competitive merger. The first scenario is of great importance if the costs of the merger are balanced against the costs of blocking the merger, where there is probability that the failing firm will survive and remain competitive. If blocking the merger implies that the failing firm's assets will exit the market and therefore the output of this firm will be lost, then allowance of the merger seems the only sensible solution. The loss to stockholders and to the community where the business operates would be less severe if the merger were allowed than if the firm exited the market.

From an economic perspective, capacity is a good predictor of output and lost output is a good measure of competitive harm. In the case of a merger increasing concentration, it is very unlikely that output will be reduced through interdependence. Output is likely to be lower if the acquired firm's assets exit the market, thus merger is the preferred possibility.[278] However, it should be noted that the current market share of the failing firm may overstate its future competitive significance and the anti-competitive effects of a merger. What would be of importance is whether the merged entity can unilaterally or collectively affect prices and output.

The failing-firm defence carries most weight when it can be shown that the merger enables productive assets to continue in productive use. The exit of the failing firm will lead to an increase in demand and an ensuing increase in production costs and prices (unless the firm is the least competitive in a declining market). If the failing firm merges or is acquired by a dominant firm, the latter will obtain assets and know-how that allow an increase in productivity, thus enhancing its competitive position. Hence, such a merger or acquisition may lead to lower production costs and prices.

However, the takeover of a failing firm by a dominant competitor may weaken the competitive position of the remaining smaller competitors and may induce them to seek merging counterparts, thus leading to further consolidation of the market. A dominant firm should be a permissible acquirer only where there is an imminent danger of liquidation of the failing firm and no other less anti-competitive purchaser is available.[279] If a non-dominant firm acquires or merges with the failing firm and becomes dominant there is high probability that the non-dominant firm's market power would have increased in any case once the failing firm exited the market. In such a case, the merger is not the cause of the adverse impact on competition. Thus the difference between allowing and blocking the merger is trivial as far as the anti-competitive effects of the merger are concerned.

In certain jurisdictions a failing-firm defence or exception is not provided for in law or in the regulations. Competition authorities should take into account the fact that the merger involves a failing firm in the estimation of the market shares before and after the merger. This approach is of great importance when the failing firm's market share appears to be in long-term decline. Furthermore, the competition authority may grant particularly generous treatment to claimed

[278] A number of authors have estimated the loss in output from a firm exiting the market with the loss in output stemming from increased concentration. See Kwoka and Warren-Boulton 1986; Friedman 1986; McChesney 1986. See further Correia 1995.

[279] Ritter and Braun 2004, at p. 594.

efficiencies when a failing firm is involved in a merger. Finally, the requirement for causation between a merger involving a failing firm and a significant reduction in competition (as is required for mergers involving failing firms that are assessed according to the European Community Merger Regulation) may be relaxed, implying that the competition authority is prone to accepting failing-firm defence or exception.

In general, in the absence of any other benefits (such as avoiding exit costs), mergers involving failing firms should not be allowed if they increase market power. The failing firm should be genuinely failing, and not merely 'ailing' ('flailing-firm defence'). Thus the merger should be allowed only when the alternative is immediate bankruptcy, and the failing firm should not receive a significant share of the gains from the merger. If it does, this should be interpreted as a signal that the firm is not failing. Finally, the greater the weight on consumer welfare and the greater the adverse effects on competition, the less likely a merger involving a failing firm is to be blocked.

The assessment of a merger involving a failing firm should not be carried out in the same way as a merger which does not involve a failing firm. Where a merging firm is failing, pre-merger competitive conditions should not be used as a benchmark. If the competition authorities reject one or more mergers falling below an unsustainable benchmark, the result could well be liquidation expected to produce greater harm to competition than is predicted to result from one or more of the rejected mergers. As the Office of Fair Trading guidelines state, if one of the parties to a merger is failing, pre-merger conditions of competition might not prevail even if the merger were prohibited. In such a case, the counterfactual might need to be adjusted to reflect the likely failure of one of the parties and the resulting loss of rivalry.[280]

A merger that would be blocked due to its adverse effect on competition is permitted when the firm to be acquired is a failing firm and a less detrimental merger is unavailable. Blocking the merger will cause the loss of jobs and assets from the market and thus possible economic and social benefits will be forgone. Therefore the merger with the failing firm leading to high concentration may be accepted under the failing-firm defence. In the assessment of a merger involving a failing-firm defence, competition authorities should take into account the conditions in the

[280] OFT, 'Mergers, Substantive Assessment Guidance', available from www.oft.gov.uk., at p. 34.

industry, potential efficiencies and the counterfactual to blocking the merger. Following the Lisbon Treaty's coming into force on 1 December 2009, interpretative issues may also arise due to the stronger references to full employment and social objectives, including the reference to a 'highly competitive social market economy', in amended Article 3 of the Treaty on European Union. This might induce arguments that broader policy standards, including employment as well as economic and social benefits, should apply.[281]

As mentioned above, one of the criteria for successfully invoking the failing-firm defence in the EU and the US requires that the assets will exit the market in the absence of the merger. This criterion reveals an exclusive focus on the failing firm's market. However, as the OECD report indicates, there is another aspect to it that merits further probing. If the failing firm's assets exit the market, there will be a tendency for supply in that market to decrease.[282] The decrease in supply resulting from the failing firm exiting the market may not always be greater than the decrease in supply after an anti-competitive merger involving the failing firm.

In addition, the assessment of the failing-firm defence in merger cases should take into account the effect of the policy rule on incentives for entry (and *ex ante* investment decisions in general).[283] A lenient approach towards mergers involving failing and financially distressed firms can balance the losses from increasing concentration after the merger with the gains from hastening entry and competition. However, the beneficial effect of a more permissive merger policy on entry is reduced if the share given to the failing firm is small. If the failing-firm defence is less likely to be accepted in cases where the share given to the failing firm is reasonably significant, the wider benefits of the policy will not be realized. In addition, a failing firm that has greater bargaining power, perhaps because it is a division of a large corporate group, gains a greater share of the surplus from merger and its entry decision will be more sensitive to the merger rule.[284] According to research

[281] See www.wilmerhale.com/publications/whPubsDetail.aspx?publication=9321.

[282] Such reductions and the welfare-reducing price increases they normally entail are virtually certain where there was little or no excess capacity in the pre-merger situation. See further OECD, 'Failing firm defence' (1996), www.oecd.org/dataoecd/35/6/1920253.pdf, at p. 19.

[283] Mason and Weeds 2003, at p. 33.

[284] The outcome of the *ICI-Kemira Oy* case (www.competition-commission.org.uk/rep_pub/reports/1991/293kemira.htm#full), assessed by the MMC (UK), in which a

conducted by Mason and Weeds, the failing-firm defence can generate greater welfare gains in cases where the target gains a substantial share of the surplus than in those where the failing firm has little bargaining power.[285]

An argument can be made in favour of a more lenient policy which could be characterized as permitting the defence to be used by severely distressed as well as by imminently failing firms and may yield social benefits through its beneficial impact on entry, resulting in more effective competition in the long run. Thus competition authorities might consider being less restrictive not only to mergers involving failing firms, but also to mergers involving divisions of failing firms, as well as failing divisions of firms. However, some assurance may be needed that the division's failing status is not merely a reflection of creative accounting as regards issues like transfer payments and the allocation of common costs.

Economic and social benefits should be taken into consideration in the assessment of the failing-firm defence. There is difficulty in determining the extent of social costs or benefits in a failing-firm context and how to account for them. The burden is borne in the form of higher prices and lost consumer surplus, while the relevant benefits relate to the failing company's workers and shareholders and the community in which the failing company's assets are located. According to Posner, the failing-firm defence is 'one of the clearest examples in antitrust law of a desire to subordinate competition to other values'.[286] The social-policy consideration regarding the merger works alongside the impact of the merger on competition. The relevant public-policy consideration regards the protection of private parties whose future depends on the existence of the failing firm as well as the protection of the welfare of the locality of the failing firm. Social costs could be considered a policy matter, since neither the legislative history of the Cellar-Kefauver amendment to §7 in 1950 nor the US Supreme Court precedent expressly precluded doing

failing division was judged more harshly than might have been the case for a stand-alone firm in a similar financial position, also threatens to undermine the benefit of the policy.

[285] Mason and Weeds 2003, at p. 3.

[286] R.A. Posner, *Antitrust: Cases, Economic Notes and Other Materials*, 2nd ed., West Publishing, 1981, at p. 472. Richard Posner was an assistant to the Federal Trade Commission and assistant to the solicitor general of the United States, and in 1981 he was appointed a judge of the US Court of Appeals for the Seventh Circuit. He was the chief judge of the Court from 1993 to 2000.

so.[287] According to Correia,[288] competition authorities should take social costs into account in adopting some general formulation of the failing-company defence, rather than taking social costs into account in individual cases.

As Fox stated, in relation to the failing-firm defence invoked in *Citizen Publishing*,[289] failing-firm defence as a matter of US Supreme Court case law is devised in the interests of stockholders and communities (e.g. jobs).[290] In addition, as was mentioned earlier in this chapter, the US Supreme Court in the *United States v. General Dynamics Corp.* case upheld that three groups – private parties, shareholders and creditors – benefit from the merger of a failing firm.[291] Major shareholder losses occur only in the case of liquidation. Shareholders are unlikely to lose their investment and are likely to reap benefits if the merger is profitable. Creditors will benefit as a result of retaining their rights against the debtor and are likely to be reimbursed for the credit they have provided to the firm. In contrast, in insolvency proceedings they are not as likely to be fully reimbursed.

Fox stressed that the case law may seem of questionable wisdom to those who believe that the job of antitrust is antitrust. Shareholders by definition take the risk of losing an investment and employment policy is not best handled by antitrust exemptions. Allowing mergers can result in job losses, as may also be the case in prohibiting mergers. If a merger is not allowed and the failing firm exits the market, the lost jobs originate from plant closure. If an anti-competitive merger is allowed, jobs may be lost when the industry raises prices and reduces output. When the failing firm disappears from the market, the employment resources of this firm are likely to be devoted to the manufacture of a completely different product or provide totally different services, perhaps not as efficiently. The likelihood of job losses, inefficient use of labour force and the political and social ramifications that such issues may have should not determine the assessment of mergers under the antitrust law.

Competition authorities (e.g. in the US and the EU) are unwilling to

[287] Federal Trade Commission (FTC), 'Competition Policy in the New High-Tech, Global Marketplace' 1996, Volume 1, Chapter 3, www.ftc.gov/opp/global/report/gc_v1.pdf, at p. 14.

[288] Correia 1995.

[289] *Citizen Publishing Co. v. United States*, (1969) 394 U.S. 131, at pp. 138–9 .

[290] 'Antitrust and Competitiveness: Efficiencies, Failing Firms, and the World Arena', statement of Eleanor Fox, 13 December 1994, www.ftc.gov/opp/global/fox.htm.

[291] *United States v. General Dynamics Corp.*, (1974) 415 U.S. 486.

extend the failing-firm defence or exception to firms which have not yet failed but are less efficient competitors. If a flailing-firm defence or exception exists, parties to competition-reducing (and thus likely profitable) mergers would have a strong tendency to claim that they are flailing even if their situation were not as severe as that of a failing firm in order to invoke the defence and be treated more leniently than they should be. In addition, as the OECD report states, even if flailing firms could be reliably identified, competition authorities may take the view that the competition such firms provide, albeit weak, benefits consumers and should be allowed to continue as long as possible. A merger involving a flailing firm might foster a considerably better competitive environment than a similar merger involving a failing firm.[292] Similar arguments can be put forward for the unwillingness of competition authorities to accept declining-industry arguments. However, what should be taken into consideration is that in declining-industry situations it is more likely that firms that are currently flailing may continue to be in an adverse situation and may not be viable at all in the near future.

As the above analysis has illustrated, the application of the failing-firm defence is highly controversial. The role of antitrust legislation in taking into consideration the phenomenon and consequences of failing firms in assessing transactions involving such firms is important in safeguarding and advancing the aims of competition law.

3.10 Concluding remarks

Mergers and joint ventures in industries may be essential during crises as a means to ensure the viability not only of the firms themselves but also of whole industries, as may be the case with the financial sector and the prevention of systemic risks resulting from the bankruptcy (rather than acquisition) of weak financial institutions. If antitrust laws are perceived to be an undue barrier to such combinations, then a legislative affirmation that this is not the case is desirable. This chapter has analysed the implications of the failing-firm defence on the restructuring process that financially distressed companies may be involved in.

Firms in financially distressed conditions may face the prospect of illiquidity and may embark on a restructuring process in order to ensure

[292] OECD, 'Failing firm defence' (1996), www.oecd.org/dataoecd/35/6/1920253.pdf, at p. 21.

their viability and profitability. 'Restructuring' is the term for the act of converting a debt into another debt that is repayable at a later time.[293] In this process of restructuring the companies may be involved in acquisitions and/or mergers. In such cases, the implications of competition legislation on the restructuring process may be severe. There may be instances where the negotiations leading to a restructuring plan have been completed successfully and the proposed solution (merger/acquisition) is to be blocked by the competition authorities. A safe harbour for such cases is the concept of failing-firm defence or failing-division defence.

Each jurisdiction has its own formulated criteria that need to be satisfied in order for the failing-firm defence to be acceptable. In general, the criteria that need to be satisfied include, among other things, that the allegedly failing firm would in the near future be forced out of the market because of financial difficulties if not taken over by another undertaking. Thus the firm must be insolvent, on the verge of insolvency or in imminent danger of financial collapse. In addition, there must be no alternative purchase less anti-competitive than the notified merger, and in the absence of a merger the assets of the failing firm would have inevitably to exit the market. Once these conditions are fulfilled the merger would not be considered to cause the deterioration of the competitive structure that follows the merger.

Hence, to qualify for the failing-firm defence, the merging undertakings must show that one of the undertakings is a failing firm and that therefore the merger itself does not bring about any anti-competitive effects. The logic in the defence is that the deterioration in the competitive structure of the market would have occurred even in the absence of the merger through the exit of the failing firm.[294]

Considering the merger with the failing firm, the economic aspects of allowing and blocking this merger, such as the loss of jobs, benefit to consumers, price maintenance and so on, should also be borne in mind. Social costs must be taken into account in adopting some general formulation of the failing-company defence, rather than taking social costs into account in individual cases.[295] The Lisbon Treaty and its reference to a 'highly competitive social market economy' might induce argu-

[293] *Oxford English Dictionary*, available at www.askoxford.com.

[294] A. MacCulloch and B. Rodger, *Competition Law and Policy in the EC and UK*, 3rd ed., Cavendish Publishing, 2004, at p. 221.

[295] Correia 1995.

ments that broader policy standards, including employment as well as economic and social benefits, should apply.[296]

The courts, mainly in the EU, have in most instances been negative towards the failing-firm defence.[297] However, there have been some landmark cases in the EU and US mentioned above and analysed in this chapter which have formulated the development of the concepts of failing-firm defence and failing-division defence. These decisions by the competition authorities and courts, along with the guidelines issued by the competition authorities, have provided the framework within which the request for such a defence must be assessed.

Deciding when and how to apply the defence is difficult in part because the facts underlying the failing-company claim may be closely intertwined with other claims, which are analytically distinct. For example, it may seem that current policy benefits alternative purchasers that are unlikely to offer the same efficiencies that a competitor purchaser may offer. In addition, the failing-firm defence can be assumed to constitute an efficiency claim, since the acquiring company argues that it can ensure the viability and profitability of the failing company. As Correia argues, a failing-company claim may also occur in the context of a declining industry where capacity is certain to exit the market. If that is the case, a merger may be justified both on efficiency grounds and on grounds of failing-firm defence, which must be analysed separately. In general, only if the merger risks substantial harm to competition must the failing-firm defence be assessed.[298]

In an interesting UK case,[299] the criteria for failing-firm defence were not satisfied, even though the target would exit the market in the near future, and the prevention of the merger would lead to harm to consumer welfare due to the discontinuity of the supply of the service.

Orbital Marketing Services Group Ltd (OMSG) ran marketing services operations specializing in the travel/tourism, education and health-care sectors. OMSG also had general direct-mail and fulfilment businesses. One of OMSG's trading divisions, BP Travel Marketing Services, provided brochure distribution and mailing services to travel principals, primarily servicing travel retailers with brochures and information. It generated around 45 per cent of OMSG's turnover. Ocean

[296] See www.wilmerhale.com/publications/whPubsDetail.aspx?publication=9321.

[297] Albeit a small number of cases where the defence has been invoked.

[298] Correia 1995.

[299] *Orbital/Ocean Park*, www.oft.gov.uk.

Park Ltd (OP) was the holding company for Au Logistics Ltd (Au) and also provided brochure distribution and mailing services to travel principals, primarily servicing travel retailers with brochures and information.

This market was under severe pressure for a number of reasons:

- There was a dramatic decrease in the number of travel brochures over the previous few years as consumers shifted from seeking paper-based holiday information to using the Internet. Tour operators were redeploying marketing budget away from brochures and into new media.
- Simple point-to-point products (such as ferries) were almost exclusively sold on the Internet rather than via brochures.
- There was a consequent fall in the number of high street travel agents (delivery points).
- There was pressure on the role of the traditional tour operator as consumers 'self-packaged' using the websites of low-cost airlines and accommodation providers.
- The top four UK tour operators responded to this pressure on their business model by merging in 2007 to create the 'top two'. They integrated products and rationalized their estate of high street travel shops – exacerbating the decline in brochure print runs.
- The top two continued to acquire other tour operators, reducing the number of customers for the distributors and adding to the volume within the top two's 'bulk-buying' rates.
- It was highly unlikely any substantial new tour operators would enter the market – in fact several had gone out of business (including XL Holidays – a top-twenty customer representing over 1 per cent of brochure volumes) and the economic downturn would adversely affect others.

The ongoing decline in brochure volumes threatened the viability of both distributors' business models. This was based on a weekly delivery by both distributors to each travel agent of a reasonable volume of brochure packs, with the resulting economy of scale leading to fixed 'lower-than-alone' pack delivery rates for each participating tour operator.

It was therefore inevitable that ultimately there would only be sufficient volume to support one company at current pricing. As volumes declined, the sector saw strong competition, meaning that contract prices (apart from two 'legacy' contracts with the original top four distributed by Au) were held down – further reducing the viability of two distributors continuing in this market.

According to the merging parties, in the face of continuing decline in brochure volumes towards sub-critical mass, the inevitable 'two distributors into one' would occur. This merger would provide for an orderly transition and a continuity of service to both customers and travel agents. In the alternative scenario of one of the distributors ceasing to trade or choosing to exit the market, the affected customers would face considerable disruption and risk. For these customers their existing fixed-price contracts would cease to apply, leaving them open to cost increases. They would incur the costs of transfer, interruption to supply (i.e. of keeping their products on sale) and a lack of continuity in management information. Also, there would not necessarily be sufficient capacity suddenly available at the remaining company for all the affected tour operators – particularly at peak distribution times.

The parties argued that although not immediately a failing firm, the financial viability of Au as a stand-alone business in its existing structure over the contract life-cycle was in some doubt. The parties maintained that there was no longer the critical volume of brochures necessary to sustain two distributors throughout the year. Increasingly there were distribution weeks with low volume driving costs up. The pricing scale was not uniform as the first parcel entailed a higher cost so it was not possible in high-volume weeks to recoup efficiencies lost in low-volume weeks.

BP always considered Au prices to be too low economically, and normally chose not to compete in order to keep customers at all costs. Although average distribution costs were similar, it had higher marginal distribution costs (due to Au's particular carrier arrangement) and was therefore less likely to follow prices down.

During the natural industry life-cycle either Au or BP would have become unprofitable and would have no prospects of recovery except at the expense of the other or through significantly above-inflation price increases for customers.

As mentioned above, according to the OFT's Substantive Assessment Guidance, in order to satisfy the failing-firm defence against a finding of an expected substantial lessening of competition, the following conditions need to be met.

- First, in order to rely on a failing-firm defence, the firm must be in such a parlous situation that without the merger it and its assets would exit the market and that this would occur in the near future. Firms on the verge of administration may not meet these criteria whereas firms in liquidation will usually do so. Decisions by profitable parent companies to close down loss-making subsidiaries are unlikely to meet these criteria.

- Second, there must be no serious prospect of reorganizing the business. Identifying the appropriate counterfactual in situations of these types is often very difficult. For example, even companies in receivership often survive and recover.
- Third, there should be no alternative less anti-competitive than the merger. Even if a sale is inevitable, there may be other realistic buyers whose acquisition of the plant or assets would produce a better outcome for competition. These buyers might be interested in obtaining the plant or assets should the merger not proceed; that could indeed be a means by which new entrants could come into the market. It may also be better for competition that the firm fails and that the remaining players compete for its share and assets than that the failing firm's share and assets are transferred wholesale to a single purchaser.

Strictly speaking, the merging parties did not satisfy the criteria for a failing-firm defence to apply in the consideration of this merger. The above case was cleared on the basis of the defence that the markets were of insufficient importance.[300] The OFT concluded that the evidence indicated that the impact of the merger would be relatively limited both in scope and in time. In particular, the size of the market after the removal of the top two customers was well below the UK£10 million threshold; the scale of any anti-competitive effects arising from the merger was likely to be limited by the relatively low level of customer switching and, in turn, competition between the parties; the market was shrinking and there were potential constraints from demand-side substitutes suggested by third parties, as well as by the parties. In addition, the duration of any harm was considered to be of a relatively short-term nature.

As the above analysis indicates, the prevention of this merger would lead to discontinuity of service, resulting in harm to customers who would not be able to have travel brochures delivered. Eventually either BP or Au would have withdrawn from the market, either in a planned way or by going out of business. In the latter case, brochure supplies and sales would have been disrupted whilst affected customers switched to the remaining

[300] The factors that the OFT considers in making this determination were set out in detail in the *BOC/Ineos* case and were applied again recently in *FMC/ISP* and *Stagecoach/Cavalier* (in favour of exercise of the discretion) and in *Nufarm/AH Marks* (against the exercise of the discretion). Those factors are market size; the strength of the OFT's concern (that is, its judgement as to the probability of the SLC); the magnitude of competition lost by the merger; the durability of the merger's impact; and the transaction rationale and the value of deterrence.

distributor or made arrangements elsewhere. This could be particularly problematic to their trade if it happened at peak distribution times. In this case it was extremely unlikely that there would be a buyer for the rump of the (unprofitable) exiting company. Thus in cases involving mergers which do not strictly satisfy the failing-firm defence criteria, the authorities may in certain cases need to show some leniency in assessing failing-firm defence especially where the exit of a firm from the market is not imminent but can be determined with some certainty to occur in the near future and the merger will ensure continuity of goods/services. In chapter 3 we shall analyse circumstances where such a lenient approach is justified, and, in addition, circumstances where the flailing-firm defence and/or failing-division defence should be accepted. In that respect we should emphasize one further point. A *flailing* firm is likely to become *failing* in the near future, especially when it operates in a *failing industry*.

As this chapter has indicated, the failing-firm defence, as well as the failing-division defence, are parts of the jurisprudence of competition law. With increased globalization of the marketplace and the increased competitive pressures placed on firms as a result of it, failing-firm defence will arise more frequently. Competition authorities should take into account the viability and profitability of the merging firms and assess transactions accordingly. Rigorous competitive effects analysis undertaken by the enforcement authorities is sufficient to ensure that valid claims of failure and changing market conditions are carefully considered and evaluated.[301]

In addition, derogation from suspension can be very important as there may be particular circumstances regarding the financial viability of the merging parties that may render a quick assessment of the merger a necessity. If that is the case, then derogation may be granted. Such derogation was granted in *Kelt/American Express*[302] and *ING/Barings*.[303] Similarly, in 2006, the DOJ permitted Mittal Steel Company to buy Arcelor SA before the expiration of the initial HSR waiting period and without a complete merger assessment by the DOJ.

Given the specific circumstances of such cases, especially in periods of crisis, the need swiftly to effect the restructuring operation in order

301 L. Leeds, 'The Failing Firm Defence', Federal Trade Commission Hearings on the Changing Nature of Competition in a Global and Innovation-Drive Age, www.ftc.gov/opp/global/GC111495.shtm.

302 Case No IV/M.116, *Kelt/American Express*, [1991] OJ L223/0.

303 Case M573 *ING/Barings*, 1995.

to prevent serious damage to one or more undertakings concerned by the concentration can convince a competition authority of the need for derogation from suspension.

Annex to Chapter 3

This annex will present the legal substantive test for the assessment of mergers in the two jurisdictions analysed in this chapter, as well as the relative parts of the legislation (where applicable) that refers to the failing-firm defence/failing-division defence. Notes are present in the original cited matter.

European Union

Council Regulation (EC) No 139/2004 of 20 January 2004 on the control of concentrations between undertakings (the EC Merger Regulation)

> Article 2(3)
> A concentration which would significantly impede effective competition, in the common market or in a substantial part of it, in particular as a result of the creation or strengthening of a dominant position, shall be declared incompatible with the common market.

Guidelines on the Assessment of Horizontal Mergers under the Council Regulation on the Control of Concentrations between Undertakings

> VIII. Failing firm
> 89 The Commission may decide that an otherwise problematic merger is nevertheless compatible with the common market if one of the merging parties is a failing firm. The basic requirement is that the deterioration of the competitive structure that follows the merger cannot be said to be caused by the merger.[304] This will arise where the competitive structure of the market would deteriorate to at least the same extent in the absence of the merger.[305]
>
> 90 The Commission considers the following three criteria to be especially relevant for the application of a 'failing-firm defence'. First, the allegedly failing firm would in the near future be forced out of the market because of financial difficulties if not taken over by another undertaking. Second, there is no less anti-competitive alternative purchase than the

[304] Cases C-68/94 and C-30/95, *France v. Commission, Société Commerciale des Potasses et de l'Azore (SCPA) v. Commission*, [1998] ECR I-1375, [1998] 4 CMLR 829, para. 110.

[305] Cases C-68/94 and C-30/95, *France v. Commission, Société Commerciale des Potasses et de l'Azore (SCPA) v. Commission*, [1998] ECR I-1375, [1998] 4 CMLR 829, para. 114. See also Commission Decision 2002/365/EC in Case COMP/M.2314, *BASF/ Eurodiol/ Pantochim*, [2002] OJ L132/45, points 157–60. This requirement is linked to the general principle set out in para. 9 of this Notice.

notified merger. Third, in the absence of a merger, the assets of the failing firm would inevitably exit the market.[306]

91 It is for the notifying parties to provide in due time all the relevant information necessary to demonstrate that the deterioration of the competitive structure that follows the merger is not caused by the merger.

United States of America

Clayton Act

§7 (Acquisition by one corporation of stock of another)
No person engaged in commerce or in any activity affecting commerce shall acquire, directly or indirectly, the whole or any part of the stock or other share capital and no person subject to the jurisdiction of the FTC shall acquire the whole or any part of the assets of another person engaged also in commerce or in any activity affecting commerce, where in any line of commerce or in any activity affecting commerce in any section of the country, the effect of such acquisition may be substantially to lessen competition, or to tend to create a monopoly.

No person shall acquire, directly or indirectly, the whole or any part of the stock or other share capital and no person subject to the jurisdiction of the FTC shall acquire the whole or any part of the assets of one or more persons engaged in commerce or in any activity affecting commerce, where in any line of commerce or in any activity affecting commerce in any section of the country, the effect of such acquisition, of such stocks or assets, or of the use of such stock by the voting or granting of proxies or otherwise, may be substantially to lessen competition, or to tend to create a monopoly.

This section shall not apply to persons purchasing such stock solely for investment and not using the same by voting or otherwise to bring about, or in attempting to bring about, the substantial lessening of competition. Nor shall anything contained in this section prevent a corporation engaged in commerce or in any activity affecting commerce from causing the formation of subsidiary corporations for the actual carrying on of their immediate lawful business, or the natural and legitimate branches or extensions thereof, or from owning and holding all or a part of the stock of such subsidiary corporations, when the effect of such formation is not to substantially lessen competition.

Nor shall anything herein contained be construed to prohibit any common carrier subject to the laws to regulate commerce from aiding

[306] The inevitability of the assets of the failing firm leaving the market in question may, particularly in a case of merger to monopoly, underlie a finding that the market share of the failing firm would in any event accrue to the other merging party. See Cases C-68/94 and C-30/95, *France v. Commission, Société Commerciale des Potasses et de l'Azore (SCPA) v. Commission*, [1998] ECR I-1375, [1998] 4 CMLR 829, paras. 115–16.

in the construction of branches or short lines so located as to become feeders to the main line of the company so aiding in such construction or from acquiring or owning all or any part of the stock of such branch lines, nor to prevent any such common carrier from acquiring and owning all or any part of the stock of a branch or short line constructed by an independent company where there is no substantial competition between the company owning the branch line so constructed and the company owning the main line acquiring the property or an interest therein, nor to prevent such common carrier from extending any of its lines through the medium of the acquisition of stock or otherwise of any other common carrier where there is no substantial competition between the company extending its lines and the company whose stock, property, or an interest therein is so acquired.

1992 Horizontal Merger Guidelines

5. Failure and exiting assets

5.0 Overview

Notwithstanding the analysis of Sections 1–4 of the Guidelines, a merger is not likely to create or enhance market power or to facilitate its exercise, if imminent failure, as defined below, of one of the merging firms would cause the assets of that firm to exit the relevant market. In such circumstances, post-merger performance in the relevant market may be no worse than market performance had the merger been blocked and the assets left the market.

5.1 Failing Firm

A merger is not likely to create or enhance market power or facilitate its exercise if the following circumstances are met: 1) the allegedly failing firm would be unable to meet its financial obligations in the near future; 2) it would not be able to reorganize successfully under Chapter 11 of the USBC;[307] 3) it has made unsuccessful good-faith efforts to elicit reasonable alternative offers of acquisition of the assets of the failing firm[308] that would both keep its tangible and intangible assets in the relevant market and pose a less severe danger to competition than does the proposed merger; and 4) absent the acquisition, the assets of the failing firm would exit the relevant market.

5.2 Failing division

A similar argument can be made for 'failing' divisions as for failing firms. First, upon applying appropriate cost allocation rules, the division must have a negative cash flow on an operating basis. Second, absent the

[307] 11 U.S.C., §§1101–74 (1988).

[308] Any offer to purchase the assets of the failing firm for a price above the liquidation value of those assets – the highest-valued use outside the relevant market or equivalent offer to purchase the stock of the failing firm – will be regarded as a reasonable alternative offer.

acquisition, it must be that the assets of the division would exit the relevant market in the near future if not sold. Due to the ability of the parent firm to allocate costs, revenues, and intracompany transactions among itself and its subsidiaries and divisions, the Agency will require evidence, not based solely on management plans that could be prepared solely for the purpose of demonstrating negative cash flow or the prospect of exit from the relevant market. Third, the owner of the failing division also must have complied with the competitively preferable purchaser requirement of section 5.1.

4

Efficiencies

> Experience with claims of efficiency defences . . . indicates that efficiencies are often exaggerated and, perhaps even more often, can be achieved through non-merger routes.
>
> Prof. Robert Pitofsky[1]

4.1 Introduction

Mergers consolidate the ownership and control of business assets, including physical assets (for example, plant) and intangibles (for example, brand reputation). They can enhance corporate – and wider economic – performance by improving the efficiency with which business assets are used. Further reasons for firms to engage in mergers and acquisitions include, as mentioned above, efficiencies, arising from the mergers, and the tendency of some countries to endorse the concept of 'national champions'.

However, mergers may eliminate any competition that exists between the merging parties and may lead to a reduction in the number of firms competing in the market. Where this reduction has a substantial adverse effect on overall market competition, the market will be less oriented to consumer and efficiency goals, even in the absence of breaches of competition legislation.

Mergers can induce both beneficial and adverse effects on a market. The importance of considering efficiencies in mergers cannot be underestimated. Efficiencies contribute a great deal towards achieving the goals of an antitrust system – whether promoting consumer welfare or total welfare, or providing genuine benefit to society. In addition, efficiencies which increase competition in the market should unambiguously be encouraged.

[1] Robert Pitofsky was the chairman of the Federal Trade Commission of the United States between 1995 and 2001.

The term 'efficiency defence', as defined in the *Superior Propane* case,[2] is a statutory defence whereby a merger must be permitted even if it will lessen competition, if efficiency gains due to the merger exceed or offset the effects of reduced competition.

The efficiency defence may be specified on the basis of the welfare standard.[3] In reality, however, the choice of a welfare standard does not reflect the findings of economic science, but rather has the nature of a political choice, which works against the adoption of the total surplus standard.[4] The EC has tended to adopt a consumer welfare standard.

Early European Commission reports on competition policy strongly suggested that European competition policy was aimed at the promotion of consumer welfare. The European Commission's first Report on Competition Policy in 1971, stated that

> competition policy endeavours to maintain or create effective conditions of competition by means of rules applying to enterprises in both private and public sectors. Such a policy encourages the best possible use of productive resources for the greatest possible benefit of the economy as a whole and for the benefit in particular of the consumer.[5]

Courts have also endorsed a consumer welfare standard. In *Continental Can* the Court ruled that

> abuse may therefore occur if an undertaking in a dominant position strengthens such position in such a way that the degree of dominance reached substantially fetters competition, i.e. that only undertakings remain in the market whose behaviour depends on the dominant one . . . it can . . . be regarded as an abuse if an undertaking holds a position so dominant that the objectives of the Treaty are circumvented by an alteration to the supply structure which seriously endangers the consumer's freedom of action in the market, such a case necessarily exists if practically all competition is eliminated.[6]

[2] *Canada (Commissioner of Competition) v. Superior Propane Inc.* (C.A.), 2001 FCA 104, [2001] 3 F.C. 185.

[3] A. Renckens, 'Welfare Standard, Substantive Tests, and Efficiency Considerations in Merger Policy: Defining the Efficiency Defense' (2007), available at http://jcle.oxfordjournals.org/cgi/reprint/3/2/149?ck=nck.

[4] M. Kocmut, 'Efficiency Considerations and Merger Control: Quo Vadis, Commission' (2006) *ECLR* 19.

[5] See http://ec.europa.eu/competition/publications/annual_report/index.html.

[6] Case 6/72 *Europemballage Corp. and Continental Can Co. Inc. v. Commission* (*Continental Can*), [1973] ECR I-215, para. 26.

The economic literature categorizes efficiencies resulting from a merger in many different ways.[7] Efficiencies can be based on the concept of the production function, and the efficiencies are gained by rationalization of production, economies of scale and scope, technological progress, and increased buying power.[8] Following Farrell and Shapiro,[9] a further distinction may be drawn between types of 'synergy efficiency' and types of 'non-synergy efficiency';[10] that is, rationalization and economies of scale.[11] In addition, there is a distinction between real cost savings and redistributive or pecuniary cost savings, as well as between fixed and variable costs according to the time horizon for which they are relevant.[12] Finally there are efficiencies that occur at the level of merging firms, at the industry level or in other markets.

There have been no EC cases where efficiencies were deemed the sole factor for clearing a merger case. Even though the EC has addressed efficiencies since the inception of the European Community Merger Regulation,[13] it has never cleared a merger on the basis of efficiencies. Recently the Commission has addressed efficiencies in cases such as *Inco/Falconbridge*,[14] *Korsnäs/Assidomän Cartonboard*,[15] and *Metso/Aker Kvaerner*.[16] We will briefly analyse the approach of the Directorate General for Competition (DG Competition) towards these cases and try to identify difficulties that the DG Competition faces in dealing with such cases.

The *Global/GCap* merger,[17] in a first-phase UK merger review

[7] L.-H. Röller, J. Stennek and F. Verboven, 'Efficiency Gains from Mergers', in The Efficiency Defence and the European System of Merger Control: A Study Prepared for the Directorate-General for Economics and Financial Affairs, No 5 (2001).

[8] C. Luescher, 'Efficiency Considerations in European Merger Control: Just Another Battle Ground for the European Commission, Economists and Competition Lawyers' (2004) 25 *ECLR* 72.

[9] J. Farrell and C. Shapiro, 'Horizontal Mergers: An Equilibrium Analysis' (1990) 80(1) *AER* 109.

[10] Synergies are cost savings or quality improvements based on the close integration of specific, hard-to-trade assets owned by the merging parties that would not be shared or exchanged absent the merger.

[11] Luescher 2004.

[12] Ibid.

[13] Council Regulation (EC) No 139/2004 of 20 January 2004 on the control of concentrations between undertakings (the EC Merger Regulation) (the 'recast ECMR'), OJ L24, 29 January 2004, pp. 1–22.

[14] M4000 *Inco/Falconbridge*, 4 July 2006.

[15] M4057 *Korsnäs/Assidomän Cartonboard*, 12 May 2006.

[16] M4187 *Metso/Aker Kvaerner*, 12 December 2006.

[17] *Completed acquisition by Global Radio UK Ltd of GCap Media plc*, 27 August 2008.

conducted by the Office of Fair Trading (OFT), was the first time that efficiencies evidence has made a material difference to the outcome in a horizontal merger case between competitors. To date, this case, which will be analysed below, is the clearest example of the application of the efficiency defence.

There can be cases where efficiencies are being alleged and the mergers occur in periods of crisis. Important questions are asked on whether the assessment of efficiencies should be different in these cases. Advocates of a more lenient approach argue for placing increased emphasis on preventing inefficiencies that may result from the prevention of the merger. Thus, rather than an efficiency defence, we may need to consider an inefficiency defence as well. In the penultimate chapter, we shall analyse when competition authorities should place increased emphasis on the continuity of service or product in merger assessment, even if the efficiency-defence criteria may not be strictly satisfied, in order to ensure the prevention of the resulting inefficiencies from discontinuing the product or service.

This chapter will start with a brief account of the theoretical underpinnings of efficiency assessment before presenting the European Commission's approach towards efficiencies in mergers. The three EC cases mentioned above will be analysed in order to assess the extent to which the Commission takes efficiencies into account in its merger assessment. Subsequently, the chapter will present the UK approach towards efficiencies and the OFT's policy as this has been developed in the *Global/GCap* merger. Finally, the chapter will address how the US authorities assess efficiencies.

4.2 A primer on efficiencies

In general, efficiencies have been classified as allocative, productive or dynamic.[18] Transactional efficiency has also been identified in the literature.[19] Allocative efficiency arises when resources are allocated to their highest valued use, ensuring maximization of society's welfare since the price consumers pay is equal to the marginal cost of producing the

[18] W.J. Kolasky and A.R. Dick, 'The Merger Guidelines and the Integration of Efficiencies into Antitrust Review of Horizontal Mergers' (2003) 71 *Antitrust Law Journal* 207, at p. 242.

[19] Beaton, 'Merger Efficiencies and the Problem of Static Welfare Analysis' (mimeo, 2006), says that transactional efficiencies occur where a firm is able to reduce costs associated with business transactions through business practices, contracts and organizational forms.

product. Productive efficiencies allow the firm to reap cost savings and thus exploit economies of scale and economies of scope.

Productive and allocative efficiencies are static efficiencies, since by definition they imply efficiencies at a given point in time. Static efficiencies have a static one-off benefit on costs, in contrast with dynamic efficiencies which induce a continuous reduction of costs and improvement of product quality. Dynamic efficiencies can arise as a result of the expertise the firm acquires due to its operation, due to economies of scale and scope in R & D, and due to the elimination of similar R & D strategies as well as due to the combination of complementary assets. By combining complementary assets the merging firms may also complement each other with respect to output, in the sense that the merged firm will enjoy economies of scope because producing a combination of products is less costly than producing the individual products. In addition, the Schumpeterian theory according to which market power stimulates innovation is also a relevant type of dynamic efficiency.

Indicatively, efficiencies can be gained by rationalization of production (optimal allocation of the production levels), economies of scale and scope, technological progress, purchasing power and reduction in x-inefficiency (improvement of management and administrative practices). One can also distinguish between real cost savings and redistributive cost savings, as well as between efficiencies that occur at the level of the merging firms (internal efficiencies) and at industry level (externalities).[20]

Table 4.1, produced by Neven and Seabright, illustrates the different types of static and dynamic efficiency.[21]

Methods to predict losses of productive efficiency include calculating the potential loss as a percentage of the costs of the combined entity. We should recognize that the impact from the loss of productive efficiency may build up gradually over time, rather than emerge at 'full strength' immediately following the completion of an acquisition.[22]

[20] Luescher 2004.

[21] D. Neven and P. Seabright, Synergies and Dynamic Efficiencies in Merger Analysis: Final Report to DG ECFIN, August 2003.

[22] W.J. Primeaux, 'An Assessment of X-Efficiency Gained through Competition' (1977) 59 *Review of Economics and Statistics* 105. See also the OECD report, Dynamic Efficiencies in Merger Analysis (2007), available at www.oecd.org (hereafter OECD efficiencies report). Methods that have been employed in the literature include using ranges of percentages, because of uncertainty; using alternative percentage ranges where there are grounds for believing that certain elements of cost may be susceptible to greater levels of productive inefficiency than others; and allowing for firm-specific or industry-specific factors in cases that may impact upon the level of productive inefficiency.

Table 4.1. *Different types of static and dynamic efficiency*

	Static	*Dynamic*
Rationalization and scale economies	Reallocation of production between plants of merging firms Closure of loss-making activities Merger of retail networks Improved production control methods	Implementation of systematic investment appraisal methods
Synergies	Exploitation of complementary brands	Pooling of R & D divisions Complementarities between one firm's marketing and another firm's design skills Deployment of a firm's reputation to the assets of the other Deployment of a firm's organizational assets to the operation of the other

Allocative inefficiency is measured as the net loss to society from the equilibrium price and quantity post-merger compared to those in the pre-merger market. Allocative inefficiency is measured as the difference between the maximum price which unsatisfied buyers would be willing to pay for the units no longer produced, less the value in other uses of the inputs necessary for the products or services no longer produced.

In assessing product quality, the OECD finds that factors that have been taken into account include the extent to which product or service quality has suffered in the past as a consequence of competitive pressures on companies, the extent to which the nature of the product or service may limit the scope for a deterioration in quality, indications that customers value service quality and are dissatisfied with poor service levels, the extent to which a restoration of quality may be accompanied by higher costs, and whether product or service quality is subject to regulatory oversight, which would be expected to help maintain quality.[23]

[23] OECD efficiencies report.

Turning to the distinction between static and dynamic efficiencies, static efficiencies have a static one-off benefit on costs, in contrast with dynamic efficiencies which induce a continuous reduction of costs and improvement of product quality. Dynamic efficiencies can be assessed by examining the innovative potential of the industry in which the merger takes place, and by evaluating the past innovation performance of the merging parties and the likely innovation post-acquisition due to remaining competitive constraints. There is no established model in economic theory that relates the degree of concentration in a market to the extent of innovation. In addition, innovation is uncertain, making it much more difficult to measure and quantify and also more difficult to assess the impact of the merger on innovation. As the OECD argues,[24] a static rather than a dynamic assessment of economic efficiency that does not take into consideration the flow of surplus from the introduction of new products may not be reliable for the assessment of the impact of the merger. A merger of two firms with sub-efficient research might allow the joint R & D activities to benefit from economies of scale, scope and network effects, and thus lead to enhanced efficiency.

Generally speaking, monopolies result in reduced output at higher prices. Monopolies reap above-perfect competition profits, and consumers pay higher prices for goods. Williamson has argued that efficiency gains can balance the deadweight loss that arises due to monopoly pricing that can result from a merger.[25] Some consumers who would prefer the monopolist's goods at the competitive price will opt for inferior substitutes. This loss is the deadweight loss (society's loss) and is not recouped by any part of society.

Williamson's model is diagrammatically depicted in Figure 4.1.[26] AC_1 represents the merging firms' average costs prior to the merger.[27] AC_2 depicts average costs after the merger, which are lower, to reflect static efficiencies. Pre-merger, the two merging parties are able to charge prices lower than the competitive price P_1. The merged entity has market power, giving it the ability to charge a price higher than the competitive level P_2. Area A_1 is the deadweight loss resulting from monopoly-level

[24] Ibid.

[25] O. Williamson, 'Economies as an Antitrust Defense Revisited' (1977) 125 *U. Pa. L. Rev.* 699, at pp. 729–31.

[26] The figure comes from ibid., p. 23.

[27] This paragraph is taken from ibid., p. 22.

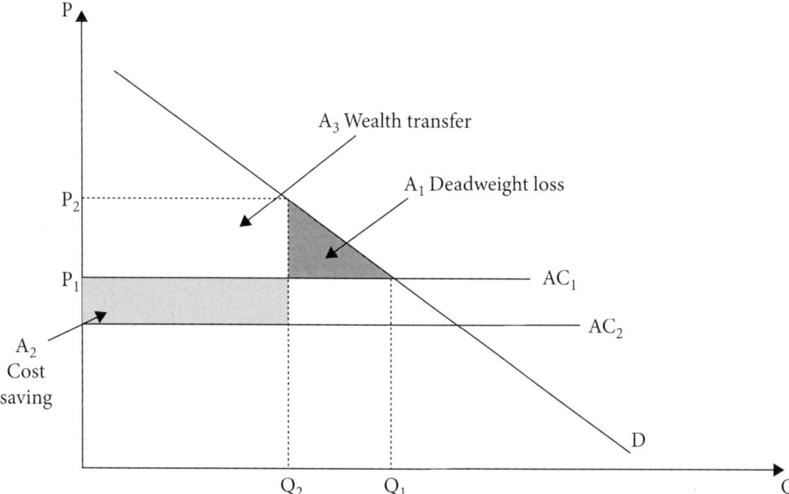

Figure 4.1. Illustration of savings arising from a merger, according to Williamson

pricing.[28] Provided the merger will induce static efficiencies, average costs will decline to AC_2. Area A_2 illustrates the related savings. Thus area A_2–A_1 provides the net allocative effect. According to Williamson's model (which follows a total surplus standard) the cost savings that result from a merger are higher than the deadweight loss resulting from the post-merger price increase.

Williamson focused on static efficiencies. Static efficiencies have a static one-off benefit on costs, in contrast with dynamic efficiencies which induce a continuous reduction of costs and improvement of product quality. A reduction in dynamic efficiencies (e.g. innovation) may reduce social welfare due to the lack of improved products. In addition, the public as a whole may fail to benefit from the introduction of improved methods of production of existing products.

Salop and Roberts have developed a technical model that balances any likely consumer harm arising from short-run price increases against consumer benefits from longer-run price decreases resulting from the benefits that competitors reap due to cost reductions induced by the merger.[29] As the OECD report states, an appropriate discount rate to

[28] Assuming that costs remained constant.

[29] G.L. Roberts and S.C. Salop, 'Efficiencies in Dynamic Merger Analysis: A Summary' (1996) 19 *World Competition*.

future time periods would ensure that greater weight is given to relatively more certain, short-run effects.[30]

Pierre-Emmanuel Noel presents a review of the literature on the evaluation of efficiencies,[31] including a case-by-case evaluation of efficiencies (Fisher and Lande[32]) and a two-stage efficiency review (Brodley[33]). Other authors have argued that as efficiencies cannot be adequately quantified, they should be presumed sufficient to overcome a presumption of illegality based on market shares, provided that they are substantial.[34] Williamson defined the task of antitrust enforcers as a case-by-case determination of the efficiencies to result from a merger.[35] Pitofsky is open to the efficiency defence on a 'probabilistic tradeoff approach',[36] resembling that used in the *Honickman* decision.[37]

Efficiencies have not been addressed extensively in case law. A number of reasons can be provided for this trend. An acquirer may not wish expressly to identify efficiencies in order to avoid a higher price being required by the target. Sometimes the parties do not devote the necessary effort to quantifying efficiencies resulting from the merger as such an argument could be taken to imply that the merger is anti-competitive. In the following part of this chapter we will analyse the most important cases in the EC, the UK and the US in which efficiency arguments have been extensively addressed.

4.3 The European Commission's approach towards efficiencies

The reform of the EC Merger Regulation (ECMR) in 2004 resulted in the adoption of Council Regulation (EC) No 139/2004 and introduced an implicit understanding that efficiencies should be taken into account

30 OECD efficiencies report.

31 P.-E. Noel, 'Efficiency Considerations in the Assessment of Horizontal Mergers under European and U.S. Antitrust Law' (1997) 18 *ECLR* 498.

32 A. Fisher and R. Lande, 'Efficiency Considerations in Merger Enforcement' (1983) 71 *Calif. L. Rev.* 1582.

33 J. Brodley, 'The Economic Goals of Antitrust: Efficiency, Consumer Welfare, and Technological Progress' (1987) 62 *N.Y.U.L. Rev.* 1020, at p. 1023.

34 T. Muris, 'The Efficiency Defense under Section 7 of the Clayton Act' (1980) 30 *Case W. Res. L. Rev.* 381, at p. 420.

35 O. Williamson, 'Economies as an Antitrust Defense Revisited' (1977) 125 *U. Pa. L. Rev.* 699, at pp. 729–31 .

36 R. Pitofsky, 'Proposals for Revised United States Merger Enforcement in a Global Economy' (1992) 81 *Geo. L.J.*, 195, at p. 208.

37 *Harold A. Honickman,* F.T.C. Docket No 9233 (16 November 1992) 5 Trade Reg. Rep. (CCH) 23, at p. 286.

in merger assessments. The treatment of efficiencies is analysed in the Horizontal Merger Guidelines.[38] The fact that the treatment of efficiencies is not mentioned in the legally binding part of Regulation 139/2004 mitigates the importance of efficiencies in the merger assessment. Thus the importance of efficiency arguments is adversely affected.[39]

In its Horizontal Merger Guidelines, the Commission explains efficiencies and their role in merger assessment:

> In order to assess whether a merger would significantly impede effective competition, in particular through the creation or the strengthening of a dominant position, within the meaning of Article 2(2) and (3) of the Merger Regulation, the Commission performs an overall competitive appraisal of the merger. In making this appraisal, the Commission takes into account the factors mentioned in Article 2(1), including the development of technical and economic progress provided that it is to the consumers' advantage and does not form an obstacle to competition. According to the Horizontal Guidelines, efficiencies should be merger-specific, verifiable, and beneficial for consumers.

The three cumulative criteria are based on work by Oliver Williamson,[40] who proposed to balance the economic pros and cons of a merger in a before-and-after approach. The positive effects a merger has on productive efficiency (e.g. cost reduction) should be compared with its negative effects on allocative efficiency (e.g. the creation of market power and the ability to increase prices or restrict quantities).

The Commission may decide that as a consequence of the efficiencies

[38] Commission Notice on the Appraisal of Horizontal Mergers under the Council Regulation on the Control of Concentration between Undertakings, COM/2002, 11 December 2002.

[39] Literature on the treatment of efficiencies in merger assessment includes P.D. Camesasca, 'The Explicit Efficiency Defence in Merger Control: Does It Make the Difference?' (1999) 1 *ECLR* 14; L. Colley, 'From "Defence" to "Attack"? Quantifying Efficiency Arguments in Mergers' (2004) 25 *ECLR* 342; Luescher 2004, at pp. 72–86; Noel 1997, at pp. 498–519; A. Burnside, 'Dance of the Veils? Reform of the EC Merger Regulation' (1996) 17 *ECLR* 371; L. Hawkes, 'The EC Merger Control Regulation, Not an Industrial Policy Instrument: The DeHavilland Decision' (1992) 13 *ECLR* 34; D. Ridyard, 'An Economic Perspective on the EC Merger Regulation' (1990) 11 *ECLR* 247; A.J. Riley, 'The European Cartel Office: A Guardian without Weapons' (1997) 18 *ECLR* 3; R. van den Bergh, 'Modern Industrial Organisation and European Competition Law' (1996) 17 *ECLR* 75; Kocmut 2006, at p. 19; I. Schmidt, 'The Suitability of the More Economic Approach for Competition Policy: Dynamic vs. Static Efficiency' (2007) 28(7) *ECLR* 408; Svetlicinii, 'Assessment of the Non-Horizontal Mergers: Is There a Chance for the Efficiency Defence in EC Merger Control?' (2007) 28(10) *ECLR* 529.

[40] O. Williamson, 'Economies as an Antitrust Defense: The Welfare Trade-Off' (1968) 58 *American Economic Review* 18.

that the merger brings about, there are no grounds for declaring the merger incompatible with the common market. This will be so when the efficiencies generated by the merger are likely to enhance the ability and incentive of the merged entity to act pro-competitively for the benefit of consumers, thereby counteracting the adverse effects on competition which the merger might otherwise have.

Furthermore, the Horizontal Merger Guidelines state that mergers may bring about various types of efficiency gain that can lead to lower prices or other benefits to consumers. For example, cost savings in production or distribution may give the merged entity the ability and incentive to charge lower prices following the merger. Cost efficiencies that lead to reductions in variable or marginal costs are more likely to be relevant to the assessment of efficiencies than reductions in fixed costs. The former are, in principle, more likely to result in lower prices for consumers. Cost reductions, which merely result from anti-competitive reductions in output, cannot be considered efficiencies benefiting consumers. The economic literature agrees with this view under the condition that greater weight is assigned by the authorities to short-term consumer welfare. Consumers may also benefit from new or improved products or services, for instance resulting from efficiency gains in the sphere of R & D and innovation.

The greater the possible negative effects on competition, the more the Commission has to be sure that the claimed efficiencies are substantial, and likely to be realized and passed on to a sufficient degree to the consumer. The Guidelines follow the reasoning established in *Accor/Wagons-Lits*,[41] *MSG/Media Service*,[42] *Aerospatiale-Alenia/De Havilland*[43] and *Saint Gobain/Wacker-Chemie/NOM*,[44] and demand that the efficiencies be passed on to consumers to a sufficient degree. In *Accor/Wagon-Lits*, the technical and economic progress factor was invoked by Accor, which claimed that the merger would enable it to improve personnel training and modernize certain facilities. In the *MSG/Media Service* decision the Commission again confirmed that the reference in Article 2(1)(b) of Regulation 4064/89 to the development of technical and economic progress was subject to the reservation that no obstacle is formed to competition.

[41] Case IV/M126 *Accor/Wagons-Lits*, [1992] OJ L204/1.

[42] M469 *MSG/Media Service*.

[43] Case IV/M053 *Aerospatiale-Alenia/De Havilland*, [1991] OJ L334/42.

[44] Case IV/M774 *Saint Gobain/Wacker-Chemie/NOM*, [1997] OJ L247/1.

Kocmut has argued that since the EU authorities appraise efficiency claims under the consumer welfare standard,[45] the requirement of passing on becomes essential.[46] We should note that if a merger generates efficiencies in one relevant market and induces anti-competitive effects in another (both product and geographical market) a trade-off 'in principle' should not be allowed.[47]

In addition, efficiencies have to be merger-specific and verifiable such that the Commission can be reasonably certain that the efficiencies are likely to materialize, and be substantial enough to counteract a merger's potential harm to consumers. As mentioned above, Farrell and Shapiro draw a distinction between efficiencies and true synergies.[48] True synergies refer to efficiencies that are uniquely accessed by a merger as opposed to efficiencies that could be accessed by the internal growth of the firm. Farrell and Shapiro emphasize that true synergies arise where the merged entity combines 'hard to trade assets' and moves on to a 'superior production function' (as opposed to a better point on an existing function).[49]

Although since the adoption of the Horizontal Merger Guidelines there have been no instances when the Commission has cleared a merger based on a successful efficiency claim, which makes it difficult to pronounce any judgement regarding practical application of the Commission's guidance, the Guidelines have been criticized on theoretical and methodological grounds by economists and legal scholars. For instance, the Guidelines were criticized for the inadequate attention they give to dynamic efficiencies that do not directly affect the price of the final product.[50]

Schmidt argues that it is doubtful whether a static theory can be applied in order to explain dynamic competitive processes appropriately. He adds that the only way to promote dynamic efficiency is to maintain effective competition as we still lack a convincing dynamic theory.[51] It is interesting to note that according to the Director General of the DG Competition, the initial competitive assessment will focus

[45] Kocmut 2006.

[46] Whether the efficiencies will be passed on depends crucially on whether the cost savings affect the pricing of the merged firm.

[47] Para. 79 of the Horizontal Merger Guidelines.

[48] Farrell and Shapiro 1990.

[49] Ibid.

[50] Kocmut 2006.

[51] Schmidt 2007.

solely on the static efficiencies and the dynamic efficiencies will come into play only in the final assessment.[52]

In the absence of the Commission's practice and of jurisprudence that would assist in the clarification of controversial issues in the application of the efficiency defence, legal and economic scholars have to rely primarily on the Guidelines and on the precedents under Regulation 4064/89. Although the case law encountered examples of efficiency claims, these were usually unsuccessful because of the presence of competitive harm and were regarded as insufficient to offset that.

The Horizontal Merger Guidelines argue that efficiencies generated by a merger might counteract negative effects on competition: 'It is possible that efficiencies brought about by a merger counteract the effects on competition and in particular the potential harm to consumers that it might otherwise have.'[53] The Preamble of the ECMR provides that 'any substantiated and likely efficiencies put forward by the undertakings concerned' will be taken into account:

> 29) In order to determine the impact of a concentration on competition in the common market, it is appropriate to take account of any substantiated and likely efficiencies put forward by the undertakings concerned. It is possible that the efficiencies brought about by the concentration counteract the effects on competition, and in particular the potential harm to consumers, that it might otherwise have and that, as a consequence, the concentration would not significantly impede effective competition, in the common market or in a substantial part of it, in particular as a result of the creation or strengthening of a dominant position. The Commission should publish guidance on the conditions under which it may take efficiencies into account in the assessment of a concentration.

The above paragraph of the Preamble indicates that efficiencies are used as a defence. However, as the Commission states in the Horizontal Merger Guidelines, the Commission considers any substantiated efficiency claim in the overall assessment of the merger.[54] Thus efficiencies may be considered a factor in the assessment of the anti-competitive effects of a merger.

If efficiencies are treated as a defence then they have to be measured in order to be compared with the competitive harm. Quantification has to use the same criteria as those used for quantifying the likely harm of

[52] P. Lowe, 'Review of the EC Merger Regulation: Forging a Way Ahead', speech delivered at the European Merger Control Conference, 8 November 2002, Conrad Hotel, Brussels.

[53] Horizontal Merger Guidelines, para. 76.

[54] Ibid., para. 77.

the merger. However, such quantification is not always possible. Due to these difficulties in quantifying efficiencies, cost-related or fixed efficiencies are treated more favourably than dynamic efficiencies, which are difficult to quantify.[55]

In an attempt to quantify efficiencies, and with regard to the benefits for consumers, Froeb and Werden have shown that in case of a merger with small market shares and a very elastic demand function,[56] cost savings of about 5 per cent are sufficient for compensation. However, even with small market shares, cost savings of more than 20 per cent are necessary to compensate the loss in competitive pressure in cases where elasticity of demand is low (for instance around unity). As Schmidt, however, argues, such cost savings are unlikely.[57] In *Aerospatiale-Alenia/De Havilland* the Commission argued that, according to the parties, cost savings to the combined entity would arise from rationalizing parts procurement, marketing and product support. Such cost savings though would have a negligible impact on the overall operation of ATR/De Havilland, amounting to around 0.5 per cent of the combined turnover. The Commission gave some indication of the requirements that this type of defence would face:

- cost savings should be substantial,
- the burden of proof should rest on the parties,
- efficiencies should be 'merger-specific' and
- efficiencies should be 'to consumers' advantage'.

Despite the fact that the Commission gives examples of efficiencies and provides guidance regarding such features as timing, verifiability, merger-specificity and so on, it does not give a clear explanation of how efficiencies will be measured against the competitive harm.

In assessing efficiencies arising from horizontal mergers, the Commission applies a 'sliding-scale' approach by linking the expected time when efficiencies are supposed to materialize to the quantity of the efficiency gains and the burden of proof that should be satisfied by the merging parties.[58] Applying the sliding scale to mergers, the Commission does not clarify the timely manner in which efficiencies

[55] Svetlicinii 2007.

[56] L.M. Froeb and G.J. Werden, 'A Robust Test for Consumer Welfare Enhancing Mergers among Sellers of a Homogeneous Product' (1998) 58 *Economic Letters* 367.

[57] Schmidt 2007, at p. 409.

[58] As will be illustrated in below in this chapter, the OFT also applies such a sliding-scale approach.

in horizontal or non-horizontal mergers are expected to materialize. In addition, the Commission applies the same timing requirement to both horizontal and non-horizontal mergers.[59]

In order to present and sustain their efficiency claims successfully, merging parties should have a clear understanding of the stage of the merger assessment at which they should be introduced, of how efficiencies will be assessed in relation to anti-competitive concerns and of what kind of evidence should be produced. The following analysis of decisional practice will shed light on how efficiencies should be invoked by parties and assessed by competition authorities.

4.4 European Commission decisional practice

The Commission has assessed efficiency claims in a number of cases.[60] However, most efficiency claims have been disregarded. In a nutshell, in *Aerospatiale-Alenia/De Havilland* efficiencies were not merger-specific, were not substantial and were not passed on to consumers. In *Accor/Wagons-Lits* efficiencies were not merger-specific and were not passed on to consumers. In *Nordic Satellite Distribution* efficiencies were considered not merger-specific.[61] In *Danish Crown/Vestjyske Slagterier* efficiencies were insufficient, were not merger-specific and were an obstacle to competition.[62] In *Gencor/Lonrho*[63] efficiencies were insufficiently verifiable and were not passed on because of the creation of a joint dominant position.

Sometimes, efficiencies have even been invoked as an anti-competitive argument (efficiency offence). In *British Telecom/MCI(II)* the more efficient use of transmission capacity was seen as a practice to strengthen the dominant position of the merging parties.[64] In *AT&T/NCR* efficiencies were rejected because they could strengthen a dominant position.[65] The following three cases are those where the Commission has placed

[59] Svetlicinii 2007.

[60] M42 *Alcatel/Telettra*, 12 April 1991; Case M315 *Mannesman/Vallourec/Ilva*, 31 January 1994; Case M477 *Mercedes-Benz/Kässborer*, 14 February 1995; Case M1025 *Mannesman/Olivetti/Infostrada*, 15 January 1998; Case M986 *Agfa-Gevaert/Dupont*, 11 February 1998; Case M1542 *Airtours/First Choice*, 22 September 1999.

[61] M490 *Nordic Satellite Distribution*, 19 July 1995.

[62] M1313 *Danish Crown/Vestjyske Slagterier*, 9 March 1999.

[63] M619 *Gencor/Lonrho*, [1997] OJ L11/30.

[64] M856 *British Telecom/MCI(II)*, 14 May 1997.

[65] M50 *AT&T/NCR*, 18 January 1991.

some importance on the existence of efficiencies. This is a very positive development in case law and one that we can hope will continue and develop.

4.4.1 Inco/Falconbridge

To date, no cases have been cleared purely on efficiency grounds.[66] In *Inco/Falconbridge*,[67] the European Commission assessed the alleged efficiencies but cleared the merger subject to conditions. Inco and Falconbridge were Canadian mining companies active in the mining, processing, refining and sale of nickel, cobalt and other metals. The merged entity would have been able to increase prices in certain nickel and cobalt markets. The merging parties committed to divest Falconbridge's sole nickel refinery and related assets, and proposed selling these assets to LionOre, an international mining company which is also active in nickel mining.

The parties indicated that the efficiencies brought about by the proposed transaction were attainable, quantifiable and transaction-specific, arising primarily from the close proximity of their respective mines or processing facilities in the Sudbury basin. According to the parties, Inco and Falconbridge had developed and operated significant assets in the Sudbury basin in Canada, and New Inco would be in a position to optimize mining and processing, which would result in increased production at lower costs, on a sustainable basis and over the long term. The parties further argued that the efficiencies were merger-specific as they related to the ability of the combined entity to shift production to the most appropriate or efficient facilities. The parties further argued that the efficiencies could not be obtained by any alternative transaction and would not be achieved by the parties individually in the absence of the merger. Finally, the parties stated that, as a result of global competition in the supply of nickel, efficiencies that resulted in an output expansion by the combined entity were likely to be passed on to the direct benefit of consumers.

The Commission concluded that while the efficiencies presented by the parties were quantified and well supported by several studies and were likely to effectively materialize, the parties did not demonstrate to

[66] D. Neven and S. Albæk. 'Economics at DG Competition 2006–2007' (September 2007) 31(2) *Review of Industrial Organization* 139.

[67] M4000.

the requisite standards that the efficiencies could not have been achieved by other means and would directly benefit end-customers in the markets where competition concerns have been identified in order to offset those concerns. The Commission relied on the sliding-scale approach and concluded that the stronger the merged entity, the more unlikely it is that it will pass on the efficiencies as lower prices to consumers. The Commission considered that the efficiencies presented by the parties could not be considered to offset the adverse effect of the proposed transaction on competition.

4.4.2 *Korsnäs/AssiDomän Cartonboard*

In M4057 *Korsnäs/Assidomän Cartonboard*, 12 May 2006, the Commission for the first time explicitly recognized merger-specific efficiencies as a countervailing factor in the competitive analysis of mergers in detail. This concentration would reduce the number of firms from three to two in the cartonboard industry, with StoraEnso being the other significant player. The Commission cleared the transaction unconditionally in the first phase. The Commission listed the claimed efficiencies as one of several factors for its unconditional approval.

The proposed transaction was likely to generate merger-specific efficiencies that would be passed on to consumers. The parties expected to save input cost, reduce personnel and improve production efficiencies.[68]

In addition, Korsnäs argued that it would be in a position to realize R & D efficiencies as well as benefit from implementing best practices across the two production sites. The Commission added that the submission by the parties raised many issues, which could not be fully assessed within the context of a first-phase investigation, in particular with respect to savings in input costs and staff reduction. It concluded that the efficiencies were likely to enhance the ability and incentive of the merged entity to act pro-competitively for the benefit of consumers.[69]

[68] The savings were estimated at between 0 and 5 per cent of the merging parties' net sales.

[69] The importance of the efficiencies was mitigated by, among other things, the significant buying power of Tetra Pak, the absence of capacity constraints due to supply-side substitutability and the conclusion that the merging parties were not each other's closest competitors.

4.4.3 Metso/Aker Kvaerner

The European Commission cleared the merger of Metso Corporation Oy and the pulp and power business of Aker Kvaerner ASA.[70] During its investigation, the Commission found that the proposed acquisition might create competition problems in a number of markets for pulp mill equipment. However, these concerns were entirely removed by Metso's commitment to divest overlapping businesses to the Canadian-based supplier GL&V. In light of these remedies, the Commission concluded that the merger would not significantly impede effective competition.

Both Metso and Aker Kvaerner are active worldwide in the development and production of equipment for pulp mills. The Commission's market investigation showed that the proposed transaction might have substantially reduced competition in those markets for pulp mill equipment in which both companies were active, namely equipment for the cooking, brown-stock washing, oxygen delignification and bleaching stages of pulp production.

Without suitable remedies, this takeover would have eliminated one of only three major players in an already highly concentrated industry with high barriers to entry. However, since the parties were willing to divest the overlapping businesses to a strong and credible competitor such as GL&V, the Commission was able to approve the operation.

The emergence of a second full-line supplier of pulp mill equipment may indeed be beneficial to customers. Customers referred to the fact that a second supplier able to provide the full range of pulp mill equipment would be created. This might enable Metso post-merger to compete more effectively with Andritz, allowing customers to choose between two suppliers offering a full product range and with experience of all these products. Customers also claimed that the merger could result in allowing the merged entity to develop better and more environmentally friendly products, to the benefit of the consumer. They also argued that they preferred having the choice between different suppliers, using their respective strengths in different markets and using competition between the suppliers to keep prices low. This would be to the benefit of customers of paper products, and would further enhance the development of environmentally and resource-friendly modern pulp and paper-making processes.

The merger between Metso and Kvaerner might hence not only create

[70] M4187 *Metso/Aker Kvaerner*, 12 December 2006.

a second full-line supplier of pulping equipment able to compete on an equal footing with Andritz, but also a manufacturer fully committed to the pulp and paper industry and having the necessary critical mass for further R & D activities.

The Commission, however, concluded that the potential efficiencies of the merger were very unlikely to counterbalance the loss of effective competition caused by the reduction of eligible supply alternatives, the removal of an important competitive constraint and the creation of the largest equipment supplier.

Although the Commission started addressing efficiency claims in each merger assessment two years after the adoption of Regulation 139/2004 and the publication of the Horizontal Merger Guidelines, the Commission's analysis in the above cases has demonstrated its increased willingness to take efficiencies into account as a balancing factor in the competitive analysis.

4.5 The UK approach towards efficiencies

4.5.1 The Enterprise Act

As the OFT's Substantive Assessment Guidance (hereafter 'Guidance') for mergers makes clear, a merger may be expected to lead to a substantial lessening of competition when it is thought to weaken rivalry to such an extent that customers would be harmed. This may come about, for example, through reduced product choice, or because prices could be raised profitably, output could be reduced and/or product quality or innovation could be reduced.[71] That is, it is adverse effects on customers that differentiate a substantial lessening of competition, warranting a reference or remedies, from a mere lessening of competition, which requires no further investigation or intervention.

As the Guidance further makes clear, the Act allows the OFT to take efficiency gains from a merger into account at two separate points in the analytical framework:

- where they avert the adverse effects of a substantial lessening of competition by enhancing rivalry, and
- where they do not avert a substantial lessening of competition but will nonetheless be passed on after the merger in the form of customer

[71] See para. 3.7 of the Substantive Assessment Guidance.

benefits that countervail the adverse effects that would arise from the substantial lessening of competition.

Consistent with the EC and other competition authority guidelines, the Guidance states that efficiency claims – at either gateway in the OFT's analysis – must meet the following cumulative criteria:[72]

- they must be demonstrable (i.e. shown to arise clearly and very likely to arise within a reasonable period of time),
- they must be merger-specific (i.e. attributable to the merger, as a direct consequence of it judged relative to what would happen without the merger) and
- they must be likely to be passed on to customers.

The latter point is relevant as it is customer welfare that is at stake in analysis of competitive effects and in the 'substantiality' of any lessening of competition, and not private gains to the merging parties.

4.5.2 Evidentiary burdens on efficiencies: a sliding-scale approach

The OFT's Guidance makes clear that the evidence required in relation to such efficiencies must be compelling if it is to be taken into account:

> where mergers raise possible competition concerns, the OFT is generally sceptical, in the absence of compelling evidence, that efficiency gains will not only arise but will also be passed on to a sufficient extent to customers, especially where there are few remaining competitive constraints on the parties. Accordingly, in these situations, the evidence presented by the parties on efficiencies and their likely impact on rivalry must indeed be compelling.[73]

This discussion of evidentiary standards equally applies to efficiencies qualifying as customer benefits.[74] Indeed, it would be odd if this were not the case given that the same efficiency claims may fall for consideration

[72] See para. 4.34 (rivalry-enhancing efficiencies) and 7.7–7.8 (customer-benefits exception) of the Substantive Assessment Guidance.

[73] See para. 4.35 of the Substantive Assessment Guidance.

[74] There is no reason to think the standard would be lower as an exception to a finding of substantial lessening of competition than in considering whether the lessening of competition is substantial in the first place. The same 'clear and compelling' evidentiary standard is cited in the customer-benefits exception with specific reference to a 'multi-market trade-off' – that is, where predicted customer harm in one market (consistent with a duty to refer and 'SLC finding') is outweighed by customer benefits in another market or other

in the substantial lessening of competition test and/or subsequently in relation to the customer benefits exception.

The importance of setting appropriate evidentiary burdens should not be underestimated, and where claims are potentially self-serving and outcome determinative to the analysis of what would otherwise be an anti-competitive merger it is appropriate that the competition authority not be easily be persuaded by unverified claims. The OFT's long line of cases involving allegedly failing firms and the evidentiary standards on counterfactuals in such cases bear this out.[75] Moreover, it is unarguable that for a claim for which the evidence can only be in the merging parties' hands, it is incumbent on those parties to furnish such evidence and meet the burden of persuasion.

At the same time, however, it is not appropriate to consider this burden in a way that is impossible in practice ever to meet or be so rigid and immutable as to be unable to vary according to context.

The gravity of the OFT's concerns as to anti-competitive effects is relevant to the overall burden such a countervailing argument must meet to overcome such concerns (and that countervailing argument itself comprises both the compelling evidentiary standard that must be met and the magnitude of efficiencies claimed). This position is consistent with the US and EC horizontal merger guidelines: that beyond meeting a suitable minimum threshold of substantiating efficiencies claims with respect to each of the above three criteria, evidence on merger-specific and 'countervailing' efficiencies should be judged on a sliding scale. That is, the greater and more powerful the case in favour of anti-competitive effects of the merger, the greater and more powerful the countervailing claims must be to meet and overcome such concerns.

As set out in the US Horizontal Merger Guidelines:

> The greater the potential adverse competitive effects of a merger . . . the greater must be cognizable efficiencies in order for the Agency to conclude that the merger will not have an anti-competitive effect . . . When the potential adverse competition effect is likely to be particularly large, extraordinarily great cognizable efficiencies would be necessary to prevent the merger from being anti-competitive. In the Agency's

Footnote 74 (*cont.*)
markets. However, the evidentiary standard applies equally to customer benefits. See para. 7.9 of the Substantive Assessment Guidance.

[75] See *Tesco/Kwik Save*, decision of 20 December 2007, citing previous cases.

> experience, efficiencies are most likely to make a difference in marginal cases when the likely adverse competitive effects, absent the efficiencies, are not great. Efficiencies almost never justify a merger to monopoly or near monopoly.[76]

According to the EC Guidelines,[77] the Commission pursues a sliding-scale approach, according to which, the greater the possible negative effects on competition, the larger the efficiencies have to be and further states that for this reason it is highly unlikely that a concentration amounting to a monopoly or near-monopoly can be saved on the basis of efficiency claims.

This clearly captures the unobjectionable notion that very large harmful effects must correspondingly be outweighed by very large countervailing benefits. But the OFT also applies the point in relation to cases where the probability of adverse effects occurring at all is small.

As should be apparent from OFT cases, including the *de minimis* line of cases,[78] what matters when considering anti-competitive effects and the welfare of customers under the substantial lessening of competition assessment is not just the size of the market (e.g. UK£10 million or UK£1 billion), the magnitude of the merger's price or non-price effect (e.g. a 3 per cent or 30 per cent price rise), or the durability of that effect (three months or three years). It also matters how likely such adverse effects are to occur at all; in other words, the confidence the OFT has in its prediction that customer harm will result from the merger. The former factors go to the question, how bad is the harm if it actually happens? The latter question is, how likely is the harm to happen at all? It would be disingenuous to ignore the fact that assessment of post-merger outcomes, both welfare-enhancing and welfare-reducing, is generally

[76] US Horizontal Guidelines (1992, efficiencies section revised in 1997), Part 4. Compare the identical point made in the subsequent 2004 EC Horizontal Merger Guidelines: 'The greater the possible negative effects on competition, the more the Commission has to be sure that the claimed efficiencies are substantial, likely to be realized and to be passed on, to a sufficient degree, to the consumer. It is highly unlikely that a merger leading to a market position approaching monopoly or leading to a similar level of market power, can be [cleared] on the grounds that efficiency gains would be sufficient to counteract its potential anti-competitive effects' (para. 84).

[77] EC Horizontal Merger Guidelines, para. 79.

[78] See in particular the OFT decision in *Anticipated acquisition by BOC Ltd of the packaged chlorine business and assets carried on by Ineos Chlor Ltd*, 29 May 2008, paras. 118–19.

an inherently predictive exercise,[79] and is based on probabilities, not certainties.[80]

This applies equally to any prediction that lost rivalry is substantial enough to result in customer harm, which explains why the OFT has deliberately taken it into account in its *de minimis* assessment.

It is appropriate, therefore, to take this variability on the facts into account in the weighing exercise of considering the evidence supporting a risk of anti-competitive effects and the evidence supporting countervailing efficiencies.

Moreover, while some efficiencies can be characterized as rivalry-enhancing and cognizable under the first gateway, and other scenarios would be cognizable only as customer benefits under the second gateway, the essential exercise of weighing evidence and considering probabilities and scale is common to both gateways. Accordingly, this point should apply to claims of rivalry-enhancing efficiency that are weighed as part of the integral assessment of the SLC test itself.

Accordingly, in keeping with a sliding-scale approach, the OFT might judge efficiencies evidence to be compelling in resolving concerns where those concerns were relatively moderate, say, based on a 25 per cent probability of future harm, but fail to do so when the probability was, say, above 90 per cent.[81] This is consistent with the notion that, in practice, efficiencies will almost never justify a merger to monopoly – because irrespective of the scale of harm, the probability of some significant degree of harm in scenarios of merger to monopoly, all else being equal, tends to be very high, which means that the probability of, say, variable cost savings that overcome the incentive to raise prices must also be correspondingly high.

In sum, then, provided always that the evidence presented by the parties on efficiencies is compelling, the OFT will have regard both to the likelihood of the benefits materializing and to the magnitude of

[79] Even in cases of completed mergers, given the OFT's statutory time limits to refer such cases and the incentives of merged firms not to raise prices pending the outcome of the OFT's investigation, the analysis is more likely to be predictive than retrospective. That said, actual post-merger price rises have been observed and taken into account in certain completed merger references under the Act: see, e.g., OFT decision *Completed joint venture between Stagecoach Bus Holdings Ltd and Braddell plc in relation to Megabus.com, Motorvator and Scottish Citylink brands*, 15 March 2006.

[80] See OFT Substantive Guidance Assessment Note on the *IBA* Case, OFT 516a.

[81] For example, in the case of a completed merger to monopoly where observable prices had in fact gone up after the merger and there were no cost-related or other reasonable alternative explanations for this, save for the elimination of pre-merger competition.

those benefits in weighing them against the magnitude and likelihood of adverse effects. The OFT will look at both demand- and supply-side efficiency arguments in assessing whether a merger should be cleared on the basis of efficiencies.

4.5.3 Demand-side efficiencies as rivalry-enhancing efficiencies

Efficiencies are often 'demand-side' efficiencies, resulting in the creation of a superior product, as opposed to simple cost savings in delivering an existing product.

OFT guidance has defined a loss of rivalry leading to customer harm as critical to the substantiality of that lessening of competition. In analysing the question of the overall effects of the merger through the prism of a process of rivalry, the relatively modest reduction in rivalry achieved by merging the two firms is outweighed by the customer benefits that enhance rivalry among remaining suppliers.

These demand-side efficiencies are known as Cournot effects and arise when products are complements such that lowering the price of one product increases demand for it and for other products that are used with (but not instead of) it. To the extent that products are complements, bringing them under common ownership (e.g. by a merger) internalizes the positive effect of a fall in the price of one on sales of the others.

Without common ownership, the firm that cuts price does not reap the full benefit of the increased sales of the other products. Consequently, internalizing this effect through a merger will result in lower prices for all products in the bundle, because it will become profit-maximizing for the firm that sells both complements to sell them at a lower combined price than the sum the customer would have paid to assemble the same package on a 'mix-and-match' basis pre-merger from two different suppliers.

The Cournot effect occurs because it solves a 'double-marginalization' problem, thus enhancing allocative efficiency. This is analogous reasoning to that which says that vertical mergers are often efficiency-enhancing because they eliminate the double mark-up; that is, pre-merger, each firm independently marks up the price of its product over marginal cost without taking into account the fact that this mark-up will adversely affect sales volumes of the complementary product it does not own. The current OFT guidelines do not explicitly capture the above points, other than to say the vertical mergers are often 'efficiency-enhancing', but the Competition Commission (the Commission) guidelines[82] and the EC non-horizontal merger guidelines develop the above point in similar terms.[83]

As suggested by the Commission guidelines, this pricing efficiency is all the more likely in instances where the merging firms had been exercising a degree of market power before the merger.[84] This holds true because if pre-merger prices were set in a perfectly competitive market – at marginal costs – there would be no 'room' for the price to go down post-merger.[85] Because in many markets for branded goods products enjoy a degree of market power, this assumes prices set significantly above marginal cost, and thus scope and incentive to lower prices post-merger.

In addition, as noted, bundling is desired by customers because it serves to reduce transaction costs through 'one-stop shopping'.

4.5.4 *Demand-side efficiencies: product repositioning*

A further demand-side merger efficiency in a two-sided market can occur as a result of post-merger product or brand repositioning.[86] The

[82] CC2: Merger References: Competition Commission Guidelines (2003), para. 3.71: 'A conglomerate merger might also involve bringing together of products that are complements. In general, the merger should then increase the incentive to lower prices', and para. 4.44.

[83] Guidelines on the Assessment of Non-Horizontal Mergers under the Council Regulation on the Control of Concentrations between Undertakings, 2007, para. 13.

[84] CC2, para. 4.44, which refers to elimination of double marginalization 'when two non-integrated firms both have significant market power'. So the third limb of the efficiency argument – that efficiencies must be likely to be passed on to customers – does not require there to be the same extent of post-merger rivalry within the market such as it may for other rivalry-enhancing efficiencies (see para. 4.34 of the OFT's Substantive Assessment Guidance for Mergers) since the pass-on of Cournot effects is in some sense 'automatic'.

[85] This argument rests on prices being linear, i.e. set on a per-unit-sold basis (or some variant thereof), rather than being non-linear, i.e. with a fixed component and then some per-unit increment. Prices for radio advertising are linear.

[86] This is also known as an indirect network effect or externality. A direct network effect in a classic market means that an individual user gains a greater benefit the greater the number of other users, the classic example being the telephone network. An indirect network effect is a benefit to users the greater the number of users on the other side of the two-sided market. In a two-sided market, economic theory supports this argument. See A. Gandhi, L. Froeb, S. Tschantz and G. Werden, 'Post-Merger Product Repositioning' (March 2008) 56(1) *Journal of Industrial Economics* 49, who find that the merged firm moves its product varieties away from each other to reduce cannibalization and that its competitors move their product varieties between those of the merged firm. Post-merger repositioning therefore benefits customers by increasing product variety. However, they

basic proposition is that by changing the features of the merging parties' products post-merger in a way that benefits consumers, the merged entity will gain customers.

4.5.5 Demonstrability of efficiency claims based on post-merger product repositioning

Efficiency claims based on post-merger product repositioning are, like any claim, susceptible to the objection that there is no guarantee that such plans will be carried out, and that, even if attempted in good faith, such plans may fail.

In addressing the issue of the demonstrability or verifiability of such claims, evidence of industry practice, and in particular efficiencies from previous acquisitions, can be particularly useful in demonstrating that, based on successful and analogous past 'experiments', efficiencies will be a plausible and potentially likely result of the merger.[87] While past success is not a guarantee of similar future benefits, a track record inspires greater confidence.

Unlike efficiencies based on the combination of complementary physical assets, product repositioning claims depend substantially more on the value of human capital, skilled staff with know-how who can manage and reposition brands and other aspects associated with the venture pre- and post-repositioning.

Although not mentioned in OFT guidance, a standard and often very valid caution in respect of know-how or managerial efficiencies is that they are not merger-specific, because managers and skilled staff are hardly unique to the merger or, in particular, to the acquiring firm. Absent the merger, the target firm could hire new comparable management and/or skilled staff. Yet it seems uncontroversial to observe that the competitive performance of a firm can vary greatly depending on its management, brand strategy and so forth, and that such skills may be in short supply. It also appears a valid general observation that a good-faith motivation for some mergers is indeed the acquiring management's

also find that repositioning affects post-merger prices in two countervailing ways: there is upward pressure on all prices as product varieties spread out but the merged firm's incentives to raise price are reduced as its product varieties move away from each other (as there is less competition between them to internalize).

[87] For an equivalent view see 'Prepared Remarks of Dr. Michael A. Salinger, Director, Bureau of Economics, Federal Trade Commission, before the Antitrust Modernization Commission: Treatment of Efficiencies in Merger Enforcement', 17 November 2005.

belief that it has the know-how to improve the target firm's proposition to customers relative to the incumbent (and any other alternative team), and in some cases that combining new management with the retention of certain key staff (and their knowledge) of the target may be a combination of human capital vital to realizing improvements in quality, progress in innovations and so forth.

It is therefore inappropriate to conclude that, in principle, managerial and know-how efficiencies are inherently not recognizable for these purposes, although they will be difficult to attest,[88] and it would be appropriate to apply the overall evidentiary safeguards discussed above in relation to all efficiencies claims: evidence of a mere good-faith belief that the acquirer's management 'can do better' will not be sufficient; compelling evidence will be required.

As to the weight to be attached to such claims, the track record of the individuals and firms they are associated with and corroboration from customers can be valuable tools in deciding whether such claims are unduly speculative or should be credited as merger-specific. The process of validating efficiencies claims requires early dialogue with the OFT to stand a proper chance of making a contribution to the analysis.

4.5.6 Supply-side efficiencies

As the OFT's Substantive Assessment Guidance for mergers makes clear, supply-side rivalry-enhancing efficiencies (e.g. cost savings) are more likely to be taken into account where they impact on marginal or variable costs. Such cost savings tend to stimulate competition and are likely to be passed more directly on to customers in terms of lower prices (because of their importance in short-run price-setting behaviour). Generally, savings in fixed costs will not be given such weight as they are not so important in short-run price formation. However, fixed costs may also be important in short-run price formation where, for example, competition takes place via a tendering process and bids reflect both the fixed and the variable costs of the tendered service.[89]

As an example of the assessment of efficiencies, this chapter analyses *Global/GCap*. This is the first case in Europe to take efficiencies into consideration, leading to the outcome of the merger assessment being changed by the efficiencies assessment.

[88] For an equivalent view, see ibid.

[89] See para. 4.33, footnote 27, of the Substantive Assessment Guidance.

As in the analysis of *Global/GCap*, in differentiated products markets, the extent of pass-through of marginal cost savings into lower prices that benefit customers is determined largely by the curvature of demand and functional forms for demand. Demand properties that lead to larger incentives to raise price from mergers also lead to greater pass-through of compensating marginal cost reductions that have the reverse incentive – to lower price.[90] In this regard, the OFT notes that if the merger does not appear to increase the parties' market power much in any event, marginal or variable cost savings do not appear more likely to be passed on as a result of the merger.

4.5.7 Global/GCap

Global Radio UK Ltd is a privately owned UK-based commercial radio group, the activities of which comprise nine local radio analogue stations grouped under three principal brands (Heart, Galaxy and LBC).[91] GCap Media plc was formed by the merger of Capital Radio plc and GWR plc in May 2005 and owns a portfolio of seventy-one local analogue radio licences across the UK, as well as the Classic FM national station.

The transaction largely combined complementary assets. Global's prime assets included relatively new and strong radio brands in Heart and Galaxy, and the corporate know-how, common programming format and consistent audience demographic associated with them; its comparative disadvantage was a lack of geographic coverage. GCap's prime assets consisted of an extensive radio network, largely of 'heritage' local radio stations, across the UK, as well as one national licence (Classic FM); its relative disadvantage was the lack of a unified and recognizable brand proposition – that is, a common programming format to attract a particular audience demographic, and a unified brand proposition to advertisers targeting that audience in a national campaign. The primary value proposition of the transaction was the combination of Global's brands and GCap's UK-wide station network.

Global had limited national coverage, being present only in London, the Midlands (where its activities overlapped geographically with those of GCap) and the North of England. Outside the Midlands and

[90] See G. Werden, L. Froeb and S. Tschantz, 'The Effects of Merger Efficiencies on Consumers of Differentiated Products' (October 2005) 1(2) *European Competition Journal*.

[91] *Global Radio UK Ltd/GCap Media plc*, www.oft.gov.uk.

in London, the transaction was best characterized as a conglomerate merger. Both parties' stations were sold as complementary products to the same class of advertising-buying agencies who purchased airtime on bundles of stations, assembled to achieve broad coverage in radio and multimedia advertising campaigns run on a 'national' – that is, UK-wide – basis.

Global offered to divest a package of radio stations to purchasers approved up front by the OFT. In principle, this would resolve the OFT's concerns by restoring competition to pre-merger levels in the Midlands. As regards the London market, the merger efficiencies tipped the balance in favour of clearance. The divestment remedies in the Midlands, where efficiencies were not sufficient, were about restoring competition to make sure customers would not be harmed.

In this case, the merger-specific efficiencies were twofold and, in the OFT's judgement, comfortably cleared the hurdle of 'tipping the balance' in the London market.

First, there was compelling evidence that Global would have the profit incentive to bundle together former GCap and Global stations at a lower package price than the equivalent mix-and-match bundled price pre-merger, when the stations were not commonly owned. The price-lowering incentive would counteract any price-increasing incentive gained from internalizing competition between the parties' stations. Unlike certain other types of efficiency, this did not require pressure from rivals to ensure pass-on to customers; it was profit-maximizing for the merged firm to lower prices of bundles independent of any rivalry.

Second, Global would reposition its commonly owned stations to attract listeners, in a way designed to increase total audience size for all stations combined, and increase the demographic focus of the respective station audiences. While directly benefiting end-consumers – who were at no risk of price effects – advertisers would also benefit: not only from the ability to reach a greater audience, but also to better target their advertising towards more focused demographics (because many product advertisements were targeted, to a greater or lesser degree, towards certain age, gender and income groups), which meant less 'wastage' of the message and better value for money for the advertising customer. Efficiencies of both types, if realized, would improve the Global/GCap station offer to listeners and advertisers. The driver of this efficiencies analysis was the net impact of the transaction on customer welfare; the OFT's overall belief was that the parties' London customers would be better off as a result of the merger, and in any event there was no realistic prospect that the parties' customers would end up worse off.

Moreover, London radio rivals like Bauer, Virgin and GMG would be obliged to respond if they wished to retain and grow both classes of customer. These efficiencies could properly be characterized as 'rivalry-enhancing' because rivals remained in the market who would need to match or better respond to the merged firm's improved offer if they were to win and retain customers made better off by the merger, and the net effect of the merger was that it would enhance – or in any event not substantially reduce – overall rivalry notwithstanding the loss of rivalry between the parties themselves.

Thus in the UK regime the current approach towards efficiencies can make a difference, even at first phase, and even in a horizontal merger with high market shares.

Before turning to the US regime and its approach towards efficiencies in merger assessment, we should mention two interesting Dutch cases. The Dutch competition authority, NMa, considered efficiencies and took them into account in conditionally clearing the merger between two hospitals, Ziekenhuis Walcheren and Oosterscheldeziekenhuizen. The merger would result in a near-monopoly position for the hospitals, with no alternative suppliers left, and no potential new entrants. In addition, even though the parties depended on large health-care insurers, the latter were not considered as having countervailing power since they would have no alternatives.[92]

The NMa considered that competition would be reduced since the hospitals in question were each other's next-best alternative, and there were no potential new entrants. The most important argument presented by the parties was that in the absence of the merger, they would have difficulty guaranteeing continuity of care, following up recent trends and developments in the field, and developing certain specialties of care. The parties argued that both hospitals operated below a scale sufficient to offer a proper degree of specialization and diversification.

As regards economies of scale and scope, the merger would create

[92] See further A. Renckens, 'The Dutch NCA Conditionally Clears a Hospital Merger Based on Efficiency Arguments, Issuing One of the First Horizontal Merger Cases in Europe Where Efficiency Gains Are the Main Argument Motivating a Merger Clearance (*Ziekenhuis Walcheren/Oosterscheldeziekenhuizen*)', March 2009, e-Competitions, www.concurrences.com.

the improvement of health-care provision referred to by the parties. Due to increased scale, emergency and intensive care services could be expanded and improved. The merger would lead to cost reductions through joint purchasing and joint investment. Finally, the attractiveness of the hospitals as an employer would increase, contributing to improvement of the development and career prospects of employees.

The parties argued that the merger would increase the quality of care provided in the hospital, which would be beneficial for patients. The competition authority was not convinced that consumers would benefit and considered a disproportionate price increase as a realistic scenario. Thus remedies were offered by the parties to make sure these efficiencies would materialize and that they would benefit consumers. First, maximum prices (equal to national average prices) were imposed on specialist medical care not part of the basic compulsory health-care insurance. The merged entity agreed to comply with minimum standards regarding the minimum size of departments and the minimum number of treatments per specialist within a six-month period. Finally, the merged entity promised to have a higher-level intensive care and emergency care unit within three years.[93]

In order to assess merger-specificity, the NMa conducted extensive research about merger-specificity in other hospital merger cases in the Netherlands and concluded that the efficiencies were deemed to be merger-specific. The NMa argued that the evidence put forward by the parties was insufficient to verify that efficiencies were likely to materialize. Remedies were imposed in order to ensure that the efficiencies would indeed materialize. The merged hospital was required to facilitate the entrance of potential new suppliers of specialist medical care and was not allowed to tie its specialists with exclusivity clauses.

As the above analysis indicates, the criteria for a successful efficiency defence were not fulfilled and thus the NMa had to rely on remedies offered by the parties to clear the merger. A factor that was given some prominence, but could not satisfy a failing-firm defence, was that there was a risk of bankruptcy for the merging parties in the absence of the merger. The hospitals incurred losses of €7 million in 2007, and were expecting losses of €5 million in 2008. The NMa was strongly concerned with maintaining service provision and thus may have accepted what would not have been accepted in other industries.

In another recent case, the NMa gave efficiencies prominence in

[93] See further ibid.

clearing the merger between European Directories (owner of De Telefoongids) and Gouden Gids (owned by Truvo).[94] The NMa noted that a small group of advertisers might be disadvantaged by the acquisition. The group of advertisers who would be disadvantaged was smaller than the group of those who would benefit from it. The acquisition would result in consumers receiving Yellow Pages Netherlands and De Telefoongids as one business directory in 2009 at the latest. Their websites would also be integrated into one online directory. The benefits to consumers were indicated by the fact that the integrated directory would be consulted by more users, which was beneficial to advertisers. In addition, users would receive a single directory with all the information they needed.

Thus in the UK and Dutch regimes, the approach towards efficiencies can make a difference. This is a very positive development in the assessment of efficiencies. One can only hope that such an approach will be continued and followed by other competition authorities.

4.6 The US approach to efficiencies

According to §7 (acquisition by one corporation of stock of another) of the Clayton Act,

> No person engaged in commerce or in any activity affecting commerce shall acquire, directly or indirectly, the whole or any part of the stock or other share capital and no person subject to the jurisdiction of the FTC shall acquire the whole or any part of the assets of another person engaged also in commerce or in any activity affecting commerce, where in any line of commerce or in any activity affecting commerce in any section of the country, the effect of such acquisition may be substantially to lessen competition, or to tend to create a monopoly.
>
> No person shall acquire, directly or indirectly, the whole or any part of the stock or other share capital and no person subject to the jurisdiction of the FTC shall acquire the whole or any part of the assets of one or more persons engaged in commerce or in any activity affecting commerce, where in any line of commerce or in any activity affecting commerce in any section of the country, the effect of such acquisition, of such stocks or assets, or of the use of such stock by the voting or granting of proxies or otherwise, may be substantially to lessen competition, or to tend to create a monopoly.

[94] See www.nmanet.nl/engels/home/News_and_publications/News_and_press_releases/Press_2008/08-24_NMa_green_light_to_acquisition_Yellow_Pages_Netherlands_by_De_Telefoongids.asp.

The approach that the EC has taken towards efficiencies is different to the US approach. The EC guidelines[95] incorporated assessment of efficiencies in the 2004 Horizontal Merger Guidelines. On the other hand, the US guidelines[96] have incorporated assessment of efficiencies since 1982.[97]

The 1992 Horizontal Merger Guidelines provide the analysis of merger enforcement and aim to provide guidance in the assessment of mergers. The Department of Justice first released merger guidelines in 1968 which needed to be replaced due to developments in legal and economic thinking about mergers. In 1982, the DOJ released revised merger guidelines which were significantly different to the 1968 guidelines and in 1984 the DOJ issued a refinement of the 1982 guidelines. The 1992 Horizontal Merger Guidelines clarify certain aspects of the 1984 guidelines that were ambiguous or were interpreted by observers in ways that were inconsistent with the actual policy of the agencies.[98]

In order for antitrust authorities to assess the anti-competitive impact of a merger they must determine the products that belong in the same market as the products of the merging firms. Market definition and the evaluation of market shares and concentration provide the starting framework for analysing the competitive impact of a proposed merger.

In addition, a merger is unlikely to create or enhance market power if entry into the relevant market is relatively easy. For entry to be considered a sufficient competitive constraint on the merging parties it must be shown to be likely, timely (within two years) and sufficient to deter or defeat any potential anti-competitive effects of the merger. In the US, the agencies take an economically driven, consumer welfare approach to merger review whereby the agencies evaluate the likely net effect of a transaction on price and output. The agencies assess whether the merger, in light of market concentration and other factors that characterize the

[95] See Guidelines on the Assessment of Horizontal Mergers under the Council Regulation on the Control of Concentrations between Undertakings, OJ C31/03; and Recital 29, Council Regulation (EC) 139/2004 of 20 January 2004 on the Control of Concentrations between Undertakings (the ECMR), [2004] OJ L24/1.

[96] See www.usdoj.gov/atr/public/guidelines/horiz_book/hmg1.html.

[97] Efficiencies were recognized in the 1982 Department of Justice (DOJ) guidelines. They were considered only in extraordinary cases based on the parties' ability to provide evidence of substantial cost savings. The 1984 DOJ guidelines maintained the requirement of clear and convincing evidence. The 1992 joint FTC/DOJ guidelines do not refer to such requirement, and the 1997 guidelines provided a fuller assessment of efficiencies. See Kolasky and Dick 2003.

[98] See www.ftc.gov/bc/docs/horizmer.htm.

market, raises concern about potential adverse competitive effects. A merger may diminish competition by enabling the incumbent firms more successfully and more completely to engage in co-ordinated interaction that harms consumers.[99]

Under the US guidelines, the enforcement agencies also examine whether a lessening of competition through either 'co-ordinated interaction' or 'unilateral effects' exists. If a merger does not pose a serious threat to competition, it is unlikely to be challenged. If a substantial threat is present, however, the enforcement agencies will assess whether net efficiencies (e.g. economies of scale, cost reduction and/or technological advancement) outweigh the likely adverse impact on competition.

The treatment of mergers and any resulting efficiencies has changed significantly over decades of jurisprudence. Judge Hand's opinion in *ALCOA*[100] states that the assessment of mergers in antitrust laws is based upon the belief that consolidation is inherently undesirable, regardless of the economic results that such consolidation may induce.

As the following analysis will illustrate, in US case law, efficiencies have played a part in, but have not constituted the only reason for, clearance. In 2005, in *Verizon Communications/MCI*, Assistant Attorney General Barnett argued that the transaction would not harm competition and would likely benefit consumers, due, among other things, to exceptionally large merger-specific efficiencies.[101] In 2006, in the approval of *Whirlpool/Maytag*, in spite of a large market share of 70 per cent of the merged entity, Assistant Attorney General Barnett allowed the transaction to proceed, taking into account efficiencies.[102] The Federal Trade Commission (FTC) has also taken efficiencies into account in merger assessment.[103] The FTC in the *General Motors/Toyota* joint venture relied on efficiencies as one of the main arguments for approving it.[104]

[99] OECD, Substantive Criteria Used for the Assessment of Mergers, www.oecd.org/dataoecd/54/3/2500227.pdf, page 293.

[100] *United States v. Aluminum Company of America*, 148 F.2d 416, 428 (2d Cir. 1945).

[101] Press Release, US Department of Justice, Justice Department Requires Divestitures in Verizon's Acquisition of MCI and SBC's Acquisition of AT&T (27 October 2005), available at www.usdoj.gov/atr/public/press_releases/2005/212407.htm.

[102] Press Release, US Department of Justice, Department of Justice Antitrust Division Statement on the Closing of its Investigation of Whirlpool's Acquisition of Maytag (29 March 2006), available at www.usdoj.gov/atr/public/press_releases/2006/215326.htm.

[103] *AmeriSource Health Corporation/Bergen Brunswig Corporation*, File No 011-0122 (24 August 2001), available at www.ftc.gov/os/2001/08/amerisourcestatement.pdf.

[104] (1984) 103 F.T.C. 374.

4.7 US case law on efficiencies

In the landmark *Brown Shoe* case, in 1962,[105] one of the first decisions of the Supreme Court to interpret the scope of §7 of the Clayton Act, Chief Justice Warren emphasized the sociopolitical considerations which almost exclusively guided Congress in the 1950 amendment, without regard to efficiency arguments. The Court held that even in an unconcentrated market, a transaction not resulting in a large post-merger market share (5 per cent in that case) may still be illegal.[106] A strict approach of horizontal mergers was also endorsed in *Philadelphia National Bank*.[107] *Philadelphia National Bank* notes that a merger, the effect of which may be substantially to lessen competition, is not saved because on some ultimate reckoning of social or economic debits and credits it may be deemed beneficial. Until the early 1980s, the efficiency defence was of no importance. In *Procter & Gamble*, the Supreme Court refused to consider promotional efficiency gains and held that 'possible economies cannot be used as a defense to illegality'.[108] In *Carilion Health System*,[109] the Court admitted defendants' evidence that the proposed merger would lead to savings in capital avoidance and to clinical and administrative efficiencies.[110]

In *Rockford*,[111] the defendants argued before the District Court that the hospital merger would generate benefits both qualitative and quantitative. But the Court, though recognizing the reality of the efficiencies created by the merger, relying on *Philadelphia National Bank*, refused to clear the transaction. *Rockford* may be read as admitting the efficiency defence, but using a strict approach: 'clear and convincing evidence' of the efficiencies has to be brought, sustained by precise dollar figures;[112] the extent of the 'sufficient' efficiencies has to be determined under the more demanding 'price standard'.[113]

[105] (1962) 370 U.S. 294.
[106] Noel 1997.
[107] (1963) 374 U.S. 321.
[108] *In re Procter & Gamble*, (1963) 63 F.T.C. 1465.
[109] *United States of America v. Carilion Health System; Community Hospital of Roanoke Valley; Lewis-Gale Hospital, Inc.; Voluntary Hospitals of America, Inc.; American Medical Association, Amici Curiae, United States Court of Appeals, Fourth Circuit.* 892 F.2d 1042.
[110] 707 F. Supp. 840 (W.D.Va), aff'd without opinion, 892 F.2d 1042 (4th Cir. 1989).
[111] *United States v. Rockford Memorial Corp.*, 717 F. Supp. 1251 (N.D. Ill. 1989), aff'd, 898 F. 2d 1278 (7th Cir.), cert. denied (1990) 111 S. Ct. 295.
[112] Noel 1997.
[113] Ibid.

4.7.1 *United States v. Mercy Health Services and Finley Tristates Health Group*

Mercy Health Centre and Finley Hospital were the only two general acute-care hospitals within a seventy-mile driving distance of Dubuque, Iowa.[114] They proposed to merge into one entity, the Dubuque Regional Hospital System.

Unless prevented, the merged entity would eliminate competition and result in higher prices and lower quality of service to patients and other health-care consumers, especially health management organizations (HMOs), insurance plans, employers and unions.

Because Mercy and Finley were each other's competitors in the provision of inpatient hospital services in the Dubuque area, their combination would result in a monopoly in the sale of acute-care inpatient hospitals in that area.

The United States filed a complaint seeking an injunction to prevent the merger under §7 of the Clayton Act and §1 of the Sherman Antitrust Act.

The defendants claimed efficiencies in the form of significant savings in their operations, especially 'best-practice' savings, capital savings, capital-avoidance savings and group-purchasing savings.

The DOJ argued that the savings claimed by the defendants were at best speculative, and that even if the consolidation occurred, the savings claimed were ill-conceived, overstated and inaccurate.

According to the DOJ,[115] for an efficiency claim to be effective, the defendants must prove with 'clear and convincing evidence' that their claimed efficiencies

(1) will actually be achieved and are not based on speculation,
(2) can be achieved only through the merger and in no other manner,
(3) will be passed on and will produce 'significant economic benefit to the consumers', and
(4) will outweigh the merger's anti-competitive effect and therefore provide a 'net economic benefit for the health care consumer'.[116]

[114] United States District Court for the Northern District of Iowa, Eastern Division. Civil Action No C94-1023. www.justice.gov/atr/cases/f0100/0141.htm. See also the Department of Justice website at www.usdoj.gov/atr/cases/f0400/0436.htm. 1994.

[115] Citing *Rockford Memorial* 717 F. Supp. at 1289.

[116] Citing *University Health* 938 F.2d at 1223.

It was pointed out that the defendants' claim was merely speculative because most of the savings were projected to occur several years into the future. Also, the savings could be achieved by other means, some of which were already being conducted unilaterally by each of the parties.

Further still, it was noted that the defendants had not been able to explain how the purported savings would be beneficial to the consumer. According to the DOJ, there was therefore serious doubt that much of the savings claimed would be achieved if competitive pressures were absent.

The District Court held that the DOJ had failed to carry its burden of proving that the merger would have anti-competitive effects and denied the injunction. The District Court also rejected the defendants' efficiency arguments. The United States appealed contending that the District Court had erred on the definition of the geographic market. The defendants cross-appealed, arguing that the District Court had erred in rejecting their efficiency arguments. However, after the appeal had been submitted, Finley formally announced that it had abandoned its proposed merger with Mercy.

From the above case, it is quite clear that the proposed merger would create no substantive efficiencies. In fact, it would appear that the efficiencies claim was only argued after the suit had been filed by the DOJ. Even if there were a substantive efficiency claim, it would still need to satisfy the 'clear and convincing' evidential test, which the defendants' claim had not been able to do.

4.7.2 Union Pacific Corp. and Southern Pacific Rail Corp.

The merger proposed by the Union Pacific Railroad Corp. (hereafter UP) and the Southern Pacific Transportation Corp. (hereafter SP) in 1995 would combine two of the three largest rail companies in the West and create the largest railroad in the US. The merging parties submitted application for prior approval by the Surface Transportation Board (STB) which was required under the Interstate Commerce Act (ICA).

The Justice Department considered that the merger would raise significant competitive concerns in a large number of markets and might result in price increases to shippers and consumers of roughly US$800 million.

The affected markets involved rail services; commodities such as wood and agricultural products, iron and steel and plastics; and intermodal traffic.

The merging parties claimed that the combination would be able to offer new and improved services to shippers, to relieve capacity constraints that UP and SP faced on certain routes, and to save US$750 million in annual expenses. In addition, the merged system would become a more effective rival to the larger, just-formed third rail company, Burlington-Northern Santa-Fe (BNSF). In order to address possible competitive concerns, UP and SP had prearranged an extensive trackage rights agreement with the BNSF.[117]

Apart from these claims concerning cost savings, the companies argued that the only solution for SP was a merger with UP because SP lacked the resources to compete with the BNSF.

The DOJ and some third parties argued that the merged entity would be able to exercise market power on a large number of routes involving shipments worth billions of dollars. They added that UP and SP's proposed remedy – the offer of trackage rights to the BNSF – was wholly inadequate, and that the alleged efficiencies were highly speculative.

The STB decided to approve the UP and SP merger, and as a condition for approving the merger the STB granted trackage rights to BNSF in order to preserve the pre-merger level of competition. With respect to cost savings, the STB endorsed UP and SP's list of 'non-quantifiable benefits' such as shorter routes and more reliable services, and assessed the quantifiable annual benefits from the merger at US$627 million.

The critics' claimed that the merger would result in two big players in the market. The merger was not allowed on the grounds that it was based on the premise that BNSF, through its trackage rights agreement, would have no effect on rates. Concerning the arrangement of trackage, the STB asserted that the full mileage charge inclusive of fixed costs was consistent with past practice and 'well within a reasonable level'.

The STB was required to apply a public-interest standard, and it considered the public benefits of a proposed merger and weighed them against any competitive harm in deciding whether the transaction would be in the public interest. The STB's public-interest standard is broader than the standard for mergers in antitrust law, allowing for consideration of other factors, including the impact of a merger on employment.

The STB's consideration of both competitive harm and efficiency gains is consistent with antitrust policy, but involves the weighing of

[117] Trackage rights are the licence granted to a rail company to use the tracks of another rail company for a fee.

economic merger benefits against competitive harms. The result was a strong presumption in favour of mergers of rail companies.

4.7.3 *FTC v. Staples Inc. and Office Depot Inc.*

Staples Inc. operated approximately five hundred retail office supply superstores in twenty-nine American states, and Office Depot Inc. also operated approximately five hundred retail office supply superstores, but in thirty-eight American states. The relevant product market was the 'retail sale of office supplies', sometimes called 'consumable office supplies'.

In September 1996 Staples and Office Depot agreed that the former corporation would acquire the stocks and assets of the latter, through a merger valued at approximately US$4 billion. The Federal Trade Commission petitioned the District Court for a preliminary injunction to prevent Staples from merging with Office Depot, on the basis that the merger would lessen competition considerably and would create a monopoly in some geographic areas within the relevant market.[118]

The injunctive relief was granted by the District Court for the District of Columbia, therefore preventing the corporations from merging.

Staples and Office Depot alleged that the merger would result in efficiencies, such as considerable cost savings. They estimated that the merger would save approximately US$5 billion to the merged corporation, of which around two-thirds would be passed on to consumers. Furthermore, they alleged that the merger would result in dynamic efficiencies, as suppliers of the merged corporation would lower prices due to the increase in their sales.

The FTC alleged that a merger between Staples and Office Depot would result in a loss of competition among office superstores in many metropolitan areas, which would increase the price of office supplies to small businesses and consumers. Furthermore, the merger would create a monopoly in some geographic areas, where Staples and Office Depot are the only office supplies superstores. Finally, FTC considered that Staples and Office Depot's claimed efficiencies were speculative, would not benefit consumers and would not overcome the anti-competitive

[118] US District Court for the District of Columbia, Case No 1:97CV00701 TFH – 10 April 1997. Details of the case obtained online at www.ftc.gov/os/caselist/cn197cv00701.shtm – Federal Trade Commission website, and also in the Westlaw database.

effects of the merger, and that the cost savings could be achieved through other methods which did not harm competition.

The Court considered that the efficiencies claimed by Staples and Office Depot did not refute the presumption that the merger might reduce competition. First of all, the Court found that the estimate of cost savings was unreliable as it exceeded almost by 500 per cent the figures presented to the boards of directors in order to obtain approval for the merger.

In addition, the Court declared that Staples and Office Depot did not demonstrate which cost savings were merger-specific and which were not. Therefore 'the calculation in the Efficiencies Analysis included product cost savings that Staples and Office Depot would likely have realized without the merger'.[119]

Finally, the Court found that the amount of cost savings that the merged company expected to pass on to consumers, through lower prices, was unrealistic, as historically Staples had passed through only 15–17 per cent. As a result, the preliminary injunction was found to be in the public interest and FTC's motion for it was granted by the Court.

The position of the Court in relation to the efficiencies defence is not clear in the judgment. Nevertheless, the Court assumes that the efficiencies defence is viable, stating that in this particular case the efficiencies evidence did not overcome the considerable anti-competitive effects of the merger.

4.7.4 *FTC v. H.J. Heinz Co. & Milnot Holding Corporation*

The US baby food market was dominated by three firms – Gerber, Heinz and Beech-Nut – with Gerber occupying 65 per cent of the market and Heinz and Beech-Nut enjoying 17.4 per cent and 15.4 per cent respectively. Despite its second place in the domestic market share, Heinz was the largest producer of baby food in the world. Beech-Nut had annual sales of US$138.7 million in baby food. Under the terms of the agreement Heinz would acquire 100 per cent of Beech-Nut's voting securities for US$185 million.[120]

The FTC argued that the merger violated §5 of the Federal Tort Claims

[119] Section 6(6), of the judgment, at p. 25, obtained at Westlaw database.

[120] Decided by the Court of Appeals for the State of Columbia, Case No 00-5632, decided on 27 April 2001.

Act (FTCA) and if consummated would violate §7 of the Clayton Act.[121] Sufficiently large Herfindahl–Hirschmann Index figures establish the prima facie case of the FTC that the proposed merger is anti-competitive at the wholesale level.

Existing firms knew that if they colluded or exercised market power to charge supracompetitive prices, entry by firms currently not competing in the market would become likely, thereby increasing the pressure on them to act competitively. Heinz and Beech-Nut did not really compete at the retail level.

There was evidence that the two did in fact compete in price against each other and that when both were present in the same area they did depress each other's prices and those of Gerber. The District Court's conclusion regarding pre-merger competition did not take into consideration the indisputable fact that the merger would eliminate competition at the wholesale level between the only two competitors for the 'second shelf' position. No court has ever held that reduction of competition at the wholesale level is irrelevant unless the plaintiff can prove impact at the retail level. The antitrust laws assume that a retailer faced with an increased cost would pass that cost on to consumers. High market concentration levels in this case require, in rebuttal, proof of extraordinary efficiencies, which the firms failed to provide. The District Court's denial of preliminary injunctive relief was reversed.

It should be noted that to determine whether the merged entity would be an efficient competitor, the cost reductions must be measured across the new entity's combined production and not just across the pre-merger output. The standard of rebuttal was high on the firm in order to establish that the merger would in fact be efficient.

4.7.5 United States v. Oracle and Peoplesoft Corp.

The product market in this merger was defined as the market for enterprise software applications (ESAs) which provide tools to automate key business processes for the running of operations.[122] Both companies

[121] Section 7 of the Clayton Act prohibits acquisitions, including mergers, 'where in any line of commerce or in any activity affecting commerce in any section of the country, the effect of such acquisition may be substantially to lessen competition or to tend to create a monopoly'.

[122] US District Court Northern District of California, San Francisco Division, Case No C04-0807 VRW, filed 1 June 2004. Details of case obtained from the plaintiff's trial brief, which can be found at www.usdoj.gov/atr/cases/f203800/203882.htm.

develop and distribute ESAs in a market in which they are two of only three companies producing such high-function products. Oracle attempted a hostile cash tender offer valued at US$7.7 billion for shares in Peoplesoft Corp.

Oracle made efficiency claims of two types: cost savings and innovation benefits. It claimed that the merger would lead to cost and innovation efficiencies through shared R & D.

The Department of Justice argued that the rivalry between the two companies provided innovative products at competitive prices to consumers and that the merger was likely to result in an increase in prices. It also argued that only 'extraordinary efficiencies' would rebut a showing that a transaction is likely substantially to reduce competition in a highly concentrated market. The defendant would have to demonstrate that the intended acquisition would result in significant economies.

Any efficiency claims test must be (1) supported by credible evidence, (2) not attributable to reduced output or quality, (3) merger-specific and (4) greater than the transaction' s substantial anti-competitive effects.

However, Oracle's claims were not supported by verifiable data and the efficiency claims were not cognizable as their core was apparently tied to reduced output and consumer choice. The DOJ argued that cost savings from anti-competitive reductions in output and services do not count as efficiencies, citing *Rockford Memorial.*[123]

The Court did not enjoin Oracle from purchasing Peoplesoft due to the existence of other competitors in the market.

However, as regards the efficiencies claimed, the Court argued that they were not verifiable and did not cure the harm to competitiveness in the industry. The standard of proof of efficiency has been set very high; it must be clearly shown that the merger will produce such levels of efficiency as would benefit consumers and reduce the harm in reduction of competition in the market. The burden of proof that the efficiencies shall reduce the anti-competitive harm produced by the merger is on the defendant company making the claims and the four-prong test discussed above must be established for the claims to stand.

4.7.6 *Whirlpool and Maytag*

The products in this case involved major household appliances, including washers and driers, refrigerators, dishwashers and ovens, as well as

[123] *Rockford Memorial* 717 F. Supp. at 1290.

other appliances such as microwave ovens and room air-conditioners. Whirlpool, based in Benton Harbor, Michigan, was the largest appliance manufacturer in the United States. Maytag, headquartered in Newton, Iowa, was the third-largest appliance manufacturer.[124]

The DOJ's public press release noted that the ability to expand sales significantly, and the large cost savings and other efficiencies that the merged firm appeared likely to achieve, indicated that this transaction was not likely to harm consumer welfare.

Despite Whirlpool and Maytag having a relatively high share of laundry products in the United States, the DOJ found that any attempt to raise prices would likely be unsuccessful, because rival appliance brands, such as Kenmore, General Electric and Frigidaire, were also well established, and newer brands such as LG and Samsung had quickly established themselves in recent years. LG, Samsung and other foreign manufacturers could increase their imports into the US and the existing US manufacturers had excess capacity and could increase production. Further, the large retailers through which the majority of these appliances were sold – Sears, Lowe's, the Home Depot and Best Buy – had alternatives available to help them resist an attempt by the merged entity to raise prices.

The DOJ also found that, despite the two companies' relatively high share of laundry product sales in the United States, any attempt to raise prices would likely be unsuccessful and that the parties were able to substantiate 'large cost savings and other efficiencies that should benefit consumers'.

To conclude the analysis of the case law, it can be argued that the US has been more open in accepting efficiencies in mergers. The European Commission, after it issued guidelines on horizontal mergers, has been adopting a more positive approach in assessing efficiencies, as the three EC cases mentioned above illustrate. The UK OFT and the Dutch NMa are the only EU competition authorities that have taken efficiencies into account in their merger assessments.

4.8 Concluding remarks

In the absence of the Commission's decisions, and judgments of the Community courts that would clarify problematic issues of the practical

[124] Department of Justice Antitrust Division Statement on the Closing of its Investigation of Whirlpool's Acquisition of Maytag', Press Release, 29 March 2006.

application of the efficiency defence, the parties and their advisers rely on guidelines. In order successfully to present and sustain their efficiency claims, merging parties should have a clear understanding of which stage of the merger assessment they should be introduced at, how efficiencies will be assessed in relation to concerns about anti-competitive behaviour and what kind of evidence should be produced.

Merging parties should be encouraged to explain and substantiate the possible efficiency motivations for their mergers and efficiencies should be the basis on which to clear an otherwise anti-competitive merger or to reduce the scope of remedies.

Simon Pritchard, OFT Senior Director of Mergers in the Global/GCap decision, mentioned that merger efficiencies benefit customers and put pressure on rivals. This shows that with the right facts, efficiencies can make a difference, even at the first phase, and even in a horizontal merger with high market shares.

Balancing efficiencies and competitive harm is not straightforward. As Ilzkovitz and Meiklejohn argue,[125] the introduction of an efficiency defence in the EU, which will require quantification of this balance, constitutes a significant change in merger assessment.

In the presence of the guidelines on horizontal and non-horizontal mergers,[126] the Commission should be open to efficiency claims by the merging parties. Recent case law has indicated that the Commission has been willing to take efficiencies into account in merger assessments and to give efficiencies more weight in decision-making.

The recent OFT Global/GCap case illustrated that a competition authority can clear a merger based on efficiencies if the 'right' evidence is available.[127] This is a very positive development in the merger case law and one which it is hoped will be followed in future by other authorities as well.

The Dutch merger between Ziekenhuis Walcheren and Oosterscheldeziekenhuizen, analysed above, is an indicative example of the need for competition authorities to assess efficiencies in mergers involving firms that are failing. According to the Dutch Health-Care Inspectorate (IGZ), which supervises the quality of care, prevention and

125 F. Ilzkovitz and R. Meiklejohn, eds., *European Merger Control: Do We Need an Efficiency Defense?*, Edward Elgar, 2006.

126 Guidelines on the Assessment of Non-Horizontal Mergers under the Council Regulation on the Control of Concentrations between Undertakings, 2007.

127 There is another case where rivalry-enhancing efficiencies have been considered by the OFT: *C&W/Thus*. See further www.oft.gov.uk.

medical products on the Dutch health-care market, the merger should have been allowed as a more intensive form of co-operation between the hospitals was found appropriate to ensure quality and continuity of hospital care in the region. The IGZ strongly recommended that the merger be cleared, as this would be the best solution for ensuring continuity of health care in Zeeland. In the absence of the merger, the parties argued, they would have difficulty guaranteeing continuity of care, following up recent trends and developments in the field, and developing subspecialties in some areas – in particular pediatrics and gynaecology. Thus the competition authority and the relevant health-care authorities placed increased emphasis on continuity of care – on continuity of the provision of service.

As we shall see in the penultimate chapter, there can be cases where efficiencies are alleged and mergers occur in a period of crisis. Important questions are asked on whether assessment of efficiencies should be different in these cases. Advocates of a more lenient approach advocate placing increased emphasis on preventing inefficiencies that may result from the prevention of the merger. Thus, rather than an efficiency defence, we may need to consider an inefficiency defence as well. This is an important consideration that was clearly taken into account in the Dutch case mentioned above. In the penultimate chapter, we shall analyse the circumstances under which the authorities should place significant emphasis on the continuity of services or products, so significant that in certain cases even if the criteria for an efficiency defence may not be strictly satisfied, the merger will be cleared on the basis of the prevention of the resulting inefficiencies from discontinuing a product or service. This argument is similar to that analysed in the discussion of failing-firm defence regarding circumstances where the authorities should be more lenient towards accepting arguments for the failing- as well as the flailing-firm defence.

5

Crisis cartels

> We rarely hear, it has been said, of the combinations of masters, though frequently of those of workmen. But whoever imagines, upon this account, that masters rarely combine, is as ignorant of the world as of the subject.
>
> Adam Smith (1723–90)[1]

> The belief persists that cartels are in some devious way 'unnatural.' Yet nothing can be further from the truth. They are but one of several kindred species of a common genus whose ancestral tree is rooted in the sanctions which underlie the modern business system as a whole. They are not strange and deformed branches ruining an otherwise symmetric tree, nor deadly fruit feeding parasitically on the benign limb. On the contrary, they are as old as the history of business enterprise, for collusion, as Adam Smith clearly recognized in his time, 'is the usual, and one may say, the natural state of things which nobody ever hears of.'
>
> Prof. Robert A. Brady (1901–63)[2]

5.1 Introduction

Cartels generally involve price-fixing, market division, control of output, mitigation of technological improvement, limiting of production. Through cartels, 'private' interests may determine the level and distribution of national income, the level of employment, the stability of markets and general economic and political stability.

[1] Adam Smith, a Scottish moral philosopher and pioneer of political economy, is widely cited as the father of modern economics. See Adam Smith, *An Inquiry into the Nature and Causes of the Wealth of Nations*, Book One: *Of the Causes of Improvement in the Productive Powers of Labour, and of the Order according to which its Produce is Naturally Distributed among the Different Ranks of the People*, Chapter 8, 'Of the Wages of Labour'.

[2] Probert A. Brady was a Professor at Columbia and a distinguished economist of the time. See his 'The Role of Cartels in the Current Cultural Crisis' (May 1945) 35(2) *American Economic Review*, Papers and Proceedings of the Fifty-Seventh Annual Meeting of the American Economic Association, 312.

The impact of cartels has been identified since the early enforcement of competition law. Brady argued that in the presence of cartels the promotion of production, economic stability, the advance of science and technology and the improvement of the common welfare 'are not – indeed, cannot be – primary but, at best, secondary objectives. They are no more and no less nefarious than this.'[3]

As regards cartelistic behaviour, most antitrust laws incorporate three elements. The element of prohibition, the element of exemption and the element of penalty. A review of antitrust legislation in relation to cartels across jurisdictions reveals that there are two principles which govern the approach that countries take towards prohibiting the anti-competitive conduct of cartels. Under the per se prohibition, cartelistic behaviour is illegal per se. On the other hand, under the 'control-of-abuse' approach, cartelistic behaviour may be permitted to some extent, but sufficient regulation is exercised to prevent any harm induced by such activities. The reason for this multitude of approaches across jurisdictions is the overriding social objectives behind some antitrust laws. For example, the adoption of the per se approach in the US emanates from the nineteenth-century Populist movement that resented the anti-competitive activities of various business trusts and therefore sought free competition at any cost. In the EC and Germany, however, the need for economic and technical development and efficiency is reflected in the view of its antitrust role as being supervisory, through the use of the control-of-abuse concept.[4]

A number of antitrust legislations incorporate exemptions as a means to avoid condemnation of certain forms of cartelistic conduct by antitrust legislation. Such legislation includes provisions which specifically exempt certain enterprises and certain conduct from the scope of the antitrust legislation because of the overriding social objectives behind antitrust legislation.

Finally, fines have a twofold role. They operate as a penalizing instrument against the conduct of a cartel, as well as a disincentive to the creation of cartelistic behaviour. The US, the UK, Ireland and Germany, for example, have criminal and civil penalties for corporate and/or individual violations of antitrust laws, while the European Commission can impose a civil penalty only against the corporation.

[3] Ibid.

[4] T. Grendell, 'The Antitrust Legislation of the United States, the European Economic Community, Germany and Japan' (January 1980) 29(1) *International and Comparative Law Quarterly* 64.

The key significance of the criminal regime from an enforcement perspective lies in its deterrence value, and in particular in its separation of the interests of individuals from those of the businesses that employ them. A report was prepared for the Office of Fair Trading (OFT) by Deloitte,[5] in which competition lawyers and companies were asked about the relative importance of various factors in deterring infringements of competition law. Both lawyers and companies surveyed regarded criminal penalties as being the most important.[6] Where cartel prohibitions are enforced with criminal sanctions on individuals (including imprisonment), the standard of proof has to be particularly high ('beyond any reasonable doubt') and it is more difficult to discharge the burden of proof without the active help of cartel members; that is, without admissions and without the agreement of the companies. These personal risks also have the effect of further destabilizing cartels, making it more likely that, once entered into, they will not be sustained. When individual sanctions operate alongside an effective leniency policy that aligns the interests of individuals with those of their employers, together with other sources of intelligence, cartels are also more likely to be detected and punished, thus reinforcing deterrence. According to Tierno, criminal sanctions would lead to underenforcement if they were to be applied where cartelists were not socially perceived as criminals.[7] The majority of countries' antitrust laws provide for enforcement by administrative agencies, with review by the courts.

Cartel justifications that have been proposed include that a cartel will prevent cut-throat competition. In industries where fierce competition would otherwise yield below-cost pricing, the cartel guarantees a 'reasonable' price. In addition, it has been argued that a cartel sustains needed capacity and prevents excess capacity. Furthermore, a cartel reduces uncertainty as regards the average price of a product. It also assists in financing desirable activities, such as R & D, and in providing countervailing power since if there is a single buyer (monopsonist/oligopsonist) or supplier (monopolist/oligopolist), there is unequal bargaining power that a cartel can address.

In periods of crisis in economies, without industry-wide agreement

[5] The Deterrent Effect of Competition Enforcement by the OFT, November 2007 (OFT962).

[6] Ibid., paras. 5.55 to 5.59.

[7] M. Tierno Centella, 'An Optimal Enforcement System against Cartels', in I. Kokkoris and I. Lianos (eds.), *The Challenge of an Optimal Enforcement System*, Kluwer, 2009.

on capacity reduction that can be achieved through a crisis cartel, smaller firms may exit the market, leaving a limited number of choices for customers as well as inducing unemployment. In such conditions, firms may operate at inefficient output levels and may even incur losses. The Treaty of Rome did not contain any clauses regarding crisis conditions. When the treaty was signed, economic expansion seemed to be likely to continue and crises were not envisaged. Due to the lack of express clauses in the Treaty of Rome, the European Commission could not justify applying the Article 101(3) criteria in periods of crisis. Thus the Commission initially reduced fines on cartels existing in crisis situations.

German legislation, the Treaty of Rome and the Treaty of Paris adopted different attitudes to the existence of crises in the economy. Their comparison is useful in assessing the need for crisis cartels. German law was more lenient towards crisis cartels by allowing structural crisis agreements. The Treaty of Paris, although not exempting crisis cartels, allows for intervention by Community institutions to ensure minimum prices.[8] In contrast, the Treaty of Rome adopts a stricter approach and does not contain any exemptions for crisis cartels.

5.2 Germany

In Germany, an abundance of cartels was induced due to the fact that during the war concentration of economic control was accelerated. The operations of Germany's army, railways and banks constituted remarkable achievements of governmental economic efficiency. Cartels proved to be the backbone of Germany's industrial development, during and after the war.

The German cartels are co-operative combination of independent enterprises for the purpose of regulating demand and supply and centralizing business management according to mutual interest.[9] Agreements to restrict competition generally were held to be legal under the principle of freedom of contract until the mid-twentieth century. A cartel ordinance, enacted in 1923, legalized all cartel agreements which did not commit abusive practices. According to the Ordinance,

[8] R. Joliet, 'Cartelisation, Dirigism and Crisis in the European Community' (1981) 3 *The World Economy* 403, at p. 405.

[9] W. Notz, 'The Cartels in War Time' (December 1915) 23(10) *Journal of Political Economy* 990.

> agreements and understandings which contain obligations regarding the manipulation of production or of sales, regarding the conditions to be observed in business transactions, regarding the method of fixing prices or regarding the demand prices (syndicates, cartels, conventions, and similar agreements), have to be executed in writing.

As Schwartz outlines, according to §§1–9 of the 1923 Ordinance,[10] all agreements and understandings falling under §1

(a) must be in writing;
(b) are void when confirmed by word of honour or when solemnly ratified in any other way;
(c) are void when they exclude or hinder an appeal to the cartel court or when they destroy the effectiveness of the cartel law or when they attempt to evade it;
(d) when endangering the common welfare or business as a whole, they may be: (a) voided by the cartel court upon application by the Minister of Economics or restricted in the ways of their execution by the court; (b) cancelled by any one of the contracting parties without prior notice upon a decree authorizing such action, which the Minister of Economics may issue; (c) investigated by the Minister of Economics in which case the agreements and understandings can come into force only after the Minister has received a copy of them;
(e) can be cancelled by any one of the contracting parties without prior notice for reason of weight;
(f) cannot be secured by a bond without the approval of the presiding judge of the cartel court. The same approval is needed where the cartel desires to take drastic steps against one or several enterprises to force them to yield. The application of the sharpest means of pressure against cartel members, outsiders or third parties is made dependent upon the approval of the presiding judge of the cartel court.

According to §10 of the 1923 Ordinance,

> Whenever the terms of delivery (standardized contracts) or the methods of price fixing adopted by enterprises or combinations of enterprises (trusts, communities of interest, syndicates, cartels, conventions, and similar combinations) are apt to endanger the economy as a whole or the common welfare (section 4, paragraph 2) through misuse of a powerful

10 See further I.E. Schwartz, 'Antitrust Legislation and Policy in Germany: A Comparative Study' (March 1957) 105(5) *University of Pennsylvania Law Review* 617.

> economic position, the Cartel Court, upon application of the Minister of Economics, may authorize any party to withdraw from any contract giving rise to such domination.

Schwartz adds that the 1923 Ordinance did not condemn cartels and other combinations per se but adopted a 'harmful-effects' approach in preventing only the abuse of economic power. Thus the legislation implicitly confirmed for the first time the right to establish cartels, subject to certain limitations resulting in 'good' cartels remaining lawful.[11]

Cartels in Germany differed from trusts (*Konzerne*) as the cartel members remain independent entities whereas in trusts the constituent firms lose their legal or economic independence or both. Trusts were a prevalent feature of markets in the US.

In the 1910s, cartels in Germany numbered about six hundred, allowing the government to control and regulate economic conditions. Thus the German government was able to estimate and control supplies of a number of products. The German government even formed compulsory cartels.[12] The importance of cartel agreements and the influence of the government is illustrated by the fact that during the first months of the First World War, the price for upper leather, which was not covered by any cartel agreement, rose by 70 per cent, whereas the price for sole leather, controlled by a cartel, increased by only about 10 per cent. As a result of the positive impact that the cartel system had, new cartels were organized after the beginning of the war, especially in those industries which had been hit the hardest.[13]

The apparent benefits that the cartels seemed to have at the time are illustrated by Notz's argument that cartels were an irreplaceable boon to small companies, which but for the existence of the cartels would have gone bankrupt. The positive attitude towards cartels at the time can be clearly illustrated by quoting Notz, who argues that in periods of peace

> the cartel organizations may be expected to make their strength felt and to act as parachutes in preventing economic disaster on a large scale – to preserve stability in general, and thus to render to the country at large, and to Germany's industries in particular, a very important service.[14]

[11] Ibid.

[12] In 1910, the potash industry was by a special law organized into a compulsory syndicate. In 1914, the potato-drying industry was placed under government supervision, and quite recently the coal cartel was continued under pressure from the government.

[13] Notz 1915.

[14] W. Notz, 'The Cartels in War Time' (December 1915) 23(10) *Journal of Political Economy* 990.

Thus cartels apparently work as a parachute in favour of economic stability. Views of cartels have changed markedly since that time, and there is a stark contrast between this approach and the way that cartels have come to be viewed in the last few decades.

Even as early as 1932, there were voices that told of the adverse effects of cartels. Bloch argued that the German cartels, created due to government control of production and the prices of raw materials, constituted a grave danger to the revival of business and to the development of the German economy.[15]

We should mention that in Germany organizations were often called 'cartel' when they had little or no relation to what is commonly understood to be a cartel. Bloch argues that the structures that were called cartels in Germany had neither the purpose of regulating the volume of production nor the object of fixing a certain sale price – the cartels mentioned above in Germany aimed at some form of control with regard to an orderly sales policy for their members (an example would be collective purchasing agreements with exclusivity clauses).

Even though the number of commodities produced by cartelized industries was limited in Germany, these cartels were essential for the German economy as cartel agreements regulated most raw materials through protective tariffs. The significance of regulating the prices of raw materials is illustrated in Table 5.1, which depicts the movement of the prices for domestic and foreign consumption. Even though we would expect commodity prices to decrease in a period of crisis (like the global financial crisis initiated in 2007), in Germany the prices of raw materials for domestic consumption illustrated resistance to the general decrease in prices. This pricing would lead to losses in the industries which do not share in the production of raw materials due to the high costs that they will pay for cartel products, thus impeding their competitive impact on the international market.

One of the most important organizations implementing a cartel agreement was the Rheno-Westphalian Coal Syndicate (Rheinisch-Westfalische Kohlensyndikat). Its aim was to settle demand and supply for coal and to stabilize prices for products. Legislation made it an obligatory cartel.[16] Without the syndicate there would have been competition

[15] K. Bloch, 'On German Cartels' (July 1932) 5(3) *Journal of Business of the University of Chicago* 213.

[16] In order to adapt the production of the Rheno-Westphalian coalfields to the demand for anthracite, an index was devised according to which at certain intervals the productive

Table 5.1. *Significance of regulating prices of raw materials – movement of raw material price for domestic and foreign consumption, 1929–30*

Year	*Raw materials for domestic consumption (US$)*	*Raw materials for foreign consumption (US$)*
1929	135.7	125.3
1930	131.2	101.2
1931	117.6	77.1

in price on the coal market; instead, with the syndicate, there was competition in productive capacity. The effect of the syndicate's stabilization of prices was that the share of the total production of each firm acquired a market value independent of the real economic value of the producing plant. As Bloch notes,[17] the coal legislation of 1919 and the following years made the formation of cartels obligatory for other mining districts, and results were very similar. Despite the trend towards overproduction of coal, government assistance sustained the inefficient plants. In all these cases of cartels imposed or sustained by the government the result was an increase in productive capacity rather than an increase in output. The 1923 Ordinance did not apply to cartels which were established by law or governmental initiative (such as the potash cartel or the Rheno-Westphalian coal cartel).

In addition, the German cement industry might be mentioned as an example of an industry in which cartels were formed. This cartel, though, more resembled the crisis cartels that were formed in later decades as their aim was to limit the creation of new capacity, which before the First World War had reached excessive levels due to the existing cartel organization. Members of the cartel, aiming at reducing or eliminating any threat of competition, prevented the construction of plants by firms outside the cartel by purchasing suitable land, or even by paying indemnities to landowners for refusing to sell. In addition, cartel members

Footnote 16 (*cont.*)
capacity of each firm was determined by experts and the actual production volume was then fixed as a percentage of the productive capacity, this percentage serving at the same time as a basis for allotting votes in the general assembly of the syndicate.

17 K. Bloch, 'On German Cartels' (July 1932) 5(3) *Journal of Business of the University of Chicago* 213.

expanded their own plants steadily.[18] They also took controlling interests in factories which supplied the machinery and apparatus for cement production in order to be able to influence firms outside the cartel agreement which might have decided to compete with cartel members.

After 1933, the government could by law establish compulsory cartels in any branch of industry and could by executive decree compel outsiders to join already-existing cartels.[19] The government's aim was to establish and maintain prices, to control raw material and production, and to promote industries that would later be essential during the Second World War.

Following the Second World War a number of industries were decartelized.[20] The aim of this deconcentration was to eliminate the excessive concentrations of economic powers, in particular in the form of cartels, syndicates and trusts. In 1947, therefore, the three Western powers acted separately and enacted military government decartelization laws in their respective zones of occupation, aiming at removing from Germany the potential and capacity for war as well as ensuring and promoting the reconstruction of the German economy.[21]

Pursuant to the the European Coal and Steel (ECSC) Treaty,[22] two factors were decisive in order for the High Authority of the Community to grant exemptions to concentrations impairing the maintenance of competition. The percentage of total Community output of the product which is controlled by the concentration in question, and the percentage of control it holds in a special market, seem to be important factors in granting such exemptions. The High Authority accepted the reconcentration of numerous German steel and coal companies. It also approved and regulated the establishment of several German coal-selling cartels

[18] Even during the boom, their plants could be operated at less than 50 per cent of their full capacity – a fact which was always threatening to break up the cartel.

[19] Law on Establishment of Compulsory Cartels (Gesetz über Errichtung von Zwangskartellen) of 15 July 1933, [1933] R.G.B. pt. 1.

[20] In the coal and steel industry, the following trusts: Vereinigte Stahlwerke, Klockner, Mannesmann, Reichs-werke, Hoesch, Gutehoffnungshütte, Otto Wolff, Ilseder Hütte, Thyssen-Bornemisza, Flick, Krupp. The big coal-selling syndicate (the former Rheno-Westphalian Coal Syndicate) was also liquidated. In the chemical industry: I.G. Farben trust. In the motion-picture industry: Cautio, UFI, UFA trust. In the banking industry: Deutsche Bank, Dresdner Bank, Commerzbank. See, for further details, Schwartz 1957.

[21] For an analysis of the Allied antitrust policy in Germany, see further H.K. Bock and H. Korsch, 'Decartelization and Deconcentration in the West German Economy Since 1945', in W. Friedmann, ed., *Antitrust Laws: A Comparative Symposium 38*, University of Toronto Faculty of Law Symposium vol. 3, 1956.

[22] Treaty of 18 April 1951.

under Article 65 of the treaty. Outside the coal, steel, chemical and motion picture industries, no new deconcentration proceedings were initiated after 1950, either by Allied or German authorities. Thus powerful enterprises continued to exist for a number of years.

The Act against Restraints of Competition, or Kartellgesetz, was promulgated in 1957 and considered cartels to be anti-competitive. This law replaced the postwar decartelization orders. Agreements made for a common purpose by enterprises or associations of enterprises were deemed anti-competitive. Substantial alterations to the law were made by the Amending Act of 1973.

The draft of the 1957 law contained exceptions for crisis, rationalization and export cartels. Following a rule-of-reason approach, three kinds of cartel agreement can be approved:

(1) crisis cartels: '[with] regard to enterprises engaged in production, ... if the applicant proves that, owing to a temporary decline of sales which is not due to a fundamental change in demand, the arrangement is necessary to prevent the total closing down of plants of the participating enterprises or of considerable parts of such plants';
(2) rationalization cartels: 'if the applicant proves that the arrangement serves to rationalize economic processes and is especially suited to raise considerably the efficiency or to foster considerably the economical operation of the participating enterprises from a technical, managerial or organizational point of view and to improve thereby the satisfaction of demand';
(3) export cartels: 'if the applicant proves that the proposed arrangement ... is suited to protect or promote foreign trade, especially by equalizing on world markets the competitive position of participating enterprises in relation to that of competitors who are not subject to this law or corresponding legislation of another country ... No [such] permission ... shall be granted for an arrangement which comprises the trade in goods or commercial services within the territory of the Federal Republic of Germany.'[23]

According to the definition of the term 'cartel' prior to the enactment of the Kartellgesetz in 1957, a cartel was deemed to be an agreement by or an association of independent enterprises engaged on the same level and in the same field of business formed for the common purpose of influencing collectively the market by regulating competition. A cartel was

[23] Draft law: Articles 2, 3, 5(1), 5(2), 7(1), 7(2). See further Schwartz 1957.

considered to be a horizontal combination, and the cartel members were legally independent entities, collectively aiming to influence the market through the regulation of competition.[24]

Earlier versions of the German legislation exempted rationalization and public-good cartels. Rationalization cartels were organized to take advantage of resources and technical improvements.[25] In public-good cartels, negative effects were outweighed by general economic advantages. Exempted enterprises had to register with the Cartel Office and were subject to regulation if they abused their position. The proponents of these exemptions argued that cartels might improve rationalization and automation, promote technical and social progress, and prevent or soften economic crisis by maintaining price levels and wages.

Schwartz argues that the main purpose of cartels in Germany was usually to protect against the risks of free competition and the dangers of economic crisis.[26] He adds that the German cartel movement began as a consequence of such a crisis. During the economic crisis of 1873, industry reacted by attempting to stabilize markets and firms. These attempts gave rise to the first cartels. Schwartz adds that German industry, protected against foreign imports by high tariffs, developed into one of the most powerful in Europe at the time.

These 'defensive' reasons for the creation of a cartel were later supplemented by such conduct as price-fixing (*Preiskartell*), allocation of quotas (*Kontingentierungskartell*); fixing of terms of payment and delivery (*Konditionenkartell*), standardization and rationalization of production (*Fertigungs und Rationalisierungskartell*), division of operation and market areas (*Gebietskartell*), and control and limitation of the use of inventions by restrictive patent-licensing agreements.

The draft 1957 Kartellgesetz declared cartel agreements null and void per se. The per se prohibition of cartels received fierce opposition, especially from German 'heavy' industry (German trade unions and the German association of trade unions also opposed the prohibition

[24] In the draft law of the 1957 Kartellgesetz, it was considered that the typical objectives and practices of cartels included price-fixing (*Preiskartell*), allocation of quotas (*Kontingentierungskartell*); fixing of terms of payment and delivery (*Konditionenkartell*), standardization and rationalization of production (*Fertigungs- und Rationalisierungskartell*), division of operation and market areas (*Gebietskartell*) and control and limitation of the use of inventions by restrictive patent-licensing agreements. See further Schwartz 1957.

[25] Grendell 1980.

[26] Schwartz 1957.

of cartels). They argued that cartel agreements should not be illegal per se when the conduct of trusts and single enterprises was not subject to such per se illegality.[27] They also added that a rationalization exemption would provide Germany with resource maximization on a national level and that a public-good exemption would grant the economics minister broad discretion to permit certain cartels in order to maintain general levels of employment, protect certain industries or strengthen domestic enterprises that compete in the international market. They added that such cartels can sustain the economy amidst an economic crisis by maintaining price levels and wages.

The 1957 legislation, which came into force in 1958, was taken as a model by advocates of relaxing the existing rules of competition in order to cope with crisis situations.[28] According to Article 4 of this legislation,

> In the case of a decline in sales due to a lasting change in demand the Federal Cartel Office may, on application, authorize production, manufacturing, jobbing or processing firms to conclude an agreement or take a decision, as specified in Article 1, if such agreement or decision is necessary for an orderly adjustment of capacity to demand and is in the interests of the general economy and the public interest.

In order for the crisis cartel to be exempted, the decrease in the sales must relate to a particular product (even if the product constitutes a market), must be market-wide and must be of long duration. Importantly, an imbalance between supply and demand at the time of applying for exemption is a necessary requirement as the aim of the agreement will be to reduce excess capacity (without necessarily eliminating it). This reduction can take place through plant closures or through a switch in the production of the plant. The statute may even allow for a price-fixing or quota allocation clause if such clauses are necessary to implement the reduction in capacity (these should not be the only means to achieve the reduction; they must play a subordinate role). Pursuant to the 1957 legislation, authorization of a crisis cartel cannot be denied because of the possibility of competitive interaction resulting in the same capacity reduction.[29] However, we should note that in periods of crisis, without an agreement on capacity reduction, as we shall see in the penultimate chapter, the firms that will survive will not necessarily be the most efficient ones.

[27] See further ibid.

[28] Joliet 1981.

[29] Ibid., at p. 409.

Judicial confirmation of the benefits of crisis cartels comes from the early case of *B. v. Saxon Woodpulp Manufacturers Association*,[30] where the former German Supreme Court argued in 1897:

> When the prices of the products of an industry fall to an unreasonably low level and the profitable operation of the industry is thereby endangered or made impossible, the resulting crisis is detrimental not only to the individual affected but also to the national economy. It is, therefore, in the interest of society that prices should not fall to an unreasonably low level. The legislature has clearly recognized this by enacting protective tariff laws designed to raise the price of certain products. It follows that it cannot be generally considered contrary to the public welfare for producers or manufacturers to combine with a view to preventing the consequent slump in prices. On the contrary, when prices continue to be so low that businessmen are threatened with ruin, combination is not merely a legitimate means of self-preservation but also serves the public interest. The formation of syndicates and cartels, such as the one here involved, has been suggested in many quarters as a means especially well adapted, if reasonably applied to the economy in general, to render a service in the prevention of uneconomic and wasteful overproduction, working at losses, and the catastrophes arising therefrom . . . Therefore cartel contracts can be objected to only from the viewpoint of public interest protected by freedom of trade, where they raise objections under the special circumstances of the individual case, particularly where the purpose of the cartel is to create monopoly and to exploit the consumers or where monopoly and exploitation of consumers actually result from the operation of such cartels.

In this case, Saxon woodpulp manufacturers formed an association aiming at ending fierce competition and at establishing a secure and reasonable price for their products. The defendant members sold directly to paper factories, thus violating the agreement, and argued that the agreement was invalid as it restricted freedom of trade. The *Saxon Woodpulp* decision provided impetus for acceptance of 'good' cartels.[31]

Significant amendments to the German Act against Restraints of Competition (*Gesetz gegen Wettbewerbsbeschränkungen* – GWB) entered into force on 1 January 1999. Unlike Article 101, the amendment to the GWB did not contain a general exemption provision. Only

[30] *B. v. den Sachsischen Holzstoff-Fabrikanten-Verband*, Reichsgericht (VI. Zivil-senat), 4 February 1897, 38 R.G.Z. 155.

[31] As Schwartz argues, having once introduced the doctrine of 'good' cartels and thus having eliminated considerations of economic policy, the Reichsgericht did not interpret freedom of trade in a manner inconsistent with legislative history and precedents. See further Schwartz 1957.

certain categories of agreement, such as joint purchasing, specialization and rationalization agreements, and so-called crisis cartels, were or could be exempted. A general exemption provision resembling Article 101(3) was introduced (§7).[32]

As regards specialization cartels, according to §3 of the 1999 amendment to the GWB,

> Agreements and decisions whose subject matter is the rationalisation of economic activities through specialisation may be exempted from the prohibition under section 1 provided the restraint of competition does not lead to the creation or strengthening of a dominant position.

As regards rationalization cartels, §5 states that

> (1) Agreements and decisions which serve to rationalize economic activities may be exempted from the prohibition under section 1 provided they are a suitable means of substantially increasing the efficiency or productivity of the participating undertakings in technical, commercial or organisational respects and of thereby improving the satisfaction of demand. The rationalisation effect should be of sufficient importance when compared with the restraint of competition connected with it. The restraint of competition shall not result in the creation or strengthening of a dominant position.
>
> (2) If the agreement or decision aims to achieve the rationalisation in conjunction with price agreements or through the establishment of joint purchasing or selling organisations, an exemption from the prohibition under section 1 may be granted, under the conditions of subsection (1), if the rationalisation effect cannot be achieved otherwise.

Structural crisis cartels are mentioned in §6, according to which,

> In the event of a decline in sales due to a lasting change in demand, agreements and decisions of undertakings engaged in production, manufacturing or processing may be exempted from the prohibition under section 1, provided the agreement or decision is necessary to systematically adjust capacity to demand, and the arrangement takes into account the conditions of competition in the economic sectors concerned.

Thus, as we can see, the 1999 amendment to the GWB maintained the exemptions for crisis cartels which were first introduced in the earlier versions of the GWB.

The German legislator in the seventh amendment of the GWB, which came into force in 2005, opted for a far-reaching harmonization

[32] D. Seeliger and D. Schroeder, 'Germany: Act against Restraint of Competition – Amendments Align Provisions with E.C. Law' (1999) 20(2) *ECLR* N26.

between the German cartel prohibition and its exemptions on the one hand and European Competition Law on the other, even for cases which stay below the threshold of affecting trade between member states. As a consequence, the wording of the current §1 GWB is very close to that of Article 101(1) of the TFEU, and §2(1) GWB mirrors Article 101(3) of the TFEU. In addition, §2(2) GWB specifies that Regulations of the Council or the Commission of the European Community on the application of Article 101(3) of the treaty to certain categories of agreements, decisions by associations of undertakings and concerted practices ('block exemption regulations') shall apply *mutatis mutandis* when applying §2(1) GWB. The provisions expressly state that this shall also apply where the agreements, decisions and practices mentioned in §2(1) GWB are inadequate to affect trade between member states.

There are still a few existing peculiarities of German competition law, such as §3 GWB, which provides an exemption from the cartel prohibition for cartels of small or medium-sized enterprises. Although the sections on rationalization cartels as well as structural crisis cartels were abolished, the seventh amendment of the GWB retained §3 applicable to small and medium-sized enterprises:

§3 Cartels of Small or Medium-Sized Enterprises

(1) Agreements between competing undertakings and decisions by associations of undertakings, whose subject matter is the rationalisation of economic activities through cooperation among enterprises, fulfil the conditions of §2(1) if:
   1. competition on the market is not significantly affected thereby, and
   2. the agreement or the decision serves to improve the competitiveness of small or medium-sized enterprises.

(2) Unless the conditions of Article 101(1) of the EC Treaty are satisfied, undertakings or associations of undertakings are – upon application – entitled to a decision pursuant to §32c, provided they demonstrate a significant legal or economic interest in such a decision. This provision becomes ineffective on 30 June 2009.

The almost complete harmonization of §§1 and 2 GWB with European competition law has rendered many former decisions of the German authorities and courts obsolete.

After looking at the legislation of Germany, which is one of the first countries to address structural crisis cartels, the chapter will now assess the legislation and case law on crisis cartels according to the European Coal and Steel Community Treaty as well as the Treaty of Rome.

5.3 The European Union

The Commission has defined structural overcapacity as existing

> where over a prolonged period all the undertakings concerned have been experiencing a significant reduction in their rates of capacity utilization, a drop in output accompanied by substantial operating losses and where the information available does not indicate that any lasting improvement can be expected in this situation in the medium term.[33]

In the European Union the problem of structural overcapacity after the second oil shock was exacerbated by increased competition at an international level that induced further reductions in capacity utilization in some industries. Such capacity reductions may not represent reductions of the least efficient capacity. Thus agreements among competitors to reduce capacity were likely to lead to better long-term prospects for the economy.

5.3.1 The European Coal and Steel Community Treaty (Treaty of Paris)

At the national and international levels, the coal and steel industries had been characterized by a high degree of concentration and cartelization. At the beginning of the Second World War, the steel market was organized into a system of national and international cartels. After the Second World War the the European Coal and Steel Community (ECSC) was created with the intention of pooling French and German coal and steel production. The ECSC Treaty was signed in Paris in 1951 and brought France, Germany, Italy and the Benelux countries together in a community with the aim of organizing the free movement of coal and steel and free access to sources of production. In addition to this, a common High Authority supervised the markets, respect for competition rules and price transparency.[34]

The ECSC Treaty sought competition in prices in industry, in contrast to the cartelization seen between the two world wars, when price competition played no part in the market for raw materials. The ECSC Treaty granted Community institutions the authority to combat crises arising from severe fluctuations of supply and demand. Mestmäcker has

[33] Twelfth Commission Competition Policy Report, points 38–9.

[34] See http://europa.eu/scadplus/treaties/ecsc_en.htm.

argued that the resulting excess capacity may have led to a kind of price competition, which in turn may be regarded as endangering the achievement of Community goals.[35]

Article 65(1) prohibits all agreements and concerted activity that would directly or indirectly prevent normal competitive conditions within the common market. Particularly offensive are agreements concerning price. Article 65(2) contains exceptions for agreements for specialization or for joint purchasing or selling, so long as these agreements contribute to an appreciable improvement in production or distribution and provided that the anti-competitive obligations of the agreement do not exceed those required for legitimate purposes.

The prohibition in Article 65 of the Treaty of Paris does not contain the same broad exceptions as are included in Article 101 of the Treaty of Rome:

> 1 All agreements between undertakings, decisions by associations of undertakings and concerted practices tending directly or indirectly to prevent, restrict or distort normal competition within the common market shall be prohibited, and in particular those tending:
> (a) to fix or determine prices;
> (b) to restrict or control production, technical development or investment;
> (c) to share markets, products, customers or sources of supply.
> However, the High Authority shall authorize specialization agreements or jointbuying or jointselling agreements in respect of particular products, if it finds that:
> (a) such specialization or such jointbuying or selling will make for a substantial improvement in the production or distribution of those products;
> (b) the agreement in question is essential in order to achieve these results and is not more restrictive than is necessary for that purpose; and
> (c) the agreement is not liable to give the undertakings concerned the power to determine the prices, or to control or restrict the production or marketing, of a substantial part of the products in question within the common market, or to shield them against effective competition from other undertakings within the common market.

If the High Authority finds that certain agreements are strictly analogous in nature and effect to those referred to above, having particular regard to the fact that this paragraph applies to distributive

[35] E.-J. Mestmäcker, 'The Applicability of the ECSC-Cartel Prohibition (Article 65) during a "Manifest Crisis"' (April–May 1984) 82(5–6) *Michigan Law Review* 1399.

undertakings, it shall also authorize them when satisfied that they meet the same requirements.

Authorizations may be granted subject to specified conditions and for limited periods. In such cases the High Authority would renew an authorization once or several times if it finds that the requirements of subparagraphs (a) to (c) were still met at the time of renewal.

The High Authority would revoke or amend an authorization if it found that as a result of a change in circumstances the agreement no longer meets these requirements, or that the actual results of the agreement or of the application thereof were contrary to the requirements for its authorization.

Decisions granting, renewing, amending, refusing or revoking an authorization would be published together with the reasons therefor; the restrictions imposed by the second paragraph of Article 47 would not apply thereto.

The High Authority could, as provided in Article 47, obtain any information needed for the application of this Article.

Any agreement or decision prohibited by paragraph 1 of Article 65 would be automatically void and may not be relied upon before any court or tribunal in the Member States.

The High Authority would have sole jurisdiction, subject to the right to bring actions before the Court, to rule whether any such agreement or decision was compatible with this Article.

On any undertaking which has entered into an agreement, or has enforced or attempted to enforce an agreement or decision, which is automatically void or an agreement for which authorization has been refused or revoked, the High Authority could impose fines or periodic penalty payments not exceeding twice the turnover on the products which were the subject of the agreement, decision or practice prohibited by this Article; if, however, the purpose of the agreement, decision or practice was to restrict production, technical development or investment, this maximum may be raised to 10% of the annual turnover of the undertakings in question in the case of fines, and 20% of the daily turnover in the case of periodic penalty payments.

As regards the steel industry, the Commission and the Council have found that the Community was facing a 'manifest crisis'[36] within the meaning of Article 58 of the ECSC Treaty. Pursuant to Article 58,

[36] *S.p.A. Ferriera Valsabbia v. Commission of the European Communities* (Case No 154/78), 1980 E. Comm. Ct. J. Rep. 907, at pp. 996–7.

1 In case of a decline in demand, if the High Authority deems that the Community is faced with a period of manifest crisis and that the means of action provided for in Article 57 are not sufficient to cope with that situation, it shall, after consulting the Consultative Committee and with the concurrence of the Council, establish a system of production quotas, accompanied, to the extent necessary, by the measures provided for in Article 74. If the High Authority fails to act, one of the member States may bring the matter to the attention of the Council which, acting by unanimous vote, may require the High Authority to establish a system of quotas.

2 The High Authority, after consultation with the enterprises and their associations, shall establish quotas on an equitable basis in accordance with the principles defined in Articles 2, 3 and 4. The High Authority may in particular regulate the rate of operation of the enterprises by appropriate levies on tonnages exceeding a reference level defined by a general decision. The sums thus obtained will be earmarked for the support of those enterprises whose production rate has dropped below the level envisaged, particularly in order to ensure as far as possible the maintenance of employment in those enterprises.

3 The system of quotas shall be terminated automatically upon a proposal to the Council by the High Authority after consulting the Consultative Committee, or by the government of one of the member States, except in the case of a contrary decision of the Council; such decision must be taken by unanimous vote, if the proposal originates with the High Authority, or by simple majority if the proposal originates with a government. The termination of the quota system shall be published by the High Authority.

4 The High Authority may impose upon enterprises violating the decisions taken by it in application of the present article, fines not to exceed a sum equal to the value of the irregular production.

As Mestmäcker has argued,[37] factors that have led to this crisis include structural peculiarities of the steel industry, an increase in production costs, a decrease in demand for steel and for steel products, and the resulting excess capacity in steel mills.

The general provisions in Article 60 concerning price are intended to prevent a deterioration of price competition. The system of setting prices in Article 60 takes into account the historical and economic peculiarities of the pricing system in the steel market, and should foster the development of an ordered and, in important respects, limited price competition:[38]

[37] Mestmäcker 1984.
[38] Ibid.

1. Pricing practices contrary to the provisions of Articles 2, 3 and 4 are prohibited, particularly:
   - unfair competitive practices, in particular purely temporary or purely local price reductions whose purpose is to acquire a monopoly position within the common market;
   - discriminatory practices involving the application by a seller within the single market of unequal conditions to comparable transactions, especially according to the nationality of the buyer.

   After consultation with the Consultative Committee and the Council, the High Authority may define the practices covered by this prohibition.
2. For the above purposes:
   (a) the prices scales and conditions of sales to be applied by enterprises within the single market shall be made public to the extent and in the form prescribed by the High Authority after consultation with the Consultative Committee; if the High Authority deems that an enterprise has chosen an abnormal base point for its price quotations, in particular one which makes it possible to evade the provisions of subparagraph (b) below, it will make the appropriate recommendations to that enterprise.
   (b) the prices charged by an enterprise within the common market, calculated on the base of the point chosen for the enterprise's price scale must not as a result of the methods of quotation:
      - be higher than the price indicated by the price scale in question for a comparable transaction; or
      - be less than this price by a margin greater than:
      - either the margin which would make it possible to align the offer in question on that price scale, set up on the basis of another point, which procures for the buyer the lowest price at the place of delivery;
      - or a limit fixed by the High Authority for each category of products, after consultation with the Consultative Committee, taking into account the origin and destination of such products.

These decisions would be taken when they appear necessary to avoid disturbances in all or any part of the common market, or disequilibria which would result from a divergence between the methods of price quotation used for a product and for the materials which enter into its manufacture.

These decisions would not prevent enterprises from aligning their quotations on the prices offered by enterprises outside the Community, provided that such transactions were reported to the High Authority; the latter may, in case of abuse, limit or eliminate the right of the enterprises in question to benefit from this exception.

The discrimination prohibition of Article 60, the duty of steel undertakings to publish a price list and the requirement that the actual prices conform to the published list modified competitive conditions in the steel market. The requirement of compliance with the published price contributed to conscious parallelism. Competition was further modified by the requirement of choosing and adhering to a certain basing point.[39]

The Treaty of Paris entitled the Commission to fix minimum prices under Article 61, as well as to establish production quotas under Article 58, but the Commission had no ability to impose capacity reduction. Quotas were established for individual undertakings to prevent increases in market share at the expense of competitors. In its Communication of 14 November 1981, the Commission argued that price competition remained possible despite the imposition of quotas.[40] Mestmäcker argued that the imposition of quotas alone did not foreclose normal competitive conditions.[41] The European Court of Justice (ECJ) confirmed this argument.[42] The ECJ emphasized that the ECSC Treaty required the Commission to consider the objectives of Articles 2, 3 and 4 in its imposition of quotas. These objectives included the protection of competition.[43]

The ECSC Treaty contained no provision that precluded the application of Article 65 to the Commission's establishment of production quotas under Article 58. If these provisions proved insufficient to combat the crisis and satisfy the aim enunciated in Article 3(c),[44] then the Commission was entitled to establish minimum prices under Article 61:

[39] Ibid.

[40] *S.p.A. Ferriera Valsabbia v. Commission of the European Communities* (Case No 154/78), 1980 E. Comm. Ct. J. Rep. 907, 1009.

[41] Mestmäcker 1984.

[42] *Maizena GmbH v. Council of the European Communities* (Case No 139/79), 1980 E. Comm. Ct. J. Rep. 3393; *Cooperatieve vereniging 'Suiker Unie' v. Commission of the European Communities* (Case No 40/73), 1975 E. Comm. Ct. J. Rep. 1663.

[43] *S.p.A. Ferriera Valsabbia v. Commission of the European Communities* (Case No 154/78), 1980 E. Comm. Ct. J. Rep. 907, 1009.

[44] Article 3:

Within the framework of their respective powers and responsibilities and in the common interest, the institutions of the Community shall: . . .

(c) seek the establishment of the lowest prices which are possible without requiring any corresponding rise either in the prices charged by the same enterprises in other transactions or in the price-level as a whole in another period, while at the same time permitting necessary amortization and providing normal possibilities of remuneration for capital invested.

> On the basis of studies undertaken in cooperation with the enterprises and their associations in accordance with the provisions of the first paragraph of Article 46 and the third paragraph of Article 48, and after consultation with the Consultative Committee and the Council as to the advisability of these measures as well as concerning the price level which they determine, the High Authority may fix for one or more products subject to its jurisdiction:
>
> (a) maximum prices within the common market, if it deems that such a decision is necessary to attain the objectives defined in Article 3 and particularly in paragraph (c) thereof;
> (b) minimum prices within the common market, if it deems that a manifest crisis exists or is imminent and that such a decision is necessary to attain the objectives defined in Article 3;
> (c) after consultation with the enterprises concerned or their associations, and according to methods adapted to the nature of the export markets, minimum or maximum export prices, if such action can be effectively supervised and appears necessary either because of dangers to the enterprises on account of the situation of the market or to pursue in international economic relations the objective defined in Article 3 paragraph (f), without prejudice, in the case of minimum prices, to the application of the measures provided for in the last paragraph of section 2 of Article 60.
>
> In fixing price limits the High Authority shall take into account the need to assure the ability to compete both of the coal and steel industries and of the consuming industries, in accordance with the principles defined in Article 3, paragraph (c).
>
> If the High Authority should fail to act under the circumstances described above, the government of one of the member States may refer the matter to the Council; the latter may, by unanimous decision, invite the High Authority to fix such maximum or minimum prices.

The Commission must consider the competitive capabilities of the relevant firms and the principles stated in Article 3(c). If these measures proved insufficient, Article 58(1) obliged the Commission to establish a system of production quotas.[45]

Thus the ECSC Treaty explicitly empowered the Commission to fix prices in periods of crisis. These minimum prices were established

[45] The Commission instituted production quotas in October 1980, under a system by which it determines appropriate production levels for individual undertakings on a quarterly basis. The regulation includes all steel undertakings within the meaning of Article 80, with the exception of small producers. Commission Decision 2794/80/ECSC, establishing a system of steel production quotas for undertakings in the iron and steel industry, 23 OJ Eur. Comm. (No L 291) 1 (31 October 1980).

pursuant to Article 61(b), according to which if the Commission finds that a manifest crisis exists, it can establish such prices in order to ensure that the objectives identified in Article 3 of the Treaty of Paris are met.[46] The Commission outlined recommended prices; it did not impose minimum prices. Non-compliance with these prices could involve sanctions according to Article 64 of the Treaty of Paris.[47] As Joliet has mentioned, once firms had increased their prices, they were asked, pursuant to Article 60(2)(b), to make these prices compulsory in the event of any price variation from the published prices, except to the extent allowed to meet a competitor's tender.[48]

The Commission established prices after consultation with steel undertakings.[49] In establishing prices, the Commission should ensure 'that the coal and steel industries and the consumer industries remain competitive, in accordance with the principles laid down in Article 3(c)'.[50] In the Commission's Communication of 14 November 1981, on the goals of its steel policy, the Commission requested steel undertakings to increase prices by specific amounts.[51] If the participating undertakings had published their price lists in accordance with price agreements, then the application of Article 60 would have led to the preclusion of all price competition. The particularly strict application of Article 60, announced by the Commission in its Communication of 14 November 1981,[52] and the sanctions to be imposed against violators, led to the conclusion that the Commission was using its power to supervise an illegal cartel.

Under the crisis conditions in the steel market, Community institutions did not feel obligated to apply the prohibition of Article 65. Instead, as Mestmäcker argued,[53] anti-competitive agreements had

[46] Although pursuant to Article 61(b) the Commission can fix prices that apply to producers, it cannot fix minimum prices for the dealers.

[47] The Commission can impose fines not exceeding twice the value of sales effected at unauthorized prices. See further OJ C133/4, 1978; OJ C182/2, 1978; OJ C103/11, 1979; OJ C277/3, 1978.

[48] Joliet 1981, at p. 429. See also OJ L114/18, 1977; OJ C174/2, 1977; OJ L352/17, 1977; OJ L87/2, 1978; OJ L176/45, 1978; OJ L370/87, 1978; OJ L344/19, 1979.

[49] Protocol of the Consultative Committee of the ECSC, Document No 9394-81, 16 November 1981, at 2 EN/ks.

[50] ECSC Treaty, Article 61(2).

[51] 'The Commission invites the steel industry to raise its list of prices for bulk products.' Communication from the Commission concerning the objectives of the steel price policy, 24 OJ Eur. Comm. (No C 294) 3 (14 November 1981).

[52] Ibid.

[53] Mestmäcker 1984.

been required as a means of combating the crisis by Community institutions. He added that the measures taken by Community institutions against the manifest crisis did not preclude the applicability of Article 65 to price agreements. The ECJ emphasized that when the Commission is empowered to take extraordinary measures that interfere with the workings of a free market, the provisions of the treaty under which the measure is taken stipulate precisely which Articles the Commission is obliged to take into account.[54]

The collapse in steel prices that resulted from excess capacity, and efforts by undertakings to recover only a portion of their overhead costs, induced the Community to accept certain measures aimed at combating the structural crisis facing the steel industry.[55] Among these measures were anti-competitive agreements among steel undertakings. Mestmäcker interestingly added that resort to concerted and voluntary action by undertakings has become a nearly routine component of the Community's steel policy.[56]

He added that undertakings cannot restrict competition, not even in order to contribute to the achievement of Community goals. Only in cases approved and controlled by the High Authority could cartels organize and operate. He further noted that undertakings were not exempt from the prohibition of Articles 4 and 65, and may not create illegal cartels.[57]

In relation to price-fixing, the ECSC Treaty prohibited practices which discriminated according to price, unfair competitive practices and discriminatory practices involving the application of dissimilar conditions to comparable transactions. In certain circumstances, though, such as a manifest crisis, the High Authority could fix maximum or minimum prices either within the Community or in relation to the export market.[58] During the coal crisis in the 1960s the High Authority of the ECSC attempted to introduce greater flexibility in the ECSC Treaty but the ECJ rejected a proposal to include in the

[54] *S.p.A. Ferriera Valsabbia v. Commission of the European Communities* (Case No 154/78), 1980 E. Comm. Ct. J. Rep. 907, 1009.

[55] The High Authority may, as provided in Article 47, obtain any information needed for the application of this Article, either by making a special request to the parties concerned or by means of regulations stating the kinds of agreement, decision or practice which must be communicated to it.

[56] Mestmäcker 1984.

[57] Ibid.

[58] See http://europa.eu/scadplus/treaties/ecsc_en.htm.

treaty clauses allowing restructuring agreements. However, as Joliet argued, Article 33 of the Treaty of Paris limited the extent of control of the ECJ. If the Commission alleged that a crisis existed, this argument could be challenged only if there was evidence of failure to comply with the treaty.[59]

As the brief analysis of the case law below illustrates, such agreements include measures that are indispensible to co-ordinated reduction in capacity. In order for such agreements to be exempt there needs to exist a detailed plan that will outline the reductions in the capacity of the undertakings as well as the timeline for reductions.

Crisis case law in the EU pursuant to ECSC Treaty

Steel cases

In 1980 the High Commission took three decisions under Article 65 of the ECSC Treaty condemning quota agreements and concerted practices.[60] Since 1974 steel prices were lower than production costs, thus steel producers were unable to cover production costs. In the French case, five of the principal French steel producers fixed prices in 1974 and 1975. Two of the undertakings were also involved in quota agreements. In the German case, eight of the principal German steel producers adopted a quota agreement. Three of the involved undertakings were repeatedly involved in similar quota agreements. In the Franco-German case, most of the French and German producers operated an interpenetration agreement to limit deliveries of steel products in each other's home markets.

As the tenth Report on Competition Policy states, in setting the fine, the High Commission took into account the financial position of the French and German steel producers. The High Commission argued that measures to combat a crisis did not entitle undertakings to apply quota agreements and concerted pricing practices in violation of competition rules. The High Commission interestingly states that the Commission may determine the measures required to deal with a crisis.

The Commission argued that the iron and steel industry should restore profitable price levels in accordance with Article 3(c) of the ECSC Treaty.

[59] Joliet 1981.

[60] Decision of 27 March 1980.

Thus through voluntary supply commitments and imposed quotas it established a better quantitative balance between supply and demand. In addition, in order to ensure the success of these quantitative measures, it ensured that producers adopted a well-ordered pricing policy.[61]

The Commission interestingly called upon the steel companies to decide on certain price rises with effect from 1 January 1982. The Commission clarified that it did not tolerate price-fixing agreements but, pursuant to the tasks of the ECSC Treaty, might play an active role as regards prices in the interest of all parties concerned.[62]

Steel flat products

The High Commission, in its 90/417/ECSC decision,[63] imposed fines on six major Community producers of stainless steel flat products for an agreement to limit deliveries for cold-rolled stainless steel flat products. The High Commission imposed a fine of ECU 425,000 for this agreement which restricted production and induced market-sharing.

The fines were lower than the usual fines in such cases, as the steel industry was in restructuring and a quota system was imposed. As the twentieth Report on Competition Policy states, all the ECSC cases after the quota system had ended would be fined along the lines of the Treaty of Rome cases.

Steel beams

In the Steel beams cases,[64] the Commission imposed fines ranging from ECU 600,000 to ECU 32 million (on British Steel) upon the major European producers for price-fixing, allocation of quotas and an extensive exchange of confidential information, dating from 1984. This decision was contentious as the sector was experiencing restructuring difficulties and controversy over state aid. The Commission, while publicly refusing a trade-off between competition and other Community policies, mitigated the severity of its approach. Interestingly, due to the difficult conditions of the industry, the Commission excluded the 'manifest crisis' period of 1980 to 1988 in determining the duration of the infringements.

[61] Eleventh Report on Competition Policy, para. 44.
[62] Ibid, para. 45.
[63] OJ L220, 15 August 1990.
[64] 16 February 1994.

5.3.2 *Treaty establishing the European Economic Community (Treaty of Rome)*

Looking at the academic literature of earlier decades, it is worthwhile examining the approach that was believed to have been taken by the EEC towards anti-competitive agreements and in competition enforcement in general. Grendell has argued that the EEC appears to have different objectives than does the US.[65] He argues that under US legislation, free competition is paramount, whereas the primary underlying goal of EEC antitrust legislation, according to Grendell, is 'rationalization'. By the latter term Grendell implies the promotion of economic development and efficiency through more rational allocation of Community resources.

Early European Commission reports on competition policy strongly suggested that European policy was aimed at the promotion of consumer welfare. The European Commission, first Report on Competition Policy, in 1971 stated that

> competition policy endeavours to maintain or create effective conditions of competition by means of rules applying to enterprises in both private and public sectors. Such a policy encourages the best possible use of productive resources for the greatest possible benefit of the economy as a whole and for the benefit, in particular, of the consumer.

The Commission and the European Court of Justice, in their fundamental decisions reached in the 1970s, interpreted the objective of protecting competition as referring to the protection of the economic freedom of market actors. These important decisions of the Commission and Community courts were not based on economics or on consumer welfare, but on the protection of the economic freedom of market players as well as on preventing firms from using their economic power to undermine competitive structures.[66]

In *Continental Can*,[67] the Court ruled that

> abuse may therefore occur if an undertaking in a dominant position strengthens such position in such a way that the degree of dominance

[65] Grendell 1980.

[66] L. Gormsen, 'Article 82 EC: Where Are We Coming from and Where Are We Going to?' (March 2006) 2(2) *Competition Law Review* 19.

[67] Case 6/72 *Europemballage Corp. and Continental Can Co. Inc. v. Commission* (*Continental Can*), [1973] ECR I-215, §26.

> reached substantially fetters competition, i.e. that only undertakings remain in the market whose behaviour depends on the dominant one . . . it can . . . be regarded as an abuse if an undertaking holds a position so dominant that the objectives of the Treaty are circumvented by an alteration to the supply structure which seriously endangers the consumer's freedom of action in the market, such a case necessarily exists if practically all competition is eliminated.

As Grendell has argued,[68] the EEC rule of reason included an assessment beyond the economic impact of the arrangement to see if the agreement was justified. Unlike the rule-of-reason approach that was taken in the US, which balances the benefits to and burdens on competition, Grendell argued that an agreement between petroleum companies to drill jointly for oil and sell such oil at a fixed price would likely be allowed by the EEC on the basis of efficient resource allocation, but that under the US per se approach it would likely be prohibited.

The thorny issue of crisis cartels in Europe was eminent in the 1960s and 1970s. Two approaches were suggested to legalize crisis cartels. One referred to a regulation enabling crisis cartels to be authorized.

In the late 1970s, the synthetic-fibres sector was under strong pressure from decreasing demand and excess capacity. The commissioner for industrial affairs, Davignon, suggested that the producers co-operate in order to withstand the crisis. The US companies would not be able to participate due to the sanctions of §1 of the Sherman Act. The agreement could not be exempt pursuant to Article 101(3). Commissioner Davignon and Commissioner for Competition Vouel produced a proposal on a draft regulation pursuant to Article 83 specifically covering crisis cartels. According to Article 103 TFEU,

> The appropriate regulations or directives to give effect to the principles set out in Articles 81 and 82 shall be laid down by the Council, acting by a qualified majority on a proposal from the Commission and after consulting the European Parliament.
>
> The regulations or directives referred to in paragraph 1 shall be designed in particular:
>
> (a) to ensure compliance with the prohibitions laid down in Article 101(1) and in Article 82 by making provision for fines and periodic penalty payments;
> (b) to lay down detailed rules for the application of Article 101(3), taking into account the need to ensure effective supervision on the one

[68] Grendell 1980.

hand, and to simplify administration to the greatest possible extent on the other;

(c) to define, if need be, in the various branches of the economy, the scope of the provisions of Articles 81 and 82;

(d) to define the respective functions of the Commission and of the Court of Justice in applying the provisions laid down in this paragraph;

(e) to determine the relationship between national laws and the provisions contained in this Section or adopted pursuant to this Article.

Under this proposed regulation, Article 101(1) would be declared inapplicable to agreements between firms aimed at balancing excess capacity with a lasting decline in demand. This reduction should be effected by means that are indispensable to the achievement of the co-ordinated reduction. The Council of Ministers would decide, upon proposal by the Commission, whether a co-ordinated reduction in the capacity of a sector was necessary.

The proposed regulation met with significant opposition from some members of the Commission. Opponents argued that such a regulation would open the floodgates of cartelization. In addition, there were concerns regarding both the success of these crisis cartels and the implications of such crisis cartels for downstream industries.[69]

The essential question was whether practices that were deemed illegal under Article 101 would be considered legal under Article 103. Articles 101(3) and 103 did not provide an adequate statutory basis for such a general regulation.[70] According to Joliet, the Council of Ministers cannot, under Article 103(c), rule out the applicability of Article 101 except within the limits imposed by the features of the sector.[71] The sectors included in the proposed regulation were not determined in advance and thus the regulation would apply to all possible sectors. Furthermore, the proposed regulation would aim at modifying the exemption criteria of Article 101(3) rather than rendering Article 101(1) inapplicable to a particular sector. However, the Council of Ministers cannot provide more flexible exemption conditions than those

[69] Joliet 1981, at p. 414.

[70] Article 85 is renumbered as Article 101 and Article 87 is renumbered as Article 83. Pursuant to the Lisbon Treaty (EC Official Journal C 306/2 of 17 December 2007, at p. 1) the provisions on anti-competitive agreements (formerly Article 81) are now in Article 101; abuse of dominance (formerly Article 82) now in Article 102; public undertakings (formerly Article 86) now in Article 106; and state aid (formerly Articles 87–8) now in Articles 107–8.

[71] Joliet 1981, at p. 419.

contained in Article 101(3). Furthermore, the proposed regulation could not be adopted pursuant to Article 231 EC as that Article enables the Council of Ministers to add new rules to the treaty (such as for mergers) rather than reduce the applicability of existing rules (such as Article 101). For such an amendment to the applicability of the competition rules there needs to be an amendment to the treaty.

It should also be noted that granting to the Commission power to suspend the enforcement of competition legislation has serious political ramifications. In 1978, the Commission announced that it would not propose to the Council of Ministers a draft regulation which would allow it to suspend application of Article 101(1) to crisis cartels for a period of one to five years.[72]

The second approach to legalizing crisis cartels relied on crisis cartels being exempt pursuant to Article 101(3). It has been argued that a crisis cartel cannot satisfy the Article 101(3) criteria as such cartels may involve restriction in output, price maintenance and market division. A crisis cartel may also not satisfy the criterion of consumer benefit envisaged in Article 101(3). A crisis cartel will require the co-ordinated reduction of capacity allowing undertakings possibly to eliminate competition. In the analysis below, but also in the penultimate chapter, we shall see cases where the above argument does not hold.

As regards crisis cartels, the Commission has, in the seventh Report on Competition Policy, announced that measures to open competition were necessary in circumstances of adverse social and regional conditions. According to Sharpe,[73] these measures were general in application and were aimed at suspending the implementation of Article 101 under certain circumstances.

In the eighth Report on Competition Policy, the Commission argued that it was inclined to accept that under certain conditions agreements between firms aimed at reducing excess capacity may be authorized under Article 101(3), but only where the firms have not simultaneously, whether by agreement or by concerted practice, fixed prices, production or delivery quotas.[74]

The Commission later indicated that agreements to reduce structural

[72] Commission statement of 26 July 1978. See further B. Hawk, *United States, Common Market and International Antitrust: A Comparative Guide*, 2nd ed., Vol. 2, Law & Business Inc./Harcourt Brace Jovanovich, 1985, at p. 146.

[73] T. Sharpe, 'The Commission's Proposals on Crisis Cartels' (1980) 17 *C.M.L. Rev.* 75.

[74] Eighth Report on Competition Policy, para. 13.

overcapacity which involve all or a majority of the undertakings in an entire sector can be accepted if they are aimed solely at a co-ordinated reduction of overcapacity and do not restrict the commercial freedom of the parties involved. Agreements involving a smaller number of firms can also be accepted if they aim at allowing reciprocal specialization in order to achieve closure of excess capacity. However, the Commission argues that such agreements must not incorporate any price-fixing, quota-fixing or market allocation.[75]

The Commission has stated that structural overcapacity occurs when, over a long period, undertakings experience a reduction in their capacity utilization and a drop in output as well as operating losses, and when there is no sign of possible recovery in the medium term.[76] In the twenty-third Report on Competition Policy,[77] the Commission argued that it may condone such agreements which aim at reducing overcapacity as long as the agreement applies to a sector as a whole. Such agreements will not involve price-fixing or quota-fixing and will not impair the free decision-making of firms.

In a case involving a restructuring plan to tackle excess capacity in bricks in the Netherlands, an agreement notified to the Commission for exemption was initially not approved as it contained several restrictions of competition, including a quota agreement. The agreement was exempted after the parties excluded any fixing of prices or output and since the agreement was in line with the criteria outlined in the twenty-third Report on Competition Policy, and will be analysed below.[78]

In the *Polypropylene* case,[79] the Commission discovered evidence in 1983 that the major polypropylene producers supplying the EEC market had been involved, since 1977, in a cartel where the firms were fixing prices, setting sales targets and allocating markets. After a meeting between producers of polypropylene and the Commission, a report on the problems facing the industry concluded that a 'crisis cartel' was not warranted and that bilateral or multilateral agreements to reduce excessive capacity would mitigate the adverse conditions of the industry. The

[75] Thirteenth Report on Competition Policy, para. 56.

[76] Twelfth Report on Competition Policy, para. 38.

[77] Point 84.

[78] Twenty-third Report on Competition Policy, para. 89. IV/34.456 – *Stichting Baksteen* OJ L 131/15.

[79] *Re Polypropylene*, OJ 1986 L230.

Commission outlined its view on crisis cartels and argued that price- and quota-fixing are usually unacceptable.[80]

The Commission will authorize a restructuring plan involving sectoral agreements if it believes that the Article 101(3) criteria are met. These criteria will be met if the reduction in the capacity of the sector will in the long term lead to more efficent capacity utilization, enhancing the competitiveness of the sector and thus benefiting consumers. Thus a detailed plan of plant closures and avoidance of the creation of new capacity are also necessary factors in the agreement being accepted by the Commission.

Furthermore, the reduction in capacity can in the long run increase profitability, restore competitiveness and mitigate adverse impacts on competitiveness.[81] The agreement must contain a detailed and binding programme of closures for each production centre in order to ensure reduction of existing capacity and to prevent the creation of new capacity. The incorporated restrictions of competition must be indispensable in order to achieve the restructuring of the sector. The agreement must be of a certain duration that will allow for the technical implementation of the capacity reduction.[82] Consumers must enjoy a share of the benefits resulting from the agreement, since in the long run they will benefit from a competitive environment while in the short run they will not have been deprived of choice of product.

Thus, in a nutshell, the conditions that need to be fulfilled before an exemption is granted (implying that the Article 101(3) criteria are satisfied) include improvement of production and distribution,

[80] See further the following Annual Reports on Competition Policy: second, points 29–31; eighth, point 42; eleventh, points 45–8; twelfth, points 38–41; thirteenth, points 56–61; fourteenth, points 80–5. See also the following cases: *Re BPCL/ICI*, OJ 1984 L212/1, [1985] 2 CMLR 330, noted (1986) 11 *E.L. Rev.* 67; *Re Synthetic Fibres*, OJ 1984 L207/17, [1985] 1 CMLR 787, noted (1986) 11 *E.L. Rev.* 64; *Re ENI/Montedison*, OJ 1987 L5/13; *Re Akzo/Shell (Rovin)* Bull. EC 5-1984, fourteenth Report on Competition Policy, para. 85, noted (1985) 10 *E.L. Rev.* 229; *Re Montedison/Hercules (Himont)*, 1988 L50/18. See also the preliminary notices in *Re Zinc Shutdown Agreement*, OJ 1983 C164/3, [1983] 2 CMLR 473 Bull. EC-1987 point 2.1.71., *Re PRB/Shell*, OJ 1984 C189/2. See further Case Comment on *Re Polypropylene*, *E.L. Rev.* 1988, 13(3), 205–9.

[81] The Commission seems to place importance on non-competition factors such as employment. The Commission clearly states that reorganization operations should be such as to secure the employment situation within the sector concerned. Twelfth Report on Competition Policy, para. 39.

[82] As the Commission states in the twelfth Report on Competition Policy, para. 39, exchange of information is acceptable provided it does not induce co-ordination either on sale conditions or on remaining capacity.

indispensability of the restrictions, incomplete elimination of competition, a fair share of the benefits to consumers, and finally the benefits outweighing the disadvantages.

The agreement aiming at the co-ordinated reduction in capacity will not be likely to restrict competition since the parties to the agreement will independently decide their strategies on elements other than the co-ordinated reduction in capacity. There may be in the market other firms not party to the agreement which may be able to provide competitive constraints. In addition, the agreement must constitute indispensable means of achieving the necessary capacity reduction. The limited duration of the agreement, the existence of firms in the industry which are not party to the agreement and the fact that the co-ordinated reduction in capacity is the only element in the business strategy of the firms constitute reassurances that competition will not be eliminated.

The Commission has faced difficulties in exempting crisis cartels pursuant to the Article 101(3) criteria. Thus the Commission has in some cases relied on the maintenance of employment in order to exempt such agreements. The ECJ in the *Metro* case[83] argued that a medium-term supply agreement was deemed to satisfy the first condition of Article 101(3) since it was considered likely to help maintain employment in situations of economic crisis. Similarly the ECJ in *Walt Wilhelm* held that

> while the Treaty's primary object is to eliminate by this means (proceedings under Article 85(1)) the obstacles to the free movement of goods within the Common Market and to confirm and safeguard the unity of that market, it also commits the Community authorities to carry out certain positive, though indirect, action with a view to promoting a harmonious development of economic activities within the whole community in accordance with Article 2 of the Treaty.[84]

[83] Case 27/76 [1977] ECR 1875.

[84] Case 14/68 *Walt Wilhelm v. Bundeskartellamt*, 13 February 1969. As S.B. Hornsby, 'Competition Policy in the 80s: More Policy Less Competition?' (1987) 12(2) *E.L. Rev.* 79, argues, this passage is increasingly used to provide a legal base for the Commission's use of the competition rules to achieve other policy objectives. Hornsby adds that decisions explicitly justifying crisis cartels by reference to distortions caused by state aid could be legally justified in appropriate cases by reference to the preliminary provisions of the treaty as indicated by the European Court in *Walt Wilhelm*. Not only have the Commission and the European Court used such a legal technique before (see Case 6/72, *Europemballage and Continental Can v. Commission*, [1973] ECR 215; Cases 6 and 7/73 *Commercial Solvents v. Commission*, [1974] ECR 223 motif 25), but also emphasis on the more economic criteria set out in the preliminary Articles would be more consistent with Article 101(3) than references to employment considerations which are not referred to at all in the rules applying to undertakings. See further Hornsby 1987, at p. 93.

As the Commission interestingly argues, a factor that will be taken into account is the impact of the capacity co-ordination on the mitigation of the adverse impact of the crisis on employment.[85] The Commission explicitly states that reorganization operations should also be used to stabilize and secure the employment situation in the sector concerned.[86] The Commission uses the positive impact of a co-ordination of business conduct of competitors on employment as a factor favouring exemption of the agreement.

However, Hornsby argues that the *Metro* judgment may not justify an exemption pursuant to Article 101(3) for industry-wide crisis cartels.[87] The maintenance of employment is mentioned neither in the competition rules applying to undertakings nor in Article 2 of the Treaty of Rome.

There have been a number of cases under the Treaty of Rome involving crisis cartels. As the following analysis will illustrate, in the majority of the cases the undertakings requested an exemption pursuant to Article 101(3).

Crisis cartel case law pursuant to the Treaty of Rome

There can be multiple types of agreement that companies may use to overcome capacity problems. Crisis cartels, through bilateral or multilateral agreements, can satisfy the conditions of Article 101(3). Bilateral agreements are more likely a form of rationalization agreement (as achieving the co-ordinated reduction in capacity among two firms is easier than among a larger number of firms) but are less likely to satisfy the conditions of Article 101(3). To satisfy the criteria of Article 101(3), such agreements should lead to a reduction in the excess capacity, rationalize production and not lead to elimination of competition. In addition, restrictions on imports imposed by intergovernmental voluntary restraint agreements may also lead to a reduction in the excess capacity of a sector.[88]

The following analysis presents cases of crisis cartels and arguments for them, where arguments were made that a crisis in a market necessitated anti-competitive conduct. More importance was placed on such arguments in some of these cases than in others.

[85] Twenty-third Report on Competition Policy, para. 85.

[86] Ibid., point 88.

[87] Hornsby 1987, at p. 93.

[88] For further information on such agreements see L. Ritter and D. Braun, *European Competition Law*, 3rd ed., Kluwer, 2004, at p. 185.

Cementregeling voor Nederland

The Commission adopted a stricter approach under the Treaty of Rome than under the Treaty of Paris. The *Cementregeling voor Nederland* case concerned an agreement within the Netherlands market.[89] Varying quantities of the product were reserved by the members of the agreement for sale, in competitive conditions. The Dutch market was sealed off to imports from other member states.[90] The Commission had forbidden these restraints as part of other proceedings[91] and in 1971 it had forbidden the dealers' price control arrangements. Although they had discontinued common price-fixing and standardized selling terms, the producers involved had applied for exemption for a limited-duration modified quota system, the CRN-1971, which they wished to maintain for a transitional period.

The Commission did not agree that the Netherlands market should remain closed to free imports of cement from other member states. The Commission argued that exemption under Article 101(3) could not be granted to an arrangement as restrictive as a quota agreement, as the quota agreement was not indispensable to the achievement of the objectives pursued by the undertakings concerned. Quota agreements are unlikely to solve the problem of surplus capacity.

The Commission also refused exemption from Article 101(1) prohibition for the Belgian La Cimenterie belge–CIMBEL SA cement industry agreement.[92]

Polyester fibres

In this case, the Commission argued that the notified agreement on cut polyester fibres did not satisfy the criteria for exemption under Article 101(3). The parties argued that the agreement was designed to ensure co-ordination of investment and rationalization of production with a view to eliminating or preventing excess capacity in the industry. In this case the Commission argued that the agreement failed to meet the criteria included in Article 101(3), since it covered a wider area and extended to the participants' production and marketing policies.[93]

[89] Commission Decision of 18 December 1972, OJ L 303, 31 December 1972, p. 7.
[90] Second Report on Competition Policy.
[91] First Report on Competition Policy, para. 9.
[92] Commission Decision of 22 December 1972, OJ L 303, 31 December 1972, p. 24.
[93] Ibid. The agreement was cancelled and the notification withdrawn.

Man-made fibres

In 1978, the leading producers of man-made fibres notified the Commission of an agreement, for exemption,[94] which provided for a reduction in capacity according to a structured plan. The Commission argued that structural crisis cartels involving an agreement to cut capacity would be exempt pursuant to Article 101(3), provided that the agreement did not involve agreements on production, sales or prices.[95]

The agreement was not at first exempted, but after the parties' amendments concerning the elimination of all clauses related to the commercial conduct of the undertakings, the agreement was exempted.

Zinc producers

The 'shutdown' agreement notified for exemption by six major producers achieved exempt status due to the heavy financial losses that the European zinc industry was facing.[96] The agreement was of fixed duration, which played a significant role in it being exempted, and the companies would voluntarily and unilaterally close capacity and notify a trustee of their closure plans. The Commission argued that if the viability of the sector improved, the agreement could not be exempted. The agreement involved voluntary closure of plants in order to reduce capacity.[97]

Synthetic fibres

As mentioned above, following the suggestion of Commissioner for Industrial Affairs Davignon, in 1977 eleven major manufacturers of synthetic fibres agreed to reduce capacity and guarantee increased sales by Italian members. The Commission was initially favourable to granting an exemption. However, it concluded that the agreement was anticompetitive as it involved market-sharing, production quotas and price provisions. Arguably, it is difficult to envisage how a co-ordinated reduction in capacity, which is the aim of a crisis cartel, can be achieved without any agreement on price or quota, since price competition between the parties to the agreement, and also from external sources, can affect the co-ordinated reduction in capacity.

In 1984, the Commission accepted that joint measures aiming at the reduction of structural overcapacity or other restructuring measures in

[94] Eighth Report on Competition Policy, para. 42.

[95] Tenth Report on Competition Policy, para. 46.

[96] *Zinc Producers*, L 362/40, 23 December 1982.

[97] Thirteenth Report on Competition Policy, para. 58.

an industry which is in a state of crisis may be accepted provided that effective competition is not eliminated, that consumers have alternative choices of suppliers and that conduct such as fixing prices or quotas is not involved.[98]

In 1984, the Commission exempted an agreement to reduce production of synthetic textiles.[99] The ten largest European manufacturers reduced their production capacity by 18 per cent. In order to exempt the agreement, the parties undertook to supply a trustee with information on the planned capacity to be reduced as well as on specific plants. In addition, compensation would be paid to the other participants to the agreement in the case of some parties not fulfilling the capacity reduction. The parties were to consult each other in cases of important changes in the market and should not fail to implement the planned reductions in capacity.

The Commission requested the deletion of some clauses in the original agreement. These clauses related to a ban on investment leading to capacity increases without the consent of all parties, as well as to a requirement not to operate a plant at more than 95 per cent capacity. The Commission did not accept the latter clause as it would have allowed the parties to monitor output and deliveries.

The Commission argued that the agreement fulfilled the Article 101(3) criteria as it contributed to the improvement of production and, importantly, allowed the restructuring process to proceed in a socially acceptable way by making suitable arrangements for the retention and redeployment of workers made redundant.[100] Thus the Commission, in exempting the agreement, took into account employment and social factors.

Futhermore, the Commission argued that consumers would receive a fair share of the benefits as, according to the Commission, the restructuring would result in an industry able to offer better products on competitive terms. In order for the Commission to satisfy itself that competition would continue to exist in spite of this agreement reducing capacity, it took into account that the agreement was of limited duration and that there were substitute products from other competitors outside the agreement and outside the involved countries.

[98] Fourteenth Report on Competition Policy. See also twelfth Report on Competition Policy, paras. 38–41, thirteenth Report on Competition Policy, paras. 56–61.

[99] *Synthetic Fibres*, OJ L207/17, 2 August 1984.

[100] Fourteenth Report on Competition Policy.

British Petroleum Chemicals/Imperial Chemical Industries

Bilateral agreements have also been used to mitigate problems of structural overcapacity. Such agreements have been a particular feature of the petrochemical sector in recent years. The effect of these arrangements is to enable petrochemical companies to specialize in products where they have a comparative advantage. Such agreements will have adverse effects on competition.

One such bilateral agreement where an agreement to reduce capacity was exempted is *BPCL/ICI*,[101] which involved two British manufacturers in the petrochemical sector. BPCL was involved in low-density polyethelene (LDPE) and ICI in polyvinylchloride (PVC). The restructuring involved the specialization of production in the UK, leading to reductions in output. The agreement concerned the reciprocal sale of ICI's production plant and goodwill as well as the licensing of technology to BPCL, giving the latter sole control. Both parties proceeded to the closure of certain plants (ICI of LDPE plants and BPCL of PVC plants in the UK), closures not provided for in the agreement but constituting a consequence of the agreement. The parties closed down two remaining plants in the markets where they considered that they suffered a comparative disadvantage. Even though the agreement concerned acquisition of sole control through a reciprocal sale, Article 101 was applied, as the agreement would restrict competition.[102]

The Commission argued that

> (34) In view of the industry-wide structural over-capacity for the products in question and the fact that the agreements and associated plant closures reduced this surplus capacity and improved plant loading without eliminating effective competition, the advantages resulting from these agreements and associated plant closures outweigh harmful effects they may entail.
>
> (35) . . . Given that the over-capacity in the industry is of a structural nature, market forces would have been too slow at bringing about the necessary radical changes. These agreements, by their immediate closure of plants, accelerate the tendency to re-establish the equilibrium in supply and demand.

The agreement was exempted pursuant to Article 101(3). The sector was characterized by excess capacity and as a result of the agreement the two firms would be able to reduce the costs of production. Thus

[101] OJ L212, 8.8.1984.
[102] Fourteenth Report on Competition Policy.

the agreement was expected to contribute to efficiency. Similar to the previous cases where the Commission has granted an exemption, the Commission added that even after the elimination of one producer consumers would still have choices of supply.

ENI/Montedison

Similar to the *BPCL/ICI* case, the Commission in *ENI/Montedison*[103] assessed a rationalization agreement arguing that pursuant to Article 101(3), the provisions of Article 101(1) were hereby declared inapplicable to the agreements between Ente Nazionale Idrocarburi and Montedison SpA involving a reciprocal transfer of certain lines of business in the petrochemical sector (base chemicals, thermoplastics and certain rubbers) and the contracts and behaviour associated with and dependent on these agreements, implying both plant closure and a de facto specialization by each party.

The agreements allowed the selection of the businesses in which ENI and Montedison would each concentrate. The selection was based on a study of their relative strengths in terms of technology, marketing expertise, production facilities, and objectives, in the main thermoplastics products.

The exemption was justified because the agreements were an essential first step in the rationalization of ENI's and Montedison's petrochemical business, which formed part of an industry suffering serious structural overcapacity in the whole Community. As a result of the agreements, the parties were able to restructure their businesses more quickly and fundamentally than would have been possible individually. According to the Commission the benefit of reducing excess capacity in an industry suffering from structural overcapacity would outweigh any restrictions of competition.

Enichem/ICI

Similarly, in *Enichem/ICI*[104] the Commission argued that agreements between Enichem and ICI continued the strategies adopted by the two companies to rationalize their respective vinyl chloride monomer (VCM)/PVC businesses. This process started in 1982 and allowed Enichem and ICI to concentrate their efforts on the sectors where their position as manufacturers was strongest. The aim of Enichem and ICI

[103] IV/31.055, *ENI/Montedison*, [1987] OJ L005/13.

[104] IV/31.846, *Enichem/ICI*, [1988] OJL 050 /18.

in setting up a jointly owned company, European Vinyls Corporation (EVC), was to complete the restructuring of their VCM/PVC business in order to regain competitiveness and progressively reduce losses. Thus, pursuant to Article 101(3), the Commission exempted, for a period from 26 March 1986 to 25 March 1991, the agreement dealing with the setting up of EVC to operate their VCM and PVC sectors, and the agreement concerning the distribution of PVC primary and secondary plasticizers.

Shell/AKZO

This joint venture, aimed at improving the utilization of capacity and thus aiding the restructuring of the petrochemical sector, was exempted by the Commission as it would sustain a choice of supply for consumers.[105] Pursuant to the joint-venture agreement, the two parties would put the PVC and VCM plants at the disposal of the joint venture.[106]

Stichting Baksteen

In *Stichting Baksteen* the Commission assessed a crisis cartel in the brick industry in the Netherlands.[107] The industry was in recession due to a combination of larger plants and a fall in demand. The undertakings were not able to balance supply and demand due to the inelasticity of price. Such balance could only be achieved by an industry-wide reduction in capacity. The Commission did not accept the original plan due to the inclusion of quota agreements. After amendments, the agreement was exempted. The application of Article 101(3) could vary depending on the economic conditions surrounding agreements that incorporate restructuring measures.

The Commission argued that

> (29) Article 85 (3) provides that an agreement must allow consumers a fair share of the resulting benefit. Consumers in the present case should benefit from the improvement in production because in the long term they will be dealing with a healthy industry offering competitive supplies and, in the short term, they will go on enjoying the advantages of continuing competition between the parties. Thanks to the agreement they can also be sure that structural adjustment keeps competitive firms or capacities on the market whilst eliminating outmoded or obsolescent capacity

105 *Shell/AKZO*, OJ C295, 2 November 1983.

106 Fourteenth Report on Competition Policy.

107 *Stichting Baksteen*, [1995] 4 CMLR 646.

> which might otherwise have affected healthy capacity through loss compensation within a group.
> (30) There are a sufficient number of producers remaining, whether or not parties to the agreement, to give consumers a choice of supplier and security of supply, while ruling out the risk of over-concentrated supply.

The commissioner for competition, Mr Van Miert, in announcing the Commission's decision in *Stichting Baksteen*, argued that cartels do not improve structures or production capacities. On the other hand, the Commission argued that the wider 'economic and legal context' within which firms' conduct must be assessed was the one where markets were expanding as liberalization occurred.[108]

Italian cast glass

In *Italian cast glass*,[109] the Commission argued that the agreements concluded between Fabbrica Pisana SpA, Società Italiana Vetro SpA (SIV), Fabbrica Lastre di Vetro Sciarra SpA and Fides-Unione Fiduciara SpA infringed Article 101(1) as regards their clauses concerning the quantitative sharing of the various kinds of cast glass, the exchange of commercial information on quantities sold and prices of each type of product, and the measures for implementing the obligations concerning the forwarding of the above-mentioned information and the supervision of compliance with the quantitative sharing between the undertakings.

Referring to the sectoral crisis situation which the parties put forward as a justification of the conclusion of their agreements, the Commission argued that the agreements cannot be considered to fall within Article 101(3) since no provision was made for a crisis situation and the agreements contained no decisions to reduce the productive capacities of the undertakings. The Commission added that such reduction might have been appropriate to a structural crisis situation. It noted that the parties decided unilaterally to set quantitative shares for sales of cast glass on the Italian market, to the benefit exclusively of the manufacturers, without any advantage to consumers. Thus the Commission could not allow, in the guise of a crisis cartel, restrictions of competition which were not indispensable.

[108] 1993 Competition Report, point 79.
[109] IV/29.869, [1980] OJ L 383/19.

Welded Steel Mesh, *Cockerill-Sambre v. Commission* and *Trefilunion*

The relevant product in this case was welded steel mesh,[110] which is a prefabricated reinforcement product made from smooth or ribbed cold-drawn reinforcing steel wires joined together by right-angle spot welding to form a network. It is used in almost all areas of construction with reinforced concrete. According to the Commission of the European Community, as of 1980 several companies, including Cockerill Sambre, formerly Steelinter SA, a company incorporated under Belgian law, established in Brussels, had breached Article 101(1) of the EC Treaty by articulating a series of deals and/or concerted practices concerning establishing quotas and prices and sharing the market for welded steel mesh.[111]

In addition, the Commission also stated that although the major targets were French, German or Benelux, the plot also affected other members states' undertakings, once they also took part in the scheme at issue. The Commission alleged that a cartel existed in the welded steel mesh sector, involving prices, and that quota agreements were being operated during the early 1980s in France, Italy, the Benelux countries and Germany.

On 31 May 1983, the Bundeskartellamt (Federal Cartel Office) granted authorization for the establishment of a structural crisis cartel of German producers of welded steel mesh, which, after being renewed once, expired in 1988. The cartel agreement included almost all German producers, and permitted organized capacity cuts, quotas and price-fixing. Authorization of price-fixing was granted only for the first two years.

For the German crisis cartel to be effective it had to include other EC producers which were able to import into Germany. The formally authorized agreement, however, included only German producers.

The Commission in the decision argued,[112]

> The cartel arrangement, and in particular subsections 5 (2) and 7 (1) thereof, not only restricted competition between the cartel members in the Federal Republic of Germany, but also distorted competition in respect of intra-Community trade because it led to artificial changes in

[110] *Welded Steel Mesh*, [1989] OJ L260/1.

[111] CFI, 11 March 1999, *Cockerill-Sambre v. Commission*, Case T-138/94, [1999] ECR II-333.

[112] *Welded Steel Mesh*, [1989] OJ L260/1, para. 131.

> the conditions for deliveries of German producers to other European markets and for deliveries of foreign producers to the German market . . . This being so, the cartel arrangement was liable to affect trade between Member States.
>
> These provisions had, moreover, as their object, or at least as their effect, the use of the structural crisis cartel as an instrument for reaching bilateral arrangements between German producers on the one hand and producers from other Member States on the other. The representatives of the German producers, in particular BStG, could now appear as representatives of the 'German cartel association' in contacts and negotiations and could thereby rely on the discipline of most members of the German structural crisis cartel . . . In this way the creation of general agreements limiting interpenetration was facilitated, as was likewise stressed by leading representatives of the German producers . . .
>
> These bilateral arrangements had the object of shutting off the German market or at least of preventing unregulated imports, so that the object of the cartel (reduction of capacity, setting of delivery quotas and price rises) should not be endangered. This was admitted by the cartel representative himself.

The Commission added that the use of the cartel to protect the German market against competition from other member states by measures which are illegal under Community law cannot be validated by the existence of a cartel authorization by the Federal Cartel Office.

Certain French producers argued that they were in fact only operating a crisis cartel in an attempt to mitigate the adverse impact of the alleged restructuring of the French welded steel mesh industry. This argument was rejected by the Commission because the cartel agreements contained no clauses on restructuring, capacity reduction and so on, which did exist in the formally approved German agreement.

The Commission took into account that at the time when the cartel was operating the industry was going through a period of crisis linked to the general crisis in the European steel industry. The industry was suffering from a structural decline in demand as well as excess capacity.

The Commission issued a notice concerning the competitive situation, which ended in fines to a number of French companies, including a fine of ECU 315,000 to Cockerill Sambre, for taking action and engaging in practices whose object or effect was to restrict or distort competition during the period from 1982 to 1984. Cockerill Sambre, along with the other companies, were involved in market-sharing for the French, German and Benelux markets and setting a common price for the

French market for welded steel mesh. As a result, they infringed Article 101(1).

The applicant appealed to the Court of First Instance (CFI) asking for an annulment of the decision. As an alternative the applicant asked the Court to annul Article 3 of the decision, imposing on the applicant a fine of ECU 315,000. He argued for a reduction in the fine to a token amount.

The Court found that the applicant had taken part in several meetings and entered into agreements on price and quotas in the French market. The Commission presented evidence for the Benelux countries' and Germany's markets, but no strong proof about the division of quotas on the same markets. Therefore the applicant breached Article 101(1). Concerning the imposed fine, the Court decided that the infringement did not cover the Germany and Benelux markets, as stated by the Commission, and reduced the fee by one-fifth to ECU 252,000.

In the appeal of Trefilunion,[113] the applicant alleged that the Commission had failed to take into account the economic context of the building and wire sector. Although the price increases were as a result of the market crisis and thus the need to ensure positive margins, and although the condition of the market was taken into account, the Commission found that this did not justify conduct which was contrary to Article 101.

The CFI, differentiating the facts of this case from other cases involving crisis cartel agreements,[114] interestingly argued,[115]

> The Court also considers that the applicant cannot rely on the three Commission decisions in the Synthetic Fibre, Zinc and Flat Glass cases since they relate to circumstances fundamentally different from those of the present case. The Synthetic Fibre Decision concerns an agreement for the coordinated reduction of capacity, which had been notified and was granted an exemption under Article 85(3) of the Treaty. In the Zinc and Flat Glass Decisions, the Commission prohibited quota and price agreements, although, as in the present case, the prevailing crisis was

[113] Judgment of the Court of First Instance (First Chamber) of 6 April 1995. *Tréfilunion SA v. Commission of the European Communities. Competition – Infringement of Article 85 of the EEC Treaty*. Case T-148/89.

[114] IV/30.350, *Zinc Producer Group*, [1984] OJ L 220/27, IV/30.988, *Agreements in and concerted practices in the flat-glass sector in the Benelux countries*, [1984] OJ L 212/13.

[115] Judgment of the Court of First Instance (First Chamber) of 6 April 1995. *Tréfilunion SA v. Commission of the European Communities. Competition – Infringement of Article 85 of the EEC Treaty*. Case T-148/89, para. 117.

> taken into account as a mitigating circumstance. The Court also considers that the applicant's alleged restructuring plan cannot be regarded as an agreement for the coordinated reduction of overcapacity and that, in any event, it was open to the producers to notify their agreements to the Commission under Article 85(3) of the Treaty, which would have enabled the Commission, if appropriate, to rule as to whether they met the criteria laid down by that provision. Since the applicant did not avail itself of that opportunity, it cannot rely on the crisis to justify setting up secret agreements contrary to Article 85(1) of the Treaty.

The CFI found that some of the arguments put forth with regard to future export quotas were not sufficiently proved and reversed them, thus reducing the fine. Nevertheless the company was found in breach of Article 101 for such conduct as price-fixing.

Limburgse Vinyl Maatschappij NV (LVM) (C-238/99 P), et al. v. Commission of the European Communities

The undertakings involved in this decision are all major petrochemical producers.[116] Seventeen undertakings participated in the infringement. PVC was one of the first bulk thermoplastic products to be developed. It is produced from vinyl chloride monomer (VCM), itself obtained from ethylene and chlorine feedstock. PVC has many important uses in heavy industry and construction, as well as varied consumer applications. It can be converted into hard material or – compounded with plasticizers – made into flexible articles, including film.

From about the end of 1980, the producers of PVC supplying the Community were parties to a complex of schemes, arrangements and measures which were worked out in the framework of a system of regular meetings.

The arrangements involved:

- the setting of target prices,
- the modalities of concerted price initiatives intended to raise price levels up to agreed targets,
- the division of the Western European markets according to annual volume targets, and

[116] *Limburgse Vinyl Maatschappij NV* (LVM) (C-238/99 P), *DSM NV and DSM Kunststoffen BV* (C-244/99 P), *Montedison SpA* (C-245/99 P), *Elf Atochem SA* (C-247/99 P), *Degussa AG* (C-250/99 P), *Enichem SpA* (C-251/99 P), *Wacker-Chemie GmbH and Hoechst AG* (C-252/99 P) and *Imperial Chemical Industries plc* (ICI) (C-254/99 P) *v. Commission of the European Communities.*

- the exchange of detailed information on their market activities in order to facilitate the co-ordination of commercial behaviour.

The basic purpose behind the institution of the system of regular meetings and the continuing collusion of the producers was to create a permanent mechanism for controlling the tonnage sold and achieving concerted price increases.

The situation did not render an exemption necessary. The Commission took into consideration the crisis but also found that the competitive forces of the market should have been maintained.

The Commission's decision was appealed to the CFI, which annulled Article 1 of the Commission's decision in so far as it held that Société Artésienne de Vinyle participated in the infringement in question after the first half of 1981. The CFI also reduced the fines.

The applicants appealed the CFI judgment that they had breached Article 101 by engaging in concerted practice. This case included several claims by the claimants but of note was the alleged claim that there was a crisis in the oil markets which had caused some companies to withdraw from the industry.

The ECJ partially annulled the CFI judgment to the extent that it dismissed the new plea raised by Montedison SpA alleging infringement of its right of access to the Commission's file and failed to respond to the plea raised by Montedison SpA alleging a definitive transfer to the Community judicature of the power to impose penalties following the Commission's decision.

Montedipe SpA v. Commission

This case involved fifteen producers of polypropelene.[117] The Commission found that the purpose of meetings that took place was to decide on price initiatives, to agree on sales volume targets, to compare market shares and to adopt accompanying measures such as the 'account leadership' system. The purpose was thus to agree on the harmonization of the sales strategies.

In this case it must be noted that all producers in the market faced constraint: the price of raw materials. However, this did not involve all other factors of production, such as taxes, wages and other expenses.

Montedipe did not deny having attended the meetings but asserted

[117] Judgment of the Court of First Instance (First Chamber) of 10 March 1992. *Montedipe SpA v. Commission*, Case T- 14/89.

that it had never considered itself bound by the results or proposals arrived at in the meetings and that it determined its own conduct in the market in complete independence.

As is clear in the case law, in order for there to be an agreement within the meaning of Article 101(1) it is sufficient that the undertakings in question have expressed their joint intention to conduct themselves in the market in a specific way. Such is the case where there are common intentions between undertakings to achieve price and sales volume targets.

The CFI argued,

> As regards the second argument put forward by the applicant, the Court considers that the economic context of the price initiatives cannot explain the manner in which the price instructions issued by the different producers correspond to each other and to the price targets set at the producers' meetings. The identical nature of the constraints faced by the various producers and the situation of market crisis cannot explain the fact that their price instructions, expressed in different national currencies, were identical, since the identical nature of those constraints was restricted to certain factors of production, such as the price of raw materials, and did not relate to general expenses, wage costs or tax rates, which meant that the profitability threshold for the various producers was significantly different.

In dismissing the appeal the Court argued that participants in a cartel which sought to raise prices from a level below cost to a level at or above cost cannot argue, in justification of their conduct, that the cartel sought to eliminate unfair competition.

Raiffeisen Zentralbank Österreich

In December 2006, the CFI in, its judgment on the Commission's decision[118] concerning the Austrian banking cartel,[119] considered that the Commission had made a mistake in assessing the market share for the fine on the Österreichische Postsparkasse and reduced its fines by half to €3,795 million.

This case concerned long-standing practices in Austria involving widespread meetings and information exchanges, which continued after Austria's accession to the European Economic Area (EEA) and the European Union. The Commission criticized a number of banks for

[118] Case COMP/36.571/D-1, *Austrian banks – 'Lombard Club'*, OJ 2004 L 56/1.

[119] *Raiffeisen Zentralbank Österreich* v. *Commission* (T-259/02, T-260/02, T-261/02, T-262/02, T-263/02, T-264/02 & T-271/02), unreported, 14 December 2006.

establishing a system of regular meetings ('the committee meetings' or 'the committees'), to which it refers as the 'Lombard network', in which they covered every conceivable subject and regularly co-ordinated their conduct with respect to the essential factors of competition in the Austrian market in banking products and services.

> As specifically regards the crisis in the banking sector, the CFI argued that it must be borne in mind that the Commission is not required to treat the poor financial health of the sector in question as a mitigating circumstance (Case T-16/99 Lögstör Rör v. Commission [2002] ECR II-1633, paragraphs 319 and 320). The fact that in previous cases the Commission took account of the economic situation in the sector as a mitigating circumstance does not mean that it must necessarily continue to follow that practice (ICI v. Commission, cited in paragraph 196 above, paragraph 372). As a general rule, cartels come into being when a sector is experiencing difficulties.

Thus the CFI confirmed that the crisis in the banking sector was not a mitigating factor that should be taken into account.

As the above analysis of the case law illustrates, the Commission has on several occasions encountered crisis cartels. During the development of case law on crisis cartels, the Commission has developed assessment criteria that it will apply to crisis cartels. In a nutshell, the conditions that need to be fulfilled before an exemption is granted (i.e. before the Article 101(3) criteria are satisfied) include improvement of production and distribution, the indispensability of the restrictions, the non-elimination of competition, a fair share of the benefits to consumers and, finally, that the benefits must outweigh the disadvantages.

After looking at the European experience this chapter now turns to the assessment of crisis cartels in the US, which has been enforcing competition legislation for more than a hundred years.

5.4 The United States of America

5.4.1 The development of crisis cartels

As mentioned above, the Sherman Act is a broad prohibition of structural anti-competitive arrangements, such as business trusts, monopolistic combinations and certain mergers.

Under the per se approach in the US, a structural anti-competitive arrangement or an anti-competitive act would be a violation of the antitrust laws without any evidence of adverse effects in the market. Horizontal arrangements, such as price-fixing, are illegal per se. For conduct that is not illegal per se the court may assess any pro-competitive effects of a given conduct and balance them against likely anti-competitive effects of the conduct. A court will not apply the rule of reason to the case if under the first step of the analysis such an arrangement is deemed a per se violation. It should be emphasized that the adoption of the per se or rule-of-reason approach depends upon the outlook of the particular Supreme Court justices. There are advantages and disadvantages to the per se approach. The per se approach provides certainty as regards conduct which is prohibited. The disadvantages of this approach include certain possibly pro-competitive conduct being branded anti-competitive without an assessment of the effects of the said conduct. As regards exemptions of cartelistic agreements, congressional exemptions can be awarded to individual enterprises or to entire categories of restrictive arrangements.

Regarding crisis cartels, the only case in which the Supreme Court applied the rule of reason to a cartel is *Appalachian Coals, Inc. v. United States*,[120] involving a price cartel established under emergency circumstances in the coal industry. A group of coal producers had established a price cartel (in the form of a syndicate) in order to prevent the harmful effects of fierce price competition. Thus the Supreme Court accepted, albeit with within narrow limits, crisis cartels. As the analysis of the US case law will indicate, this decision, which is an exception to the per se rule, was based on a detailed analysis of the extraordinary circumstances of the case. In the *Saxon Woodpulp* case that was decided by the Reichsgericht, the facts did not establish such an extraordinary situation.

Posner has presented a statistical study of antitrust enforcement in the US.[121] In his study he collected data on cartel cases in the US since the coming into force of the Sherman Act. He collected data on a number of cases and fines, and classified the cases by type of infringement, as well as by the number of firms involved. We present these tables in this chapter and shall also present conclusions regarding the 1929 crisis[122] and the Second World War.[123]

[120] *Appalachian Coals, Inc. v. United States*, (1933) 288 U.S. 344 .

[121] R.A. Posner, 'A Statistical Study of Antitrust Enforcement' (October 1970) 13(2) *Journal of Law and Economics* 365.

[122] This was represented, historically, as the most adverse crisis in the US economy. Among the consequences of this crisis, 9,036 banks collapsed in a scenario of a very steep recession in the US economy which spread to other countries. For an enlargement see Chapter 2 above.

[123] Export cartels in the US were 'allowed' under §2 of the Webb-Pomerene Act, which provided that the Sherman Act shall not apply to an association formed for the sole purpose

Table 5.2 illustrates, among other things, the number of cases involving horizontal combinations of conspiracies.[124] Horizontal conspiracy includes all cases in which competitors agreed or conspired to eliminate competition among themselves, usually, although not always, price competition. Conspiracies among retailers or other distributors are included in Table 5.3, as are conspiracies among manufacturers to establish resale prices. After the 1929 crisis, which arguably finished in 1934,[125] the number of cases that were instituted and were related to horizontal conspiracies indicated a significant increase from twenty-three in the 1930–4 period to forty-one in 1935–9. Then, during the Second World War, the number of horizontal conspiracies showed a 400 per cent increase from 41 to 192. In the postwar era, the number did not markedly decrease compared to the pre-crisis era, but remained well above a hundred (falling to 127). It is noteworthy that the number of horizontal conspiracies continued their increasing trend in the postwar era.

It is controversial to allege that this increase in the number of cartels can be attributed to crisis cartels. But the argument can be made that certain circumstances in the US market led to such a high increase in the number of alleged horizontal conspiracies. The periods of massive increase in the numbers of such allegations coincide with severe market conditions, similar to those that give rise to the 'need' for crisis cartels.

Footnote 123 (*cont.*)

of engaging in export trade. The criteria for legality were that no restraint of export trade results adversely to the interest of any domestic competitor and that there is no effect upon prices within the United States. The case law indicates though that the Act has been interpreted restrictively. In *United States v. Minnesota Mining & Mfg Co.* (92 F. Supp. 947 (D. Mass. 1950)), while the District Court indicated that an agreement by the manufacturers of coated abrasives to export exclusively through a jointly organized export company on a basis of assigned quotas was authorized by the Webb-Pomerene Act, the Court held that a combination of manufacturers controlling four-fifths of the export trade to establish jointly owned factories abroad was not 'an association entered into for the sole purpose of engaging in export trade' under §1 of the Webb-Pomerene Act.

[124] This table contains information relating to the allegations of violations in Department of Justice antitrust cases. Since most of the DOJ's antitrust suits are terminated without a determination or acknowledgement of guilt, and since in any event the factual statements in antitrust opinions cannot be assumed to be accurate without a careful examination of the record of the case, the information recorded in the table is of interest mainly for the implications about enforcement policy.

[125] In 1934 there were elements of improvement in the economy resulting from the New Deal.

Table 5.2. *Cartel cases: statistical study of antitrust enforcement in the US*[126]

Period in which case was instituted	*Cases involving horizontal combinations or conspiracies*	*Cases involving abuse*	*Percentage of abuse cases*
1890–4	5	2	29
1895–9	7	0	0
1900–4	6	0	0
1905–9	32	4	11
1910–14	78	23	23
1915–19	32	6	16
1920–4	55	5	8
1925–9	46	11	19
1930–4	23	11	32
1935–9	41	19	32
1940–4	192	75	28
1945–9	127	79	38
1950–4	137	58	30
1955–9	157	65	29
1960–4	172	66	28
1965–9	146	50	26

An indication of the 'attitude' of the Department of Justice (DOJ) towards the increased number of horizontal conspiracies is illustrated in Figures 5.1 and 5.2, which depict the US gross national product and the aggregate antitrust fines between 1890 and 1969. As the graph indicates, in the 1935–9 and 1940–4 periods, there was a massive increase in the number of fines. The increase in the number of fines coincides with the periods during which there was a significant increase in the number of horizontal conspiracies. Thus even though there was a massive increase in the number of horizontal conspiracies, it is unlikely that these conspiracies were deemed to be 'acceptable' or 'reasonable' crisis cartels.[127] However, we should note that no conclusive arguments regarding the existence of crisis cartels can be made by correlating the increase in

[126] Posner 1970.

[127] This argument cannot be proved based only on the tables included in this chapter. However, analysis of US case law confirms this argument as there is not a significant number of crisis cartel cases.

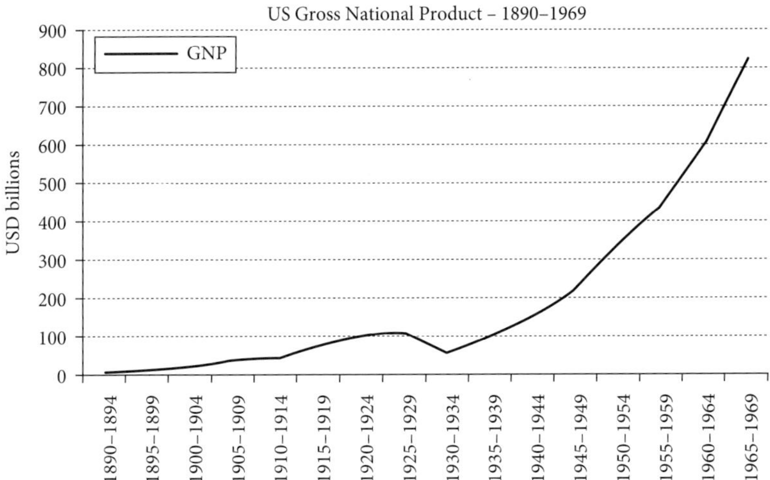

Figure 5.1. US gross national product. From R.A. Posner, 'A Statistical Study of Antitrust Enforcement' (October 1970) 13(2) *Journal of Law and Economics* 365.

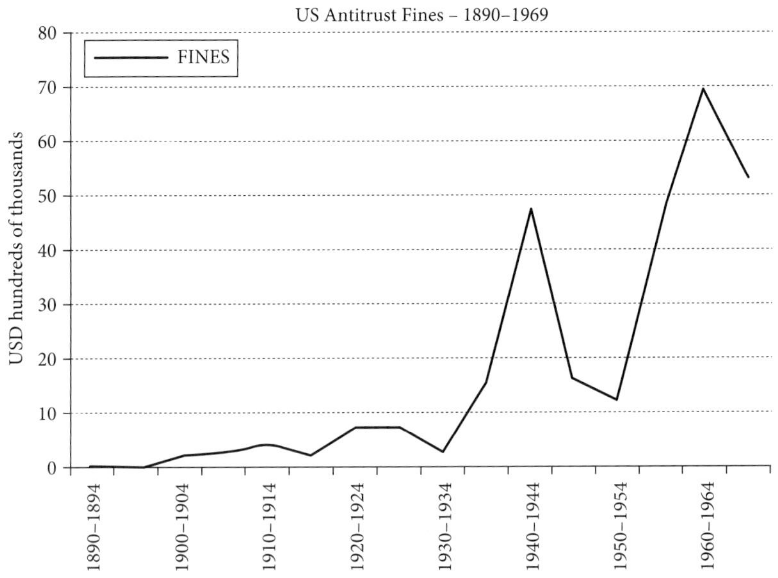

Figure 5.2. Aggregate antitrust fines between 1890 and 1969. From R.A. Posner, 'A Statistical Study of Antitrust Enforcement' (October 1970) 13(2) *Journal of Law and Economics* 365.[128]

[128] Ibid.

the number of horizontal conspiracy cases with the total level of fines imposed. The level of fines and the number of horizontal conspiracy cases are not necessarily proportional.[128]

Table 5.3 provides a more detailed account of alleged anti-competitive conduct as it illustrates the number of horizontal conspiracies (this includes conduct such as price-fixing, market-sharing and so on). Such conspiracies increased from nineteen in the 1930–4 period, to thirty-four in the 1935–9 period, and then indicated a significant increase to 179 during the Second World War (1940–4). They remained above a hundred until the mid-1960s.

Tables 5.4 and 5.5 depict some characteristics of the price-fixing conspiracies addressed by the DOJ.[129] In Table 5.4 we should note the frequency with which more than a simple agreement to fix prices is involved (for example, a division of territories, a system of fines and audits, a patent agreement or an agreement on resale prices) and, in particular, the large proportion of cases involving trade associations. This table indicates either that conspiracies to fix prices are difficult to effect without such ancillary arrangements, or that the adoption of such arrangements increases the probability of detection.

As Table 5.5 illustrates, there is a large number of regional or local conspiracies. Such conspiracies are the most frequent. In addition, the table indicates a small number of conspiracies by purchasers. Although monopsony is considered the opposite of monopoly and is treated symmetrically with monopoly in academic literature, its incidence appears to be far less than monopoly.

Table 5.6 illustrates that the vast majority of cases involve twenty or fewer conspirators and almost two-thirds involve ten or fewer; where large numbers are involved, invariably a trade association, commodity exchange, patent pool or other organization is instrumental in effecting the conspiracy.

Even though crisis cartels are not prevalent in the US case law,[130] there have been voices in the academic literature that advocate the positive impact of crisis cartels. Tobriner and Jaffe argued that voluntary planned production should be tried tentatively in industries in which a condition of overproduction is chronic. They added that in those industries where disparity between production and

[129] The source of these tables is Posner 1970.

[130] Although, as the above tables show, crisis cartels, even if they existed, were not deemed acceptable.

Table 5.3. *Topical classification of US Department of Justice antitrust charges between 1890 and 1969*

	Period in which charge was instituted																
Antitrust charge	*1890–4*	*1895–9*	*1900–4*	*1905–9*	*1910–14*	*1915–19*	*1920–4*	*1925–9*	*1930–4*	*1935–9*	*1940–4*	*1945–9*	*1950–4*	*1955–9*	*1960–4*	*1965–9*	*Total*
Horizontal conspiracy	3	7	5	28	62	29	50	36	19	34	179	114	122	122	104	75	989
Monopolizing	3	n.a.	1	9	25	3	7	8	9	14	65	60	62	45	40	19	370
Acquisitions short of monopoly	n.a.	n.a.	1	2	3	1	1	5	1	3	2	5	3	26	61	80	104
Boycott	n.a.	1	n.a.	2	15	9	10	20	5	8	43	20	44	38	18	12	245
Resale price maintenence	n.a.	n.a.	n.a.	n.a.	2	4	2	n.a.	n.a.	n.a.	1	n.a.	4	4	8	2	27
Vertical integration	n.a.	n.a.	n.a.	2	3	n.a.	1	1	2	7	6	11	6	6	7	1	53
Tying arrangements	n.a.	n.a.	n.a.	n.a.	3	2	n.a.	1	1	4	8	23	12	5	4	2	65
Exclusive dealing	1	n.a.	n.a.	1	9	1	3	1	1	4	16	24	29	23	22	6	140
Territorial and customer limitations	n.a.	n.a.	n.a.	n.a.	n.a.	n.a.	n.a.	n.a.	n.a.	n.a.	8	2	4	28	24	13	74
Violence	4	n.a.	n.a.	n.a.	2	n.a.	8	3	10	7	7	n.a.	n.a.	4	n.a.	2	47

Price discrimination	1	n.a.	1	3	6	2	1	4	n.a.	5	29	20	16	15	14	6	123
Other predatory or unfair practice	1	n.a.	n.a.	3	2	3	1	2	1	5	27	17	7	4	11	4	88
Interlocking directorates	n.a.	n.a.	n.a.	n.a.	n.a.	n.a.	n.a.	2	n.a.	1	n.a.	5	4	2	2	n.a.	16
Clayton Act §10	n.a.	n.a.	n.a.	n.a.	n.a.	n.a.	n.a.	n.a.	n.a.	n.a.	n.a.	n.a.	n.a.	n.a.	n.a.	n.a.	n.a.
Labour cases	3	n.a.	n.a.	2	6	n.a.	16	6	7	18	35	2	17	7	5	1	125
Patent and copyright cases	n.a.	n.a.	n.a.	n.a.	6	1	8	3	2	3	36	45	22	15	13	11	165
Total cases in period	9	1	6	39	91	43	66	69	30	57	223	157	159	195	215	195	1551

Table 5.4. *Horizontal conspiracies before the US DOJ (by means employed) between 1890 and 1969*

	Period in which case was instituted																
Description of horizontal conspiracies	*1890–4*	*1895–9*	*1900–4*	*1905–9*	*1910–14*	*1915–19*	*1920–4*	*1925–9*	*1930–4*	*1935–9*	*1940–4*	*1945–9*	*1950–4*	*1955–9*	*1960–4*	*1965–9*	*Total*
Number of cases	3	7	5	28	62	29	50	36	19	34	179	114	122	122	104	75	989
Exclusive sales agency or protocol	n.a.	1	1	n.a.	5	2	3	4	1	4	6	4	7	8	5	4	55
Production or sales quota	n.a.	n.a.	n.a.	n.a.	n.a.	n.a.	n.a.	n.a.	n.a.	n.a.	11	1	1	n.a.	2	1	16
Trade association or equivalent	2	6	n.a.	3	19	13	22	18	12	17	96	41	62	60	28	32	431
Policing, fines, audits, etc.	n.a.	n.a.	n.a.	n.a.	n.a.	n.a.	n.a.	1	1	3	7	5	8	10	5	3	43
Division of product markets	n.a.	n.a.	n.a.	n.a.	n.a.	n.a.	n.a.	n.a.	n.a.	n.a.	3	5	7	n.a.	n.a.	3	18

Division of territories	n.a.	n.a.	n.a.	1	2	1	n.a.	1	2	n.a.	32	31	30	24	15	5	144
Allocation of customers	n.a.	n.a.	n.a.	1	1	n.a.	2	3	n.a.	4	11	8	15	14	7	11	77
Collusion on terms besides basic price	n.a.	n.a.	n.a.	n.a.	n.a.	n.a.	7	4	7	3	32	25	18	23	7	13	139
Exchange of information	n.a.	n.a.	n.a.	n.a.	n.a.	2	18	2	3	2	14	5	9	n.a.	5	1	61
Delivered pricing	n.a.	n.a.	n.a.	n.a.	n.a.	1	1	n.a.	1	n.a.	5	4	4	1	5	n.a.	22
Resale prices or other restricted distribution	n.a.	n.a.	1	n.a.	2	1	1	3	1	1	26	6	9	8	9	3	71
Patents or copyrights	n.a.	n.a.	n.a.	n.a.	1	n.a.	6	2	n.a.	1	28	27	13	7	5	6	96

Table 5.5. *Horizontal conspiracies before the US DOJ between 1890 and 1969: other characterizing elements*

	Period in which case was instituted																
	1890–4	*1895–9*	*1900–4*	*1905–9*	*1910–14*	*1915–19*	*1920–4*	*1925–9*	*1930–4*	*1935–9*	*1940–4*	*1945–9*	*1950–4*	*1955–9*	*1960–4*	*1965–9*	*Total*
Number of cases	3	7	5	28	62	29	50	36	19	34	179	114	122	122	104	75	989
Sales to government involving bidding	n.a.	n.a.	n.a.	n.a.	n.a.	n.a.	n.a.	n.a.	n.a.	1	6	5	5	14	29	13	73
Other bidding cases	n.a.	1	n.a.	n.a.	n.a.	n.a.	1	n.a.	n.a.	9	18	11	8	4	10	4	66
Buying conspiracy	n.a.	n.a.	1	n.a.	3	4	n.a.	2	1	n.a.	23	6	8	8	5	3	64
Average number of conspirators	n.a.	14	24	35	28	14	53	95	56	14	19	13	21	15	21	15	n.a.
Average duration of conspiracy (years)	n.a.	n.a.	n.a.	n.a.	n.a.	n.a.	n.a.	n.a.	n.a.	n.a.	n.a.	n.a.	11	7	6	6	n.a.
Average annual sales affected (US$million)	n.a.	n.a.	n.a.	n.a.	n.a.	n.a.	n.a.	n.a.	n.a.	n.a.	n.a.	n.a.	55.3	27	161.5	166.7	n.a.
Nationwide conspiracy	n.a.	n.a.	1	3	13	9	28	10	8	10	86	59	45	41	38	21	372
Local or regional	3	7	3	14	24	11	11	16	3	19	74	38	71	73	57	45	469
Foreign trade involved	n.a.	n.a.	n.a.	n.a.	6	n.a.	n.a.	n.a.	n.a.	3	24	28	13	10	2	n.a.	86

Table 5.6. *Frequency distribution of number of conspirators in horizontal conspiracy cases before the DOJ – 1890–1969*[132]

Period in which case was instituted	*0–5*	*6–10*	*11–20*	*21–50*	*51–100*	*100+*	*Number of observations*
1890–4							
1895–9			1				1
1900–4				1			1
1905–9		1			1		2
1910–14				4			4
1915–19		1	1				2
1920–4		1		1		1	3
1925–9			1		1	2	4
1930–4		2	1			1	4
1935–9	1	5	2	2			10
1940–4	20	9	10	3	4	1	47
1945–9	19	10	10	4	4	1	48
1950–4	21	18	13	2	2	2	58
1955–9	29	18	19	5	1	1	73
1960–4	28	23	10		1	3	65
1965–9	12	16	7	6	1	1	43
Total	130	102	76	29	15	13	365

consumption causes waste and harms the public, co-operation among producers should not be illegal. They provide the examples of the oil, gas, lumber and many natural-resource industries, where competition has not only produced enormous wastage, but the illegality of cartel agreements has prevented co-operation to avoid this loss. The authors are radical enough to propose that that the law should validate plans aimed to assist in the stabilization of an industry through the balancing of production against consumption, whereby economic waste in such an industry will be reduced. They believe that such agreements should be excepted from the Sherman Act.[131]

According to this radical proposal, each industry, if it felt the need,

[131] They should be expected from the Cartwright Act. See further M.O. Tobriner and L.L. Jaffe, 'Revision of the Anti-Trust Laws' (September 1932) 20(6) *California Law Review* 585.

could petition Congress for such treatment. The authors point to a speech at Tulsa, Oklahoma, where Secretary Hoover said, 'An amendment to the Sherman Act permitting oil companies to curtail their drilling activities in small localized fields, which may threaten to upset the condition of the entire country, seems to be advisable.'[133]

As is clear in the case law, monopoly as such is not condemned by the Sherman Act. When it results from 'normal growth' it does not offend the law. 'Monopolization' (prohibited by the Sherman Act) is, though, prohibited. In some of the decisions of the lower federal courts there appears the phrase 'reasonable monopoly'.[134] The term 'reasonable monopoly' can either be attributed to monopolization or can result from 'normal growth'. Tobriner and Jaffe argue that assuming that the term implies that the 'rule of reason' as such is applicable to monopolies is wrong. According to the authors, a consolidation, to be 'reasonable', must not control the market.

Tobriner and Jaffe suggest that as the courts are not likely to take the burden of adopting a new approach, an amendment to the antitrust laws is required in order to uphold production agreements in prostrate industries. The authors outlined the following proposed amendment to the Sherman Act:[135]

> Provided that no existing or proposed contract, combination in the form of trust or otherwise, or conspiracy, in restraint of trade or commerce among the several States, or with foreign nations and no monopoly or attempt to monopolize, or combination or conspiracy to monopolize any

[132] Ibid.

[133] As the above argument illustrates, the controversial nature of the oil industry has been recognized for many decades. More recently, according to J.A. Pratt, 'The Petroleum Industry in Transition: Antitrust and the Decline of Monopoly Control in Oil' (December 1980) 40(4) *Journal of Economic History* 815, proponents of antitrust have largely ignored the historical record, which offers little encouragement for free competition in the energy industries. Defenders of the existing market structure in oil have treated oligopoly and vertical integration as inevitable products of the evolution of the oil industry. They argue that economics, not politics, have determined the structure of the industry. Thus any governmental policy aiming at promoting competition will likely induce an imbalance in contrast to the fundamental economic realities of the industry. Thus, according to their view, the cartelized nature of the oil industry should be left unharmed.

[134] See *United States v. International Harvester Co.* (D. Minn. 1914) 214 Fed. 967, 1011, 1012; *United States v. Eastman Kodak Co.* (W. D. N. Y. 1915) 226 Fed. 62, 65.

[135] The authors emphasize that the Committee on the Anti-Trust Laws of the State Bar of California has approved a statute embodying the principles of that suggested in their proposed text.

> part of the trade or commerce among the several States or with foreign nations, shall be deemed illegal or within the provisions of this Act, the plan and details of which shall have been submitted to and approved by the Federal Trade Commission as tending to assist in the stabilization of an industry through the balancing of production or distribution of goods or performance of services with demand therefore whereby economic waste in such industry is or will be reduced.

5.4.2 US case law on crisis cartels

The US authorities have tackled crisis cartel arguments but have been hesitant in accepting such arguments, as the following analyses illustrate.

Addyston Pipe & Steel Co. v. United States

The background of this case was an agreement held among six companies manufacturing iron pipes in the US, which decided to combine their efforts in order to fix prices and avoid competition between them.[136]

The case was originally decided by the Court of Appeals of the Sixth Circuit,[137] and was later appealed to the Supreme Court.

During the trial, the defendants argued that their activities were legitimate, because the object of the association was to prevent ruinous competition. They claimed that the bonuses charged were not exorbitant profits but simple deductions from a reasonable price – a penalty intended for each member in case any market player decided to get more than his due proportion.

On these grounds, the defendants stated that their activities involved a reasonable restraint of trade. Nevertheless, the Sixth Circuit deemed that the joint activities were contrary to the Sherman Act, which only allows a restraint of trade when (i) it is ancillary to the main purpose of the lawful contract, and (ii) it is necessary to protect enjoyment of legit fruits or to protect from dangers.

The Supreme Court later confirmed the illegality of the defendants' activities, based on the fact that the manufacturers and sellers of cast-iron pipes were in a concerted action to fix prices.

[136] *Addyston Pipe & Steel Co. v. United States*, US Supreme Court (1899) 175 U.S. 211.
[137] *Addyston Pipe & Steel Co. v. United States*, 85 F. 271, 1898.

Window glass

In the *Window Glass* case,[138] machine manufacturers sought to put hand manufacturers out of business. The hand manufacturers were saved by the hand-workers, who accepted wage cuts and part-time work to enable the hand manufacturers to cut costs. To keep the industry functioning, the labour unions and manufacturers in the hand trade agreed that the various plants were to be run part-time only, that working hours were to be apportioned among all workers, and that production quotas were to be assigned to the manufacturers. The question presented to the Court was whether the agreement between the hand-workers and the producers providing for periodic shut-downs and apportionment of hours among workers was an unreasonable restraint of trade. The motive, said the Court, was the workers' desire to protect their jobs, and this was not unreasonable.[139] However, the arrangement between the labour unions and manufacturers in the hand trade was sanctioned by the Supreme Court.

United States v. Socony-Vacuum Oil Co.

In 1926 there was an overproduction of crude oil in the US that affected crude oil and petrol markets, and drove the price of oil to levels below the cost of production. To face this situation, the defendants created and participated in a General Stabilization Committee, with the object of eliminating price wars by negotiation.[140]

Major oil companies selling gasoline conspired to raise, fix and maintain at non-competitive levels car tank prices for gasoline in the 'spot market' in the East Texas and Mid-continent fields for jobbers and consumers.

Basically, the cartelists were buying up surplus oil to stabilize price and output, which was regarded as a co-ordinated effort devoid of any economic, pro-competitive justification, other than that it would stabilize prices.[141]

The conclusion was that defendants' purpose was not merely to raise the spot market prices, but to raise the price of gasoline in their sales to consumers as well. The alleged conspiracy was not registered

[138] *National Association of Window Glass Mfrs. v. United States*, (1925) 263 U.S. 403, 44 Sup. Ct. 148.

[139] Tobriner and Jaffe 1932.

[140] *United States v. Socony-Vacuum Oil Co.*, US Supreme Court (1940) 310 U.S. 150.

[141] F. Alese, *Federal Antitrust and EC Competition Law Analysis*, Ashgate, 2008, at p. 50.

in any formal contract or agreement, but was based on testimonies and on thousands of exhibits. This case was originally decided by a District Court which found twelve corporations and five individuals guilty of violations of Article 1 of the Sherman Act. This decision was appealed and the Seventh Circuit reversed and remanded the case for a new trial. Finally, the Supreme Court ruled that a price-fixing agreement is per se illegal under §1 of the Sherman Act and that the elimination of 'competitive evils' is not a legal justification for such agreements.

United States v. Civil Aeronautics Board

The United States argued that the Board,[142] faced with a shortage of fuel for commercial aeronautical use, instinctively reacted anti-competitively by permitting three major air carriers to agree among themselves as regards the number and scheduling of flights in twenty major markets. The US wanted each carrier to take action individually. The Board rejected unilateral reductions as being inconsistent with the public interest because, it thought, it would have left some markets with little or no service and would have resulted in a 'bottleneck' of flights at peak demand times.

The Court held that while there were emergency conditions that provided a justification for the Board's summary course in approving capacity reduction agreements in October 1973, its continuance of that approach in its July 1974 order was not legal. Where an agreement has among its significant aspects elements which are plainly repugnant to established antitrust principles, approval should not be granted unless it can be illustrated that the agreement will secure important public benefits.

Blomkest Fertilizer, Inc. v. Potash Corp. of Saskatchewan, Inc.

The case revolved around potash,[143] an essential ingredient in fertilizer. The American potash market was mostly dominated by Canadian producers. One of defendants, Potash Corp. of Saskatchewan (PCS), was a principal Canadian potash producer selling potash to America. Due to a slump in agriculture, the demand for potash fell dramatically during the 1980s. The subsequent oversupply caused a potash price war and a crisis across the entire industry in Canada. The president of PCS sales

[142] *United States v. Civil Aeronautics Board*, 511 F.2d 1315 C.A.D.C. 1975.

[143] *Blomkest Fertilizer, Inc. v. Potash Corp. of Saskatchewan, Inc.*, 176 F.3d 1055.

announced that 'the industry wouldn't be able to end the price war without joint action'.[144]

The whole industry was forced to form a cartel to stabilize the price at a low level in 1986. The new CEO of PCS kept the same price-fixing policy.[145] In 1986, PCS and the whole industry were investigated by the US Department of Commerce in respect of possible dumping in the American market. They were ordered to post bonds on all exports to the United States. PCS then announced it would increase its price according to the bond expense. Other Canadian companies also followed the price increase. As a result, the average price of potash was higher than would be expected based on market value during the 1988–93 period. Prices also remained significantly higher than the minimum prices imposed by the suspension agreement reached earlier by the Canadian producers and the Department of Commerce. The plaintiffs sued the Canadian producers and two American affiliated producers, alleging a conspiracy to raise and stabilize prices. The defendants moved for summary judgment on the ground that 'the plaintiffs had not produced any evidence that showed the defendants had conspired, rather than setting their prices individually taking into account their competitor's probable responses'.[146] The District Court gave the summary judgment in favour of the defendants.

The plaintiffs appealed and the Court of Appeals held that there was no evidence that one producer supplied price information to other defendants and no showing of parallel pricing by two producers.[147] Thus the Court of Appeals affirmed in part and reserved in part. After the rehearing was granted, the circuit judge of the Court of Appeals affirmed that evidence was insufficient to support a claim of a price-fixing conspiracy based on the theory of conscious parallelism.[148]

[144] *Blomkest Fertilizer, Inc. v. Potash Corp. of Saskatchewan, Inc.*, 176 F.3d 1055, 1999–1 Trade Cases P 72, 515, 1058.

[145] *Blomkest Fertilizer, Inc. v. Potash Corp. of Saskatchewan, Inc.*, 176 F.3d 1055, 1999–1 Trade Cases P 72, 515, 1059.

[146] *Blomkest Fertilizer, Inc. v. Potash Corp. of Saskatchewan, Inc.*, 176 F.3d 1055, 1999–1 Trade Cases P 72, 515, 1060.

[147] *Blomkest Fertilizer, Inc. v. Potash Corp. of Saskatchewan, Inc.*, 176 F.3d 1055, 1999–1 Trade Cases P 72, 515, 1056.

[148] *Blomkest Fertilizer, Inc. v. Potash Corp. of Saskatchewan, Inc.*, 203 F.3d 1028, 2000–1 Trade Cases P 72,812, C.A.8 (Minn.), 17 February 2000 (NO. 97-1330).

Morgan Stanley Capital Group, Inc., v. Public Utility District No 1 of Snohomish County et al., Supreme Court of the US

The California Legislature deregulated the power industry in 1996, establishing a so-called 'spot market' in which utilities purchased electricity on the day it was needed. In 2000 and 2001, during exceptionally hot summers, wholesale electricity prices skyrocketed. In response, several utilities on the Western power grid, such as Snohomish County, determined that they could no longer afford the spot market, and instead negotiated less expensive but still inflated long-term contracts with power suppliers, such as Morgan Stanley. Snohomish signed a nine-year contract to purchase electricity from petitioner Morgan Stanley at a rate of US$105 per megawatt hour (MWh), whereas prices in the Pacific Northwest have historically averaged US$24/MWh.[149] Not only was Morgan Stanley charging these new prices, but also most players in the market had done the same (e.g. Enron and other players). Once the crisis had passed, the utilities asked the government to let them change the contracts to reflect the new lowered electricity prices. The government refused, citing a long-standing Supreme Court doctrine presuming that utilities' contracts were reasonable and did not harm the public interest. The Ninth Circuit ultimately ordered the government to permit the changes.[150]

As the above analysis of the case law illustrates, the US competition authorities and courts have been less apprehensive of crisis cartels than the European Commission and the CFI or ECJ. The US has been more strict on enforcing the per se illegality of crisis cartels. The only case in which the Supreme Court did apply the rule of reason to a cartel is *Appalachian Coals, Inc. v. United States*,[151] involving a price cartel established under emergency circumstances in the coal industry. Thus the Supreme Court has accepted, albeit with within narrow limits, crisis cartels. This decision, which is an exception to the per se rule, was based on a detailed analysis of the extraordinary circumstances of the case.

[149] See www.solarbuzz.com/CaliforniaEnergyCrisis.htm for details on the 2001 energy crisis in the US.

[150] *Morgan Stanley Capital Group, Inc., v. Public Utility District No 1 of Snohomish County et al.*, 19 February 2008, decided 26 June 2008, No 06–1457. 2008.

[151] *Appalachian Coals, Inc. v. United States*, (1933) 288 U.S. 344 .

5.5 Crisis cartels in other jurisdictions

In order to complete the analysis of crisis cartels in the major jurisdictions, we should include the crisis cartels that have been alleged in other jurisdictions.[152]

5.5.1 *Ireland*

The Competition Authority v. The Beef Industry Development Society Ltd

The issue in this case is whether the arrangements by the members of the Beef Industry Development Society Ltd (BIDS), for the purposes of the rationalization of the beef processing industry in Ireland through a mechanism of reduction of the overall capacity in the industry, have as their object or effect the prevention, restriction or distortion of competition in the common market and therefore fall within the prohibition under Article 101(1) TFEU.

BIDS was an industrial and provident society established by fifteen beef processing companies in 2002, the members of which represented approximately 93 per cent of the market for beef supply in Ireland. The second defendant was a beef processing company which reached an agreement with BIDS but had not taken an active part in the proceedings.[153]

The overcapacity in the Irish beef processing industry could be attributed to some historic reasons, including the considerable subsidies granted by the government to the industry which resulted in

[152] For further details on important case law and legislation in the UK and Ireland, see further the chapters on the United Kingdom and Ireland in I. Kokkoris, *Competition Cases from the European Union: The Ultimate Guide to Leading Cases of the EU and All 27 Member States*, Sweet and Maxwell, 2007. In Spain, Law 52/1999 (the LDC) took effect on 29 March 2000. The LDC maintained three reasons for authorization of agreements and collusive practices. These reasons are the promotion of exports, increase in the economic level of depressed zones, and incapacity to significantly affect competition. E.N. Varona, 'Amendments to the Spanish Law for the Defence of Competition' (2000) 21(4) *ECLR* 235, at p. 235. The excess capacity which constituted a reason for authorizing an agreement or collusive practice in the previous LDC was deleted in the amended LDC. Thus pursuant to the amendment to the LDC crisis cartels are not likely to be authorized. We briefly look at crisis cartels in Argentina below.

[153] *The Competition Authority v. The Beef Industry Development Society Ltd and Another*, [2008 E.C.C. 6, 113].

the construction of plants irrespective of actual demand for beef.[154] In addition, significant seasonality of production in the industry also led to the capacity reaching a level which should have been able to meet demand in the peak season. However, with the implementation of the reform of the Common Agricultural Policy in 1992, under which financial support was no longer granted through the processors and a deseasonalization premium was introduced for the purposes of reducing seasonal variation in production, there was substantial overcapacity in the beef processing industry.[155] As found in a report in 1998 presented by a consultant commissioned by the government and the industry, the industry had an estimated overall capacity to kill 66,000 head of cattle a week, while actual maximum output was 45,000 a week and average output was 32,000 a week. The report also predicted that overcapacity was very likely to increase, and if so, it would have an adverse effect on the profitability of the industry as a whole.[156] The report proposed that rationalization of the players and plants in the industry be implemented, reducing the number of the processors; those processors staying in the industry ('stayers') compensating the processors exiting the industry ('goers'). A Beef Task Force was then established by the minister for agriculture and food. It issued a report in 1999, acknowledging the findings and proposals in the consultant's report above and recommending that a special fund be set up to facilitate the rationalization.[157]

In 2002, BIDS was established for such a purpose. It prepared the arrangements for rationalization, which provided, among other things, the following: (1) 'the goers would voluntarily agree to exit the beef industry' and be bound by a two-year non-compete covenant; (2) 'the processing plants of the goers would be decommissioned'; (3) 'land associated with the decommissioned plants would not be used for the purposes of beef processing for a period of five years'; (4) the goers would be compensated by the BIDS with the fund set up by the stayers; (5) 'a levy system would be established under which the stayers would pay BIDS

[154] *The Competition Authority v. The Beef Industry Development Society Ltd and Another*, [2008 E.C.C. 6, 113], at p. 117.

[155] *The Competition Authority v. The Beef Industry Development Society Ltd and Another*, [2008 E.C.C. 6, 113].

[156] *The Competition Authority v. The Beef Industry Development Society Ltd and Another*, [2008 E.C.C. 6, 113], at p. 118.

[157] *The Competition Authority v. The Beef Industry Development Society Ltd and Another*, [2008 E.C.C. 6, 113], at p. 119.

levies based on an agreed formula, i.e., a GBP2 levy on the traditional (percentage) cattle kill level of stayers and an GBP11 levy on cattle kill above the traditional (percentage) cattle kill level'; and (6) 'the equipment of goers used for primary beef processing would only be sold to the stayers for use as back-up equipment or spare parts or otherwise sold outside Ireland'.[158]

During its preparation of the above arrangements, BIDS consulted with the Competition Authority. The Competition Authority filed an application to the Irish High Court on 30 June 2003, on the ground that the BIDS arrangements were prohibited under Article 101(1), and sought restraining orders. It was alleged that the BIDS arrangements were intended to restrict and control production and capacity of the beef supply in the Irish market, which would ultimately have an impact on pricing and lead to increased prices for consumers.[159] BIDS denied the allegation of the Competition Authority, arguing that 'the arrangements did not have, either as object or effect, the prevention, restriction or distortion of competition', but acknowledged that 'the arrangements were liable to have an appreciable effect on the trade between Member States for the purposes of Article 101(1)'.[160]

The High Court dismissed the claim of the Competition Authority. It found that no provision of the BIDS arrangements could be considered plainly or evidently a limitation on output, a sharing of the market or a prohibition on investment, and held that they 'did not have either as their object or their effect the prevention, restriction or distortion of competition'. In the meantime, although it was not necessary for the High Court to consider whether the arrangements should be exempt under Article 101(3) if they did not fall within the prohibition of Article 101(1), it nevertheless examined the applicability of Article 101(3) and found that the arrangements satisfied three of its four requirements, excluding the requirement of a fair share of the resulting benefits to consumers, which BIDS did not discharge its burden to prove.[161] However, since the arrangements did not infringe

[158] *The Competition Authority v. The Beef Industry Development Society Ltd and Another*, [2008 E.C.C. 6, 113], at p. 121.

[159] *The Competition Authority v. The Beef Industry Development Society Ltd and Another*, [2008 E.C.C. 6, 113], at p. 122.

[160] *The Competition Authority v. The Beef Industry Development Society Ltd and Another*, [2008 E.C.C. 6, 113].

[161] *The Competition Authority v. The Beef Industry Development Society Ltd and Another*, [2008 E.C.C. 6, 113], at pp. 122–3.

Article 101(1), there was no need for the High Court to rule on the applicability of Article 101(3).[162]

The Competition Authority appealed the judgment of the High Court to the Supreme Court. They argued that the arrangements were restrictive by object because they involved a restriction of capacity, which should be equated with a restriction of output for the purposes of Article 101(1); a reduction in capacity by itself should also be considered restriction by object. BIDS contended that a reduction of excess capacity should not be necessarily regarded as a restriction of output in every case and therefore constituted a restriction of competition by object prohibited under Article 101(1).[163] They argued that as long as there was no output limitation in the market as a whole, there would be no output limitation within the meaning of Article 101(1). The BIDS arrangements did not restrict the stayers' ability to increase their capacity or production and they could do so at their own discretion, and the High Court found that the exit of the goers would not restrict the overall output of the industry. BIDS also contended that a reduction in capacity could not be equal to a limitation on output, especially when it was a reduction of excess capacity.[164]

The arrangements would not result in the insufficiency of the remaining capacity, but were intended to 'reduce the excess capacity in the industry to achieve an efficient allocation of resources and make it more competitive in the international markets'. Furthermore, BIDS argued that a reduction in capacity was not a 'hardcore' restriction like price-fixing, output limitation or market-sharing, and that therefore the Competition Authority should go further to consider the effect of such a reduction in its legal and economic context.

The Supreme Court considered that the appeal was concerned with the interpretation of 'the arrangement or decision which were restrict [*sic*] by object' provided in Article 101(1).[165] Depending on the interpretation, if Article 101(1) is applied in the first stage in this case, then it would be necessary for it to consider the applicability of Article

[162] *The Competition Authority v. The Beef Industry Development Society Ltd and Another*, [2008 E.C.C. 6, 113], at p. 123.

[163] *The Competition Authority v. The Beef Industry Development Society Ltd and Another*, [2008 E.C.C. 6, 113], at p. 124.

[164] *The Competition Authority v. The Beef Industry Development Society Ltd and Another*, [2008 E.C.C. 6, 113], at p. 125.

[165] *The Competition Authority v. The Beef Industry Development Society Ltd and Another*, [2008 E.C.C. 6, 113], at p. 126.

101(3). The Supreme Court was not referred to any clear interpretation of Article 101(1) for the purposes of this case by the European Court of Justice, so it decided to stay the proceedings and referred the following question to the ECJ for a preliminary ruling on whether

> where it is established to the satisfaction of the Court that:
>
> (a) there is overcapacity in the industry for the processing of beef, which calculated at peak throughput, would be approximately 32%;
> (b) the effect of this excess capacity would have very serious consequences for the profitability of the industry as a whole over the medium term;
> (c) while, as reported, the effects of surplus requirements have not been felt to any significant degree as yet, independent consultants have advised that, in the near term, the overcapacity is unlikely to be eliminated by normal market measures, but over time the overcapacity will lead to very significant losses and ultimately to processors and plants leaving the industry;
> (d) processors of beef representing approximately 93% of the market for the supply of beef of that industry have agreed to take steps to eliminate the overcapacity and are willing to pay a levy in order to fund payments to processors willing to cease production, and the said processors, comprising ten companies, form a corporate body, for the purpose of implementing an arrangement with certain features, and that it is agreed that such an agreement is liable, for the purpose of application of Article 101(1) to have an appreciable effect on trade between Member States, is such an arrangement to be regarded as having as its object, as distinct from effect, the prevention, restriction or distortion of competition within the common market and therefore as incompatible with Article 101(1).[166]

According to the ECJ, when deciding whether an agreement will be caught by Article 101(1), it is not necessary to further consider its actual effect if it seems to have as its object to prevent, restrict or distort competition within the common market.[167] The Competition Authority, the Belgian government and the Commission of European Communities submitted written observations to the ECJ with a view that the BIDS arrangements were anti-competitive (thus there was no need to examine their actual effect) and that they should fall within the prohibition under

[166] *The Competition Authority v. The Beef Industry Development Society Ltd and Another*, [2008 E.C.C. 6, 113], at p. 127.

[167] Case C-209/07 *The Competition Authority v. The Beef Industry Development Society Ltd and Barry Brothers (Carrigmore) Meats Ltd*, [2008, ECR 00], para. 16.

Article 101(1).[168] BIDS argued that the arrangements did not fall within the scope of infringement by object under Article 101(1), and therefore should be examined in light of their actual effect on the market.[169] It also argued that the purpose of the arrangements was to 'rationalise the beef industry in order to make it more competitive' through a mechanism of reduction of excess capacity in the industry, and therefore they were not anti-competitive in purpose and they did not cause adverse effect on the consumers and on competition in general. The ECJ did not accept the arguments put forward by BIDS. According to the ECJ, close attention must be paid to the wording and the objective of an agreement when determining whether it falls within the prohibition of Article 101(1).[170] Even if it can be established that the parties have no 'subjective intention to restrict competition, but with an object to remedy the effects of a crisis in the industry', it is irrelevant for the purposes of applying Article 101(1). It may only be taken into account when considering whether an exemption under Article 101(3) could be granted.

The ECJ stated,[171]

> In fact, to determine whether an agreement comes within the prohibition laid down in Article 81(1) EC, close regard must be paid to the wording of its provisions and to the objectives which it is intended to attain. In that regard, even supposing it to be established that the parties to an agreement acted without any subjective intention of restricting competition, but with the object of remedying the effects of a crisis in their sector, such considerations are irrelevant for the purposes of applying that provision. Indeed, an agreement may be regarded as having a restrictive object even if it does not have the restriction of competition as its sole aim but also pursues other legitimate objectives (General Motors v. Commission, paragraph 64 and the case-law cited). It is only in connection with Article 81(3) EC that matters such as those relied upon by BIDS may, if appropriate, be taken into consideration for the purposes of obtaining an exemption from the prohibition laid down in Article 81(1) EC.

The ECJ has stated in past decisions that the existence of a crisis in the market cannot in itself preclude the anti-competitive nature of an

[168] Case C-209/07 *The Competition Authority v. The Beef Industry Development Society Ltd and Barry Brothers (Carrigmore) Meats Ltd*, [2008, ECR 00], para. 18.

[169] Case C-209/07 *The Competition Authority v. The Beef Industry Development Society Ltd and Barry Brothers (Carrigmore) Meats Ltd*, [2008, ECR 00], para. 19.

[170] Case C-209/07 *The Competition Authority v. The Beef Industry Development Society Ltd and Barry Brothers (Carrigmore) Meats Ltd*, [2008, ECR 00], para. 21.

[171] Case C-209/07 *The Competition Authority v. The Beef Industry Development Society Ltd and Barry Brothers (Carrigmore) Meats Ltd*, [2008, ECR 00], para. 21.

agreement, although the existence of a crisis might have been relied upon in order to seek an exemption under Article 101(3).[172] The ECJ in this case, as well, does not prohibit the existence of crisis cartels per se, but argues that the legality of such cartels needs to be assessed pursuant to the exemption criteria of Article 101(3). This view confirms the practice, in relation to crisis cartels, that we have seen in the enforcement of Article 101 since the early 1960s.

The ECJ found that the BIDS arrangements were intended to allow the processors who represented more than 90 per cent of the beef supply in the Irish market to achieve their minimum efficient scale and thereby improve the overall profitability of those processors; by doing so, market concentration would be increased and almost 75 per cent of the excess capacity would be reduced.[173] The ECJ concluded that such arrangements contradicted the fundamental principle in the EC Treaty regarding competition that each undertaking should be able to make an independent decision regarding their activities in the common market.[174] The ECJ also found that the measures adopted under the BIDS arrangements included restrictions with anti-competitive object.[175] The levy of UK£11 beyond the usual volume of production of a stayer would discourage the stayer to produce beyond its usual level of production and therefore the natural development of the market share might be affected.[176] Restrictions imposed on disposal and use of the processing plants of the goers would make it impossible for the new entrants into this industry to compete with the stayers and therefore such restrictions had as their object a restriction of competition.[177]

172 Court of Justice in Joined Cases C-238/99 P, C-244/99 P, C-245/99 P, C-247/99 P, C-250/99 P to C-252/99 P and C-254/99 P *LVM and Others v. Commission*, 16 October 2002, para. 487.

173 Court of Justice in Joined Cases C-238/99 P, C-244/99 P, C-245/99 P, C-247/99 P, C-250/99 P to C-252/99 P and C-254/99 P *LVM and Others v. Commission*, 16 October 2002, para. 32.

174 Court of Justice in Joined Cases C-238/99 P, C-244/99 P, C-245/99 P, C-247/99 P, C-250/99 P to C-252/99 P and C-254/99 P *LVM and Others v. Commission*, 16 October 2002, para. 34.

175 Court of Justice in Joined Cases C-238/99 P, C-244/99 P, C-245/99 P, C-247/99 P, C-250/99 P to C-252/99 P and C-254/99 P *LVM and Others v. Commission*, 16 October 2002, para. 36.

176 Court of Justice in Joined Cases C-238/99 P, C-244/99 P, C-245/99 P, C-247/99 P, C-250/99 P to C-252/99 P and C-254/99 P *LVM and Others v. Commission*, 16 October 2002, para. 37.

177 Court of Justice in Joined Cases C-238/99 P, C-244/99 P, C-245/99 P, C-247/99 P, C-250/99 P to C-252/99 P and C-254/99 P *LVM and Others v. Commission*, 16 October 2002, para. 38.

Based on the above, the ECJ replied that the BIDS arrangement 'had as its object the prevention, restriction or distortion of competition within the meaning of Article 101(1)'.[178]

5.5.2 *The United Kingdom*

The Yarn Spinners' Agreement

The Yarn Spinners' Agreement was concluded among the members of the Yarn Spinners Association, providing for a minimum-price scheme for the yarn consisting of 85 per cent cotton or more. Yarn is sold by weight and the price varies significantly according to quality and count. Nevertheless, members of the association were bound not to sell their products of the described specification at a price lower than that in the agreement. The association alleged that the terms of the agreement were not contrary to the public interest; in fact they insisted that the removal of price restrictions had direct adverse consequences on unemployment levels.

By the terms of the Trade Restrictive Act, the scheme was, prima facie, contrary to the public interest, unless the association could prove the existence of the circumstances defined in one or other of the seven categories in §21. The association contended that the Court should be satisfied either with the circumstances set out in category (b) or with those in category (e). Similar claims under categories (a) and (f) were abandoned in the course of the hearing.[179]

Category (b) states that the removal of the restriction would deny to the public as purchasers, consumers or users of any goods other specific and substantial benefits or advantages enjoyed or likely to be enjoyed by them as such, whether by virtue of the restriction itself or by virtue of any arrangements or operations resulting therefrom. The association contended that by virtue of the scheme a number of benefits were enjoyed by the shopping public which purchases cotton goods. Further, it contended that benefits were enjoyed by purchasers of yarn; these were all trade purchasers, mainly weavers, and it was submitted that they constitute the yarn-buying public.

[178] Court of Justice in Joined Cases C-238/99 P, C-244/99 P, C-245/99 P, C-247/99 P, C-250/99 P to C-252/99 P and C-254/99 P *LVM and Others v. Commission*, 16 October 2002, para. 40. Odudu (2008) 'Restrictions of Competition by Object – What's the Beef?' (2009) 9(1) *Competition Law Journal* 11.

[179] Restrictive Trade Practices Act, 1956, s. 21.

The requirement in category (e) is that, having regard to the conditions actually obtaining or reasonably foreseeable at the time of the application, the removal of the restriction would likely have a serious and persistent adverse effect on the general level of unemployment in an area, in which a substantial proportion of the trade or industry is situated.[180]

The members of the association were mainly the spinners of the Lancashire cotton industry. Public consumers were receiving yarn in the form of cotton goods and its price was directly affected by the per-pound price of yarn, which in theory, according to the agreement, was calculated on a hypothetical average cost and did not represent the cost actually incurred by any individual mill; every mill would, therefore, be above or below it by a smaller or larger margin. The industry itself was in recession; mills were closing in spite of the agreement that facilitated higher prices than those that would have pertained in a free market. Without the agreement the number of mills put out of business would have increased, nevertheless the agreement itself only postponed the inevitable shutdown. However, in both cases the public interest would not be affected as the industry had stable demand and the capacity of manufacturers was enough to meet almost any fluctuations in demand, with the exception of an increase of export market share.

The spinning industry employed around 100,000 people and was concentrated in a small area within Lancashire. If the agreement were to be abrogated, the industry would, in order to survive, have to get rid of a redundant 20 per cent or so of the workforce, which in turn, according to the Ministry of Labour, would increase the unemployment level in the region from 4.3 per cent to 5.9 per cent. The majority of employees were women and elderly people, whose opportunities for re-employment were not too bright.

The association had not presented enough evidence to prove that the removal of the agreement would result in any loss of benefit to the public. The agreement itself was contradictory of the concept of free trade; although it might have provided some advantages in the form of price stability its merits to consumers remained arguable. The benefit to the public of the free market, on the other hand, was a general presumption. Therefore the question was whether the benefits of the agreement outweighed the benefits of the free market in the specific circumstances

[180] Restrictive Trade Practices Act, 1956, s. 21.

of the present case. The association was not able to convince the Court on that specific issue of price stability.

Considering the association's point about adverse unemployment consequences for the eleven areas, the Court had to consider factors such as the number of mills that would be closed if the agreement were overruled, the number of mills to be closed irrespective of the decision, the number of workers who would lose their jobs and the time it might take them to find new ones. The Court had to base its decision on a number of assumptions, as there was no possibility of obtaining more precise information. It was agreed that the consequences of the abrogation would have adverse affects on the unemployment situation in the region.

There was no perceivable reduction in the availability of cotton goods, unless the lowering of the price of yarn might trigger it. It might have resulted in a price reduction that was beneficial to the public, therefore the association's agreement would have been detrimental to a free-market price that would have been lower without any such restrictions. The redundant workforce was also a concern, but it would have only local ramifications, contrary to the global consequences that might have been induced by the restriction. The benefits to the yarn purchasers were obvious, although this was only for a rather small class of traders. Based on the above analysis the Court concluded that the restrictions would be unreasonable. Thus the association was not able to refer to §21 of the Act as a whole and the restrictions were declared contrary to the public interest.[181]

5.5.3 *Argentina*

It is widely accepted that success in the application of competition legislation appears to be due in significant part to a policy consensus within government. In countries where political and social commitment to competition law enforcement is more ambivalent, or where other priorities prevail, such as in Argentina, competition agencies appear to have been less successful in enforcing competition legislation.[182]

The Argentine government, concerned about the crisis in 2005,

[181] Yarn Spinners' Agreement, the Westlaw database.

[182] For a general overview of competition law enforcement in Latin American countries, see further B.M. Owen, Competition Policy in Latin America, Stanford Law School John M. Olin Program in Law and Economics Working Paper 268, 2003.

intended to promote the conclusion of 'price agreements' with supermarkets and dairy and meat producers. These agreements were intended to fix the retail and wholesale prices of some key products for a given period of time. The government used high export tariffs to ensure supply in the domestic market. More recently, though, the government has started an active 'pro-antitrust' campaign, accusing supermarkets of being involved in unlawful collusive practices.[183]

After looking at crisis cartels in a number of jurisdictions, this chapter now turns to addressing the concept of 'financial constraints' in cartel cases. Undertakings raise this argument in order to achieve a reduction in imposed fines. The European and US authorities and courts have accepted such arguments in a number of cartel cases and have imposed lower fines than those that would have been imposed had the 'financial-constraints' defence not been raised.

5.6 Financial-constraints defence

The 'financial-constraints' consideration reflects a concern that high fines might force an offending firm into insolvency. The EC and the US have wide discretion as well as lack of transparency in awarding these discounts. However, factors external to competition policy, in particular the social objectives of the EC Treaty, may determine how they are granted. Following the Lisbon Treaty's coming into force on 1 December 2009, interpretative issues could also arise due to the stronger references to full employment and social objectives, including the reference to a 'highly competitive social market economy', in amended Article 3 of the Treaty on European Union. This might induce arguments that a broader industrial policy standard should apply.[184]

So firms can be involved in cartels and not ending up paying fines in crisis situations, thus increasing their profits from collusion, and increasing their tendency to be in cartels (in the absence of criminal sanctions like those the UK competition authorities can impose). The Commission has accepted such discounts in crisis industries, rather than for individual firms in crisis.

[183] P.I. Colomo, 'The Revival of Antitrust Law in Argentina: Policy or Politics?' (2006) 27(6) *ECLR* 317.

[184] See www.wilmehale.com/publications/whPubsDetail.aspx?publication=9321

5.6.1 *Seamless steel tubes*

Eight undertakings producing seamless steel tubes (four European, four Japanese) concluded an agreement not to sell tubes of another party to the agreement in their respective domestic markets.[185] The Commission found that the undertakings respected each other's domestic markets for standard steel borehole pipes and project transportation pipes used in the exploration and transport of oil and gas. The Commission concluded that the agreement had an anti-competitive effect on the common market. The cartel lasted from 1977 to 1994, meeting twice each year. The market was defined as that for the manufacturing and distribution of seamless steel tubes for the oil and gas industries.

The Commission argued that the parties were guilty of anti-competitive practices including price-fixing, partitioning of domestic territories and the making of an agreement to share the remainder of the world markets for seamless steel tubes.

The Commission considered that 1990 should be taken as the starting point of the cartel for the purpose of fixing the amount of the fines, owing to the existence, between 1977 and 1990, of an agreement between the European Community and Japan on the voluntary restraint of exports. According to the Commission, the infringement came to an end in 1995. However, in the case of different undertakings, the infringement time varied, starting in 1990 and 1991 and finishing between 1994 and 1997.

Setting the amount of fines, the Commission took into account the fact that the steel pipe and tube industry had been in crisis for a long time and that the situation in the sector had deteriorated since 1991. The Commission reduced the basic amounts by 10 per cent, on the ground of attenuating circumstances.[186]

The Court of First Instance (CFI) refused to annul the Commission's decision but reduced the fines imposed on three European and four Japanese producers as the Commission had not shown that it should have set the starting date for the infringement earlier than 1991, and, in relation to the Japanese producers, the Commission had wrongly assessed the gravity of the infringement.

[185] Decision 2003/382, [2003] OJ L140/1. See appeals: *Mannesmannröhren-Werke AG v. EC Commission* (T-44/00); *Corus UK Ltd v. EC Commission* (T-48/00); *Dalmine SpA v. EC Commission* (T-50/00) and *JFE Engineering Corp. and Others v. EC Commission* (T-67/00, T-68/00, T-71/00 and T-78/00), *Salzgitter Mannesmann GmbH v. European Commission* (Case C-411/04 P) [2007] All ER (D) 196 (Jan).

[186] Commission Press Release IP/99/957, 8 December 1999

5.6.2 French Beef

In the *French Beef* case the Commission alleged that French federations in the beef sector were involved in a price-fixing cartel.[187] Following deflated prices for beef in France as a result of the BSE crisis, the French agriculture minister actively encouraged an agreement between four French farmers' unions and two French slaughterhouse unions. This agreement provided for the purchase of beef at fixed minimum prices and for the boycott of imports in order to stabilize and maintain the level of prices. Although the actual agreement was of short duration, in practice it continued as a recommendation from the unions. The Commission argued that the infringement continued from October 2001 until January 2002.

The Commission underlined that even these special circumstances cannot entitle private parties to pursue anti-competitive conduct.[188] However, the imposed fines were very low, as the Commission gave extensive credit for the exceptional economic context. The fines were reduced by 60 per cent, rather than the more usual 10–15 per cent that is the usual reduction in cases of sectors in crisis.

The Commission considered the specific economic context of the case. It emphasized that measures had already been taken under the Common Market organization for beef in order to attenuate the crisis in the sector, and thus additional initiatives involving anti-competitive conduct could not be justified.

As the CFI states,

> the economic context was characterised by the following factors: first, the drop in the consumption of beef as a result of the 'mad cow' crisis, which affected a sector already in a difficult situation; second, intervention measures taken by the Community and national authorities aimed at restoring balance in the beef market; third, the loss of consumer confidence, linked to the fear of 'mad cow' disease; fourth, the situation of farmers who, despite Community adjustment measures applied by France, were faced with slaughterhouse entry prices for cows which were falling again, while consumer prices remained stable.[189]

In December 2006, the CFI reduced the fines imposed by the Commission on the main French federations in the beef

[187] Decision, [2003] OJ L209/12.IP/03/1105, 23 July 2003.
[188] Commission Press Release IP/03/479, 2 April 2003.
[189] Para. 356 of the Commission's decision.

sector.[190] The overall fines concerned were reduced from €15.96 million to €11.97 million.

The CFI rejected the appeals but argued that reduction of the fine by 60 per cent for exceptional circumstances by the Commission was not enough.

The CFI stated,

> It must be borne in mind that, while the Commission has discretion in setting the amount of fines, the Court has, by virtue of Article 17 of Regulation No 17, unlimited jurisdiction within the meaning of Article 229 EC to review decisions whereby the Commission has fixed a fine and may, consequently, cancel, reduce or increase the fine imposed.[191]
>
> In the present case, the Court considers that the different consequences identified and taken into account by the Commission in the contested decision pursuant to section 5(b) of the Guidelines are very exceptional. Their exceptional nature arises from the particular characteristics of the applicants, their functions and their respective spheres of activity, as well as from the circumstances inherent in the economic context of this particular case.
>
> The Court considers that the 60% reduction in the fines decided upon by the Commission pursuant to Section 5(b) of the Guidelines, although substantial, does not take sufficient account of all those exceptional circumstances.
>
> Therefore, to take full and proper account of all the circumstances identified by the Commission in the contested decision and in consideration of the fact that this is the first time that the Commission has sanctioned this type of anti-competitive conduct, the Court, asserting its unlimited jurisdiction, considers it appropriate to set at 70% the reduction to be allowed in the applicants' fines pursuant to Section 5(b) of the Guidelines.

The CFI first emphasized the Commission's discretion to set fines, and the CFI's unlimited jurisdiction under Article 229 EC Treaty and Article 17 of Regulation 17/62.[192] Taking into account the severe crisis in the sector the CFI reduced the fine by 70 per cent for 'very exceptional' circumstances.[193]

[190] *Fédération nationale de la coopération bétail et viande (FNCBV) and Fédération nationale des syndicats d'exploitants agricoles (FNSEA) v. Commission of the European Communities* (T-217/03 & T-245/03), 13 December 2006.

[191] Paras. 358–61 of the judgment of the CFI.

[192] J. Ratliff, 'Major Events and Policy Issues in EC Competition Law, 2006–2007: Part 1' (2008) 19(2) *I.C.C.L.R.* 29.

[193] *Fédération nationale de la coopération bétail et viande* (T-217/03), 13 December 2006, paras. 358–61.

5.6.3 *Bolloré SA v. Commission of the European Communities*

In autumn 1996 the Commission suspected the existence of a cartel in the market for carbonless paper.[194] According to the Commission decision,[195] the parties to the cartel agreed on an overall anti-competitive plan aiming essentially at improving the profitability of the participants by collectively increasing prices. The principal objective of the cartel through that plan was to agree price increases and also the timing of those increases. To that end, various meetings were organized at different levels – general, national and regional. The general cartel meetings were followed by a series of national or regional meetings, the purpose of which was to ensure market-by-market implementation of the price increases agreed at the general cartel meetings. During these meetings the participants exchanged detailed and individual information on their prices and sales volumes. In order to ensure implementation of the agreed price increases, in some national cartel meetings sales quotas were allocated and market shares were fixed for each participant.

The Commission took the view that the cartel arrangements involved all major operators in the EEA and were conceived, directed and encouraged at high levels in each participating company. By its very nature, the implementation of that type of cartel leads automatically to an important distortion of competition. Taking into account the nature of the behaviour under scrutiny, its actual impact on the carbonless paper market and the fact that it covered the whole of the common market and, following its creation, the whole EEA, the Commission considered that the undertakings concerned by the decision had committed a very serious infringement of Article 101(1).

In order to establish the starting amount of the fine according to the gravity of the infringement, the Commission put the undertakings concerned into five categories according to their relative importance in the market concerned. In order to ensure that the fine had a sufficient deterrent effect, it then increased the starting amount of the fine thus determined by 100 per cent for AWA, Bolloré and Sappi. The Commission then took into account the duration of the infringement committed by each undertaking in order to fix the basic amount of the fines imposed.

As regards aggravating circumstances, the Commission increased the basic amount of the fine imposed on AWA by 50 per cent on account

194 T-109/02, *Bollore SA v. Commission of the European Communities*, [2007] ECR II-947.

195 Case COMP/E-1/36.212 – *Carbonless Paper*, OJ 2004 L 115/1.

of its position as cartel leader. The Commission did not establish any extenuating circumstances in the present case.

The Commission adopted the final amounts to take into account the provisions of Article 15(2) of Regulation 17 (recital 434), then applied the Leniency Notice which justified a reduction in the amount of the fines by 50 per cent for Mougeot, 35 per cent for AWA, 20 per cent for Bolloré (Copigraph) and by 10 per cent for Carrs, MHTP and Zanders.

The parties sought annulment of the decision and/or cancellation or reduction of the fine. Regarding the economic situation of the carbonless paper sector, a number of applicants (Bolloré; Zanders; Mougeot; AWA, supported by the Kingdom of Belgium; Koehler) complained that the Commission did not, in contrast to its previous established practice, take account of the crisis which the carbonless paper sector was going through at the material time.

It is apparent from the decision that the carbonless paper market was characterized by structural overcapacity and reduced demand on account of the use of electronic media. Several undertakings claimed to have suffered significant losses during the period in question.

The Commission itself accepted that, during the period covered by the decision, the carbonless paper market was declining. It found, however, at recital 431, that the information received in the replies to the Statement of Objections and the report of Mikulski Hall Associates (MHA) commissioned by the Association of European Manufacturers of Carbonless Paper (AEMCP) did not support the conclusion that during the infringement period, from 1992 to 1995, the carbonless paper sector was in a serious crisis comparable to the sectors concerned in the previous cartel cases mentioned by the undertakings.

The Commission maintained that cartels often originate at times of economic crisis, so that the possibility of taking into account the economic difficulties of the sector concerned can be envisaged only in entirely exceptional circumstances. However, the infringement period could not be described as a particularly serious period of crisis. Notwithstanding the start of a period of decline, sales were maintained at high levels.

The Court of First Instance has stated that just because in earlier cases the Commission had taken the economic sector into account as an attenuating circumstance it did not necessarily have to continue to observe that practice.[196] As the Commission observed, as a general rule

[196] Case T-13/89, *ICI v. Commission*, para. 372.

cartels come into being when a sector encounters problems. If the applicants' reasoning were to be followed, the fine would have to be reduced as a matter of course in virtually all cases.

It must be stated as well that although growth in demand slowed from 1990–91, the real decrease occurred during 1995, towards the end of the infringement established in the decision. The parties adduced no evidence such as to cast doubt on that data. However, the data suggested that whilst it is true that the market was in decline, the start of the crisis coincided with the end of the infringement.

The Commission was therefore right to find that the situation of the carbonless paper sector did not constitute an attenuating circumstance.

5.6.4 *Cartonboard, Finnboard v. Commission, Metsä-Serla Sales v. Commission*

The infringement in these cases[197] consisted of participating in an agreement and concerted practice by which the producers supplying cartonboard in the Community, in concert and contrary to Article 101,

- met regularly in a series of secret and institutionalized meetings to discuss and agree a common industry plan to restrict competition,
- agreed regular price increases for each grade of the product in each national currency,
- planned and implemented simultaneous and uniform price increases throughout the Community,
- reached an understanding on maintaining the market shares of the major producers at constant levels (subject to modification from time to time),
- took concerted measures to control the supply of the product in the Community in order to ensure the implementation of the said concerted price rises, and
- exchanged commercial information (on deliveries, prices, plant standstills, order backlogs, machine utilization rates and so on) in support of the above restrictions.

The agreement included the 'freezing' of the west European market shares of the major producers at existing levels, with no attempts to be

[197] *Cartonboard*, [1994] OJ L243/1, *Finnboard v. Commission*, T-338/94 [1998] ECR II-1617, *Metsä-Serla Sales v. Commission*, C-298/98 P [2000] ECR I-10157.

made to win new customers or extend existing business through aggressive pricing. In the context of the successful implementation of price initiatives, it was considered essential to develop a comprehensive system for the reporting and monitoring of production, sales volumes and capacity utilization.

The basic objective of the producers in setting up their scheme of institutionalized collusion was artificially and secretly to regulate the market and co-ordinate their behaviour in such a way as to ensure that their concerted price initiatives would be successful.

The Commission collectively imposed a fine of ECU 138 million. Seventeen of the companies held responsible for the infringement subsequently brought actions to contest the decision.

The Court added that the fact that the undertakings participating in the collusion on prices orchestrated the announcement of the concerted price increases, and the fact that they were discouraged from taking notes at meetings to discuss this, prove that they were aware of the unlawfulness of their conduct and that they took steps to conceal the collusion. The Commission is entitled to hold these steps to be aggravating circumstances when assessing the gravity of the infringement. The absence of official minutes and the almost total absence of internal notes relating to the meetings constituted sufficient proof that the participants were discouraged from taking notes, bearing in mind the number of such meetings, the length of time for which they continued and the nature of the discussions in question.

The CFI largely upheld the decision. The ECJ in turn dismissed the appeal. Fiskeby Board AB, a Swedish member of the cartonboard cartel, was fined ECU 1 million. Fiskeby Board argued that, following the *Polypropylene* decision,[198] the fact that it made losses during the period of the infringement should have been taken into account in the calculation of the fine. The CFI argued that the difference is that in the *Polypropylene* case the difficulties were encountered across the whole sector. The crisis that adversely influenced the cartonboard sector was

[198] *Polypropylene Cartel*, [1986] OJ L230/1; *Rhône-Poulenc v. Commission*, T-1/89 [1991] ECR II-827; *Petrofina SA v. Commission*, T-2/89 [1991] ECR II-1087; *Atochem v. Commission*, T-3/89 [1991] ECR II-1177; *Enichem v. Commission*, T-6/89 [1991] ECR II-1623; *SA Hercules NV v. Commission* T-7/89 [1991] ECR II-1711; *ICI v. Commission* T-13/89 [1992] ECR II-1021; *Commission v. Anic Partecipazioni*, C-49/92P, [1999] ECR I-4125; *Hercules Chemicals NV v. Commission*, C-51/92P [1999] ECR I-4235; *Hüls AG v. Commission*, C-199/92P [1999] ECR I-4287; *ICI v. Commission* C-200/92P, [1999] ECR I-4399.

not similar to that which affected the market in the *Polypropylene* case. The ECJ has argued that an individual loss-making situation will not be deemed to mitigate the illegality of a conduct as such a policy would confer an unjustified competitive advantage on undertakings that are least adapted to market conditions.[199] Thus a crisis cartel in a loss-making industry may be treated more leniently.

5.6.5 *Graphite Electrodes, Specialty Graphites, and Carbon & Graphite*

As this analysis shows, the European Commission has accepted a 'financial-constraints' mitigating factor in several cartel cases. This mitigating factor led to reductions in fines in a number of cases. The financial-constraints factor is important in ensuring that the imposition of a fine will not induce the insolvency of the firm. The Commission in a number of cases in the graphite industry took financial constraints into account, including *Graphite Electrodes*,[200] *Specialty Graphites*[201] and *Carbon & Graphite*.[202]

In *Graphite Electrodes*, the Commission rejected arguments from the involved undertakings concerning their ability to pay the fine. The Commission argued that taking account merely of an undertaking's loss-making financial situation would confer an unjustified competitive advantage on undertakings least adapted to the conditions of the market. In contrast to this 'harsh' approach, the Commission in *Specialty Graphites* and *Carbon & Graphite* reduced the fine by 33 per cent due to the financial constraints of the undertakings.

In *Carbon & Graphite*, the Commission stated that SGL was granted a 33 per cent reduction of its fine for the reason that SGL both was undergoing serious financial constraints and had relatively recently had imposed on it two significant fines by the Commission for participation in simultaneous cartel activities.[203] In imposing fines, the Commission has discretion to impose fines that will induce adequate deterrence. The Commission argued that even after the discount to

199 Joined Cases 96/82 to 102/82, 104/82, 105/82, 108/82 and 110/82, *IAZ v. Commission*, [1983] ECR 3369; [1984] 3 CMLR 276, para. 55.

200 Commission Decision of 18 July 2001, Case C-36/490, [2002] OJ L100/1.

201 Commission Decision of 17 December 2002, Case C-37/667, COM (2002) 5083 final.

202 Commission Decision of 3 December 2003, Case C-38/59, [2004] OJ L125/45.

203 [2004] OJ L125/45, para. 360.

SGL due to its financial constraints, the imposed fine would ensure adequate deterrence.[204]

In its appeal against the *Graphite Electrodes* decision to the CFI,[205] SGL argued that the Commission's failure to take account of its poor financial situation was contrary to the Commission's *Speciality Graphites* decision, where the Commission expressly reduced the fine imposed on SGL owing to its serious financial situation. The CFI argued that the latter decision took into consideration both SGL's financial situation and the fact that a large fine had already been imposed on SGL for its participation in the cartel in the graphite electrodes market, so that the Commission considered that 'in these particular circumstances, imposing the full amount of the fine did not appear necessary in order to ensure effective deterrence' (recital 558).[206]

Stephan has argued that the Commission may be influenced by factors that have nothing to do with competition policy.[207] The CFI in the *Graphite Electrodes* appeal, after stating that the Commission is not required to take into account the financial situation of an infringing firm,[208] argued that an undertaking's

> real ability to pay must be taken into consideration. That ability applies only in a 'specific social context' consisting of the consequences which payment of the fine would have, in particular, by leading to an increase in unemployment or deterioration in the economic sectors upstream and downstream of the undertaking concerned.

During the proof stage of this book, on 23 June 2010, the European Commission published its decision in a cartel investigation involving seventeen companies in the bathroom-fitting sector. Five of the smaller companies received lower fines, taking into account their inability to pay due to the recession and in order to prevent their going into insolvency. The Commission looked at recent financial statements, provisional current-year statements and future projections, and at several financial ratios that measure a company's profitability and liquidity.

[204] 'The Speciality Graphite Price Fixing Cartels', *Competition Policy Newsletter* No 1, Spring 2003, at p. 66.

[205] *Tokai Carbon v. Commission* (T 236, 239, 244, 251 & 252/01): [2004] ECR II-1181.

[206] *Tokai Carbon v. Commission* (T 236, 239, 244, 251 & 252/01): [2004] ECR II-1181, para. 374.

[207] A. Stephan, 'The Bankruptcy Wildcard in Cartel Cases' (August 2006) *J.B.L.* 511.

[208] *Tokai Carbon v. Commission* (T 236, 239, 244, 251 & 252/01): [2004] ECR II-1181, para. 370.

Commissioner Almunia noted that the inability to pay would become more prevalent for struggling businesses. This is a very positive development during this period and one we hope will be enhanced (see press release 18/10/790).

This argument by the CFI allows the Commission to take into account the 'specific social context', thus granting the Commission discretion over the factors that it will consider necessitates a reduction in the fine due to financial constraints that the undertaking may be experiencing.

We should reiterate the argument of the CFI that, according to settled case law, the Commission is not required when determining the amount of the fine to take account of an undertaking's financial losses since recognition of such an obligation would have the effect of conferring an unfair competitive advantage on the undertakings least adapted to the conditions of the market.[209] In spite of the above case law, we should note that the CFI noted in *Lögstör Rör v. Commission*[210] that the Commission is not required to regard as an attenuating circumstance the poor financial state of the sector in question and added that just because the Commission has taken account in earlier cases of the economic sector as an attenuating circumstance it does not necessarily have to continue to observe that practice.[211] The CFI stressed that as a general rule cartels come into being when a sector encounters problems, and thus if the Commission was required to take such attenuating circumstances into account, fines would have to be reduced as a matter of course in the majority of cartel cases.

Turning to practice in the USA, the US Department of Justice (DOJ) has invoked an exception similar to the financial-constraints mitigating factor that the European Commission takes into account. The DOJ can take into account the inability of the firm to pay the fine. That may lead, among other things, to a reduction in the level of the fine, as well as to a favourable payment schedule.

The aim of Chapter 11 bankruptcy in the US is to sustain firms in order to prevent the costs related to liquidation. Stephan has mentioned that following the imposition of a US$135 million fine by the DOJ in spring 1998 for price-fixing in the graphite electrodes industry,

[209] Case T-23/99, *LR AF 1998 v. Commission*, [2002] ECR II-1705, para. 308; T-9/99, *HFB and Others v. Commission*, [2002] ECR II-1487, para. 596; and T-213/00, *CMA CGM and Others v. Commission*, [2003] ECR II-913, 'the *FETTCSA* judgment', para. 351.

[210] Case T-16/99, *Lögstör Rör v. Commission, [*2002] ECR II-1633, paras. 319 and 320.

[211] Case T-13/89, *ICI v. Commission*, [1992] ECR II-1021, para. 372.

SGL faced substantial private actions for treble damages. In December 1998, it ordered its US subsidiary to file a voluntary Chapter 11 bankruptcy petition in the US District Court to safeguard itself from these damages claims which could have severely affected its financial viability. The application was not accepted as the Court considered that the firm was on the verge of insolvency in spite of the extent of the likely damages claims that would ensue. However, SGL agreed with the DOJ to pay its fine in five-yearly instalments. In addition, the DOJ requested that the Court waive the requirement for interest due to SGL's inability to pay.[212]

The DOJ reached an agreement with Hynix Semiconductor (which pleaded guilty to price-fixing DRAM computer chips and agreed to pay US$185 million), according to which the fine would be reduced to the ability of the firm to pay; in addition, it would be paid over five years. Stephan makes, however, the interesting argument that the firm would spend US$250 million on a business venture in China.[213]

As this brief account of the treatment of the inability-to-pay exception by DOJ illustrates, we can argue that similar to the Commission's approach, the DOJ is vague on the factors that it will into account in reducing the fine due to the inability of the firm to pay.

Other US cases where the inability to pay has been considered and accepted as a mitigating factor include *UCAR* (US$110 million),[214] *DUCOA* (US$500,000)[215] and *Tokai* (US$110 million).[216]

In *DUCOA* the DOJ argued that beginning in January 1988 and continuing until September 1998, the defendant and co-conspirators entered into and participated in a combination and conspiracy to suppress and eliminate competition by fixing the price and allocating the volume of, as well as customers for, choline chloride manufactured by the defendant and its co-conspirators.

In *UCAR* the DOJ charged the defendant with participating in a conspiracy to suppress and eliminate competition by fixing the price and

[212] *USA v. SGL Carbon Aktiengesellschaft*, Criminal No 99-244, US District Court, Pennsylvania. See further Stephan 2006, at p. 530.

[213] Stephan 2006, quoting H. Mutchnik and C. Casamassima, '*United States* v. *Hynix Semiconductor, Inc*: Opening the Door to the Inability-to-Pay Defence?' (2005) *Antitrust Source* 4.

[214] *USA v. UCAR International Inc.*, Criminal No 98-177, 13 April 1999, US District Court, Pennsylvania; *USA v. Mitsubishi Corp.*, Criminal No 00-033, 19 April 2001.

[215] *USA v. DUCOA, LP*, Criminal No 3-02CR0029IN, 30 September 1999, US District Court, Texas.

[216] *USA v. Tokai Carbon Co. Ltd*, Criminal No 99-233, 18 May 1999, US District Court, Pennsylvania.

allocating the volume of graphite electrodes sold in the United States and elsewhere in unreasonable restraint of trade and commerce beginning at least in July 1992 and continuing until June 1997. As regards the calculation of the fine, the DOJ argued that

> Pursuant to 18 U.S.C. §3612(f)(3)(A), the Government respectfully requests that the Court waive the requirement for interest due to UCAR's inability to pay . . . In essence, the below-Guidelines minimum fine (but still $10 million larger than the previous highest Sherman Act fine), the payment schedule, and the absence of interest reflect a public-interest balancing of the need to punish UCAR for its participation in this egregious conspiracy against the need to avoid jeopardizing the company's continued viability in light of its extensive liabilities.
>
> The United States also recommends that the Court impose no order of restitution because UCAR has been sued by the victims of this conspiracy – all sophisticated companies represented by knowledgeable, private antitrust counsel. There are class actions, as well as suits instituted by other groups of graphite electrodes customers, which seek treble damages and attorneys fees as provided for persons damaged by violations of the antitrust laws under Section Four of the Clayton Act, 15 U.S.C. §4. Given the remedies afforded victims of antitrust crime and the active involvement of private antitrust counsel representing the victims of this case, the need to fashion a restitution order is outweighed by the difficulty the Court would encounter in attempting to determine the losses suffered by all of the many victims and the undue complication and prolongation of the sentencing process.

In *Tokai* the DOJ stated that the defendant had participated in a conspiracy to suppress and eliminate competition by fixing the price and allocating the volume of graphite electrodes beginning in 1992 and continuing until 1997. The DOJ argued that although Tokai played an active role in the illegal conduct, other conspiring competitors, including the leaders and organizers of the conspiracy, were substantially larger in terms of worldwide production and sales, and Tokai's share of the United States market was extremely small. The DOJ added that the Court should impose no order of restitution because Tokai had been sued by the victims of this conspiracy in class actions. In reducing the fine for *Tokai* the DOJ referred to the *UCAR* decision and to UCAR's inability to pay a high fine without jeopardizing its continued viability.

Thus, as the above analyses illustrate, both EU and US authorities have accepted the financial-constraints argument in their assessment of cartels and have thus been lenient when imposing fines. The existence of such an argument may, in the absence of criminal sanctions, incentivize parties in industries experiencing difficulties to conclude cartel agreements and then, once caught, invoke this argument and achieve a reduced fine. Thus the likely payoff of such a cartel agreement is higher than would be the case without invoking the financial-constraints argument. However, a pragmatic balance needs to be struck, as the penultimate chapter of this book will show, between referring a cartelist and inducing its bankruptcy.

5.7 Concluding remarks

As the case law illustrates, crisis cartels are likely to appear in industries where production facilities are durable and specialized and consumer demand falls due to adverse market conditions.

The Commission and the CFI or ECJ will authorize a restructuring plan involving sectoral agreements if they consider that Article 101(3) criteria are met. These criteria will be met if the reduction in the capacity of the sector will in the long term lead to more efficent capacity utilization, enhancing the competitiveness of the sector and thus benefiting consumers. In addition, as the Commission interestingly argues, a factor that will be taken into account is the impact of the capacity co-ordination on the mitigation of the adverse impact of the crisis on employment.[217]

The Commission explicitly states that reorganization operations should also be used to stabilize and secure the employment situation in the sector concerned.[218] Again the Commission uses the positive impact on employment of a co-ordination of the business conduct of competitors as a factor favouring exemption of the agreement. Thus a detailed plan of plant closures as well as avoidance of the creation of new capacity are also necessary factors in the agreement being accepted by the Commission.

In addition, the agreement must constitute indispensable means of achieving the necessary capacity reduction. The limited duration of the agreement, the existence of firms in the industry which are not party to the agreement, and the fact that the co-ordinated reduction in capacity is only one element in the business strategy of firms constitute reassurance that competition will not be eliminated.

The Commission, the CFI, the ECJ, and the US and German authorities and courts have been somewhat lenient towards crisis cartels.

[217] Twenty-third Report on Competition Policy, para. 85.
[218] Twenty-third Report on Competition Policy, para. 88.

Germany recently abolished the sections on rationalization cartels as well as structural crisis cartels. US authorities and courts have always been stricter than Germany and the EU on such cartels, assessing them pursuant to an approach of per se illegality. Thus in periods where undertakings are experiencing severe difficulties as a result of systemic crisis conditions in a market, allowing crisis cartels under certain conditions may prove an effective way to tackle the further deterioration of the market due to excessive capacity. Sustaining excessive capacity may lead to markets with a small number of firms, thus the result may be worse than would occur if crisis cartels were allowed.

Intuitively, between a market with a small number of remaining firms and a market with a significant number of firms which, in periods of severe crisis threatening the sustainability of whole sectors of the economy, decide to co-ordinate in the reduction of capacity, the latter alternative may be more beneficial to the market. We should note that in the latter scenario, as soon as the adverse conditions in the market cease to exist, the structure of the market that results after the expiration of the crisis cartel agreement (which should follow positive developments in the market) is likely to have a greater potential to return to pre-crisis competition levels due to the survival and existence of a larger number of firms. Of course, any likely adherence (either intentional or due to undertakings becoming used to behaving in a certain way) of the undertakings to the crisis cartel agreement should be assessed by the competition authorities and should be fined accordingly. As we shall see in the penultimate chapter, this balance is a sensitive one.

In spite of the strict assessment of crisis cartels, both the US and the EU, as the above analysis has indicated, have been more lenient in reducing the fines on cartelists operating in industries experiencing crisis. Competition authorities and courts should follow a pragmatic approach when dealing with crisis cartels, taking into account the long-term sustainability of competitive conditions in markets by ensuring the long-term viability of incumbents in markets experiencing severe crisis.

6

State aid

PHEDON NICOLAIDES

> In Europe the provision of subsidies and other forms of aid by the State still forms an accepted part, indeed often a central part, of economic policy, even in those countries most attached to the model of the free market. Yet the very existence of State aid poses obvious problems for the single market for which the European Union is striving. The EC law of State aid therefore raises issues of the greatest social, economic and political importance as well as a great variety of difficult and fascinating legal problems. Seldom have the rules of Community law on State Aids been invoked more frequently than at present. Seldom has the definition of a State aid presented more difficulty.
>
> Andrea Biondi, Prof. Piet Eeckhout and James Flynn[1]

6.1 Introduction

This chapter explains in detail the concept of state aid. In the penultimate chapter we shall examine how the state aid rules of the European Union have been applied during the financial crisis, and we present there a critical assessment of the role and effectiveness of state aid policy during the crisis.

The control of state aid is an important component of the competition policy of the European Union. State intervention influences the way markets operate by favouring certain undertakings and causing, as a result, serious damage to their competitors operating in the same and/or different member states.

State intervention may thus undermine the achievement of a market economy with free and undistorted competition. Indeed, Protocol 27 of the Treaty on the European Union (TEU) and the Treaty on the Functioning of the European Union (TFEU) recognizes that the

[1] A. Biondi, P. Eeckhout and J. Flynn, *The Law of State Aid in the European Union*, Oxford University Press, 2004.

establishment of an internal market, as provided by Article 3 TEU, requires 'a system ensuring that competition is not distorted'.

Therefore the state aid policy of the EU prohibits in principle state aid and allows, exceptionally, only the kind and amounts of state aid that pursue common policy aims and do not cause excessive distortion between member states.

The principle of the incompatibility of state aid with the internal market is laid down in Article 107(1) TFEU. Exceptions are provided by Article 93 TFEU for public transport, Article 106 TFEU for services of general economic interest and Article 107(2) and (3) for the rest of the economy.

The assessment of whether state aid is compatible with the internal market is the exclusive competence of the European Commission. Member states are under obligation, stemming from Article 108(3) TFEU, to notify the Commission of all new state aid measures. Failure to do so renders state aid automatically illegal.

EU courts (the Court of Justice (ECJ) and the CFI or the General Court) confine their role to verifying that the Commission complies with the rules of procedure and the duty to give reasons; that the facts are accurate; that there is no manifest error in assessing facts, no error of law and no misuse of powers.

The Commission also issues guidelines to member states on the types and amounts of aid that it regards as compatible with the internal market. During the financial crisis, the Commission issued several such guidelines which are reviewed below.

The chapter is structured as follows. The next section presents the latest statistics on the amount of state aid granted by member states. Then it is explained when a public measure is categorized as state aid.

6.2 How much state aid?

Between 2002 and 2007, the amount of state aid to industry and services decreased annually on average by 2 per cent and stood at €65 billion. That amount corresponded to less than 0.5 per cent of GDP in 2007. The financial crisis led to an explosion of state aid. The overall level of state aid almost quintupled in 2008 compared to 2007 and increased to 2.2 per cent of GDP, almost exclusively as a result of crisis aid to the financial sector. Crisis aid to the real economy through the 'Temporary Framework' started to be implemented by member states only in 2009 and therefore is not reflected in the 2008 statistics.

Total state aid (excluding railways) granted by the member states amounted to €279.6 billion in 2008, or, in relative terms, to 2.2 per cent of the GDP of the twenty-seven member states. Crisis measures reported by member states in 2008 amounted to €212.2 billion or 1.7 per cent of GDP. In 2008, thirteen member states implemented crisis aid in favour of the financial sector (Belgium, Denmark, Germany, Ireland, Spain, France, Latvia, Luxembourg, the Netherlands, Portugal, Finland, Sweden and the United Kingdom).

By the end of October 2009, all EU-15 member states and Hungary, Latvia and Slovenia had financial crisis measures approved by the Commission. When excluding the crisis measures, total state aid amounted to around €67.4 billion in 2008 or 0.54 per cent of EU-27 GDP.

However, the total amount of aid for the following twelve months expanded exponentially. The maximum volume of crisis measures approved by the Commission between October 2008 and October 2009 amounted to around €3,632 billion, corresponding to 29 per cent of the EU-27 GDP. With regard to guarantee schemes, the maximum volume amounted to €2,738 billion, which corresponds to 22 per cent of the EU-27 GDP. Recapitalization measures amounted to €231 billion, corresponding to 2 per cent of EU-27 GDP. General liquidity measures and asset relief interventions amounted to €76 billion and represented 0.6 per cent of EU GDP. In addition, the Commission took decisions in several ad hoc interventions in favour of individual financial institutions amounting to a total volume of €587 billion.

When confidence collapsed and inter-bank lending dried up in September 2008, member states injected large amounts of aid to the banking sector in order to prevent financial meltdown. Guarantees, recapitalization measures and risk shields for financial institutions were put in place by member states to ensure that lending to the economy could continue. Then, on the basis of the Temporary Framework, member states started to provide additional incentives to the real economy to continue or resume investment.

During the period from 2008 to 2010, the European Commission's state aid policy has had several objectives. The first was a co-ordinated rescue and restructuring process for banks and the avoidance of discriminatory provisions in the granting of deposit guarantees. The second was to allow the recapitalization of fundamentally sound banks on an equitable basis. The third was the avoidance of undue distortion of competition caused by incentives to increase credit in the real economy. The fourth, which has only recently come into play, is the review of the various support measures and their gradual withdrawal. This is also known as the 'exit' strategy.

6.3 The concept of state aid

State aid is in principle prohibited. Article 107(1) TFEU declares any aid which distorts competition and affects trade between member states to be incompatible with the internal market, unless the treaty dictates otherwise. This qualification implies that certain exceptions are possible to this general prohibition of state aid. In this respect, the second and third paragraphs of Article 107 define certain categories of aid that are either compatible or may be declared compatible with the common market. In addition, there are the exceptions in Articles 93 and 106(2).

Article 108 TFEU defines the procedure on the basis of which member states are required to report all new state aid (in schemes or individual awards) or amendments to existing state aid schemes to the Commission, for assessment. State aid cannot be granted or put into effect unless it has been approved or is deemed to have been approved by the Commission. The procedure of Article 108 has been extended and elaborated by Council Regulation 659/99 laying down detailed rules for the application of that Article.

Article 107(1) TFEU provides that:

> Save as otherwise in this Treaty, any aid granted by a Member State or through state resources in any form whatsoever which distorts or threatens to distort competition by favouring certain undertakings or the production of certain goods shall, in so far as it affects trade between Member States, be incompatible with the common market.

Article 107(1) TFEU does not present a concrete definition of the concept of state aid by reference to its cause or objective but rather defines it by reference to its effect.[2] A measure of public support is classified as state aid only if the conditions defined in that paragraph are all satisfied. They are cumulative and not alternative. This means that not all measures of public support, even those that may involve public subsidies, are necessarily classified as state aid.

The five conditions that must all hold are the following:

(1) aid must be granted by the state or through state resources,
(2) this aid must confer an advantage to the recipients,

[2] Case 30/59, *Steenkolenmijnen v. High Authority*, [1961] ECR 1, at p. 19.

(3) the advantage must favour certain (selected) undertakings or economic activities,
(4) aid must affect trade between member states and
(5) aid must distort competition in the common market.

Aid must be granted 'by a Member State or through state resources'. The term 'member states' includes central governments and their ministries or departments, regional and local governments or councils and municipalities.

The term 'state resources' refers to public or private bodies established or designated by the state and which use resources which belong to the state or are controlled by the state.[3] Any aid given by private entities (such as privately owned companies) is not considered to be state aid and thus falls outside the scope of Article 107 TFEU. In the *Preussen Elektra* case, the European Court of Justice ruled that the obligation imposed by the German government on distributors of electricity to purchase 'green' electricity had no impact on the public budget and merely regulated transfers between private entities. It was, therefore, not state aid.[4]

This means that regulatory or administrative measures are not considered to be state aid even if they confer a commercial advantage to certain undertakings. Such measures do not normally have a budgetary effect for the state.

The recipients of aid must be 'undertakings' which are natural or legal persons engaging in economic activities. An undertaking for the purposes of Article 107 TFEU can be a professional self-employed person (such as a lawyer or accountant), a partnership, a private company, a group of companies[5] or a public company wholly or partially owned or controlled by the state.

[3] Case C-72-73/91, *Sloman Neptun Schiffahrts AG v. Seebetriebsrat Bodo Ziesemer*, [1993] ECR I-887, para. 19. Case C-290/83, *Commission v. France*, [1985] ECR 439, para. 14.

[4] Case C-379/98, *Preussen Elektra AG v. Schleswag AG*. See also C-482/99, *France v. Commission* (*Stardust Marine*), para. 52, where the ECJ stated that 'it is also necessary to examine whether the public authorities must be regarded as having been involved, in one way or another, in the adoption of those measures'.

[5] Case C-303/88, *Italy v. Commission*, [1991] ECR I-1433, concerning aid granted to ENI, a state holding company, owning the Lanerossi group of companies. In this case the ECJ stated that the Commission was entitled to regard the funds provided by ENI through Lanerossi to four of its subsidiaries as state aid, without it being necessary to establish that the capital funds received by ENI from the Italian government were specifically intended to make up losses of the subsidiaries. It was sufficient to observe that in any event the receipt of the capital funds enabled ENI to release other resources to make up for the losses of the subsidiaries (para. 14).

The concept of an undertaking is not defined anywhere in the treaty. It refers broadly to any natural or legal person, regardless of legal status and means of being financed, who carries out economic activities of certain regularity and duration and which could be done for remuneration.

According to settled case law an 'economic activity' is 'any activity consisting in offering goods and services on a given market'.[6] An economic activity presupposes the assumption of risk for the purpose for remuneration.[7] Remuneration constitutes consideration 'normally agreed upon between the provider and the recipient'.[8]

For some activities there cannot be a market because they belong to the sphere of exclusive competence of the state, such as the issuing of passports or birth certificates, irrespective of the fact that normally one has to pay to obtain such documents. Moreover, only the state has the prerogative to impose regulatory requirements such as broadcasting or banking licensing. Not only are these activities reserved for the state, but one cannot obtain certificates or licences unless one qualifies by satisfying certain legal criteria or fiduciary requirements.[9]

It follows that an activity is non-economic when there can be no market for comparable goods and services either because there is no voluntary participation, interaction or transactions by sellers and buyers (because costs cannot be covered), or because the state has reserved it for itself.[10] Public funding of non-economic activities is not state aid.

State aid exists when the transfer of state resources favours one or more undertakings, resulting in a competitive advantage that could not have been obtained under normal market conditions, where recipients of the aid do not have to provide anything in return. Aid itself is any relief from the expenses which are normally borne by undertakings in their daily operations. As the General Court (GC), formerly the CFI, stated,

[6] Case C-35/96, *Commission v. Italy*, [1998] ECR I-03851, para. 36. See also cases C-180/98 to C-184/98, *Pavel Pavlov and Others*, [2000] ECR I-6451, para. 75; Case C-222/4, *Ministerio dell'Economia e delle Finanze*, judgment of 10 January 2006, para. 108.

[7] Case C-184/98, *Pavel Pavlov and Others*, [2000] ECR I-6451; C-475/99, *Ambulanz Glöckner*, [2001] ECR I-09089.

[8] Case C-263/86, *Humbel and Edel*, [1988] ECR I-05365, para. 17.

[9] Case C-30/87, *Bodson*, [1988] ECR I-2479; Case C-364/92, *Eurocontrol* [1994] ECR I-43; Case C-96/94, *Centro Servizi Spediporto*, [1995] ECR, I-2883.

[10] Commission Decision of 6 April 2005, N 244/2003, United Kingdom – *Credit Union Provision of Access to Basic Financial Services – Scotland.*

> Article 107(1) TFEU is aimed merely at prohibiting advantages for certain undertakings and the concept of aid covers only measures which lighten the burdens normally assumed in an undertaking's budget and which are to be regarded as an economic advantage which the recipient undertaking would not have obtained under normal market conditions.[11]

Article 107(1) TFEU applies to aid in any form. The concept of aid is very wide and includes any advantage of a monetary nature conferred by the state or state resources which would not have otherwise been enjoyed by the recipient. Such advantages encompass not only grants, subsidies, loans and guarantees actually given by the state, but also anything owed to the state which the latter fails to collect or receive, such as taxes, social security payments, interest on loans and dividends on invested public capital, as well as anything that the state gives up without objective reason such as products and services it sells at excessively low prices and anything the state gives away without objective reason such as products and services it purchases at excessively high prices.

The actual form of the aid or the intentions and the formal objectives of the public policies of the authority granting the aid are irrelevant for the purposes of Article 107(1) TFEU. Even if a policy has no formal objective of conferring an advantage or assisting an undertaking, its application may still inadvertently favour certain undertakings over others. Article 107(1) TFEU bans aid according to its actual or potential effects, rather than according to the declared intentions of the granting authority.[12]

It follows that the notion of state aid is very wide. It includes a large variety of measures, such as:

- grants;
- loans at below-market rates of interest from the state, interest subsidies;
- guarantees by the state for which the beneficiary does not pay a market fee;
- tax advantages: tax base reductions, tax deferment, tax cancellation, tax rate reduction, tax exemptions;
- reductions of social security contributions;

[11] Case T-157/01, *Danske Busvognmænd v. Commission*, [2004] ECR II-917, para. 57. The implication from this case was that lightening of 'abnormal' burdens is not aid. Combus, a bus company, was compensated by the Danish government for its extra costs of employing civil servants after it was privatized.

[12] Case C-173/73, *Italy v. Commission*.

- provision of goods and services by the state at below-market prices;
- sale of public land at below-market prices;
- purchase of goods and services by the state at above-market prices;
- capital injections which are not in conformity with the market economy investor principle (lower expected return than a private investor would demand at similar market conditions and risk).

In cases concerning the injection of public capital into companies, the Commission has developed the 'private investor' principle in order to be able to assess whether the actions of a government indirectly constitute state aid by conferring an advantage on certain undertakings. To establish the existence of aid, the Commission compares the situation in question under the prevailing market conditions with the behaviour of private investors in similar circumstances. The ECJ has also held in this regard that, in order to determine whether a state measure constitutes state aid, it is necessary to establish whether the recipient undertaking receives an economic advantage which it would not have obtained under normal conditions.[13] According to this principle, public authorities may give loans and guarantees, inject capital and otherwise be involved in commercial ventures, but they must behave in the same way as a private investor would behave in similar circumstances.

A private investor would never provide an advantage to someone else without demanding compensation for the value that its actions generate for the beneficiary company. This is because a private investor is motivated solely by the possibility of making profits or returns on investment and ignores all other policy objectives, irrespective of how laudable or worthy they may be, such as lowering unemployment, raising productivity, improving training, expanding research, increasing regional investment, protecting the environment and so on.[14]

The hypothetical private investor does not need to pursue the most profitable investment or maximize returns on investment. It is sufficient that the rate of profit or the return is on a par with the average in the particular sector where the investment takes place, without running excessive risk in relation to other investors in comparable situations. However, he may not wilfully forgo any obvious opportunity for profit.[15]

[13] Case C-39/94, *SFEI v. La Poste*, [1996] ECR I-3547, para. 60.

[14] Case C-278/92, *Spain v. Commission*, [1994] ECR I-4103; T-358/94, *Air France v. Commission*, [1996] ECR II-02109.

[15] Case T-228/99, *WestLB v. Commission*, [2003] ECR I-435.

Also, a private investor does not have to pursue short-term profits. He may be guided by the same objective as a group of companies that tolerate short-term losses by one of the subsidiaries in order to achieve long-term profits for the group as a whole, possibly because this protects the image of the group.

A private investor that already owns shares in a company may also tolerate short-term losses and behave differently than a new investor in order to protect his existing investment or in order to avoid paying any extra costs or incurring penalties from liquidating his shareholding.

As in all state aid cases, the Commission assesses whether a public authority acts like a private investor on the basis of the facts available at the time the public authority adopts the measure in question (such as to invest, to extend a loan, to write off debt and so on). It is irrelevant whether the investment turns out to be profitable or not. Measures that may constitute state aid are not assessed with the benefit of hindsight.[16]

The onus of proof is on the public authority which alleges to act as a private investor. The Commission does not accept uncorroborated claims, speculations or hunches (private investors gambling with their own money may make risky bets, but authorities using public money should act with due prudence). Any claims or expectations as to how the investment is likely to turn out must be reasonable.[17] What is reasonable in this context is what the rest of the market believes. Since the test of the private investor is a comparison between the behaviour of a public authority and that of a hypothetical investor, the corroborative evidence that is accepted by the Commission constitutes analyses, reports or declarations from independent banks, venture capital companies, consultants or other economic experts.[18]

'General' measures of economic policy are not aid. Article 107(1) TFEU refers to advantages favouring 'certain' undertakings or the production of 'certain' goods. This has been interpreted over the years to mean that aid must be 'selective' or 'specific' rather than general. As the CFI ruled in the *CETM* case,

> The fact that the aid is not aimed at one or more specific recipients defined in advance, but that it is subject to a series of objective criteria pursuant to which it may be granted, within the framework of a predetermined overall budget allocation, to an indefinite number of beneficiaries

16 C-482/99, *France v. Commission* (*Stardust Marine*).

17 T-152/99, *Molina v. Commission*, [2002] ECR II-3049.

18 Case T-228/99, *WestLB v. Commission*.

> who are not initially individually identified, cannot suffice to call into question the selective nature of the measure, and, accordingly, its classification as state aid within the meaning of Article 107(1) of the Treaty. At the very most, that circumstance means that the measure is not an individual aid. It does not, however, preclude that public measure from having to be regarded as a system of aid constituting a selective, and therefore specific, measure if, owing to the criteria governing its application, it procures an advantage for certain undertakings or the production of certain goods, to the exclusion of others.[19]

No concrete definition of 'general measures' has been given either in the practice of the Commission or in the jurisprudence of EU courts. However, it is understood, for example, that reduction of corporate taxation across the board does not constitute state aid.[20] Further, measures which apply to persons in accordance with objective criteria, without regard to the location, sector or undertaking in which the beneficiary may be employed, are not considered to be state aid.[21]

On the other hand, however, general measures which are implemented on a discretionary basis would fall within Article 107(1) TFEU. A scheme operated by Finland and intended to boost employment by subsidizing new jobs was found to be incompatible with the internal market because the public authorities had discretion in confirming eligibility and thus in disbursing the subsidies. Hence for a policy measure to escape Article 107 TFEU its application must be general and without any discriminatory effect among undertakings, and its benefits must be readily or automatically available to any undertaking.

Measures which appear to be general may still be found to favour certain undertakings or certain goods. For example, a general export credit scheme operated by France in respect of all national products which were exported was found to be state aid.[22] The same was found for a scheme of interest rate subsidies on all exports from Greece[23] and for a scheme that exempted all Greek export undertakings from a special single tax on undertakings.[24] The reasoning of the Commission in these cases

[19] Case T-55/99, *Confederación Española de Transporte de Mercancias (CETM) v. Commission*, [2000] ECR II-3207, para. 40.

[20] Commission notice on the application of the State aid rules to measures relating to direct business taxation, OJ C384, 10 December 1998, para. 14.

[21] Commission notice on co-operation between national courts and the Commission in the state aid field, OJ C312, 23 November 1995, para. 7.

[22] Case C-11/69, *Commission v. France*, [1969] ECR 523.

[23] Case C-57/86, *Greece v. Commission*, [1988] ECR 2855.

[24] Commission Decision 89/659, OJ L394, 30 December 1989.

was identical. Certain products were subject to more favourable treatment by the mere fact that they were sold to customers outside France and Greece. This not only discriminated against identical products sold to domestic customers (e.g. shirts), but it also discriminated against products that could only be offered to local customers, such as many services.

Given the fact that not all undertakings operate under identical conditions, in principle there is no such thing as a general scheme that can apply equally to all undertakings. The Commission and the ECJ, however, do not attempt to examine the precise *ex post* effects of a general scheme on company competitiveness. They consider instead whether in principle it applies to all sectors of the economy (i.e. whether it discriminates *a priori* between sectors) and whether any company may, in theory, be legally eligible to benefit from it.

In *Unicredito*, Italy introduced a law which, among other things, provided that banks which merged or engaged in similar restructuring would benefit from a tax advantage. Unicredito argued that the measure was not selective since it constituted a measure of general character and that the differentiations were 'justified by the nature and general scheme of the tax system'. The ECJ did not accept this argumentation. First, the measure was selective since it only applied to the banking sector and only to certain undertakings carrying out certain activities within this sector. The measure was, therefore, held to be 'selective in relation to other economic sectors and within the banking sector itself'. Therefore it could not be regarded as a general measure. Moreover, the 'nature and overall structure of the [Italian] tax system' did not justify the tax reduction in question.[25]

The conditions under which trade between member states is affected and competition is distorted for the purposes of Article 107(1) EC are as a general rule inextricably linked. For this reason, if aid is found to have an appreciable effect on trade, it is inevitably found to distort or to threaten to distort competition.[26] Confirming its earlier case law,[27] the ECJ stated in the *Philip Morris v. Commission* judgment that when state aid strengthens the position of an undertaking compared with other undertakings competing in intra-Community trade, the latter must be regarded as affected by that aid.[28]

[25] Case C-148/04, *Unicredito Italiano*, [2005] ECR I-11137, paras. 44–54.

[26] Case T-288/97, *Regione Autonoma Friuli Venezia Giulia v. Commission*, [2001] ECR II-1169, paras. 49–50.

[27] Case C-173/73, *Commission v. Italy*.

[28] Case 730/79, *Philip Morris v. Commission*, [1980] ECR 2671, para. 11.

There is no definition or quantitative measure of when aid is capable of affecting trade. It is settled case law, however, that aid may affect intra-Community trade even if it is of relatively small amounts. In the *Altmark* case, which concerned local/regional transport services, the ECJ held,

> In this respect, it must be observed, first, that it is not impossible that a public subsidy granted to an undertaking which provides only local or regional transport services and does not provide any transport services outside its State of origin may none the less have an effect on trade between Member States. Where a Member State grants a public subsidy to an undertaking, the supply of transport services by that undertaking may for that reason be maintained or increased with the result that undertakings established in other Member States have less chance of providing their transport services in the market in that Member State . . . In the present case, that finding is not merely hypothetical, since, as appears in particular from the observations of the Commission, several Member States have since 1995 started to open certain transport markets to competition from undertakings established in other Member States, so that a number of undertakings are already offering their urban, suburban or regional transport services in Member States other than their State of origin. Next, the Commission notice of 6 March 1996 on the de minimis rule for State aid (OJ 1996 C 68, p. 9), as its fourth paragraph states, does not concern transport. Similarly, Commission Regulation (EC) No 69/2001 of 12 January 2001 on the application of Articles 87 and 88 of the EC Treaty to de minimis aid (OJ 2001 L 10, p. 30), in accordance with the third recital in the preamble and Article 1(a), does not apply to that sector. Finally, according to the ECJ's case-law, there is no threshold or percentage below which it may be considered that trade between Member States is not affected. The relatively small amount of aid or the relatively small size of the undertaking which receives it does not as such exclude the possibility that trade between Member States might be affected.[29]

Any aid, in turn, is presumed to affect trade unless

- it is *de minimis*;
- the market is affected only at national level; or
- the situation is wholly outside the EU, provided that there is no indirect impact on the common market.

Small amounts of aid that do not affect trade are regarded to be *de minimis* aid. Regulation 1998/2006 defines *de minimis* amounts to be less than €200,000 over a period of three fiscal years per undertaking.[30]

[29] Case C-280/00, *Altmark*, [2003] ECR, I-7747, paras. 77–81.

[30] OJ L379, 28 December 2006.

Similarly to other Treaty provisions, Article 107 TFEU does not cover situations which are purely domestic or completely outside the EU. For example, subsidies granted to hairdressers would not be considered to be state aid because individuals do not normally buy hairdressing services from other member states.[31]

However, even if aid is received by an undertaking which sells its products exclusively within the domestic market of a member state, intra-EU trade may still be indirectly affected, if it becomes more difficult for similar products from other member states to enter that market. A situation of this kind may arise in cases of overcapacity in a particular market, as a result of which domestic production may be maintained or increased, with the end result that undertakings established in other member states have less chance of exporting their products to the market in that member state.[32]

Also, aid which is given to an undertaking that exports exclusively to a non-EU country may still have an indirect impact on intra-EU trade, if it displaces exports by companies in other member states, which are then redirected towards the internal EU market.[33] Similarly, in *AITEC v. Commission*, the CFI annulled the Commission's decision to approve an aid scheme on the grounds that the latter should have considered the foreseeable effects of the aid on competition and on intra-EU trade.[34] There is always a need to examine how trade is likely to be affected.

However, unlike antitrust cases, the Commission is not required to define markets in detail or to analyse rigorously their structures and the ensuing competitive relationships in order to establish a real effect on trade between member states, which would anyway be impossible if aid has not yet been implemented. If new aid has been granted without prior notification having been given, the Commission is not required to

[31] Twenty-sixth Report on Competition Policy, at p. 230. The Commission decided to terminate proceedings on aid for firms providing only local passenger transport services in Italy, since the measure was not liable to distort competition in that it did not affect trade between member states. See also Commission Decision N 377/2007 – support to Bataviawerf (reconstruction of a vessel from the seventeenth century), where support in favour of the Batavia shipyard (local musem), located in Lelystad, the Netherlands, was found to fall outside Article 87(1) EC as not affecting intra-Community trade due to the very local demand that the museum addressed. Also see Commission Decision 465/2005 – school support services, where aid granted to school support providers escaped Article 87(1) EC due to the specific/local characteristics of the Dutch educational system.

[32] Case 102/87, *France v. Commission*, [1988] ECR 4067, para. 49.

[33] Case C-142/87, *Belgium v. Commission*, [1990] ECR I-959, para. 38.

[34] Cases T-447 and 449/93, *AITEC v. Commission*, [1995] ECR II-1971, paras. 139–40.

establish whether the aid has a real effect on trade and competition. According to well-established case law, such a requirement would favour member states which grant aid in breach of the obligation to notify, to the detriment of those which do notify aid at the planning stage.[35] However, the Commission is obliged to justify its decisions and not conclude on the existence of effect on trade outright, without proper reasoning.[36]

For aid to be caught under Article 107 TFEU, it must also be capable of distorting competition. As mentioned above, the conditions under which trade between member states is affected and competition is distorted are as a general rule inextricably linked. The test defined by the Commission and the courts for determining the effect on trade and competition is not strict. Small effects on trade are sufficient to conclude distortion. Similarly, anything that actually disturbs or threatens to disturb the conditions of competition between undertakings from different member states is sufficient for Article 107 TFEU to apply.

Competition is distorted if the aid in question strengthens the competitive position of the recipient, say by reducing its operating or investment costs, in relation to its rivals.[37] The relevant question is always, what would be the competitive position of the recipient in the absence of aid? If this would be worse in relation to its rivals, then aid distorts competition.

Article 107(1) TFEU is not confined to large amounts of aid, significant distortions of competition or substantial disturbance to trade. Given that that Article requires no quantitative tests, it applies to both direct and indirect effects, and to both actual and potential effects, and provided that it focuses on effects rather than on the intentions of public policies it is very difficult for an aid scheme to escape being caught by it, even if it appears to be of a modest amount. It is settled case law that even aid of a relatively small amount is liable to affect trade between member states and strengthen the position of the recipient as compared to its competitors.[38]

The argument often advanced by member states that aid aims to offset

[35] Case T-55/99, *CETM v. Commission*, para. 103, and the case law cited therein.

[36] Case T-304/04, *Italy v. Commission (Wam)* (not yet published), where the CFI annulled the Commission's decision, finding aid worth €105,000 for the export-related activities of Wam to Shanghai and Korea to be a measure affecting trade between member states, for lack of motivation.

[37] Case 234/84, *Belgium v. Commission*, [1986] ECR 2263, para. 22. See also cases C-148/04, *Unicredito Italiano*, and C-71/04, *Xunta de Galicia*, [2005] ECR I-7419.

[38] Case T-214/95, *Vlaams Gewest v. Commission*, [1998] ECR II-717, para. 49.

alleged competitive disadvantages of recipient undertakings has never been accepted as such by the courts or the Commission.

In addition, the fact that a member state seeks to approximate, by unilateral measures, conditions of competition in a particular sector of the economy to those prevailing in other member states cannot deprive the measures in question of their character as distorting competition. It follows that aid cannot be justified either by the existence of more favourable conditions for undertakings in other member states or by the competition from those undertakings.[39]

6.4 Possible exceptions (compatible aid)

Article 107(1) TFEU provides that state aid is considered incompatible with the internal market and thus prohibited, 'save as otherwise provided in this Treaty'. Exemption is therefore possible.

There are four possibilities of exception in the treaty, other than Article 107(2) and (3). First, Article 42 TFEU limits the application of the rules on competition to the extent that it is necessary for the operation of the Common Agricultural Policy. In particular, state aid may in certain situations be permitted by the Council for the protection of enterprises handicapped by structural or natural conditions or within the framework of economic development programmes. There are specific provisions for state aid to agriculture in Council Regulation 1184/2006.

Second, Article 93 TFEU considers as compatible with the treaty aid which meets the need of co-ordination of public transport services or represents a reimbursement for the discharge of certain obligations inherent in the concept of public service. There are specific provisions for state aid to public transport in Council Regulation 1370/2007.

Third, Article 106(2) TFEU exempts from the rules of competition undertakings providing services of general economic interest (SGEIs) in so far as compliance with competition rules would prevent them from fulfilling the obligations imposed on them by law. There are specific provisions on state aid to SGEIs in Commission Decision 2005/842 and the Commission Framework on SGEIs of December 2005.

Fourth, Article 346 TFEU excludes armaments from the treaty. This means that member states may subsidize the manufacturing of weapons.

However, the provisions of Article 107(2) and (3) TFEU remain the main categories of exception. Article 107(2) lays down that certain aid

[39] Joined cases 6 and 11/69, *Commission v. France*, [1969] ECR 523, para. 20.

is automatically compatible with the internal market. Article 107(3) TFEU defines certain categories of aid that may be considered compatible with the internal market. This is the job of the Commission. Finally, according to Article 107(3)(e), the Council of the EU, acting by qualified majority on a proposal from the Commission, may decide in exceptional instances that certain aid may also be considered compatible with the internal market.

It is a well-established principle in the case law that no aid may be exempted under Article 107(2) or (3) TFEU when it violates any other provision in the treaty. Examples of such violations are restrictions on the nationality of beneficiaries, restrictions on the mode of establishment of beneficiaries in the region that grants the aid, restrictions on where the results of subsidized R & D may be commercially exploited, obligations on the use of domestic products by beneficiaries, and measures that promote domestic products at the expense of products from other member states.[40]

The second paragraph of Article 107 TFEU defines three instances in which state aid is automatically compatible with the common market. In practice, very few cases of aid are authorized on the basis of that paragraph. Article 107(2) TFEU provides that

> 2 The following shall be compatible with the internal market:
> (a) aid having a social character, granted to individual consumers, provided that such aid is granted without discrimination related to the origin of the products concerned;
> (b) aid to make good the damage caused by natural disasters or exceptional occurrences;
> (c) aid granted to the economy of certain areas of the Federal Republic of Germany affected by the division of Germany, in so far as such aid is required in order to compensate for the economic disadvantages caused by that division.

Aid to individuals must not be linked to their employer. Any such link will be considered as conferring an indirect advantage to certain firms and therefore will have to be examined in the context of the exceptions allowed by Article 107(3) TFEU. Taken that the basic characteristic of this category is the social character of the aid, the beneficiaries are normally lower-income groups which need financial assistance, such as the

[40] Case C-21/88, *Du Pont de Nemours*, [1990] ECR I-0889; Case C-225/91, *Matra*, [1991] ECR I-05823; Case C-307/97, *Compagnie de Saint Gobain*, [1999] ECR I-06161; Case C-156/98, *Germany v. Commission*, [2000] ECR I-06857.

elderly, children and handicapped persons or citizens of specific categories such as those who live in remote places and may need assistance when they travel to the national capitals.

The natural disasters or exceptional occurrences for which aid may be given under Article 107(2)(b) TFEU must be out of the ordinary, substantial and unpredictable. Thus, for example, rainfall below normal rates that has a negative effect on agricultural production is not considered to be a natural disaster. By the same token, above-normal rainfall that ruins a holiday season is also not considered to be a natural disaster for tourist operators. Natural disasters include droughts, tornadoes, major forest fires, earthquakes, volcanic eruptions and diseases of plants and animals of catastrophic proportions.[41] Also, as the Commission has stated in its guidelines on state aid to the agriculture sector, adverse weather conditions such as frost, hail, ice, rain or drought may be upgraded to natural disasters once the level of damage reaches a certain threshold, which has been fixed at 20 per cent of normal production in the less-favoured areas and 30 per cent in other areas.[42]

Exceptional occurrences include war, internal civil disturbances or strikes, and with certain reservations and depending on their extent, major nuclear or industrial accidents and fires which result in widespread loss. They do not include high interest rates or a crisis in the market, since those 'are the expression of the market forces which must be faced by any business'.[43] Most notably, Article 107(2)(b) TFEU has been the basis for the authorization of aid to businesses affected by flooding of rivers and by marine pollution caused by the sinking of oil tankers and to airlines to compensate them for the losses suffered as a result of the closure of US airspace and the increase in insurance premiums in the aftermath of the terrorist attacks on New York in September 2001.

Aid in relation to the division of Germany under Article 107(2)(c) TFEU has not been authorized since the reunification of Germany.[44] The Treaty of Lisbon has introduced the possibility for repeal of this provision.

[41] Eighth Report on Competition Policy, at p. 164.

[42] Community Guidelines for State Aid in the Agriculture Sector, OJ C28, 1 February 2000.

[43] Case C-346/03, *Atzeni and Others*, [2006] ECR I-1875, para. 80.

[44] See in this respect joined cases C-57/00 and C-61/00, *Freistaat and Volkswagen v. Commission*, [2003] ECR I-9975.

Needless to mention, the mere fact that state aid is always compatible with the internal market in all the instances mentioned above does not relieve member states from their obligation to notify.

Article 107(3) TFEU defines five instances in which state aid 'may be' compatible with the common market. In particular, it provides that

> 3 The following may be considered to be compatible with the internal market:
> (a) aid to promote the economic development of areas where the standard of living is abnormally low or where there is serious underemployment;
> (b) aid to promote the execution of an important project of common European interest or to remedy a serious disturbance in the economy of a Member State;
> (c) aid to facilitate the development of certain economic activities or of certain economic areas, where such aid does not adversely affect trading conditions to an extent contrary to the common interest;
> (d) aid to promote culture and heritage conservation where such aid does not affect trading conditions and competition in the Union to an extent that is contrary to the common interest;
> (e) such other categories of aid as may be specified by decision of the Council acting by a qualified majority on a proposal from the Commission.

The Commission has wide discretion to decide on the compatibility of aid schemes with the common market. Responsibility for making that determination rests exclusively with the Commission. This is the reason why Article 108 TFEU and Regulation 659/99 define a procedure whereby member states must first notify the Commission of their proposed aid schemes or individual aid and obtain its authorization before they implement them. The Commission is free to authorize outright, demand changes or reject completely a notified aid scheme if it does not satisfy the requirements of existing guidelines or of Article 107(3) TFEU itself.

When the Commission examines aid schemes notified by member states, it is bound by EU law to authorize only those schemes which fall within the categories defined in Article 107(3) TFEU. Any other kind of aid must be rejected. This principle was established in the case law by the ruling in the landmark case involving Dutch aid granted to Philip Morris in the late 1970s. The Court ruled that Article 107(3) did not allow member states to 'make payments which would improve the financial situation of the recipient undertaking although they were not necessary for the attainment of the objectives specified in Article 107(3)'.[45]

This principle has frequently been restated in the case law. More recently, for example, the CFI ruled that 'the Commission is entitled to refuse the grant of aid where that aid did not induce the beneficiary undertakings to adopt conduct likely to assist attainment of one of the objectives mentioned in Article 107(3) TFEU'.[46]

Therefore, in order for state aid to be exempt it must be shown to be necessary for the undertakings that receive it. These undertakings have to do something extra with the aid they obtain. That 'extra' must go beyond their normal practices. In other words, the aid must have an 'incentive effect'.[47]

As put by the Commission in its decision concerning aid proposed to be granted by Belgium to GM Europe,[48]

> an aid measure can be found compatible with the common market pursuant to Article 107(3)(c) TFEU only when it is necessary for the beneficiary to undertake the activity in question. The Commission notes that the necessity of the aid is a general compatibility criterion. Where the aid does not lead to additional activities being undertaken by the beneficiary that would have not been achieved by the market forces alone, the aid cannot be authorised. With regard to compatibility on the basis of Article 107(3)(c) TFEU, the aid does not 'facilitate' the development of economic activities if the company would have undertaken the supported activities in any event, and notably in the absence of aid.

State aid is found to be necessary in the following situations:

- the recipient undertaking carries out extra or additional investment;
- the aided project is high-risk, as is often the case in research;
- the aided project is of long duration and therefore the results are more uncertain or may become outdated; or
- counterfactual analysis shows that the profitability of the project is low or negative without aid.

[45] C-730/79, *Philip Morris v. Commission*, para. 17.

[46] Case T-126/99, *Graphischer Maschinenbau v. Commission*, para. 34.

[47] With some exceptions (aid to remote regions and areas eligible for aid under Article 87(3)(a), EC maritime transport and environmental taxes), the Commission has always regarded operating aid as lacking incentive effect. Both the Commission and Community courts have repeatedly declared operating aid to distort competition 'in principle' because it keeps companies artificially afloat by covering costs they should be able to cover themselves. See, for example, Case T-459/93, *Siemens v. Commission*; Case T-214/95, *Vlaamse Gewest v. Commission*.

[48] Commission Decision 2007/612 on training aid to General Motors, para. 24.

In general, the Commission will conclude that aid is unnecessary when market forces alone are sufficient to induce companies to carry out investment, research, training and so on.[49]

This approach has been recently made more explicit and systematic in the so-called 'balancing test' that was introduced by the State Aid Action Plan of 2005. Demonstration of the incentive effect or the necessity of state aid is an intrinsic component of the balancing test, as discussed below.

Article 107(3)(a) TFEU refers to regional aid and is applicable to regions that are disadvantaged in comparison with the rest of the EU. According to the Commission guidelines on regional aid,[50] eligible regions must have a per capita GDP of less than 75 per cent of the EU average.

Until 2008, aid under Article 107(3)(b) TFEU was mostly used to support large R & D projects with common European interest, such as projects which aim to strengthen the European electronic industry by creating know-how and research networks throughout Europe in which scientists, producers of components and system users work together in order to ensure an independent European position on basic microelectronics technology.[51]

Aid under this Article is also permitted for the purpose of remedying a serious disturbance in the economy of a member state. Until the outbreak of the financial crisis this provision was used only once in the history of the EU. Most measures to counter the crisis, however, have been approved by the Commission on the basis of Article 107(3)(b). Its application will be examined in more detail below.

Article 107(3)(c) TFEU covers aid both to certain regions and to certain economic activities. The regions which are eligible for aid are those which are disadvantaged in comparison with the national average standard of prosperity as measured by income and unemployment level.

Most state aid given to horizontal policy objectives is authorized on the basis of Article 107(3)(c) TFEU. Examples of such horizontal objectives are training, employment, environmental protection, research and investment in small and medium enterprises (SMEs). Most of the guidelines issued by the Commission concern these types of aid.

[49] See Commission Decision 2007/612 on training aid to General Motors (Belgium) and Commission Decision 2006/938 on training aid for Ford Genk (Belgium).

[50] OJ C54, 4 March 2006, p. 13.

[51] Twenty-fifth Report on Competition Policy, at p. 238.

Lastly, aid is also possible under Article 107(3)(d) for the promotion of culture and the preservation of heritage.

It should be noted that both the Commission and the Courts have taken a very negative position on operating aid. This is defined as aid which relieves an enterprise of the expenses it normally has to bear in its day-to-day management or its usual activities. Such aid is not linked to a specific purpose and has no incentive effect on enterprises. It is considered to be very distorting, and the distortion is normally not justified by any EU objective. Therefore operating aid can only exceptionally be authorized.

Under current rules, operating aid may be authorized under certain conditions only in regions eligible for aid under Article 107(3)(a) TFEU, provided that it is justified in terms of its contribution to regional development and that its amount is proportional to the handicaps it seeks to alleviate (e.g. relief of extra transport costs in remote regions).[52] Operating aid is also exceptionally allowed to relieve ecotaxes and in maritime transport.[53]

Export aid is already forbidden under the WTO rules and therefore it is never allowed by the EU.

6.5 Concluding remarks

Competition policy has been one of the most important areas of EU concern and a pillar of its internal market. The prohibition in principle of state aid has protected the internal market from unwarranted state intervention to prop up inefficient companies and create national champions.

The concept of state aid is evolving. Public authorities have been quite adept at devising new measures to support companies or whole industrial sectors. As a consequence, EU courts have had to refine the definition of what constitutes state aid and the Commission has had to sharpen its investigative methods.

Not surprisingly, state aid policy has played an important role during the financial crisis. It has allowed member states to support, initially, financial institutions and then the real economy while at the same time it has strived to prevent excessive distortion of competition and disruption to the flow of resources between member states.

[52] Regional Aid Guidelines, http://eur-lex.europa.eu/LexUriServ/site/en/oj/2006/c_054/c_05420060304en00130044.pdf.

[53] See the guidelines on environmental aid and on maritime transport.

At this stage it is not possible to know whether indeed the distortion has been kept to a minimum. No cost-benefit analysis has been carried out so far. However, it is possible to surmise with a fair degree of confidence that certain forms of distortion have been avoided. Member states have not been allowed to discriminate in favour of their banks. They have not been allowed to grant unlimited amounts of aid. They have been required to submit realistic restructuring plans which in some cases have led to the sale of the beneficiaries or even to their closure.[54]

The more difficult question is whether the permitted amount of aid was excessive. There is no doubt that the special rules that were issued by the Commission were accommodating. Given that similar and even more generous measures have been adopted by countries outside the European Union, it is not unreasonable to conclude that the special rules merely reflect the exceptional nature and unprecedented magnitude of the crisis.

The question for the near future is how quickly the special rules will be phased out. The Temporary Framework for aid to the real economy expires at the end of 2010. It is not yet clear what the 'exit' strategy is likely to be for aid to financial institutions. Table 6.1 illustrates the state aid measures that member states implemented and the different types of aid included in these measures. Table 6.2 indicates the decisions on state aid measures that were taken by the European Commission in 2008 and 2009. Table 6.3 outlines the national state aid measures that are still under review by the European Commission. Table 6.4 illustrates the national measures that aimed at improving the sustainability of the real economy. Table 6.5 identifies the decisions of the European Commission regarding the measures aiming at improving the viability of the real economy in member states. Finally, Table 6.6 outlines the outstanding cases regarding measures pursuant to the Temporary Framework that the European Commission is investigating.

[54] For example, the liquidation aid to Roskilde Bank in Denmark (NN 39/2008).

Table 6.1. *State aid for financial institutions, 2008–9 (amounts in billions of euros)*

	Measure				
Member state	*Guarantee*	*Recapital-ization*	*Liquidity*	*Asset relief*	*Individual cases*
Austria	70.6	13.8	4.4	1.2	0.1
Belgium					288.3
Cyprus	3				
Denmark	580	13.5			6.3
Finland	50	4			n.a.
France	265	21.5			59.5
Germany	400	80	1.5		107.6
Greece	15	5	8		
Hungary	4.99	1			
Ireland	376				
Italy	n.a.	20			
Latvia	4.24				3.2
Luxembourg					7.3
Netherlands	200				40.5
Poland	10				
Portugal	20	4			0.5
Slovenia	12				
Spain	200		50		
Sweden	150	4.8			0.5
UK	376.75	63	11.3		61.2
TOTAL	2737.6	230.6	75.2	1.2	587.4

Source: European Commission

Table 6.2. *Decisions adopted by the Commission in 2008–9 (as of 16 December 2009)*

Member state	*Type of measure/ beneficiary*	*Type of decision*	*Date of adoption*
Austria	N 557/2008 – aid scheme for the financial sector (guarantees and recapitalization)	No objection	9 December 2008
	Prolongation		30 June 2009
Austria	N 214/2008 – recapitalization of Hypo Tirol	No objection	17 June 2009
Belgium/ France/ Luxembourg	NN 45-49-50/2008 – guarantee on liabilities of Dexia	No objection	19 November 2008
	Prolongation		30 October 2009
Belgium/ France/ Luxembourg	C 9/2009 – guarantee in favour of Dexia on certain assets in FSA	No objection	13 March 2009
Belgium/ Luxembourg/ Netherlands	N 574/2008 – measures in favour of Fortis	No objection	19 November 2008
Belgium/ Luxembourg/ Netherlands	NN 42-46-53A/2008 – restructuring aid to Fortis Bank and Fortis Bank Luxembourg	No objection	3 December 2008
Belgium/ Luxembourg	N 255/2009 and N 274/2009 – additional aid measures in favour of Fortis Bank and Fortis Bank Luxembourg	No objection	12 May 2009
Belgium	N 602/2008 – recapitalization measure in favour of KBC	No objection	18 December 2008
Belgium	NN 57/2008 – capital injection for Ethias Group	No objection	12 February 2009

Table 6.2. *(continued)*

Member state	*Type of measure/ beneficiary*	*Type of decision*	*Date of adoption*
Belgium	C 18/2009 – recapitalization and asset relief for KBC Group	No objection	30 June 2009
Belgium	C 18/2009 – asset relief and restructuring package for KBC	Conditional decision after formal investigation	18 November 2009
Cyprus	N 511/2009 – support of credit institutions (guarantee)	No objection	22 October 2009
Denmark	NN 36/2008 – rescue aid to Roskilde Bank	No objection	31 July 2008
Denmark	NN 39/2008 – liquidation aid Roskilde Bank	No objection	5 November 2008
Denmark	NN 51/2008 – guarantee scheme for banks	No objection	10 October 2008
Denmark	N 31a/2009 – recapitalization scheme and amendment of the guarantee scheme	No objection	3 February 2009
	Prolongation		17 August 2009
Denmark	NN 23/2009 – rescue aid for Fionia Bank	No objection	20 May 2009
Finland	N 567/2008 – guarantee scheme	No objection	14 November 2008
	N 239/2009 – prolongation and modification		30 April 2009
Finland	NN 2/2009 – guarantee for Kaupthing Bank Finland	No objection	21 January 2009

Table 6.2. *(continued)*

Member state	*Type of measure/ beneficiary*	*Type of decision*	*Date of adoption*
Finland	N 329/2009 – capital injection scheme	No objection	11 September 2009
France	N 548/2008 – financial support measures to the banking industry	No objection	30 October 2008
	N 251/2009 – extension of the scheme		12 May 2009
France	N 613/2008 – financial support measures to the banking industry	No objection	8 December 2008
	N 29/2009 – amendment to the decision		28 January 2009
	N 164/2009 – amendment to the decision		23 March 2009
France	N 249/2009 – capital injection for Caisse d'Épargne and Banque Populaire	No objection	8 May 2009
Germany	C 9/2008 – restructuring aid to Sachsen LB	Conditional decision after formal investigation procedure	4 June 2008
Germany	C 10/2008 – restructuring aid to IKB	Conditional decision after formal investigation procedure	21 October 2008
Germany	NN 44/2008 - Rescue aid to Hypo Real Estate Holding	No objection	2 October 2008

Table 6.2. *(continued)*

Member state	*Type of measure/ beneficiary*	*Type of decision*	*Date of adoption*
Germany	N 512/2008 – aid scheme for financial institutions (guarantees and recapitalizations)	No objection	27 October 2008
	N 330/2009 – prolongation		22 June 2009
Germany	N 615/2008 – guarantee and recapitalization for Bayern LB	No objection	18 December 2008
Germany	N 655/2008 – guarantee for NordLB	No objection	22 December 2008
	N 412/2009 – prolongation		10 September 2009
Germany	N 639/2008 – guarantee for IKB	No objection	22 December 2008
Germany	N 17/2009 – guarantee for SdB	No objection	22 January 2009
Germany	N 244/2009 – Commerzbank capital injection	No objection	7 May 2009
Germany	C 43/2008 – aid for the restructuring of WestLB	Conditional decision after formal investigation procedure)	12 May 2009
Germany	N 531/2009 – temporary additional aid to WestLB	No objection	7 October 2009
Germany	N 264/2009 – recapitalization of HSH Nordbank	No objection	29 May 2009
Germany	C 17/2009 – recapitalization and asset relief for LBBW (Landesbank Baden Württemberg)	No objection	30 June 2009

Table 6.2. *(continued)*

Member state	*Type of measure/ beneficiary*	*Type of decision*	*Date of adoption*
Germany	N 314/2009 – asset relief scheme	No objection	31 July 2009
Germany	N 400/2009 – additional aid (guarantees) for IKB	No objection	17 August 2009
Germany	N 456/2009 – export credit scheme	No objection	15 September 2009
Germany	C 17/2009 – restructuring plan and impaired assets relief measure for LBBW	No objection	15 December 2009
Greece	N 560/2008 – aid scheme to the banking industry in Greece (guarantees and recapitalization)	No objection	19 November 2008
	Prolongation and modification		18 September 2009
Hungary	N 664/2008 – financial support measures to financial industry (recapitalization and guarantee scheme)	No objection	12 February 2009
	N 355/2009 – prolongation and modification		3 September 2009
Hungary	N 358/2009 – mortgage support scheme	No objection	13 July 2009
	N 603/2009 – prolongation		24 November 2009
Ireland	NN 48/2008 – guarantee scheme for banks	No objection	13 October 2008

Table 6.2. *(continued)*

Member state	*Type of measure/ beneficiary*	*Type of decision*	*Date of adoption*
Ireland	N 9/2009 – recapitalization of Anglo Irish Bank	No objection	14 January 2009
Ireland	N 356/2009 – recapitalization of Anglo Irish Bank	No objection	26 June 2009
Ireland	N 61/2009 – change of ownership of Anglo Irish Bank	No objection	17 February 2009
Ireland	N 149/2009 – recapitalization of Bank of Ireland	No objection	26 March 2009
Ireland	N 241/2009 – recapitalization of Allied Irish Bank	No objection	12 May 2009
Ireland	N 349/2009 – revised guarantee scheme for financial institutions	No objection	20 November 2009
Italy	N 520a/2008 – guarantee scheme for banks	No objection	14 November 2008
	N 328/2009 – prolongation		16 June 2009
Italy	N 648/2008 – recapitalization scheme	No objection	23 December 2008
	N 466/2009 – prolongation		6 October 2009
Latvia	NN 68/2008 – public support measures to Parex Banka	No objection	24 November 2008
	N 189/2009 – amendment to the decision		11 May 2009
Latvia	N 638/2008 – guarantee scheme for banks	No objection	22 December 2008

Table 6.2. *(continued)*

Member state	*Type of measure/ beneficiary*	*Type of decision*	*Date of adoption*
	N 326/2009 – prolongation		30 June 2009
Latvia	NN 60/2009 – capital injection for Mortgage Bank of Latvia	No objection	19 November
Luxembourg	N 344/2009 and N 380/2009 – restructuring aid for Kaupthing Bank Luxembourg	No objection	9 July 2009
Netherlands	N 524/2008 – guarantee scheme for financial institutions	No objection	30 October 2008
	N 379/2009 – prolongation		7 July 2009
Netherlands	N 528/2008 – measure in favour of ING	No objection	13 November 2008
Netherlands	N 569/2008 – measure in favour of Aegon	No objection	27 November 2008
Netherlands	N 611/2008 – SNS Reaal (new capital injection)	No objection	10 December 2008
Netherlands	C 10/2009 – ING illiquid asset facility	No objection	31 March 2009
Netherlands	C 10/2009 – ING restructuring plan and illiquid asset back-up facility	Conditional decision after formal investigation procedure	18 November 2009
Poland	N 208/2009 – support scheme for financial institutions (guarantee and liquidity support)	No objection	25 September 2009

Table 6.2. *(continued)*

Member state	*Type of measure/ beneficiary*	*Type of decision*	*Date of adoption*
Portugal	NN 60/2008 – guarantee scheme for credit institutions	No objection	29 October 2008
Portugal	NN 71/2008 – state guarantee for Banco Privado Português	No objection	13 March 2009
Portugal	N 556/2008 – bank recapitalization scheme	No objection	20 May 2009
Slovakia	N 392/2009 – bank support scheme	No objection	8 December 2009
Slovenia	N 531/2008 – guarantee scheme for credit institutions	No objection	12 December 2008
	N 331/2009 – prolongation		22 June 2009
Slovenia	N 637/2008 – liquidity scheme for financial sector	No objection	20 March 2009
	N 510/2009 – prolongation		19 October 2009
Spain	NN54a/2008 – Fund for the Acquisition of Financial Assets	No objection	4 November 2008
	N337/2009 - Prolongation		7 August 2009
Spain	NN 54b/2008 – guarantee scheme for credit institutions	No objection	22 December 2008
	Prolongation		25 June 2009
	N 588/2009 – second prolongation		1 December 2009
Sweden	N 533/2008 – support measures for the banking industry	No objection	29 October 2008
	N 26/2009 – amendment to the decision		28 January 2009

Table 6.2. *(continued)*

Member state	*Type of measure/ beneficiary*	*Type of decision*	*Date of adoption*
	N 154/2009 – amendment and prolongation		28 April 2009
	N 544/2009 – prolongation		26 October 2009
Sweden	NN 64/2008 – emergency rescue measures regarding Carnegie Investment Bank	No objection	15 December 2008
Sweden	N 69/2009 – recapitalization scheme	No objection	11 February 2009
	N4 36/2009 – prolongation		5 August 2009
United Kingdom	NN 41/2008 – rescue aid to Bradford and Bingley	No objection	1st October 2008
United Kingdom	N 507/2008 – aid scheme to the banking industry (guarantees and recapitalization)	No objection	13 October 2008
	N 193/2009 – prolongation		15 April 2009
	N 537/2009 – prolongation		13 October 2009
United Kingdom	N 111/2009 – working capital guarantee scheme	No objection	24 March 2009
United Kingdom	N 65/2009 – asset-backed securities guarantee scheme	No objection	21 April 2009
	Prolongation		27 October 2009

Table 6.2. *(continued)*

Member state	*Type of measure/ beneficiary*	*Type of decision*	*Date of adoption*
United Kingdom	C 14/2008 – restructuring package for Northern Rock	Conditional decision after formal investigation procedure	28 October 2009
United Kingdom	N 428/2009 – restructuring plan of Lloyds Banking Group	No objection	18 November 2009
United Kingdom	N422/2009 and N621/2009 – Royal Bank of Scotland, impaired asset relief measure and restructuring plan	No objection	14 December 2009

Note: As a general rule, each of these schemes is reviewable after six months. This means that the first wave of reviews started in April 2009.

Source: European Commission

Table 6.3. *Cases of financial institutions currently under formal investigation*

Country	*Type of measure/beneficiary*	*Date of decision to open formal investigation*
Belgium/France/ Luxembourg	Restructuring of Dexia	13 March 2009
Germany	Aid for Hypo Real Estate	7 May 2009
	Prolongation	13 November 2009
Germany, Austria	Aid for Bayern LB and its Austrian subsidiary Hypo Group Alpe Adria	12 May 2009
Germany	Aid for HSH Nordbank AG	22 October 2009
Germany	Support for German savings bank Sparkasse KölnBonn	5 November 2009

Table 6.3. *(continued)*

Country	*Type of measure/beneficiary*	*Date of decision to open formal investigation*
Latvia	Aid for JSC Parex Banka	29 July 2009
Netherlands	State measures in favour of Fortis Bank Nederland (FBN) and the activities of ABN Amro	8 April 2009
Portugal	State guarantee for Banco Privado Português	10 November 2009

Table 6.4. *Real economy measures, 2009*

	Measure					
Member state	*€500,000 per company*	*Guarantees*	*Subsidized loan*	*Reduced-interest loans for production of green products*	*Risk-capital schemes*	*Export-credit schemes*
Austria	2				1	
Belgium		1				1
Czech Republic	1	1				
Denmark						2
Finland	1	1				1
France	1	1	1	1	2	1
Germany	3	1	2	1	1	1
Greece	1	1	1			
Hungary	1	3	1			
Ireland	1					
Italy	1	1	1	1	1	
Latvia	1	1				
Lithuania	1					
Luxembourg	1	1				1
Malta	1					
Netherlands	1					1
Poland	1					
Portugal	1					
Spain	1			1		

Table 6.4. *(continued)*

	Measure					
Member state	*€500,000 per company*	*Guaran-tees*	*Subsidized loan*	*Reduced-interest loans for production of green products*	*Risk-capital schemes*	*Export-credit schemes*
Estonia	1					
Romania		1				
Slovakia	1					
Slovenia	1	1				
Sweden		1				
UK	1	1	2	1		

Source: European Commission

Table 6.5. *Real economy cases under the Temporary Framework (as of 16 December 2009)*

Member state	*Type of measure/ beneficiary*	*Type of decision*	*Date of adoption*
Austria	N 47/a/2009 – aid up to €500,000	No objection	20 March 2009
	N 317/2009 – amendment		18 June 2009
Austria	N 47/d/2009 – risk capital	No objection	25 March 2009
Belgium	N 117/2009 – subsidized guarantees	No objection	20 March 2009
Belgium	N 532/2009 – export-credit insurance	No objection	6 November 2009
Czech Republic	N 237/2009 – subsidized interest rates	No objection	6 May 2009
Czech Republic	N 236/2009 - Aid up to €500,000	No objection	7 May 2009

Table 6.5. *(continued)*

Member state	*Type of measure/ beneficiary*	*Type of decision*	*Date of adoption*
Denmark	N 198/2009 – temporary scheme (export-credit insurance)	No objection	6 May 2009
	N 554/2009 (amendment)		29 October 2009
Estonia	N 387/2009 – temporary scheme (aid up to €500 000)	No objection	13 July 2009
Finland	N 224/2009 – aid up to €500,000	No objection	3 June 2009
Finland	N 82b/2009 – guarantees	No objection	9 June 2009
Finland	N 258/2009 – export-credit insurance	No objection	22 June 2009
France	N 7/2009 – aid up to €500,000	No objection	19 January 2009
France	N 15/2009 – reduced interest rates	No objection	4 February 2009
France	N 11/2009 – reduced interest rates to producers of green products	No objection	3 February 2009
France	N 23/2009 – subsidized guarantees	No objection	27 February 2009
France	N 119/2009 – modification of risk-capital scheme	No objection	16 March 2009
France	N 609/2009 – aid up to €15,000 for the agricultural sector	No objection	2 December 2009
France	N 36/2009 – risk capital	No objection	30 June 2009
France	N 449/2009 – export-credit insurance	No objection	5 October 2009

Table 6.5. *(continued)*

Member state	*Type of measure/ beneficiary*	*Type of decision*	*Date of adoption*
Germany	N 661/2008 – KfW-run special programme 2009 (interest subsidies)	No objection	30 December 2008
Germany	N 668/2008 – limited amount of compatible aid	No objection	30 December 2008
	N 299/2009 – amendment		4 June 2009
	N 411/2009 – amendment		17 July 2009
Germany	N 39/2009 – temporary adaptation of risk-capital schemes	No objection	3 February 2009
Germany	N 27/2009 – guarantees	No objection	27 February 2009
Germany	N 38/2009 – reduced interest rates	No objection	19 February 2009
Germany	N 426/2009 – green products	No objection	4 August 2009
Germany	N 384/2009 – export-credit insurance	No objection	5 August 2009
Germany	N 597/2009 – aid up to €15,000 for the agricultural sector	No objection	23 November 2009
Greece	N308/2009 – guarantees	No objection	3 June 2009
Greece	N309/2009 – subsidized interest rates	No objection	3 June 2009
Greece	N 304/2009 – aid up to €500,000	No objection	15 July 2009
Hungary	N 114/2009 – guarantees	No objection	10 March 2009
Hungary	N 77/2009 – aid up to €500,000	No objection	24 February 2009

Table 6.5. *(continued)*

Member state	*Type of measure/ beneficiary*	*Type of decision*	*Date of adoption*
Hungary	N 78/2009 – subsidized interest rates	No objection	24 February 2009
Hungary	N 203/2009 – guarantees	No objection	24 April 2009
Ireland	N 186/2009 – aid up to €500,000	No objection	15 April 2009
Italy	N 279/2009 – risk capital	No objection	20 May 2009
Italy	N 266/2009 – guarantees	No objection	28 May 2009
Italy	N 248/2009 – aid up to €500,000	No objection	28 May 2009
Italy	N 268/2009 – subsidized interest rates	No objection	29 May 2009
Italy	N 542/2009 – aid for green cars	No objection	26 October 2009
Latvia	N 124/2009 – aid up to €500,000	No objection	19 March 2009
Latvia	N 139/2009 – temporary scheme (guarantees)	No objection	22 April 2009
Latvia	N 670/2009 – guarantee to JSC Liepājas Metalurgs	No objection	15 December 2009
Lithuania	N 272/2009 – aid up to €500,000	No objection	8 June 2006
	Amendment		13 November 2009
Luxembourg	N 99/2009 – aid up to €500,000	No objection	26 February 2009
Luxembourg	N 128/2009 – guarantees	No objection	11 March 2009
Luxembourg	N 50/2009 – export-credit insurance	No objection	20 April 2009
Malta	N 118/2009 – aid up to €500,000	No objection	18 May 2009

Table 6.5. *(continued)*

Member state	*Type of measure/ beneficiary*	*Type of decision*	*Date of adoption*
Netherlands	N 156/2009 – aid up to €500,000	No objection	1 April 2009
Netherlands	N 409/2009 – export-credit insurance	No objection	2 October 2009
Poland	N 408/2009 – aid up to €500,000	No objection	17 August 2009
Portugal	N 13/2009 – aid up to €500,000	No objection	19 January 2009
Romania	N 286/2009 – guarantees	No objection	5 June 2009
Romania	N 547/2009 – aid up to €500,000	No objection	3 December 2009
Romania	N 478/2009 – guarantee in favour of Ford Romania	No objection	13 November 2009
Slovak Republic	N 222/2009 – aid up to €500,000	No objection	30 April 2009
Slovenia	NN 34/2009 – guarantees	No objection	12 June 2009
Slovenia	N 228/2009 – aid up to €500,000	No objection	12 June 2009
Spain	N 140/2009 – aid for green cars	No objection	29 March 2009
Spain	N 307/2009 – aid up to €500,000	No objection	8 June 2009
Sweden	N 80/2009 – guarantees in favour of Volvo cars	No objection	5 June 2009
Sweden	N 605/2009 – export-credit insurance	No objection	25 November 2009
United Kingdom	N 43/2009 – aid up to €500,000	No objection	4 February 2009
United Kingdom	N 71/2009 – guarantees	No objection	27 February 2009

Table 6.5. *(continued)*

Member state	*Type of measure/ beneficiary*	*Type of decision*	*Date of adoption*
United Kingdom	N 72/2009 – aid to businesses producing green products	No objection	27 February 2009
United Kingdom	N 257/2009 – subsidized interest rates	No objection	15 May 2009

Source: European Commission

Table 6.6. *Cases under the Temporary Framework which are being formally investigated (as of 16 December 2009)*

Country	*Type of measure/beneficiary*	*Date of decision regarding opening of formal investigation*
Romania	C 36/2009 – state guarantee in favour of Oltchim	19 November 2009

Source: European Commission

7

Competition enforcement in periods of crisis

The Chinese use two brush strokes to write the word 'crisis.' One brush stroke stands for danger; the other for opportunity. In a crisis, be aware of the danger – but recognize the opportunity.

John Fitzgerald Kennedy (1917–63)[1]

In the present crisis, government is not the solution to our problem; government is the problem

Ronald W. Reagan (1911–2004)[2]

7.1 Introduction

The global recession illustrates that assumptions of market efficiency are misplaced where systemic uncertainty roams the marketplace. As Devlin argues, 'it reveals that macroeconomic fluctuations cannot be controlled by monetary policy alone'.[3] This chapter will therefore address whether competition policy has or should have a different role in periods of crisis. It will examine in detail the application of competition legislation on crisis cartels, mergers and state aid. The aim of the chapter is to present how competition enforcement should be applied on these issues in periods of crisis.

As John Fingleton, the chairman of the OFT, argues, the crisis brought its own challenges in the temptation to form cartels or to engage in other forms of permissible or non-permissible horizontal competition. In addition, more failing-firm defence arguments in mergers were

[1] John Fitzgerald Kennedy was the thirty-fifth president of the United States.

[2] Ronald W. Reagan was the fortieth president of the US and the thirty-third governor of California.

[3] A. Devlin, 'Antitrust in an Era of Market Failure' (1999), available at http://ssrn.com/abstract=1429539.

likely, and the view that loss of competitive rivalry was not significant in the existing economic conditions was advanced.[4]

In the past, economic recessions have often been followed by efforts to change the legal framework of competition, in order to preserve people's faith in the free-market system. Perhaps the most prominent example of such efforts was the National Industrial Recovery Act (NIRA) in the US, at the time of the Great Depression in the early 1930s. In trying to contain the damage of the Great Depression, this Act allowed hundreds of industries legally to meet and agree upon rules limiting 'excessive' competition. However, subsequent historical analysis has shown that an adverse impact on the economy was the actual result of these efforts.[5] Pursuant to this legislation, there was full suspension of the enforcement of competition law combined with collective bargaining in setting the wages. Had there not been full suspension and had the US government followed European Community policy of the 1980s and 1990s, the outcomes of the recovery of the economy might not have been so slow.

In every crisis, there will be a push for a regulatory response and a political response, which would lead to a restructuring of regulation but restrict competition even further.[6] It is obvious that the European Commission (and all competition authorities in the EU), under the current economic crisis, have to be very cautious with the application of competition rules. They must consider not only the short-term restabilization of the economy but also the long-term development of competition as well. According to Nadia Calvino (deputy director-general for Competition at the European Commission (EC)),

> There are clear challenges in the policy landscape: there is a financial crisis which leads to systemic risks and is now turning also into a real economic recession. The European Commission has a significant role to play in the current economic environment but; [*sic*] we have to protect the

[4] OECD, Summary Record of the Discussion on Competition and Financial Markets, DAF/COMP/M(2009)1/ANN4, 10 April 2009, Roundtable 3 on Real Economy and Competition Policy in a Period of Retrenchment, available at www.oecd.org.

[5] See K. Heyer and S. Kimmel, 'Merger Review of Firms in Financial Distress' (2009), available at www.usdoj.gov/atr/public/eag/244098.htm.

[6] Professor Petzman's speech at the OECD, Summary Record of the Discussion on Competition and Financial Markets, DAF/COMP/M(2009)1/ANN5, 10 April 2009, Roundtable 4 on Going Forward: Adaptation of Competition Rules, Processes and Institutions to Current Financial Sector Issues, available at www.oecd.org.

> short-term stability of markets while also keeping in mind the importance of a long-term perspective.[7]

European Union governments have also been sensitive to the crisis initiated in 2007, judging it appropriate to intervene in the distressed situation. They felt the need to protect depositors in banks and financial institutions whose failure affects various sectors of the economy and society in general. In fact, their interventions included 'nationalizations, recapitalizations, guarantees, loans, and state acquisition of toxic assets'.[8] What is exceptional in these measures is that usually state aid (Article 87 of the EC Treaty or 107 pursuant to the Lisbon Treaty) is only allowed after approval from the Commission, which chose to be flexible in its assessment of state aid by accelerating its decision-making and by introducing a new basis on which state aid can be cleared. The European Commission has shown sensitivity to the difficulties deriving from the recent worldwide financial crisis. State aid has been one of the main means through which the Commission has responded to the financial crisis. Companies in urgent need of money sought support from member states in order to overcome their liquidity crisis. The greater availability of state aid is obvious in the number of approvals of such measures by the Commission between September 2008 and January 2009 – nearly sixty national state aid measures were approved, compared to the thirteen aid measures that were approved over the same period the previous year.

This chapter will initially provide a brief account of competition enforcement during other crises. Then it will present the objectives of competition legislation and analyse the welfare standards that competition authorities use in enforcement. Subsequently, it will delve into the enforcement of competition legislation on crisis cartels, mergers and state aid in periods of crisis.

7.2 Experience of other crises

During past crises where whole economies experienced times of recession and/or depression, competition authorities were under strong

[7] EU, Competition & Public Law Report, Brussels Focus (2009), 'Brussels: Part of the Problem or Part of the Cure', available at www.abreuadvogados.com/xms/files/05_Comunicacao/Artigos_na_Imprensa/Iberian_Lawyer_Artigo_MMP_Fev.2009.pdf.

[8] 'Antitrust Implications of the Financial Crisis: A UK and EU View' (Spring 2009) 23(2) *Antitrust*.

political pressure to subordinate competition policy to other policies. This was accomplished either by allowing governments to support companies in distress with public subsidies, and/or by assessing mergers or cartels more leniently.

As regards mergers, there was a trend towards protectionist policies endorsing the creation of national champions. As regards cartels, undertakings were allowed to organize themselves to promote mutually agreed rules of conduct to compensate for the deterioration of the market. Such restrictions, which were often established and enforced by trade associations, eliminated the normal risk associated with business activity as they concerned prices, quantities and other competitive factors.

During the Korean crisis, government agencies tended to overlook the potential beneficial effects of competitive markets in times of economic crisis. The OECD report notes that a lesson that arose from the Korean crisis was that competition authorities should be more vigorous in their competition advocacy efforts and that active enforcement against cartels was necessary during periods of retrenchment. In Japan, policy measures taken to counter recessions in the 1950s and 1960s included the introduction of rationalization cartels, which allowed firms to co-ordinate production and services, reduce capacity or even co-ordinate price levels.[9] As the OECD report states, these measures were considered to have serious anti-competitive effects on the economy in the medium and long term and were later abolished.

Fingleton identified empirical evidence showing that the suspension of competition laws in the US during the 1930s made the Great Depression last longer.[10] This suspension of the competition rules by the Roosevelt administration in 1933 is argued to have added to the duration of the Great Depression – one of the most important crises that has been experienced worldwide; and arguably government intervention to restrict competition in structurally depressed industries enhanced the Japanese recession in the 1990s.

Professor Gerber, in his presentation to the OECD Roundtable,[11] provided a historical analysis of the enforcement of competition laws in periods of crisis. He argued that in times of difficulty, competi-

[9] OECD, Competition and Financial Markets (2009), available at www.oecd.org.

[10] J. Fingleton, 'Competition Policy in Troubled Times' (20 January 2009), available at www.oft.gov.uk.

[11] OECD, Summary Record of the Discussion on Competition and Financial Markets, DAF/COMP/M(2009)1/ANN4, 10 April 2009, Roundtable 3 on Real Economy and Competition Policy in a Period of Retrenchment, available at www.oecd.org.

tion law enforcement suffered. During the US depression in the 1930s the Roosevelt administration had not been interested in supporting competition law, and thus enforcement fell away and the courts were less likely to support it. The New Deal, which was implemented by the Roosevelt Administration, incorporated NIRA in 1933. NIRA suspended antitrust law and permitted collusion in some sectors, provided that that industry raised wages above market clearing levels and accepted collective bargaining with independent labour unions.[12]

As the OECD report states,[13] a number of studies have concluded that these New Deal policies were important contributory factors to the persistence and depth of the Great Depression. Cole and Ohanian concluded that New Deal policies reduced consumption and investment during 1934–9 by about 14 per cent relative to levels prevalent in competitive markets.[14]

Ohanian and Cole develop a theoretical model of New Deal policies, and quantitatively evaluate their macroeconomic effects. As they argue, recovery from the Great Depression was weak. Their depiction of real output, real consumption and hours worked is presented here in Figure 7.1. Real GDP per adult, which was 39 per cent below the trend value (based on the development of real GDP prior to the Depression) in 1933, remained 27 per cent below trend in 1939.[15]

As Cole and Ohanian argue,[16] the large negative shocks that caused the 1929–33 downturn, including monetary shocks, productivity shocks and banking shocks, reversed after 1933. This reversal should have induced a rapid recovery with output and employment returning to the trend values (prior to the crisis) by the late 1930s. The authors' main finding is that New Deal cartelization policies were a key factor behind the weak recovery, accounting for 60 per cent of the difference between actual output and trend output.

Interestingly, the authors note that the key feature of the policies involved in the New Deal was not government-sponsored collusion

12 The Act was declared unconstitutional in 1935.

13 OECD, Competition and Financial Markets.

14 H. Cole and L. Ohanian, 'New Deal Policies and the Persistence of the Great Depression: A General Equilibrium Analysis' (2004) 112 *Journal of Political Economy* 779.

15 Ibid.

16 H. Cole and L. Ohanian, New Deal Policies and the Persistence of the Great Depression: A General Equilibrium Analysis, Federal Reserve Bank of Minneapolis, Research Department Staff Report 30, 2003.

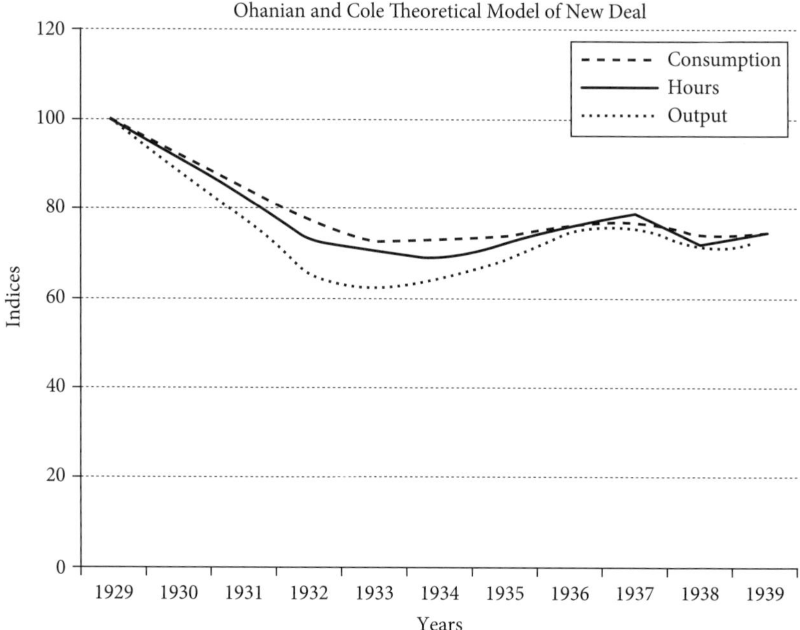

Figure 7.1. Real output, real consumption and hours worked during the Great Depression.

per se, but rather the policies linking high wages and the ability to collude – the policies behind sustaining high wages. The authors' model shows that high wages reduced employment in the cartelized and non-cartelized sectors of the economy.

The coincidence of high wages, low consumption and low hours worked indicated that the labour market was not in equilibrium during the New Deal. President Roosevelt believed that the severity of the Depression was due to excessive business competition, which reduced prices and wages, which in turn lowered demand and employment. Roosevelt aimed at promoting economic recovery through raising prices and wages, thus the Congress passed industrial and labour policies to limit competition and raise labour bargaining power. As mentioned above, NIRA suspended antitrust law and permitted collusion in some sectors, provided that industry raised wages above market clearing levels and accepted collective bargaining with independent labour unions. The cornerstone of NIRA was a Code of Fair Competition for each industry. Firms and workers negotiated these codes under the guidance of the National Recovery Administration (NRA). Presidential approval was granted only if the industry raised wages and accepted collective bargaining. In return, NIRA suspended antitrust law and each industry was encouraged to adopt trade practices that limited competition and raised prices. Codes of Fair Competition endorsed practices including minimum prices, restrictions on production and investment, resale price maintenance, and so on. Ohanian and Cole note that minimum price was the most widely adopted provision. In some codes, the authority determined the minimum price directly, either as the authority's assessment of a 'fair market price' or as the authority's assessment of the 'minimum cost of production'. By 1934, they were applied in over five hundred industries, which accounted for nearly 80 per cent of private, non-agricultural employment.[17]

In 1935, the US Supreme Court ruled that NIRA was unconstitutional primarily due to the the Act's suspension of the antitrust laws. The government passed the National Labor Relations Act (NLRA), which strengthened several of NIRA's labour provisions and granted even more bargaining power to workers than NIRA had, as well as the right to organize and bargain collectively. Roosevelt's views changed in the late 1930s, and he argued that cartelization was contributing to the persistence of the Depression and in response he strengthened competition enforcement. In addition, bargaining power was weakened. Ohanian and Cole argue that the DOJ was not active in antitrust enforcement after 1935, and maintain that the government ignored collusive arrangements in industries that paid high wages.

The authors present evidence that New Deal policies significantly increased wages and prices in the relevant industries. Real wages in the three covered sectors rose after NIRA was adopted and remained high through the rest of the decade. The wage and price data from manufacturing, energy, mining and agriculture indicated that New Deal policies raised relative prices and real wages in those industries covered by these policies. An additional source of evidence supporting the authors' conclusions is FTC analyses of manufacturing industries, which concluded that there was little competition in many concentrated industries, including autos, chemicals, aluminium and glass.[18]

Recovery from the adverse market conditions during the Depression should address the low levels of consumption, investment and

[17] See further Cole and Ohanian 2004.

[18] Ibid., at p. 31.

employment, as well as high real wages and reduced competition in the labour market. Importantly, the authors add that the key depressing element behind New Deal policies – the link between collusion and high wages – reduced output, consumption and investment. The adoption of these industrial and trade policies coincided with the persistence of the depression through the late 1930s. In addition, the abandonment of these policies coincided with the strong economic recovery of the 1940s.

As regards Europe, according to Gerber,[19] there was also less enforcement in Europe in the crisis of the late 1970s and 1980s, when competition authorities were seldom powerful and were susceptible to direct political and economic pressure. Mergers and cartels were the areas of competition law closest, and most susceptible, to industrial policy and therefore with the greatest vulnerability to pressure.[20]

As the above analysis illustrates, evidence of previous crises shows that unreserved relaxation of competition enforcement can prolong the adverse effects of a crisis.

We should stress that we are not advocating in this book that competition policy be automatically relaxed. The premise behind the analysis presented herein is that competition authorities should be pragmatic in identifying instances where, even if some of the strict failing-firm defence criteria or some of the assessment criteria for efficiencies are not satisfied, the competition authorities, rather than prohibiting an anti-competitive merger outright, should consider whether this prohibition may induce severe harm to consumer welfare, which will be more severe than any likely anti-competitive impact of the merger. Thus, as we shall see later in this chapter, a balancing of the two post-merger situations needs to be considered in order to ensure that the conclusion of the merger assessment will induce as beneficial a result as possible. Similarly, regarding cartels, certain agreements can have beneficial effects on markets during a crisis. Adopting a strict approach to such agreements and/or imposing high fines may risk the long-term viability of undertakings and/or industries as a whole.

[19] D.J. Gerber, *Law and Competition in Twentieth Century Europe: Protecting Prometheus*, Oxford University Press, 1998.

[20] See further OECD, Summary Record of the Discussion on Competition and Financial Markets, DAF/COMP/M(2009)1/ANN4, 10 April 2009, Roundtable 3 on Real Economy and Competition Policy in a Period of Retrenchment, available at www.oecd.org.

In the following sections of this chapter, we shall analyse how competition law should be enforced in periods of crisis. A pragmatic competition policy which takes into account the implications of crises will ensure the maximization of consumer welfare in cases where, unless some competition principles are applied more leniently, the result will be the creation of inefficiencies in the market, inefficiencies that can have long-term adverse implications after the crisis has come to an end.

7.3 The objectives of competition law

Turning briefly to the objectives of competition legislation, in the EU the notion of harm to consumers should be read in conjunction with that of harm to the process of competition, although the two notions are quite distinct. Moreover, consumer welfare is an aim which should be viewed dynamically, by examining also its dimensions on a mid- and long-term basis.[21]

In contrast to US antitrust law, there has been continuing debate over a narrower or a broader meaning of the concept of consumer welfare. There are three components of consumer welfare.[22] The first component is value for money. Consumer welfare is enhanced if the prices of goods or services are reduced or the quality of those goods is increased while the price does not change. Price and quality are connected. However, a consumer is not interested in the quality of a good or service unless they also know its price. Quality is important because if prices in a market reach marginal costs, this may lead to a switch from higher quality to lower quality goods or services; indeed, this situation depends on the consumers and their sensitivity to price. The second component is consumer choice. Choice does not have value in itself; nonetheless, if consumers have different tastes, then consumer welfare may increase if they can choose from a wider variety of products. The last component is innovation. Consumers may benefit and consumer welfare may increase

[21] V. Mertikopoulou, 'DG Competition's Discussion Paper on the Application of Article 102 of the EC Treaty to Exclusionary Abuses: The Proposed Economic Reform from a Legal Point of View' (2007) 28(4) *ECLR* 241, at p. 242. In competition law the primary role of the consumer welfare standard is to verify the goals of competition policy and to delineate the general legal framework of competition law enforcement by establishing the basis for the standard of proof required in investigation and litigation.

[22] A. Lindsay, *The EC Merger Regulation: Substantive Issues*, Sweet and Maxwell, 2003.

if new products or services are developed, on the basis that there is actual or potential demand for the new products or services.[23]

Promotion of consumer welfare has traditionally been considered one of the aims, not the sole aim, of antitrust, both in the United States and in Europe.[24] In the US the FTC acts to ensure that markets operate efficiently to benefit consumers. In the UK the OFT declares that its goal is to make markets work well for consumers. Most academics seem to agree that consumer protection is the prevailing aim of antitrust legislation.[25]

Early European Commission reports on competition policy strongly suggested that that policy was aimed at the promotion of consumer welfare. The European Commission's 1st Report on competition policy, in 1971, stated that

> competition policy endeavours to maintain or create effective conditions of competition by means of rules applying to enterprises in both private and public sectors. Such a policy encourages the best possible use of productive resources for the greatest possible benefit of the economy as a whole and for the benefit, in particular, of the consumer.

The Commission and the ECJ in their fundamental decisions reached in the 1970s interpreted the objective of protecting competition as referring to the protection of the economic freedom of market actors. These important decisions were not based on economics or consumer welfare. In these early cases the Commission and the Community's courts focused more on the protection of the economic freedom of market players, as well as on preventing

[23] J. Malinauskaite, 'The Development of 'Consumer Welfare' and its Application in the Competition Law of the European Community and Lithuania' (2007) 18(10) *ICCLR* 354, at p. 355.

[24] R. Whish, *Competition Law*, 5th ed., Butterworths, 2003, at p. 15 et seq.

[25] A report of the ICN Unilateral Conduct Working Group (hereafter ICN report) presents the objectives of laws covering unilateral conduct identified in the responses of jurisdictions surveyed as part of the ICN report. The report, prepared for the Sixth Annual Conference of the ICN in May 2007 in Moscow, consists of three chapters, which address the objectives of unilateral conduct laws, the assessment of dominance/substantial market power, and state-created monopolies. The report describes the approaches of competition agencies around the world to these issues, and distils themes that may assist in promoting convergence in these areas. The report is based on the responses of ICN members and of non-governmental advisers (NGAs) to a questionnaire developed by the working group. See www.internationalcompetitionnetwork.org/media/library/unilateral_conduct/Objectives%20of%20Unilateral%20Conduct%20May%2007.pdf.

firms from using their economic power to undermine competitive structures.[26]

In *Continental Can*, the Court ruled that

> abuse may therefore occur if an undertaking in a dominant position strengthens such position in such a way that the degree of dominance reached substantially fetters competition, i.e. that only undertakings remain in the market whose behaviour depends on the dominant one . . . it can . . . be regarded as an abuse if an undertaking holds a position so dominant that the objectives of the Treaty are circumvented by an alteration to the supply structure which seriously endangers the consumer's freedom of action in the market, such a case necessarily exists if practically all competition is eliminated.[27]

The European Commission Notice on the Application of Article 81(3) provides:

> The concept of 'consumers' encompasses all direct or indirect users of the products covered by the agreement, including producers that use the products as an input, wholesalers, retailers and final consumers, i.e. natural persons who are acting for purposes which can be regarded as outside their trade or profession. In other words, consumers within the meaning of Article 101(3) are the customers of the parties to the agreement and subsequent purchasers. These customers can be undertakings as in the case of buyers of industrial machinery or an input for further processing or final consumers as for instance in the case of buyers of impulse ice-cream or bicycles.[28]

The Commission has stated that the objective of Article 101 is to protect competition in the market as a means of enhancing consumer welfare,[29] which must be the same for Article 102, as both Articles 101 and 102 seek to achieve the same aim.[30]

Advocate General Jacobs has stated that

> it is important not to lose sight of the fact that the primary purpose of Article 82 is to prevent distortion of competition – and in particular to

[26] L. Gormsen, 'Article 82 EC: Where Are We Coming From and Where Are We Going To?' (March 2006) 2(2) *The Competition Law Review* 19.

[27] Case 6/72, *Europemballage Corp. and Continental Can Co. Inc. v. Commission* (*Continental Can*), [1973] ECR I-215, §26.

[28] European Commission Notice Guidelines on the Application of Article 101(3), [2004] OJ C101, para. 84.

[29] European Commission Notice Guidelines on the Application of Article 101(3), [2004] OJ C101, paras. 13 and 33.

[30] Case C-6/72 *Continental Can v. Commission*, [1973] ECR 215, §25.

> safeguard the interest of consumers – rather than to protect the position of particular competitors.[31]

The Court of First Instance (CFI) in *British Airways* explained,

> Article 82 EC does not require it to be demonstrated that the conduct in question had any actual or direct effect on consumers. Competition law concentrates upon protecting the market structure from artificial distortions because by doing so the interests of the consumer in the medium to long term are best protected.[32]

It is noteworthy that Commissioner Kroes argued that

> consumer welfare is now well established as the standard the Commission applies when assessing mergers and infringements of the Treaty rules on cartels and monopolies . . . An effects-based approach, grounded in solid economics, ensures that citizens enjoy the benefits of a competitive, dynamic market economy.[33]

In addition, Commissioner Kroes, in her speech of 23 September 2005 to the Fordham Corporate Law Institute, mentioned that the objective of Article 82 is the protection of competition in the market as a means of enhancing consumer welfare and ensuring an efficient allocation of resources.[34]

Consumer harm is the overall criterion for deciding whether a dominant firm's behaviour is abusive or not. Fjell and Sorgard propose an effects approach, implying that the appropriate test for abuse would be to check whether consumers are harmed.[35]

According to Cseres,

> the adoption of the consumer welfare standard vis-à-vis the total welfare standard places consumers' economic needs and responses to firm behaviour further into the focus of competition law enforcement. It

[31] Opinion in the *Oscar Bronner* case, para. 231 (C-7/97, *Oscar Bronner v. Mediaprint*, [1998] ECR I-7791).

[32] Case T-219/99, *British Airways v. Commission*, para. 264.

[33] N. Kroes, 'European Competition Policy: Delivering Better Markets and Better Choices' (15 September 2005), available at http://europa.eu/rapid/pressReleasesAction.do?reference=SPEECH/05/512 &format=HTML&aged=0&language=EN&guiLanguage=en.

[34] N. Kroes, 'Preliminary Thoughts on Policy Review of Article 102', speech given on 23 September 2005 at the Fordham Corporate Law Institute New York, available at http://europa.eu/rapid/pressReleasesAction.do?reference=SPEECH/05/537&format=HTML&aged=0&language=EN&guiLanguage=en.

[35] K. Fjell and L. Sorgard L., 'How to Test for Abuse of Dominance' (July 2006) 2 *European Competition Journal* 69.

> counterbalances firms' information advantages, lobbying advantages, the fact they are better represented, as well as their first mover advantages in selecting the strategic moves they pursue. The consumer welfare standard seems, from both the legal and political aspect, an appropriate standard of enforcement.[36]

All thirty-two agencies responding to a report on unilateral conduct prepared by the International Competition Network (ICN) argued that ensuring an effective competitive process is an objective in its own right; a means to achieve other desirable goals such as consumer welfare, economic freedom or efficiency; or both an objective and a means to achieve such objectives. Of the nine other items that respondents identified as objectives in and of themselves, a significant number[37] of respondents relied on the promotion of consumer welfare and on maximizing efficiency.[38]

Summing up this brief account of the objectives of competition law we should stress that the director general of the Directorate General for Competition, Philip Lowe, has emphasized that 'competition is not an end in itself, but an instrument designed to achieve a certain public interest objective, consumer welfare'.[39]

7.4 Welfare standards

This section will present a brief analysis of the welfare standard that is relevant for competition enforcement. In the European economic and antitrust literature, the question of welfare standards hinges on whether the consumer welfare model or the total surplus model constitutes the relevant welfare standard.

There have been arguments in the welfare standards theory that competition rules should pursue the total surplus standard. However, the present development of competition law would not allow policy-makers to take the radical step of adopting the total surplus standard. For example, a merger which would cause severe harm to consumers would not be allowed even if total welfare were enhanced as a result of larger profits to the producers.

The OECD report analysed whether, in the financial sector,

36 K.J. Cseres, 'The Controversies of the Consumer Welfare Standard' (2007) 3(2) *Competition Law Review* 170.

37 Thirty agencies.

38 See further ICN report, at p. 5.

39 'Preserving and Promoting Competition: A European Response', EC Competition Policy Newsletter, No 2, summer 2006.

competition policy should focus exclusively on consumer welfare or also pursue other objectives like general economic and systemic stability.[40] One way to accomplish that would be to explicitly incorporate other objectives into competition policy. Similar to the exceptions that UK legislation has for, among other things, financial stability, the institutional and legislative framework of competition policy could incorporate an objective of financial stability rather than an exception of financial stability, an exception that was inserted 'at the last minute' in the Enterprise Act 2002, in an attempt by the UK government to sustain financial stability.

The OECD report outlines an additional way to include other objectives in competition enforcement by granting the competition authority the task of safeguarding consumer welfare and having another decision-making body to weigh this objective against other objectives that may be or may become prevalent at times.

Examples of both systems can already be found in existing institutional designs across countries. An example of a competition authority explicitly incorporating in its analysis objectives other than consumer welfare is Austria, where a merger can be cleared if it is indispensable to the international competitiveness of the undertakings concerned and justifiable on macroeconomic grounds.[41] An example of a separate decision-making body which balances the importance of consumer welfare against other objectives is the UK, where the Secretary of State retains the decision-making power for mergers involving the public interest, as is specified in the Enterprise Act 2002, with the OFT and the Competition Commission having only advisory powers.

As the OECD report states, an enlargement of the objectives of competition authorities beyond consumer welfare has the benefit of keeping potential trade-offs between competition concerns and other concerns within the same competition authority, with the advantage that competition may be given higher weight.[42] Due, however, to the lack of expertise or lack of information about non-competition-related policies (e.g. financial stability, macroeconomic policy) that a competition authority may have, the OECD advocates that some form of co-operation between competition authorities and sector regulators should take place.

Thus non-competition-related objectives are, under certain circumstances, essential in the enforcement of competition law. This approach

[40] OECD, Competition and Financial Markets.

[41] Ibid.

[42] Ibid., at p. 38.

should not provide a motive for relaxing competition standards, but should be given prominence in situations such as the current financial crisis, where competition policy should be balanced against other policies. Depending on the welfare standard we adopt, competition policy induces different results.

In periods of crisis, the consumer welfare standard may need to be prioritized below, among other things, the total welfare standard. As we shall see below, assessing mergers under considerations not related to consumer welfare may have different implications for the application of the failing-firm defence and/or for the assessment of efficiencies. For example, assessing a merger under a total welfare standard implies that a merger inducing benefits to the total surplus will be cleared, while at the same time it may harm consumer welfare. In addition, taking other considerations into account in the assessment of mergers, such as job losses, will lead competition authorities to clear mergers the prohibition of which may entail severe job losses. Ensuring the continuation of supply of a product or service, or continuation of the research on a particular product or process, may necessitate the clearance of a merger which may have anti-competitive effects or the enactment of an agreement ensuring rationalized reduction of the excess capacity of undertakings.

As mentioned above, such an approach should be used cautiously and by no means universally. Not all anti-competitive mergers or crisis cartel agreements merit approval due to non-competition-related aims. However, as we shall see below in this chapter, competition policy needs to be pragmatic, and flexible enough to address sudden exogenous shocks and the wide-ranging implications of such shocks to whole markets. After all, the ultimate and undoubted aim of competition should be to enhance the operation of a market, in order to improve consumer welfare. On a number of occasions it is thus essential to subordinate competition policy if such an approach will ensure sustainability and improvement of consumer welfare, or alternatively if such an approach will prevent deterioration of consumer welfare through means irrelevant to competition policy (e.g. systemic crisis, macroeconomic instability and so on).

7.5 Merger enforcement amidst crises

According to the OECD report,[43] merger activity is expected to increase once financial markets are restored. The crisis is likely to result in

[43] Ibid.

a higher incidence of failing-firm defences put forward as a reason to clear anti-competitive mergers. Mergers and acquisitions become very difficult to fund due to the credit crunch and, at the same time, the crisis is likely to increase the number of failing firms and lead to attempts to consolidate certain sectors of the economy.

In a period of crisis the most sensible mergers and those most frequently presented to competition authorities are strategic mergers and thus are likely to be horizontal, enhancing the ability of the merged entity and in some cases its competitors to impose higher prices (or adopt other types of anti-competitive conduct, such as reducing quality) than would be possible under normal competition.

The New Zealand submission to the OECD report on enforcement of competition in a financial crisis suggests that competition authorities should consider the trade-off between reductions in competition from mergers on the one hand and stability gains in the broader economy on the other. The issue of merger enforcement amidst the financial crisis was also addressed by, among others, the Canadian and Irish submissions.[44]

The Canadian submission to the OECD suggested that competition authorities need to co-ordinate the definition and application of the failing-firm concept in multi-jurisdictional cases. One measure that might deal effectively with some of the immediate demands of the crisis was the treatment of the failing-firm defence doctrine. The failing-firm defence is normally difficult to apply successfully, and in times of economic crisis succeeding in that defence might be even harder. The Canadian submission adds that greater co-ordination in dealing with the failing-firm issue could lead to a decrease in the prospect of unjustified inconsistent results, to increased certainty for business and to more effective resolutions and credibility for the authorities.[45]

The Irish submission to the OECD noted in its contribution that 'measures put in place by the Irish government to ensure the stability of the financial services sector are capable of putting aside domestic competition rules'. The Irish submission noted that emergency legislation was enacted in October 2008 in about thirty-six hours. There was no time for extensive debate, especially in a context that was described as 'an

[44] Ibid.

[45] Summary Record of the Discussion on Competition and Financial Markets, DAF/COMP/M(2009)1/ANN4, 10 April 2009, Roundtable 3 on Real Economy and Competition Policy in a Period of Retrenchment, available at www.oecd.org.

enormous systemic risk' to a number of Irish financial institutions. The principal feature, according to the Irish submission, was not an exemption from competition rules or the movement of the merger function away from the competition authority, but a guarantee not only of deposits but also of the liabilities of Irish institutions. There was a lacuna in Irish merger legislation which prohibited a weekend transaction, and there was no way to clear a merger with the provision that the analysis could be done subsequently. The legislation provided that the minister of finance should seek advice from the competition authority so the authority engaged with ministry officials, attempting to educate them on merger assessment and intending to exert influence in favour of structural remedies that could, if appropriate, be put in place after the crisis had passed.[46]

In Switzerland the Financial Market Supervisory Authority was responsible for assessing mergers in the interest of creditors. The Swiss legal framework, for more than ten years, provided for an exception for forced bank mergers by dismissing competition assessment. That did not result from any systemic crisis. The provision notes that the interests of creditors take priority over competition concerns in banking mergers, but only where the creditors' interests are in clear danger. There was also a shift of decisional jurisdiction from the competition agency to the financial supervision authority. The competition agency had to be heard but the interests of the creditors were predominant. The Financial Market Supervisory Agency can carry out constant monitoring, and, having an information advantage, it can act rapidly and make an early intervention if necessary.

7.5.1 *Failing-firm defence*

The question arises as to the extension of the 'sensitivity' and flexibility of the European Commission in respect of the application of the failing-firm defence when assessing mergers, given the current economic crisis. In other words, how lenient must the Commission be? Ought the conditions for the application of the defence, or more generally the competition policy rules, to be loosened during difficult economic times? What does a crisis imply for the failing-firm defence criteria?

To the question whether the current distressed economic environment makes securing antitrust approval for mergers or acquisitions easier than it otherwise might be, Akin Gump argued that 'antitrust

[46] Ibid.

principles will take into account the weakened financial condition of a merging party'.[47]

The Lloyds/HBOS merger is a clear example of the intervention of the UK government in the assessment of mergers in exceptional circumstances. In this case the government intervened and allowed the merger despite the fact that the merger was capable of giving rise to competition concerns.[48] The OFT took into account the bad financial situation of HBOS, along with the disadvantages that a failure of a bank entails in terms of consumer confidence and costs, but did not clear the merger.[49] In fact, the government enabled the Secretary of State to get involved with the merger and temporarily countervail competition rules in order to maintain general financial stability. There were multiple press articles talking about this unusual involvement of the government in competition law. Andrea Gomes Da Silva and Mark Sansom said,

> In the UK, at the height of the turmoil in the banking sector last Fall, the British government brokered a merger between the struggling HBOS banking group and its competitor LloydsTSB, creating a new banking giant – the country's largest bank and mortgage lender.[50]

Many have even viewed this involvement of the government in the assessment of mergers as 'ripping up Britain's competition law'.[51] The UK's contribution to the OECD said, 'the market failure in these circumstances is a mismatch of incentives or incorrect signaling – not an 'excess' amount of competition . . . suspending competition law itself creates a market failure and this is not a sound policy response to an existing market failure'.[52]

[47] Akin Gump, Strauss Hauer & Feld LLP, 'Acquisitions of Distressed Companies: Obtaining Antitrust Merger Clearance Using the Failing and Weakened Firm Defenses', available at www.akingump.com.

[48] The UK government could intervene in merger-control decisions only in relation to national security and media-related mergers, but in this case the government decided to extend the situations where it could intervene by including in the Enterprise Act the category of 'maintaining the stability of the UK financial system' in order to be able to intervene in Lloyds TSB/HBOS.

[49] It has to be stressed, though, that in this particular case the failing-firm defence was not applicable and therefore was not the basis for the clearance of the merger.

[50] A. Gomes Da Silva and M. Sansom, 'Antitrust Implications of the Financial Crisis: A UK and EU View' (Spring 2009) 23(2) *Antitrust*.

[51] 'HBOS Takeover Fails to End Global Panic on Financial Markets', *The Guardian*, 26 September 2008, available at www.guardian.co.uk/business/2008/sep/17/lloydstsbgroup.hbosbusiness2.

[52] UK Submission to the OECD.

The UK government introduced an additional public-policy consideration providing for the stability of the UK financial system to be introduced as a policy exception, along with national security, to the referral of relevant merger situations to the Competition Commission (the Commission) under §58 of the Enterprise Act 2002.[53]

The Act permits the Secretary of State to intervene in a merger if he or she believes that one or more defined public interest considerations may be relevant to the consideration of a merger.[54] These considerations, as currently defined in the Act, are:[55]

- the interests of national security (including public security),
- various considerations relating to the media, and
- the interest of maintaining the stability of the UK financial system.[56]

If the Secretary of State believes that public interest considerations are relevant in a merger case, he or she may give an intervention notice to the OFT.[57] It is the Secretary of State who decides whether a merger should be referred to the Commission for investigation once an intervention notice has been given.[58]

[53] Summary Record of the Discussion on Competition and Financial Markets, DAF/COMP/M(2009)1/ANN2, 10 April 2009, Introduction and Roundtable 1 on Principles: Financial Sector Conditions and Competition Policy, available at www.oecd.org.

[54] Sections 42 and 58 of the Enterprise Act. See also the joint substantive merger guidelines at www.oft.gov.uk/www.competition-comission.org.uk.

[55] See also the OFT's Mergers – Jurisdictional and Procedural Guidance, Chapter 9.

[56] This exception was added to the Enterprise Act by Order No 2645, 2008: The Enterprise Act 2002 (Specification of Additional Section 58 Consideration) Order 2008; for text see www.opsi.gov.uk/si/si2008/uksi_20082645_en_1. The Secretary of State issued an intervention notice specifying this consideration in the context of the proposed merger between Lloyds TSB Group plc and HBOS plc. On 31 October 2008, the Secretary of State exercised his discretion not to refer the merger to the Competition Commission on the basis that the merger would result in significant benefits to the public interest as it related to ensuring the stability of the UK financial system and that these benefits outweighed the potential for the merger to result in anti-competitive outcomes identified by the OFT. See www.berr.gov.uk/files/file48745.pdf.

[57] Intervention notices issued in relation to mergers with a national security element are listed at www.bis.gov.uk/policies/business-law/competition-matters/mergers/mergers-with-a-public-interest. Information and documents in relation to the issuing of an intervention notice in respect of the acquisition by BSkyB plc of 17.9 per cent of the shareholding of ITV plc are at www.berr.gov.uk/whatwedo/businesslaw/competition/mergers/public-interest/broadcasting/index.html.

[58] Save where the Secretary of State subsequently decides that there is no relevant consideration of public interest, in which case the decision on whether or not to refer the merger to the Competition Commission reverts to the OFT under §56.

Lord Mandelson cleared the merger on public interest grounds,[59] rather than refer the merger to the Competition Commission, ranking competition concerns behind financial stability.[60] He argued that the benefits of the transaction for the stability of the UK financial system outweighed the potential for the merger to result in anti-competitive outcomes, which was therefore deemed to be in the public interest.

Thus the Secretary of State made the final assessment of whether to refer the merger to the Competition Commission. As we saw earlier in the analysis of the failing-firm defence, the OFT recommended reference but the Secretary of State decided to clear the merger. This unusual procedure could not until then be justified for mergers in the financial industry. In fact, the OFT and the Competition Commission were the only qualified and independent authorities specializing in competition issues. However, when the financial stability of the economy is at stake, it becomes understandable, and to an extent necessary, for governments temporarily to adopt measures necessary to avoid a deepening of the crisis or the crisis becoming systemic.

The Merger Action Group, an association of persons and businesses in Scotland,[61] appealed the decision to the Competition Appeal Tribunal on, among others, the ground that Secretary of State

- had his discretion unlawfully fettered by statements of 18 September by senior ministers stating that the merger would be cleared under a public interest criterion not then in law, and
- acted irrationally and without proper regard to relevant considerations in clearing the merger on the basis of the changed circumstances of late October. The plaintiffs claimed that the Financial Services Authority's statement before the OFT was filled with factual and legal errors and that the Secretary of State relied excessively

[59] He used powers under the Enterprise Act, which contains provisions under which the Secretary of State can intervene on grounds of public interest in the merger-control process where a merger is subject to review by the OFT. He has the power to decide, on grounds of public interest, to clear a merger despite a substantial lessening of competition – or to prohibit a merger or to subject it to conditions – even where such measures are not justified by competition concerns alone. Decision by Lord Mandelson, Secretary of State for Business, not to refer to the Competition Commission the Merger between Lloyds TSB Group plc and HBOS plc under section 45 of the Enterprise Act 2002, 31 October 2008, available at www.berr.gov.uk/files/file48745.pdf.

[60] BERR, 'Peter Mandelson Gives Regulatory Clearance to Lloyds TSB Merger with HBOS', press release, 2008/253, 31 October 2008.

[61] See www.mergeractiongroup.org.uk.

on its findings whereas the OFT's report should have been given precedence.[62]

In its judgment given on 10 December 2008, the Competition Appeals Tribunal dismissed the appeal, finding no basis for the allegation that the Secretary of State had not given proper consideration to the continuing need for the merger.[63]

The treatment of the Lloyds/HBOS merger has been deemed 'the rather pragmatic approach adopted by some Member States, most notably the United Kingdom'.[64] Sir Callum McCarthy, former president of the UK Financial Services Authority, having been involved himself in the Lloyds/HBOS decision-making process, said that the decision was based on an acute crisis of confidence, of which the most obvious sign was an abrupt and very large movement in the HBOS share price. This decision was also criticized commercially when it was announced that HBOS had made losses of around UK£10 billion, putting in doubt the commercial arguments about the deal which, Lloyds TSB claimed, had the prospect of UK£1.5 billion savings a year.[65]

A merger involving a failing firm should not be assessed in the same way as a merger which does not involve a failing firm. Where a merging firm is failing, pre-merger competitive conditions should not be used as a benchmark. If the competition authorities reject one or more mergers falling below an unsustainable benchmark, the result could well be a liquidation, which is expected to produce greater harm to competition than is predicted to result from one or more of the rejected mergers. If one of the parties to a merger is failing, pre-merger conditions of competition might not prevail even if the merger were prohibited. In such a case, the counterfactual might need to be adjusted to reflect the likely failure of one of the parties and the resulting loss of rivalry.[66] When the

[62] D. Gerard, 'EC Competition Law Enforcement and Financial Crisis' (2009) 1 *Concurrences* 46.

[63] J. Vickers, 'The Financial Crisis and Competition Policy: Some Economics', *Global Competition Policy*, December 2008.

[64] D. Gerard, 'Managing the Financial Crisis in Europe: Why Competition Law Is Part of the Solution, Not of the Problem', *Global Competition Policy*, December 2008.

[65] Summary Record of the Discussion on Competition and Financial Markets, DAF/COMP/M(2009)1/ANN4, 10 April 2009, Roundtable 2 on Crisis: The Role of Competition Policy in Financial Sector Rescue and Restructuring, available at www.oecd.org.

[66] OFT, 'Mergers, Substantive Assessment Guidance', available at www.oft.gov.uk., at p. 34.

Australian competition authority, the ACCC, looked at the proposed takeover of BankWest by the Commonwealth Bank, it looked at the counterfactual in a slightly different way by assuming that BankWest would continue to be owned by HBOS if it were not sold because it could not identify any other buyers. That, in the ACCC's view, meant that BankWest would no longer be an aggressive bank building market share and that its aggressive market price would change.

We should emphasize that once a bank or a financial institution of the size of HBOS or Lehman Brothers is involved, there are few banks big and strong enough to act as an acquirer and hence the choice open to the authorities is extremely limited. Thus the strict application of failing-firm defence criteria becomes more complicated and likely to be unsuccessful, resulting in the bankruptcy of the failing undertaking and in the ensuing adverse implications for the relevant market (such as systemic crisis).

The change in the approach towards mergers, during the recent crisis, is clearly illustrated by the treatment of the Lloyds/HBOS merger. In looking at the Lloyds/HBOS merger the OFT's counterfactual was its assumption that in the short run the bank would continue to operate with government support. In the long run they assumed it would either be sold or become independent again. Archie Kane, a main board member of Lloyds, said that HBOS had 'basically shut down' to the corporate and small-business market as it was close to running out of funds. He added, 'It is quite clear that HBOS could not have survived on its own', that 'HBOS was finished as an [independent] entity'.[67] Mr Kane admitted that the takeover by Lloyds would not have happened had the government 'not taken the extraordinary step of waiving competition concerns'.[68]

[67] See *The Scotsman*, 3 December 2009, available at http://thescotsman.scotsman.com/news/Lloyds-chief-insists--HBOS.5879387.jp.

[68] Lloyds' chief executive, Eric Daniels, said that 80 per cent of the write-off on bad loans, equal to £10.7 billion, came from HBOS, with as much as £9 billion related to lending on commercial property. The majority of loans made by the Bank of Scotland side of the business before the takeover were 'outside the traditional Lloyds low-risk appetite'. Disposals by Lloyds and Royal Bank of Scotland as a way to create more competition in retail banking were ordered by the European Commission to compensate for the huge amounts of state aid the banks have received. The European competition commissioner, Neelie Kroes, again made it clear that Lloyds would not be allowed to remain dominant in areas where it is already strong. Lloyds Banking Group would have to sell six hundred branches and its Cheltenham and Gloucester and TSB brands after the European Commission gave its approval to its state-aid settlement. The sign-off by Brussels ends

In 2001 the Secretary of State had adopted a diametrically opposite view in the planned acquisition of Abbey National by Lloyds. The merger would lead to efficiency gains but the Commission was not convinced that these would be passed on to consumers in the form of reduced prices. The merger would, moreover, have an adverse effect on consumer choice, which would be material in relation to the personal current accounts and small- and medium-enterprise (SME) markets.[69] The concern at the time was that no remedies could have offset the potential anti-competitive effects deriving from this acquisition due to the highly oligopolistic structure of the British banking sector. In that case, the post-merger entity would have a lower market share than did Lloyds/HBOS. As the OECD report states, the dramatic shift observed in the case of Lloyds/HBOS is witness to the extraordinary difficulty of the situation and the consequent subordination of competition concerns to stability concerns, at least in the short run.[70]

We should note at this point that Anthony Stern, a member of the UK Competition Commission, noted at the Members' Roundtable: Competition in Recession, at the Competition Commission, that we may expect further 'public interest' considerations to be added to the present list (for example, 'effect on employment').[71] Christopher Smallwood,

months of wrangling between the bank, the Treasury and the Commission and clears the way for Lloyds to raise £21 billion through a rights issue and a debt-for-equity swap by the end of the year. Under the agreement with Brussels, Lloyds will cut its share of the market in current accounts and mortgages from 30 per cent to 25 per cent. The bank has four years to unload the assets. Commissioner Kroes noted that the new focus of Lloyds will be core corporate and retail banking activities and the application of Lloyds TSB's more prudent risk-management methods. The Commission supported Lloyds' capital-raising exercise as a solid alternative to the UK government's Asset Protection Scheme, as it minimizes taxpayer burdens. The proposed divestments will create an entity with a market share of around 5 per cent in the retail banking market, and a solid footing in mortgage and SME markets. See further www.guardian.co.uk/business/2009/sep/29/royal-bank-of-scotland-eu; www.guardian.co.uk/business/2009/oct/26/lloyds-rbs-eu-bail-outs; www.telegraph.co.uk/finance/breakingviewscom/6495177/Britain-only-half-undoes-LloydsHBOS-mess.html; http://article.wn.com/view/2009/11/18/The_wait_is_over_for_Lloyds_as_Brussels_gives_green_light_to/; and http://europa.eu/rapid/pressReleasesAction.do?reference=SPEECH/09/541&format=PDF&aged=0&language=EN&guiLanguage=en, Neelie Kroes, Speech/09/541, 18 November 2009.

[69] DTI Press Notice, Reference Made to the Competition Commission on 23 February 2001, (P/2001/100) Excerpts from the Report Summary, Lloyds TSB Group plc/Abbey National plc published on 10 July 2001. Available at www.competitioncommission.rg.uk/inquiries/completed/2001/index.htm.

[70] OECD, Competition and Financial Markets, at p. 32.

[71] See further A. Stern, 'Implications for the Wider Economy' (March 2009), at www.competition-commission.org.uk.

another member of the UK Competition Commission, put forward the view that the current competition regime was one for good times and that a broader, refashioned public interest test might be more appropriate to these changed times, with value judgements being left to the Secretary of State. Thus in this crisis which led to the introduction of the financial stability public interest consideration, or during future crises, we may not yet have seen the final act in the involvement of the Secretary of State in competition proceedings.

The OFT has stated that it will take account of prevailing economic and market conditions when assessing evidence put forward by merging parties. A contextual evaluation of evidence will be important in relation to, for example,

- the inevitability of the target business exiting the market and
- the realistic availability of alternative purchasers for the target business.

The OFT adds, though, that it will not relax the standard of 'sufficient compelling evidence' that it applies to the failing-firm defence.[72]

One of the criteria of the failing-firm defence – the lack of an alternative purchaser – must be established by good-faith efforts to find another purchaser. It is required that the failing firm has made an effort in good faith to obtain offers from other firms that would keep the failing firm in the market while constituting a less serious threat to competition. Thus the failing firm must explore alternative merger possibilities and seek out bona fide offers. Current policy towards failing-firm defence may systematically prefer alternative purchasers (weaker competitors or potential entrants) that are unlikely to offer the same efficiencies that a strong competitor purchaser may offer. In addition, the defence requires companies to be in a severe state of decline before they qualify for it.

The requirement to make good-faith efforts to find an alternative purchaser safeguards against loss in competition. However, the alternative purchaser may have much less to offer in the way of improving the efficiency of the acquired firm than the prospective competitor purchaser. In addition, there is concern that the competitor's offer may be higher because it includes a market-power premium, a payment for anticipated gains in market power. There could be a market-power premium, or an efficiency premium, or both. The problem is that it is difficult to separate

[72] See further OFT Restatement of OFT's Position Regarding Acquisitions of 'Failing Firms', December 2008 (OFT1047).

them. Overestimating the market-power premium means underestimating the efficiency premium. The willingness of the acquirer to buy a company that is heading towards failure justifies giving its efficiency claims some additional credence.[73] The Supreme Court interpretation of the alternative-buyer condition was presented in the case of *Citizen Publishing Co. v. United States*.[74]

Satisfaction of the failing-firm defence criteria is biased in favour of non-market participants. Any efficiencies that a potential competitor purchaser might generate from the merger may be unnecessarily sacrificed. Furthermore, a non-market participant may simply be seeking a revenue stream rather than to operate as an effective competitor by making long-term investment plans.[75] Many firms that purchase a distressed business may be seeking a revenue stream and thus may not compete vigorously. In situations of severe financial crises and lack of available capital, the identification of alternative purchasers may be very difficult as the lack of capital will create an insurmountable barrier to entry into the market.

Fingleton argues that crises induce long-term benefits by facilitating the exit of inefficient firms from the market while facilitating the entry of new and better competitors.[76] Considerations of entry have always been essential in competition enforcement. Assumptions of prompt entry into some markets may have to be revisited throughout the duration of the credit crisis.[77] In situations where prompt entry is a condition for post-merger competition, or in conglomerate mergers where rivals' access to capital is an important consideration in analysing the danger of cross-subsidization, the likelihood of entry may be highly relevant to the decision. Although entry may not be likely or is indeed limited during the crisis, competition authorities need to assess the likelihood of entry once the crisis is over. Competition authorities may wish to mitigate the adverse effects of an anti-competitive domestic merger by preferring international takeovers of domestic firms where domestic mergers risk increasing market power. If the sustainability of a domestic firm needs to be maintained through its acquisition, then competition

[73] F. Correia, 'The Failing Company Defence' (1995), available at www.ftc.gov/opp/global/final.htm.

[74] *Citizen Publishing Co. v. United States*, (1969) 394 U.S. 131, 138–9 .

[75] D. Valentine, 'Horizontal Issues: What's Happening and What's on the Horizon' (1995), available at www.ftc.gov/speeches/other/dvhorizontalissues.htm.

[76] Fingleton 2009.

[77] Devlin, 'Antitrust in an Era of Market Failure'.

authorities and governments can promote new entry, which reduces the competitive concerns of such mergers, by reducing regulatory barriers to entry, increasing the availability of information to consumers and ensuring that switching costs are limited.

A firm's willingness to enter a market may decline where profits within that market have become less attractive, as a result of a decline in customer demand.[78] The ability of firms to enter certain markets may also be more limited under more restricted wholesale funding, particularly where potential entrants who may previously have been able and willing to enter on leveraged business models can no longer do so. Thus purchasers may not be able to raise the necessary funds for the acquisition of the firm, and competition authorities should not expect a long list of alternative purchasers and should be ready to accept a less anti-competitive purchaser in conditions of severe liquidity shortage.

A lenient approach towards mergers involving failing and financially distressed firms can balance the losses from increasing concentration after the merger against the gains from hastening entry and competition. The assessment of the failing-firm defence in merger cases should take into account the effect of the policy rule on the incentives for entry (and *ex ante* investment decisions in general).[79] According to research conducted by Mason and Weeds, the policy towards failing firms that competition authorities may adopt affects entry decisions.[80] A firm entering a market also considers its ease of exit, foreseeing that it may later wish to leave should market conditions deteriorate. One way of entering a market is the acquisition of or a merger with an incumbent. Such a merger or acquisition will allow the entrant to benefit from the infrastructure, expertise and customer base of the incumbent. In addition, by facilitating exit in times of financial distress, the failing-firm defence can encourage entry so as to increase overall welfare. Even if welfare is decreased when the firm enters the market by merging with or acquiring an incumbent, the increase in welfare resulting from earlier entry may more than offset this loss.

Apart from the importance and implications of entry in a merger involving a failing firm, competition authorities should also pay attention

[78] Although falling interest rates may partially counteract this by making profitable low-return investments which otherwise would not have been.

[79] R. Mason and H. Weeds, 'The Failing Firm Defence: Merger Policy and Entry' (2003), available at repec.org/res2003/Mason.pdf, at p. 33.

[80] Ibid.

to potential dynamic or innovative efficiencies in assessing a merger involving a failing firm. Dynamic or innovative efficiencies may make a particularly powerful contribution to competitive dynamics, R & D and welfare, but are not readily verifiable and quantifiable because they tend to focus on future products. Merger analysis should give efficiencies more weight if the profitability of a failing industry can be improved by the merger (e.g. by lowering fixed costs) even if the price effects are not immediate. Thus there is a trade-off between, on the one hand, the viability of the failing firm and the positive impact that it may have on competition due to the existence of one additional competitor in the market and, on the other, further consolidation in the market (if a competitor merges with or acquires the failing firm) due to the merger, which may, however, also result from the exit of the failing firm from the market.

As we have seen, in the application of the failing-firm defence, one of the criteria is also that the allegedly failing firm would in the near future be forced out of the market because of financial difficulties if not taken over by another undertaking. Furthermore, in the absence of a merger the assets of the failing firm would inevitably exit the market. Thus, for the failing-firm defence to apply, a merger, acquisition and/or sale should be the only viable method of corporate restructuring. Otherwise, the failing-firm defence cannot be applicable. A tentative conclusion can be made that lack of alternative means of reorganization is a vital criterion for the success of the failing-firm defence. However, there is substantial uncertainty surrounding the reorganization scenario. A significant problem in applying the reorganization consideration, especially in crisis periods, is that it may be impossible to make reliable predictions at the time of assessing the merger as regards the likelihood that alternative restructuring methods will be successful. Thus competition authorities should be careful in assessing the availability and likelihood of alternative reorganization scenarios.

It is natural that the failing-firm defence may be closely intertwined with other considerations, such as social, public-policy and employment issues. Competition authorities in assessing mergers involving failing firms should, to an extent, take into account such issues as they are likely to affect the outcome of the merger assessment. As regards economic and social benefits, there is an inherent difficulty in determining the extent of social costs or benefits in a failing-firm context and how to account for them. The burden is in the form of higher prices and lost consumer surplus, while the relevant benefits concern the failing company's workers and shareholders and the community in which the failing company's assets are located. More importantly, amidst periods of crisis systemic stability concerns are of the utmost importance. According to Correia, competition authorities should take also social costs into account in adopting some general formulation of the failing-company defence, rather than take social costs into account in individual cases.[81] Such concerns may lead to a different interpretation of consumer welfare, thus entitling competition authorities to take social, public-policy and employment issues into consideration in defining their consumer welfare objective of merger assessment. Following the Lisbon Treaty's coming into force on 1 December 2009, interpretative issues could also arise due to the stronger references to full employment and social objectives, including the reference to a 'highly competitive social market economy' in amended Article 3 of the Treaty on European Union. This might induce arguments that a broader industrial policy standard should apply, and some of the issues mentioned above may be given enhanced importance.[82]

The policy towards mergers may have an impact on the employees of the merging firms. Allowing mergers can result in job losses, as may also be the case in prohibiting mergers. If a merger is not allowed and the failing firm exits the market, the lost jobs originate from plant closures. When the failing firm disappears from the market, the employment resources of this firm are likely to be devoted to the manufacture of a completely different product or to the provision of totally different services or goods.

There are advocates who argue that the likelihood of job losses, inefficient use of labour force and the political and social ramifications that such issues may have should not determine the assessment of mergers under antitrust law. Issues relating to employment safety should be dealt with by employment policy and should not influence competition policy. However, according to Posner, the failing-firm defence is 'one of the clearest examples in antitrust law of a desire to subordinate competition to other values'.[83] The social-policy consideration regarding the merger works alongside the impact of the merger on competition.

In addition to economic and social concerns, the relevant public-policy considerations are related to the protection of private parties whose future depends on the existence of the failing firm as well as to the

[81] Correia 1995.

[82] See www.wilmerhale.com/publications/whPubsDetail.aspx?publication=9321.

[83] R.A. Posner, *Antitrust: Cases, Economic Notes and Other Materials*, 2nd ed., West Publishing, 1981, at p. 472.

welfare of the locality of the failing firm. The shareholders are unlikely to lose their investment and are likely to reap benefits if the merger is profitable. The creditors will benefit as a result of retaining their rights against the debtor and are likely to be reimbursed for the credit they have provided to the firm.

As the analysis of case law indicates, arguments such as that the target company will exit the market if it becomes independent, and that jobs will be lost, will not constitute reasons for clearance of the concentration. However, as Ritter and Braun have argued, revitalization of the target company to operate more efficiently may constitute a reason for the concentration to be cleared.[84] Amidst crises such considerations are essential.

Considering the likely anti-competitive outcome of allowing a merger involving a failing firm and the counterfactual of blocking the merger and the firm exiting the market, an argument can be made in favour of a more lenient policy towards the failing-firm defence which could be characterized as permitting the defence to be used by severely distressed as well as by imminently failing firms, which may yield social benefits through its positive impact on entry, resulting in more effective competition in the long run.

Thus competition authorities might consider being less restrictive not only towards mergers involving failing firms, but also towards mergers involving divisions of failing firms, as well as failing divisions of firms. However, some assurance may be needed that the division's failing status is not merely a reflection of creative accounting as regards issues like transfer payments and the allocation of common costs. With a more lenient approach to failing divisions, the outcome of the *Bertelsmann*[85] and *Rewe/Meinl*[86] mergers might have been different. The Commission took a more lenient approach towards a failing division in the *Newscorp/Telepiù* merger,[87] where it considered the overall conditions of the Italian market in clearing the merger.

Thus the failing-firm defence might also be applied when a subsidiary or division of the company is failing. Refusal of such defence would force the parent company either to cease the operations of a subsidiary or to keep it operating at a loss. This requirement was widely discussed

[84] L. Ritter and D. Braun, *European Competition Law: A Practitioner's Guide*, 3rd ed., Kluwer Law International, 2004, at p. 597.

[85] Case No IV/M.993, *Bertelsmann/Kirch/Premiere*, [1999] OJ L 053/1.

[86] Case No IV M.1221, *Rewe/Meinl*, [1999] OJ L 274/1.

[87] Case COMP/M.2876, *Newscorp/Telepiù*, [2004] OJ L110/73.

by the Supreme Court in the case of *International Shoe Co. v. FTC*.[88] In addition, the presence of distressed-industry conditions could also affect the speed of the investigation as a prolonged merger review may harm the firm to be acquired and could weaken it to the point where the merger no longer makes sense to the purchaser.[89] The Supreme Court rejected the failing-industry defence in *Socony-Vacuum*.[90] However, the DOJ in *United States v. LTV Corp.*[91] considered the weakened state of the companies and the efficiencies that would result from the transaction.

Accepting distressed-industry arguments could help revitalize failing industries by lowering their overall costs and enabling them to compete more efficiently. In moderately concentrated industries exhibiting excess capacity, the ease of entry in combination with the increased threat of import competition would render any anti-competitive impact of the merger unlikely. However, the difficulty of identifying a distressed industry and the distinction between a distressed industry and one experiencing a downturn may make it unlikely that crucial weight is placed on consideration of distressed-industry circumstances. In the distressed-industry defence there is a consensus that mergers are strong candidates to achieve efficiencies.[92] Thus efficiencies which may not be credible in booming industries may be applicable when the distressed-industry defence is invoked.

In this part of the chapter, we will use certain examples of mergers cleared by the authorities in the US, the UK and the EU during the crisis to demonstrate our argument of the necessary flexibility in the application of the failing-firm defence in the EU.

In *United States v. General Dynamics*,[93] the concerned firm was not failing in the sense of the failing-firm defence. The lack of resources of the firm was considered enough for the Court to clear the merger. If, under normal circumstances, the firm had to be failing for the merger to be cleared, during a crisis a new notion was introduced, at least temporar-

[88] (1930) 280 U.S. 291.

[89] B. Nigro, 'The Effect of Market Conditions on Merger Review: Distressed Industries, Failing Firms, and Mergers with Bankrupt Companies, available at www.abanet.org/antitrust/committees/communication/distressedindustry.pdf.

[90] *U.S. v. Socony-Vacuum Oil Co.*, (1940) 310 U.S. 150. See further Valentine (1995).

[91] 1984-2 Trade Cas. (CCH) 66,133 (D.D.C.) appeal dismissed, 746 F.2d 51 (D.C.Cir.1984).

[92] Federal Trade Commission (FTC), 'Competition Policy in the New High-Tech, Global Marketplace, Volume 1' (1996), Chapter 3, available at www.ftc.gov/opp/global/report/gc_v1.pdf.

[93] *United States v. General Dynamics Corp.*, (1974) 415 U.S. 486.

ily, generally known the 'flailing-firm defence'. The *General Dynamics* case provided the definition of the 'flailing', 'quasi-failing', or 'weak-competitor' defence, which was first applied by the lower courts in *United States v. International Harvester Co.*[94] The Court held that the acquisition did not violate §7 because the acquired company did not have sufficient financial resources to compete effectively. The claim that the firm to be acquired is a weak competitor is made in order to show that the merger is less troubling than the combined market shares may imply. A 'weak-competitor claim' can be made in circumstances that are difficult to evaluate. In the case of *United States v. International Harvester Co.*, the acquired company's 'weak-competitor claim' arose from its difficulty in borrowing the capital. The Court allowed the acquisition because the acquired company lacked the financial resources necessary to operate competitively. Nevertheless, a weak-competitor claim does not circumvent the requirement of the alternative purchaser. In *FTC v. Warner Communications Inc.*,[95] the Court noted that a weak-company defence would expand the strict limits of the failing-company doctrine.

The spirit of the *General Dynamics* decision has been incorporated into the US merger guidelines by language acknowledging that 'recent or ongoing changes in the market may indicate that the current market share of a particular firm either understates or overstates the firm's competitive significance' and committing to take into consideration 'reasonably predictable effects of recent or ongoing changes in market conditions in interpreting market concentration and market share data'.[96]

Furthermore, in *United States v. General Dynamics Corp.*, although the Supreme Court rejected a distressed-industry defence, it emphasized the importance of considering all relevant facts, especially in cases where the relevant market or industry exhibits fluctuations as well as dynamic features.[97] Antitrust authorities could also consider industry conditions as an argument in favour of approving a transaction. However, distressed-industry conditions could lead to increased entry barriers and, therefore, make it more difficult for a transaction to obtain approval. In spite of that, antitrust authorities take into account the impact of economic conditions on the ability of firms to raise capital and make investments, which they need in order to be more effective competitors. Thus despite the fact that

[94] *United States v. International Harvester Co.*, 564 F.2d 769 (7th Cir. 1977).
[95] 742 F.2d 1156 (9th Cir. 1984) (per curiam).
[96] Nigro, 'The Effect of Market Conditions on Merger Review'.
[97] *United States v. General Dynamics Corp.*, (1974) 415 U.S. 486, 504–6.

courts still follow a case-by-case approach, they consider the relevant market, the financial distress of the firm and the crisis (almost regarded as force majeure) to be more welcoming of attenuated versions of the failing-firm defence (such as flailing or even simply weakened) and clear mergers that would have been, in non-crisis circumstances, blocked due to their incompatibility with antitrust law.

In certain cases, competition authorities should treat flailing-firm defence arguments with great caution. If underperforming, inefficient and poorly managed firms are bailed out simply because of the crisis and because they are large employers, then the message to industry will simply be to become too big to fail and not be concerned about being efficient.

As regards the financial industry, central banks had long struggled to prevent the 'too-big-to-fail' thesis becoming a moral hazard and had attempted to avoid any definition of whether any given institution fell into that category. As Sir Callum McCarthy, former chair of the UK's Financial Services Authority, argues, the general view is that there is a real problem with the 'too-big-to-fail' concept and that it would be perfectly rational for depositors and counterparties to trade preferentially with larger firms, thus squeezing out the smaller ones. Preventing that would be a real issue in terms of competition policy.[98]

The 'too-big-to-fail' doctrine is understood to mean that if a bank were big enough, it would receive financial assistance to the extent necessary to keep it from failing.[99] It implies that all deposit obligations would be met by some form of government pledge or guarantee without the fact of there being a deposit insurance scheme in place or not making any difference.[100] In other words, taxpayers would bail out the failing bank.[101] Recently, the 'too-big-to-fail' doctrine has evolved and been broadened to 'too-interconnected-to-fail', 'too-complex-to-fail' or 'too-global-to-fail'.[102]

[98] Presentation to the OECD, Summary Record of the Discussion on Competition and Financial Markets, DAF/COMP/M(2009)1/ANN5, 10 April 2009, Roundtable 4 on Going Forward: Adaptation of Competition Rules, Processes and Institutions to Current Financial Sector Issues, available at www.oecd.org.

[99] See P. Molyneux, 'Banking Crises and the Macro-Economic Context', in R. Lastra and H. Schiffman, eds., *Bank Failures and Bank Insolvency Law in Economies in Transition*, Kluwer Law International, 1999, at pp. 5–6.

[100] Some illustrative examples in this sense are Continental Illinois in the USA (1984), Banesto in Spain (1993), Banco di Napoli in Italy (1996) and Credit Lyonnais in France (1997).

[101] See Molyneux, at p. 6.

[102] See M.D. Knight, 'Mitigating Moral Hazard in Dealing with Problem Financial Institutions: Too Big To Fail? Too Complex To Fail? Too Interconnected To Fail?', in

If some banks are too big to be allowed to fail, it naturally suggests that those banks are safer than others,[103] which evidently distorts the market because large banks will have an *ex ante* competitive advantage over smaller banks that are not too big to fail. In this respect it is worth noting that there is no set criterion to mark a bank as too big to fail, which grants discretion to government officials. Molyneux argues that central banks should always continue to maintain a policy of ambiguity associated with the provision of support for troubled banks,[104] strongly rejecting the idea of making guarantees explicit *ex ante* because regulators will wish to avoid weakening market discipline (moral hazard) and they will not want to commit themselves to future courses of action which they subsequently might prefer not to take. The 'too-big-to-fail' doctrine should be used only in exceptional circumstances because it might result in the medicine doing more harm than the illness. The knowledge that the authorities will allow a bank, even a big bank, to fail is an important mechanism of market discipline.[105]

In certain circumstances, the social cost of rescuing the relevant institutions will be less than the ruinous cascade effects that may surge through the financial sector. This is the state of being too big to fail, which both the FTC and the DOJ have identified as an outcome that antitrust law could and should prevent.[106]

If competition authorities wish to prevent companies becoming too big to fail, they may have to put less emphasis on efficiency arising

J.R. LaBrosse, R. Olivares-Caminal and D. Singh, eds., *Financial Crisis Management and Bank Resolution*, Informa, 2009, at p. 257.

103 See P. Molyneux, 'Banking Crises and the Macro-Economic Context', in R. Lastra and H. Schiffman, eds., *Bank Failures and Bank Insolvency Law in Economies in Transition*, Kluwer Law International, 1999, at p. 4.

104 P. Molyneux, 'Banking Crises and the Macro-Economic Context', in R. Lastra and H. Schiffman, eds., *Bank Failures and Bank Insolvency Law in Economies in Transition*, Kluwer Law International, 1999.

105 Discretion by the central bank authorities creates uncertainty. Therefore the 'great task' of central banks has to be performed prior to a crisis of a given institution by strict supervision of the banks. To achieve this, what is also required is improvement in accounting standards to reflect the 'real' situation of banks. Financial disclosure is increasingly favoured by banks, by their supervisors and by international organizations as an instrument promoting transparency without adding undue regulatory burdens or creating competitive distortions for banks compared to other financial institutions. R.M. Lastra, *Central Banking and Banking Regulation*, Financial Markets Group, 1996, at pp. 112, 123.

106 Interview with Thomas Rosch, commissioner, Federal Trade Commission (2009) 23 *Antitrust* 32, at p. 41 .

from mergers. On the one hand, the change in the focus of competition authorities is likely to create harm to consumer welfare, as efficiencies enhancing consumer welfare will not be allowed to materialize. On the other hand, such an approach towards efficiency may discourage firms from investing in order to achieve such efficiencies in the first place.

Summing up the above analysis, amidst crises saving unproductive companies may harm long-term growth; only when a business goes bankrupt do its competitors pick up its market share and only then does the sector continue to function. In some cases new firms may enter and create new jobs over a short duration, contributing to positive employment effects. However, the potential for job losses may lead to pressure on governments to adopt measures against the closure of the flailing firm. Philip Collins, the chairman of the OFT, argues that in the current crisis governments were under pressure to preserve jobs; to retain skills, manufacturing bases and supply chains; and to intervene more in markets such as the automotive market.[107] As the OECD states in its report,[108] 'governments need to make a case-by-case call on whether and how to provide some kind of assistance, depending on an analysis of the systemic, economy-wide implications of failure in a particular industry'. With the Lisbon Treaty there are stronger references to full employment and social objectives, including the reference to a 'highly competitive social market economy' in amended Article 3 of the Treaty on European Union.[109] As the above analysis illustrates, failing-firm defence arguments should be treated leniently in periods of crisis affecting whole markets or economies.

Turning to the derogation possibilities, there are, as mentioned above, a number of cases where a merger is the only means for a company to avoid bankruptcy. Sometimes, this decision has to be made within a very short period of time. For example, Bear Stearns' liquidity deteriorated in a matter of days as the market speculated that it would not be able to make delivery of securities or cash. Just three days earlier the firm had appeared to have sufficient capital to continue operating. Once it lost the confidence of investors and trading counterparties, the firm was no longer able to sustain operations.

[107] OECD, Summary Record of the Discussion on Competition and Financial Markets, DAF/COMP/M(2009)1/ANN4, 10 April 2009, Roundtable 3 on Real Economy and Competition Policy in a Period of Retrenchment, available at www.oecd.org.

[108] OECD, Competition and Financial Markets.

[109] See www.wilmerhale.com/publications/whPubsDetail.aspx?publication=9321.

Washington Mutual was unable to continue as a going concern when it experienced a bank run.[110] In such situations the bank can immediately lose access to funding and can no longer trade and undertake any business that requires capital. Derogation from the general rule of suspension of the concentration's realization is taken after a request by the participating (to the concentration) undertakings or even after a request by interested third parties,[111] with the intention of avoiding harm to their interests. In cases where a derogation has been requested, the European Commission is obliged, in order to decide if the realization of the concentration is permissible, to balance not only the interests of the merging parties and those of interested third parties, but also the possible harm to competition as a consequence of the immediate completion of the merger.[112] During crisis periods such derogations are essential in promoting mergers that can sustain the viability of undertakings and sectors as a whole. Between September 1990 and November 2008 the European Commission issued around a hundred decisions about derogation from suspension of concentrations.[113] According to Article 7(3) of Regulation 139/2004, derogation constitutes the European Commission's practice only in exceptional circumstances. Nevertheless, derogation has been issued for a variety of reasons that interested undertakings usually provide.[114] Between 1990 and November 2008 there have been 101 decisions where derogation has been granted by the European Commission.[115]

In periods of crisis, there would be a legitimate concern that the timetable for investigating an issue and reaching a resolution could be too long to prevent an undertaking from collapsing. The merger of an undertaking whose viability is at stake must be completed in a matter of

[110] Depositors grew concerned that their funds were endangered and began to withdraw money rapidly.

[111] Interested third parties could include, for instance, creditors, employees and so on.

[112] This is the reason why 'such a derogation may be made subject to conditions and obligations in order to ensure conditions of effective competition'. On this point see G. Karydis, 'Le contrôle des concentrations entre enterprises en vertu du règlement 4064/89 et la protection des intérêts légitimes des tiers' (1997) 1–2 *Cahiers de droit Européen* 81, mainly at p. 92, point 24.

[113] See Article 7(4) of the precedent Regulation 4064/1989. See in comparison http://ec.europa.eu/comm/competition/mergers/statistics.pdf.

[114] About the derogation issue, see O. Blanco, ed., *EC Competition Procedure*, 2nd ed., Oxford University Press, 2006, paras. 16.07–16.09; and N. Levy, *The Control of Concentrations between Undertakings*, Matthew Bender, 2002, para. 5.13.

[115] Full statistics can be found at the DG Competition website: http://ec.europa.eu/competition/index_en.html.

days or weeks rather than the months that an antitrust review normally requires. The European Commission has shown willingness to be flexible in its usual requirement to wait for clearance before closing.[116] The Commission has announced its readiness to grant derogations to the standstill obligation enshrined in Article 7 of the EC Merger Regulation (ECMR): 'where there is urgency and where there are no "a priori" competition concerns'.[117] The derogation enables the immediate implementation of transactions that are part of rescue operations, pending merger-control clearance, such as to enable acquirers to monitor the nature and structure of the target's risks portfolio and take appropriate measures to protect the value of certain assets.[118]

The Commission, in the *Bradford and Bingley* case,[119] has proven to be realistic since it made a concession by allowing the closing of the deal even before a merger clearance. Santander, the leading bidder, was allowed to close the deal immediately. Otherwise, real damage might have occurred: 'Where a rescue package has to be put together very swiftly, the suspensory effect of the European Community merger rules could seriously hamper rescue acquisitions.'[120]

As was noted earlier in this book, the US DOJ can use a 'pocket decree' – a similar arrangement to the derogation that is provided for in the ECMR. A pocket degree can enable a merger to complete prior to clearance and require a divestiture at a later date if necessary. In 2006, Mittal Steel Company pursued a hostile takeover of Arcelor SA. Mittal entered, prior to the completion of the merger assessment by the DOJ, into a letter agreement with the DOJ agreeing to divest specific assets (including a hold-separate agreement) if the acquisition were found to result in a substantial lessening of competition.[121] However, the pocket decree might not always present a viable solution in cases where the

[116] Freshfields Bruckhaus Deringer, 'Antitrust in the Downturn' (November 2008).

[117] N. Kroes, 'Dealing with the Current Financial Crisis', address before the Economic and Monetary Affairs Committee, European Parliament, Brussels, 6 October 2008, Speech/08/498, available at http://ec.europa.eu/comm/competition/speeches/index_2008.html.

[118] Gerard 2008.

[119] See 'State Aid: Commission Approves UK Rescue Aid Package for Bradford & Bingley' press release, IP/08/1437, 1 October 2008.

[120] 'Antitrust Implications of the Financial Crisis: A UK and EU View' (Spring 2009) 23(2) *Antitrust* 125.

[121] 'U.S. DOJ Requires Divestiture in Mittal Steel's Acquisition of Arcelor', 1 August 2006, available at www.usdoj.gov/atr/public/press_releases/2006/217516.htm; *United States v. Mittal Steel Co.*, No 06-1360, 2007 U.S. Dist. LEXIS 45386, at p. 25 (D.D.C. 23 May 2007).

competition problem relates to a substantial portion of the target. In 1995, Hoechst was given a 'blank cheque' (with a hold-separate agreement) by the FTC to acquire Marion Merrell Dow,[122] provided that, once the FTC concluded its investigation, Hoechst would follow the FTC's recommendations. The use of such measures is encouraged during periods of crisis, as they are essential in the viability of a merger during such times.

In a speech concerning the financial crisis, Neelie Kroes,[123] European commissioner for Competition Policy during the peak of the crisis, said the following:

> The Commission is committed to continue applying the existing rules, taking full account of the economic environment.
>
> That means the Commission can and will take into account the evolving market conditions and, where applicable, the failing-firm defence.
>
> - The existing rules allow the Commission to permit take-overs to be implemented without having to wait for the Commission's approval in cases where there is urgency and where there are no 'a priori' competition concerns.
> - The Commission can indeed grant derogations from the standstill obligation, pending a definitive outcome of the proceedings, so as to enable the immediate implementation of the transactions which are part of rescue operations.

Similarly, in the UK, the intervention of the Secretary of State in order to accelerate the process and the lack of referral to the Commission has to be based on serious grounds. The Enterprise Act of 2002 clearly separated competition authorities from the government by making the OFT an independent entity. However, the Act includes an exception to this principle since the government, through the Secretary of State, can sometimes get involved in merger cases on the ground of public interest.[124] What was, until the crisis that was initiated in 2007, understood from the notion of 'public interest' was grounds of 'national security' and

122 Proposed Consent Agreement with Analysis to Aid Public Comment, 60 Fed. Reg. 49,609, 49,615 (FTC Sept. 26, 1995). W. Baer, director of the FTC at the time, argued that in order to employ the blank-cheque option, a party would need to satisfy the following criteria: (1) the 'relevant markets must be easily defined', (2) the maximum necessary relief must be readily identifiable with specificity and (3) the parties must be willing to let the agency decide unilaterally how much of the maximum remedy is necessary. See further J. Rich and T. Scriven, 'Bank Consolidation Caused by the Financial Crisis: How Should the Antitrust Division Review "Shotgun Marriages"'? (December 2008) 8(2) *The Antitrust Source*.

123 N. Kroes, European commissioner for European Policy, 'Dealing with the Current Financial Crisis', available at http://ec.europa.eu/competition.

124 Section 42 of the Enterprise Act.

'media plurality'. Nevertheless, 'public interest' today includes financial stability, since the UK government decided to get involved, despite the general rule of non-involvement, in a merger case (Lloyds/HBOS) that affected neither national security nor media plurality:

> The Secretary of State announced his intention, having consulted with the UK Treasury, the Bank of England, and the Financial Services Authority (FSA), to intervene in the merger on public interest grounds to ensure the stability of the UK financial system.[125]

On 7 October 2008, the UK government explained its involvement and the reasons behind the newly introduced public-interest ground (financial stability) in the draft financial stability order. The reasons found in the document are the importance of a healthy economy in general (financial institutions and banks) and the stability of the UK financial system. These reasons explain the extraordinary procedure justified by the urgency of the situation. Although the OFT published a restatement of its position on the failing-firm defence in merger assessment, underlining that this is just a restatement and not a change of position, this does not exclude that the antitrust authority might expect, under a certain economic climate, the defence to be used more often.

According to Peter Freeman, chairman of the Commission, the general principle adopted by both the OFT and the Commission is that the rules are unchanged. He adds, though, that the facts to which they are applied may be altered. Interestingly, he adds that this may affect the analysis, and possibly the outcome. This may take the form of acceptance that the assets of a failing firm are likely to leave the market and that this is a less competitive outcome than its acquisition by a competitor.[126] Freeman thus acknowledges that the application of the failing-firm defence can be different once the specific facts (e.g. a crisis) are taken into account. Such facts can include crisis situations where competition policy should not threaten the stability of markets.

The report of the US authorities to the OECD Competition Committee – Competition and the Financial Markets[127] – states that since September 2008, financial markets in the United States and around

[125] See www.freshfields.com/publications/pdfs/2009/apr09/Spring09-daSilvaC.pdf.

[126] P. Freeman, 'We Are Here in a Very Melancholy Situation: Financial Crisis and Competition Policy', 3 November 2009, David Hume Institute. He mentions the OFT clearance of the HMV/Zavvi merger (analysed in Chapter 3 above) as an example of this approach.

[127] Submission to OECD, Competition and Financial Markets.

the world have experienced significant turmoil. In 2008, twenty-five banks in the United States failed and, as of the end of the third quarter of 2008, 171 banks had been identified as 'troubled'.[128] In addition, since the beginning of October 2008, over twenty transactions have been addressed under the emergency provisions of the federal bank statutes that govern mergers of banks and bank holding companies.[129]

As the US report to the OECD states,[130] bank mergers are subject to concurrent competitive review by either the Federal Reserve, the Office of the Comptroller of the Currency (OCC), the Federal Deposit Insurance Corporation (FDIC) or the DOJ. Antitrust review of bank mergers in the United States is governed by the Bank Holding Company Act (BHCA),[131] the Bank Merger Act (BMA),[132] and the Home Owners Loan Act.[133] Bank mergers are exempt from the merger review process under the Hart-Scott-Rodino (HSR) Act of 1976.[134] Banks must file with the relevant bank regulatory agency applications for approval of their proposed mergers. These applications are forwarded to the DOJ for competition review.[135]

[128] J. Adler, 'Success with Failures', *American Banker*, 29 December 2008.

[129] 12 U.S.C. §§1828(c), 1842, and 1849(b).

[130] Submission to OECD, Competition and Financial Markets.

[131] 12 U.S.C. 1842, 1849.

[132] 12 U.S.C. 1828(c).

[133] 12 U.S.C. 1467a(e)(2). Statutes specific to the banking industry, including also the Change in Bank Control Act, 12 U.S.C. §1817(j), govern most bank merger reviews. The BMA requires that, except where the relevant banking agency determines that 'it must act immediately in order to prevent the probable failure of one of the banks . . . involved', both the banking agency and the Antitrust Division assess the competitive impact of the transaction – 12 U.S.C. §1828(c)(6); the Federal Reserve (the Fed) reviews transactions involving bank holding companies and banks that are members of the Federal Reserve System – 12 U.S.C. §1842(a)(3)–(4); the FDIC reviews transactions in which the acquirer is a state bank that is not a member of the Federal Reserve System – 12 U.S.C. §1828(c)(2)(C); the OTS reviews acquisitions of savings associations and savings-and-loan holding companies (unless the acquirer is a bank holding company, in which case the Fed is responsible) – 12 U.S.C. §1828(c)(2)(D); and the OCC reviews transactions in which the acquirer is a national bank – 12 U.S.C. §1828(c)(2)(A). Rich and Scriven 2008.

[134] 15 U.S.C. §18. Note that the procedures described here apply only to transactions involving bank depository institutions. The passage of the Gramm-Leach-Bliley Act in 1999 has allowed bank holding companies to own non-bank financial subsidiaries. Mergers of holding companies with both bank subsidiaries and non-bank financial subsidiaries are considered 'mixed transactions' under the Hart-Scott-Rodino (HSR) Act. The non-bank component is subject to the reporting requirements of the HSR Act and its waiting periods. These HSR Act procedures also apply to acquisitions of financial companies (such as investment banks) that do not include a depository institution.

[135] As between the DOJ and the US Federal Trade Commission, the DOJ has exclusive jurisdiction to review bank mergers and acquisitions. 12 U.S.C. 1828(c), 1849.

The emergency provisions of the BHCA have been invoked for numerous transactions during the economic crisis. Most of the banking mergers during the crisis, such as the acquisition of Wachovia Corporation by Wells Fargo & Co. were approved under the emergency provisions of the BHCA with a five-day post-approval waiting period. The DOJ received prior notification, conducted an expedited competition review, and provided comments to the bank regulatory agency prior to approval of the application.[136] Press reports have speculated that the Wells Fargo acquisition of Wachovia could raise issues in California, where both institutions have a substantial presence.[137] Other bank mergers presented direct horizontal combinations (e.g. JP Morgan Chase/Washington Mutual) that could have resulted in extensive review and possible demands for remedies.[138] The Federal Reserve reviewed Wells Fargo's application to acquire Wachovia Corporation[139] and Bank of America's acquisition of Countrywide.[140] The FDIC handled the JP Morgan Chase acquisition of Washington Mutual because the bank was in FDIC receivership.[141]

As we demonstrated above, it is a difficult task for the parties to prove that one of the firms is failing (in order to satisfy the failing-firm defence) by demonstrating that the requirements are all met. In times of crisis, the emergency created by financial distress requires fast and effective measures. Authorities must be able to act effectively and in the shortest time possible. Therefore competition rules must be flexible and the application of the failing-firm defence must be accepted when the considerations at hand are more important than the blind application of the

[136] For those transactions that have a non-bank portion subject to the reporting requirements of the HSR Act, the DOJ also received and reviewed the HSR notifications.

[137] See V. Colliver and J. Temple, 'Wells Fargo, Citigroup Vie for Wachovia', *San Francisco Chronicle*, 8 October 2008, at p. C1. Bank of America currently already controls 10.9 per cent of US bank deposits following its acquisition of Countrywide Financial Corp. in June 2008. See Federal Reserve System, Order Approving the Acquisition of a Savings Association and Other Nonbanking Activities, 5 n. 13 (5 June 2008) (order approving Bank of America's acquisition of Countrywide), available at www.federalreserve.gov/newsevents/press/orders/orders20080605a1.pdf. See further Rich and Scriven 2008.

[138] Freshfields Bruckhaus Deringer 2008.

[139] See press release, Federal Reserve Board, Approval of Proposal by Wells Fargo & Company to Acquire Wachovia Corporation, 12 October 2008, available at www.federalreserve.gov/newsevents/press/orders/20081012a.htm.

[140] Federal Reserve Board, Approval of Proposal by Bank of America (5 June 2008), available at www.federalreserve.gov/newsevents/press/orders/20080605a.htm.

[141] FDIC, JPMorgan Chase Acquires Banking Operations of Washington Mutual (25 September 2008), available at www.fdic.gov/news/news/press/2008/pr08085.html.

texts. In other words, the application of the criteria with more flexibility than under non-crisis conditions causes less damage than does their strict application. The Commission, after the meeting held in Brussels on 29 October 2008, through the speech of its president, made it clear that flexibility is inevitable when the situation is of certain gravity. We should note that 'in declining industry situations it is more likely that firms flailing today will be failing tomorrow'.[142] Flexibility implies that a court accepts the defence despite the fact that the allegedly failing firm is not likely to exit the market in the near future but is in financial distress, which makes it difficult for it to exercise real and effective competition.

The UK government and the European Commission seem to have outlined their priorities: competition laws are very important. However, in times of crisis, they must be applied with flexibility and interpreted largely to leave room for more effective measures intended to maintain financial stability and rescue different entities such as banks and financial institutions. Fingleton has argued that the fact that banks are different from other businesses may exceptionally justify intervention.[143] However, Lowe has argued that it is necessary to recognize the systemic and special features of the banking sector,[144] the reality that the banking sector is no different from any other sector in terms of the need to restructure, and to plan out what constitutes a return to viability.[145] Elena Carletti, a consultant to the OECD, argued in a similar vein that it was not clear whether a distinction could be made between the financial sector and the real sector in considering how to apply competition policy in a systemic crisis.[146] Bank failure risks systemic effects (i.e. the failure of one bank may lead to a run on others, as opposed to other sectors where the removal of one player may not induce such adverse effects on incumbents). As the OECD argues, the loss of confidence in one major

[142] Oxera, 'Failing, or just Flailing? The Failing-Firm Defence in Mergers', available at www.oxera.com.

[143] Fingleton 2009.

[144] C. Borio and P. Lowe, 'Assessing the Risk of Banking Crisis', (December 2002) *BIS Quarterly Review* 43.

[145] OECD, Summary Record of the Discussion on Competition and Financial Markets, DAF/COMP/M(2009)1/ANN5, 10 April 2009, Roundtable 4 on Going Forward: Adaptation of Competition Rules, Processes and Institutions to Current Financial Sector Issues, available at www.oecd.org.

[146] OECD, Summary Record of the Discussion on Competition and Financial Markets, DAF/COMP/M(2009)1/ANN2, 10 April 2009, Introduction and Roundtable 1 on Principles: Financial Sector Conditions and Competition Policy, available at www.oecd.org.

financial institution in a financial crisis can snowball into a loss of confidence in the entire market, because the inability of one bank to meet its obligations can drive other, otherwise healthy, banks into insolvency.[147] The collapse of confidence in turn can cause liquidity to disappear, and thus remove an essential element for the banking system to function, almost inducing a systemic collapse. In this sense, the credit crunch resulted from an exceptional implosion of supply, and not simply a cost increase or a contraction of demand.

In relation to the application of the defence in a crisis situation, Francisco Enrique Gonzales Diaz, competition partner at Cleary Gottlieb Steen & Hamilton in Brussels, noted,

> The failing firm defence is one that has however previously proved difficult to apply in practice in a merger scenario . . . Despite the crisis M&A activity will continue and therefore we hope that the EC will take account of the current economic environment in situations where the 'failing firm defence' may apply. I am not suggesting that the rules should not be applied in the same way but rather that the Commission uses its margin of discretion flexibly to take account of present market conditions.[148]

Professor Ito, in his submission to the OECD, said that he questioned the perceived view that a merger was necessarily bad for competition simply because it reduced competition.[149] He questioned how many firms could exist in any one industry in any one country, and considered that more was not necessarily better, even given scale economies. The Japanese recovery from the problems of the 1990s was very protracted because there were too many small construction companies in the industry. Mergers should have been one of the answers (the other being bankruptcies, according to the author) because there were too many inefficient companies. He adds that the financial industry was a special case. Following on from this argument, we should note that if there were too many companies in one industry and more firms than the optimal number, then mergers should be allowed, especially if imports were liberalized at the same time. Thus, in such industries, especially in periods of crisis, failing-firm defence arguments should be viewed with

[147] OECD, Competition and Financial Markets.

[148] EU, Competition & Public Law Report, Brussels Focus (2009), 'Brussels: Part of the Problem or Part of the Cure', available at www.abreuadvogados.com/xms/files/05_Comunicacao/Artigos_na_Imprensa/Iberian_Lawyer_Artigo_MMP_Fev.2009.pdf.

[149] OECD, Summary Record of the Discussion on Competition and Financial Markets, DAF/COMP/M(2009)1/ANN4, 10 April 2009, Roundtable 3 on Real Economy and Competition Policy in a Period of Retrenchment, available at www.oecd.org.

an even more positive attitude not only in order to sustain the viability of some of the incumbents but also in order to reduce the number of the sustainable firms in an industry.

A more lenient approach to mergers involving the failing-firm defence on the part of the competition authorities in Europe might play a crucial role in recovering from the crisis. But while this approach might be helpful for the companies to overcome their difficulties it might have adverse effects on future and long-term competition. The unstable economic climate might constitute a window of opportunity for pursuing more difficult deals 'since the downturn is likely to have produced more fertile ground for "failing firm" arguments'.[150]

In addition, a relaxation of the application of the failing-firm defence may lead to dangers for competition, and also to a weakening of the credibility of the competition law regimes:

> Relaxation of the requirements of this defence in times of financial trouble would pose the same problems as relaxing competition law more generally. In an economic downturn more firms may be 'failing' making the defence potentially available to a greater number of companies. But that does not suggest that the requirement that the merging firm must show there were no other less anticompetitive alternatives is automatically satisfied.[151]

The European Commission (and competition authorities in the EU as well), when considering the application of the defence in a proposed merger, also examine the reason for the failure:

> The reason for the greater number of failing firms in times of economic crisis also should be considered. In some instances, firms fail because they are inefficient or because demand for their products or services has declined. In such cases, firms should either exit the market or merge with firms that remain competitive. In other situations firms may be failing because of inefficiencies in financial markets. In those circumstances, the better course is to address the inefficiency in the financial markets that is creating the underlying problem, rather than altering merger policy as a way of managing the consequences.[152]

150 Baker & McKenzie Global Antitrust & Competition Group (2009), 'Opportunities in M&A: Doing Difficult Mergers in Difficult Times', available at www.bakernet.com/NR/rdonlyres/EA24139B-C82F-4A22-B63E-DFC43BFECECA/0/eu_opportunitiesmergers_ca_jan09.pdf.

151 OECD, Competition and Financial Markets, Note by the United States (2009), DAF/COMP/WD(2009)11/ADD1, available at http://ftc.gov/bc/international/docs/09financialcrisis.pdf.

152 OECD, Competition and Financial Markets, Note by the United States, available at http://ftc.gov/bc/international/docs/09financialcrisis.pdf, at p.5.

In the presence of a severe crisis, e.g. a financial crisis affecting a whole economy and carrying the risk of systemic crisis, the different markets and the financial stability and welfare of consumers, employees and competitors are all affected. If the credit market has ceased to function effectively, then firms struggle to obtain financing. Banks or other providers of finance normally play a crucial role in sorting out efficient from inefficient players. Hence competition rules fail to achieve their original goal in the presence of a stronger and more urgent priority called 'crisis'. Consequently, it is completely understandable to substitute, for a short time only and until the problem is resolved, exceptional competition rules, decided by the competition authorities or courts on a case-by-case basis, in order to provide a solution that benefits the economy in general, including consumers, shareholders (of the failing firms) and employees (even though social issues are usually intentionally neglected in competition law).

Deciding when and how to apply the defence is difficult in part because the facts underlying the failing-company claim may be closely intertwined with other claims, which are analytically distinct. A merger that would be blocked due to its adverse effect on competition is permitted when the firm to be acquired is a failing firm and when a less detrimental merger is unavailable. Blocking the merger will cause the loss of jobs and assets from the market and thus possible economic and social benefits will be forgone. Therefore a merger with a failing firm leading to high concentration may be accepted under the failing-firm defence. In the assessment of a merger involving a failing-firm defence, competition authorities should take into account the conditions in the industry, potential efficiencies and the counterfactual to blocking the merger.

In sum, considering a merger with a failing firm during a crisis, the economic aspects of allowing and blocking this merger – such as the loss of jobs, benefit to consumers, price maintenance – should also be borne in mind. Social costs must be taken into account in adopting some general formulation of the failing-company defence, rather than taking social costs into account in individual cases.[153] Thus in the assessment of a merger the overall conditions of the market should be taken into account, as well as the social and economic implications of allowing or blocking the merger. As promoting employment and social protection are two tasks that are central to the EC Treaty, the European Commission is not entirely free of the influence of wider policy agendas.

[153] Correia 1995.

We should note that the Lisbon Treaty includes stronger references to full employment and social objectives, including the reference to a 'highly competitive social market economy', in amended Article 3 of the Treaty on European Union. This might induce arguments that a broader industrial policy standard should apply.[154] However, the likely anti-competitive effects of the merger should be one of the leading influencing factors in assessing the transaction, rather than other considerations of social and public policy.

Furthermore, if the merger with or acquisition of a failing firm is not allowed and the failing firm exits the market, any technical or productive achievements of the failing firm will be lost. Hence there may be adverse welfare implications. However, exit of the failing firm may be preferable from a competition perspective if the remaining firms may compete more aggressively to counteract the decrease in supply due to the loss of the failing firm's capacity and in order to win the failing firm's customers. In crisis conditions such aggressive competition is questionable.

The failing-firm defence carries most weight when it can be shown that the merger enables productive assets to continue in productive use. The exit of the failing firm will lead to an increase in demand and an ensuing increase in production costs and prices (unless the firm is the least competitive in a declining market). If the failing firm merges with or is acquired by a dominant firm, the latter will obtain assets and know-how that allow an increase in productivity, enhancing its competitive position. Hence such a merger or acquisition may lead to lower production costs and prices.

The next few years seem likely to see consolidation mergers in many sectors; for example, there is talk of consolidation in the US automotive industry. As Correia has argued,[155] a failing-company claim may also occur in the context of a declining industry where capacity is certain to exit the market. If that is the case, a merger may be justified both on efficiency grounds and on grounds of the failing-firm defence, which, however, must be analysed separately. As mentioned above, regulators will often be faced with a case that presents challenging competition issues but a strong commercial imperative to get the deal done quickly.[156] It should be noted that in the assessment of the failing-firm defence the overall conditions of the market should be taken into account, as

[154] See www.wilmerhale.com/publications/whPubsDetail.aspx?publication=9321.

[155] Correia 1995.

[156] Freshfields Bruckhaus Deringer, 'Antitrust in the Downturn'.

well as the social and economic implications of allowing or blocking the merger. Antitrust policy and the likely anti-competitive effects of the merger should be one of the leading influencing factors in assessing the transaction.

In general, the financial crisis does not entail that there should be a change in the fundamentals of competition law as regards the application of the failing-firm defence since drastic and excessive changes would pose a danger to the structure of the economy. However, a pragmatic approach must be adopted. The OECD report states that international co-operation in setting and enforcing competition policy, especially in relation to failing-firm defence claims, is essential for ensuring consistency in troubled times, speeding up the enforcement process and giving clarity to enforcement activities.

Although competition authorities will be asked to clear an anti-competitive deal, it is not realistic to expect that competition authorities would necessarily have a place at the table discussing sensitive issues that arise amidst crises. Of course it would be preferable to be at the table when issues are discussed across governments. The Business and Industry Advisory Committee to the OECD (BIAC), in its presentation to the OECD,[157] argued that competition authorities should do all they can to ensure that they are called to the table, that they accept the invitation and ensure that their analytical presentations are carried out within the necessary time frame, and with the degree of flexibility that the situation warrants. Thus BIAC stresses, in addition to the fully fledged competition analysis, the necessary flexibility that competition authorities should have in tackling issues that arise during a crisis.

According to the OECD report, the principles and objectives of the enforcement of competition law therefore must not change, but the analysis has to be realistic about conditions in the market. That means a shift from a form-based analysis to a case-by-case analysis in which the context and effects of actual practices and behaviour are very much taken into consideration. The Commission can use its margin of discretion flexibly in the assessment of the failing-firm defence to take account of the market conditions. The conditions of the failing-firm defence are

[157] OECD, Summary Record of the Discussion on Competition and Financial Markets, DAF/COMP/M(2009)1/ANN5, 10 April 2009, Roundtable 4 on Going Forward: Adaptation of Competition Rules, Processes and Institutions to Current Financial Sector Issues, available at www.oecd.org.

justified strictly under market conditions. In fact, it would be too easy for firms to fake financial distress in order to succeed in a merger that would otherwise have been blocked unless the evidential burden were substantial. However, in crisis situations, competition authorities and courts in the EU must take into consideration the grounds on which the failing-firm defence was introduced in merger legislation and temporarily apply it with more flexibility in order to achieve those same original goals. We should emphasize that any flexibility shown by the European Commission and the competition authorities in the EU during a crisis must be considered exceptional and temporary.

7.5.2 Ensuring efficiencies or preventing inefficiencies

Even when efficiencies are taken into account, the approach of competition authorities of various jurisdictions may vary considerably.[158] The reason for this divergence is that systems of competition law may adhere to different welfare standards, which in practice define what types of efficiency will be considered and how they will be evaluated.

As submitted, economists favour the total surplus standard over the consumer welfare standard, because the latter severely narrows the scope for considering efficiencies. Nevertheless, despite its obvious limitations, the consumer welfare standard has been retained as the relevant standard for appraising efficiencies.[159] While the Commission has not opted for an explicit confirmation of the relevant welfare standard, the Horizontal Merger Guidelines do not leave much doubt. In sum, because European competition policy regards consumer interests as being of primary importance,[160] any trend towards the adoption of a total surplus standard remains unlikely.[161]

According to the Commission, the initial competitive assessment of mergers will focus solely on static efficiencies; dynamic efficiencies

[158] M. Kocmut, 'Efficiency Considerations and Merger Control: Quo Vadis, Commission' (2006) 27(1) *ECLR* 19.

[159] C. Luescher, 'Efficiency Considerations in European Merger Control: Just Another Battle Ground for the European Commission, Economists and Competition Lawyers' (2004) 25 *ECLR* 72.

[160] M. Monti, 'A Reformed Competition Policy: Achievements and Challenges for the Future' (2004) 3 *Competition Policy Newsletter* 2.

[161] F. Ilzkovitz and R. Meiklejohn, 'European Merger Control: Do We Need an Efficiency Defense?', in European Commission, *European Economy: The Efficiency Defence and the European System of Merger Control*, European Communities Belgium, 2001, Reports and Studies No 5.

will come into play only in the final assessment.[162] It is questionable whether the limitation of the initial assessment to static efficiencies is justified.

Economics literature warns that since 'the theoretical distinction between fixed and variable costs blurs almost beyond recognition in real firms and markets . . . a long-run approach' is recommended.[163]

Under the consumer welfare standard, real efficiencies ought to be preferred to pecuniary or redistributive efficiencies, which are those reductions that cannot be deemed to be real resource savings.[164]

As mentioned above, the primary objective of the efficiency goal of European competition policy is to protect consumer interests. The focus on consumer welfare restricts the analysis of the price effects of a merger even in the presence of efficiency and excludes an analysis of the effects of efficiency under a total welfare model.

Under the total welfare standard a merger is approved if the sum of consumer's plus producer's surplus increases after the merger. The total surplus standard has been advocated by most economists, who argue that other standards will sometimes sacrifice social surplus. In some circumstances the single-market imperative might induce that efficiency achieved by merger should be evaluated under a total surplus standard rather than under a consumer welfare standard.[165] The total welfare standard was also advocated by Williamson.[166]

Given this latter rationale, an anti-competitive merger may only be approved if the merged entity achieves substantial gains in productive or dynamic efficiency. Röller, Stennek and Verboven argue that for prices to decrease after a merger in a Cournot or Bertrand competition model, the merged firm must achieve significantly lower marginal cost than did either of the merging firms prior to the merger.[167] The required reduction in marginal cost depends on the firms' pre-merger market shares and the firms' elasticity of demand.

[162] P. Lowe, 'Review of the EC Merger Regulation: Forging a Way Ahead', speech delivered at the European Merger Control Conference, 8 November 2002, Conrad Hotel, Brussels.

[163] M. de la Mano, For the Customer's Sake: The Competitive Effects of Efficiencies in European Merger Control, Enterprise Papers No 11, European Commission, 2002.

[164] L.H. Röller, J. Stennek and F. Verboven, 'Efficiency Gains from Mergers', in European Commission, *European Economy: The Efficiency Defence and the European System of Merger Control*, European Communities Belgium, 2001, Reports and Studies No 5.

[165] Luescher 2004.

[166] Williamson 1968.

[167] Röller, Stennek and Verboven 2001.

As Luescher argues,[168] most economists take the view that competition policy should not be designed to protect consumer interests alone but should be directed to maximize 'total surplus'.[169] According to the total surplus standard, even a merger leading to higher prices may be cleared if the efficiency gains realized by the merged entity exceed the losses suffered by consumers. Williamson argued that efficiency gains can balance the deadweight loss that arises due to monopoly pricing that can result from a merger.[170] Some consumers who would prefer the monopolist's goods at the competitive price will now look for inferior substitutes. This loss is the deadweight loss – society's loss – and is not recouped by anybody. The Williamson-style total surplus standard does not take into account the wealth transfer implied by price increase from consumers to producers and, as a consequence, efficiency does not have to be passed on to consumers. In contrast, according to the consumer welfare standard, it appears that the merged entity should be required to pass on efficiency gains to consumers. Furthermore, it suggests that, in many cases, relatively modest efficiency gains, implying an average cost reduction, would be sufficient to compensate for deadweight loss induced by a price increase.

As the above analysis indicates, the assessment of efficiency claims and of their importance for the competitive assessment of a merger is based on a balance between efficiency gains and losses due to expected reduced competition as well as on the welfare standard.

Apart from the consumer and total welfare standards, there are two more different standards that have been advocated in the academic literature: the price standard and the weighted surplus standard. Under a price standard, a merger is approved if the price will not increase as a result. In order for efficiencies to clear a merger, they must lead to a reduction or to no change in prices. As the consumer welfare standard encompasses price and non-price elements, the differences between the consumer surplus standard and the price standard arise due to a deterioration of the quality of the product after the merger (due to a reduction in quality, choice and so on). Under the weighted surplus standard, the various effects of the merger are summed, but each gets multiplied by a social weight reflecting the importance attached to that group's welfare.[171]

[168] Luescher 2004.

[169] Röller, Stennek and Verboven 2001.

[170] O. Williamson, 'Economies as an Antitrust Defense: The Welfare Trade-Off' (1968) 58 American Economic Review 18

[171] Luescher 2004.

Some jurisdictions consider other effects of mergers than on consumers and producers. Effects on employment and local or regional development are often taken into account. A standard reflects the way in which authorities conceive the competition policy and its objectives. Jenny argued that if merger control aims at promoting economic efficiency, then the competition authority will clear (with remedies) a merger having anti-competitive effects as well as efficiencies – in order for these efficiencies to materialize.[172] If the sole aim of merger control is to promote competition, a competition authority is likely to block an anti-competitive merger even if the merger has efficiency benefits. With the Lisbon Treaty there are stronger references to full employment and social objectives, including the reference to a 'highly competitive social market economy' in amended Article 3 of the Treaty on European Union. Thus this might induce arguments that a broader industrial policy standard should apply affecting the standard of merger assessment.[173]

In the Orbital/Ocean Park Ltd merger that we analysed previously, the merging parties did not satisfy the criteria for a failing-firm defence to apply in consideration of this merger. The merger was cleared on the basis of the defence of markets of insufficient importance.[174] The prevention of this merger would lead to discontinuity of the service, resulting in consumer harm to customers who would not be able to have travel brochures delivered. Eventually either party would withdraw from the market, either in a planned way or by going out of business. If the latter, then brochure supplies and sales would be disrupted whilst the affected customers would not switch to the remaining distributor or make arrangements elsewhere. This could be particularly problematic to their trading if it happened at peak distribution times. In this case it was extremely unlikely that there would be a buyer for the rump of the (unprofitable) exiting company. Thus in cases involving mergers the prohibition of which can induce significant inefficiency in the market

[172] OECD Competition Committee, Competition and the Financial Markets, www.oecd.org.

[173] See www.wilmerhale.com/publications/whPubsDetail.aspx?publication=9321.

[174] The factors that the OFT considered in making this determination were set out in detail in the *BOC/Ineos* case and were applied again recently in *FMC/ISP* and *Stagecoach/Cavalier* (in favour of the exercise of discretion) and in *Nufarm/AH Marks* (against the exercise of discretion). Those factors are: market size, strength of the OFT's concern (that is, its judgement as to the probability of substantial lessening of competition), the magnitude of competition lost by the merger, the durability of the impact of the merger, transaction rationale, and the value of deterrence.

(as regards, for example, service and security of supply), competition authorities should consider whether the prevention of inefficiency should be taken into account in the assessment of a merger. Such inefficiencies are likely to be more important during periods of crisis.

In addition, the Dutch merger between Ziekenhuis Walcheren and Oosterscheldeziekenhuizen, which was analysed earlier in this book, is an indicative example of the need for competition authorities to assess efficiencies in mergers occurring in industries experiencing crisis. According to the Dutch Health-Care Inspectorate (IGZ), which supervises the quality of care, prevention and medical products on the Dutch health-care market, the merger should have been allowed as a more intensive form of co-operation between the hospitals was found appropriate to ensure quality and continuity of hospital care in the region. The IGZ strongly recommended that the merger would be cleared, as this would be the best solution for ensuring continuity of health care in Zeeland. In the absence of the merger, the parties argued, they would have difficulty guaranteeing continuity of care, following up recent trends and developments in the field, and developing subspecialities in some areas, in particular paediatrics and gynaecology. Thus the competition authority as well as the relevant health-care authorities placed more emphasis on the continuity of care and the continuity of the provision of service.

In cases where efficiencies are alleged and the mergers occur in a period of crisis, important policy questions should be asked concerning whether the assessment of efficiencies should be different. Advocates of a more lenient approach recommend placing increased emphasis on preventing inefficiencies that may result from the prevention of the merger. Thus rather than an efficiency defence we may need to consider an inefficiency defence as well. This is an important consideration that was clearly taken into account in the Dutch case mentioned above. In periods of crisis competition authorities should place significant emphasis on the continuity of service or product, so significant that in certain cases even if the criteria of the efficiency defence are not strictly satisfied, the merger will be cleared on the basis of preventing resulting inefficiencies from discontinuing the product or service. In crisis situations, competition authorities should allow the lack of resulting inefficiencies to be a factor, especially if consumer harm results from such discontinuation.

The emphasis of Williamson's basic static model of efficiencies was on cost and price in one market.[175] Williamson's model would permit

[175] Williamson 1968.

mergers that increase total surplus despite any increase in price above the competitive level, which would cause consumer harm. Under a consumer welfare standard, in contrast to the total welfare standard, wealth transfers from consumers to producers would not be allowed; additionally, any cost savings that are not passed on to consumers would not be taken into account. Thus assessing a merger under a total welfare standard could allow a merger if it increased total surplus despite a price increase, whereas assessing a merger under a consumer welfare standard would in most cases require at least no, or limited, change in the post-merger price. As a result of the different focus that the two standards have, the consumer welfare standard would require greater efficiencies than would the total surplus standard.

Adopting a total welfare standard in periods of crisis may allow a competition authority to clear mergers the prohibition of which could inhibit efficiency in the provision of the goods or services. Competition authorities can permit such mergers on the condition that the parties actually achieve the efficiencies which they claim will occur and on which basis the mergers are cleared. The merging parties would be granted a probation period within which to realize the efficiencies. As the OECD report on efficiencies notes,[176] if the firm fails to deliver the promised level of efficiencies, the competition authority may break up the company, impose fines, or adopt remedies that will restore the degree of competition to previous levels. Thus parties will no longer have incentive to inflate their efficiency claims, since they will be penalized for not achieving them.

Turning to the criteria of assessment efficiencies in mergers, the Commission considers alternatives that are reasonably practical in the business situation faced by the merging parties, having regard to established business practices in the industry concerned.[177] This approach can be tailored in periods of crisis to incorporate changed business situations and business practices as a result of the crisis. In such cases competition authorities could adopt a total welfare standard, especially in cases where prohibiting the merger would induce inefficiencies in production or distribution methods.

In addition, the criterion concerning the pass-on requirement that

[176] OECD, Competition and Financial Markets.

[177] Guidelines on the Assessment of Horizontal Mergers under the Council Regulation on the Control of Concentrations between Undertakings, OJ C 31, 5 February 2004, pp. 5–18, para. 85.

needs to be satisfied for efficiencies claims to be accepted is only relevant when the merger is assessed under the consumer welfare standard. Under a total surplus standard it would be irrelevant whether cost savings are passed on to consumers or not. This criterion is the one that is normally not satisfied in efficiency claims and causes the prohibition of the respective mergers. Thus adopting a total welfare standard enables a competition authority to clear a merger and safeguard the viability and development of the involved undertakings. Adopting a total welfare standard in certain mergers during a crisis and thus allowing them to complete will ensure and/or enhance the viability of the involved undertakings and prevent deteriorations of service, as well as of firms. In addition, consumer welfare will not be adversely affected as a result of the inefficiencies provoked from prohibiting the merger.

Competition authorities require that efficiencies be substantial. Thus the value of efficiencies must exceed the competition authorities' assessment of the merger's anti-competitive effects. Williamson argued that a sliding scale should be used, depending on how speculative the claimed efficiencies are.[178] Highly speculative claims should yield high net benefits, whereas efficiencies that can be easily and objectively verified could yield lower net benefits.[179]

According to the EC Guidelines,[180] the Commission pursues a sliding-scale approach, according to which, the greater the possible negative effects on competition, the larger the efficiencies have to be and further states that for this reason it is highly unlikely that a concentration amounting to a monopoly or near-monopoly can be saved on the basis of efficiency claims.

As set out in the US Horizontal Merger Guidelines,

> The greater the potential adverse competitive effects of a merger . . . the greater must be cognizable efficiencies in order for the Agency to conclude that the merger will not have an anticompetitive effect . . . When the potential adverse competition effect is likely to be particularly large, extraordinarily great cognizable efficiencies would be necessary to prevent the merger from being anticompetitive. In the Agency's experience, efficiencies are most likely to make a difference in marginal cases when the likely adverse competitive effects, absent the efficiencies, are

[178] Williamson 1968.

[179] OECD, Competition and Financial Markets.

[180] Guidelines on the Assessment of Horizontal Mergers under the Council Regulation on the Control of Concentrations between Undertakings, OJ C 31, 5 February 2004, pp. 5–18, para. 79.

> not great. Efficiencies almost never justify a merger to monopoly or near-monopoly.[181]

As should be apparent from recent OFT cases, including the *de minimis* line of cases,[182] what matters when considering anti-competitive effects and the welfare of customers under the substantial-lessening-of-competition assessment is not just the size of the market, but also the magnitude of the merger's price or non-price effect, and the durability of that effect. It also matters how likely such adverse effects are to occur at all; in other words, the confidence the OFT has in its prediction that customer harm will result from the merger. The former factors go to the question, how bad is the harm if it actually happens? The latter question is, how likely is the harm to happen at all? It would be disingenuous to ignore the fact that assessment of post-merger outcomes, both welfare-enhancing and welfare-reducing, is generally an inherently predictive exercise,[183] and is based on probabilities, not certainty.[184] In periods of crisis we should also add the question, how likely is harm to materialize as a result of the inefficiencies from blocking a merger?

Thus, as the above analysis illustrates, in periods of crisis, competition authorities should consider whether strict application of the consumer welfare standard will induce the most beneficial impact in the market. There may be instances where the total welfare standard will induce better results in the post-merger market by ensuring the viability of the supply of goods or services. The UK and Dutch competition authorities in the *Orbital/Ocean Park* and the *Ziekenhuis Walcheren/Oosterscheldeziekenhuizen* cases respectively took into account the

[181] U.S. Horizontal Guidelines (1992, efficiencies section revised in 1997), Part 4. Compare the identical point made in the subsequent 2004 EC Horizontal Merger Guidelines, para. 84: 'The greater the possible negative effects on competition, the more the Commission has to be sure that the claimed efficiencies are substantial, likely to be realized and to be passed on, to a sufficient degree, to the consumer. It is highly unlikely that a merger leading to a market position approaching monopoly or leading to a similar level of market power, can be [cleared] on the grounds that efficiency gains would be sufficient to counteract its potential anti-competitive effects.'

[182] See in particular the OFT decision in *Anticipated acquisition by BOC Ltd of the packaged chlorine business and assets carried on by Ineos Chlor Ltd*, 29 May 2008, paras. 118–19.

[183] Even in the case of completed mergers, given the OFT's statutory time limits to refer such cases and the incentives of merged firms not to raise prices pending the outcome of the OFT's investigation, the analysis is more likely to be predictive than retrospective.

[184] See OFT Substantive Guidance Assessment Note on the IBA Case, OFT 516a, available at www.oft.gov.uk.

continuation of supply of the product or service as one important factor in the clearance of the case.

We should also refer to the approach that the Canadian competition authority uses in merger assessment. The authority uses a weighted-surplus or balancing-weights approach in evaluating efficiencies claims.[185] Relevant consideration factors include productive, distributive, administrative and dynamic efficiency gains; consumers' and producers' deadweight loss; socially adverse wealth transfers; and other socioeconomic effects stemming from either the enhanced market power or the efficiencies that a transaction is expected to generate. According to this approach,[186] if it is found that the merger will likely result in a wealth transfer between different income groups that will adversely affect social welfare, the competition authority can alter the weights that will be placed on the different welfare standards in order to prevent adverse effects on social welfare. Pursuant to the balancing-weights approach, if the income effect on some purchaser groups would be more severe than on others, different weights can be allocated among the groups. Thus a competition authority can safeguard against consumer harm arising from inefficiencies due to the prohibition of a merger. The authority will need to balance this harm with the consumer welfare harm that is induced from a likely price increase of the merged entity. A competition authority must determine the weight that would have to be given to the aggregate reduction in consumer surplus in order for it to equal the increased producer surplus that would result from the merger.

Pursuant to the weighted-surplus standard that the Canadian authority uses, if the adverse welfare effects of a price increase are significant enough, a competition authority is free to vary the weights ascribed to different relevant factors so that the analysis accurately reflects a proposed merger's real-world implications. This approach can be beneficial in periods of crisis, where authorities can use different weights for producer and consumer welfare and thus can alternate between total and consumer welfare standards in an attempt to ensure that the result will best address the merger's implications in the crisis market, which can include severe consequences such as product or service discontinuation and quality deterioration. Adopting such an approach amidst crises will prevent inefficiencies resulting from prohibiting the merger.

[185] OECD, Competition and Financial Markets.

[186] Ibid., Canadian submission.

As mentioned earlier in this book, applying the total welfare standard is preferred by economists who argue that other standards will sometimes sacrifice social surplus. In some circumstances the efficiency achieved by merger, or the inefficiency that will result from preventing the merger, must be evaluated under a total surplus standard rather than under a consumer welfare standard.[187]

However, the above approach should be used with caution and only when the adverse effects of a crisis are felt in an economy. The total welfare standard and the balancing of the consumer and producer's surplus should apply in cases where the prohibition of the merger would induce greater harm to consumer welfare than the merger might induce. The competition authority, by applying a total welfare standard or by placing different weights on the total and consumer welfare standards, in periods of crisis can clear a merger which could not be cleared under a consumer welfare standard,[188] and prohibition of which would, as illustrated above, induce inefficiencies. This approach should not provide an excuse for relaxing competition standards, but should be given prominence in situations such as the current financial crisis, where competition policy should be balanced against other policies.

7.5.3 *Other considerations in merger assessment*

An additional area where a crisis can influence merger assessment is remedies. Before we assess the implications of a crisis for the imposition of remedies, this section provides a brief analysis of remedies. Modifications of concentrations in the process of competition assessment are more commonly described as 'remedies' since their object is to eliminate the competition concerns identified by the European Commission. The Commission may attach to its decision conditions and obligations intended to ensure that the undertakings concerned comply with the commitments they have entered into vis-à-vis the Commission with a view to rendering the concentration compatible with the common market.

It is more common that the parties submit commitments with a view to rendering the concentration compatible with the common market and that those commitments are implemented following clearance. Whereas

[187] Luescher 2004.

[188] And at the same time the merger does not satisfy any defence to the prohibition (e.g. failing-firm defence).

the parties have to propose commitments sufficient to remove the competition concerns and submit the necessary information to assess them, it is for the competition authorities to establish whether or not a concentration, as modified by commitments validly submitted, must be declared incompatible with the common market because it leads, despite the commitments, to a significant impediment to effective competition.

Structural commitments

Structural commitments, in particular divestitures, proposed by the parties will be accepted only in so far as the Commission is able to conclude with the requisite degree of certainty that it will be possible to implement them and that it is likely that the new commercial structures resulting from them will be sufficiently workable and lasting to ensure that the significant impediment to effective competition will not materialize. The divestiture has to be completed within a fixed time period agreed between the parties and the Commission. In the Commission's practice, the total time period is divided into a period for entering into a final agreement and a further period for the closing of the transaction.

Divestiture is the most common form of structural remedy. Basically, it seeks to preserve competition in a relevant market following a merger either by creating a new source of competition through the sale of business or of a set of assets to a new market participant or by strengthening an existing source of competition through sale to an existing market participant independent of the merging parties.[189] It can involve the sale of a complete business,[190] the sale of an existing business of one of the parties merging,[191] the sale of parts of both parties' businesses,[192] the sale of parts of a business,[193] or the severance of links with competitors.[194] Structural remedies offer advantages from an enforcement perspective. Once a purchaser has been finalized, no further monitoring is needed by the competition authority, in contrast to behavioural or quasi-structural remedies. The effectiveness of structural remedies is endangered by the risks concerning composition, purchaser and assets. Omission of key assets necessary for the viability of the business is one of the sources of

[189] International Competition Network, 'Merger Remedies Review Project', para. 3.8, available at www.internationalcompetitionnetwork.org.

[190] E.g. M214, *DuPont/ICI*.

[191] E.g. M1795, *Vodafone Airtouch/Mannesmann*; M2016, *France Telecom/Orange*.

[192] M2544, *Masterfoods/Royal Canin*.

[193] M190, *Nestle/Perrier*; M3436 *Continental/Phoenix*.

[194] M1182, *Akso Nobel/Courtaulds*; M3436 *Continental/Phoenix*.

inadequacy. Parties are not obliged to disclose the information on which parts of the business are essential for its viability. This may allow for opportunistic behaviour of the seller, with the buyer frequently ending up in *ex post* hold-ups.[195]

The divested activities must consist of a viable business that, if operated by a 'suitable purchaser', can compete effectively with the merged entity on a lasting basis. A viable business is a business that can operate on a stand-alone basis, which means independently of the merging parties as regards the supply of input materials or other forms of co-operation other than during a transitory period.

The suitable-purchaser requirements are the following:

- the purchaser is required to be independent of and unconnected to the parties;
- the purchaser must possess the financial resources, proven relevant expertise and the incentive and ability to maintain and develop the divested business as a viable and active competitive force in competition with the parties and other competitors; and
- the acquisition of the business by a proposed purchaser must neither be likely to create new competition problems nor give rise to a risk that the implementation of the commitments will be delayed. Therefore the proposed purchaser must reasonably be expected to obtain all necessary approvals from the relevant regulatory authorities for the acquisition of the business to be divested.

There are cases where only the proposal of an up-front buyer will allow the Commission to conclude, with the requisite degree of certainty, that the business will be effectively divested to a suitable purchaser. The parties therefore have to undertake in the commitments that they are not going to complete the notified operation before entering into a binding agreement with a purchaser for the divested business, approved by the Commission.

In fix-it-first remedies, the parties identify and enter into a legally binding agreement with a buyer outlining the essentials of the purchase during the Commission's procedure. The Commission will be able to decide in the final decision whether the transfer of the divested business to the identified purchaser will remove the competition concerns.

[195] D. Went, 'The Acceptability of Remedies under the EC Merger Regulation: Structural versus Behavioural' (August 2006) *European Competition Law Review* 455, at pp. 464–74.

If the Commission authorizes the notified concentration, no additional Commission decision for purchaser approval will be needed and the closing of the sale of the divested business may take place shortly afterwards.

Commitments which are structural in nature, such as the commitment to sell a business unit, are, as a rule, preferable from the point of view of the merger regulation's objective, inasmuch as such commitments prevent, durably, the competition concerns which would be raised by the merger as notified, and do not, moreover, require medium- or long-term monitoring measures.

The most effective way to maintain effective competition, apart from prohibition, is to create conditions for the emergence of a new competitive entity or for the strengthening of existing competitors via divestiture by the merging parties. The Court of First Instance (CFI) has argued that commitments which are structural in nature are as a rule preferable from the point of view of the ECMR's objectives.[196] However, the ECJ also mentioned in *Tetra Laval/Sidel* that there should not be an automatic presumption in favour of structural remedies.[197] It added that behavioural remedies can be used to prevent a loss of competition as well as to control the effects of a loss of competition.

In *Babyliss v. Commission*,[198] the CFI said that the Commission was bound to accept the least onerous set of remedies which was likely to resolve the competition concerns referring expressly to the principle of proportionality.

In the *Unilever/Amora Maille* case,[199] the competition concern related to the merging parties' dominant position in the French market for mayonnaise and salad dressings. The divestiture of the Benedicta brand was much wider, including other products (such as mustard) and covering all territories where the brand was registered. It was held that the new entrant would need to offer the full range of Benedicta products and to be present internationally in order to compete effectively with Unilever.

The Commission also considers the use of 'crown jewels' undertakings, namely a commitment to set out an alternative proposal in order to

[196] T102/96, *Gencor v. Commission*.

[197] M2416, *Tetra Laval/Sidel*; T-5/02, *Tetra Laval v. Commission*; C-12/03, *Commission v. Tetra Laval*.

[198] T-114/02, *Babyliss v. Commission*.

[199] M1802, *Unilever/Amora Maille*.

render the divestiture packages more effective, especially in cases where the Commission is uncertain of the likelihood of a successful divestment (third-party pre-emption rights, transferability of key contacts, intellectual property rights).[200]

The Commission therefore may accept commitments of other types, but only in circumstances where the other remedy proposed is at least equivalent in its effects to a divestiture.

As we shall see below, the Commission has accepted remedies foreseeing the granting of access to key infrastructure, networks, technology (including patents, know-how or other intellectual property rights) and essential inputs. Normally, the parties grant such access to third parties on a non-discriminatory and transparent basis.

Behavioural commitments

The Commission may examine other types of non-divestiture remedies, such as behavioural commitments, only exceptionally in specific circumstances, such as in respect of competition concerns arising in conglomerate structures. Behavioural remedies consist of commitments aimed at guaranteeing that competitors enjoy a level playing field in the purchase or use of some key assets, inputs or technologies that are owned by the merging parties.[201] In *Newscorp/Telepiù*[202] and *Telia/Sonera*,[203] non-structural remedies were deemed appropriate (as is frequently the case in transactions raising vertical or interoperability concerns). There are sectors where behavioural remedies may be preferable. In telecommunication sector mergers, the Commission has approved remedies such as granting access to the network.[204] In the energy sector appropriate remedies have been related to providing access to capacity (such as to electricity generation capacity via auctions over a certain period).[205] Some cases involved an increase in capacity in order to open the network and

[200] M291, *KNP/Buhrman Tetterode/VRG*; M938, *Guiness/Grand Metropolitan*; M1467, *Akzo Nobel/Courtaulds*; M3225, *Alcan/Pechiney (II)*; M2337, *Nestle/Ralston Purina*; M2922 *Pfizer/Pharmacia*; M1813, *Industri Kapital (Nordkem)/Dyno*; M3687, *J&J/Guidant*.

[201] M. Motta, M. Polo and H. Vasconcelos, 'Merger Remedies in the EU: An Overview', contribution prepared for the Guidelines for Merger Remedies symposium, Ecole des Mines, Paris, 2002, pp. 11–12.

[202] M2876, *Newscorp/Telepiù*.

[203] M2803, *Telia/Sonera*.

[204] M1439, *Telia/Telenor*; M1795, *Vodafone Airtouch/Mannesmann*.

[205] M1853, *EDF/EnBW*; M2947, *Verbund/Energie Allianz*; M2389, *Shell/DEA*; M2533, *BP/E.ON*; M1383, *Exxon/Mobil*.

provide access for potential entrants.[206] Access remedies have also been accepted in mergers in the air passenger transport as well as media sectors.[207] In *Air France/KLM*,[208] the Commission accepted a commitment that whenever the merged entity published a reduced fare on the Paris–Amsterdam route, it would apply an equivalent reduction on the Lyon–Amsterdam route.

Appropriate remedies may also consist of vertical firewalls (Chinese walls), which aim at ensuring the independence of different units.[209] The Commission may require that no information be circulated within the different units of the merged entity and thus impose non-disclosure provisions.[210] However, their implementation can be problematic since it is impossible to guarantee that no communication between different units of the same entity will happen. This remedy is particularly appropriate when a merger creates a vertically integrated firm where the upstream unit supplies not only the downstream unit but also the competitors and it is therefore possible that competitively sensitive information about downstream rivals is passed from the upstream to the downstream unit of a merged entity.

Another type of remedy has been identified which can be grouped with the structural remedies despite their nature because they may be equivalent in terms of effect by modifying the structure of the market. These behavioural–structural hybrids are often called quasi-structural remedies.[211] They can be aimed at granting an exclusive license of intellectual property rights. In addition, they may involve exit from long-term exclusive contracts in which the parties may be involved. Quasi-structural remedies are behavioural remedies that, once implemented, induce an immediate and permanent change in the market.[212]

Behavioural remedies have a number of drawbacks. In some cases

[206] M2434, *Grupo Villar Mir/EnBW/HidroelectricadelCantabrico*; M2684, *EnBW/Cajastur/Hidrocantabrico*.

[207] M157, *AirFrance/Sabena*; M259, *British Airways/TAT*; M616, *Swissair/Sabena, KLM/Alitalia*; M2041, *United Airlines/US Airways*; M3280, *Air France/KLM*; M3770, *Lufthansa/Swissair*. Merger cases in the media sector include M2050, *Vivendi/Canal+/Seagram*; M2876, *Newscorp/Telepiù*.

[208] M3280, *Air France/KLM*.

[209] K. Paas, 'Non-Structural Remedies in EU Merger Control' (2006) 27(5) *ECLR* 209.

[210] M3099, *Areva/Urenco/ETC*.

[211] Lindsay 2003.

[212] ICN Merger Working Group, Analytical Framework Subgroup, Merger Remedies Review Project, Report for the fourth ICN annual conference, Bonn, Germany, June 2005.

where granting access to infrastructure was used, expansion of the market was not as important as originally expected. Thus their design was not adaptable. In addition, the proper definition of access posed implementation problems. Behavioural and quasi-structural remedies require ongoing monitoring to assess the compliance of the merged entity with its commitments. The direct intervention in the market that behavioural remedies entail may distort competition and generate inefficiencies.[213]

By their nature, behavioural remedies are more vulnerable to manipulations by a merged entity attempting to evade the spirit of the remedy. The merging parties may increase prices, reduce quality or cause delay, conduct which is inconsistent with the objective, but may not always constitute a breach, of the remedy.

The implementation problems of behavioural remedies can be prevented by precisely outlining the scope of the remedy. Review clauses (incorporating any necessary amendments due to changes in market conditions) allow the Commission to grant an extension of deadlines or, in exceptional circumstances, to waive, modify or substitute the commitments. The involvement of trustees in the monitoring process and the possibility of arbitration in case of disputes is likely to make the enforcement of behavioural remedies smooth.

In accepting commitments the Commission must ensure that there is effective implementation and the ability to monitor commitments.[214]

[213] A. Ezrachi, Under- (and Over-) Prescribing of Behavioural Remedies, Working Paper L 13/05, University of Oxford, Centre for Competition Law and Policy.

[214] As the Commission cannot, on a daily basis, be directly involved in overseeing the implementation of commitments, the parties have to propose the appointment of a trustee to oversee the parties' compliance with their commitments, in particular with their obligations in the interim period and the divestiture process (the so-called 'monitoring trustee'). The parties thereby guarantee the effectiveness of the commitments submitted by them and allow the Commission to ensure that the modification of the notified concentration, as proposed by the parties, will be carried out with the requisite degree of certainty. The monitoring trustee will carry out its tasks under the supervision of the Commission and is to be considered the Commission's 'eyes and ears'. It shall be the guardian of the business being managed and properly kept on a stand-alone basis in the interim period. The Commission may therefore give any orders and instructions to the monitoring trustee in order to ensure compliance with commitments, and the trustee may propose to the parties any measures it considers necessary for carrying out its tasks. The parties, however, may not issue any instructions to the trustee without approval by the Commission. For divestitures, the parties have to propose to appoint a divestiture trustee in order to make the commitments submitted by them effective and allow the Commission to ensure that the modification of the notified concentration, as proposed by them, will be carried out. If the

Whereas divestitures, once implemented, do not require any further monitoring measures, commitments of other types require effective monitoring mechanisms in order to ensure that their effect is not reduced or even eliminated by the parties. Irrespective of the type of remedy, commitments will usually include a review clause. This may allow the Commission, upon request by the parties showing good cause, to grant an extension of deadlines or, in exceptional circumstances, to waive, modify or substitute the commitments.

Turning to the approach that competition authorities should adopt in periods of crisis, such as the current one, the availability of buyers of divested assets at those prices which prevailed before the crisis may not always be possible. Potential buyers may have the relevant expertise and the incentive and ability to maintain and develop the divested business as a viable and active force in competition with the parties and other competitors, but they may not possess the financial resources that will enable them to acquire the business.

Thus companies may find it harder to dispose of assets as part of a structural remedy, or to do so within the specific time frame, because they cannot find a buyer. Implementing divestments may be more difficult in the current financial environment of low liquidity, and in any crisis affecting liquidity in a market. The possibility that no buyer might step forward, even at a negative price, is real and likely to induce complications in the assessment of a merger. This risk of lack of potential purchasers may increase as the credit crunch develops.

In a period of financial instability, the relative attractiveness of behavioural remedies increases compared to that of structural remedies.

parties do not succeed in finding a suitable purchaser within the first divestiture period then, in the trustee divestiture period, the divestiture trustee will be given an irrevocable and exclusive mandate to dispose of the business to a suitable purchaser, under the supervision of the Commission, within a specific deadline, at no minimum price. Parties have to fulfil certain obligations in the interim period. The following should normally be included in the commitments in this respect: (i) safeguards for the interim preservation of the viability to the business; (ii) the necessary steps for a carve-out process, if relevant; and (iii) the necessary steps to prepare the divestiture of the business. In order to maintain the structural effect of a remedy, the commitments have to foresee that the merged entity cannot subsequently acquire influence over the whole or parts of the divested business. The intended effect of the divestiture will only be achieved if and once the business is transferred to a suitable purchaser in whose hands it will become an active competitive force in the market. The M877 *Boeing/McDonnell Douglas* case illustrates the circumstances where there is no suitable purchaser for the divested assets.

Behavioural remedies have the particular feature that they can be reviewed and revised as the market evolves.[215]

Structural commitments will usually also include a review clause. This may allow the competition authorities, upon request by the parties showing good cause, to grant an extension of deadlines or, in exceptional circumstances, to waive, modify or substitute commitments. As regards the review provisions of both behavioural and structural remedies, competition authorities should follow a flexible, pragmatic approach, taking into account the practical difficulties that the circumstances of a crisis impose on the implementation of remedies.

Thus in a period of crisis the challenge to competition authorities is to devise appropriate remedies that account for both static and dynamic concerns. In such periods, it may be harder to implement structural remedies because the market itself is changing and a structural remedy that does not acknowledge this may lead to a suboptimal equilibrium in the market that will result from the crisis. Behavioural remedies have the advantage of not being static – they can be reviewed and revised as the market evolves. Behavioural remedies might also be designed to accommodate wider policy concerns which may vary depending on the priorities that a crisis sets.

In its report to the OECD, the UK argued that its approach towards merger remedies in times of crisis was a combination of principle and pragmatism. It noted that, in a recession, there might be no purchaser for a potential disposal, or it might take longer to find one, and the purchaser might not compete effectively even if found. It was very important for authorities to give a clear message that merger remedies and policy would remain robust, without involving excessive measures. Similarly, with remedies such as divestments, competition authorities may have to accept more flexible time frames.

BIAC supported the continued use of conventional competition principles but importantly it added that there was no time for excessive regulation, which would impose extra costs on businesses in excessive fines and remedies.[216] The EU acknowledged the need for authorities to be realistic about the impact of remedies on markets, and added that remedies must be clear as white knights are unlikely to materialize every

[215] See further UK Response to OECD, Competition and Financial Markets.

[216] Summary Record of the Discussion on Competition and Financial Markets, DAF/COMP/M(2009)1/ANN4, 10 April 2009, Roundtable 3 on Real Economy and Competition Policy in a Period of Retrenchment, available at www.oecd.org.

time a remedy anticipated an entry in the market or required the purchase of a divestment.[217]

Thus, as the above analysis illustrates, in periods of severe crisis competition authorities should be pragmatic in identifying remedies of either a structural or a behavioural nature that can be effectively implemented and can effectively address the anti-competitive concern. In addition, in such crises, competition authorities ought to be pragmatic, among other ways, in the satisfaction of the 'suitable-purchaser' criteria especially as regards the requirement for financial resources. In addition, the dynamic aspects of markets should be taken into account as well as the necessary flexibility in time frames for the assessment of the submitted undertakings. As the above analysis illustrates, competition authorities must illustrate substantial flexibility in their willingness to adopt a more lenient approach in merger assessment during periods of crisis.

Before moving on to the assessment of crisis cartels, we should very briefly note an argument that was echoed in the OECD report and regards national champions. Germany argued that there was a gap between theory and practice regarding the issue of national champions.[218] The benefits of forming a national champion included enhancing national presence and ensuring effective competitive power abroad, safeguarding jobs, and taking advantage of economies of scale vis-à-vis other multinational firms. The main drawback in the creation of national champions was the distortion of national competition. In Germany, the Bundeskartellamt blocked the merger of E.ON and Ruhrgas but was overruled by the German government on political grounds.[219] The merger contributed to the security of supply in Germany during the gas quarrel between Ukraine and Russia. Frederic Jenny has argued that it was clear from the German submission that government intervention for national champions may in some cases be useful even if it had or might create competition problems.[220]

[217] Summary Record of the Discussion on Competition and Financial Markets, DAF/COMP/M(2009)1/ANN4, 10 April 2009, Roundtable 3 on Real Economy and Competition Policy in a Period of Retrenchment, ibid.

[218] On the issue of national champions see the related proceedings of the 2009 GFC roundtable: DAF/COMP/GF/M(2009)1/ANN1, available at www.oecd.org.

[219] Summary Record of the Discussion on Competition and Financial Markets, DAF/COMP/M(2009)1/ANN4, 10 April 2009, Roundtable 3 on Real Economy and Competition Policy in a Period of Retrenchment, www.oecd.org.

[220] OECD Competition Committee, Competition and the Financial Markets, www.oecd.org.

It would be interesting to mention the case of national champions in Argentina, a country that has experienced several crisis events. Following the 2001 collapse in the Argentine economy, antitrust law faced new challenges. As a consequence of the violent devaluation of the national currency (the peso), Argentine firms became very exposed to takeovers from foreign companies. The main concern after the devaluation was whether antitrust rules were going to protect national interests. During the opening of the economy in the 1990s many national companies were taken over by multinational groups. In 2003, the Petrobras/Pecom merger was cleared after a final approval decision adopted by the government, which was politically motivated. This case illustrated the shift towards a more political approach in the enforcement of antitrust rules.[221] It concerned the takeover by Petrobras, the incumbent Brazilian oil company, of Pecom, an Argentine company active in different segments of the energy sector. According to the Comision Nacional de Defensa de la Competencia (CNDC), the merger did not give rise to competition concerns, given the limited market share of both undertakings in the relevant markets. The president of Argentina publicly considered Transener a strategic company and required Petrobras to sell Pecom's stake in Transener.[222]

In concluding this part of the chapter, we should echo the Court of First Instance, which stated in *Nestlé/Perrier* that the Commission should take taking into consideration the social effects of merger decisions if they can adversely affect the social objectives referred to in the Treaty on European Union.[223] The Commission may therefore have to ascertain whether the concentration is liable to have consequences, even if only indirectly, on the position of employees in the undertakings in question, such as to affect the level or conditions of employment in the Community or in a substantial part of it.[224] In the Lisbon Treaty there are stronger references to full employment and social objectives. This

[221] Case No S01:0257793/02, 28 April 2003, *Petrobras/Pérez Companc*, available at www.mecon.gov.ar/download/cndc/dictamenes/c388_petrobras.pdf.

[222] P.I. Colomo, 'The Revival of Antitrust Law in Argentina: Policy or Politics?' (2006) 27(6) *ECLR* 317.

[223] *Comité Central d'Entreprise de la Société Générale des Grandes Sources v. Commission* (T-96/92), [1995] ECR II-1213.

[224] L. McGowan and M. Cini, 'Discretion and Politicization in EU Competition Policy: The Case of Merger Control' (1999) 12 *Governance: An International Journal of Policy and Administration* 175. See also A. Stephan, 'The Bankruptcy Wildcard in Cartel Cases (August 2006) *J.B.L.* 511.

might induce such arguments being taken into consideration more often in merger assessment.[225]

After the above analysis of the approach towards mergers in periods of crisis, and addressing the several implications that merger assessment has in such periods, the chapter turns to the assessment of crisis cartels.

7.6 Crisis cartels amidst crises

As we have seen in the chapter addressing crisis cartels, without industry-wide agreements on capacity reduction that can be achieved through a crisis cartel, smaller firms may exit the market, leaving a limited number of choices for customers as well as inducing unemployment. In such conditions, undertakings may operate at inefficient output levels and may even incur losses.

Arguments for ordered restructuring of industries or firms colluding on the removal of spare capacity are typical of the forms of cartelization that are likely to be seen in a recession. Many collusive agreements have been formed amidst adverse market conditions. In addition, the conduct of executives may change in situations of crisis, inducing them to put their own job safety over any concerns they may have with price-fixing. However, the possibility of criminal or director disqualification sanctions in some jurisdictions may dissuade such executives from engaging in cartelistic behaviour. In addition, the possibility of demand increasing in the future increases incentives to deviate from cartelistic conduct.

BIAC supported the continued use of conventional competition principles in periods of crisis, but importantly it added that there was no time for excessive regulation, which would impose extra costs on businesses in excessive fines and remedies.[226] The EU added that it was right for authorities to be realistic about the impact of remedies or fines on markets, and was clear that full account needed to be taken of a firm's ability to pay a fine, especially where imposition of a fine led to a lessening of competition.

Difficult economic times often lead to increased temptations for competitors to reach anti-competitive agreements that will allow them to sustain their viability. Thus an increase in cartel occurrence is likely to

[225] See www.wilmerhale.com/publications/whPubsDetail.aspx?publication=9321.

[226] Summary Record of the Discussion on Competition and Financial Markets, DAF/COMP/M(2009)1/ANN4, 10 April 2009, Roundtable 3 on Real Economy and Competition Policy in a Period of Retrenchment, available at www.oecd.org.

materialize.[227] Crisis conditions may make it more difficult for antitrust authorities to obtain the amount of fines that will ensure deterrence. Such difficulties that are due to crisis conditions could lead competition authorities to look for other methods of deterrence, such as jail sentences or other sanctions for individuals.

The OECD report mentions that the political measures taken to counter Japanese economic recession had implications for competition policy.[228] A series of economic recessions since the 1970s had led to the 1990s being called a 'lost decade' for the Japanese economy. The growth rate had been very low for more than fifteen years and policy measures taken to counter recessions in the 1950s and 1960s included a system of so-called rationalization cartels, introduced in 1953 as an exemption to anti-monopoly legislation to allow companies to co-ordinate production or service volumes, to reduce capacity or even to co-ordinate price levels.

Energy-intensive industries lost their competitiveness in the 1970s because of the oil crises, and a series of temporary laws covering structurally depressed industries were introduced throughout the late 1970s and 1980s to reduce excess capacity, allowing joint sales and providing some financial assistance. These measures had serious anti-competitive effects and were abolished in 1999, although in any case they were rarely used after the 1980s. Competition policy had to give way to industry rescue policy measures that harmed competition, but the Japan Fair Trade Commission (JFTC), in order to ensure that the proposed provisions did not compromise the Anti-monopoly Act and the spirit of competition policy, acted by strengthening competition enforcement in the 1980s and 1990s and by reviewing measures every five years. With every review the measures were made less anti-competitive. The lost decade of the Japanese economy was not a lost decade for competition policy in Japan, however. On the contrary, competition policy was strengthened in a major way during the 1990s.

The crisis cartels that were allowed in Japan were contrary to the rationale behind the institution of such radical measures. During the so-called 'lost' decade of the 1990s competition-reducing measures such as exemption cartels were much used and targeted towards

[227] G. Addy, A. Banicevic and M. Katz, 'Antitrust Legislation and Policy in a Global Economic Crisis—A Canadian Perspective', *Global Competition Policy*, December 2008, available at www.globalcompetitionpolicy.org.

[228] OECD, Competition and Financial Markets.

specific individual firms rather than towards industries. Philip Lowe, at the OECD Roundtable,[229] argued that on cartels, if co-ordination of output or price by producers themselves was allowed, the more likely it was that crisis measures aimed at reducing capacity would be accompanied by collusion, detrimental to everyone – including consumers and taxpayers – and to competitiveness. We should emphasize that as the EU experience has shown,[230] such agreements should not be applied to specific firms but to the majority of firms or to industries as a whole. As the EC has indicated, agreements to reduce structural overcapacity which involve all or a majority of the undertakings in an entire sector can be accepted if they are aimed solely at a co-ordinated reduction of overcapacity and do not restrict the commercial freedom of the parties involved.[231]

As regards crisis cartels, the Commission has, in the seventh Report on Competition Policy, announced that measures to stimulate competition were necessary under adverse social and regional circumstances. In the eighth Report on Competition Policy the Commission argued that it is inclined to accept that under certain conditions agreements between firms aimed at reducing excess capacity may be authorized under Article 101(3) but only where the firms have not simultaneously, whether by agreement or concerted practice, fixed either prices or production or delivery quotas.[232]

The Commission has stated that structural overcapacity occurs when, over a long period, undertakings experience a reduction in their capacity utilization and a drop in output and rise in operating losses, and when there is no sign of possible recovery in the medium term.[233] As mentioned above, in the Twenty-third Report on Competition Policy the

[229] Summary Record of the Discussion on Competition and Financial Markets, DAF/COMP/M(2009)1/ANN4, 10 April 2009, Roundtable 3 on Real Economy and Competition Policy in a Period of Retrenchment, available at www.oecd.org.

[230] See further Chapter 5 above on crisis cartels.

[231] Agreements involving a smaller number of firms can also be accepted if they aim at allowing reciprocal specialization in order to achieve closure of excess capacity. See further thirteenth Report on Competition Policy, para. 56. An indication of political involvement in competition enforcement is illustrated by the promotion of price agreements by the Argentinian government in response to heightened concerns of inflation. Argentina had shown robust growth rates but the government was concerned about the negative effect of high inflation. The government concluded price agreements with supermarkets, dairy producers and meat producers in order to freeze the retail and wholesale prices for a given period of time. Colomo 2006.

[232] Eighth Report on Competition Policy, para. 13.

[233] Twelfth Report on Competition Policy, para. 38.

Commission argued that agreements to reduce structural overcapacity which involve all or a majority of the undertakings in an entire sector can be accepted if they are aimed solely at a co-ordinated reduction of overcapacity and do not restrict the commercial freedom of the parties involved.[234] Agreements involving a smaller number of firms can also (and to some extent exceptionally) be accepted if they aim at allowing reciprocal specialization in order to achieve closure of excess capacity. However, the Commission argues that such agreements must not incorporate any price-fixing, quota-fixing or market allocation.[235]

Chapter 5 above, addressing crisis cartels, analysed a number of cases involving a restructuring plan to tackle excess capacity.[236] In the *Polypropylene* case,[237] the Commission outlined its view on crisis cartels and argued that price-fixing and quota-fixing are usually unacceptable.[238] There have been a number of cases under the Treaty of Rome involving crisis cartels where, in the majority, the undertakings requested an exemption pursuant to Article 101(3). The Commission will authorize a restructuring plan involving sectoral agreements if it believes that the Article 101(3) criteria are met. These criteria will be met if the reduction in the capacity of the sector will in the long term lead to more efficient capacity utilization, enhancing the competitiveness of the sector and thus benefiting consumers. Thus a detailed plan of plant closures as well as avoidance of the creation of new capacity are also necessary factors in the agreement being accepted by the Commission.

Furthermore, reduction in capacity can in the long run increase profitability, restore competitiveness and mitigate the adverse impacts on competitiveness.[239] The agreement must contain a detailed and binding

[234] See twenty-third Report on Competition Policy, para. 84.

[235] Thirteenth Report on Competition Policy, para. 56.

[236] IV/34.456, *Stichting Baksteen*, OJ L 131/15.

[237] *Re Polypropylene*, OJ 1986 L230.

[238] See further the following annual reports on Competition Policy: second, points 29–31; eighth, point 42; eleventh, points 45–8; twelfth, points 38–41; thirteenth, points 56–61; fourteenth, points 80–5. See also the following cases: *Re BPCL/ICI*, OJ 1984 L212/1, [1985] 2 CMLR 330, noted (1986) 11 *E.L. Rev.* 67; *Re Synthetic Fibres*, OJ 1984 L207/17, [1985] 1 CMLR 787, noted (1986) 11 *E.L. Rev.* 64; *Re ENI/Montedison*, OJ 1987 L5/13; *Re Neickem/ICI*, OJ; *Re Akzo/Shell* (*Rovin*), Bull. EC 5-1984; fourteenth Report on Competition Policy, para. 85, noted (1985) 10 *E.L. Rev.* 229; *Re Montedison/Hercules* (*Himont*), 1988 L50/18. See also the preliminary notices in *Re Zinc Shutdown Agreement*, OJ 1983 C164/3, [1983] 2 CMLR 473, point 2.1.71; *Re PRB/Shell*, OJ 1984 C189/2. See further case comment on *Re Polypropylene* (1988) 13(3) *E.L. Rev.* 205.

[239] The Commission seems to place importance on non-competition factors such as employment. The Commission clearly states that reorganization operations should be

programme of closures for each production centre in order to ensure reduction of existing capacity and to prevent the creation of new capacity. The incorporated restrictions of competition must be indispensable in order to achieve the restructuring of the sector. The agreement must be of a duration that will allow for the technical implementation of the capacity reduction.[240] Consumers must enjoy a share of the benefits resulting from the agreement, since in the longer run they will benefit from a competitive environment while in the short run they will have not been deprived of choices of product.

Thus, in a nutshell, the conditions that need to be fulfilled before an exemption is granted (i.e. satisfying the Article 101(3) criteria) include that production and distribution are improved, that the restrictions are indispensable, that elimination of competition is not complete, that consumers take a fair share of the benefits, and finally that the benefits outweigh the disadvantages.

The agreement aiming at the co-ordinated reduction in capacity will not be likely to restrict competition since the parties to the agreement will independently decide their strategies on elements other than the co-ordinated reduction in capacity. There may be other firms in the market not party to the agreement which may be able to provide competitive constraints. In addition, the agreement must constitute an indispensable means of achieving the necessary capacity reduction. The limited duration of the agreement, the possible existence of firms in the industry which are not party to the agreement, and the fact that the co-ordinated reduction in capacity is the only element in the business strategy of firms constitute reassurances that competition will not be eliminated.

The Commission has faced difficulties in exempting crisis cartels pursuant to the Article 101(3) criteria. Thus the Commission has sometimes relied on the maintenance of employment in order to exempt such agreements. The ECJ in the *Metro* case argued that a medium-term supply agreement was deemed to satisfy the first condition of Article 101(3) since it was considered likely to help maintain employment in situations of economic crisis.[241] Similarly, the ECJ in *Walt Wilhelm* held that

such as to secure the employment situation within the sector concerned. Twelfth Report on Competition Policy, para. 39.

[240] As the Commission states in the twelfth Report on Competition Policy (para. 39), exchange of information is acceptable provided it does not induce co-ordination either on sale conditions or on the remaining capacity.

[241] Case 27/76, *Metro*, [1977] ECR 1875.

> while the Treaty's primary object is to eliminate by this means (proceedings under Article 85(1)) the obstacles to the free movement of goods within the Common Market and to confirm and safeguard the unity of that market, it also commits the Community authorities to carry out certain positive, though indirect, action with a view to promoting a harmonious development of economic activities within the whole community in accordance with Article 2 of the Treaty.[242]

According to the ECJ, when deciding whether an agreement will be caught by Article 101(1), it is not necessary to consider its actual effect further if it seems to have as its object to prevent, restrict or distort competition within the common market.[243] Close attention must be paid to the wording and the objective of an agreement when determining whether it falls within the prohibition of Article 101(1).[244] Even if it can be established that the parties have no 'subjective intention to restrict competition, but . . . an object to remedy the effects of a crisis in the industry', this is irrelevant for the purposes of applying Article 101(1). It may only be taken into account when considering whether an exemption under Article 101(3) might be granted. The Supreme Court remitted the issue to the High Court to assess whether an exemption can be granted. The Supreme Court argued that the agreement could realize substantial efficiencies, no customers had complained and the restraints to prevent players who had been paid to leave the industry from re-entering seemed indispensable to the access of the arrangements. As the ECJ has eloquently stated,[245]

[242] Case 14/68, *Walt Wilhelm v. Bundeskartellamt*, [1969] ECR 1 motif 11. As Hornsby has argued, this passage is increasingly used to provide a legal base for the Commission's use of the competition rules to achieve other policy objectives. See further S. Hornsby, 'Competition Policy in the 80s: More Policy Less Competition?' (1987) 12(2) *E.L. Rev.* 79. Hornsby adds that decisions explicitly justifying crisis cartels by reference to distortions caused by state aid could be legally justified in appropriate cases by reference to the preliminary provisions of the treaty as indicated by the European Court in *Walt Wilhelm*. Not only have the Commission and the European Court used such a legal technique before (see Case 6/72, *Europemballage and Continental Can v. Commission*, [1973] ECR 215; Cases 6 and 7/73, *Commercial Solvents v. Commission*, [1974] ECR 223, motif 25), but also emphasis on the more economic criteria set out in the preliminary Articles would be more consistent with Article 85(3) (or 101(3) pursuant to the Lisbon Treaty) than are references to employment considerations which are not referred to at all in the rules applying to undertakings. See Hornsby 1987, at p. 93.

[243] Case C-209/07, *The Competition Authority v. The Beef Industry Development Society Ltd and Barry Brothers (Carrigmore) Meats Ltd*, [2008] ECR 00, para. 16.

[244] Case C-209/07, *The Competition Authority v. The Beef Industry Development Society Ltd and Barry Brothers (Carrigmore) Meats Ltd*, [2008] ECR 00, para. 21.

[245] Case C-209/07, *The Competition Authority v. The Beef Industry Development Society Ltd and Barry Brothers (Carrigmore) Meats Ltd*, [2008] ECR 00, para. 21.

> In fact, to determine whether an agreement comes within the prohibition laid down in Article 81(1) EC, close regard must be paid to the wording of its provisions and to the objectives which it is intended to attain. In that regard, even supposing it to be established that the parties to an agreement acted without any subjective intention of restricting competition, but with the object of remedying the effects of a crisis in their sector, such considerations are irrelevant for the purposes of applying that provision. Indeed, an agreement may be regarded as having a restrictive object even if it does not have the restriction of competition as its sole aim but also pursues other legitimate objectives (General Motors v. Commission, paragraph 64 and the case-law cited). It is only in connection with Article 81(3) EC that matters such as those relied upon by BIDS [Beef Industry Development Society Ltd] may, if appropriate, be taken into consideration for the purposes of obtaining an exemption from the prohibition laid down in Article 81(1) EC.

The ECJ has argued in past decisions that the existence of a crisis in the market cannot in itself preclude the anti-competitive nature of an agreement. The existence of a crisis might have been relied upon in order to seek an exemption under Article 101(3).[246] The ECJ does not prohibit the existence of crisis cartels per se, but argues that the legality of such cartels needs to be assessed pursuant to the exemption criteria of Article 101(3). This view confirms the practice, in relation to crisis cartels, that we have seen in the enforcement of Article 101 since the early 1960s.

There can be multiple types of agreement that companies may use to overcome capacity problems. Crisis cartels through bilateral or multilateral agreements can satisfy the conditions of Article 101(3). Bilateral agreements are a more likely form of rationalization agreement (as achieving the co-ordinated reduction in capacity among two firms is easier than among a larger number of firms), but are less likely to satisfy the conditions of Article 101(3). To satisfy the criteria of Article 101(3) such agreements should lead to a reduction in excess capacity and rationalize production, and should not lead to full elimination of competition.[247]

As the Commission interestingly argues, a factor that will be taken into account is the impact of the capacity co-ordination on the mitigation

[246] Court of Justice in Joined Cases C-238/99 P, C-244/99 P, C-245/99 P, C-247/99 P, C-250/99 P to C-252/99 P and C-254/99 P, *LVM and Others v. Commission*, 16 October 2002, para. 487.

[247] In addition, restrictions on imports imposed by intergovernmental voluntary restraint agreements may also lead to a reduction in the excess capacity of a sector. For further information on such agreements see Ritter and Braun 2004, at p. 185.

of the adverse impact of the crisis on employment.[248] The Commission explicitly states that reorganization operations should also be used to stabilize and secure the employment situation in the sector concerned.[249] The Commission uses the positive impact of a co-ordination of business conduct of competitors on employment as a factor favouring exemption of the agreement. The stronger references to full employment in, and the social objectives of, the Lisbon Treaty might induce arguments that a broader industrial policy standard should apply, rendering the above considerations more important.[250]

Turning to the consideration of 'financial constraints', this consideration reflects a concern that high fines might force an offending firm into insolvency. The EC and the US competition authorities have wide discretion and apparent lack of transparency in awarding these discounts. However, factors external to competition policy, in particular the social objectives of the EC Treaty, may determine how they are granted.

The Commission has accepted such discounts in crisis industries, but in general not for firms in crisis. In crisis situations firms can be involved in cartels and may end up not paying a fine, thus increasing their profits from collusion and their tendency to be in cartels (in the absence of criminal sanctions). The US, the UK, Ireland and Germany, for example, have criminal and civil penalties for corporate and/or individual violations of their antitrust laws, while the EC has a civil penalty only against the corporation. A possible compensation for the lack of deterrence due to the reduction in the fine is criminalization. With criminalization, the financial viability of the firm is not adversely affected, while at the same time deterrence is maintained, if not increased. The key significance of the criminal regime from an enforcement perspective lies in its deterrence value and, in particular, its separation of the interests of individuals from those of the businesses that employ them. A report was prepared for the OFT by Deloitte,[251] in which competition lawyers and companies were asked about the relative importance of various factors in deterring infringements of competition law. The lawyers and companies surveyed regarded criminal penalties as being the most important.[252]

[248] Twenty-third Report on Competition Policy, para. 85.

[249] Twenty-third Report on Competition Policy, para. 88.

[250] See www.wilmerhale.com/publications/whPubsDetail.aspx?publication=9321.

[251] The deterrent effect of competition enforcement by the OFT, November 2007 (OFT962), available at www.oft.gov.uk.

[252] The deterrent effect of competition enforcement by the OFT, November 2007 (OFT962), available at www.oft.gov.uk, paras. 5.55–5.59.

Where cartel prohibitions are enforced with criminal sanctions on individuals (including imprisonment), the standard of proof has to be particularly high ('beyond any reasonable doubt') and it is more difficult to discharge the burden of proof without the active help of cartel members; that is, without admissions and without the agreement of the companies. These personal risks also have the effect of further destabilizing cartels, making it more likely that, once entered into, they will not be sustained. When operating alongside an effective leniency policy that aligns the interests of individuals with those of their employers, together with other sources of intelligence, it also means that cartels are more likely to be detected and punished, thus reinforcing deterrence, especially in the presence of reduced fines that will ensure the viability of undertakings.

The imposition of fines that risk driving companies out of business is not acceptable to competition authorities for four main reasons. Stephan has argued that anything that increases the risk of bankruptcy imposes a social cost,[253] which, according to Posner,[254] consists of the transfer of wealth away from shareholders, managers, employees and creditors; reductions in efficiency of asset use; cost to creditors who will not be paid; and cost to other firms who relied on the bankrupt firm as a customer.[255]

A high fine may induce severe liquidity problems to firms, some of which may go bankrupt. In such a case, the resulting increase in concentration in the market renders collusion more likely. As the market becomes more concentrated firms may use this increased concentration in order to reap benefits from anti-competitive conduct. A high fine is likely to induce intensive political lobbying against its imposition. In addition, if firms go bankrupt then parties injured by collusion will not be able to claim damages.

A firm's fine for its infringement in Europe is calculated as a percentage of its annual turnover. Firms in a market experiencing crisis are likely to face liquidity problems and the fine will be calculated on a lower turnover, thus it will be lower than would have been the case had the crisis not occurred. We should note that the lower magnitude of the fine does not eliminate the risk that the firm may go bankrupt as a result of the fine.

[253] Stephan 2006.

[254] R.A. Posner, *Antitrust: Cases, Economic Notes and Other Materials*, 2nd ed., West Publishing, 1981.

[255] The cost of professional services such as lawyers and bankers that are related to the bankruptcy proceedings can run into hundreds of millions of dollars. See further Stephan 2006.

On the other hand, the availability of a financial-constraint defence aiming at reducing fines encourages the creation of cartels as actual levels of fines are reduced. When a cartelist knows that the fine will never be high enough to threaten its financial viability, there is an incentive for it to intensify the infringement as the fines are reduced due to the financial-constraint defence. According to paragraph 35 of the EC guidance on fines,

> In exceptional cases, the Commission may, upon request, take account of the undertaking's inability to pay in a specific social and economic context. It will not base any reduction granted for this reason in the fine on the mere finding of an adverse or loss-making financial situation. A reduction could be granted solely on the basis of objective evidence that imposition of the fine as provided for in these Guidelines would irretrievably jeopardise the economic viability of the undertaking concerned and cause its assets to lose all their value.

To understand the importance of the 'social context', one must review the Treaty establishing the European Community. In addition, according to Article 3 of the Lisbon Treaty,

> The Union shall establish an internal market. It shall work for the sustainable development of Europe based on balanced economic growth and price stability, a highly competitive social market economy, aiming at full employment and social progress, and a high level of protection and improvement of the quality of the environment. It shall promote scientific and technological advance.
>
> It shall combat social exclusion and discrimination, and shall promote social justice and protection, equality between women and men, solidarity between generations and protection of the rights of the child.
>
> It shall promote economic, social and territorial cohesion, and solidarity among Member States.
>
> It shall respect its rich cultural and linguistic diversity, and shall ensure that Europe's cultural heritage is safeguarded and enhanced.

Bankruptcy of firms resulting from the imposition of high fines has, of course, adverse effects on employment. As mentioned above, promoting employment and social protection are two tasks that are central to the EC Treaty. This might induce arguments that a broader industrial policy standard should apply.[256]

The drawback of the financial-constraints defence is that it leads to lower fines and, in the absence of other penalties such as criminal sanctions, may lead to decreased deterrence and to increased likelihood of cartel formation. In addition, the lack of transparency and absence of

[256] See www.wilmerhale.com/publications/whPubsDetail.aspx?publication=9321.

clear criteria for the financial-constraints defence may lead to an exploitation of the Commission's discretion, resulting in fines that do not endanger the viability of the firm.

The case law analysed earlier in this book illustrates the approach the US and the EU competition authorities take in relation to this consideration. In the US, the DOJ can impose criminal sanctions, as well as treble damages in civil antitrust actions, which can 'compensate' for any reduction in fines. As Stephan notes, in the DOJ's *Graphite Electrodes* case, two executives of UCAR were jailed for seventeen months and nine months respectively and a total of seven other executives were prosecuted and fined.[257] As mentioned in the chapter analysing crisis cartels, UCAR received a reduction in its fine. However, cartel deterrence was enhanced by the imposition of the jail sentences.

In the *French Beef*[258] case the Commission alleged that French federations in the beef sector were involved in a price-fixing cartel. Considering the specific economic context of the case, the Commission emphasized that measures had already been taken under the Common Market organization for beef in order to attenuate the crisis in the sector, and thus additional initiatives involving anti-competitive conduct could not be justified.

As the CFI stated regarding the economic context,[259]

> the economic context was characterised by the following factors: first, the drop in the consumption of beef as a result of the 'mad-cow' crisis, which affected a sector already in a difficult situation; second, intervention measures taken by the Community and national authorities aimed at restoring balance in the beef market; third, the loss of consumer confidence, linked to the fear of 'mad cow' disease; fourth, the situation of farmers who, despite Community adjustment measures applied by France, were faced with slaughterhouse entry prices for cows which were falling again, while consumer prices remained stable.

In December 2006, the CFI reduced the fines imposed by the Commission on the main French federations in the beef sector.[260] The

[257] Stephan 2006.

[258] Decision, [2003] OJ L209/12.IP/03/1105, 23 July 2003.

[259] *Fédération nationale de la coopération bétail et viande (FNCBV) and Fédération nationale des syndicats d'exploitants agricoles (FNSEA) v. Commission of the European Communities* (T-217/03 and T-245/03), 13 December 2006, para. 356.

[260] *Fédération nationale de la coopération bétail et viande (FNCBV) and Fédération nationale des syndicats d'exploitants agricoles (FNSEA) v. Commission of the European Communities* (T-217/03 and T-245/03), 13 December 2006.

overall fines concerned were reduced from €15.96 to €11.97 million. The CFI rejected the appeals ruled but argued that

> the 60% reduction in the fines decided upon by the Commission pursuant to Section 5(b) of the Guidelines, although substantial, does not take sufficient account of all those exceptional circumstances.[261]

As the above analysis illustrates, the EU and the US authorities have accepted the financial-constraints argument in their assessment of cartels and have thus been lenient when imposing fines. The existence of such an argument may incentivize parties in industries experiencing difficulties to conclude cartel agreements and then, once caught, invoke this argument and achieve a reduced fine. Thus the likely payoff of such a cartel agreement is higher than would be the case without invoking the financial-constraints argument, and is likely to induce parties to engage in cartel agreements – the defence induces enhanced incentives as well as decreased deterrence. Thus it should be used with caution. However, the viability of a company is a factor that should be taken into consideration by competition authorities when setting the level of a fine.

A market in which the number of firms will have been reduced due to bankruptcy of incumbents as a result of high fines far from enhances consumer welfare. To the extent that the firms that exit the market are the least efficient ones, consumer welfare is enhanced. Fines that cause a firm to go out of business may be beneficial to competition policy only if bankruptcies lead to a reduction in overcapacity and to a mitigation of inefficiencies.

However, in periods of crisis, firms may face liquidity constraints as well as decrease in demand that mitigates their efficiency. Thus although in the absence of the crisis these firms could be operating efficiently, due to the crisis they face difficulties in their operation. Once the crisis is over, however, these firms are likely to return to efficient operation. Thus although during a crisis a firm may appear to be inefficient and should not be prevented from exiting the market as a result of a high fine, in reality the exit of this firm may adversely affect efficiency in the market once the crisis is over. Otherwise efficient firms (which appeared inefficient due to the crisis) will have exited the market once the crisis is over.

[261] *Fédération nationale de la coopération bétail et viande* (T-217/03), 13 December 2006, paras. 358–61.

Without industry-wide agreement on capacity reduction that can be achieved through a crisis cartel, smaller firms may exit the market, thus leaving a limited number of choices for customers as well as inducing unemployment. In such conditions, firms may operate at inefficient output levels and may even incur losses. The Treaty of Rome did not contain any clauses regarding crisis conditions. When the treaty was signed, economic expansion seemed likely to continue. Due to the lack of express clauses in the Treaty of Rome the Commission could not justify applying the Article 101(3) criteria. Thus the Commission initially merely reduced fines on cartels in crisis situations.

As the above analysis illustrates, crisis cartel agreements should not be automatically prohibited and the financial-constraints defence should be taken into consideration during periods of crisis. Intuitively, given a choice between a market with a small number of remaining firms and a market with a significant number of firms which have decided to co-ordinate capacity reduction during the crisis, the latter alternative may be more beneficial to the market in the long term. We should note that in the latter scenario, as soon as the adverse conditions in the market under the crisis cease to exist, and following expiration of the crisis cartel agreement, the structure of the resulting market is likely to have a greater potential to return to pre-crisis competition levels due to the survival and existence of a larger number of firms. Of course, any likely adherence (either intentional or due to undertakings becoming used to behaving in a certain way) of the undertakings to the crisis cartel agreement should be assessed by the competition authorities and should be penalized accordingly. Existence of criminal sanctions, as well as of leniency programmes, can ensure deterrence once the crisis is over and normal market conditions resume.

As analysed herein, crisis cartel agreements can ensure the sustainability of an industry that is in crisis. Such agreements need to satisfy the criteria the Commission outlined in the twenty-third Report on Competition Policy. The Commission argued that it may condone such agreements which will aim at reducing overcapacity as long as the agreement applies to a sector as a whole. Such agreements will not involve price-fixing or quota arrangements and will not impair the free decision-making of firms.[262]

[262] Twenty-third Report on Competition Policy, para. 84.

Such agreements need to operate within a specific time frame, which will not exceed the duration of the crisis. As regards the identification of the end of the crisis, economists argue that once the results at the end of a quarter show positive growth (irrespective of how low), the economy, which has been experiencing negative growth for two or more consecutive quarters (and thus is in recession), has overcome the crisis.[263] The equivalent analysis may apply to particular sectors of an economy if those sectors are experiencing a severe crisis. Thus the duration of a crisis cartel agreement can match the duration of the crisis that harms the sector or the whole economy. Alternatively, depending on the case at hand, the cartel crisis agreement may implement a co-ordinated one-off decrease in capacity, and then the firms will return to normal competitive interaction. The limited duration of the crisis cartel agreement will prevent both adherence of the undertakings to the cartelistic conduct and the repetition of such conduct.

Competition authorities should, of course, adopt a case-by-case approach in assessing crisis cartel agreements. As mentioned above, they should focus on the economic context of each case. The Advocate General in *Montecatini v. Commission* argued that it follows from the scheme of Article 101 that account is to be taken under Article 101(1) only of the elements of the legal and economic context which could cast doubt on the existence of a restriction of competition.[264] He added (and then explained),

> In examining whether agreements like the BIDS agreements have as their object the restriction of competition, the following approach is to be taken. First of all, it must be considered whether such agreements have restrictions of competition as their necessary consequence or are aimed at limiting the freedom of the parties to determine their policy on the market independently (1) and thereby at affecting market conditions (2). Subsequently it must be examined as part of an overall assessment whether the restrictive elements are necessary in order to achieve a pro-competitive object or a primary objective which does not come under the fundamental prohibition contained in Article 101(1) EC (3).

[263] Technically speaking, a growth in the gross domestic product will evidence an end of the recession. However, since a crisis is usually accompanied by a recession, the fact that the recession is over is considered a strong indicator that the crisis is over. Unfortunately, there is no precise measuring element to determine when a crisis is over, which is not the case with a recession.

[264] See, in particular, C-235/92 P, *Montecatini v. Commission*, [1999] ECR I-4539, paras. 114–28.

According to the ECJ, the BIDS arrangements were intended to enable several undertakings to implement a common policy which had as its object the encouragement of some of them to withdraw from the market and the reduction, as a consequence, of the overcapacity which affected their profitability by preventing them from achieving economies of scale. In addition, the means put in place to attain the objective of the BIDS arrangements included restrictions whose object was anti-competitive.[265] Thus a crisis cartel agreement that will not lead to exit of firms may not be deemed to have as its object the restriction of competition.

The Advocate General set out three categories in which the assumption of a restriction of competition may be rejected, or at least doubted, on the basis of the factual or legal context.[266] The first category of cases includes those where a limitation of the freedom of undertakings to determine their policy in the market independently has no effects in relation to competition. This may be the case where it is doubtful whether the undertakings party to the agreement are competing among themselves,[267] as well as where it is doubtful whether there is actually sufficient competition which can be restricted by the agreement.[268] In periods of crisis, the competitive interaction of undertakings may be at best limited. Due to adverse market conditions and stagnated demand, competition between firms may not be sufficient, and thus, even if it is restricted, the assumption of a restriction of competition may be rejected or at least doubted.

The second category concerns cases in which an agreement is ambivalent in terms of its effects on competition. If the object of an agreement is to promote competition, for example by strengthening competition in a market, opening up a market or allowing a new competitor to access a market, the necessary restriction of the requirement of independence can give way to the aim of promoting competition.[269] Thus if the object of a crisis cartel agreement is to sustain the viability of the firms in the

[265] Including the levy of €11 per head of cattle slaughtered beyond the usual volume of production of each of the stayers, restrictions imposed on the goers as regards the disposal and use of their processing plants and a non-competition clause imposed on the goers.

[266] See further the Advocate General's Opinion.

[267] Case T-374/94, *European Night Services*, [1998] ECR II-3141.

[268] T168/01, *GlaxoSmithKline Services v. Commission*.

[269] Case 258/78, *Nungesser and Eisele v. Commission*, [1982] ECR 2015; Case 26/76, *MetroSB-Großmärkte v. Commission*, [1977] ECR 1875.

market, then again the assumption of a restriction of competition may be rejected or at least doubted.[270]

Finally, the Advocate General added that factors which are not capable of casting doubt on the existence of a restriction of competition, such as improvements in the production of goods as a result of economies of scale, may not be taken into account in the context of Article 101(1), but only in the context of Article 101(3), even where they are ultimately to be assessed positively in terms of an agreement's compatibility with Article 101.

Crisis cartel agreements should not automatically be deemed illegal; rather, their aims and effects should be assessed in order to balance the negative impact of crisis cartel agreements against the positive effects of sustaining the viability of undertakings in the market, which can ensure the availability of consumer choices once the crisis is over. Assessment of such agreements can thus proceed pursuant to Article 101(3) in balancing the positive and negative effects of the agreement. Factors which are not capable of casting doubt on the existence of a restriction of competition, such as improvements in the production of goods as a result of economies of scale, may not be taken into account in the context of Article 101(1), but only in the context of Article 101(3), even where they are ultimately to be assessed positively in terms of an agreement's compatibility with Article 101.

This strict case-by-case approach and the justification of the treatment of a crisis cartel agreement will prevent adverse precedential issues for competition authorities. Competition authorities need to make clear in their decisions that the approach they adopt in allowing a crisis cartel agreement has, as mentioned above, limited duration, applies to specific sectors and is justified by the adverse impact of the crisis on the specific sector. Following such an approach will prevent setting precedents

[270] The advocate general added a third category concerning ancillary arrangements which are necessary in order to pursue a primary objective. If the primary objective pursued does not come under the fundamental prohibition contained in Article 101(1) because it is neutral as regards competition or because it promotes competition, the ancillary arrangements which are necessary to achieve that objective do not come under the fundamental prohibition in Article 101(1) either. A restriction of competition cannot be taken to exist in such cases. If, on the other hand, the primary objective pursued comes under the fundamental prohibition laid down in Article 101(1), there is a restriction of competition. See further Case 42/84, *Remia and Others v. Commission*, [1985] ECR 2545; C-250/92, *DLG*, [1994] ECR I-5641; C-309/99, *Wouters and Others*, [2002] ECR I-1577; C-519/04 P, *Meca-Medina and Majcen v. Commission*, [2006] ECR I-6991.

which may unnecessarily complicate enforcement of competition in periods not characterized by crisis.

It is essential for competition authorities to consider such issues carefully, following a pragmatic approach, as there is the risk of harm to consumer welfare as a result of strict and non-pragmatic enforcement of competition legislation. The chairman of the Competition Committee of the OECD, Frederic Jenny, noted, 'the biggest problem is to convince legislators or executive branches of the government that competition authorities can make positive contributions during crises and that competition law can be adapted in scope, time and focus'.[271] Thus competition policy should be adapted along the lines suggested in the analysis here in crisis situations in order to prevent the market from worsening further.

7.7 State aid amidst crises

When the financial crisis broke out in September 2008,[272] member states and EU institutions responded with a variety of policy instruments. Member states primarily injected capital into banks and raised deposit guarantees to reassure the public and prevent runs on banks.[273]

European institutions also acted, but with varying degrees of speed and effectiveness. The European Central Bank immediately extended credit lines and increased liquidity in financial markets to prevent them from freezing up completely.

The European Commission intervened to ensure that national measures to prop up banking activities were not discriminatory. Then it issued new guidelines on state aid to banks and committed itself to deal with notified measures within record time, normally not more than two days. In December 2008 it broadened the new rules to cover the real economy as well.

The Council recommended that member states increase public spending by about €200 billion. However, most of that money was not new; it was to come from accelerated uptake of structural funds.

[271] Summary Record of the Discussion on Competition and Financial Markets, DAF/COMP/M(2009)1/ANN4, 10 April 2009, Roundtable 2 on Crisis: The Role of Competition Policy in Financial Sector Rescue and Restructuring, available at www.oecd.org.

[272] This part of this chapter is authored by Professor Phedon Nicolaides.

[273] UK, NN 41/2008; Ireland, NN 48/2008; Denmark, NN 51/2008; Sweden and Spain, N 337/2009.

The policy measures mentioned above have been coupled with proposals for significant institutional change. In 2009 the EU began discussion on possible reform of the regulatory framework for financial services. On the basis of recommendations made by the so-called 'de Larosière' report,[274] the Commission proposed in the autumn of 2009 the establishment of four new institutions: a European Systemic Risk Board, a European Banking Authority, a European Insurance and Occupational Pensions Authority and a European Securities Authority.[275] Deliberations on the structure and mandate of these new entities are still ongoing.

However, of all policy instruments at the disposal of EU institutions, the most extensively used were the rules on state aid. The Commission had to intervene on a number of occasions to prevent distortions in the internal market and then to lay down new rules concerning aid to financial institutions and enterprises in the real economy.

The first challenge to the functioning of the internal market came in mid-September 2008 with the announcement of the Irish government that it would cover only six Irish banks with a state guarantee scheme. That presented the serious risk of a large outflow of capital from non-eligible competitors. The Commission asked the Irish government to broaden the coverage of the scheme so that the guarantee would be available to all banks with subsidiaries or branches in Ireland having a significant presence in the domestic economy.[276]

Similarly, when France announced its planned aid to the automotive sector, which originally raised concerns concerning state aid and the integrity of the internal market (because it was offered on condition that the recipients repatriated their activities to France), the Commission stated without ambiguity that any aid granted under additional non-commercial conditions concerning the location of investments (and/or the geographic distribution of restructuring measures in another case) could not be regarded as compatible. After intensive discussion between the Commission and the French authorities, France committed itself to avoiding any conditions contrary to the rules of the single market. This

[274] See http://ec.europa.eu/internal_market/finances/docs/de_larosiere_report_en.pdf.

[275] Proposal for a Regulation on Community macro prudential oversight of the financial system and establishing a European Systemic Risk Board, 2009/0140 (COD).

[276] NN 48/2008. The original Irish scheme had to be modified, in order to delete any discriminatory coverage of banks with systemic relevance to the Irish economy. See press release MEMO/08/615.

line has been maintained in all other cases, in particular with regard to the German plans in relation to Opel.

Within a mere couple of weeks from the outbreak of the crisis, it became obvious that existing state aid rules were not suitable for dealing effectively with the problems facing financial markets. The Commission, therefore, proceeded to adopt new rules in relation to the following:

- the application of state aid rules to measures taken in relation to financial institutions in the context of the current global financial crisis, 13 October 2008;
- the recapitalization of financial institutions in the current financial crisis: limitation of aid to the minimum necessary and safeguards against undue distortions of competition, 5 December 2008;
- the treatment of impaired assets in the Community banking sector, 25 February 2009;
- a temporary framework for state aid measures to support access to finance in the current financial and economic crisis, adopted on 17 December 2008 (see as amended on 25 February 2009, 28 October 2009 and in December 2009); and
- the return to viability and the assessment of restructuring measures in the financial sector in the current crisis under the state aid rules, 23 July 2009.

7.7.1 The new state aid rules

The Banking Communication

The Commission published, on 13 October 2008, a Communication on the application of state aid rules to measures taken in relation to financial institutions.[277] The aim was to return financial institutions to long-term viability in as orderly a manner as possible through restructuring operations, rather than their being liquidated.

According to the Communication, support schemes introduced by the member states, such as guarantees to cover their liabilities or recapitalization schemes, can be approved by the Commission in an accelerated procedure if they fulfil conditions which guarantee that they are well targeted and proportionate (paragraph 15) to the objective of stabilizing financial markets, and that they contain certain safeguards against unnecessary negative effects on competition.

[277] OJ C 270/8, 2008.

The Commission first reiterates the general principles governing the aid to individual undertakings in difficulty (i.e. Article 107(3)(c) and Rescue and Restructuring Guidelines). In addition, aid under Article 107(3)(b) is recognized, in the light of the seriousness of the crisis of the financial markets, as a possible legal basis for exemption (paragraph 9) if member states declare to the Commission that there is a risk of serious disturbance. Ad hoc intervention of the member states under Article 107(3)(b) is not excluded (paragraph 10).

However, the Commission emphasizes the exceptional character of this exemption and that it cannot be used as a matter of principle in other sectors in the absence of a risk that they have an immediate impact on the economy of the member state as a whole (paragraph 11) and that the measures can be applied only as long as the crisis situation persists (paragraph 12). Therefore reviews carried out at least every six months, as well as reports to the Commission, are prescribed for the member states (paragraph 13).

The Communication distinguishes between illiquid but otherwise fundamentally sound financial institutions and financial institutions characterized by endogenous problems. The former category requires less substantial restructuring, whereas the latter fits within the normal framework of rescue aid (paragraph 14).

Allowable measures are divided into two groups: guarantees covering the liabilities of financial institutions and recapitalization of financial institutions.

As regards the category of guarantees covering the liabilities of financial institutions, objective and non-discriminatory eligibility criteria are required (paragraph 18). With respect to the material scope of the guarantee, general guarantees protecting retail deposits (and debt held by retail clients) are accepted as a legitimate component of the public-policy scheme. Additional criteria are laid down for guarantees going beyond retail deposits (paragraph 20), wholesale deposits and short and medium debt instruments (paragraph 21). Any extension to other types of guarantee beyond those mentioned above requires closer scrutiny. Subordinated debt or an indiscriminate coverage of all liabilities is explicitly excluded.

National schemes must be limited in time. This means that their duration should not go beyond the minimum necessary and member states are obliged to carry out reviews every six months, assessing the justification and the potential need for adjustment (paragraph 24). In addition, aid must be limited to the strict minimum, and a significant contribution from the beneficiaries and/or the sector should be ensured. In order to avoid undue distortion of competition, member states must include a combination of behavioural constraints or appropriate provisions enforcing behavioural constraints, ensuring that the beneficiary does not engage in aggressive expansion (paragraph 27). Another instrument for avoiding distortions of competition is adjustment measures for the sector as a whole and/or the restructuring or liquidation of individual beneficiaries.

As regards the recapitalization of financial institutions, the rules on the general guarantee schemes regarding non-discrimination, temporal limitations, necessity of aid and safeguards apply *mutatis mutandis* (paragraph 36).

A special section of the Communication deals with the controlled winding-up of financial institutions (paragraph 43(f)). The rules set out for guarantee schemes apply. In the context of a liquidation, the possibility of a benefit of any aid to shareholders or creditors should be excluded (paragraph 46). The document lists the criteria taken into account by the Commission in determining the potential existence of aid to the buyers of the financial institution or of parts of it (paragraph 49).

The Commission expects member states to inform it of their intentions and notify their measures as early as possible, in any event before the implementation of the measures in question. Such notifications could be dealt with, if necessary, within twenty-four hours or over a weekend.

The Recapitalization Communication

The deterioration of credit-lending conditions in autumn 2008 threatened to affect the real economy and many states decided to support financial institutions with capital injections, in order to induce them to continue lending to the real economy. On 5 December 2008, the Commission adopted a Communication on the Recapitalization of financial institutions in the current crisis.[278]

Up to that date, the Commission had approved recapitalization schemes in three member states,[279] as well as individual recapitalization measures based on the Banking Communication.[280] However, the latter document proved insufficient, as many states envisaged the

[278] OJ C 16, 2009, pp. 2–10, consolidated version OJ C 83, 2009.

[279] N507/08, N512/08, N560/08.

[280] N528/08, NN68/08.

recapitalization of banks not primarily as a rescue but rather to ensure lending to the real economy.

The common objectives of the Communication are to restore the financial stability of the banks, to ensure lending to the real economy and to avoid the systemic risk of possible insolvencies.

The Commission stated that as a result of a recapitalization scheme or measure, distortions of competition can arise cumulatively on three levels (paragraph 7(f)). First, the bank would get an undue competitive advantage over banks in other member states and this could lead to a subsidy race among member states. Second, schemes targeting all banks within a member state without any degree of differentiation according to risk profiles may give an advantage to distressed or less-well-performing banks. Third, recapitalization should not put banks that do not have recourse to public funding but seek additional capital on the market in a significantly less competitive position.

In order to strike a balance between these concerns and the need to restore financial stability, state interventions must be therefore proportional and temporary (paragraph 11) and they must distinguish between fundamentally sound and less-well-performing banks (paragraph 12). The Commission pointed out that it will pay particular attention to the risk profile of the beneficiaries (paragraph 13) and that it will need a basis for a differentiation of remuneration rates for different banks such as compliance with regulatory solvency requirements and prospective capital adequacy, pre-crisis spreads and ratings (paragraph 14).

The Communication took into account the methodology for benchmarking the state recapitalization measures for fundamentally sound institutions in the euro area adopted by the Governing Council of the European Central Bank (ECB) on 20 November 2008 (paragraph 16). The latter document proposed a pricing scheme for capital injection based on a corridor for rates of return for beneficiary banks which, notwithstanding variations in their risk profile, are fundamentally sound (paragraph 17). The Commission Communication extended the guidance to cover conditions other than the remuneration rates and terms under which banks which are not fundamentally sound may have access to public capital. The Commission expressed the view that recapitalization measures by member states should take into account the underestimation of risk in the pre-crisis period (paragraph 18).

The document details the principles governing the different types of recapitalization, i.e. recapitalization at current market rates (point 2(1)) and the temporary recapitalization of fundamentally sound banks in order to foster financial stability and lending to the real economy (point 2(2)). The first category deals with capital injections on equal terms with significant participation of private investors. As regards the second category, a distinction between fundamentally sound and other banks is made. The conditions for an overall remuneration (paragraph 23) and the total expected return on capitalization (paragraph 25) are presented in detail.

As regards the method for determining the price of recapitalization for fundamentally sound banks, the Eurosystem recommendation of 20 November 2008 is mentioned (paragraph 26).

The Communication contains incentives for state capital redemption (paragraph 31(f)) which must be used by member states in order to force banks to redeem state capital when the market allows. A clear exit mechanism will be assessed on a case-by-case basis and is more necessary the higher the size of recapitalization and the higher the risk profile of the bank.

The Communication refers to the safeguards against possible abuses and distortions of competition mentioned in the Banking Communication (paragraph 35). High remunerations require fewer safeguards; however, safeguards may be necessary to prevent aggressive commercial expansion financed by state aid (paragraph 37) and mergers and acquisitions should be organized on the basis of a competitive tendering process.

As in the Banking Communication, a regular review is prescribed (paragraph 40). Stricter requirements apply to banks which are not fundamentally sound (paragraph 43(f)).

The Impaired Assets Communication

State aid offered to banks proved to be an important tool in coping with the crisis, but it could not avoid the structural reform of individual banks. In addition to restructuring measures, cleaning up impaired assets was necessary for many banks. In order to provide guidance to the state interventions for financial institutions to clean their balance sheets of 'toxic assets', the Commission adopted, on 25 February 2009, a Communication on the treatment of impaired assets in the EU banking sector.[281]

The Communication offers specific guidance on the application of state aid rules to asset relief. Asset relief can be a measure to safeguard

[281] OJ C 72, 26 March 2009, pp. 1–22.

financial stability and underpin the supply of credit to the real economy, as it directly addresses uncertainty regarding the quality of bank sheets and revives confidence in the sector (paragraph 7). Not only should the immediate objectives of safeguarding financial stability (paragraph 8) be pursued, but also such long-term considerations as behavioural safeguards and restructuring should be included in a government intervention (paragraph 9).

As regards the application of state aid rules to asset relief measures, public asset relief measures constitute state aid if they free the beneficiary bank from the need to register a loss or a reserve for a possible loss on its impaired assets and/or free regulatory capital for other purposes (paragraph 15). Asset relief measures must comply with the general principles of necessity, proportionality and minimization of competition; distortion should be clearly defined and identified (paragraph 19(f)) and based on objective criteria in order to avoid individual banks taking unwarranted advantage. The Communication defines criteria for minimizing the risk of or recurrent need for state interventions in favour of the same beneficiary (*ex ante* transparency and disclosure of impairments by eligible banks and a viability review) (paragraph 20) as well as the rules on the sharing of the burden of costs between the state, shareholders and creditors (paragraph 21). State aid in the form of guarantee or asset purchase can be awarded to banks if putting a bank into administration or its orderly winding up appear inadvisable for reasons of financial stability (paragraph 23). In this case, the aid is meant to allow the bank to operate for the period necessary for a restructuring or winding-up plan to be devised.

In order to give incentives for banks to participate in asset relief with public-policy objectives, an enrolment window limited to six months from the launch of the scheme by the government should be introduced (paragraph 26). Participation in the scheme may be mandatory or voluntary. In the latter situation, additional incentives may be provided to the banks so as to facilitate take-up. However, the principles of transparency and disclosure, fair valuation and burden-sharing must be respected (paragraph 28). Behavioural constraints should always condition access to asset relief.

The Communication introduces criteria for eligibility (paragraph 32(f)), valuation, pricing (paragraph 37(f)) and management of assets (paragraph 44(f)).

In the context of asset relief measures, state aid rules aim at ensuring the minimum and least-distortive support in order to prepare solid ground for a return to long-term viability without state support. However, the banks themselves have to take appropriate measures to avoid recurrence of similar problems and ensure future profitability. The Communication details the general rescue and restructuring conditions in the particular context of asset relief (paragraph 49(f)).

The Restructuring Communication for Financial Institutions

The Restructuring Communication complements the previous guidance on the assessment of state aid for banks concerning guarantees, recapitalization and the treatment of impaired assets. These communications have explained in particular the conditions under which banks are required to submit a restructuring plan. The new Communication adopted on 14 August 2009 outlines how the competition rules will be applied to support financial stability, as the return of banks to viability is the best guarantee for stability and for their sustained ability to lend to the economy.[282]

Restoring the long-term viability of financial institutions is the central issue of this Communication. However, criteria for restructuring have been detailed in the Banking Communication, the Impaired Assets Communication and the Recapitalization Communication. The present Communication complements the existing criteria and explains how the Commission will asses the compatibility of restructuring aid to financial institutions under Article 104(3)(b) (paragraph 4). The restructuring plans submitted by member states should be comprehensive, detailed and based on coherent concepts, and must include a comparison with alternative options (paragraph 9). When a bank cannot be restored to viability, the restructuring plan will indicate how to wind it up in an orderly fashion.

The Communication outlines the information necessary to be included in a restructuring plan (paragraph 11). A return to viability should mainly derive from internal measures and banks are expected to withdraw in the medium term from activities which remain structurally loss-making (paragraph 12).

The criteria for determining the long-term viability of a bank are presented in detail (paragraph 13). The Commission requires not only base scenarios, but also 'stress' scenarios and worst-case assumptions. Long-term viability requires either that the aid is redeemed over time, or that a remuneration according to normal market conditions is paid (paragraph

[282] OJ C 195, 19 August 2009, pp. 9–20.

14). Although the restructuring period should be as short as possible, the Commission may allow structural measures to be completed within a longer time horizon, in order to avoid depressing the markets (paragraph 15). Aid initially not foreseen in the plan but which appears necessary during the restructuring period is subject to individual *ex ante* notification (paragraph 16).

The second possibility for the return to viability – that is, viability through the sale of a bank – is permitted if a viable purchaser is found (paragraph 17) through a transparent, objective, unconditional and non-discriminatory procedure (paragraph 18). However, requirements of viability, own contribution and limitation of the distortion of competition need to be respected.

As regards the state aid issues concerning the buyer and/or the sold activity, an open and unconditional competitive tender in which the assets go to the highest bidder excludes state aid for the buyer (paragraph 20). Exceptionally, a negative price may involve no state aid if the seller would have to bear higher costs in the event of liquidation.

If a return to long-term viability is not possible, a winding-up should be considered. The criteria set up in the Banking Communication will apply (paragraph 21). Acquisition of 'good' assets and liabilities or the creation of a 'good bank' may also be acceptable for viability (paragraph 21).

In order to ensure that rescued banks bear adequate responsibility for the consequences of their past behaviour and in order to create incentives for future behaviour, aid should be limited to covering costs which are necessary for the restoration of viability (paragraph 23) and the bank's own contribution to restructuring should be significant (paragraph 24(f)). However, an *ex ante* fixed threshold for burden-sharing is not required.

Banks are not allowed to use state aid to remunerate their own funds if these do not generate sufficient profit (paragraph 26). When justified by reasons of financial stability, provision of additional aid during the restructuring period is permitted (paragraph 27).

Although aid has positive spillover effects and is designed to support financial stability in times of systemic crisis, it can create distortions of competition in many ways: prolongation of past distortions created by excessive risk-taking and unsustainable business models, undermining the single market by shifting the share of the burden of structural adjustment to other member states, creating entry barriers and undermining incentives for cross-border activities (paragraph 28). In order to limit the distortions of competition, the Commission will assess the need for such a measure, the nature and form of the measure depending on the amount of the aid and the conditions under which it is granted (paragraph 31), and the characteristics of the market in which the beneficiary will operate (paragraph 32).

The Commission considers adequate remuneration of state interventions one of the most appropriate limitations of distortion of competition. However, an entry price at a level significantly below the market price may be accepted for reasons of financial stability if the terms of the financial support are revised in the restructuring plan so as to reduce the distortive effect of the subsidy (paragraph 34). Banks benefiting from state aid may be required to divest subsidiaries or branches, portfolios of customers or business units (paragraph 35) or to limit their expansion in certain business or geographical areas (paragraph 36). The Commission committed to paying attention to the need to avoid retrenchment within national borders and fragmentation of the single market.

As regards the time limit for the implementation, this can be extended if a buyer cannot be found and if a binding timetable for scaling down the business is provided (paragraph 37).

State aid cannot be used to fund anti-competitive behaviour such as acquisition of competing businesses (paragraph 40) or offering other terms which cannot be matched by competitors which do not receive aid (paragraph 44).

The Commission will request regular detailed reports on the implementation of the restructuring plan (paragraph 46). In case of doubts as to the compliance of the restructuring plan with the relevant requirements, the Commission will open a formal investigation (paragraph 47).

This Communication applies to restructuring aid notified before 31 December 2010.

The Temporary Framework for the real economy

The first actions taken by the Commission targeted the state aid rules in relation to financial institutions. The impact of the economic crisis was also felt in the private sector, a serious downturn affecting the wider economy and hitting households, businesses and jobs. Banks became much more risk-averse than in previous years and this led to a credit squeeze, which threatened to affect healthy companies. Therefore a framework setting up the rules for state intervention in this sector became necessary.

On 17 December 2008, the Commission adopted a Communication

setting up an EU Framework for state aid measures to support access to finance in the current financial and economic crisis which allowed member states to grant aid under existing instruments for all sectors of the economy through higher limits on grants, credit guarantees, risk capital and loans.[283]

While recognizing the need for new temporary state aid, the Commission pointed out that the challenge for the EU at that time was to avoid as much as possible public interventions which would undermine the objective of less and better-targeted state aid. Recognizing that state aid is no miracle cure for the current difficulties, the document states that competition rules should ensure a level playing field for European companies and avoid member states engaging in a subsidy race.

The objectives of this document are twofold: unblock bank lending to companies (especially small and medium enterprises – SMEs), and encourage companies to continue investing in the future, in particular in a sustainable growth economy.

The document groups the possible means of intervention into three categories: general measures which are not state aid, state aid on the basis of existing instruments and use of Article 107(3)(b) TFEU.

General economic policy measures are not considered state aid. For example, they may take the form of extension of payment deadlines for social security or taxes; granting financial support directly to the consumer, for instance for scrapping old products and/or buying new products; and using general EU programmes such as the Competitiveness and Innovation Framework Programme (2007–13)[284] and the Seventh Framework Programme of the European Community for research, technological development and demonstration activities (2007–13).[285]

The document makes reference to possible state aid under existing instruments: the general block exemption regulation, the *de minimis* regulation, the guidelines on state aid for environmental protection, the framework for state aid for research and development and innovation, the notice on the application of Articles 107 and 108 TFEU to state aid in the form of guarantees, the guidelines on state aid to promote risk capital

[283] Communication from the Commission – Temporary Framework for State Aid Measures to Support Access to Finance in the Current Financial and Economic Crisis, OJ C 16/01, 2009.

[284] OJ L 310, 9 November 2006, at p. 15.

[285] OJ L 412, 30 December 2006, at p. 1.

investments in SMEs, the guidelines on regional aid, and the guidelines on state aid for rescue and restructuring.

Concerning the applicability of Article 107(3)(b) TFEU, under the category of aid to remedy a serious disturbance in the economy of a member state, the Commission restates previous practice according to which the disturbance must affect the whole territory of the state concerned.[286] So in the light of the seriousness of the financial crisis, it concludes that support for the economy is needed beyond support for the financial system, and that certain categories might be justified, for a limited period of time, and declared compatible with the internal market on the basis of Article 107(3)(b) TFEU (point 4(1)). Article 107(3)(b) was previously used only once,[287] and was rejected on several occasions.[288]

An amendment of the Temporary Framework adopted on 25 February 2009 introduced the obligation of member states to show that the state aid measures of which the Commission has been notified under this Framework are necessary, appropriate and proportionate to remedy a serious disturbance in the economy of the member states concerned and that all conditions are fully respected.[289]

The aid granted under this legal basis was further divided into aid falling under the existing rules (e.g. *de minimis* regulation, state aid in the form of guarantees, aid in the form of subsidized interest rates, aid

[286] Joined Cases T-132/96 and T-143/96, *Freistaat Sachsen and Volkswagen AG v. Commission*, [1999] ECR II-3663, para. 167; Commission Decision 98/490/EC in Case C 47/96, *Crédit Lyonnais*, OJ L 221, 8 August 1998, p. 28, point 10.1; Commission Decision 2005/345/EC in Case C 28/02, *Bankgesellschaft Berlin*, OJ L 116, 4 May 2005, p. 1, points 153 et seq.; and Commission Decision 2008/263/EC in Case C 50/06, *BAWAG*, OJ L 83, 26 March 2008, p. 7, point 166. See Commission Decision in Case NN 70/07, *Northern Rock*, OJ C 43, 16 February 2008, p. 1; Commission Decision in Case NN 25/08, *Rescue aid to WestLB*, OJ C 189, 26 July 2008, p. 3; and Commission Decision of 4 June 2008 in Case C 9/08, *SachsenLB*, not yet published.

[287] As a result of the oil crisis, but only for the territory of Greece, (1987) OJ L 76/18. Greek privatization programme, XXI Competition Report, 1991, §251.

[288] *Crédit Lyonnais*, (1995) OJ L 308/92, *GAN*, (1997) OJ L 78/1, *Northern Rock* (NN70/07), *WestLB* (NN25/08), *Sachsen LB* (C9/08). A rise of 45 per cent in the fuel prices in Spain in the year 2000 was not considered to be a serious disturbance in the sense of this Article (C-73/03, *Spain v. Commission*), nor was the reunification of Germany a serious disturbance for the economy of Germany as a whole (joined Cases T-132/96 and T-143/96, *Freistaat Sachsen and Volkswagen AG v. Commission*, [1999] ECR II-3663, para. 170; C-301/96, *Germany v. Commission*, [2003] ECR I-9919, para. 105).

[289] Communication from the Commission – Amendment of the Temporary Framework for State Aid Measures to Support Access to Finance in the Current Financial and Economic Crisis, adopted on 25 Febuary 2009.

for the production of green products and risk capital measures) and new measures of aid falling under a temporary adaptation of the existing rules.

In the chapter dealing with *de minimis* aid, the Commission mentions a new form of aid amounting to €500,000 which, although falling within the scope of Article 107(1) TFEU, will be compatible on the basis of Article 107(3)(b) TFEU provided that a few conditions are met. The additional conditions for compatibility were the following:

- The aid does not exceed a cash grant of €500,000 per undertaking; all figures used must be gross – that is, before any deduction of tax or other charges; where aid is awarded in a form other than a grant, the aid amount is the gross grant equivalent of the aid.
- The aid is granted in the form of a scheme.
- The aid is granted to firms which were not in difficulty on 1 July 2008; it may be granted to firms that were not in difficulty at that date but entered in difficulty thereafter as a result of the global financial and economic crisis.
- The aid scheme does not apply to firms active in the fisheries sector.
- The aid is not export aid or aid favouring domestic over imported products.
- The aid is granted no later than 31 December 2010.
- Prior to granting the aid, the member state obtains a declaration from the undertaking concerned, in written or electronic form, about any other *de minimis* aid and aid pursuant to this measure received during the current fiscal year, and checks that the aid will not raise the total amount of aid received by the undertaking during the period from 1 January 2008 to 31 December 2010 to a level above the ceiling of €500,000.
- The aid scheme does not apply to undertakings active in the primary production of agricultural products; it may apply to undertakings active in the processing and marketing of agricultural products unless the amount of the aid is fixed on the basis of the price or quantity of such products purchased from primary producers or put on the market by the undertakings concerned, or the aid is conditional on being or entirely passed on to primary producers.

Mentioning this new form of compatible aid in the chapter regarding the *de minimis* regulation was rather confusing, as the maximum amount of aid was not set at €200,000 as in the former regulation, but at €500,000. The later amendments of the Temporary Framework did not shed light on this matter. However, it is now clear from the practice of the Commission that the two types of aid are different even though, until 31 December 2010, any *de minimis* award will have to be subtracted from the amount of €500,000 received by any single undertaking.

In addition, new aid in the form of guarantees (point 4(3)(2)), aid in the form of subsidized interest rates (point 4(4)(2)), aid for the production of green products (point 4(5)(2)), and risk capital measures (point 4(6)(2)) can be considered compatible with the common market on the basis of Article 107(3)(b) TFEU subject to some conditions.

As regards cumulation, the aid ceilings established in the Temporary Framework apply regardless of the origin of the aid (state or EU resources). However, the temporary aid measures cannot be cumulated with *de minimis* for the same eligible costs.

Application of the special state aid rules

Table 6.1 in the previous chapter shows the total reported amount of state aid in various forms for financial institutions. By the end of 2009 it had reached a staggering €3,630 billion. Table 6.2 lists the Commission decisions per member state and their outcomes. It is worth noting that of a total of eighty-one measures, seventy-five have been approved with no objections and only six have been approved conditionally. Table 6.3 lists eight measures concerning which the Commission had concerns and which were, as of December 2009, still under investigation. Even if Tables 6.2 and 6.3 are combined to give a grand total of eighty-nine measures, it is still possible to conclude that the Commission has approved unconditionally more than 85 per cent of national measures to combat the financial crisis.

Tables 6.4 and 6.5 show the number and type of measures adopted by each member state to support the real economy. There are sixty-six such measures. Table 6.6 lists the single case which was being investigated by the Commission. That is, of a grand total of sixty-seven measures, the Commission had concerns in only one case.

These statistics raise a fundamental question: has state aid control become too permissive as a result of the financial crisis? Certainly the outcome of the Commission's assessment of each notified case is a combination of two factors: (i) the requirements laid down by Commission guidelines and (ii) the contents of the measures which are formulated and notified by the member states. There is no doubt that the special rules for the financial-services sector are quite permissive. The mere fact that they exist at all signifies the intention of the Commission to allow aid for that particular sector. In addition, the Commission has been willing to apply laxer rules in view of the gravity of the situation in that sector. For example, and as will be shown in the two case studies below, banks that receive public funds for restructuring may not be required to undertake divestments to the same extent as other undertakings that had received aid for the same purpose in the past.

With regard to the real economy, the aid that is allowed by the Temporary Framework is mostly operating aid that would normally not be authorized. But here, again, the avowed intention is not to induce beneficiaries to undertake new investment but to release liquidity so that they are able to cover their day-to-day costs and remain in business.

As regards the design of the various national measures, the statistics reveal that member states have been quite adept at complying with the requirements of the new rules. The vast majority of their notifications have been approved by the Commission without objection. Given the fact that the new rules are very accommodating, one wonders why there was even a small minority of measures about the compatibility of which with the internal market the Commission expressed doubts. Again, as shown by the case studies below, the answer is likely to be that certain banks found themselves in such a complex situation and faced such difficult problems that the solutions they devised in co-operation with the member state authorities could not fit well into any set of EU rules. Therefore it was perhaps inevitable that the Commission would have concerns and would want to launch formal investigations.

Case studies

The two cases reviewed below demonstrate two important aspects of the application of state aid rules during the financial crisis. First, the Commission has been willing to adjust the rules to enable member states to address the crisis speedily and effectively. Not only did the Commission change the legal basis for assessing many of the emergency measures put in place by the member states (i.e. from Article 107(3)(c) to Article 107(3)(b) TFEU), but, probably more importantly, it also relaxed existing rules to give more leeway to the member states and the beneficiaries of state aid. For example, it did not insist that beneficiary banks would have to make large contributions to their own restructuring plans or that they should sell assets immediately as that would further depress their prices.

Second, the complexity of the problems facing financial institutions meant that member states had a difficult task in designing appropriate measures. Consequently, the Commission's task of assessing the various schemes was equally difficult. In many cases, such as Sachsen LB, WestLB, Dexia and Fortis, the issue was not just recapitalization. The real problem was to remove non-performing assets from the balance sheets of the banks to enable them to start lending again. It was not always easy to identify all the beneficiaries and calculate the amount of aid in the various state guarantees and capital injections.

Commission Decision C 9/2008 of 4 June 2008 on state aid to Sachsen LB This case involved a package of two different measures in favour of Sachsen LB. First, a number of German *Landesbanken* agreed to offer liquidity to Sachsen LB through a commitment to buy the commercial paper that was to be issued by one of its subsidiaries. The commitment would come into effect only if the commercial paper could not be placed on the market. The subsidiary in question functioned as a special conduit for the trading of asset-backed securities and found itself in trouble when the American subprime mortgage market collapsed. Second, Sachsen LB was to be sold to LBBW, which is the *Landesbank* of Baden-Württemberg. The sale was accompanied by a guarantee of €2.75 billion to cover potential losses.

In addition, Sachsen LB was to be restructured. The restructuring plan was produced by LBBW.

The Commission regarded the liquidity measure as state aid for the following reasons. First, the *Landesbanken* who committed themselves to buying the commercial paper of Sachsen LB's subsidiary were part of the state as they were closely affiliated with public authorities. Second, the market for that kind of commercial paper had dried up. Since no private investor would grant such liquidity, the Commission concluded that there was an advantage for Sachsen LB.

The sale of Sachsen LB to LBBW could involve state aid in two respects. First, to the buyer (i.e. LBBW), if too low a sales price were accepted, and second, to Sachsen LB, if liquidation would have been less costly than accepting and going through with the sale. While an open, transparent and unconditional sale signifies the absence of state aid, it does not follow that a negotiated sale necessarily contains state aid.

The Commission considered that the sale price paid by LBBW corresponded to the market value of Sachsen LB and that the State of Saxony conducted negotiations with several potential buyers and in the end decided to sell Sachsen LB to LBBW because it had made the best offer.

The Commission found no reason to suspect that Sachsen LB was sold at a price below its market value. Its conclusion was that there was no state aid to LBBW.

However, it also found that there was state aid to Sachsen LB because it would have been cheaper to the State of Saxony to liquidate the bank instead of selling it with the guarantee.

The next step in the Commission's analysis was its assessment of the compatibility of the aid with the internal market. It rejected German arguments for the aid to be declared compatible on the basis of Article 107(3)(b). The Commission decided that

> a serious economic disruption is not remedied by an aid measure that 'resolve[s] the problems of a single recipient . . . as opposed to the acute problems facing all operators in the industry'. Also in all cases of banks in difficulty, the Commission has to date not relied on this provision of the [EU] Treaty [paragraph 94].

It went on to observe that

> the investigation has confirmed the Commission's observation that the problems of Sachsen LB are due to company-specific events. Moreover, the information provided by the German authorities has not convinced the Commission that the systemic effects that might have resulted from a bankruptcy of Sachsen LB could have reached a size constituting 'a serious disturbance in the economy' of Germany within the meaning of Article 107(3)(b). Therefore, the present case must be regarded as based on individual problems, and thus requires tailor-made remedies, which can be addressed under the rules on firms in difficulty. The Commission therefore finds no grounds for compatibility of the measures on the basis of Article 107(3)(b) TFEU [paragraph 95].

These two paragraphs from the Commission's decision reveal the extent of the change in the Commission's attitude that occurred a mere two months later. In the first instances of support to financial institutions in late 2007 and early 2008, such as the rescue of Northern Rock, the Commission insisted on relying on Article 107(3)(c) TFEU and the Rescue and Restructuring Guidelines. However, as of September 2008, it changed tack and recognized the wider possibilities offered by Article 107(3)(b). While Article 107(3)(c) requires the 'development' of certain economic activities or sectors, Article 107(3)(b) allows for aid which is neither for rescuing or restructuring, nor for development. For example, state guarantees to creditors of banks or state guarantees for the debt held by banks would more naturally fall under Article 107(3)(b) rather than Article 107(3)(c).

In applying the conditions of the Rescue and Restructuring Guidelines, the Commission had to determine whether the bank would be returned to viability within a reasonable period of time (normally five years), whether the bank itself made a significant contribution to its restructuring and whether there were sufficient compensatory measures to reduce distortions to competition.

The Commission was satisfied that the restructuring plan addressed the source of the problems facing the bank and that Sachsen LB contributed more than 50 per cent of the cost of restructuring through its own resources.

With respect to the compensatory measures, as is normally the case with restructuring aid, the Commission asked for divestment. Sachsen LB sold a number of foreign subsidiaries and withdrew from certain international activities, mainly in real estate. It was probably quite natural for Sachsen LB to focus on its own domestic market, where it had a stronger presence.

Commission Decision 2009/971 (ex C 43/2008) of 12 May 2009 on state aid to WestLB The notified measure involved the restructuring and sale of WestLB. The sale would be effected through an open, transparent and non-discriminatory procedure. In order to facilitate the sale, the restructuring plan foresaw cost-cutting and downsizing through divesture and closure of operations in certain locations. WestLB would close down five of its eleven locations in Germany and twenty-three of its thirty locations outside Germany. It would also abstain from external growth through mergers or acquisitions.

A significant aspect of the restructuring was the transfer of impaired assets with a nominal value of €23 billion to a special-purpose vehicle. This transfer would be accompanied by a guarantee of €2 billion issued by the owners of WestLB and an additional guarantee of €3 billion issued by the Land of North Rhine–Westphalia.

The Commission first had to determine the existence or non-existence of state aid. There was agreement with Germany that the guarantees constituted state aid. However, there was a significant difference of opinion with respect to the amount of aid. Given that the impaired assets of WestLB hardly had any marketable value and that, in view of WestLB's troubles, it was unlikely that any private investor would agree to providing such a guarantee, the Commission concluded that the amount of state aid was equal to the total amount covered by the guarantee – €5 billion.

Once it established that the measure contained state aid, the next step in its analysis was the assessment of the compatibility of the aid with the internal market. In the opening of the formal investigation the Commission declared that Article 107(3)(c) TFEU was the legal basis for the compatibility assessment of the aid measure in question. However, in the meantime the Commission acknowledged that there was a threat of serious disturbance in the German economy and that measures supporting banks were apt to remedy that serious disturbance. Therefore it accepted that the legal basis for the assessment of the aid measure was Article 107(3)(b) TFEU.

The Commission then explained how it would assess aid granted to banks. According to paragraph 63 (internal references omitted), such aid would be

> assessed in line with the principles of the R&R [Rescue and Restructuring] Guidelines: taking into consideration the particular features of the systemic crisis in the financial markets. The R&R Guidelines require that State aid is accompanied by thorough restructuring to restore viability, by an adequate contribution of the beneficiary to the restructuring costs and by measures to remedy the potential distortions of the competition. They therefore also offer an appropriate framework for dealing with the restructuring of WestLB in the context of the crisis situation. However, the nature and the scale of the present crisis call for further specific elements related to the current market conditions to be taken into account. Therefore the principles of the R&R Guidelines have to be modulated when applied to the restructuring of WestLB in the context of the crisis situation . . . Special attention should be given to the rules set out in the R&R Guidelines for the own contribution of the beneficiary. Given the fact that the external financing for WestLB has *[. . .] [sic]*, the 50% target set in R&R Guidelines appears very difficult to achieve, the Commission accepts that it may during the systemic crisis in the financial markets not be appropriate to request a precise quantification of the own contribution. Furthermore the design and implementation of measures to limit distortion of competition may also need to be reconsidered in so far as WestLB may need more time for their implementation due to market circumstances.

With respect to the return of WestLB to viability, the Commission observed that one of the reasons for WestLB's problems was the ownership structure of the bank and the different interests of the respective owners. Therefore the Commission considered that the change of ownership, to be achieved until the end of 2011 in the form of an open, transparent and non-discriminating tender procedure, was a key element to solving the difficulties. It made the sale of the bank a condition for the approval of the state aid.

It was also satisfied that the planned cost-cutting, the removal of impaired assets from the balance sheet of the bank, the sale of nearly all its subsidiaries and the closure of the majority of its locations would be capable of restoring its viability. These actions would eliminate loss-making and non-core activities and would refocus the bank on its core customers.

In addition, these measures would reduce any distortions to competition as they would limit the presence of the bank in various markets.

Lastly and as mentioned above, the Commission accepted that WestLB did not have to make an own contribution of at least 50 per cent of restructuring costs, as required by the Rescue and Restructuring Guidelines.

Are state aid rules a threat to the integrity of the internal market?

Before concluding the review of the application of state aid rules during the financial crisis, it is necessary to consider a complaint voiced primarily by some German officials.[290] It has been reported in the press that the Commission has been criticized for its handling of certain cases of aid to financial institutions because the beneficiaries were allegedly forced to withdraw from other member states and that that was damaging the integrity of the internal EU market.

First of all, it is true that the Rescue and Restructuring Guidelines require that the recipients of aid compensate their competitors. This requirement is intended to minimize the distortive effect of aid. The typical compensatory measure is divestment, closure of capacity or withdrawal from certain markets or activities. Therefore there was nothing unusual in the Commission's demands.

Second, the internal market concept has been defined as an area without barriers or frontiers. The rules of the internal market are phrased in the form of prohibitions. They stipulate the removal of barriers but not the presence of companies in the markets of other member states. It cannot be expected that in an integrated market all companies

290 According to the *Financial Times*, 'Weber Hits out at Brussels', 22 April 2009, 'Europe's competition authorities risk throwing the continent's economic integration into reverse with their response to the financial crisis, [Axel Weber,] the head of Germany's Bundesbank, has warned in rare public criticism of Brussels.'

will be present in all locations. Their choice of location depends on their competitiveness and business model. In the same way that companies choose not to locate in certain areas within a country, they also choose not to operate in all countries of the EU.

Third, getting rid of loss-making assets, disengaging from marginal activities and focusing on core business and customers make companies stronger. Such kinds of restructuring intensify competition and in the longer term enable companies to offer better products and to enter new markets. The viability of the internal market very much depends on the strength of competition.

Fourth, the compensatory measures included in restructuring plans are defined first by the beneficiaries themselves and then proposed by the corresponding member states. The Commission does not request that companies exit the markets of other countries. However, the Commission does expect to see exit from unprofitable markets (so that companies can return to viability) and substantial limitation of the activities of aid recipients so that their competitors are disadvantaged to the smallest possible extent. Therefore it is unfair to accuse the Commission of having acted in a way that undermined the cohesion of the internal market.

Not surprisingly, state aid policy has played an important role during the financial crisis. It has allowed member states to support financial institutions initially and then the real economy while at the same time it has strived to prevent excessive distortion to competition and disruption to the flow of resources between member states. There is no doubt that the special rules that were issued by the Commission were accommodating. Given that similar and even more generous measures have been adopted by countries outside the European Union, it is not unreasonable to conclude that the special rules merely reflected the exceptional nature and unprecedented magnitude of the crisis. The more difficult question is whether the permitted amount of aid was excessive.

7.8 Concluding remarks

Before presenting some concluding thoughts let us briefly present an interesting Article 102 case illustrating how the Commission addressed abusive conduct amidst a crisis. In *ABG*,[291] the court argued that in order to be safe from the accusation of abuse under Article 102, a dominant

[291] IV/28841, Official Journal L 117 – 9 May 1977.

undertaking must allocate any available quantities to its several buyers on an equitable basis when there is a general supply crisis. In order to calculate the reduction made in supplies to each buyer during the period of scarcity, the same reference period must be chosen for all buyers; it must be a recent period, yet long enough to reflect seasonal variations in the market. It should also take account of the latest changes in dealings between buyers and sellers.

The relevant market was that of premium- and standard-grade motor spirit for carburation in four-stroke engines. The relevant geographical market was that of the Netherlands, where ABG members did all their distribution business. In the last quarter of 1973, when the oil crisis began, national motor spirit production rose slightly in comparison with the corresponding quarter of 1972, while domestic deliveries fell slightly and imports fell by some 25 per cent. The crisis originated in the limitation of production which occurred in November 1973 in many producing countries. There was a simultaneous reduction in the supply of oil combined with a substantial increase in its price. The supply crisis was rendered particularly acute in the Netherlands, which brought imports of crude down by nearly 50 per cent. By January 1974, however, supplies picked up again as the major oil companies made arrangements to divert to their Rotterdam refineries certain quantities transiting through other countries. The fear of a scarcity of petroleum products led to shortage concerns. At the time of the crisis, the seven companies which were directly engaged in the production of premium and regular motor spirit in the Netherlands were Esso, Shell, BP, Mobil, Chevron, Texaco and Gulf Oil.

Following the November 1973 crisis, ABG's situation became very difficult as regards both the volume of supplies and the terms on which it was able to obtain them. Before the crisis, up to 1968, BP supplied ABG on the basis of a short-term contract under which the two sides annually set price, quantities and other terms. When reorganizing its operational departments in November 1972, BP terminated the agreement with ABG. During the twelve months before the crisis, BP was ABG's principal supplier, and accounted on average for 81 per cent of its inputs, and for 100 per cent in October 1973, the month immediately preceding the beginning of the crisis. During the crisis from 1 November 1973 the quantities and the origin of the products supplied to ABG changed radically. The Dutch authorities recommended a reduction of between 15 and 20 per cent of consumption in the Netherlands. BP cut its supplies of motor spirit to ABG even more. During the crisis BP and Gulf had made greater reductions in their deliveries to ABG than to their other customers and ABG had great difficulty obtaining supplies.[292]

As the court stated, from the Community law point of view, it is the extent, regularity and continuity of commercial relationships which ought to be taken into consideration. The court argued that it is not to say that in a period of crisis dominant firms are not entitled to take into consideration particularities which may exist in the commercial circumstances of their customers. The court further added that even supposing that BP might have had grounds for supplying contractual and non-contractual customers in different ways, it should have treated ABG without discrimination relative to its other non-contractual customers. It follows, therefore, that BP abused its dominant position during the period of shortage by reducing its supplies to ABG not only substantially but also to a proportionately much greater extent than to its other clients. Thus, as the court makes clear, in periods of crisis a dominant undertaking can reduce supplies without being found to have abused its dominant position. What it should not do is discriminate in the reductions that it gives and be disproportionate. The crisis conditions can provide an objective justification for conduct that would otherwise be deemed abusive.

An additional implication of a crisis on abuse of dominance cases is that the existence of significant barriers to entry which are a result of the crisis, as explained above, may lead to incumbents being deemed dominant undertakings.

In concluding this chapter we should note that Fingleton has distinguished between banks and other sectors of the economy as bank failure risks systemic adverse effects in markets.[293] 'Weekend' decisions on the sustainability of financial institutions, such as HBOS, Bear Stearns and Lehman Brothers, were political decisions that were taken with financial stability as the overriding concern. Competition issues were left behind.[294] Professor Vives, in his presentation to the OECD,[295] interestingly argued that there is a trade-off between competition and stability. Bank runs could happen independently of the level of competition

[292] The attempts to buy on the free market failed by virtue of the difference between Dutch domestic prices and world prices, which made imports virtually impossible.

[293] Fingleton 2009.

[294] Summary Record of the Discussion on Competition and Financial Markets, DAF/COMP/M(2009)1/ANN4, 10 April 2009, Roundtable 3 on Real Economy and Competition Policy in a Period of Retrenchment, available at www.oecd.org.

[295] Ibid.

but an excessive level of competition tended to worsen co-ordination problems. Systemic crises tend to be less likely in concentrated banking systems. He added that institutions close to insolvency have incentives to gamble for resurrection and must be restrained in their competitive ability.

Concerns whether competition policy should be flexible enough to support other objectives are important and likely to have wide ramifications given the governmental intervention in the financial markets, which has increased since the collapse of Lehman Brothers. The essential question is whether the usual framework for regulation of the competition impact of mergers and state aid is flexible enough to deal with such adverse situations or whether it has simply been ignored in an attempt to restore tranquility in the financial markets. Competition authorities in the EU should tend towards more flexibility in their application of competition rules during a crisis, in order to overcome and soften the hard consequences that the latter entails for the European single market.

The chairman of the OFT, Philip Collins, in his presentation to the OECD, argued that the established principles of competition policy could not be disregarded because of the recession, but competition agencies and policies needed to adapt the way in which interventions were made, the kinds of investigation carried out and the kinds of instrument used, so that they are demonstrably relevant, timely and beneficial both in retrenchment and in recovery.[296]

The UK response to the OECD states that competition law and policy should be flexible enough to accommodate a range of policy objectives. It adds that there may be compelling reasons to accept other concerns. In this changed climate, competition authorities will need to demonstrate pragmatism, but equally they will need to be effective advocates of competition within government and across the wider economy to ensure that the competition process is not compromised in the long term. Competition authorities will need to adapt quickly to changing priorities, and to display a degree of pragmatism by recognizing occasions when other policy interests may, or rather should, override competition policy.

Professor Ito argues that competition should be set aside during a systemic crisis.[297] He adds that in an acute crisis, protecting financial

[296] Ibid.

[297] T. Ito, Global Financial Crisis of 2008: Crisis Management and Competition Policy, OECD, 17 February 2009.

stability is of paramount importance to the economy. Vives notes that competition has to be restricted or regulated for companies close to insolvency and for those which have received subsidies.[298] According to Vives, the main aim of competition policy in times of crisis should be to preserve long-term viability and strength of competition in the financial sector. Thus measures including merger policy should be flexible in the short term. He adds that a systemic crisis overrides competition policy concerns, and importantly adds that banking is not like any other sector as regards competition policy. According to Vives, merger policy should be more lenient in banking but consistent over time since the banking sector's systemic character, and thus its specificity, in competition policy should be acknowledged. Lowe, though, has argued that it is necessary to recognize the systemic and special features of the banking sector, and the reality that the banking sector is no different from any other sector in terms of the need to restructure. It is necessary also to plan out what constitutes a return to viability.[299]

As the OECD report states, competition authorities have to remain firm on the principles and continue their efforts to promote and safeguard competition.[300] It adds that competition policy issues were not quite the same as they used to be and some adaptation to new tools and new pressures coming from policies other than competition policy will be needed.

Professor Peltzman, in his presentation to the OECD,[301] argued that the regulation that tried to head off a financial crisis was inherently anti-competitive, even in normal times. The tension between competition and solvency regulation, which is permanent, was resolved in favour of stability. He added that

> in the last few months, the ten biggest banks in the US had been told to sign an agreement which amounted to collusion. Both the US and the UK had, in effect, nationalized their banking systems and the banks were now

[298] X. Vives, Competition and Stability in Banking: A New World of Competition Policy? OECD, 17 February 2009.

[299] Summary Record of the Discussion on Competition and Financial Markets, DAF/COMP/M(2009)1/ANN5, 10 April 2009, Roundtable 4 on Going Forward: Adaptation of Competition Rules, Processes and Institutions to Current Financial Sector Issues, available at www.oecd.org.

[300] Ibid.

[301] Presentation to OECD Competition Committee, Competition and the Financial Markets, www.oecd.org.

> effectively agents of the government. Firms that were deemed systemically important were subsidised, clearly against the spirit of the WTO and the EC. All this meant that the world had moved a long way from the tenets of competition policy in the crisis . . . For the future, it is clear that substantial government intervention in any future crisis is an absolute certainty and that intervention will be unrestrained by competition law.

As the analysis in this chapter has illustrated, competition authorities should be pragmatic in enforcing competition legislation against mergers, cartels and state aid in periods of crisis. In adopting such an approach, competition authorities should, as emphasized above, aim at minimizing adverse precedential issues as well as adverse effects on competition, effects that can sustain after the crisis is over. Competition policy needs to be pragmatic, and flexible enough to address sudden exogenous shocks and the wide-ranging implications of such shocks to whole markets. After all, the ultimate and undoubted aim of competition should be to enhance the degree of competition in a market, leading to improvement of consumer welfare. On a number of occasions, it is essential thus to subordinate competition policy if such an approach will ensure sustainability and enhancement of consumer welfare, or, alternatively, if such an approach will prevent a deterioration of consumer welfare through means irrelevant to competition policy (such as systemic crisis, macroeconomic instability and so on).

Short-term anti-competitive measures introduced to counter a financial and economic crisis should not harm current and future market competition, must be as temporary and as limited in scope as possible, and should promote resource reallocation rather than maintaining the status quo. Peter Freeman, chairman of the UK Competition Commission, has argued that competition authorities should not expand their remit but rather look at and try and understand the full policy context.[302] Competition authorities must be allowed to focus on promoting competition through well-targeted interventions while remaining mindful of the situation in the wider economy and the broader policy concerns that governments may need to address. Public policies should not aim at supporting firms who were in distress independently of the crisis.

Frederic Jenny, opening the discussion in the Role of Competition

[302] P. Freeman, Competition Policy after the Credit Crunch: The view from a UK competition authority, Chatham House Conference, 26 June 2009.

Policy in Financial Sector Rescue and Restructuring roundtable,[303] mentioned that as regards the management of the crisis from the point of view of competition policy, competition law enforcement might be too narrowly focused in the financial sector and the concept of efficiency might need to be enlarged to include stability. Competition policy played a useful role in a period of crisis but may need to be of secondary concern during such times. This approach is key to the long-term benefits of competition for consumers and for the economy as a whole in terms of growth and increased productivity.

We should emphasize that the Lisbon Treaty's references to full employment and social objectives may induce arguments that a broader industrial policy standard should apply, an approach that can prove influential in enforcing competition policy in periods of crisis.[304]

[303] Summary Record of the Discussion on Competition and Financial Markets, DAF/COMP/M(2009)1/ANN4, 10 April 2009, Roundtable 2 on Crisis: The Role of Competition Policy in Financial Sector Rescue and Restructuring, www.oecd.org.

[304] See www.wilmerhale.com/publications/whPubsDetail.aspx?publication=9321.

8

Conclusion

> Of all the human powers operating on the affairs of mankind, none is greater than that of competition.
>
> Henry Clay (1777–1852)[1]

As a result of the recent crisis, we have experienced instances where competition policy has been set aside due to special and exceptional circumstances. These special and exceptional circumstances can be the collapse of a bank that can trigger a systemic crisis. Therefore it is important to have a clear understanding of the rules (competition law) and the exceptions to those rules, especially in the presence of such exceptional circumstances. In addition, it is important for distressed entities and policy-makers to understand clearly the array of options that they have in advance since these can be used as part of their 'crisis toolkit'. The aim of this book has been to provide an analysis of such exceptions to competition law and policy, particularly in the context of a financial crisis.

The key issue that this book has addressed is whether the risk of a systemic crisis can justify the adoption of a more lenient approach. In summary, the book has provided a comprehensive understanding of the rationale of competition law in the light of conflicting interests (promoting competition versus the collapse of a firm that might result in a systemic crisis). It has analysed the foundations of concepts such as failing-firm defence, efficiency defence, crisis cartels and state aid and assessed how these concepts should apply in periods of crisis. During a crisis, concepts such as failing-firm defence and efficiency defence are essential in effective and pragmatic enforcement of merger legislation. In addition, the treatment of state aid as well as of crisis cartels is essential in ensuring the sustainability of undertakings and whole industries during periods of distress.

1 Henry Clay, American statesman, Secretary of State and presidential candidate, speech to the American Senate, 1832.

8.1 Control of state aid

State aid has negative effects on competition and on trade between member states. It is widely accepted that state aid might also generate serious inefficiencies and consequences for the economy as a whole. In addition, state aid allows firms which are less efficient to survive in the market at the expense of firms which are more efficient. By providing state aid, the market power of the selected undertaking can be created, maintained or strengthened by providing economic advantages to that benefit from state support. State aid can be a source of market failure.[2]

Subsidization might give rise both to allocative and to technical inefficiencies, and subsidization of investments in long-term growth is ambiguous. Granting of state aid might cause pricing that is likely to distort competition. It may distort competition or harm competitors not only due to pricing, but also due to non-price effects that seriously harm non-recipients. The distortion of competition arises because the recipient could use the aid to invest, for example in R & D, and become able to provide a higher-quality product. Competing firms could be harmed and forced to reduce their price, output and investment.[3]

Government provision of state aid weakens incentives for firms to improve efficiency. The expectation that aid might be granted – government tendency to grant state funds – changes the behaviour of firms. The negative effects of state aid on welfare must be outweighed by benefits from granting state aid. There must be overall positive effects from the correction of the market failure. Only in such cases does economic justification for granting state aid exist, namely to raise efficiency by correcting market failures. This is, for example, when markets fail to deliver the optimal level of goods or services: only in such cases can state aid be expected to improve welfare and only then should it be authorized by the EC.

State aid and merger control are the two core sectors through which the Commission has responded to the global crisis by taking a more flexible stance on competition policy. In particular, as Biondi, Eckhaut and Flynn argue,

> in Europe the provision of subsidies and other forms of aid by the State still forms an accepted part, indeed often a central part, of economic

[2] J. Kornai, *Economics of Shortage*, North Holland, 1980.

[3] P. Møllgaard, 'Competitive Effects of State Aid in Oligopoly', unpublished mimeograph, 2005.

> policy, even in those countries most attached to the model of the free market. Yet the very existence of State aid poses obvious problems for the single market for which the European Union is striving. The EC law of State aid therefore raises issues of the greatest social, economic and political importance, as well as a great variety of difficult and fascinating legal problems. Seldom have the rules of Community law on State Aid been invoked more frequently than at present. Seldom has the definition of a State aid presented more difficulty.[4]

State aid policy has played an important role during the financial crisis. It has allowed member states to support financial institutions initially and then the real economy while at the same time it has strived to prevent excessive distortion to competition and disruption to the flow of resources between member states.

During the recent financial crisis, in the area of state aid, the Commission has been swiftly approving national state aid measures,[5] a large percentage of which were directed to financial institutions.[6] This constitutes a dramatic increase over 2007 levels.

EU control of state aid has thus the potential to significantly constrain the level of subsidies in the member states. Control of state aid *ex ante* can allow state aid's opportunity costs to be considered and the aid itself to be directed towards activities where more positive externalities can be expected. During crises, the provision of rescue of firms in difficulty may be justified by social or regional policy considerations, by the need to take into account the beneficial role in the economy of small and medium-sized enterprises, or, exceptionally, by the desirability of maintaining a competitive market structure when the insolvency of firms could lead to monopolistic or oligopolistic market structures.

Member states have not been allowed to discriminate in favour of their banks. They have not been allowed to grant unlimited amounts of aid. They have been required to submit realistic restructuring plans, which in some cases have led to the sale of the beneficiaries or even to their closure.[7] The more difficult question is whether the permitted amount of aid was excessive. There is no doubt that the special

[4] A. Biondi, P. Eeckhout and J. Flynn, *The Law of State Aid in the European Union*, Oxford University Press, 2004.

[5] For example, the Commission approved the UK support scheme for financial institutions in less than two working days, while such decisions normally take about six months.

[6] European Commission, Tackling the economic crisis: The real economy – State aid. Available at http://ec.europa.eu/competition/state_aid/overview/tackling_economic_crisis.html.

[7] For example, the liquidation aid to Roskilde Bank in Denmark (NN 39/2008).

rules that were issued by the Commission were accommodating. Given that similar and even more generous measures have been adopted by countries outside the European Union, it is not unreasonable to conclude that the special rules merely reflected the exceptional nature and unprecedented magnitude of the crisis. With the Temporary Framework for aid to the real economy expiring at the end of 2010, the question for the near future is how quickly the special rules will be phased out.

Thus it is important for competition policy that such subsidies are well targeted and closely monitored by the Commission. Member states should only grant aid that is non-discriminatory, limited in time and carefully designed to target the problem for which it was sought.[8]

8.2 Merger control

As regards the assessment of mergers in periods of crisis, according to Lisa Rabbe, managing director of Goldman Sachs International,[9] the failing-firm doctrine has to be applied flexibly and competition authorities should not engage in brinksmanship where the bank is about to go bankrupt. In addition, issues such as efficiencies and remedies are also affected by crisis conditions in markets.

The US Federal Trade Commission acknowledged that the fact that the country is in an overall economic crisis would not be a 'get-out-of-jail-free' card for any particular merger.[10] In the UK, the merger between Lloyds TSB and HBOS was cleared after the introduction of a

[8] The American International Group (AIG) benefited from more than US$170 billion in a federal rescue (A. Beattie and J. MacIntosh, 'Summers "outrage" at AIG bonuses', *Financial Times*, March 2009, available at www.ft.com/cms/s/0/31bafc52-1192-11de-87b1-0000779fd2ac.html) and is a clear example that if state aid is not well enough planned, as well as monitored by the competition authorities so as to promote development in the economy, it is likely to create more harm than the originally envisaged benefit. See further N. Kroes, 'The Road to Recovery', address at 105th meeting of the OECD Competition Committee, 17 February 2009, available at http://europa.eu/rapid/pressReleasesAction.do?reference=SPEECH/09/63&format=HTML&aged=0&language=EN&guiLanguage=en.

[9] Summary Record of the Discussion on Competition and Financial Markets, DAF/COMP/M(2009)1/ANN4, 10 April 2009, Roundtable 2 on Crisis: The Role of Competition Policy in Financial Sector Rescue and Restructuring, available at www.oecd.org.

[10] A. Gump, 'Acquisitions of Distressed Companies: Obtaining Antitrust Merger Clearance Using the Failing and Weakened Firm Defenses', Resource Centre, available at http://agmarketcrisis.com/?p=703.

new public-interest ground enabling the Secretary of State to allow this merger in order to protect the stability of the UK financial system. On the same day financial stability became a consideration of public interest in UK merger law, thereby allowing ministers lawfully to override a merger reference by the Office of Fair Trading (OFT) to the Competition Commission, the OFT published its competition assessment of the proposed merger between Lloyds and HBOS. Despite the conclusions of the OFT that the merger was likely to lead to a substantial lessening of competition, Lord Mandelson cleared the merger on public interest grounds,[11] rather than refer the merger to the Competition Commission, thus ranking competition concerns behind financial stability.[12]

Such high-profile government intervention and swift legal reform – introducing a new public-interest consideration of the maintenance of the stability of the UK financial system – has been heavily criticized. Newspapers reported that 'Gordon Brown intervened to broker a solution to HBOS and Downing Street made clear it was prepared to rip up Britain's competition laws to allow the takeover'.[13] The BBC reported that the government had 'said it would overrule any concerns that competition authorities may raise'.[14] *The Economist* questioned the wisdom of allowing the takeover to proceed, noting that 'shotgun weddings rarely make for happy marriages'.[15] We should note that the public interest ground based on the financial crisis is currently not recognized by the European Commission; however, it will be interesting to see how the Commission reacts to a pressing need for clearing a merger that may sustain financial stability or the stability of any other sector affecting more than one economy amidst a severe crisis.

[11] He used his powers under the Enterprise Act, which contains provisions under which the Secretary of State can intervene on grounds of public interest in the merger-control process where a merger is subject to review by the OFT. He has the power to decide, on grounds of public interest, to clear a merger despite there being a substantial lessening of competition, or to prohibit a merger (or to subject it to conditions) even where such measures are not justified by competition concerns alone. Decision by Lord Mandelson, the Secretary of State for Business, not to refer to the Competition Commission the merger between Lloyds TSB Group plc and HBOS plc under section 45 of the Enterprise Act 2002, 31 October 2008, available at www.berr.gov.uk/files/file48745.pdf.

[12] BERR, 'Peter Mandelson Gives Regulatory Clearance to Lloyds TSB Merger with HBOS', Press Release 2008/253, 31 October 2008.

[13] *The Guardian*, international edition, 18 March 2009.

[14] The BBC News Channel, 17 September 2008, available at http://news.bbc.co.uk/1/hi/business/7621151.stm.

[15] *The Economist*, 25 September 2008, available at www.economist.com/world/britain/displaystory.cfm?story_id=12305706.

In the presence of a financial crisis affecting a whole economy and inducing the risk of systemic collapse, different markets and the financial stability of consumers, employees and competitors are all affected. Hence competition rules fail to achieve their original goal in the presence of a stronger and more urgent priority – crisis. Consequently, it is completely understandable to adapt the application of competition rules, for a short time only and until the problem is resolved, on a case-by-case basis, in order to provide a solution that benefits the economy in general, including consumers, shareholders (of the failing firms) and employees (even though social issues are usually intentionally neglected in the application of competition law). The notion of 'public interest' should include, for all these reasons, financial stability.

In general, the financial crisis does not entail that there should be a change in the fundamentals of competition law as regards the application of the failing-firm defence since drastic and excessive changes would be dangerous for the structure of the economy. As the OECD states in a report,[16] 'governments need to make a case-by-case call on whether and how to provide some kind of assistance, depending on an analysis of the systemic, economy-wide implications of failure in a particular industry'. The Commission can use its margin of discretion flexibly in the assessment of the failing-firm defence to take account of market conditions in a crisis. The conditions of the failing-firm defence are difficult to justify under normal market conditions. However, in crisis situations, competition authorities and courts in the EU must be pragmatic and take into consideration the grounds on which the failing-firm defence was introduced in the merger legislations and apply it temporarily with more flexibility in order to achieve those same original goals of competition enforcement. We should emphasize that any flexibility shown by the European Commission and the competition authorities in the EU during the credit crunch must be considered exceptional and temporary.

Considering a merger with a failing firm during a crisis, the economic aspects of allowing or blocking this merger – such as the loss of jobs, benefit to consumers, price maintenance – should also be borne in mind. Social costs must be taken into account in adopting some general formulation of the failing-company defence, rather than taking social costs into account in individual cases.[17] Thus, in the assessment of a merger,

[16] OECD, Competition and Financial Markets, 2009.

[17] E. Correia, 'The Failing Company Defence' (1995), www.ftc.gov/opp/global/final.htm.

the overall conditions of the market should be considered, as well as the social and economic implications of allowing or blocking the merger. As promoting employment and social protection are two tasks that are central to the EC Treaty, the European Commission is not entirely free from the influence of wider policy agendas. As noted above, the Lisbon Treaty includes stronger references to full employment and social objectives, including the reference to a 'highly competitive social market economy'. This might induce arguments that a broader industrial policy standard should apply.[18] However, the likely anti-competitive effects of the merger rather than other social and public-policy considerations should be one of the leading factors influencing assessment of the transaction.

As regards the efficiency defence, applying the total welfare standard is preferred by economists who argue that other standards will sometimes sacrifice social surplus. In some circumstances the efficiency achieved by merger or the inefficiency that will result from preventing the merger should be evaluated under a total surplus standard rather than under a consumer welfare standard.[19]

However, the above-mentioned approach should be used with caution. The total welfare standard and the balancing of the consumers' and producers' surplus should apply in cases where the prohibition of the merger would induce greater harm to consumer welfare than would the merger itself through disruptions in the supply of a good or service or the worsening of other factors important for consumer choice. The competition authority, by applying a total welfare standard or by placing different weights on the total and consumer welfare standards, can clear a merger that could not be cleared under a consumer welfare standard and prohibition of which would, as illustrated in Chapter 4, induce inefficiencies.[20] This approach should not provide a panacea for relaxing competition standards, but should be given prominence in situations such as the current financial crisis, where competition policy should be balanced against other policies.

[18] See www.wilmerhale.com/publications/whPubsDetail.aspx?publication=9321.

[19] C. Luescher, 'Efficiency Considerations in European Merger Control: Just Another Battle Ground for the European Commission, Economists and Competition Lawyers' (2004) 25 *ECLR* 72.

[20] Where the merger does not satisfy any defence to the prohibition (e.g. failing-firm defence).

8.3 Crisis cartels

Crisis cartels are allegedly justified by the fact that collusive behaviour is the only means for the survival of the cartelists. Crisis cartel agreements should not be automatically deemed illegal; rather the aims and effects of these should be assessed in order to balance their negative impact against the positive effects of sustaining the viability of undertakings in the market, which can ensure the availability of customer choice once the crisis is over. Assessment of such agreements can thus be made pursuant to Article 101(3), balancing the positive and negative effects of the agreement. Factors which are not capable of casting doubt on the existence of a restriction of competition, such as improvements in the production of goods as a result of economies of scale, may not be taken into account in the context of Article 101(1), but only in the context of Article 101(3), even where they are ultimately to be assessed positively in terms of an agreement's compatibility with Article 101.

As analysed in Chapter 5, crisis cartel agreements can ensure the sustainability of an industry that is in crisis. Such agreements need to satisfy the criteria the Commission outlined in the twenty-third Report on Competition Policy. The Commission argued that it may condone such agreements which aim at reducing overcapacity as long as the agreement applies to a sector as a whole.[21] Such agreements will not involve price-fixing or quota agreement and will not impair the free decision-making of firms.

This strict case-by-case approach and the justification of the treatment of a crisis cartel agreement will prevent adverse precedential issues for competition authorities. Competition authorities need to make clear in their decisions that the approach they adopt in allowing a crisis cartel agreement, as mentioned above, has limited duration, applies to specific sectors and has as its justification the adverse impact of the crisis on the specific sector. Following such an approach would prevent setting precedents which may unnecessarily complicate enforcement of competition in periods not characterized by crisis.

In addition, the 'financial-constraints'consideration reflects a concern that high fines might force an offending firm into insolvency. The EC and the US have wide discretion and apparent lack of transparency in awarding these discounts. Following the Lisbon Treaty's coming into force, arguments that a broader industrial policy standard should apply

[21] Twenty-third Report on Competition Policy, para. 84.

may become more relevant.[22] Thus firms can be involved in cartels and not end up paying a fine in crisis situations, thus increasing their profits from collusion, and thus increasing their tendency to be in cartels (in the absence of criminal sanctions).

However, as analysed in Chapter 5, the financial-constraints defence should be used in circumstances where a high fine will mitigate the viability of an undertaking and may lead to an apparently inefficient firm exiting the market. A market in which the number of firms has been reduced due to the insolvency of incumbents as a result of high fines does not enhance consumer welfare. To the extent that the firms that exit the market are the least efficient ones, consumer welfare is enhanced. However, in periods of crisis firms may face liquidity constraints and decrease in demand, both of which mitigate their efficiency. Thus although in the absence of the crisis these firms would be operating efficiently, due to the crisis they face difficulties in their operation, and once the crisis is over they are likely to return to efficient operation. Thus although during a crisis a firm may appear to be inefficient and in theory should not be prevented from exiting the market as a result of a high fine, in reality the exit of this firm may adversely affect the efficiency of the market once the crisis is over.

According to Lisa Rabbe, the application of competition law must not exacerbate systemic risks. There are two key objectives for financial institutions and policy-makers in distinguishing between a short-term approach and a medium- and longer-term approach. The first is to do no further harm, to ensure that there is no further erosion of confidence in the market and no greater systemic risk. The second is to do everything possible to restore credit flows and facilitate access to capital in order to mitigate the damage to the real economy.[23] Thus any measures that in the short term can ensure no further erosion of confidence in the market and no greater systemic risk are necessary, including mergers involving failing firms, or crisis cartels. In the short term, stability (macroeconomic, financial) should take priority over competition enforcement in an attempt to prevent further adverse effects in a market amidst a financial crisis.

22 See www.wilmerhale.com/publications/whPubsDetail.aspx?publication=9321.

23 Summary Record of the Discussion on Competition and Financial Markets, DAF/COMP/M(2009)1/ANN4, 10 April 2009, Roundtable 2 on Crisis: The Role of Competition Policy in Financial Sector Rescue and Restructuring, available at www.oecd.org.

The OECD has argued that even during the crisis, competition authorities should continue to act independently, examining issues such as transparency and switching costs in retail banking.[24] Easier switching and increased transparency could increase the competitiveness of current market structures and facilitate new entry and expansion.

According to the OECD report, the principles and objectives of competition law enforcement therefore must not change, but the analysis has to be realistic about market conditions.[25] That means continuing the shift from a form-based analysis to a case-by-case analysis in which the context and effects of actual practices and behaviour are very much taken into consideration.

We should note that the Lisbon Treaty aims at a more democratic, efficient and transparent Union. Pursuant to Article 3(3) of the consolidated version of the Treaty on European Union,[26]

> The Union shall establish an internal market. It shall work for the sustainable development of Europe based on balanced economic growth and price stability, a highly competitive social market economy, aiming at full employment and social progress, and a high level of protection and improvement of the quality of the environment. It shall promote scientific and technological advance.

Article 3 of the Treaty on the Functioning of the European Union[27] no longer includes the words 'a system ensuring that competition in the internal market is not distorted' as a policy objective of the EU. Instead, the reference to undistorted competition has been moved to a protocol annexed to the treaty. The Lisbon Treaty now refers to 'competition rules necessary for the functioning of the internal market'.

Following the Lisbon Treaty's coming into force on 1 December 2009, interpretative issues could also arise due to the stronger references to full employment and social objectives. As mentioned above, this might induce arguments that a broader industrial policy standard should apply.[28]

The chairman of the Competition Committee of the OECD, Frederic Jenny, noted that the biggest problem is to convince legislators or execu-

[24] Ibid.

[25] Ibid.

[26] See http://eur-lex.europa.eu/LexUriServ/LexUriServ.do?uri=OJ:C:2008:115:0001:01:EN:HTML.

[27] See http://eur-lex.europa.eu/LexUriServ/LexUriServ.do?uri=OJ:C:2008:115:0001:01:EN:HTML.

[28] See www.wilmerhale.com/publications/whPubsDetail.aspx?publication=9321.

tive branches of the government that competition authorities can make positive contributions during crises and that competition law can be adapted in scope, time and focus.[29]

In the EU, the president of the Commission said, in his speech concerning the financial crisis on 29 October 2008, 'Our top priority is to minimize the impact on jobs, purchasing power and prosperity of our citizens'.[30] Hence the basis on which the Commission will be willing temporarily to adapt its competition rules is public interest.

As the analysis in this book illustrates, competition authorities should be pragmatic in enforcing competition legislation in periods of crisis. As emphasized above, in adopting such a pragmatic approach, competition authorities should aim at minimizing adverse precedential issues as well as adverse effects on competition – effects that can sustain after the crisis is over. Such an approach should be used cautiously and by no means universally. Not all anti-competitive conduct or practices (such as mergers, crisis cartels, state aid) merit approval due to aims related to non-competition. Competition policy must be able to address sudden exogenous shocks and the wide-ranging implications of such shocks for whole markets. After all, the ultimate and undoubted aim of competition should be to improve consumer welfare through enhancing the degree of competition in a market. On a number of occasions, it is thus essential to cautiously subordinate competition policy if such an approach will ensure sustainability and the enhancement of consumer welfare, or alternatively if such an approach will prevent a deterioration of consumer welfare through means irrelevant to competition policy (such as systemic crisis, or macroeconomic instability). Thus competition policy should be adapted in crisis situations in order to prevent markets and economies from worsening further. A fine balance needs to be struck between competition policies and other policies ensuring economic and market stability. Such a balance is an imperative amidst crises in order to ensure long-term consumer welfare.

[29] Summary Record of the Discussion on Competition and Financial Markets, DAF/COMP/M(2009)1/ANN4, 10 April 2009, Roundtable 2 on Crisis: The Role of Competition Policy in Financial Sector Rescue and Restructuring, available at www.oecd.org.

[30] J.M.D. Barroso, president of the European Commission, 'From Financial Crisis to Recovery: A European Framework for Action', 29 October 2008.

INDEX